THE DE HAVILLAND MOSQUITO

A COMPREHENSIVE GUIDE FOR THE MODELLER

Richard A. Franks

SAM Publications

Modellers Datafile No.20
The De Havilland Mosquito
by Richard A. Franks

First published in Great Britain, 1998 by SAM Publications.
Second edition published 2013 by Media House, under licence from SAM Publications Limited
Media House,
21 Kingsway,
Bedford,
MK42 9BJ,
United Kingdom

This edition reprinted 2013 with additional material edited by Gary Hatcher and featuring the work of:
Nick Greenall, Graham Marsh, Alec Smith and Ted Taylor
© 2013 John Fox - Cover

© 1998 Richard A. Franks
© 1998 Richard J. Caruana - Colour side-views and scale plans
© 1998 Steve Benstead - Colour interior artwork
© 1998 Anthony Oliver - Interior artwork and sketches

All rights reserved. No part of this publication may be reproduced or transmitted in any form or by any means, electronic or mechanical, including photocopy, recording, or any other information storage and retrieval system, without permission in writing from the publishers.

ISBN 978-1-906959-3-33

Studio Manager – Jonathan Phillips
Typeset by SAM Publications, Media House, 21 Kingsway, Bedford, MK42 9BJ, United Kingdom
Printed and bound in the United Kingdom.

The MDF Series

- No.1 – De Havilland Mosquito *
- No.2 – Hawker Hurricane *
- No.3 – Supermarine Spitfire (Part 1: Merlin-Powered) *
- No.4 – Avro Lancaster (Inc Manchester & Lincoln)
- No.5 – Supermarine Spitfire (Part 2: Griffon-Powered)
- No.6 – Bristol Beaufighter *
- No.7 – English Electric Lightning
- No.8 – Gloster (& Armstrong-Whitworth) Meteor
- No.9 – Messerschmitt Bf 109 (Part 1 Prototype to E Variants)
- No.10 – Messerschmitt Bf 109 (Part 2 F to K Variants)
- No.11 – British Aerospace Sea Harrier
- No.12 – The F-4 Phantom II (Part 1: USAF)
- No.13 – The F-4 Phantom II (Part 2: US Navy & Marine Corps)
- No.14 – The F-4 Phantom II (Part 3: Overseas Operators)
- No.15 – The Grumman F-14 Tomcat
- No.16 – The Hawker Hunter
- No.17 – The BAe (Hawker Siddeley) RAF Harrier
- No.18 – The Vought F4U Corsair
- No.19 – The General Dynamics F-111 Aardvark
* Out of print

Acknowledgements
A word of thanks must go to the following people and organisations, without whose help and encouragement this title would never have happened: The Department of Information Services, Royal Air Force Museum, Hendon; The Aircraft & Exhibits Department, Royal Air Force Museum, Hendon; The Aerospace Museum, Cosford, with a special note of thanks to Keith and Phil; Phil Birtles and all the staff at The Mosquito Museum, Salisbury Hall, London Colney; Rolls-Royce Heritage Trust, Derby; Trevor Snowden, Airfix Ltd; Neil Burkill, Paragon Designs; Gaston Bernal, AeroMaster Products; Stuart Howe; Michael Payne; and Ken Real.

Contents

Glossary 5
Preface 6

The Mosquito - A Concise History

Chapter 1 — **The Concept** 7
The birth of the D.H.98 design

Chapter 2 — **Concept Becomes Reality** 10
From drawing board to production

Chapter 3 — **Into Action** 14
The arrival of the Mosquito in RAF service

Chapter 4 — **The Multi-role Combatant** 18
The ability of the Mosquito is finally realised

Chapter 5 — **Special Operations** 24
The Mosquito's use for a number of special tasks

Chapter 6 — **All at Sea** 30
The Mosquito's use by the Banff Wing and the Royal Navy

Chapter 7 — **Worldwide Service** 35
A look at the Mosquito's use around the globe

Chapter 8 — **Post-War Operations** 39
Post-war RAF operations and foreign and civil operators of the Mosquito

Colour Side-views 49
Colour Interior Views 55

Modelling the Mosquito

Chapter 9 — **The Basics** 59
The starting point for modelling the Mosquito in 1/72nd, 1/48th and 1/32nd scales

Chapter 10 — **Understanding the Subject** 65
A detailed analysis of all the different versions of Mosquito, and how to model them

Contents

Chapter 11 — **Detailing** 81
A detailed look in and around the Mosquito

Chapter 12 — **Building the Mosquito** 115
Nine different versions of the Mosquito are built in 1/48th scale

Colour Photographs 128

Chapter 13 — **Colour & Marking Notes** 129
A modeller's guide to the colour and markings applied to the Mosquito throughout its career

Appendix I **Kit Listing** 141
A complete listing of all the Mosquito construction kits

Appendix II **Conversions & Accessories** 142
A complete listing of conversions and accessories produced for the Mosquito

Appendix III **Decals** 143
A concise listing of all Mosquito decal sheets

Appendix IV **Powerplants** 144
Technical specifications of all Rolls Royce Merlin engines used in the Mosquito, including Packard-built versions

Appendix V **Variants** 145
A complete listing of the technical specifications of the different Mosquito variants

Appendix VI **Genealogy** 148
The genealogy of the Mosquito from Prototype to final production

Appendix VII **Squadrons** 149
A complete listing of Mosquito Squadrons

Appendix VIII **Chronology** 153
A concise chronology of the Mosquito's history

Appendix IX **Production** 155
A complete listing of Mosquito production

Appendix X **Bibliography** 157
Mosquito Bibliography

Index 158

Fold-out scale plans

Preface

Welcome to this, the first in our new Modellers Datafile series. This series of books has been conceived from the outset with the static scale model maker in mind, although I am sure that they will prove as popular with aviation enthusiasts and historians. In the past there have been a number of titles which looked at a specific subject, but they offered only the historical and technical information. The Modeller's Datafile series has been created to offer the modeller information which he will find of use when building the type. Each title will contain a short historical text describing the design's evolution, technical data, scale plans, colour interior drawings, black and white sketches, details of how to make most versions in the major scales, a list of all known kits of the type, accessories and decals and finally a comprehensive bibliography to help the reader decide on other suitable titles should he wish to do further research.

The choice for this first volume is a purely personal one. My great affection for the Mosquito was founded on the admiration that my late father had for it. He had been a carpenter and joiner by profession and therefore he truly appreciated the beauty and grace of such an elegant wooden aircraft. As a child I attended many airshows in the south of England with my father and my general scanning of the skies was suddenly focused when he would say 'there she is!", as this indicated that the Mosquito had arrived to display. Having been surrounded with the craft of carpentry all my life I have become a lifelong fan of the Mosquito and seeing it reminds me very much of those early

A very atmospheric shot of B Mk 35 TA634 at the Mosquito Museum during the winter months before it was afforded hanger protection. Can't recall the horses name!
(S.Howe)

days at airshows and of my father.

Many of you may well recall the series of features I wrote in *Scale Aviation Modeller International* magazine way back in 1996 (Vol 2 Iss 7, 8, 9 &10). Although this formed the basis of this book in some respects, all of the artwork, sketches and models used in this title are new. A great deal of research has gone into this title and although I do not feel it is 'definitive' (what title ever is?), I hope that you will all find it an invaluable tool in identifying the numerous marks of Mosquito. I also hope that it forms the basis of many a model creation and that in various ways it will allow you to appreciate the true beauty and grace of the Mosquito, a type which has never been equalled in the Royal Air Force.

Richard A. Franks

Glossary

The sad end of a Mosquito. This machine, all identity gone, looks like a night fighter variant, so is most likely an NF Mk 30 or 36 and is seen here in a sorry state in the late 1950s at an unknown location *(via S.Howe)*

AA	Anti-Aircraft
A.&A.E.E.	Aircraft & Armament Experimental Establishment
ACM	Air-Chief Marshal (RAF)
A.I.	Airborne Interception (radar)
AM	Air Marshal (RAF)
ASH	Air to Surface Home (AN/APS-4) radar
ASV	Air to Surface Vessel
AVM	Air Vice Marshal (RAF)
B	Bomber
BAFO	British Air Forces of Occupation
BS	British Standard
BSDU	Bomber Support Development Unit
CAACU	Civilian Anti-Aircraft Co-operation Unit
CAT	Clear-air Turbulence
D.H.	De Havilland Ltd.
D.H.C.	De Havilland Canada Ltd.
Do	Dornier
FB	Fighter-bomber
Fg. Off.	Flying Officer (RAF)
Flt. Sgt.	Flight Sergeant
FRU	Fleet Requirements Unit
FS	Federal Standard
Gp. Cpt.	Group Captain (RAF)
HQ	Headquarters
IFF	Identification Friend or Foe
kg	Kilogram
KG	Kampfgeschwader (Luftwaffe)
lb	Pound
lt	Litre
Lt. Cdr.	Lieutenant Commander (Royal Navy)
MAC	Mediterranean Air Command
MAP	Ministry of Air Production
Me.	Messerschmitt
Mk	Mark
ML	ML Aviation Ltd.
MU	Maintenance Unit (RAF)
NF	Night Fighter
No.	Number
OTU	Operational Training Unit
PFF	Pathfinder Force
Plt. Off.	Pilot Officer (RAF)
PR	Photographic reconnaissance
PRU	Photo-reconnaissance Unit
RAAF	Royal Australian Air Force
RAE	Royal Aircraft Establishment
RAF	Royal Air Force
RATO	Rocket Assisted Take-Off
RCAF	Royal Canadian Air Force
RNAS	Royal Naval Air Station
Sgt.	Sergeant
Sqn.	Squadron
Sqn. Ldr.	Squadron Leader (RAF)
T	Trainer
TF	Torpedo/Fighter
TI	Target indicator
TR	Torpedo/Reconnaissance
TT	Target Tug
UK	United Kingdom
USAAF	United States Army Air Force
VJ-Day	Victory in Japan Day
Wg. Cdr.	Wing Commander (RAF)
W/O	Warrant Officer
/G	Suffix letter added to aircraft serial number denoting that it carried special equipment and was to be guarded at all times

A sad sight, a line up of T Mk IIIs and FB Mk VIs await final scrapping at Seletar, Singapore in the late 1940s *(via S.Howe)*

The Concept

Chapter 1

The idea of an unarmed bomber, which could survive in an operational wartime environment was, during the 1930s, one which the Air Staff simply could not accept. Some of these men had been in service during the First World War and they remembered the losses suffered by unarmed machines in the face of faster enemy fighters. Prior to the D.H.98, De Havilland's designs had been mainly for civilian application, although the D.H.82 Tiger Moth was supplied to the RAF for crew training duties. During the severe financial constraints of the 1920s and 30s, De Havilland had concentrated on the civil sector and had only looked at military specifications in a very limited way. The famous Moth series, which included the D.H.60 Moth, Gipsy Moth, Tiger Moth, Puss Moth, Fox Moth, Leopard Moth and Hornet Moth, were all designed for the private owner and the many flying clubs and schools which operated during this period. For the fledgling civil airlines, De Havilland offered the D.H.84 Dragon, D.H.89 Rapide, D.H.90 Dragonfly and the four-engined D.H.86. At this stage it should be remembered that airlines were very much in their infancy and were unable to operate without the benefit of subsidies from the government. This of course meant that only limited purchasing finance was available to such firms and it was here that De Havilland found a ready market for their economical designs.

The concepts which led to the Mosquito are usually linked directly with the D.H.88 Comet racer and D.H.91 Albatross airliner, but to be truthful they arose much farther back than that. Captain (later Sir) Geoffrey de Havilland had, during the First World war, concluded that superior speed, range and operational altitude were virtues in a bomber which offered far greater survival rates than purely defensive armament could ever hope to achieve. Without the added weight penalty of gun turrets and the crew to operate them, the aircraft would be lighter and therefore able to operate at higher speeds. To this end the D.H.4 design was created towards the end of the war and it is from this original background that the D.H.98 emerged. After the First World War and during the inter-war period, De Havilland and his company had remained very much in the civil sector of the aviation market, although occasionally they had offered prototypes for various military specifications. It was during the 1930s that a De Havilland design was to capture the world's imagination, and make the firm a household name. This design was the D.H.88.

Sir MacPherson Robertson, a wealthy Australian confectionery magnate, decided to celebrate the centenary of the state of Victoria in 1934 by offering £15,000 in prize money for an air race. This event was to become known as the MacRobertson Trophy and it was staged between Mildenhall and Melbourne, a distance of 12,300 miles. At this time it was an unprecedented distance and there were no British aircraft types which seemed able to complete the course. The race was split into two parts, the first being a straight speed dash offering £10,000, while the other was a handicapped section with £2,000 worth of prize money. De Havilland considered this race and its requirements and decided that a small aircraft powered by two

The DH-4 high-speed bomber of WWI, was the basis from which the D.H.98 design originated

Gipsy Six 200hp engines, and a crew of just two, could go the course. The design and building of the type, plus its field support throughout the race, would cost £20,000 to £30,000 and this was only if three could be utilised. At this stage one should consider the great financial constraints that were imposed throughout the world, and with only the possibility of £12,000 worth of prize money, could De Havilland truly afford to invest £30,000 in a project which would basically be just for PR and prestige? There seemed to be little time wasted in deciding to go ahead with the idea, (which was also to prove the case with the D.H.98 design), and in late 1933 adverts were placed in *The Aeroplane* and *Flight* offering to build aircraft for the race at a unit price of £5,000 each. From these adverts De Havilland received three orders; the first was from Amy (*nee Johnson*) and James Mollison, another from a wealthy racing motorist, Bernard Rubin, and the third from A.O.Edwards, the managing director of the Grosvenor House Hotel in London. By February 1934 design and construction of these racers had begun and over the next seven months the three machines were built in great secrecy. On the 8th September 1934, just six weeks before the race, the first D.H.88 Comet was flown. The type was powered by two 230hp Gipsy Six R engines and was of all-wood construction. Fuel tankage for the race consisted of 258 gal in two tanks forward of the pilot. This was supplemented by a third tank of just 20 gal behind the cockpit. Looking back on the type from today's perspective, it seems to have followed a well thought-out route to achieve success. However, ideas such as a retractable undercarriage, variable-pitch propellers and a totally streamline shape, were not the 'norm' of this era and the design was therefore very much a trend-setter, not a 'follower'. The use

The De Havilland D.H.88 Comet (G-ACSS) was the progenitor of the Mosquito
(Hawker-Siddeley)

of variable-pitch propellers at this time was a great step forward, and in February 1934, Messrs F.T.Hearle and A.E.Hagg of De Havilland visited Hamilton Standard in the USA to try to negotiate license production of their variable-pitch propellers for the D.H.88. In the end however, just prior to the race, the D.H.88 was fitted with Ratier propellers from France, as the Hamilton ones had proved unsuitable. However, the negotiations and license agreement with Hamilton were to allow De Havilland to become one of the leading propeller manufacturers during the Second World War, which was to be of great benefit to a number of designs, including the D.H.98.

The race itself had initially been lead by the Mollinsons in G-ACPS *Black Magic,* but they had to pull out at Allahabad, India and the lead was taken by C.W.A.Scott and Tom Campbell-Black in G-ACSS *Grosvenor House*. Despite low oil pressure on one engine, this team went on to win the race in a time of 70hr, 54min, 18sec. The third Comet, flown by O. Cathcart Jones and E. N. Waller, ended the race in fourth position overall. With the success of G-ACSS *Grosvenor House* against such advanced airlines as the Douglas DC-2 and Boeing 247, the idea of a fast streamlined airliner came into the fertile minds of the design team at De Havillands. At this time no thought was given to a military aircraft utilising the aesthetically pleasing lines, wooden construction and advanced features of the D.H.88; instead thoughts turned to a new four engine airliner. This machine, which was to become the sleek D.H.91 Albatross, was proposed to the Air Ministry just three weeks after the success of the D.H.88 in the MacRobertson race. The initial reception at the ministry was icy, but eventually an order did arrive and it was for two experimental mailplanes able to carry 1,000lb of payload over 2,500 miles against a 40mph headwind. The D.H.91 made its first flight on the 20th May 1937 and it cruised at 210mph and offered a far superior gross ton-mile per gall of fuel than both the D.H.88 and D.H.66 Hercules airliner. This was achieved thanks to the type's extremely streamlined shape and the use of advanced wooden construction. The type used four Gipsy 12 engines and these adopted reverse-flow cooling via leading-edge radiators, a feature which was to soon appear on the D.H.98. Imperial Airways ordered five of a 23-seat passenger version of

The sleek D.H.91 Albatross, an all-wooden airliner. De Havilland made a number of studies relating to the possible conversion of this type for military use *(BAe)*

the Albatross and these began operations on the 25th November 1938. At this time however more and more airlines were turning to the American Douglas and Lockheed designs, so the market for the D.H.91 was very limited and only a few saw operational service, with Imperial Airways. These were impressed into RAF service after the start of WWII.

During the 1930s the Royal Air Force was in the midst of its Expansion Scheme and by 1934 it was obvious to those in the Air Ministry that the current bomber types would need to be replaced by 1940. To this end a new specification, B.1/35, was drawn up for a medium bomber and this was followed in August 1936 by a revised specification, B.13/36. It called for a two-engined medium bomber, with a crew of four or six, that would require good range, speed and bomb load. These factors all meant that the type was to have a high cruising speed, to reduce the amount of time spent over enemy territory. At this stage tail and nose gun-turrets were specified and the type was to have a range of 3,000 miles, a top speed of 275mph at 15,000 feet and a bomb-load of 4,000lb. On top of this the Air Ministry hoped that the type could be adopted and converted for bomber, general reconnaissance or general purpose duties, and to make matters worse, they also wanted it to carry two torpedoes. De Havilland had already been looking at two-engine developments of the D.H.91 and these included the D.H.96 transport and D.H.97 trainer projects. They concluded that they could meet the requirements of specification P.13/36 with a twin-engined version of the D.H.91, if catapult assisted launch was used to achieve the required range. In the end however, other commitments meant that the type was not continued with and the Air Ministry sought tenders without taking much notice of the D.H. design. In the end B.13/36 lead to the Avro Manchester and, in its initial form, the Handley Page Halifax, both types being powered by the Rolls Royce Vulture engine.

By April 1938, De Havilland had decided that a twin engine version of the D.H.91, powered by the Rolls Royce Merlin, would meet the needs of the RAF's next generation bomber. They did not feel that specification B.13/36 would produce a good bomber, and it certainly could not be met with a twin-engine type. Design ideas continued to be studied on the new twin-engine type, but because of the limited power offered by the Rolls Royce Merlin at this time, other engines were also considered. These included the Bristol HE 1M radial and the complex Napier Sabre 24-cylinder 'H' engine. Both would offer greater power than the current Merlin, but the extra weight of each was considered a penalty. By October 1938, De Havilland had once again turned their attention to an unarmed bomber which utilised the speed of a fighter to evade enemy interception. The design was to be of wooden construction, with a span of 61ft 6in and a crew of three. Initial armament layouts included six or eight forward firing machine-guns, plus one or two manually operated guns and a tail turret. The inclusion of all this 'standard equipment' as the Ministry called it, was totally unacceptable to De Havilland and therefore the design reverted to its unarmed layout. The use of wood in the construction of the type was based on its success in the previous D.H.88 and D.H.91 designs, but also for a number of other reasons. The first was that other than in a torsion plane, wood had the same strength as steel. The bonded wooden surface would be completely smooth, therefore offering far less wind resistance and so offering better top speed and fuel consumption. De Havillands had massive experience with wooden construction and in the event of a war, wood was not a strategic material and would continue to be in ample supply. They knew all too well that if war occurred, the metal industry would be fully committed, but the wood-working industry would not and therefore many subcontractors in the form of coach builders and furniture makers could be utilised to produce components for the type.

During 1938 De Havillands had also been working on their new all-metal airliner, the D.H.95 Flamingo, and consideration was given to adapting this design to meet the bomber specification. By now all work on the unarmed wooden bomber had been designated 'D.H.98 Reconnaissance-Bomber' and it was obvious that the only way to make this design work was to remove the armament and reduce the crew to two. This idea was continually raised with the officials at the Air Ministry, but fell on increasingly deaf ears. The officials at the Air Ministry at this time were very concerned that the enemy would develop a fighter faster than this radical new bomber, and the thought of sending crews out in an unarmed bomber in that situation was totally unacceptable to them. The other factor, not often considered when looking at official resistance to this design, is the fact that the type was to utilise the new Rolls Royce Merlin engine, and it was known that types already in service, or about to join, were nearly all using this engine, and there was simply no additional production capacity to allow another Merlin-powered design to be considered.

In September 1938 the situation in Europe worsened and De Havilland Ltd. was moved to approach the Air Ministry with a view to discussing their radical new design. Both Geoffrey de Havilland and Charles Walker went to the Air Ministry during this month and they were met by considerable scepticism from officials. The Ministry seemed to take a dim view of De Havillands, as they saw it as a firm which had shunned official specifications in the 1920s and 30s, and the whole idea of an unarmed, wooden bomber was just too radical for them. It was turned down. When war finally broke out in September 1939, Geoffrey de Havilland once again went to the Air Ministry to propose his radical new bomber. At this stage production of all the civil types produced by De Havilland had ceased, with production of the Moth Minor moving to Australia and the only production being undertaken by the parent firm consisting of the sub-contracted construction of 150 Airspeed Oxford aircraft and an order for 660 Tiger Moth trainers and 130 Queen Bee target drones. To undertake detailed design and development of the D.H.98 was well within the capacity of De Havilland at this time, and during September 1939 two new studies were instigated. Each looked at an aircraft which could carry 1,000lb of bombs for 1,500 miles and had two engines offering a maximum take-off power of 1,300hp each. The first design had a span of 48ft and was estimated to have a cruising speed of 332mph at 15,00ft and a top speed of 419mph. The second design had a span of 51ft 3in and offered a cruising speed of 325mph and a top speed of 409mph. Once again other powerplants were considered and the use of the new Rolls Royce Griffon or a 16-cylinder development of the Napier Dagger was considered, along with the Napier Sabre once again. Visits to the Air Ministry at this time no longer met with outright rejection, but the Air Staff were still very sceptical. To understand why the Air Staff were so sceptical one must consider that at this point they already had front-line bombers in service and new designs underway, which were faster than the front-line fighters of the day. The problem with this thinking was that one of the front-line fighters of the day was the Gloster Gladiator, a biplane with a top speed of just 253 mph. Designs such as the Blenheim were indeed quicker than this type, but when one considers that the current new fighter in the Luftwaffe was the Messerschmitt Bf 109, a monoplane with a top speed of 354 mph (570 km/h), over 100mph faster than the Gladiator, one can see that the Air Staff seemed to be living in a bit of a dream world. The arrival of the Bf 109 in the Spanish Civil War had awoken their ideas and it was obvious that new designs with far greater top speeds would be required. The Air Staff did not however see the need for fighter speed to evade interception, instead they felt that good defensive armament would protect the bombers as they flew to and from the targets. Not every company was thinking along these lines though and in late 1939 other companies were also looking at the fast bomber concept. De Havilland had already done the basic design work to create this fast bomber and by November they handed detailed design investigations to the Air Ministry and these included the addition of the tail turret, just in case the Air Ministry had to have this defensive armament in place. The inclusion of such a contraption reduced the top speed by nearly 60 mph, so during a meeting with ACM (later Sir) Wilfred Freeman KCB, DSO, MC, the Air Member for Research and Development, on the 22nd November 1939, De Havilland stressed how important it was not to include a turret and that fighter speed could only be achieved if this were the case. This was agreed and tests in the wind tunnel at RAE Farnborough were started. Two initial designs were considered; the first had a crew of three, with the third member sitting aft of the wing and having viewing panels with rearward and downward vision. This type was to carry two 500lb or four 250lb bombs or four 20mm cannon, provision for which had been made in the lower fuselage. The other design was to have a crew of two seated in tandem and either four 20mm cannon or three F.24 cameras. By December 1939 however the design suffered a serious setback, as officers of Bomber Command stated that they had no place for an unarmed bomber in their force. The heavy losses being suffered by armed types such as the Wellington in operations over Europe, made an unarmed type seem totally ridiculous. They did however agree that if the type could fly fast and high that they would have a use for it as a reconnaissance platform. The armed twin-seat version of the design was now discarded, although provision for the cannon

The D.H.95 Flamingo. Studies were also carried out to convert this type for military use, however its metal construction would have placed a considerable extra burden on the metal-airframe industry *(BAe)*

was retained, and development of the reconnaissance version started. On the 12th December 1939 the Air Ministry decided to order a prototype and this was followed on the 29th December by another conference in which the speed, bomb-load and operational range of this new design was discussed. All of this formed the basis of a new specification, B.1/40, and this called for a two-engine design powered by the Rolls Royce RM3SM Merlin engines, a loaded weight of 17,150lb for the PR version and 18,845lb for the bomber version. The cruising speed was set at 327mph at 26,600ft, with a maximum speed at 23,700ft of 397mph. Fuel tankage was to be 555 gal and this would offer a range of 1,480 miles at 343mph and 24,900ft. The service ceiling of this new design was to be 32,100ft. No other restricting factors, such as turrets etc, were imposed by the Air Ministry and therefore the design team at D.H., consisting of R.E. Bishop (chief designer), W.A. Tamblin (senior designer) and R.M. Clarkson (head of aerodynamics), plus the men from Rolls Royce, swung into action.

By October 5th 1939, the design team working on the D.H.98 had moved from Hatfield for security from bombing raids, to a moated manor house, called Salisbury Hall, near London Colney. Nell Gwynne and Charles II had spent time in this house some 300 years previously and now the D.H. team moved in to develop the new design. A hanger, disguised as a barn, was erected on the cabbage patch across the moat from the house and it was here that the D.H.98 was born. By now, with official backing, it was time to consider a name. The true story behind the choice of the name for the D.H.98 will never be known, as it has faded into the mists of time, but it seems likely that the name reflected the nature of the machine. The team must have thought 'what was fast, small, has a lethal sting and can strike over a wide area?': of course, the MOSQUITO!

Concept Becomes Reality

Chapter 2

After all the uncertainty about the future of the D.H.98 throughout the previous two years, an official order for fifty Mosquito bombers and reconnaissance aircraft was placed with De Havilland by the Air Ministry on the 1st March 1940. These machines (serialled W4050-4099) included the prototype, which was under construction at Salisbury Hall. Many wood-working firms, hitherto limited in their war work commitments, were contacted to undertake, sub-contract, the construction of this new type. These included Gommes, the maker of 'G Plan' furniture at High Wycombe, Dancer & Hearne and Mulliners of Chiswick.

With the fall of France in 1940, the newly created Ministry of Aircraft Production, under Lord Beaverbrook, re-appraised all new aircraft designs and attempted once again to axe the Mosquito. Production was to be concentrated on five major types: the Hurricane, Spitfire, Wellington, Whitley and Blenheim. De Havillands were instructed to drop the Mosquito and concentrate on Tiger Moth and Airspeed Oxford production, which was considered to be of far greater importance. On three separate occasions Lord Beaverbrook told ACM Freeman to stop work on the Mosquito. He omitted to actually issue a firm instruction however and at no time was an official order passed to Hatfield or, therefore, to the team at Salisbury Hall. Because of the limited use of strategic material in the design and the fact that the small team were working at a remote site, the construction of the prototype was able to continue. The project was reinstated however in July 1940, but not until De Havilland had proved that the type did not use excessive amounts of strategic material and had promised (with some reservation) that they could deliver 50 Mosquitoes to front line service by July 1941!

The greatest strength of the design at this stage was certainly the limited amount of strategic material that it used. The use of wood really was the saving grace of the type, but D.H. also used castings in place of machined components, therefore reducing the work and time involved in producing these parts. Previously De Havilland had used a rubber-in-compression suspension system and this was reinstated for the D.H.98 design in place of any oleo-pneumatic system. The use of such a system, considering the weight of the D.H.98, may seem odd, but the system was to prove extremely effective and far more resilient to the operational rigours of a war environment than any oleo-pneumatic system.

On the 18th July 1940, De Havilland was instructed to finish one of the prototypes as a fighter and this was to become the F.II (W4052). Interest in a fighter version of the Mosquito design had been limited, but you will recall that one of the bomber options was armed with four cannon and the area for the installation of these guns was retained, so modification to a fighter was quite easy for the D.H. team. The F.II was eventually fitted with four 20mm Hispano cannon in the ventral fuselage and four Browning .303in machine-guns in the nose, and a production contract for this version was eventually issued on the 16th November 1940. By the beginning of August 1940 the

The mock-up of the Mosquito takes shape on the 16th June 1940. This mock-up is made of wood 'skinned' with brown paper (De Havilland)

second fuselage shell had been completed and the wings were about to be skinned by Vanden Plas at Hendon, North London. Many of the metal fittings were being produced at Hatfield and all looked to be going well when, on the 3rd October 1940, Hatfield was bombed. The raider, a Ju 88 of KG 77, had set out from France on a bombing run to a biscuit factory in Reading and being unable to find the primary target due to bad weather, the pilot set course east and came right across the airfield at Hatfield, which he bombed. The raid left 80% of the finished castings for the Mosquito destroyed as well as resulting in the death of 21 and injury of 70 workers. There was little other damage to dispersed Mosquito production, but the raid was a setback. The loss of so many people was felt personally by all the team at D.H. and this gave them far greater impetus to develop a type which would hit back hard. The raid also highlighted the need to disperse production and although this had already been in the minds of the executives for a while before the raid, the aftermath of it also gave them greater resolve to set up production of Mosquito in a large number of satellite premises.

On November 3rd, the first prototype was loaded onto a trailer at Salisbury Hall and sent the short distance by road to

The prototype (W4050) lands at Hatfield on the afternoon of the 10th January 1941 at the end of the trials to investigate the airflow break-up around the rear of the engine nacelles (S.Howe)

The prototype (W4050) fitted with a mock-up of a turret behind the cockpit. The aircraft flew with this installation in July 1941 *(De Havilland)*

Hatfield. The components were placed in a bomb-proof hanger and assembled. The aircraft was to carry a B-class registration, E0234, and was painted bright yellow to aid AA gunners' recognition of the type during test flights. The first flight was drawing near and taxying trials began on the 24th. All was well, so Geoffrey de Havilland Jnr and John E. Walker climbed aboard the aircraft and at 3.45 on the afternoon of the 25th, the aircraft flew for the first time. This initial test lasted for 30 minutes and during this time an indicated air speed of 220 mph was achieved. At the time of this first flight the aircraft featured Handley Page leading-edge slats, although these were locked shut and taped over during the initial flight. As the aircraft showed no tendency to dip a wing near the stall during further flights, the use of these slats was considered unnecessary and they were not fitted to any of the production aircraft.

Throughout December 1940 and the beginning of 1941, the prototype flew regularly and production of components for the production versions was moving apace. Fourteen fuselage shells had been produced by the middle of December, and although the sub-contractors who were making the wings had to deal with working to much finer tolerances and using glue in the correct amount and manner, some 16 sets of wings were also completed. It was during this period that blistering, caused by heat build-up, was noted for the first time on the engine cowlings of the Mosquito. This was a problem which was to continue for some considerable time during the type's development and was only fully rectified when the engine nacelle shape was revised and new exhaust systems were used. In the first month of 1941, De Havilland was informed that the prototype was to be followed by a photo-reconnaissance aircraft. The Mosquito was designed as a bomber by De Havilland, but Bomber Command wanted to use the type for photo-reconnaissance and therefore the next aircraft was built for this role. This machine, serial W4051, was to be followed by the pure fighter prototype (W4052) and then 19 production PR Mk 1s. The remainder of the initial order of 50 was to be made up of fighters and the Ministry of Aircraft Production informed De Havilland that the next order for 150 machines would all be bombers. By the end of January the prototype, now coded W4050, had been painted with camouflage (Dark Green and Earth Brown) over the yellow under surfaces, to allow the aircraft to fly to A.&A.E.E (Aircraft & Armament Experimental Establishment) Boscombe Down, near Salisbury in Wiltshire, to undertake service acceptance trials. The aircraft arrived on the third Wednesday of the month and the next day it was subjected to a precise weighing before flight testing could begin. At this stage the 'boffins' were extremely dubious about what De Havilland claimed this aircraft could do, but during flight trials over the next few days the claims were all proven to be true. With a wetted wing area nearly twice that of a Spitfire, this two-engined machine could out-fly that type by over 20 mph and at a much higher altitude as well (22,000 ft). Late in the afternoon on the 24th February however, disaster struck when the aircraft was being taxied across the airfield at Boscombe and the tail wheel caught in a rut. The difficulties already experienced with the type's castoring tailwheel compounded this problem when it locked and the resulting force fractured the rear fuselage aft of the access door on the starboard side. Initially De Havilland thought that this would kill the project, as the machine seemed too fragile to be used operationally. However this was not the case and the ease of repair which was to return so many damaged Mosquitoes to action later in the war was shown to good effect now. The fuselage of the second prototype (W4051) was shipped to Boscombe to replace the damaged one on W4050 and this therefore meant that W4051 was now fitted

The second aircraft (W4051) served as the PR Mk 1 prototype and was fitted with a production fuselage, after its original was used to replace the damaged one on W4050 *(De Havilland)*

Concept Becomes Reality 11

The prototype in the new hanger erected for it at Salisbury Hall, photographed here in 1974 when the aircraft was still in a camouflage and yellow colour scheme *(S.Howe)*

The prototype at Salisbury Hall as she is today, in an overall yellow scheme *(S.Howe)*

with a production fuselage and could go directly into service with the RAF, one of the very few prototypes ever to have achieved this. W4050 now continued its trial work and it was soon apparent that this new aircraft could fly at 392 mph TAS at 22,000 ft and achieve a ceiling of 34,000 ft.

During these trials one of the only vices in the design was found. This was some severe buffeting of the tail, which was encountered at about 240 mph. The cause of this was traced to the break-up of the airflow around the rear of each engine nacelle. A number of different methods were tried to cure this. Initially wool tufts were fixed to the nacelle sides to study the airflow characteristics and these were followed by slipstream rectifiers, which were basically metal strips fitted to the rear of the nacelle and under each wing, to act as a slot and give a cleaner airflow. In the end however further trials showed that the best way to overcome this problem was to extend the nacelle back past the wing trailing edge, and this solution was adopted for all marks after the initial bomber series. The fitment of ejector style exhaust pipes did raise the top speed, so they were also fitted to all production versions. During the initial trails of W4050 however, cooling intakes were added to the front edge of each nacelle and these took cold air over the exhaust manifolds in an attempt to cure the blistering problems which had occurred right from the start of flight testing.

By the end of 1940, the 'Scourge of the Atlantic', in the form of the long range Focke Wulf Fw 200 Condor, had become such a great threat that the Air Ministry issued a specification (F.21/40) for a long-range night and escort fighter. De Havilland were asked if the Mosquito could meet this requirement and with the fitment of four machine-guns and the ventral armament of four 20mm cannon, the type seemed admirably suited. The Ministry however wanted the machine-guns in a turret (Bristol B Mk XI), as this offered far great operational flexibility than fixed guns. To prove the effect of such an item, W4050 was fitted with a mock-up, just aft of the cockpit. The aircraft flew for the first time in this configuration on the 24th July and it reduced the TAS by some 20 mph; it also generally reduced some areas of performance and endurance fell below five hours. Further trials with a turret were requested and two F.IIs, W4053 and W4057, were flown from Salisbury Hall to Hatfield to undertake these trials and were fitted with mock-ups of the Bristol B Mk IX turret. Both two and four gun turret arrangements were considered along with six fixed machine-guns in the dorsal spine of the Mosquito, which fired upwards, in a manner similar to the German Schräge Musik system. In the end however the Mosquito was never used as an escort fighter, as this role was initially met by catapult-launched Hurricanes from merchant ships and later from the fighters aboard escort carriers.

One of the most famous incidents in the Mosquito's history was to occur just a few days before the fighter prototype flew out of Salisbury Hall. On the 13th May 1941 a German spy, Karel Richter, parachuted into a field close to Salisbury Hall. Having

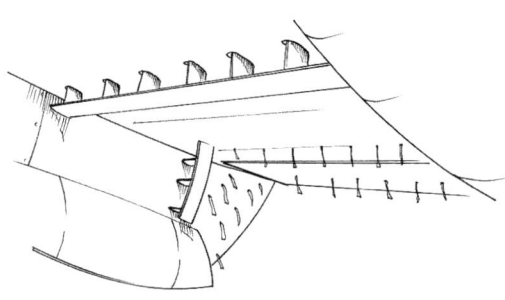

These were the 'Flamingo-type slots' fitted to the prototype, which were tested in an attempt to reduce the breakup of the airflow at the end of the engine nacelles. The area was covered in wool tufts, as depicted here, for flight trials on the 10th January 1941 *(© A.Oliver)*

laid low for a few days, he started to move towards London, unaware of the significance of Salisbury Hall. He walked down the main road towards London in the early hours of the 15th and was unfortunate enough to be asked the way by a passing lorry driver. Richter could not help and was quite aggressive towards the driver, so when the driver came across a Police Constable further down the road, he informed him of the strange gentleman he had just met. Richter was soon apprehended by the P.C. and was taken into custody. As a result of this Richter was executed as a spy at Wandsworth Prison on the 10th December 1941. Had Richter just waited a few hours more he would have witnessed the first flight of the fighter prototype, because on the evening of the 15th May, Geoffrey de Havilland flew the overall black fighter out of the meadow alongside Salisbury Hall. The reason for this odd location for the first flight was a simple one: taking the aircraft apart and shipping it to Hatfield, then re-assembling it all took time, and this would all be saved if the aircraft could be flown at Salisbury Hall. The problem was that the meadow alongside offered just a 450 yard run and there were both hedgerows and a tree to consider. To allow the aircraft to cope with the very soft ground in the meadow, it had been fitted with over-sized tyres from the D.H.95 Flamingo for this initial flight. The type also differed in having larger tailplanes than W4050, which were to become common to all future production Mosquitoes, and extended

The frill style of Youngman airbrake is shown here fitted to W4052. In the end the idea was dropped as lowering the undercarriage was found to be as effective
(Hawker Siddeley Ltd)

wing tips which brought the span up to 52 ft 2 in (16.25m). Other differences between the fighter and the PR version included the armoured bulkhead in the nose, strengthened wing-spars, a flat bullet-proof windscreen, the repositioned crew-access door and a stick-type control column in place of the 'spectacle' version. By the 20th May this machine was at Hatfield undergoing firing tests of the cannon in the firing butts. On the 18th June 1942 it was passed to A.&A.E.E Boscombe Down for handling trials, and during later flight trials achieved a top speed of 378 mph. Development of the type now followed two different paths; the prototype was designed as an F Mk II, but with the fitting of A.I. radar in July it became a night fighter and therefore was also the prototype for the NF Mk II. Only the NF.II saw service with the RAF, as the F Mk II was not required by them and only one was ever built. This machine was passed to D.H. in Australia and was used as a pattern aircraft for them to start production. Initially the A.I. Mk IV radar was fitted to the NF Mk II, but this was later replaced by the Mk V version. Each type used the 'arrowhead' antenna in the nose (transmitter) and the angled twin dipoles on the starboard upper and lower mainplane (receiver). Production NF Mk IIs also featured shrouded exhaust units in place of the 'saxophone' type used in previous examples. A number of early NF Mk IIs were converted with the removal of the radar and fitment of *Gee* radio navigation aids and were operated by No. 23 Squadron from Malta. These machines were known as the NF Mk II (Intruder).

The top speed of a Mosquito was always a problem for airborne interception, and methods of slowing the aircraft down during the attack were considered. One such scheme was the fitment of a Youngman segmented air-brake around the rear mid-fuselage. This unit was tried in many forms with 'frills' from 10in to 16in lengths, with and without the 'frills' and even with a section cut out of the top to reduce the effect on the vertical fin. In the end however the brake was found to reduce the time taken to decelerate from 250mph to 150mph in level flight by a third and this was considered too small a margin to take the item into production. In the end lowering the undercarriage was settled upon as a suitable method of slowing down during an interception.

The photo-reconnaissance version of the Mosquito was hot on the heels of the fighter and was ready for flight trials to commence on the 24th May. It should be noted that at this time the first production PR Mk I was entering the paint shop at Hatfield, so this type was set to be the first available for RAF operational use. The prototype (W4051) however started trials work and although some problems with the powerplants were experienced during the initial flights, these were overcome and the aircraft then underwent a series of trials connected with different styles of exhaust stacks, camera fits and fuel consumption tests. Fitting a camera to the Mosquito was not that easy and trials were conducted to deal with the many complex problems including camera lens misting, vibration and even heating. By the middle of September 1941, however, most of these problems had been solved and therefore W4055, one of the first production PR Mk Is delivered to No.1 PRU (Photo-Reconnaissance Unit) RAF Benson, undertook the first operational sortie by a Mosquito.

It had taken just over eight months since the prototype flew to achieve this goal and the Mosquito had indeed proved itself to be a 'Wonder'.

The prototype NF Mk II (W4052) flew for the first time from a meadow at the back of Salisbury Hall on the 15th May 1941 (via S.Howe)

Concept Becomes Reality | 13

Into Action

Chapter 3

So much interest had been shown in the photo-reconnaissance version of the Mosquito, that the prototype (W4051) was test flown on the 12th June 1941 by the commanding officer of No.1 PRU, RAF Benson (Wg. Cdr. G. Tuttle), before the aircraft had even started its service trials at Boscombe Down on the 25th June. Because this machine was fitted with a production fuselage, since its original one had been used to repair the first prototype after its taxying accident at Boscombe Down, it was able to be used operationally. On the 13th July 1941, W4051 landed at RAF Benson and by 17th September this machine had been joined by a further four production PR Mk 1s. These production PR Mk 1s featured a few changes from the prototype and these included the replacement of the metal-skinned ailerons with fabric ones and the fitment of 700-gallon long-range internal tanks, instead of the 550-gallon tanks of W4051. The first two machines, W4060 and W4061 were fitted with this equipment, but the next two, W4062 and W4063, were also tropicalised. This modification included the fitment of different radiator-flap settings as well as some revisions in the intake and coolant systems which would allow the type to operate in the Mediterranean. All of the production PR versions could carry one oblique and three vertical cameras and they featured the short nacelles and smaller tailplanes of the prototype. It was at 11.30 am on the 17th September that W4055, a production PR Mk I, flew the first ever operational sortie by a Mosquito. Piloted by Sqn. Ldr. Clerke the aircraft set course for a photographic sortie to Brest and then on to the Franco-Spanish border. Unfortunately an electrical fault meant that the camera installation did not operate properly during this flight, but the aircraft itself proved to be admirably suited to the task. The speed and operational ceiling of the Mosquito made it almost impossible for the Luftwaffe to catch and No 1 PRU at Benson used the early PR Mk Is singly on operations with great success. The first operational loss of a Mosquito occurred in December 1941, when W4055 was shot down by AA fire near Bergen in Norway.

Operations with the PR versions were intense and during the next few months sorties were mounted to Stavanger, Bergen and other sites in Norway and to Keil and Wilhelmshaven, where photographs of the *Scharnhorst* and *Gneisenau* were obtained. Operations were also undertaken to Poland and East Prussia, the flight to East Prussia being the longest PR sortie of the war in Europe. Prior to the Commando raids on St Nazaire W4051 photographed the French coast, and on the 24th April W4059 reached Augsburg to obtain clear photographs of the damage inflicted by Bomber Command on the MAN diesel engine works within the city.

During January 1942 W4062 and W4063, the tropicalised PR Mk 1s, left the UK for operational use in Malta and Egypt. Photo-reconnaissance missions continued and by 1942 eighty-eight had been completed with the loss of only the one airframe. Supply of the PR versions was a problem, however, as many of the initial order had been diverted and converted to bombers. No 1 PRU at Benson did however obtain two NF Mk IIs (DD615 and DD620) which were at an MU having their AI Mk V radar fitted, and fitted these with cameras at Benson on the 12th & 17th April, to supplement their small number of operational PR machines. These two converted airframes were later joined by two others, DD659 and W4089. It was in W4089 that Flt. Lt. Victor Ricketts DFC and Sgt. Boris Lukhmanoff were lost during

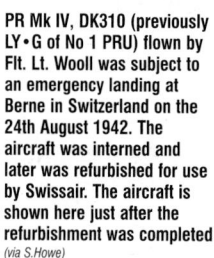

PR Mk IV, DK310 (previously LY•G of No 1 PRU) flown by Flt. Lt. Wooll was subject to an emergency landing at Berne in Switzerland on the 24th August 1942. The aircraft was interned and later was refurbished for use by Swissair. The aircraft is shown here just after the refurbishment was completed *(via S.Howe)*

This side view of DK310 has been retouched, as the original included a long pitot tube extending out of the nose glazing *(via S.Howe)*

an operation to Starsborg and Ingolstadt on the 11th June 1942. This was the unit's second operational loss.

Development of the Williamson F.52 aerial camera had been completed by the RAE and this type entered RAF service in the summer of 1942, quickly being adopted for use in the PR Mk I and PR Mk IV now in operational use by No.1 PRU at Benson. With the shortage of PR versions, it was decided to allow a small number of the fifty B Mk IV bombers currently in production to be released and converted, to PR standard. Initially DZ411 and DZ419 were converted and this proved to be so successful that a further twenty-seven were also converted. These machines became the PR Mk IV. Two additional B MK IVs, DK284 and W4067, were also converted at Benson by No 1 PRU and W4067 was to be the only PR Mk IV Series I ever produced.

Long-range flights were becoming the trade-mark of the PR Mosquito, and on the 8th July 1942 a number of flights were started to and from Russia. The target for these operations was the battleship *Tirpitz*, and during one flight a Mosquito found the ship and photographed it, before landing to refuel at Murmansk and flying straight back to RAF Leuchars. Flights of four to six hours were commonplace for the PR Mosquitos and improvements in the type were always being made. The fitment of ejector-style exhausts to the PR Mk IVs, in place of the 'saxophone' versions in the PR Mk I,

resulted in an increase in top speed of some 10 mph, and PR Mk IV DZ523 was experimentally fitted with a blister in the upper canopy to increase rearward vision By the middle of 1943 the PR Mk Is and Mk IVs were becoming vulnerable to the new German fighters and all operations transferred were to night, while day operations were undertaken by the new generation of PR Mosquito.

It was during an operation to Venice that Flt. Lt. Wooll in DK310 (LY·G) experienced cooling problems and had to shut down an engine. Being too far from home, he realised that he would have to make an emergency landing and therefore decided to land at Belpmoos airfield, near Berne in Switzerland. Attempts to destroy the machine failed and it was interned by the Swiss authorities. This machine was the first intact Mosquito to fall into the hands of anyone outside the Allies, and although the Swiss were neutral the Air Ministry feared that the Mosquito would be passed into German hands. The crew were soon exchanged for two German fighter pilots, but the aircraft remained at Berne. High level talks between the Swiss and British resulted in an agreement on the 1st August 1943, which allowed the Swiss government to fly DK310 in Swiss markings. Initially the aircraft was coded B-4 and was operated to train crews for the Swiss A.F. On 13th October 1943 the aircraft was handed over to Swissair, registered HB-IMO, who intended to use it for night mail flights. In the end this idea came to nothing, and after six pilots had been trained on the type it was handed back to the Swiss A.F. in February 1944.

Production of the bomber version of the Mosquito had been very restricted and although this was the task De Havilland had always envisaged for the type, it was not until July 1941 that an official order for the bomber was received. Delay in the placement of an order for the type as a bomber was due mainly to the fact that the Air Ministry could not believe that the

aircraft would achieve the performance claimed by de Havilland. To this end W4050 underwent a lengthy series of trials at Boscombe Down and it was only once the superior performance of the type was apparent that an order was placed. This order came in the form of a revision to the existing agreement for the PR version and was issued on the 19th July 1941. The revision called for nine machines, W4064 to W4072, to be converted to what was initially known as the PRU/Bomber Conversion, although they later became the B Mk IV Series I. These machines featured the short nacelles of the PR Mk I and as they were converted from PR machines, they were able to carry both bombs and cameras. The first true bomber prototype, as W4050 was purely an aerodynamic test bed, was W4057 and this machine was completed in the third week of September 1941 and was flown to Boscombe Down on the 27th. After trials at A.&A.E.E Boscombe Down the aircraft returned to Hatfield to undergo further development trials. One of the big problems with the type was the limited bomb-load and so De Havilland started to look at ways in which this could be increased. The hope was that the current bomb-load of four 250lb bombs could be increased to four 500lb versions. The problem was the overall length of the current GP bombs used by the RAF, which meant that four simply could not be accommodated in the bomb-bay. Initially C.T.Walker, Assistant Chief Designer, thought about the provision of telescopic fins. These fins were tested in drop trials from W4064 at Hatfield on the 31st October, and although the

Another view of DK310 in Switzerland (via S.Howe)

DZ313, a B Mk IV is shown here on a pre-delivery flight with Pat Fillingham (?) in the pilot's seat (M.Payne)

The cockpit of a B Mk IV (© A.Oliver)

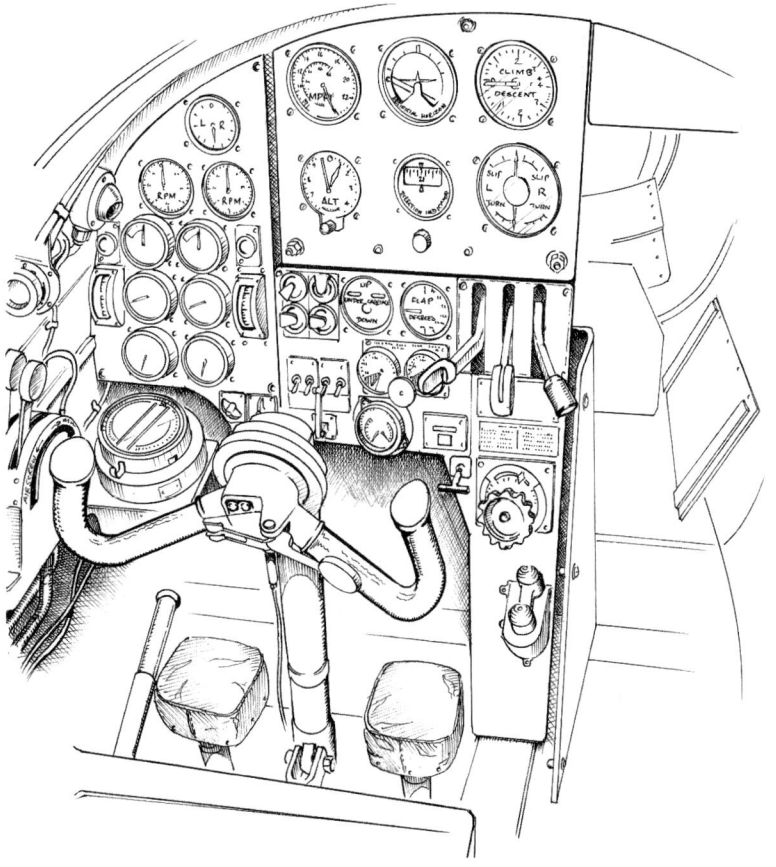

Into Action **15**

DZ367 (GB•J) of No.105 Squadron banking nicely away from the camera-ship to show the camera ports in the forward bomb bay and the tactical camera in the aft fuselage (C.E.Brown)

Indicator and control for A.I. Mk IV fitted to the NF Mk II (© A.Oliver)

B Mk IV Series II, DK338 is shown here on a pre-delivery flight (C.E.Brown)

fins had little adverse effect on the trajectory of the bombs, the system was a bit too technical. In the end the simple method of shortening the existing No.26 tail on the 500lb GP was introduced. Trials with this new style of tail were conducted using the only B Mk V, W4057, and after similar trials were conducted from Boscombe Down over Salisbury Plain ranges, the type was introduced into service. This allowed four 500lb bombs to be fitted with the new No.28 tail and resulted in the Mosquito's bomb-load being doubled, without any major change in the construction of the airframe. It should be noted that due to production build-up, supplies of these new-style tails did not reach operational squadrons until April. After the first nine B Mk IV Series Is had been completed, the B Mk IV Series II entered production. These machines differed from the previous examples by having the extended engine nacelles which had been adopted in an effort to cure the airflow around the rear of each unit. As part of the development with the bomber, and to look at the effect of the greatly increased bomb-load, DK290/G was tested with a tailplane of 10° of dihedral, to move it out of the slipstream. In the end the standard tailplane proved to be as effective and the dihedral unit was not adopted. DK290/G was later to become a development airframe for the B Mk IV. Tests alongside the captured Focke Wulf Fw 190A-3, which had landed in error at RAF Pembrey on the 23rd June 1942, made it obvious that the Mosquito still had the edge, but the speed margin was small and therefore tests including the fitment of wing root fillets, ejector exhaust units and even a high gloss finish, were tried to see just how much faster the type could be

made to go. In the end DK290/G had the bomb-bay doors removed and it was fitted with the dropping equipment for two of the new *Highball* bouncing bombs which had been developed from the *Upkeep* weapon devised by Sir Barnes Wallis. Another idea tested in these early stages was the use of 'scare' guns in the airframe. This idea had been thought of before by the Air Ministry, but De Havilland was against it. This time however De Havilland submitted three ideas; the first being for a belt-fed machine-gun in the tail-cone, the second called for guns in the back of each nacelle which were manually set on the ground, and the final option was for a single machine-gun in the rear canopy, which was fired by the navigator. In the end none of these were proceeded with, but Rose Bros. of Scampton did fit a trial set-up of guns in the rear nacelles of one B Mk IV and it did undertake successful ground firing trials.

The first squadron chosen to operate the new Mosquito bombers was No.105, which was based at Swanton Morley in Norfolk. Geoffrey de Havilland Jnr took W4064 to Swanton on the 15th November 1941 and gave a dazzling display of its performance to the assembled crews, although he had to return to Hatfield with the aircraft the next day due to oil and hydraulic leaks. By 22nd November W4066 was with the squadron and W4064, which was still at Hatfield, was due within the week. By the time the squadron moved to Horsham St Faith in December, it had four Mosquitoes on strength. The squadron now started to undertake all the training which would be required before they could become operational on the type. Production of the B Mk IV had started on the Hatfield production line by February 1942 and by May eight machines were being operated

by No.105 Squadron. Most of these were PRU/Bomber conversions (B Mk IV Series I), but they also included the first B Mk IV Series II, DK288. This machine featured the extended engine nacelles which reduced the airflow breakup and therefore buffeting, which had been experienced with the early production models. During March 1942, W4065 was pitted against a Spitfire Mk V by the Air Fighting Development Unit at RAF Duxford, and even with the Mosquito carrying full operational load and the Spitfire at emergency boost settings, the Mosquito out-paced the Spitfire below 24,000 ft.

The first operational bombing sortie by a Mosquito was undertaken on the 31st May 1942, when Sqn. Ldr. Oakshott of No 105 Squadron took off in W4072 (GB•D) from Colerne at 04.00hr and was followed by W4064 at 11.40hr flown by Plt. Off. Kennard and Plt. Off. Johnston and followed by W4065 (GB•N) and W4071 (GB•L) at 11.45pm. This operation was to be a harassing raid following on from the 1,000 bomber raid on the previous day. On arriving at the drop zone, Oakshott discovered that smoke obscured the city up to 14,000 ft and they all had to fly above it and aim by dead reckoning to attempt a bombing run. Later that afternoon W4069 (GB•M), flown by Sqn. Ldr. Channer, took off for a low-level reconnaissance sortie over the city. He flew in cloud until 60 miles from the target and then dived at 380mph to take his pictures and therefore escaped unscathed. Unfortunately for the bombers they did suffer at the hands of the flak and W4064 fell to AA fire. The shattered wreckage was examined by the Germans, but all they learned was that the aircraft was made of wood.

Right up until September 1942 the Mosquito had remained a secret from the British public, but all this changed with the events of the 25th September. On this day four B Mk IVs (DK296:G, DK313:U, DK328:V and DK325:S) of No.105 Squadron took off from Leuchars and headed towards Oslo. The target was to be the Gestapo Headquarters and the aircraft flew in fast and low along the Oslo Fjord to drop their bombs on the target. One machine (DK325) was shot down by Focke Wulf Fw 190s on the way, but the others placed four bombs into the target. Unfortunately three went straight through the building before exploding and the fourth one did not go off. By this time No 105 Squadron was joined by the second Mosquito bomber squadron, in the form of No.139 (Jamaica) Squadron at Horsham St Faith, and by the end of the month No.105 Sqn. had nineteen Mosquitoes on strength.

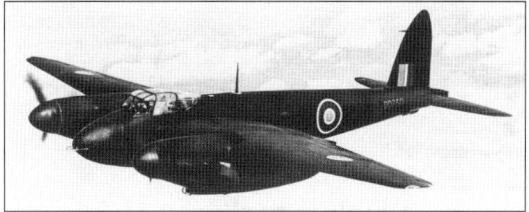

The fighter version of the Mosquito was the last type into operational use, when in January 1942 W4073 (an ex-turret armed machine) flew into Castle Camps to join the newly formed No.157 Squadron. This squadron's C.O. was Wg. Cdr. Gordon Slade, who had flown the Mosquito prototype (W4050) during trials at Boscombe Down. This first Mosquito was a dual-control Mk II (NF Mk II (DC)). Due to the short runway at this new station, night flying training was not started until March and it was a few weeks later before the first Mk IIs (W4087 and W4098) with their secret A.I. Mk V radar arrived at the squadron from No.32 MU. By 9th March the squadron had fourteen Mosquitoes, but only one night training flight had been made by the 13th March. By mid-April the squadron had nineteen NF Mk IIs (Including dual-control examples) and a T Mk III trainer. Only B Flight of this squadron converted to the Mosquito, while A Flight retained its Defiants. The next squadron to get this type was No.151, which soon received sixteen at their Wittering base. Throughout April 1942 both units worked towards full operational status, and it was during this time that the problems with heat build-up in the area of the exhausts became apparent once again. It was a while before De Havillands could introduce a system which overcame this and on the 11th April No.157 Squadron had grounded its Mosquitoes due to a cowling burning through during flight. The tailwheel troubles, which had led to the damage of the prototype, were at long last cured when the unit was fitted with the twin-contact Marstrand type 'anti-shimmy' tyre, and all modifications were completed by the 27th May. It was during April and May of 1942 that the famous 'Baedeker' raids took place, as Hitler ordered the systematic bombing of historic cities throughout England, using a pre-war tourist guide (The Baedeker Guide) to determine which cities to hit. Many of these

Bombing-up, the B Mk IVs of No.105 Squadron at Horsham St Faith (C.E.Brown)

raids came within the range of both No.157 and No.151 squadrons, but neither of them had much success initially. The first victory occurred on the night of the 29th May 1942, when Flt. Lt. Pennington (flying DD628) of No.151 Squadron made contact, and claimed a Do 217E (although originally the claim was for an 'He 111' and it was only listed as a probable) of KG 2 during that unit's raid on Grimsby. Plt. Off. Wain of No.151 Squadron (in DD608) was also to claim a Do 217 on this night. Just before dawn on the 30th May Sqn. Ldr. Ashfield of No.157 Squadron (flying W4099) was guided by the A.I. radar onto a Do 217E and although he fired for a considerable time at the aircraft, he was unable to confirm a kill due to its diving for cloud cover. The coastal tracking station also lost track of the machine some ten miles from the coast, but German records of this time state that four machines were lost during that night's operations, so this may well have been one of them. Strangely German records do not confirm the earlier claim by No.151 Squadron, though it is obvious that by the 30th May 1942, the Mosquito had achieved its first kill.

So by June 1942, just nineteen months after the flight of the prototype, the photo-reconnaissance, bomber and fighter versions of the Mosquito had all made their operational debut and achieved operational success. The stage was now set for the full potential of this machine to be realised; the 'Wooden Wonder' had been born.

An NF Mk II (DD750) which served with No.157, 25, 239 and 264 Squadrons shows off its sleek line in its overall 'Night' scheme (Real Photos)

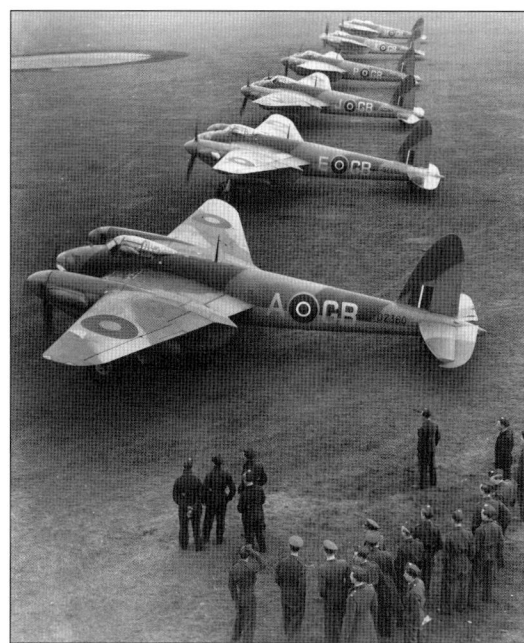

A line-up of No.105 Squadron B Mk IV Series IIs at Horsham St Faith for a press day in early 1942 (C.E.Brown)

The Multi-role Combatant

Chapter 4

Development and service use of all three main types of Mosquito were well established by the end of 1942 and from these the type was to develop into the first and only true 'Multi-role' combat aircraft.

The early night fighter operations by No.157 and No.151 Squadrons had proved the type suitable for night interception by radar, and so the development of new versions fitted with more advanced radar was commenced. The next NF series type produced was the NF Mk XII and this was fitted with the new A.I. Mk VIII centimetric radar unit. Conversion of the NF Mk II with the addition of the new radar was undertaken by Marshall of Cambridge, who received the first airframe in January 1943. The type was to enter service very quickly and the first (HK107) arrived with 85 Squadron, commanded by Wg. Cdr. John Cunningham, on the 28th February. Success with this type was quite swift and the first two kills were achieved on the night of the 14/15th April, when Sqn. Ldr. Green (VY•F) and Flt. Lt. Howitt (VY•L) shot down a Do 217 each during a raid on Chelmsford. The Mosquito proved a match for most types, including Fw 190As, the first of which was shot down at night by Flt. Lt. H.E.Tappin of No.157 Squadron near Evreux on the 14th May and the type was also responsible for shooting down the first Me 410 on the 13/14th July (by Flt. Lt. Bunting in VY•T) and the first Ju 188 (by Sqn. Ldr. Maquire) on the 15/16th October over England.

The next night fighter variant was the NF Mk XIII and this was based on the FB Mk VI airframe and therefore had the strengthened wings which allowed for the fitment of 50-gallon drop-tanks on the outer wing panels. The type carried the same AI Mk VIII radar of the previous version, in the pointed 'thimble' type radome. Powerplants included the Merlin 25, although the Merlin 21 and 23 could also be utilised. The use of the FB Mk VI airframe as the basis for this type also meant that it could carry bombs and the 5$^{3}/_{4}$hr endurance made the type ideally suited to the intruder and bomber escort roles. This type became operational with No.488 (New Zealand) Squadron and the unit made its first operational patrol on the 8th October 1943. The first victory for this type came just a month later on the 8th of November 1943, when HK369 destroyed an Me 410 of KG 2 off Clacton. Operational use of the NF series Mosquito had shown that there were some areas which needed improvement. The first was for better speed at around 20,000ft, but also a steeper climb was required to get the aircraft up to the interception point sooner. A quick method of clearing ice from the flat armoured windscreen was also needed, as icing

problems had been encountered on many operations. To give the Merlin 21/23/25 engines more power for short periods, a nitrous-oxide (N_2O) injection system was developed. The system was fitted to two machines, one from the Fighter Interception Unit and the other (HK374) of 85 Sqn, by the RAE and this resulted in an increase in speed of up to 47mph at 27,000ft. The system was to be retro-fitted to fifty NF Mk XIIIs and this work was carried out by Heston Aircraft Ltd. Most of these machines were operated by No.96 and No.410 (Cougar) Squadrons. With the strengthened wing of the fighter/bomber series, NF Mk XIIIs were also able to carry bombs under the outer wing panels, and HK508 of No.256 Sqn. was even modified in the field to carry two 500lb bombs on these points, instead of the more usual 250lb examples. Wg. Cdr. John Cunningham flew an NF Mk XIII

(HK374) for the first time on the night of the 2/3rd January 1944 and successfully shot down an Me 410.

The next night fighter variant was to have been the NF Mk XIV, powered by Merlin 67s or 72s, but this type was superseded by the NF Mk XIX and NF Mk 30. The arrival of American radar equipment in the form of the SCR 720/729 system was soon adopted as the AI Mk X by the RAF and utilised in the Mosquito. Trials with this new system were carried out in NF Mk II (DZ659) and the scanner was carried inside the 'Bullnose' universal style of radome. Initially 100 NF Mk IIs were converted by Marshalls Flying Services Ltd to carry the A.I. Mk X and they therefore became NF Mk XVIIs. The true prototype for this series was HK195/G. Operational use of the type was to be undertaken by No.25 Sqn.. on the 4th January 1944, and on the 20th February the squadron scored its first victory when a Ju 188 was shot down by Plt. Off. J.R.Brockbank (in HK285) during a raid on London. By the middle of 1944 the UK was under increasing attack from Hitler's new 'Vengeance

DZ659 was originally built as an NF Mk II, but was fitted with the SCR720/729 in the universal radome to become an NF Mk XIII. This machine was operated by the Fighter Interception Unit from April 1943 to May 1945
(Real Photos)

MM652 is a Leavesden-built NF Mk XIX and it is seen here prior to its delivery to the RAF
(Real Photos)

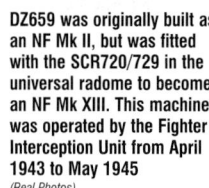

Another view of DZ659
(Real Photos)

Weapons', and the NF Mk XVII scored a number of successes against V-1s. Many methods were tried to deal with the V-1 threat and this included photo-cell indicators to assist ranging and one NF Mk XVII, HK324/G, was even fitted with a backward-looking radar, housed in a perspex tailcone. The first V-1 kill by a Mosquito was achieved by Flt. Lt. J.G.Musgrove in an FB Mk VI of No.605 Sqn. on the 15th June 1944.

The next night fighter into operational use was the NF Mk XIX. This was identical to the NF Mk XVII but it was able to carry either the AI Mk VIII or the A.I. Mk X (SCR 720/729) in a universal 'Bullnose' radome or the more pointed 'Thimble' style unit. The prototype for this series was HK364 and the type was powered by the Merlin 25. Radar developments at this stage meant that this type was to carry a number of different systems. Some machines of No.85 and No.157 Squadrons were fitted with *Monica I* or *Monica VI* rearward-looking radar to supplement the American SCR 720/729 radar, and it was housed in a small blister aft of the tailwheel. During November 1944 some of No 85 Squadrons NF XIXs were also fitted with *Perfectos Mk II*, which homed into the IFF sets of German aircraft. At the start of 1945, the new *Serrate Mk IV* unit, which homed in on SN-2 transmissions of German night fighters, was fitted to NF Mk XIXs of No.157 Squadron.

The last night fighter Mosquito type of the war was the NF Mk 30, which also doubled as a high-altitude night fighter.

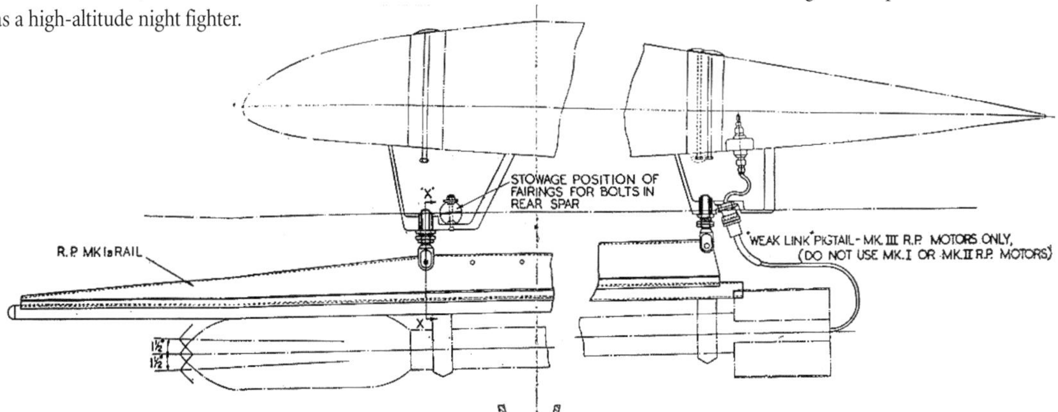

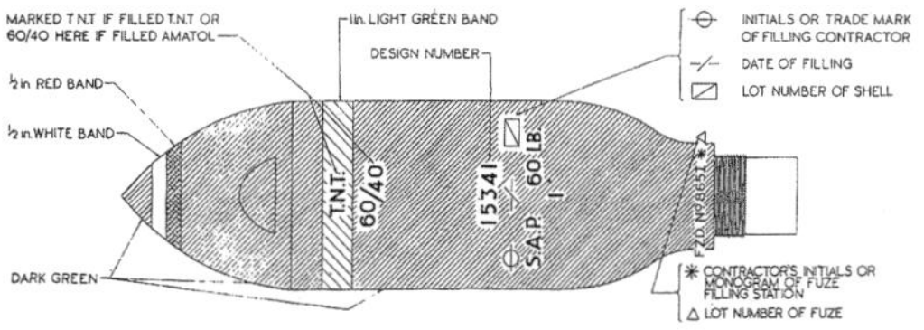

Ground crews prepare to load bombs onto FB Mk VIs of No.487 (RNZAF) Squadron *(via S.Howe)*

was to merge the bomber and fighter versions together, retaining as much bomb load capability as the design would allow. This type was to become the FB Mk VI and the prototype for the series was HJ662/G which was converted from a B Mk IV (DZ434). After this conversion to the FB Mk VI, another B Mk IV was allocated serial DZ434 on the De Havilland production line. The FB Mk VI had the strengthened wing of the proposed B Mk V which allowed it to carry 50-gallon drop-tanks or two 250lb

Rocket projectile installation details

The type was similar to the NF Mk XIX, with the same AI Mk X radar, however its high altitude performance came from the two-stage Merlin 72 engines fitted to the initial production versions. On later production versions these were replaced by the Merlin 76 and 113. The prototype for this series was MM686 and the type was able to carry either two 250lb bombs or 50- or 100-gallon drop tanks on the outer wing panel hard points. The first operational NF Mk 30 was delivered to No.219 Sqn. on the 13th June 1944 and the first operation kill was achieved by a machine of No.410 Sqn. (MM744) on the night of the 19/20th August that year. Once again this type was fitted with a number of the new radar systems used in the NF Mk XIX and these included the *Perfectos Mk IV* and the *Monica Mk VI*. Initially the exhaust flame-damper units on the NF Mk 30 caused problems and although they were modified, the inner shrouds started to burn and so the entire NF Mk 30 fleet was grounded in November for rectification work. New louvered shrouds were fitted retrospectively to all NF Mk 30s.

With the Mosquito in the night fighter, bomber and fighter roles and the NF Mk II (Intruders) with their intruder ability roaming the whole of Europe, the idea of a fighter-bomber version of the Mosquito was considered in July 1941. The theory

bombs. The prototype first flew on the 1st June 1942 and was then flown to Boscombe Down on the 13th June for acceptance trials. Initially there were also two other versions of the Mk VI; the first being the NF Mk VI (previously called the 'Mk VIA') with 403 gallons of fuel and no capacity to carry bombs, and the LRF Mk VI (previously the 'Mk VIB') which was a long-range fighter and intruder with 530 gallons of fuel. Neither of these types was proceeded with, as the FB Mk VI and NF versions were found to be capable of their perceived roles.

The initial versions of the FB Mk VI were called 'Series I', as they could only carry two 250lb bombs in the bomb bay and two under the wings. Strengthening was carried out and this resulted in the 'Series II' version which could carry two 500lb bombs in the bomb bay with two more under the wings. Other operational configurations included a 250lb bomb and 50-gallon

Identification markings on the 60lb S.A.P/H.E No.1 Mk.I rocket projectile head

The Multi-role Combatant 19

Col Davies, Bill Pawson (rear) and 'Pop' Fisher (right) re-arm NS994 (SB•F) of No.464 (RAAF) Squadron at Thorney Island in June 1944
(Sport & General via S.Howe)

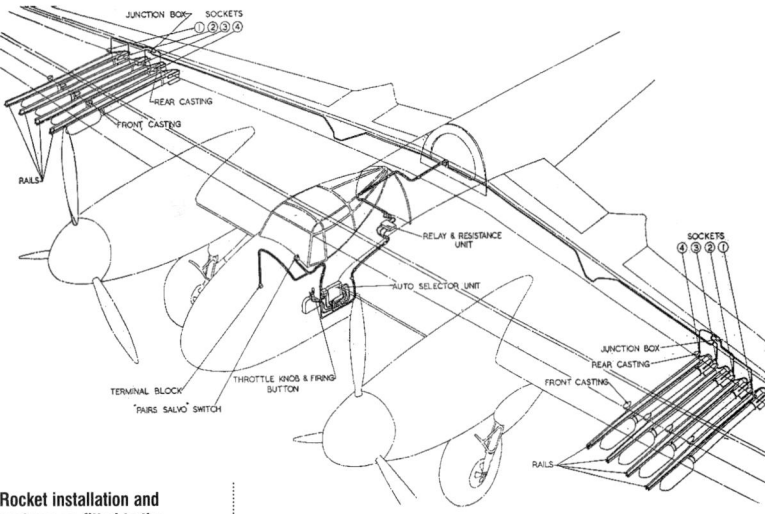

Rocket installation and systems as fitted to the fighter-bomber versions of the Mosquito

NS881 (SM•O), an FB Mk VI of No.305 (Polish) Squadron. This squadron, along with No.107 and No.618 Squadrons formed No.138 Wing in late 1943
(Polish Aircraft Archives)

tank under the wings on intruder operations and a 151-gallon fuel cell could replace the internal bomb load on long range operations. Trials were also conducted with a smoke-screen generating device, called SCI, which could be carried on the bomb-racks under the wings of the FB Mk VI and was designed for use as a screen to cover advancing ground forces, or to cover an amphibious landing. The FB Mk VI was fitted with the Merlin 21, 23 or 25 and the 25 series engine was fitted with a higher boost level (18lb/in) for better operational performance at low and medium levels. The first production FB Mk VI did not fly until February 1943, because of other Mosquito production commitments. The type was able to carry bombs, a Mk XI depth-charge and even a Mk VIII mine under the wings, although trials with HR135 at Boscombe Down soon proved that the mine could not be dropped above 250 mph without the risk of a 'hang-up' and therefore the operational use of mines on the Mosquito was not proceeded with. The fitment of rocket projectiles however was to prove most successful on the FB Mk VI. The standard RAF 3in rockets had already been used with great success by Hurricanes, Beaufighters and Hudson aircraft and the system was first fitted to HJ719 in October 1943. A blast plate was attached to each wing panel and the rockets themselves were initially the 25lb-armour piercing versions, although the 60lb semi-armour-piercing versions were also fitted. The destructive force of a salvo of 60lb rockets from a Mosquito was equal to that of a broadside from a cruiser. In the end all FB Mk VIs were fitted with four of these weapons under each outer wing panel, although later trials also considered the fitment of a two-tier rack which allowed four rockets and a 50 gallon drop-tank to be carried for long-range operations. The first unit to get the FB Mk VI was No.418 (City of Edmonton), based at Ford, and they received their first machine on the 11th May 1943. This was followed by No.605 (County of Warwick) Sqn., at Castle Camps which got its machines in July. Overseas use of the type was started by No.23 Sqn. on Malta who received their first FB Mk VIs at the end of May, replacing their NF Mk II (Intruders). Operations from Malta with the FB Mk VI, fitted with 50 gallon drop-tanks, allowed attacks as far as Rome and Foggia and No 23 sqn. was joined by No.108 Sqn. in February 1944, when they received Mosquitoes to supplement their existing fleet of Beaufighters.

By the June 1943 the 2nd Tactical Air Force (2TAF) had been formed to concentrate operations against tactical targets, while Bomber Command concentrated on strategic bombing. No.464 (RAAF) and No.487 (RNZAF) Squadrons were the first 2TAF units to re-equip with the FB Mk VI, receiving the first machines on the 21st August 1943 and being joined by No.21 Sqn. a few months later. These units became No.140 Wing and started operations on the 2nd October, when twelve machines of No.464 and No.487 Sqn. attacked the power stations at Pont-Château and Guerleden. Operations against the V-1 bases in France began in December 1943 and by the 21st of this month a fourth squadron, No.613, made its operational debut with the FB Mk VI in a mission flown by Wg. Cdr. K.H.Blair DFC and Fg. Off. J.G.Majer in LR271. This unit, plus No.107 and No.305 (Polish) squadrons, formed the basis of No.138 Wing, while No.140 Wing

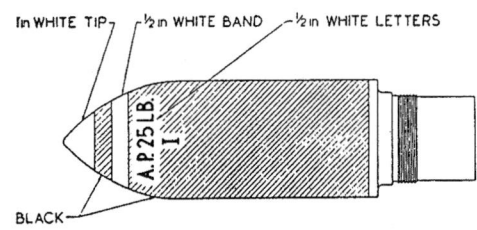

Identification markings on the 25lb SHOT A.P. rocket projectile head

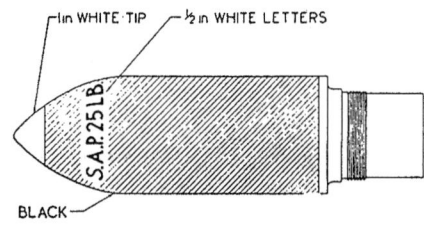

Identification markings on the 25lb SHOT S.A.P. rocket projectile head

moved south to a new base at Hunsdon, Herts over the New Year period.

The FB Mk VI will always be remembered for a number of daring low-level raids against pin-point targets and the first was *Operation Jericho*. In January 1944 information was received that over 100 French resistance members were being held in the Amiens jail and the French government asked if the RAF would attack the jail, breech the walls, and therefore give the resistance

Left: An FB Mk VI of No.613 Squadron swoops low (left) during the attack by this squadron on the Scheveningsche Wegg on the 11th April 1944 *(via S.Howe)*

Far left: The Dutch Central Population Registry burns after the successful pin-point attack by No.613 Squadron on the 11th April 1944 *(via S.Howe)*

members a chance of escape. Originally the mission was planned for the 17th January, but it was postponed due to bad weather. Therefore just before 11am on the 18th February, eighteen Mosquitoes of No.140 Wing and a B Mk IV (DZ414) of the Wing's Film Unit, took off from Hunsdon lead by Grp. Cpt. P.C.Pickard DSO and two bars, DFC and Flt. Lt. J.A.Broadley DSO, DFC, DFM. The attack was divided into three waves; the first (No.487 Sqn.) was to breech the 20ft high, 3ft thick walls on the north and east sides, the second (No.464 Sqn.) was to attack the quarters of the German guards at either end of the prison and a third wave stood by in case they were required to take any follow-up action. The group was escorted by Typhoons to the prison and the attack followed a strict-time table, as the waves would cross each other at right angles, and collisions had to be avoided. The first wave breached the walls as planned and the second wave attacked the guard barracks as the Film Unit B Mk IV circled the prison taking pictures. The third wave was not therefore required and they flew off at low level. Gp. Cpt. Pickard (in HX922 EG•F) was lost when the tail of his machine was shot off by defending Fw 190s. The only other losses of the operation were two of the Typhoons which were shot down by AA fire and MM404, whose navigator (Flt. Lt. R.W.Simpson) was killed by flak and whose pilot (Sqn. Ldr. McRitchie) managed to crash-land in a snow storm, even though his right arm was paralysed. The operation was considered a success, as 258 prisoners had escaped, although 102 were killed by either the bombs or machine-gun fire from the German guards. A similar low-level raid took place against the Dutch Central Population Registry in the Scheveningsche Wegg in the Hague on the 11th April 1944. The attacking force comprised six FB Mk VIs, lead by Wg. Cdr. R.N.Bateson of No.613 Sqn., and the five-storey building in a block was successfully destroyed with a combination of 500lb bombs and incendiaries without the loss of a single Mosquito (although NS844 was slightly damaged by flak). The Gestapo barracks at Bonneuil Matours was destroyed by No.487 Squadron on the 14th July. FB Mk VIs next attacked the Gestapo HQ at Jutland on the 31st October 1944. This operation was to assist the Danish resistance and twenty-four machines of No.21, 464 and 487 Sqns. undertook the mission. The target comprised two buildings in the Aarhus University campus and the group was lead by Gp. Cpt. P.G.Wykeham DSO and bar, DFC. The aircraft, escorted by Mustangs, reached the target and delivered 11sec delay bombs into the building without any opposition from the German AA crews. Only one machine was lost on this operation (PZ164), and that had to force land in Sweden. A similar operation was undertaken on the 21st March 1945 against the Gestapo HQ in the Shellhaus building in Denmark. The raid was lead by Gp. Cpt. Bateson (in RS570:X) and the aircraft sped in at 10ft to deliver the bombs directly on target. Unfortunately one machine crashed on an adjacent school-house killing a number of children, and four Mosquitoes and two Mustangs were lost to AA fire.

The use of the Mosquito in pin-point raids did make Bomber command consider the FB Mk VI as a type which was ideally suited to the precise placement of markers for bomber raids and the first use of the type for this operation was attempted by Gp. Cpt. Leonard Cheshire DSO and two bars, DFC on the marshalling yards at Juvisy, Paris, although this was unsuccessful, as the marker flare hung-up in the bomb-bay. On the 24th April 1944, Cheshire flew NS993 (•N) again and this time marked Munich for the 200 Lancasters of No.617 Sqn. Cheshire dived on the target from 10,000ft and placed the flare right on the rail yards, then circled the area to relay information to the bombers about the fall of their bombs. For this action, Cheshire was later awarded the VC.

Use of the Mosquito for high level photographic work had been continuing and the prototype PR Mk VII, DK324, made its maiden flight on the 20th October 1942. This machine was based on the PR Mk IV, but was fitted with the two-stage Merlin 61 engines, was not pressurised and could carry 50 gallon drop-tanks. The initial order was for ten machines, but this was soon reduced to five. These machines comprised the prototype, DZ342, DZ364, DZ404 and DZ424, each of which had initially been laid down as a B Mk IV. The type entered operational service at RAF Benson, equipping No.540 Squadron, which had been formed from No.1 PRU. The first operational use of this Mark was by DZ342, flown by Sqn. Ldr. G.E.Hughes and Sgt. H.W.Evans, which flew a sortie to La Rochelle and St Nazaire on the 19th February 1943 even though mud on the camera shutter rendered the mission useless. It was to a PR Mk VIII that the honour of the first photo sortie over Berlin would fall (even though DZ364, flown by Flt. Lt. K.H.Bayley DFC, had tried on the 3rd March), when DZ404 (HS•Z), flown by Wg. Cdr. M.J.B.Young DFC, took off for the German capital on the 8th March 1943. With the next PR version, the PR Mk IX, coming into service, all of the PR Mk VIIIs were withdrawn by November 1943.

The next type to enter service for photo-reconnaissance work

An FB Mk VI of No.613 Squadron, with bomb doors open, pulls out after dropping its bombs on the Dutch Central Population Registry on the 11th April 1944 *(via S.Howe)*

PR Mk XVI NS705 is shown here on a pre-delivery flight. This aircraft was later delivered to RAF Benson, before it went to the Mediterranean, ultimately to go missing on the 20th January 1945. *(C.E.Brown)*

ML926/G was the first production B Mk XVI and after initial trials this machine was used for Oboe and H2S trials. The machine is depicted here with the H2S scanner radome fitted under the bomb-bay during trials with this at Defford *(Hawker Siddeley)*

The B Mk IX was a bomber version of the PR Mk IX and it utilised the two-stage Merlin engines. LR495 depicted here was the first of the type produced and is shown here with 500lb bombs under the wings. This aircraft was retained for development work and crashed during overload take-off trials on the 29th January 1944 *(De Havilland)*

A B Mk XVI, either of No.105 or No.109 Squadrons, is shown here along with its crew and other members of the squadron. The mission tally and the dragon motif are noteworthy, as is the painted-out nose glazing, a sure sign of an Oboe-equipped machine *(Stan Wright via R.W.Edwards)*

was therefore the PR Mk IX and this was based on the new B Mk IX. The first two machines, LR405 and LR406 were finished in April 1943, and they were delivered to RAF Benson on the 29th May to equip No.540 Squadron which flew its first mission with the type (LR408) on the 20th June. The next unit to form from No.1 PRU was No.544 Squadron and this too was equipped with the PR Mk IX, makings its operational debut with them on the 13th September 1943 during a sortie to Vannes. One of the most graphic illustrations of the Mosquito's great range and immunity to fighters was made by Flt. Lt. Merrifield DSO, DFC of No.544 Squadron when he flew PR Mk IX LR417 1,900 miles non-stop in 6$^{1}/_{2}$ hours. This flight encompassed Trier in the Rhineland, Regensburg in Bavaria, Linz and Vienna in Austria, Budapest, back to Vienna, Sarbono, Bucharest and via Foggia in southern Italy to Catania in Sicily. PR Mk IXs of No 540 Squadron obtained the pictures of Peenemünde on the 3rd October 1943 which confirmed that a new pilotless aircraft (the V-1) was being developed there. Once again electronic devices in the form of *Gee* and *Rebecca H* could be carried, as well as *Boozer*. Production of this mark reached ninety in May to November 1943 and the type was then replaced by the PR Mk XVI.

Development of the PR Mk XVI started when PR Mk IX, MM229, was fitted with the new RM10SM Merlin 67 engines in December 1943. Another PR Mk IX, MM235, was fitted with Merlin 76 and 77 engines, driving Hamilton Standard paddle-blade propellers and this was found to increase the ceiling by as much as 3,000ft as well as giving greater speed at around 35,000ft. Eight other PR Mk IXs were modified in this manner and MM235 was later fitted with an F.52 camera in each drop-tank to take tactical photos of the V-weapon sites in Northern France. The first production PR Mk XVIs reached operational service in December 1943 and they equipped Nos.140 and 400 Squadrons, although a lack of heat exchangers resulted in no

cabin heating and the type suffered from canopy icing. The first operational sortie by a PR Mk XVI was by MM279 of No.140 Sqn. on the 4th February 1944, when it flew to the Cabourg-St Aubin region of northern France. Once again, as with the B Mk IX, this version could carry *Gee*, *Rebecca H* and *Boozer* devices. The canopy icing problems were soon cured, after development work undertaken with MM352, and the type undertook many reconnaissance missions during the D-Day landings. Operations in the Mediterranean theatre were mainly the domain of No.60 Sqn. (SAAF), which had operated PR Mk IXs since August 1943. They were joined in February 1944 by another squadron, No.680, which received some PR Mk IXs in February and some PR Mk XVIs shortly afterwards. This squadron went into action for the first time on the 7th May. The operational radius of these two squadrons increased and by the middle of 1944 they were roaming as far north as Bilzna in Poland to photograph the V-2 testing ground there.

Development of the bomber versions was also going at a pace and the next version after the B Mk IV was the B Mk IX. The prototype PR Mk VIII, DZ324, was converted to become the prototype for this series and it was followed in March 1943 by the first production B Mk IX, LR495, which first flew on the 24th of that month. This new version was fitted with the new Merlin 72 engine and could carry two 500lb bombs under the

wings, as well as four more in the bomb-bay. On top of this the type could replace the bomb-load with extra fuel-tankage giving a maximum fuel capacity of 627 gallons. Later a small number of B Mk IXs were converted with the bulged bomb-bay doors which allowed the 4,000lb HC 'Cookie' to be carried. The prototype for this series was ML915, although the use of the 4,000lb bomb did raise the all-up weight to 24,385lb compared to the 22,823lb of the standard version. It was the B Mk IX that was to be of great use as a Pathfinder and all machines operated as such were fitted with a number of special electrical guidance and bombing aids, including *Oboe* and *Gee-H*. A small number of B Mk IXs were also fitted with *H2S Mk VI* bombing radar and the nose transparency was painted over on all these machines. The first operational squadron to have the B Mk IX was No.109 at RAF Wyton, who received examples on the 21st April 1943. This squadron used the type operationally for the first time on the 11th June 1943, during a raid on Düsseldorf, when LR497:Z was flown by Sqn. Ldr. F.A.Green. Five of these machines were passed over to No.105 Squadron on the 5th July 1943, as this unit had been training for some while with the Oboe system. The first flight by a B Mk IX of this unit was against Cologne on the 13th July. Operations against V-1 sites by FB Mk VIs were often marked by B Mk IXs of No.109 Squadron. A small number of the type was also used for weather reconnaissance and No.1409 Flight at Oakington received examples on the 21st and 23rd May.

A pressurised version of the B Mk IX followed and this was to become the B Mk XVI. This machine was similar to the B Mk IX, but was fitted with a Marshall cabin supercharger, driven off the port Merlin 73 or 77, which maintained the cockpit pressure at 2lb/sq.in above the outside atmospheric pressure. Initial production versions had the Merlin 73 on the port side and Merlin 72 on the starboard, but later ones used the Merlin 76/77 combination. To seal the interior of a Mosquito for pressurised operations did not prove too difficult and a sealing membrane was added forward of the bomb-bay, with all control cables and tubes carefully sealed with rubber and jointing compound. This variant also saw the addition of an upwards-hinged door inside the cockpit, above the downward-hinging crew-access door, once again to help seal the cockpit interior. The prototype B Mk XVI was DZ540, a B Mk IV, and this machine made its first flight in late July 1943. The first production B Mk XVI was ML926/G and this aircraft was to be used in *Oboe* repeater equipment, radar bombsight and H_2S bombing radar trials. The first unit to receive this version was No.109 squadron, who received their first examples (ML928 & ML930) on the 19th December 1943 and undertook their first operational sortie to Deelen on the night of the 1/2nd March. Soon No.105 squadron joined in B Mk XVI operations, flying their first on the 3rd March, although this machine (ML928:D) flown by Wg. Cdr. H.J.Cundall had its *Oboe* equipment fail and was unable to mark the target. Initially the first twelve machines were designed to carry four 500lb bombs in the bomb-bay, but after the 13th production machines (ML937) the fitment of the bulged bomb-bay doors for the 4,000lb HC 'Cookie' was

standard. The first successful use of this weapon was by ML941 (XD•N) and ML942 (XD•F) of No.139 Sqn., when they were dropped on München Gladbach on the 2/3rd March 1944.
The use of the new Avro-type bomb carriers developed for the B Mk IX were adopted for the B Mk XVI and these allowed six 500lb bombs to be carried in the bulged bomb-bay. Developments in electronic equipment were such that the B Mk XVI carried *Gee, Gee-H* or *Oboe* equipment as well as the newer types such as *Boozer*, a system designed to home in on the Germans *Würzburg* radar, and *Fishpond*, a device which issued a transmission on the same band as the H_2S system, but which identified aircraft on the same level or lower than the carrier, always a useful idea, as so many German fighter attacks were from astern. The use of the H_2S bombing radar had been trial tested in a B Mk IV (DZ476 XD•U) of No.139 Squadron, when it flew to Berlin on the 1st February 1944. The squadron then fitted the device to a number of their Canadian built B Mk XXs (first of all in KB329 XD•L) and finally to a small number of their B Mk XVIs. The first operational use of this device in a B Mk XVI was on the 10th February 1944 when ML940 (XD•O) was flown by Flt. Lt. E.A.Holdaway DFC to Berlin. The use of H_2S continued operations with No.139 squadron throughout 1944 and into 1945. With an improvement in the range of *Oboe*, Berlin was within range by April 1945, and two B Mk XVIs of No.105 Squadron (LR513 & LR507) and three of No.109 Squadron (ML927, RV308 & RV318) visited the capital for the first time on the 8th April 1945. This first operation to the capital by *Oboe*-equipped B Mk XVIs was followed by a further ninety such flights during the rest of April. One of the last uses of the *Oboe*-equipped Mosquito squadrons in World War II was for them to drop medical supplies and information

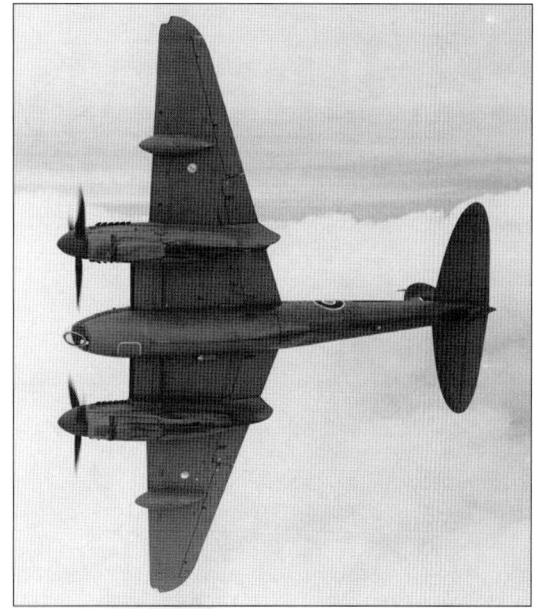

pamphlets to POWs at eight camps within the German capital on the 24th April 1945, and this was followed by their marking various sites in Holland so that Lancasters could drop much needed food supplies into this country.

As well as being used as Pathfinders for Bomber Command, the B Mk IX and B Mk XVI were also used by the Command's Light Night Striking Force. The first unit to re-equip with the modified B Mk IX (4,000lb) was No.692 Sqn. and they used the type for the first time on the 23rd February 1944, when Fg. Off. Hassell (DZ647), Flt. Lt. Moore (DZ534) and Flt. Lt. McKeard (DZ637) attacked Düsseldorf. This was followed by a similar raid on Kiel on the 24th February. The B Mk XVI was used operationally for the first time by No.692 Sqn. on the 5th March 1944, when Flt. Lt. V.S.Moore and Fg. Off. P.F.Dillon attacked Duisburg. This was followed by a new squadron, No.571, which made a raid on Osnabruck on the night of the 12/13th April 1944 with their B Mk XVIs (ML942 & ML963). On the 7th February 1945, this squadron used the new *Loran* navigational aid for the first time during a raid on Magdeburg. Two Canadian squadrons, No.608 and No.627 had also equipped with the B Mk XVI in March 1945 and they joined No.571 and No.692 squadrons in the sustained bombing campaign against the German capital throughout the final months of the war. By the 21st April 1945, 1,459 'Cookies' had been dropped by these Mosquitoes. It was to eight squadrons of Bomber Command that the honour of making the last operational sortie of the war was to fall, when this group attacked Kiel on the night of the 2/3rd May 1945.

This pleasing view of B Mk XVI (ML963) clearly shows the bulged bomb-bay of the type. The lighter colour around the crew-access hatch is the sealing strip, which was required on this pressurised version of the Mosquito *(C.E.Brown)*

An FB Mk VI, in the form of TA122, is based at the Mosquito Museum and it is hoped that restoration work on this machine will someday result in a complete fighter-bomber on display in the UK *(S. Howe)*

This B Mk XVI (ML963: 8K•K) was operated by No.571 Squadron. The unit, along with seven other squadrons of Bomber Command carried out the last operation of the war, when they bombed Kiel on the 2/3rd May 1945 *(C.E.Brown)*

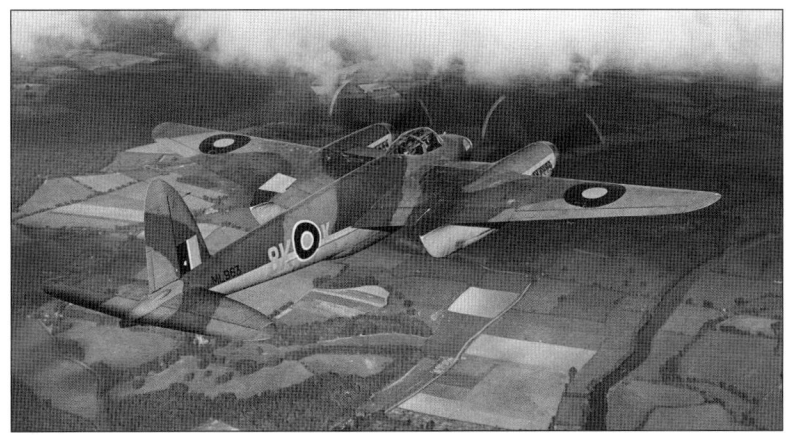

Special Operations

Chapter 5

The NF Mk II (Intruder)

The Mosquito was to be used for a number of highly specialised tasks, on top of the more usual photo-reconnaissance, bomber and fighter roles. The first was that of an intruder. During June 1940, No.604 Squadron had started to use its Bristol Blenheims for intruder missions over occupied airfields in France. The idea was for the intruders to shoot down the returning German bombers when they were at their most vulnerable and No.23 Sqn. using Blenheims, Havocs and Bostons did a large number of this type of operation during 1941.

The Mosquito was in service by the end of 1941 and its speed, range and armament made it ideally suited to the intruder role. No.23 Squadron, as the most experienced in this field, was therefore the ideal choice to trial the type for this style of operation and they received their first Mosquito, a T Mk III trainer, on the 7th June 1942. This was followed on the 2nd July 1942 by their first operational machine, an NF Mk II (DD670, YP•S). Just four days later the squadron mounted its first patrol with this aircraft over Caen and the first confirmed victory (a Do 217 over Montdidier) was achieved on the following night, with a Do 217 and He 111 claimed on the 5th July. The squadron claimed a number of victories throughout December and their NF Mk IIs were given greater range by the fitment of a 150-gallon fuel-tank in the bomb-bay aft of the cannon. In the afternoon of the 6th December however the squadron was stood down, while their aircraft were fitted with long-range tanks, tropical equipment and the Marstrand tailwheels for their new operational theatre: Malta. These modifications were completed by the 13th December and the squadron set out for Malta via Gibraltar on the 20th December. Once they arrived on the island on the 27th December, the squadron started operations against the retreating German troops heading towards Tunisia. The squadron made night-intruder flights to harass the German convoys and by September 1943 they had destroyed twenty-four aircraft, 172 trains and attacked twenty-five ships. At this time the unit was re-equipped with the FB Mk VI and it continued to operate these machines in the intruder role until they returned to England in May 1944.

As well as the squadron's nineteen NF Mk IIs, six aircraft from Nos 25, 85, 151, 157 and 264 Squadrons were modified with the addition of the long-range tanks, the removal of the A.I. Mk V radar and the fitment of *Gee* navigational aids, and these aircraft thereafter became known as the NF Mk II (Special). The Mosquito's intruder role was soon divided into several different types. The first was the *Instep* mission, which was flown over the Bay of Biscay against German fighters which were operating against Coastal Command's anti-U-boat patrols. The next type was the *Ranger* mission and this was for a flight to a specified target, with the crew given a free hand to attack any target considered worthwhile and this sort of mission was just to ensure the Luftwaffe kept a sizable fighter force in the west. This type of operation was done in two forms, being the *Day Ranger* or *Night Ranger*, each mission setting out at preset

times, so they would be over the target by day or night. The first *Instep* and *Ranger* missions were flown by No.264 Squadron, on the 15th December 1942 and the 4th February 1943 respectively. With the extended range offered by the use of the Mosquito, intruder missions after about June 1942 were able to expand, covering Germany, Denmark and even Czechoslovakia. Once the aircraft were based in Europe after D-Day, operations as far as East Prussia could be undertaken.

DZ716, an NF Mk II (Intruder) of No.605 Squadron, depicted here at dusk at Castle Camps prior to the start of another operation *(via S.Howe)*

The NF Mk XV

The advent of Junkers Ju 86P aircraft on reconnaissance flights over England in 1942, at heights in excess of 40,000ft, had highlighted the need for a high-altitude interceptor to counter this new threat. The development of the new two-speed two-stage Merlin 61 series by Rolls Royce had allowed for consideration of the use of this powerplant in the Mosquito for high altitude operations. The first installation of this powerplant was in the prototype W4050, which received a pair in early 1942 and flew with them for the first time on the 20th June 1942. Demand for the new Merlin 61s in Spitfire Mk IXs meant that the Mosquito took a back seat for a while, but the prototype continued to fly with these powerplants and it was soon joined by another machine, MP469. This machine was similar to the B Mk XVI, with a pressurised canopy and a bomber nose. Initially it did not have a mark number, it was simply known as the 'pressure-cabin bomber prototype'. It first flew on the 8th August 1942 and it started test flying from Hartford Bridge on the 27th. The arrival of the Ju 86P and R over the UK coincided with the start of MP469's trials and

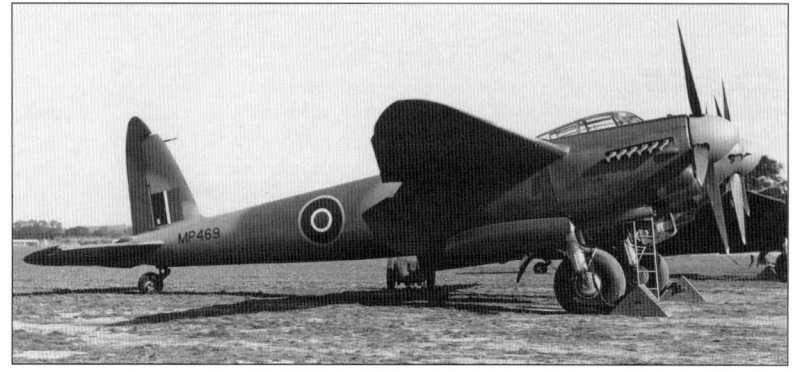

A view of the NF Mk XV prototype (MP469) in its initial form, with the fighter nose grafted onto the high-altitude bomber airframe *(BAe)*

The NF Mk XV prototype (MP469) photographed once it had been painted 'Deep Sky' overall (via S.Howe)

Last of the five production PR Mk 32s, NS589 is shown sitting on the airfield at Hatfield after conversion. Note the extended wing tips which were fitted to this variant and the NF Mk XV high-altitude interceptor

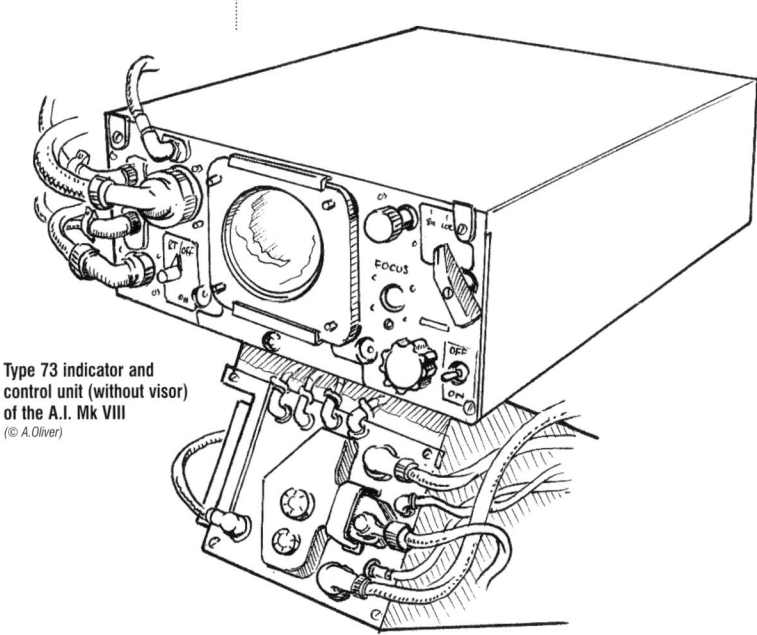

Type 73 indicator and control unit (without visor) of the A.I. Mk VIII (© A.Oliver)

De Havilland's design staff was asked whether they could develop a new high-altitude pressurised fighter from their new bomber by Mr N.E.Rowe, the Director of Technical Development. Initially, the nose of an NF Mk II (DD715), which had been removed to be replaced by an A.I. Mk VIII radar so this machine could become the prototype NF Mk XII, was fitted. The forward bulkhead (usually armoured in a fighter) was fabricated from duraluminium, the bomber's 'spectacle' control yoke was replaced by a fighter-style stick and the headrest, which was usually armour plate, was replaced by a sheet of plywood. The aircraft also featured three-bladed propellers initially, but on the 13th September these were replaced by the four-blade units from the prototype, which had been used to test them. One of the most noticeable changes to the type was the extension of the wing tips. The standard units were removed and extended versions, taking the span up to 59ft, were installed. The airframe also had to be considerably lighter and therefore the outer wing and fuselage fuel-cells were removed, reducing the total fuel capacity to just 287 gallons. Some of the radio equipment was also removed and the bullet-proofing was removed from the fuel and oil tanks. The final modifications made were the fitment of lightened bomb-bay doors and the use of simplified hydraulic jacks for them. Just a week after Mr Rowe's request, MP469 was ready. This new machine was called the NF Mk XV and it weighed just 16,200lb with the pilot, 200 rounds of ammo, fuel and oil, which compared with the 22,485lb of the aircraft in its earlier bomber configuration. The type first flew on the 14th September with John de Havilland at the controls and the next day it climbed to 43,500ft. The type was sent to the newly formed High Altitude Flight at RAF Northolt on the 16th and there it waited for the next Ju 86. Unfortunately they never came. Fg. Off. Sparrow (ex-No.151 Squadron), the chosen pilot for this operation, did manage to test the type during this inactive period and the aircraft is reported to have achieved a maximum height of no less than 45,000ft, which was about 300ft higher than the maximum height attainable by the new Spitfire Mk VIII which was just entering service. With the Ju 86s obviously withdrawn, MP469 was returned to De Havillands in October, where it was fitted out with A.I. Mk VIII radar in a new 'thimble' nose radome. Because of the fitment of the radar, the machine-guns were now unusable, so the D.H. team lead by Fred Plumb designed a new ventral gun-pack to fit these under the belly of the new NF Mk XV. In this 'operational' format the second crew-member was carried once again and the 24-gallon wing tanks were re-fitted. Although four guns had been designed to go into the ventral pack, normally only two were carried. By the end of November it had been decided to build four more NF Mk XVs and these were DZ366, DZ385, DZ409 and DZ417, all of which had originally started on the production line as B Mk IVs. These machines were similar to the final version of MP469, but only DZ366 had the Merlin 61s fitted, while the others had Merlin 77s. These were finished in a special overall 'Deep Sky' colour and were initially based with the Fighter Interception Unit at RAF Ford. Later all five became C Flight of No.85 Sqn. based at RAF Hunsdon. The Ju 86 threat never reappeared and although flights and interceptions in excess of 44,000 ft were achieved, most of the NF Mk XVs went on to become testbeds for pressurised cockpits, or instructional airframes.

The PR Mk 32

Another very special high-altitude version of the Mosquito was the PR Mk 32. This type started out as a PR Mk XVI, MM328, which had been used for four-blade propeller trials in connection with the new Westland Welkin F Mk I fighter. This machine was fitted with the new Merlin RM15SM engines and the span extended to 59ft 2in in early 1944. It was passed to the PR Development Unit at RAF Benson on the 20th May 1944 and then to Rolls-Royce Ltd. on the 4th June for engine trials. It returned to No.1 PRU on the 3rd July for operational use. Tests showed that the altitude was increased by some 5,000ft and during August and September, five production versions were constructed. All of these, NS582, NS586, NS587, NS588 and NS589, were taken from a PR Mk XVI production batch and completed as PR Mk 32s. The type equipped No.540 Sqn., where NS589 made the first operational sortie on the 5th December 1944, flown by Wg. Cdr. H.W.Ball DSO DFC and Flt. Lt. E.G.Leatham DFC. No. 540 Squadron had only two PR Mk 32s (NS589 & NS582), while No.544 Squadron had just one (NS587). They used this machine for the first time on the 23rd December on a sortie to Hamburg and Magdeburg. This version was almost a ton lighter than the PR Mk XVI and had a reduced fuel capacity of 660 gallons which allowed it to reach a ceiling of 42,000ft, whilst still being faster than the PR Mk XVI.

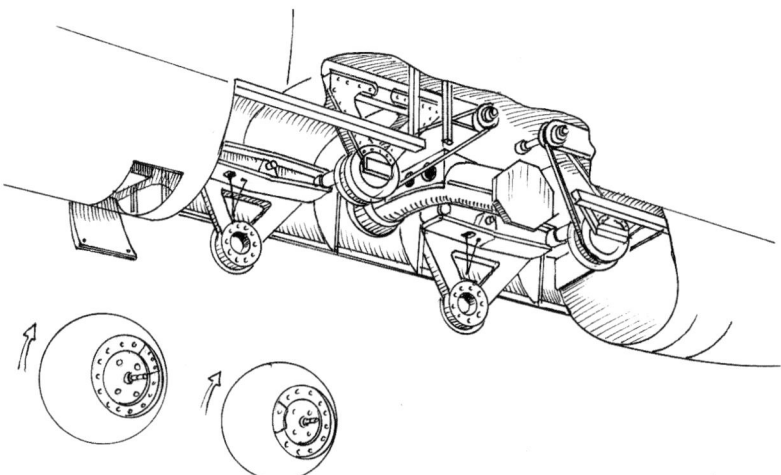

This diagram shows the twin Highball installation in the B Mk IV *(© A.Oliver)*

'Highball'

The *Highball* weapon was devised by Dr Barnes Wallis and this spherical bouncing bomb was developed alongside the famous *Upkeep* weapon used by the Dambusters (No.617 Sqn.). The B Mk IV was destined to be modified to carry this weapon, although it was never to be used in anger. The weapon was originally intended to sink the *Tirpitz*, which was anchored in the Alten Fjord and to this end No.618 Sqn. was formed at Skitten on the 1st April 1943 and was commanded by Sqn. Ldr. C.F. Rose DFC DFM.

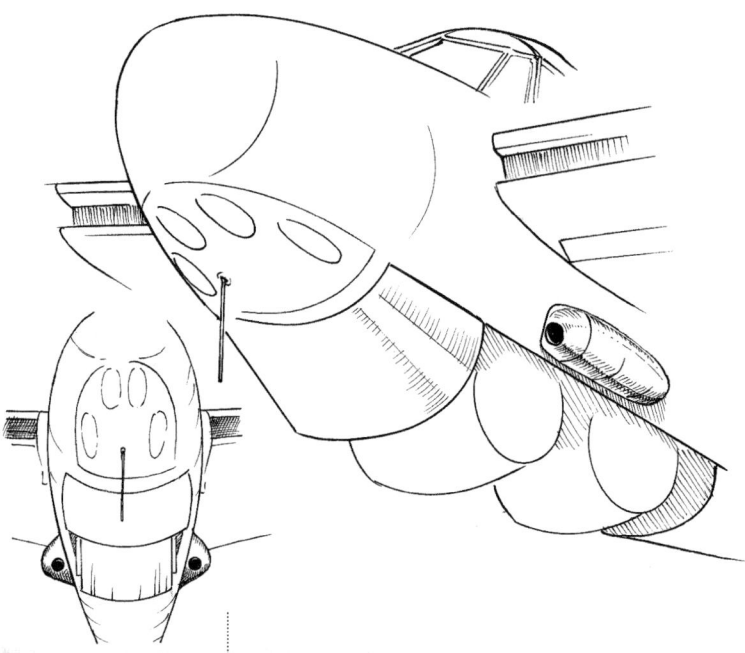

These two views depict the large air intakes fitted to the Highball Mosquitos when the air-turbine was installed *(© A.Oliver)*

Initially the Beaufort had been considered for the task, but by the time the weapon was sufficiently developed in 1942 the Mosquito B Mk IV was modified to carry two of them, one behind the other. The bomb-bay doors were removed and the bomb-bay was widened to accept the weapons. Each was suspended in an inverted 'A' frame and they were spun anticlockwise at nearly 700rpm before release. These booms could be spun thanks to a turbine, which had air scoops on either side of the bomb-bay, and they could be activated any time during the Mosquito's decent to 25ft above the water. Drive from the turbine to the bomb was via a simple pulley and belt assembly and each weapon was a 32in sphere with a stub-axle suspended in the 'A' frame. Trials with this weapon were carried out by DK290/G in late March 1943. This machine had been sent to Heston on the 24th March and converted to carry this new weapon. The initial trials were carried out at Reculver, and twenty-three *Highballs* were dropped between the 13th and 29th April. Initially the weapons were clad in wood, but these were found to explode on impact with the water and were therefore later reclad with steel. The trials were undertaken by No.618 squadron against a target ship, the *Bonaventure*, moored in Loch Cairbawn. The attack on the *Tirpitz* was planned for the 15th May 1943, so the squadron had to hurry with its preparations. In the end however problems with the dropping gear, plus the bomb casing, meant that this timescale was not achieved. The squadron had fifteen aircraft by the end of May, but the use of the weapon and its further development did mean that its was not used operationally. There had been plans to use *Highball* as a depth charge, although this was cancelled and they even trialed the weapon for anti-train operations, bouncing it up a railway line into a tunnel. By May 1944 an air-turbine system was developed for the spinning gear and fifty-four weapons had been dropped during development of a new sighting device. By this time No.618 squadron no longer had any operational requirement, so the crews were often seconded to No.248 Sqn. to operate the FB Mk XVIII with its 57mm cannon.

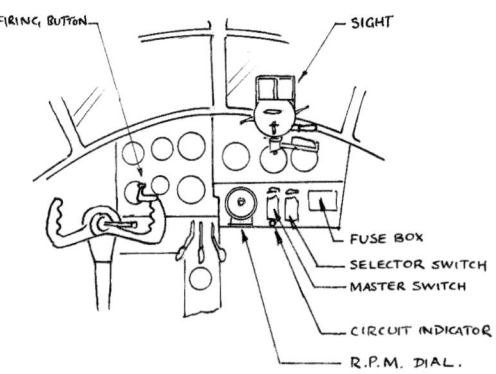

This sketch shows the cockpit layout of the equipment fitted for Highball operations *(© A.Oliver)*

On the 9th July 1944, No.618 squadron was re-formed and its operational task was revised, as it was decided that the unit could be used for carrier-based anti-shipping operations in the Pacific under the code name *Oxtail*. All of the squadron's machines were now modified to meet this new task. Vickers-Armstrong Ltd and Marshalls Flying Services Ltd undertook the modification work which included the fitment of armour plate, revised canopy glazings, the fitment of Merlin 25s in lieu of the previous Merlin 21s or 23s and the fitment of an arrestor hook and four-blade propellers for carrier operations. It is not known if the aircraft were fitted with the extended tailplanes of the TR Mk 33 Sea Mosquito, but it seems likely

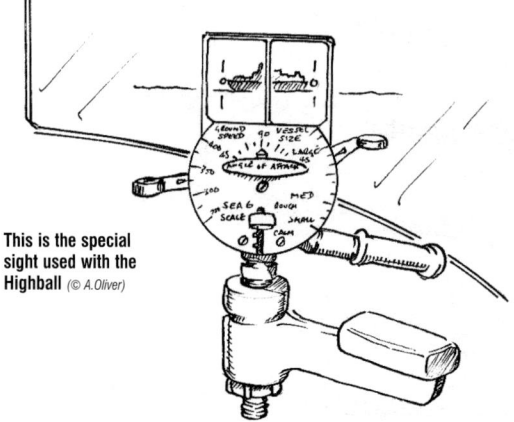

This is the special sight used with the Highball *(© A.Oliver)*

that this might be the case. The unit started to train for deck landings at Crail in Fairey Barracudas and once they had been equipped with three PR Mk XVIs (NS729, NS732 and NS735) as well as their special B Mk IVs, the unit started deck landings with the Mosquito on the 10th October. On the 31st October the B Mk IVs and three PR Mk XVIs departed the UK aboard HMS *Fencer* and *Striker*, and arrived in Melbourne on the 23rd December. In the end the unit was never used in anger, and on the 29th June 1946 was disbanded. The *Highball* weapons were all destroyed in-situ for security reasons and the squadron's Mosquitos were scrapped.

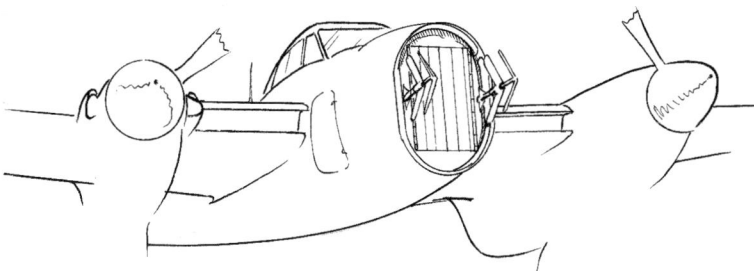

Turbinlite installation in Mk II (W4087) *(© A.Oliver)*

Turbinlite

The Helmore Turbinlite was an airborne searchlight of some 2,600 million candle-power and it was developed by General Electric Co under the sponsorship of A.C.W.Helmore CBE FRAES, the Ministry of Aircraft Production Scientific Adviser. The unit was fitted into a number of Douglas Havoc I and II aircraft and it was not long before the Mosquito was also considered for this equipment. An NF Mk II (W4087) was fitted with the unit by Alan Muntz at Heston between 14th October and 31st December, the power for the light being supplied by 26 battery units housed in the rear of the cannon bay, while the Turbinlite was fitted into a re-profiled nose. The power of this unit was massive, being the most powerful searchlight in the world at this time at 1,400 amps in comparison to the standard Army units which were 150 amps. The Turbinlite unit was fitted with a para-elliptical reflector unit and this gave a long beam of some 950 yards wide at 1 mile distance. The idea was to use the aircraft (fitted with A.I. Mk V radar) to vector onto a raider, then illuminate it for the other Mosquito NF Mk IIs or Defiant and Hurricane night fighters to attack it. By this time the idea had been surpassed by the new centrimetric radar units, such as the Mk VIII in the Mosquito NF Mk XII, and the whole thing was finally dropped, without the Mosquito Turbinlite ever having been used operationally.

Tse-Tse

Right at the beginning of the Mk II's development it had been considered for convoy operations, and the NF Mk IIs and FB Mk VIs had proved themselves very suitable for anti-shipping work in the Mediterranean. It was a letter to R.E.Bishop, the chief designer at De Havilland, from the Ministry of Aircraft Production on the 10th March 1943, which first asked about the fitment of a six-pounder cannon

MM424, an FB Mk XVIII depicted prior to delivery *(Real Photo)*

into the Mosquito airframe. To see what effect the 8,000lb of recoil force would have on a Mosquito airframe, De Havilland used the nose of a crashed Mosquito and fitted a six-pound field gun into it. The weapon was then fired, while the effects were recorded on ciné film. Final design work was carried out in another damaged airframe, to clear up areas such as the mounting and ammo feed for the weapon. Just three months

The front end of an FB Mk XVIII. The muzzle of the Molins 57mm cannon can be seen at the bottom of the nose, with the bulge for the breech mechanism just behind it *(Hawker Siddeley)*

Special Operations 27

A BOAC operated FB Mk VI comes in to land at Leuchars
(British Airways)

G-AGGF (HJ720), an FB Mk VI of B.O.A.C is depicted taxing out for another flight

later, an FB Mk VI (HJ732/G) had been fitted with the Molins 57mm quick-firing cannon. In this configuration the aircraft was known as the FB Mk XVIII. The aircraft was intended for use on anti-U-boat operations and the initial order was for thirty machines, all to be converted from an existing order for FB Mk VIs, although in the end just eighteen machines, plus the prototype, were made. The type was designed to keep its four machine-guns in the nose, although many users just retained two to aid aiming the 57mm cannon. Fuel tankage was supplemented by either 50- or 100-gallon drop-tanks and a 65-gallon long-range tank in the bomb-bay. With the addition of this tank the type could range right into the Bay of Biscay and with the ability to carry either two 500lb bombs or eight 3" rocket projectiles, the FB Mk XVIII had a formidable bite.

The first prototype was test firing the 57mm cannon by the 6th June and on the 8th came its debut flight. The aircraft was flown to A.&A.E.E. Boscombe Down for service evaluation on the 12th. Trials here were satisfactory, but there were problems with the ammo-feed system and some modifications had to be made to this before the type could be accepted. Because of the shortage of FB Mk VIs, the initial batch produced was just three (HX902, HX903 & HX904). These machines were issued to a Beaufighter unit, No.248 Sqn., who were based at Predannack, Cornwall on the 22nd October 1943. The first operational sortie, with HX902 (DM•E) and HX903 (HX•I), was made over the Bay of Biscay on the 24th October. As noted in the *Highball* section, many No.618 squadron crews were seconded to this squadron and on the second operational sortie on the 4th November, the CO of No.618 Squadron, Sqn. Ldr. C.F.Rose DFC DFM, was killed when his aircraft disintegrated during an emergency ditching. The squadron changed from Beaufighter to Mosquito FB Mk VIs in December 1943 and in March 1944 the FB Mk XVIIIs came under a separate detachment within the squadron. In January 1945 the squadron's FB Mk XVIIIs were withdrawn from service, as the 3" rocket projectile was more effective. Five FB Mk XVIIIs did serve from March to May 1945 with No.254 Sqn., at North Coates alongside the unit's usual Beaufighters. In the end the FB Mk XVIII had helped to account for ten U-boats in co-operation with other FB Mk VIs and Beaufighters. At the end of the war two FB Mk XVIIIs were fitted with arrestor hooks and sent for evaluation at NAS Patuxent River test facility in the USA. These machines later became NX66422 and NT220.

BOAC

During the war the UK needed to keep contact with Sweden, which was neutral, mainly for the supply of high-quality precision-machined products such as ball-bearings and springs as well as the supply of machine-tool steel. Initially BOAC had operated two Lockheed Lodestars from Leuchars to Stockholm. Because of the war situation and the poor performance of the type, they had to use bad weather and cloud cover as protection and by 1942 BOAC was pressing for the supply of Mosquitoes to run this route. Initially the government did not want to offer a front-line type, so the Whitley and Albemarle were offered instead. BOAC was not interested and still pressed for some Mosquitoes. The route had already been proven by a Mosquito, when a B Mk IV (DK292) of No.105 Sqn. had flown to Stockholm on the 6th August 1942 to deliver a diplomatic bag. For this flight the RAF crew wore civilian clothes and the aircraft had all roundels, serials and squadron markings removed.

The BOAC received its first Mosquito on the 15th December 1942, in the form of a B Mk IV DZ411, which became G-AGFV. The first flight to Stockholm was made by Capt. C.B.Houlder and R/O. F. Frape on the 4th February 1943, with another twelve being completed by the end of April. This first machine was then followed by another six aircraft, all FB Mk VIs; HJ680, HJ681, HJ718, HJ720, HJ721 and HJ723. They each went into BOAC service with the following registrations; G-AGGC (HJ680), G-AGGD (HJ681), G-AGGE (HJ718), G-AGGF (HJ720), G-AGGG (HJ721) and G-AGGH (HJ723). The first machine, G-AGFV, was badly damaged on the night of the 22/23rd April, when it was attacked by Focke Wulf Fw 190s, and had to make an emergency landing at Barkaby near Stockholm. The aircraft was eventually repaired in-situ but it was the 10th December before she was ready to fly again. The type was also used to carry a passenger in the bomb-bay and this modification was carried out in literally a few hours, so a negotiator could be rushed out to arrange the purchase of all Sweden's ball-bearing production in advance of the Germans, whose own production had just been severely effected by the USAAF raid on their factories at Schweinfurt on the 17th August 1943. Operations with a passenger became quite common, but the poor passenger had a nerve-racking flight sitting on top of the bomb-bay doors with only an intercom mic. to communicate with the pilot and no idea of what was happening outside. In the end the BOAC only lost two passengers, one being a BOAC pilot (Capt. B.W.B.Orton) who was travelling as a passenger when G-AGKP crashed mysteriously on the 18/19th August 1944. The other was a Mr Carl Rogers who was killed when G-AGGG crashed about a mile from Leuchars on the 25th October 1943, due to an engine failure. G-AGGF was also lost when it crashed at Invermaik on the 17th August 1943, killing the pilot Capt. L.A.Wilkins and R/O. Beaumont. During January 1944, G-AGGD was damaged beyond repair in a landing accident and this machine was reduced to spares on-site at Leuchars. During April 1944 three more Mosquito FB Mk VIs were delivered, these were G-AGKO (HJ667), G-AGKP (LR296) and G-AGKR (HJ792). These were supplemented by three T Mk IIIs which were loaned by the RAF for pilot training. The final loss of a Mosquito in BOAC service was when G-AGKR disappeared without trace after leaving

Gothenburg on the 29th August 1944. The pilot, Capt. White and R/O. Gaffney were never found.

The final BOAC flight to Sweden was on the 17th May 1945 after 520 flights had been achieved. G-AGGE, G-AGGH and G-AGKO were handed back to the RAF on the 22nd June and were followed by G-AGGC on the 9th January 1946.

100 Group

During 1942 the Commander-in-Chief of Bomber Command, Sir Arthur Harris, had suggested that the Mosquito should mix in with the bomber streams, so they could attack and destroy the German night fighters which were inflicting such grievous losses on the heavies. On the 8th November 1943 No. 100 (Bomber Support) Group was formed. Initial trials were carried out with No.141 Squadron Beaufighters fitted with A.I. radar and *Serrate*. This device could get a fix on the German *Lichtenstein* radar from about 100 miles, although this was confined to a bearing and no range. These flights were followed by the adoption of No.605 (County of Warwick) Sqn. for the task. They made their first sortie on the 31st August 1943 with *Serrate*-equipped NF Mk IIs. No.239 Sqn. soon joined the group and they had NF Mk IIs fitted with the early A.I. Mk IV and these machines had antenna on the leading-edges of the wings. The next squadron to join was No. 169, which also had *Serrate*-equipped NF Mk IIs. The first kill was to be claimed by No.141 Sqn. on the 20th January 1944 by HJ711. Attacks from the rear were a common Luftwaffe night fighter tactic and to this end rearward-looking radar was developed and this was first tried on two Mosquito NF Mk IIs (DZ299 & HJ902), followed by another (HJ705), which were all operated by the Fighter Interception Unit based at Ford. The first operational use of these machines was on a mission to Maastricht and Paris on the 25th August 1943, by HJ702. These offensive operations were code-named *Mahmoud* and they consisted of the Mosquitoes either getting amongst the bomber streams, or circling the German night fighter assembly points.

Radar-jamming work by the group did require the operating frequencies to be discovered and therefore radar monitoring became a task for the group as well. To do this three Mosquito B Mk IVs, DZ375, DZ376 and DZ410, were specially modified and passed to No.1474 Flight in November 1942. This unit started to train with the new equipment and on the 4th January 1943, the flight was renumbered as No.192 Sqn. The complexity of the equipment aboard these machines was such that the squadron did not become operational until the 11th June 1943, when DZ410 patrolled between Texel and Calais. This unit was supplemented by another 'jammer' when No.515 Sqn. (which formed on the 1st October 1942) became operational with the Mosquito in March 1944. By early 1944, the NF Mk IIs of the group were becoming increasingly unreliable and therefore they were re-engined with newer Merlin 22s. All *Serrate*-equipped units within the group also had their NF Mk IIs replaced with FB Mk VIs during 1944. By this time however two night fighter squadrons, No.85 and No.157, had been moved over to assist with the protection of the bomber streams. These squadrons operated the A.I. Mk X equipped NF Mk 30 and they also had *Monica I* (later *Monica VI*) rearward-looking radar. The units first became operational in this role in May 1944, but by the end of June they had both been diverted to anti-V-1 operations. The space left by the loss of these units was filled by the first intruder unit, No.23 in July. During April and May the new Bomber Support Development Unit (BSDU) had been set up at Foulsham to deal with the radar-equipment installations in all 100 Group machines and in June the unit received its first A.I. Mk XV from America. This unit was also known as ASH, for Air to Surface Home, and initially the installation of this

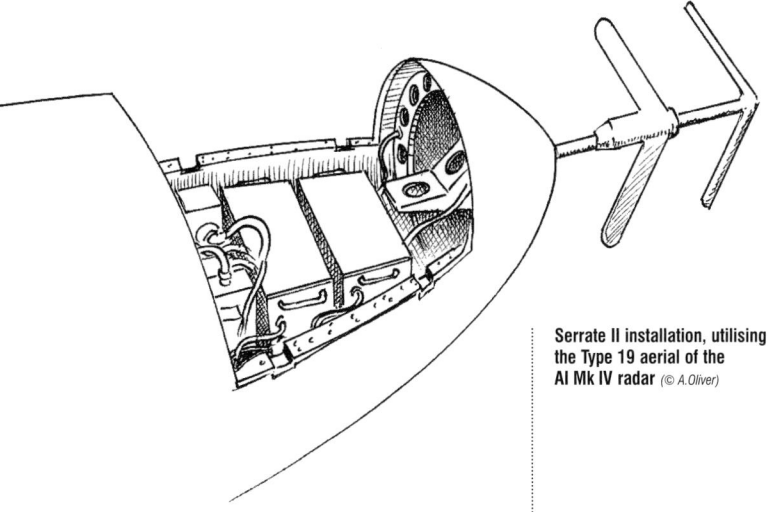

Serrate II installation, utilising the Type 19 aerial of the AI Mk IV radar (© A.Oliver)

equipment in a Mosquito had been thought of as a separate pod on the starboard wing leading-edge. However, in the end, the BSDU devised a new radome for the radar's scanner unit and this was to become universally known as the 'thimble' nose radome. It was fitted to a number of FB Mk VIs of No.23, 141 and 515 squadrons. The first success with this radar was achieved on the 1st January 1945, when Sqn. Ldr. Tweedale and Flt. Lt. Cunningham in RS507 downed a Ju 88 near Ahlhorn. 100 Group Mosquitos were also the first to use a new weapon in operations code-named *Firebash* during the latter stages of the war when seven Mosquitoes of No.141 Sqn. dropped 100-gallon

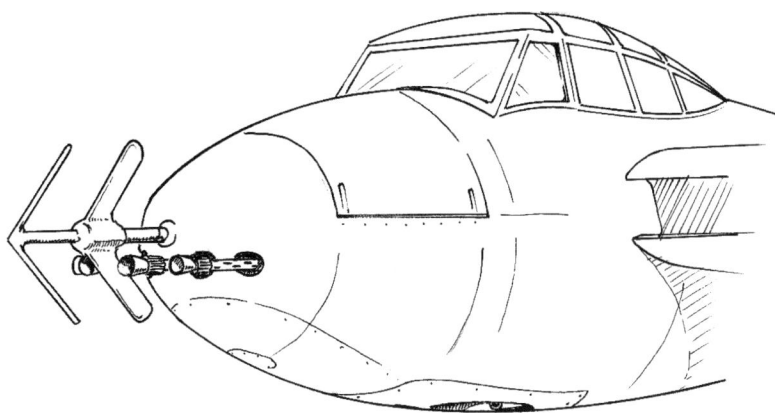

A.I. Mk IV installation in the NF Mk II (note, Serrate II aircraft had no machine guns) (© A.Oliver)

tanks containing *Napalm* gel on the airfield at Neubiburg on the 14th April 1945, heralding this weapon's use in future conflicts.

A good indication of the longevity of the Mosquito design is shown by a B Mk IV, W4071. This machine was issued to No.192 Sqn., in the radar monitoring role, although originally it had taken part in the first Mosquito sortie of the war (to Cologne in May 1942) and it was also to undertake the last operational B Mk IV sortie of the war, on the 9th April 1945!

All at Sea

Chapter 6

The Mosquito was used by the Coastal Command for the first time in an offensive role form when No.333 (Norwegian) Squadron was formed, from No.1477 (Norwegian) Flight at Banff, by Gp. Cpt. Max Aitken DSO DFC on the 10th May 1943. Operations by No.333 Sqn. started that month, using their NF Mk IIs, when they carried out reconnaissance and anti-shipping duties along the Norwegian coast, of which they had intimate, personal knowledge. In September they were re-equipped with the FB Mk VI and at Predannack, Cornwall, No.248 Squadron received the FB Mk VI in December. No.248 Squadron was to start operations with the 57mm Molins armed FB Mk XVIII in March 1944. The operation of this type is covered in Chapter 5, but alongside the FB.XVIII they operated the FB Mk VI. On the 16th June No.248 Squadron was joined by a second FB Mk VI equipped squadron, No.235. This squadron had swapped its Beaufighters for the Mosquito and both it and No.248 Sqn. moved to Banff in Scotland during September, having flown their last operational sortie from Predannack on the 7th. These two squadrons joined No.333 (Norwegian) Sqn. and began operations against enemy shipping along the Norwegian coast. On the 28th September, the Wing's aircraft were modified to carry eight of the new 3" rocket projectiles. Trials with these rockets on the Mosquito had been carried out on an FB Mk VI (HJ719) in October 1943 and due to its rocket-propulsion system, the weapon did not have the recoil stresses associated with a big gun such as the Molins 57mm cannon. The rocket projectile was also far easier and cheaper to produce and therefore was made in larger quantities. Four of these weapons were carried on Mk 1 rails under each outer wing panel and they had to be placed parallel with the airflow, otherwise, once launched, the rockets would weathercock and veer off course. Use of this weapon was not as simple as it may seem, as they had to be launched within a certain speed envelope and it was also found that an attack angle of about 20° was the best. Initially the rockets carried the 60lb (27kg) semi-armour-piercing heads, which had been utilised against armour with excellent success by the Hurricane and Beaufighter, although these were found to have little effect on shipping and were soon replaced with the 25lb (11kg) armour-piercing heads. The first operational use of these new weapons was undertaken by the Wing on the 26th October. The two Beaufighter squadrons at Banff left on the 22nd October for Dallachy, and

No.143 Squadron moved up from North Coates to join the rest of the Wing. This squadron flew its first operation on the 7th November, with a mission between Obrestad and Lindesnes. The operational size of the Banff Wing increased during the latter part of the year, and combined operations with the Beaufighters based at Dallachy were not uncommon. Operations included the squadron's FB Mk VIs as well as the FB Mk XVIII of the special detachment in No.248 Sqn. The commander of No.235 Squadron, Wg. Cdr. R.A.Atkinson DSO DFC, was killed on the 13th December, when his Mosquito crashed during a sortie against a merchantman in Ejdsfjord. Operations during late

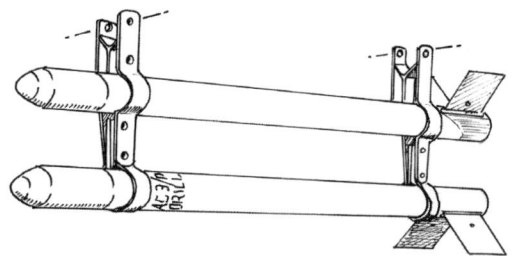

1944 and early 1945 had led to quite a high loss rate, as the fjords and ships were well protected with both flak and fighters. The 57mm armed FB Mk XVIIIs were withdrawn in January 1945 and sent south to North Coates, and in February No.235 Squadron took their FB Mk VIs into action armed with the 3" rockets for the first time. By March the Mosquitoes of the Wing

PZ202 was an FB Mk VI built at Hatfield during May 1944 to June 1946. This machine was issued to A.&A.E.E. Boscombe Down and was used for rocket projectile and drop-tank trials. This machine is fitted with a twin-tier rocket installation and 100-gallon drop tanks. The camera mounted in the nose is noteworthy, as production FB Mk VIs carried their camera off-set to port, not centrally *(BAe)*

This sketch shows the trial two-tier arrangement tested on PZ202. This system, when used operationally, had the standard four-fin units installed *(© A.Oliver)*

Far left: A view from the back of the rocket installation on the FB Mk VI *(C.E.Brown)*

Left: In this view of the 3" rockets under the FB Mk VI's wing the 'T' aerial of the radio altimeter fitted to the type can also be seen *(C.E.Brown)*

started to operate freelance from the Beaufighters, and it was not long after that the new Mk 1b rocket rails were available. These rails allowed the fitment of a two-tier arrangement of the rockets and this in turn meant that long-range drop-tanks could be fitted. During the early part of 1945, the Wing operated on a number of anti-shipping missions along the coast and over Denmark. On the 9th April a formation of thirty-one FB Mk VIs, all rocket armed, set out for the Kattegat in Denmark and once there, they discovered three U-boats (804, 843 and 1065) on the surface in a neat line astern. Sqn. Ldr. Bert Gunnis DFC, ordered No.143 Sqn. to attack and during the next few minutes the Mosquitoes sunk all three of the U-boats. To give some idea of the low-level at which such attacks were carried out, in this one the PR Mosquito which had accompanied the Wing on the sortie was brought down by the explosion of one of the submarines and three other Mosquitoes had to crash-land in Sweden because of damage to their engines caused by flying debris.

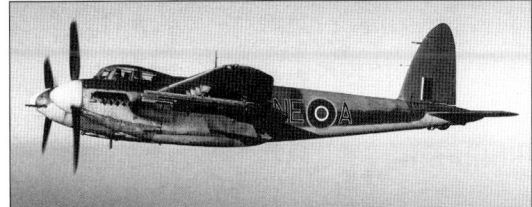

Although a well known photograph, this shot of FB Mk VI (HR405), nonetheless shows the overall finish of a Banff Strike Wing aircraft to perfection (C.E.Brown)

On the 22nd April, No.404 (Buffalo) Squadron flew its first mission with the Wing, having re-equipped with the Mosquito in early March. The war was now drawing to a close and although the U-259 was sunk at Kattegat on the 2nd May, the last operational strike by the Wing was carried out on the 4th May. On this day forty-eight machines of Nos.143, 235, 248, 333 and 404 Squadrons undertook a sortie to Kiel Bay and it was during this sortie that Flt. Lt. Gerry Yeates of No.248 Squadron managed to come back with the top of a flag pole embedded under the nose of his Mosquito, German Naval flag and all! With the anti-U-boat patrols at an end, the Wing concentrated on operations against the remaining E-boats, but by the end of May 1945 coastal strikes were coming to a close.

A very atmospheric shot that shows a formation of Banff Wing FB Mk VIs setting out for another mission (via S.Howe)

The Royal Navy had been interested in the Mosquito throughout the war. However, due to the RAF's demand on the type, they were not able to obtain any quantity. Design studies for a naval Mosquito had been undertaken by D.H. Ltd for a number of specifications, including S.11/43. A naval version of the Mosquito with the A.I. Mk VIII was considered, but

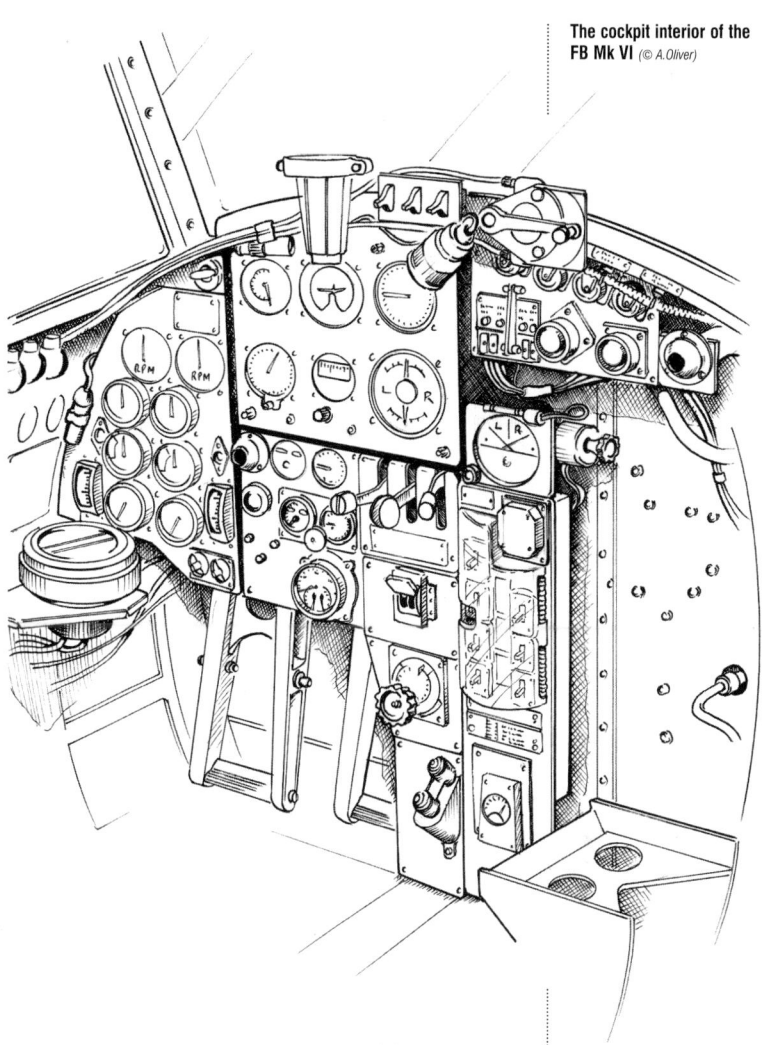

The cockpit interior of the FB Mk VI (© A.Oliver)

Below: This is another view of HR405 and it shows the amount of dirt and oil underneath the type during operations. The repair patches over the control pulleys for the port elevator are noteworthy (C.E.Brown)

All at Sea

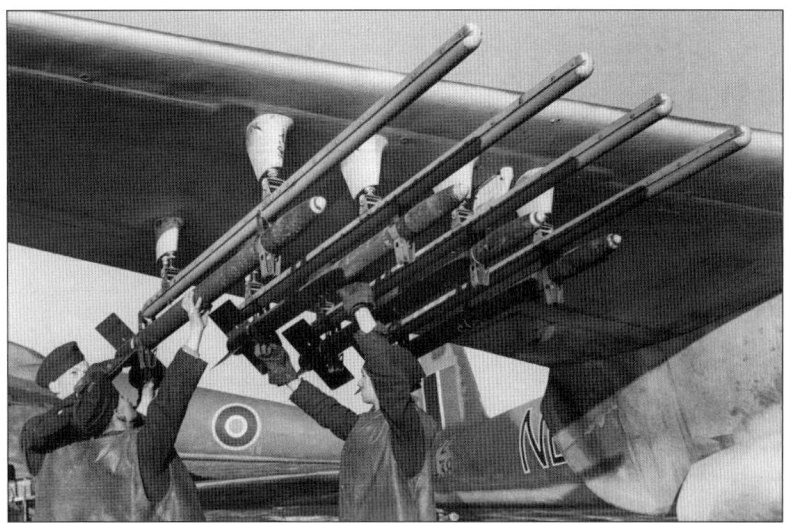

Armourers fit 3" rocket projectiles, with 25lb A.P. heads under the wings of an FB Mk VI of the Banff Wing *(C.E.Brown)*

HR632 was a Standard Motor-built FB Mk VI which saw service with No.248 Squadron based at Banff. This machine was lost in action on the 13th March 1945 *(C.E.Brown)*

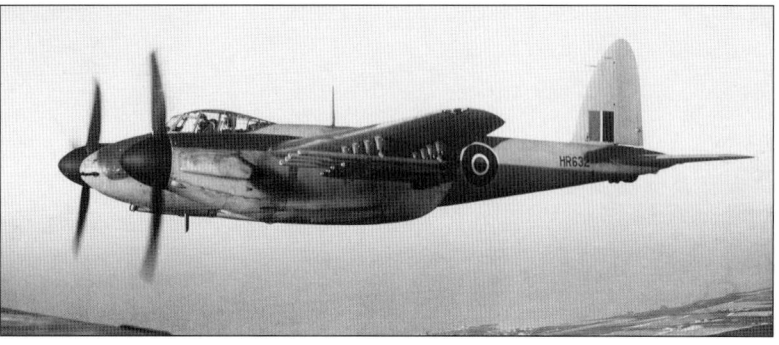

The 18" Mk XV torpedo fitted under the centreline of a TR Mk 33 Sea Mosquito *(BAe)*

by some 10%. This first version of a Naval Mosquito did not feature folding outer wing panels. Evaluation of the type's suitability for carrier operations was undertaken by Lt. Cdr. Eric 'Winkle' Brown OBE DSC, who was asked to land the type on a carrier. These trials took place in March 1944 on *HMS Indefatigable*, which although it had a 766ft (233m) long deck, was only 95ft (30m) wide and narrower (80ft, 24m) at the island. Landing an aircraft with a 54ft (16.5m) span on an 80ft (24m) deck was hard enough, but one that was pitching in a swell? Lt Cdr. Brown undertook the first landing on the 25th March and his main concerns were about the strength of the arrestor hook and unmodified undercarriage, because the Mosquito weighed 16,000lb (7,260kg), even without any armament fitted. The landing itself was achieved at 78mph (125kph) without a hitch and successive landings were made with the aircraft getting heavier and heavier. The only problem occurred at a weight of 18,000lb when the arrestor hook claw

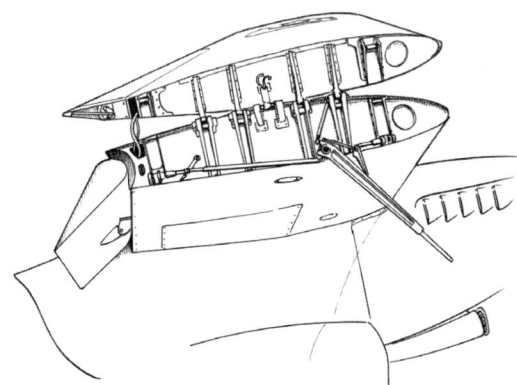

This sketch illustrates how the outer wing panels on the TR Mk 33 fold *(© A.Oliver)*

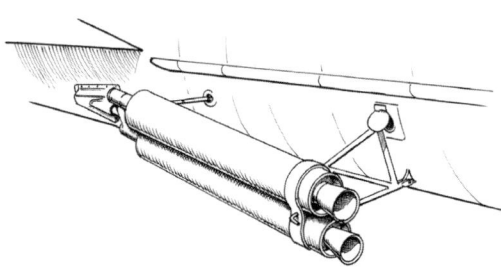

A sketch of the twin (detachable) RATO bottles carried by the TR Mk 33 *(©A.Oliver)*

sheared a bolt and rotated, slipping the wire, and Lt. Cdr. Brown had to push the throttles through the stops and make a hasty getaway from the carrier deck to avoid going over the side. The second prototype was another FB Mk VI (LR387) and this machine featured manual wing-fold for the outer wing panels. Converting the Mosquito for Naval use was difficult and many elements of the design were not suited to carrier operations. The fitment of a hydraulic wing-folding system was out of the question, as this would have necessitated a complete redesign of the entire hydraulic system. Even with the wing folded, its span (27ft 3in), was still too large for the standard lifts (20ft) fitted to the carriers then operated by the navy.

Production of the new TR Mk 33 was started in late 1945 and the first production TR Mk 33 (TW227) off the assembly line at Leavesden flew on the 10th November 1945. Although a wing-fold had been specified originally, the first thirteen machines did not have this facility. The fourteenth TR Mk 33 emerged not only with a wing-fold but with a new undercarriage system. The rubber-in-compression system of the Mosquito had too much rebound for deck landings and so it was replaced with a Lockheed system with oleo-pneumatic legs. At the same time

eventually the Navy decided that a simple 'navalised' version of the successful FB Mk VI would meet their needs. Nineteen FB Mk VIs had been delivered to the Royal Navy as crew trainers for proposed operations in the Pacific. This type was also to be used later for the training of the new TR Mk 33 crews and at least one machine (PZ281) had an arrestor hook fitted.

During 1944 the Admiralty had issued a specification (N.15/44) which called for a twin-engine aircraft capable of operating from a carrier. De Havilland considered that their FB Mk VI was up to the task and to this end they converted one, LR359, to the prototype TR Mk 33. This machine featured an A-frame arrestor hook, strengthened fuselage, more powerful Merlin 25 engines, enlarged elevators and non-feathering four-blade De Havilland propellers of 12ft 6in diameter. The use of the more powerful engines coupled with the larger-diameter propellers meant that the overall thrust achieved was increased the diameter for the mainwheels was reduced slightly. The type had been designed from the outset to carry a torpedo in the form of an 18in (46cm) diameter Mk XV or XVII unit which was carried under the fuselage on the centreline. There was also provision for a depth charge or 2,000lb (910kg) A.P. bomb to be carried in the same location. As usual, two 500lb (230kg) bombs could be carried in the aft bomb bay and although the prototype did not carry any armament, production machines retained the four 20mm cannon. Fuel tankage could be supplemented with either two 50-gallon (230 lt) or two 30-gallon (136 lt) drop tanks on the outer wing pylons. When the 30-gallon tanks were fitted two 3" rocket projectiles could also be carried under each wing, outboard of the tanks. The type also used the ASH (Air to Surface Home) radar pod that had first been used in No.100 Group FB Mk VIs and this was housed in the 'thimble' nose

TS449 is one of two Sea Mosquitoes operated by the Royal Navy for handling trials. This machine is shown here fitted with RATO bottles *(De Havilland)*

radome. Because of the need for overload take-off ability, the type was also stressed for RATO (Rocket Assisted Take-Off) bottles and these were carried on either side of the lower rear fuselage, two per side. The type also featured the revised fighter canopy with the glazing alongside the navigator 'blown' to allow better forward and rear vision for that crew member. This style

A view of TF Mk 37, VT724 *(Francis Bergese)*

of canopy was also used on the J 30, all FB Mk VIs sold to foreign countries post-war and in most fighter types produced in Canada and Australia. Two TR Mk 33s (TS444 and TS449) were used for handling trials by the Navy and in total fifty production TR Mk 33s were constructed. These machines were allocated serial numbers TW227 to TW257 and TW277 to TW295. With the cessation of hostilities another order for forty seven machines was cancelled.

Equipping a squadron with the TR Mk 33 began in August 1946, when No.811 Sqn., based at RNAS Ford (*HMS Peregrine*), received the first of fifty machines. This unit was no stranger to the Mosquito, as it had operated some fifteen FB Mk VIs supplied in September 1945. It continued to operate the type during the next 11 months, moving to RNAS Brawdy in January 1947, and eventually disbanding there in July 1947. Other operators of the type included No.771 Training Squadron at RNAS Lee-on-Solent (*HMS Daedalus*), who operated the type from 1947 to 1950, No.772 Training Squadrons at RNAS Arbroath during 1946 and 1947, No.762 Squadron at RNAS Ford

(1946-1949) and No.778 and No.790 Squadrons.

The TR Mk 33 Sea Mosquito was also used for development work on the improved version of the *Highball* weapon, called *Highball 2*. The weapon was envisaged for use in the TR Mk 33 as well as the new Sea Hornet and it was to be carried in a removable crate. Tests were carried out using two TR Mk 33s, TW230/G and PZ281. A further revision of the weapon called *Card*, was tested in TW228, but in the end neither of these weapons saw operational service.

The next Naval Mosquito was the TF Mk 37. This machine was only slightly revised from the TR Mk 33, in that it had the British ASV (Air to Surface Vessel) Mk XIII radar fitted. This unit required a more elongated radome, which changed the contour of the Sea Mosquito's nose. The prototype, TW240, was converted from a TR Mk 33 and only fourteen of the production version (VT724 -VT737) were ever constructed, all being made at Chester. Six saw service with No.703 squadron, while the rest were used for crew training and development work with the new radar system.

The navy can claim to have had the only 'ugly' Mosquito, in the form of the TT Mk 39 target tug. This type was designed as a shore-based, high-speed target-towing aircraft and the two prototypes were converted from B Mk XVIs by General Aircraft Ltd to specification Q.19/45. This variant, designated GAL 59 by General Aircraft Ltd, featured some radical changes to the shape of the type, not least of which was the huge extension to the nose which increased the overall length to 43ft 4in and which was extensively glazed with optically-flat panels. The crew of this new version was increased to four, with the new nose designed to house a camera operator and a compartment in the rear fuselage for the winch operator. The type also featured the four-blade non-feathering propellers of the TR Mk 33/TF Mk 37,

TW240, the prototype TF Mk 37. This machine was converted from a TR Mk 33 *(Real Photos)*

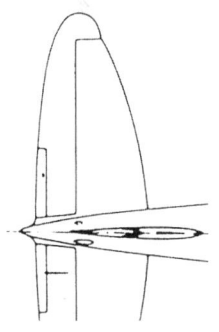

Enlarged elevator of Sea Mosquito

A line-up of TR Mk 33s (and a single Hornet), possibly at Hurn or St. Davids. These machines feature the revised nose fairing over the ASH pod. Note also the Lockheed oleo legs and the smaller mainwheels *(John English)*

VT724 was one of the Chester-built TF Mk 37s and it is shown here prior to delivery. Of note are the pitot tube on the starboard wing tip, the smaller mainwheels (with tread) and the revised radome *(Francis Bergese)*

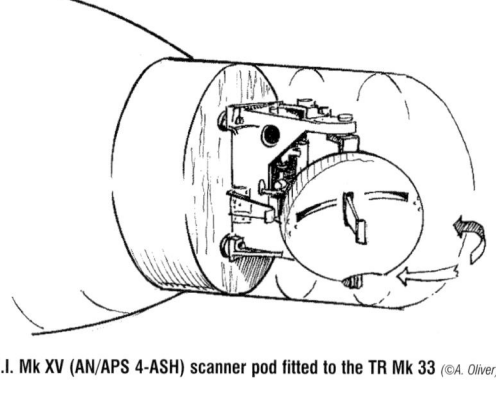

A.I. Mk XV (AN/APS 4-ASH) scanner pod fitted to the TR Mk 33 *(©A. Oliver)*

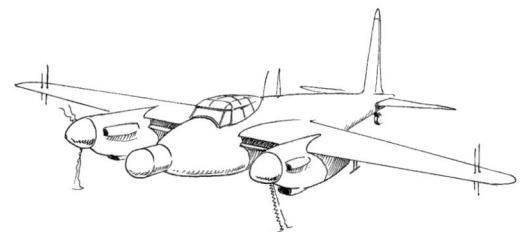

ASH pod and associated aerials of the TR Mk 33 *(©A. Oliver)*

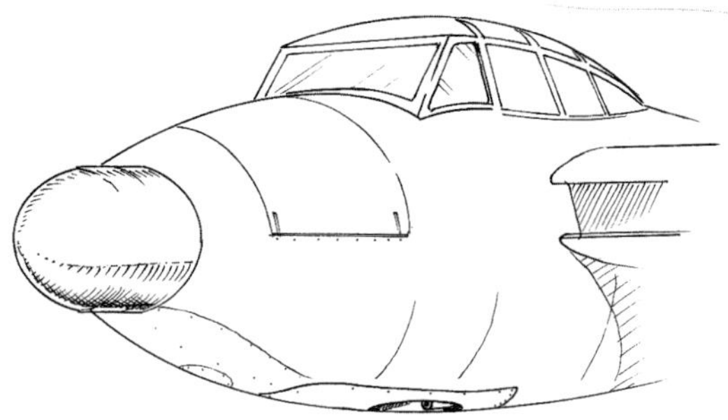

but because of the wider nose, each blade was cropped. The drogue winch was housed in the bomb bay and was only lowered when required. Six targets could be carried by this type and both winged (32ft or 16ft span versions) or sleeve (M3 or M4) types could be carried, with up to 6,000ft of cable available. The winch operator in the rear fuselage, aft of the rear spar, gained access through a new door in the undersurface of the rear fuselage. A glazed cupola was installed on the upper decking of the rear fuselage, so that he could see the drogue and

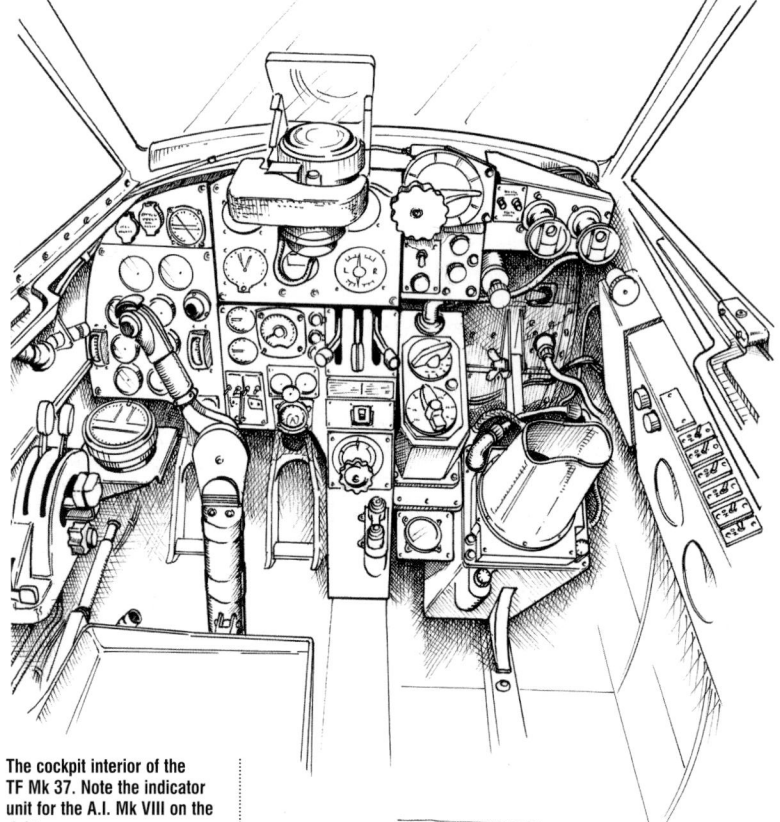

The cockpit interior of the TF Mk 37. Note the indicator unit for the A.I. Mk VIII on the right *(© A.Oliver)*

A.I. Mk VIII ASH pod in the nose of the Mosquito *(©A. Oliver)*

control its winch-out. Wire guards around the tail unit were installed as per the TT Mk 35 conversions and the only other modification carried out to the type was the strengthening of the entire rear fuselage, with reinforcing strips of a larger size on each side. The prototypes for this type were ML995 and PF569, both originally B Mk XVIs, and another twenty-four airframes were converted by General Aircraft Ltd at Hanworth. This type served with the Fleet Requirements Units (FRU) and with No.728 FRU at Hal Far, Malta from 1948, until they were replaced by the Sturgeon TT.2 in 1950.

PF606 was originally built as a B Mk XVI, but was converted to a TT Mk 39 by General Aircraft Ltd *(via S.Howe)*

34 Chapter 6

Worldwide Service

Chapter 7

The Mosquito design was intended for use in all theatres. Although it had mainly been used in Europe, its initial form of gluing did not lend itself to use in hot and humid climates. The type was, however, to see service all around the world, and in all types of climate.

The Far East

Climatic trials were conducted with four NF Mk IIs in India during February 1943 and they were followed by four more during May. Two of these machines used the new formaldehyde glue, instead of the usual casein version. This glue resisted tropical and humid environments far better as well as being far less susceptible to insect damage. An FB Mk VI also arrived in India on the 10th August for climatic trials. By this time the NF Mk IIs had been fitted with cameras and had joined No.681 Sqn. in Calcutta and were later joined by an FB Mk VI (HJ730) fitted with a camera in the nose. The first operational use of these machines also marked the first use of the Mosquito against the Japanese and this was a PR mission over the Mandalay region on the 23rd August by DZ697. A second unit, No.684, formed in Calcutta in October and they operated two NF Mk IIs, three FB Mk VIs, four North American Mitchells and a small number of the new PR Mk IX Mosquito, which were delivered on the 18th October 1943. The first operational sortie of the new PR Mk IX was undertaken by No.681 Sqn., when

LR440 flew on a mission to Rangoon and Magwe on the 21st October. This unit was to cease using the Mosquito in December and thereafter No.684 Sqn. became the principal PR Mosquito unit in this theatre, starting operations on the 1st November. On the second, DZ697, the Mosquito which had carried out the first PR mission against the Japanese in August, failed to return from a PR mission over Rangoon.

Use of the Mosquito in this area had shown that the type could stand humidity of over 78%, although repair was proving a bit of a problem, as the units could only do minor work in the field and stocks of wood could not be stored in any quantity at the store in Bengal. Two RAF MUs (Maintenance Units) near Calcutta undertook all major work and De Havilland Ltd had a subsidiary at Karachi which produced major components.

The FB Mk VI was soon to re-equip No.45 and No.82 Squadrons, which had previously used the Vultee Vengeance, and No.1672 Conversion Unit was set up at Yellahanka in January to train the crews. No.45 Squadron was the first to use the type operationally, with a tactical reconnaissance mission on the 28th

September and No.82 Sqn. followed with strike missions from October. On the 20th October however disaster struck, when an FB Mk VI of No.82 sqn, while attacking a target in a shallow dive at Random Range, had an outer wing panel fail and crashed. The wreckage was examined and it was found that the climate had indeed started to effect the structure of the Mosquito. There were cracks in both glue joints and the fabric and some outer skinning had separated from the spars. At once, all the Mosquitoes in India were grounded, with all machines which had been in use for three months flown to No.1 MU at Kanchrapara for inspection. All of those which used the new formaldehyde glue were found to be unaffected, but those with casein showed signs of deterioration. No major modifications were needed on any of the intact machines and they returned to operational use in November 1944, with No.45 Squadron and with No.82 Squadron on the 19th December. During this month No.684 Sqn. and its PR Mosquitoes had moved to Comilla in Bengal to undertake operations over northern Thailand and Burma. The FB Mk VIs of No.684 Sqn. undertook both PR and ground attack operations and in January 1945 the squadron returned to Calcutta. No.45 and No.82 squadrons were joined by a third FB Mk VI squadron, No.47. Initially the squadron had been instructed to re-equip with the Mosquito on the 19th September. It had sent back all its Beaufighters by the 5th October and had a full complement of Mosquitos. The failure of the wing of the Mosquito at the Random Ranges lead to an urgent signal on the 19th October which grounded the entire squadron's strength and so on the

DZ895, an F Mk II of a batch of eighty which were passed to Mediterranean Air Command (M.A.C) during early 1943. This machine is depicted here without squadron codes, so it was probably photographed during its delivery flight *(Crown Copyright)*

The disposal of Mosquitoes never posed a problem due to their wooden construction and KA158, a Canadian T Mk 29 is seen here being 'disposed of' at RAF Kasfarit, Egypt in late 1945 *(M.Payne)*

The first Canadian built B Mk VII (KB300), shown here during its first flight on the 24th September 1942. It is being flown by DH Canada Chief Test Pilot, Ralph Spradbrow *(Public Archives of Canada)*

Worldwide Service 35

Depicted here are three B Mk XXs of No.627 Squadron at Woodhall Spa in 1944. It was KB267 'E' of this squadron which crashed near Steenbergen on the 19th September 1944, killing the pilot Wg. Cdr. Guy P.Gibson VC DSO DFC and his navigator Sqn. Ldr. J.B.Warick DFC *(B.E.B.Harris)*

Canadian-built B Mk XX KA970 had an air bottle explode in flight during its Atlantic delivery flight. The pilot managed to make a successful crash landing at Prestwick. *(via S.Howe)*

This close-up of KA970s fuselage gives you an idea of the extent of the damage caused by the exploding air bottle *(BAe)*

This shows the third F-8-DH (43-4926), which was flown back to the UK by De Havilland Test Pilot, Pat Fillingham

30th November the Beaufighters returned! By February 1945 the machines of this squadron had been modified with the addition of a F.24 camera in the nose, so that the type could also undertake tactical reconnaissance missions to supplement the work of the PR Mk IXs and PR Mk XVIs of No.684 Sqn. A number of the new PR Mk XVIs to supplement their PR Mk IXs were supplied to No.684 Sqn. in February 1945 and they began operations in March. During this month two new fighter-bomber squadrons, No.84 and No.110 started to work up on the FB Mk VI and a sixth, No.211, joined the group in June, although it did not see operational use before VJ-Day. In May No.684 Sqn. moved once again, this time to Alipore, to fly operations over Bangkok and as far south as Singapore. Operations in this theatre were long and arduous, and the longest, a flight of 8hr 48min duration, was flown by Flt. Lt. Irvine on the 9th March 1945 in PR Mk XVI, NS695.

On the 16th June 1945, Flt. Lt. Irvine and Sqn. Ldr. Andrews flew a PR Mosquito on a mission to photograph Mount Everest. The type had been specially fitted with 14in F.52 cameras in the drop tanks and during the flight the aircraft circled the mountain for some 20 minutes. Another such mission was undertaken on the 1st July but heavy snow storms obscured the view. The last operational use of the Mosquito in the theatre was a mission by No.110 Sqn., which took place on the 20th August 1945 (five days after the end of the war) against a target at Tikedo.

Production Abroad

The De Havilland company had subsidiaries in both Canada and Australia, which were to produce the Mosquito in large numbers.

The decision to make the Mosquito in Canada had been made in 7th July 1941, after the Canadian Minister of Munitions and Supply, the Hon. C.D. Howe, saw the prototype Mosquito fly on the 29th December 1940. Production was to take place at the De Havilland Aircraft of Canada Ltd plant at Downsview, near Toronto. Prior to this in September 1940, the Packard Motor Co. of Detroit had undertaken licensed production of the Rolls Royce Merlin engine and these powerplants were to be used in all Canadian and Australian produced Mosquitoes. Detailed plans for the production of forty Mosquitoes a month were discussed throughout August 1941 and it was decided that two machines should been completed by September 1942, with the production rate rising to fifty per month by 1943. In September 1943 two De Havilland Hatfield-based engineers were sent to Canada, Mr Harry Povey (Chief Production Engineer) and Mr W.D.Hunter (Senior Designer). Their task was to adapt the standard De Havilland design for the use of Canadian materials and equipment, without major redesign. Setting up production at Downsview was protracted, with some material and tools being lost to enemy action at sea, and many of the parts required for the type were not as readily available from Canadian sources as had originally been hoped. The original fuselage jigs took three months to get from Hatfield to Downsview, by which time D.H.C. Ltd had made their own. Many new production processes were developed by Harry Povey, the De Havilland representative with D.H.C., and these included the use of concrete fuselage moulds. This system was later to be adopted by De Havilland in the UK.

The first production version from Canada was designated the B Mk VIII and twenty-five were produced (KB300-KB324). These machines still retained a large amount of British equipment, but were powered by the Packard Merlin 31s and had Hamilton Standard propellers, otherwise they were basically similar to the proposed B Mk V version. The first flight of the B Mk VII was undertaken by D.H.C. Chief Test Pilot, Ralph Spradbrow, on the 24th September 1942. Prior to this a B Mk IV (DK287) had been shipped to Canada as a pattern. The aircraft arrived late, just a few days before the B Mk VII's first flight, and was also damaged during shipment. This first production B Mk VII (KB300) was also flown in America, at Wright Field by Geoffrey de Havilland on the 29th October 1942.

Canadian-produced Mosquitoes had been allocated marks in the 20-29 series and the next production version was therefore the B Mk XX. In total 245 B Mk XXs were completed and they were basically a B Mk VII with the inclusion of far more American and Canadian equipment. Initially the first eight (KB100-179) had Packard Merlin 31 engines, as per the B Mk VII, but the remainder (KB180-299 and KB325-369) had the improved Packard Merlin 33s plus the provision for 50- or 100-gallon drop tanks. The first two machines supplied to the RAF, *New Glasgow* and *Acton*, flew via Greenland, Iceland and Prestwick and arrived at Hatfield on the 12th August 1943. These were followed by a further three in November. All of the Canadian-supplied machines were converted to RAF standard at No.13 MU, RAF Henlow and by VE-Day over 350 Canadian-built Mosquitoes had been sent to the RAF. The first unit to have the

36 Chapter 7

B Mk XX was No.139 Sqn. in November 1943 and these were later supplemented by B Mk 25s during October 1944.

The second unit to be equipped with Canadian machines was No.627 Sqn. which became operational with the B Mk XX on the 7th July 1944 with a mission to the V-1 depot at St Leu d'Esserent. No.608 Sqn. was the next unit to become operational with the B Mk XX, when it flew an operation to Wanne Eickel on the 5th August 1944. No.128 Sqn. followed when they became operational on the type on the 10th September with a mission to Berlin and No.142 Sqn. became operational with the B XX on the 28th October with a mission to Cologne. It was on the 19th September 1944, that a B Mk XX (KB627) was to be lost and with it its pilot Wg. Cdr. Guy Gibson VC, DSO DFC. The exact reason for the loss of this machine is still unclear, but it is likely that it suffered an engine failure at low level near the Dutch village of Steenbergen. In October 1944, No.608, 142 and 128 Squadrons received the new B Mk 25, while No.627 Sqn. received theirs in November.

The first Australian-built Mosquito, FB Mk 40 (A52-1), which flew for the first time on the 23rd July 1943 *(Frank F.Smith via S.Howe)*

The fitment of the new Packard version of the Merlin 25 (225) to the B Mk XX resulted in the B Mk 25. The proposed high-altitude B Mk 23 version with Packard Merlin 69s had never been put into production, so the B Mk 25 was the next production variant. Four hundred B Mk 25s were produced (KA930-999 and KB370-699), the first being KB370 and over 340 of them were used by Bomber Command. Approximately seventy of these machines were turned over to the Royal Navy in 1945 and were operated by the Fleet Requirements Unit (No.771 Sqn). The fitment of two-stage Merlin engines to the Canadian-produced machines was considered, but none were ever used and in the end the only modification carried out on the B Mk 25 was the fitment of the bulged bomb-bay door to five machines (KB409, KB416, KB490, KB561 and KB625), which were used by No.627 Sqn. to carry two 1,000lb Target Indicators.

The FB Mk 21 was the Canadian version of the FB Mk VI and it utilised the Packard Merlin 31 engines. Only three of these machines were built (KA100 to KA102), as with the arrival of the Packard Merlin 225 this type was superseded by the FB Mk 26. The FB Mk 21 was also developed into a two-seat trainer and this type, the T Mk 22, was powered by Packard Merlin 33s. Just six of these machines were built and they were allocated serial numbers in the KA873-KA876 and KA896-KA897 ranges. Due to a shortage of cannon and radio equipment a number of the FB Mk 26s were finished as

An Australian-built FB Mk 40 (A52-75) of No.94 Squadron photographed in 1945 *(Frank F.Smith via S.Howe)*

A line-up of Mosquitoes alongside some Oxfords at No.36 OTU. Greenwood, Novia Scotia, in June 1944. Visible are a B Mk XX (KB140) and two T Mk IIIs (HJ879 '6' and HJ883 '8') and points to note include the yellow wing leading-edges *(R.H.Dargue via S.Howe)*

The RCAF wanted to fly 'home-produced' Mosquitoes and asked if the first fifty machines could be issued to them. The Ministry of Aircraft Production in the UK decided that they would release twenty-four British-built T Mk III dual-control trainers to the RCAF and these were used for converting both RCAF pilots to the type and for training ferry crews who would fly the Canadian examples to the UK. During October 1943 Britain had agreed to allocate 120 machines to the USAF, although this was revised to just 40, and they were designated the F-8-DH. Unlike the PR Mk XVI, the F-8-DH had its cameras installed in the nose and in operational use the USAF preferred the PR Mk XVI with its camera in the bomb-bay. Of the forty F-8s, six were converted from the B Mk VIII, while the remaining thirty-four were all converted B Mk XXs. Serial numbers 43-4924 to 43-4963 were allocated for these machines and by December 1943 about twelve were with No.375 Servicing Squadron at Watton. The quality of some of these machines was not up to standard and eleven of them were returned to the RAF by the USAAF, in exchange for PR Mk XVIs. These machines were later repaired and reverted to their 'KB' serial number for use with the RAF.

An American F-8-DH, converted to USAAF standard by Bell Aircraft, is shown here picketed outside at an unknown location in the USA, possibly post-war *(U.S. Air Force)*

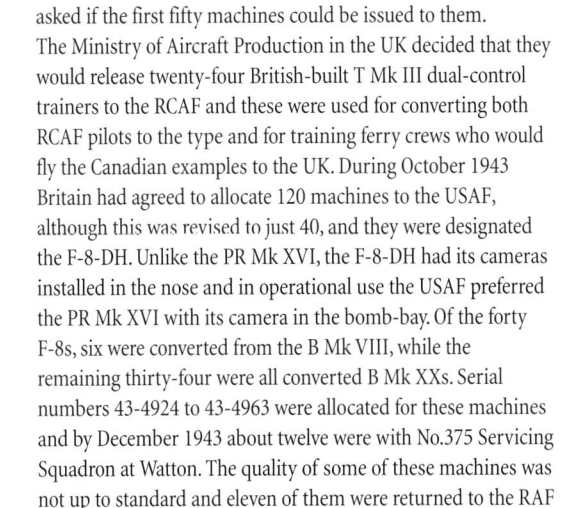

Worldwide Service 37

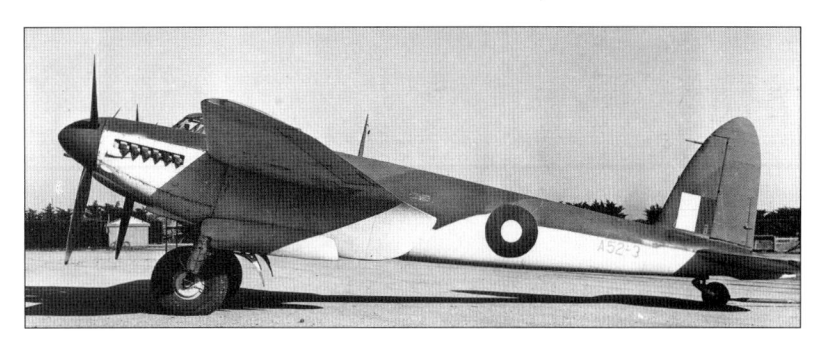

The third FB Mk 40 (A52-3) after it was rolled out at Bankstown. This machine was later converted to a T Mk 43 and re-serialed A52-1050 *(RAAF Photo)*

A formation of three British-built FB Mk VIs of No.1 Squadron, RAAF *(RAAF Photo)*

T Mk 27 trainers and the T Mk 27 was later replaced by the Packard Merlin 225 powered T Mk 29. There were 300 FB Mk 26s completed, of which forty-nine into T Mk 27s and thirty-seven were converted into T Mk 29s. By May 1945 fifty-nine FB Mk 26s had been delivered to the RAF and many of these were passed to No.249 Sqn. based at Habbaniya, India during 1946.

Production at the D.H.C. Downsview plant ceased in October 1945 and in all 1,065 had been built. Of these 396 were delivered to the RCAF, while the rest were sent to the RAF.

Australia

Within a very short space of time after the japanese attack on Pearl Harbour, the plans for the production of the fighter-bomber version of the Mosquito at the Mascot, Sydney, plant of De Havilland Pty Ltd. had been finalised. Construction of the Mosquito in Australia was on a smaller scale than that in Canada as there were far fewer sub-contractors available. By the end of March 1942 official government approval was given for production to start. The provisional first-flight date was set as the 31st August 1943 during a meeting at the Ministry of Aircraft Production on the 31st March. During June 1942 the only F Mk II (DD664) was shipped to Australia and in the meantime parts and jigs were shipped from both De Havilland in England and Canada. On arrival DD664 was allocated RAAF serial number A52-1001 and on the 17th December 1942 it made its first flight with Bruce Rose at the controls. The Rolls Royce engines were soon replaced by Packard Merlin 31s and it flew in this configuration on the 23rd March 1943. By the end of April 1943 a new assembly hanger at Bankstown was nearly completed and the infrastructure to commence serial production of the type was almost in place.

The Australian-built versions of the Mosquito were allocated marks in the 40 series and the first machine was an FB Mk 40 (A52-1) which made its maiden flight on the 23rd July 1943, and it was powered by the Merlin 31s removed from DD664. The FB Mk 40 was based on the British FB Mk VI and originally four versions were considered; a fighter-bomber, long-range fighter, reconnaissance, and night-fighter. The first 100 FB Mk 40s featured the narrow propeller blades and Packard Merlin 31 engines. Later production versions had the 'paddle' propellers and the Packard Merlin 33. Production of The FB Mk 40 totalled 212, of which 108 had been completed by VJ-Day. This figure represents all the Australian production as all subsequent marks were converted from the FB Mk 40. Deliveries of the type to RAAF service were delayed by the shortage of some components and the change from casein to formaldehyde glue in the construction. The first machine arrived with the RAAF on the 4th March 1944 and there were a further six delivered by June. The second FB Mk 40 (A52-2) and five others (A52-4, 6, 7, 9 & 26) were all completed as PR Mk 40s with a vertical camera in the nose instead of the machine-gun armament, two more cameras in the bomb-bay and two oblique cameras. This type became operational with No.1 Photo Reconnaissance Unit at the end of May.

Production of the type was delayed when the twenty-second machine was found to have a fault in a glued joint in the wing. Modifications were carried out on all completed wings, but this problem once again elongated the delivery schedule of the type into RAAF service. The failure of A52-12 on a pre-acceptance flight lead to modifications being carried out on the detachable wing-tip and this also caused delay. To overcome this delay thirty-eight British-built FB Mk VIs were imported into Australia and they were allocated serial numbers in the A52-500 to A52-537 range. In addition twenty-two PR Mk XVIs were shipped out to fill the gap until the PR Mk 41 was in production and these were allocated serials in the A52-600 to A52-622 range. All the FB Mk VIs were operated by No.1 Sqn. who gained their machines from January 1945, while most of the PR Mk XVIs were used by No.87 Sqn. The Mosquito did not really play a key part in the Pacific campaign, as production in Australia was slow and it was not until January 1945 that No.1 Sqn., started to be equipped with the FB Mk VI and FB Mk 40. The squadron moved to Morotai off western New Guinea for operations over the Dutch East Indies and they later assisted with the recapture of Borneo. The other main squadron operating the type was No.87 Sqn. whose PR Mk XVIs and PR Mk 41s were supplemented by three PR Mk 40s, a few FB Mk 40s and even a couple of T Mk III trainers. This squadron helped the RAF in its operations over the Dutch East Indies and Java during 1945. The only other squadrons to operate the type during the war were No.94 Sqn., which used the FB Mk 40 and No.5 Operational Training Unit, which used both FB Mk 40s, T Mk 43s and some T Mk IIIs.

Post-War Operations

Chapter 8

One of the first tasks of the Mosquito, post-war, was that of a courier aircraft. FB Mk VIs of No.21 Sqn. flew between Fürth and Blackbushe throughout the Nuremburg war crime trials. The squadrons operating with the British Air Forces of Occupation (BAFO) after the war included a number of FB Mk VI units, namely No.21, 107 and 613 Squadrons.

In India No.684 Sqn. began an aerial survey of Indo-China from a base in Saigon in November 1945 and they also completed a similar survey of Cambodia from a base at Bangkok in January 1946. This was followed in early February with the initial survey of the whole of India.

The situation in the Dutch East Indies after the cessation of hostilities was such that this area proved to be a problem for some considerable time. An independent Republic of Indonesia had been proclaimed by Dr Sukarno upon the defeat of the Japanese and it was not long before guerrilla action began to take place by rebels using ex-Japanese weapons and even aircraft. The RAF response to this was to send No.84 and No.110 Squadrons in to fly reconnaissance missions from the 9th November 1945. These machines were soon backed up with five FB Mk VIs of No.82 Sqn. and four from No.47 Sqn. Attacks by these machines were mainly on radio stations and guerrilla forces, as well as flying protection flights over British ground forces. The use of the Mosquito in this area had ceased by March 1946.

Post-War Variants

The three main types developed after the end of World War Two were the PR Mk 34, B Mk 35 and NF Mk 36. The PR Mk 34 was a development of the PR Mk XVI and it featured the new Merlin 113/114 engines with improved high–altitude performance and the SU fuel–injection pump. As with the PR Mk XVI, the port engine drove the cabin supercharger. The limited range of existing PR types operating from India and by the RAAF meant that the RAF could see a large gap in its photographic coverage towards the end of the war. To overcome this a number of designs were considered and these even included a PR Mk XVI converted to have in-flight refuelling capacity. In the end the new PR Mk 34 was created to meet the needs of such operations and it achieved the extra range thanks to the fitment of a large fuel tank in the swollen–bomb bay, as well as carrying the new 200–gallon drop–tanks. It should be noted that although similar, the bomb–bay in the PR Mk 34 was actually slightly bigger than the standard bulged bomb–bay of the types able to carry the 4,000lb 'Cookie'. Two vertical F.52 cameras were carried forward of the large fuel tank and two more vertical F.52s and an oblique F.24 were mounted aft of the bomb–bay. The F.24 could be swapped for an American K.17 camera for aerial survey work. The removal of all fire-proofing and armour plate allowed this mark to fly 3,600 miles at 25,000ft cruising at 300mph. In total 181 PR Mk 34s were built; fifty of these were constructed by Percival Aircraft Ltd at Luton with the rest being made by D.H. at Hatfield. The prototype for this series was RG176 and it made its first flight on the 4th December 1945. A small number of PR Mk 34s were converted by Marshall's Flying Services Ltd to the improved PR Mk 34A configuration. This involved the fitment of the new Merlin 114A engines with their anti-surge supercharger diffusers, the more advanced *Gee* navigational aids and improvements to the undercarriage retraction and locking mechanism.

The first production PR Mk 34 delivered to the RAF was RG179, which went to No.544 Sqn. based at RAF Benson and which was flown from there for the first time on the 21st April 1945. No UK based PR Mk 34s were ever used in the war. However, a special detachment of PR Mk 34s with No.684 Sqn. did go to the Cocos Islands in June 1945. The first operational sortie by the type was made on the 3rd July 1945, when Wg. Cdr. W.E.M.Lowry DFC and Flt. Sgt. Pateman flew RG185 ('Z') to Morib, Point Pinto, the Port Swettenham area and on to parts of Sumatra. By the end of the war thirty-eight sorties had been undertaken by this squadron and on the 20th August Flt. Lt J.R.Manners and W/O F.A.Burley, in RG210 ('J'), flew the longest flight from the Cocos islands with a 2,600 mile trip which took 9hr 5min. By the end of August 1945 No.684 Sqn. had seven operational PR Mk 34s.

In September 1946 No.684 Sqn. was renumbered No.81 Squadron. During the late 1946 period No.540 Sqn. at RAF Benson was equipped with the PR Mk 34 and in April 1947 Transport Command set up a team of two machines for an attempt at the London-Cape Town record. This record had been set by D.H.88 Comet *The Burberry* in November 1937. The attempt was made by RG238, the other machine being a reserve, and it was flown by Sqn. Ldr. H.B.Martin DSO, DFC (of Dambusters fame) with navigator Sqn. Ldr. E.B.Sismore DFO, DFC.

Although this PR Mk 34's serial number is not visible (probably in the VL613-60 batch), the bleak surroundings make it likely that this machine is being operated in the Middle East
(via D.Welch)

This FB Mk VI (RF773: UX•P) of No.82 (United Provinces) Squadron is displayed at St. Thomas' Mount in January 1946. Cpl. Hilditch is in line for a charge, as he is standing on the horizontal tailplane with his boots on!
(via S.Howe)

Post War Operations **39**

This PR Mk 34 (RG300) is shown here in 1957 being prepared for its flight to the USA, where it became N9871F *(via S.Howe)*

They started from Heathrow Airport at 6.04pm (GMT) on 30th April and the aircraft touched down at Cape Town at 3.35pm (GMT) 1st May, breaking the record comfortable with an average speed of 279.256 mph.

In the Middle East No.680 Sqn. became No.13 Sqn. in September 1946 and continued to use the PR Mk 34 until 1952. This unit operated in the Suez Canal zone, as well as over Palestine during the troubled period before the state of Israel was established.

Operation Firedog

The proposed Malayan Union was not well received by the UK Government and the Communists soon reactivated the Malayan guerrilla army to mount a campaign of terrorism to force the British out of Malaya. A state of emergency was declared on the 17th June 1948 and *Operation Firedog* began. No.81 Sqn. was equipped with the PR Mk 34 and operated from Tengah, Singapore island. This unit did photo-reconnaissance missions to aid anti-terrorist operations and its first was on the 9th July using one of its Spitfire PR Mk XIXs. By the end of 1952 the Sqn. had photographed some 34,000 square miles of the territory in over 4,000 flights. By this time the Mosquito was reaching obsolescence and it was No.81 Sqn. which was to make the last operational RAF sortie with a Mosquito when RG314 flown by Fg. Off. A.J. Knox set out on a reconnaissance flight over two terrorist camps on the 15th December 1955.

Some of the more unusual uses of the PR.34 included the coverage of the floods which hit the English East Coast in 1953. The PR Mk 34s of No.540 and the PR Mk 34s and PR Mk 35s (converted B Mk 35s) of No.58 Squadron flew some 4,000 miles to survey the damage to coastal defenses etc and to help direct rescue operations. No.81 Sqn. also flew a number of missions to Christmas Island in the Pacific prior to the H-bomb trials in 1956, and they also did some anti-piracy patrols over Borneo for a time which even resulted in the capture of a number of pirates!

Gust Research

British European Airways formed the Gust Research Unit to find out more about clear-air turbulence (CAT) at high altitude. This research was in connection with the new jet airliners such as the D.H.106 Comet and at this time little was known about the problem. Two PR Mk 34s were employed (RG238 and RG231); these machines became G-AJZF and G-AJZE (respectively) and although owned by the Ministry of Supply were leased to BEA. The unit was based at Cranfield and the two machines were delivered there on the 8th September 1947. The College of Aeronautics based at Cranfield undertook all work to make the aircraft pass a Civil Certificate of Airworthiness and each machine was fitted with beam approach and *Gee* navigational aids. The internal fuel tank of the PR Mk 34 was removed and external 100-gallon drop-tanks were fitted, although these were fixed and could not be jettisoned, to comply with ARB regulations. All the cameras, the cabin heater and certain radio equipment were removed and replaced with gust-research equipment. This work involved a considerable number of man-hours and G-AJZE did not fly until January 1948, with G-AJZF following it on the 3rd June 1948.

The research was planned to take the form of a 'saw-tooth' pattern of consecutive climbs and descents between 20,000 and 37,000ft to find areas of CAT. If turbulence over a set amount was encountered this region was investigated. The flights were long and took a great deal of concentration on the part of the crew; trouble was also encountered with the canopies, which cracked at altitude. By January 1949, seven areas of CAT had been encountered. Financial constraints lead to the closure of the unit in January 1950 after some 92,300 miles had been flown. The results were far from conclusive, but this work pioneered further research into an area of aeronautics which is still not fully understood. Both machines were refurbished by Marshall's Flying Services Ltd and returned to the RAF in 1950. Later, during 1954, RG238 was to become a film star, when it was repainted and starred in the film based on the H.E.Bates's novel *The Purple Plain*.

A number of other PR Mk 34s were later converted for civil use by D.H. at Hatfield, in 1955-56, and these included examples operated by Jack Amman Photogrammetric Engineers Inc of Los Angeles. These machines were fitted with new cameras plus a D/F loop and a number of radio navigation aids, and were registered N9910F (ex-PF678), N9911F, N9868F (ex-PF670), N9869F, N9870F (ex-RG233) and N9871F (ex-RG300). Two of these (N9910F and N9868F) were used by IREX Survey Co for a series of survey flights over Libya during 1957, being eventually broken up at Cambridge in March 1960.

The Last Bomber

The B Mk 35 was a development of the B Mk XVI and this also featured the improved Merlin 113/4 engine's SU injector system. The prototype made its first flight on the 12th March 1945 was too late to see operational service in the war. In total 274 were built at Hatfield and later versions featured the improved Merlin 113/114A engines with the anti-surge systems as per the PR Mk 34A.

The type entered operational service with No.109 and No.139 Squadrons at Hemswell in mid-1945 and also saw service with the British Air Forces of Occupation (BAFO) in Germany. No.69 Sqn. (previously No.619 Sqn.) was based at Wahn from August 1945 to November 1947 when it was disbanded. Other units in this area included No.14 Sqn. at Wahn and No.98 Sqn. at Celle. A number of non-operational units used the B Mk 35 and these included the Central Bomber Establishment and the Radio Warfare Establishment. Those with the Central Bomber Establishment were fitted with H2S radar in a ventral radome aft of the bomb-bay. The B Mk 35 was not replaced in No.109 and No.139 squadrons until the arrival of the Canberra in (respectively) July 1952 and June 1953. Ten B Mk 35s were modified by De Havilland at

PR Mk 34 RG231 is shown here in its civilian markings (G-AJZE) after conversion for Gust Research by B.E.A, outside the hanger at Cranfield in 1948 *(British Airways)*

Target Tugs, clockwise from top right:

TA724 is seen here in September 1957, taxying out at Biggin Hill, where the aircraft was displayed during an air show (P.Clifton)

VP191 was flown by the commander of No.3 CAACU at Exeter and is seen here on the 5th July 1961 being refuelled (via S.Howe)

VP191 is seen here banking away and this shot illustrates the black and yellow undersurfaces, along with the ML winch and the banners in the rear of the bomb bay (M.Payne)

Not all target towing operations went smoothly, as can be seen in these two shots of TT Mk 35 (RV367), which was operated by No.2 CAACU at Langham and is shown here looking very sorry for itself after a forced landing on rough ground caused by the failure of the starboard engine (note feathered propeller) (K.H.Jackson)

Three TT Mk 35s (TK606:C, TA703:F and TA633:E) are seen here awaiting disposal at RAF Shawbury in 1959. These machines had all been operated by No.2 CAACU at Langham (C.Foulds)

TA639 is seen at an air display at Exeter in July 1960. This machine was operated by No.3 CAACU, which was based at Exeter Airport (M.Payne)

Leavesden for night photo–reconnaissance using flash lights and they were designated PR Mk 35. The prototype for this type was RS700 and four of these machines equipped B Flight of No.58 Sqn. from 1951.

Supersonic Research

With the advent of the jet and rocket engine towards the end of the war, the need for research into the aerodynamic effects of supersonic flight was paramount. Both the UK and America were trying to be the first to attain supersonic flight, not knowing that the Russians were to achieve it first.

In the UK the Miles M.52 supersonic research aircraft was designed to specification E.24/43 and it was powered by the Power Jets (Whittle) W.2/700 fitted with an afterburner. To test the aerodynamics of such a design the Ministry of Supply contracted Vickers-Armstrong Ltd to carry out a number of air–dropped model tests. These tests were carried out from Farnborough and the model used was a 3/10th scale version of the M.52. The type was initially considered for solid-fuel rocket power, but this proved to have too low a power output and in the end the RAE developed a new rocket motor called the *Alpha*, which was based on the German Walther 109-509 unit used to propel the Messerschmitt Me 163B 'Komet'. Because of the duration of the flight, telemetry and radio guidance were required and these factors all contributed to delay the programme. The 3/10th scale model was 11.74ft long with a span of 8.07ft and it was to be carried under a specially modified B Mk XVI (PF604). This machine had the bulged bomb bay doors removed and replaced with the standard flush examples.

A slot was cut in the rear of the doors for the model's vertical fin and slots were also cut in each side of the door to accommodate the special carrier framework which held the model under the aircraft. The Mosquito was also fitted with a ciné camera and telemetry in the nose, as well as the guidance control–unit in the cockpit. In the end only three complete models were constructed. The flights were carried out over the ocean from St Eval in Cornwall and a Meteor Mk IV acted as a chase plane. Many test drops were made with dummy models, but unfortunately on the

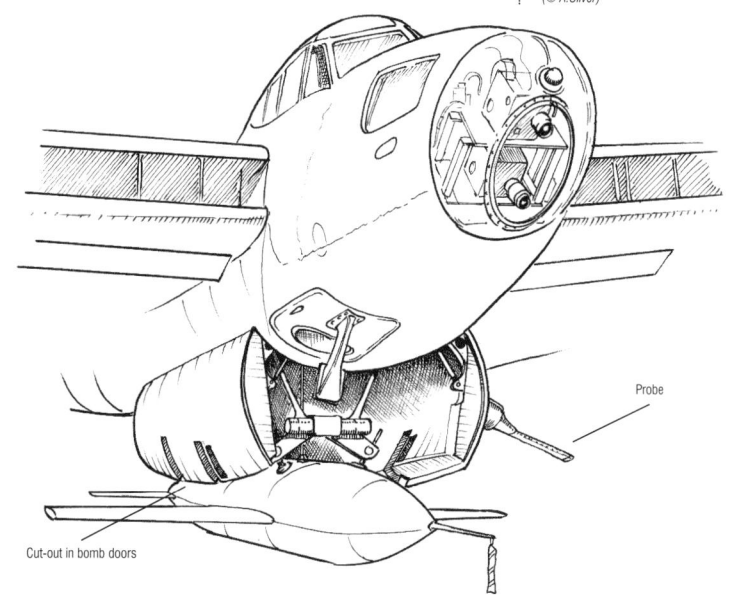

This sketch shows the installation of the Vickers A.2 (Miles M.52) supersonic research model being fitted into the bomb bay of PF604 (© A.Oliver)

Cut-out in bomb doors

Probe

Post War Operations **41**

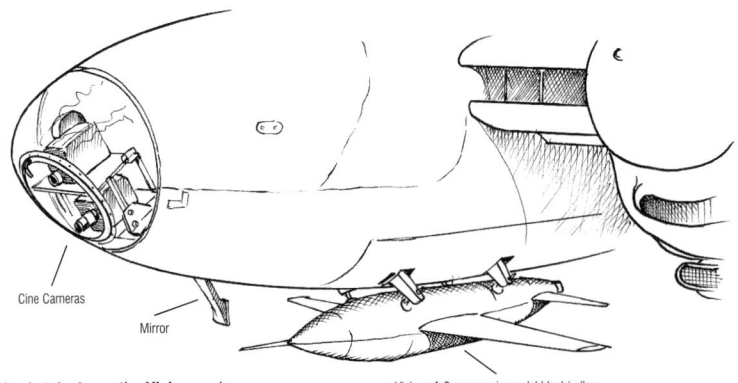

This sketch shows the Vickers A.2 supersonic research model attached under the bomb bay of PF604 *(© A.Oliver)*

Vickers A.2 supersonic model black/yellow (Othochromic film shows this as yellow/black)

The prototype TT Mk 35 (RS719) was used for development trials with the ML Type G winch *(Real Photos)*

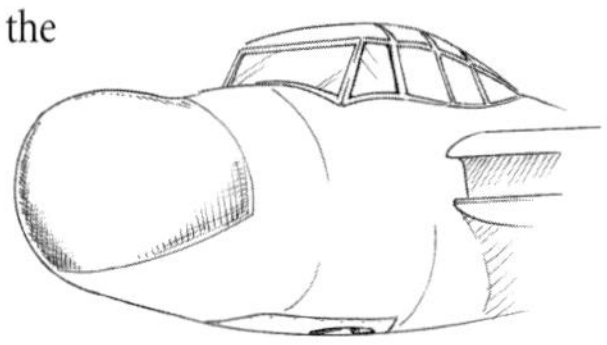

Far right: The Bullnose radome of the NF 30/36/38 *(© A. Oliver)*

Right: The NF Mk 36 was the last night–fighter variant of the Mosquito to be operated by the RAF and RL146 depicted here was operated by No.85 Squadron based at West Malling *(Real Photos)*

This NF Mk 38 (VT653) is shown here without the upper perspex cover of the radar unpainted. This machine was used for development work for a while, before being sold to Yugoslavia in 1952 *(Real Photos)*

Another view of NF Mk 38 VT653, although this shot is of the machine in its standard RAF camouflage prior to delivery *(via Francis Bergese)*

30th May 1947 the Mosquito crew lost control of PF604 and in the ensuing roll the model broke away and was lost. The next example was not ready until the 8th October and when it was finally dropped from 35,000ft the rocket motor failed to fire and the model exploded. In the USA however the goal of a manned flight through the sound barrier was realised on the 14th October 1947, when Capt. Charles 'Chuck' Yeager flew the Bell X-1 (46-602) faster than the speed of sound. In the UK much testing followed the loss of the second model to cure the ignition failure and eventually the third and final model was launched on the 9th October 1949. This time it was a complete success and the model achieved a maximum speed of Mach 1.38 (approx 900 mph), making it the first British built aircraft to exceed the speed of sound in level flight. The breaking of the sound barrier in the USA did mean that interest in the M.52 was very limited and although detailed design for the type was completed the Government decided that manned supersonic flight was too dangerous and the entire project was cancelled in early 1948.

The Target Tug

A second-line task undertaken by converted B Mk 35s was that of target tug. One hundred and five B Mk 35s were converted to target–tug configuration by Brooklands Aviation Ltd in 1952/3. The official modification included the carrying of three towed targets in the bomb-bay, although some versions were fitted with the ML Type G winch and carried four targets on the outside of the bomb–bay and lower rear fuselage. Alternatively the ML winch could be omitted. The tail was protected from fouling the 6,000ft of cable with wire guards, similar to the naval TT Mk 39. The prototype for the winch–equipped version was RS719, while the non-winch version was developed from VR793 which was converted by Marshall's Flying Services Ltd and first flown in July 1952. Eight TT Mk 35s were operated from RAF Schleswigland and this was the last operational RAF Mosquito unit. The last two operational Mosquitoes with the RAF were two T Mk IIIs operated by the Home Command Examining Unit based at White Waltham. The last operational use of the Mosquito, however, was by the Civilian Anti-Aircraft Co-Operation Units (CAACU), which were civil operations run on contract to the Air Ministry. The ground crew and pilots were civilians, and all the aircraft were supplied by the RAF. No.3 CAACU was operated by Exeter Airport Ltd and it started to use

the Mosquito TT.35 in January 1953, until 1963, when all of the aircraft were returned to the Air Ministry.

In 1956 a number of TT Mk 35s were converted for meteorological use and these were designated Met Mk 35s.

Post war Night Fighters

The NF Mk 36 was based on the NF Mk 30 and this version had the Merlin 113/114 engines with their SU injector system, although unlike the PR Mk 34 and B Mk 35, this mark was not pressurised. Some later NF Mk 36s had the Merlin 113A engines fitted and the American A.I. Mk X (SCR720/729) radar was still carried, as per the NF Mk 30. The prototype NF Mk 36 (RK955) first flew in May 1945 and the type entered service with Nos.23, 141, 25, 29, 85 and 264 Squadrons. Night Defence in the Suez Canal area was undertaken by the NF Mk 36s of No.39 squadron during the 1949 to 1953 period from bases at Fayid and Kabrit. Like the B Mk 35, some NF Mk 36s were converted to target–tug configurations and some later became weather–reconnaissance machines under the designation Met Mk 36.

The last Mosquito

The last production version of the Mosquito was to be a night fighter and it was the NF Mk 38. The prototype was RL248 and this was converted from an NF Mk 36. Its first flight was on the 18th November 1947 and although the type was evaluated by the Central Fighter Establishment, the NF Mk 38 was never destined to see RAF service. It suffered from stability problems brought about by the longer engine nacelles of the Merlin 113 engines and the movement forward, by 5 inches, of the entire cockpit area. In all 101 NF Mk 38s were built and sixty of these were passed to the Yugoslavian Air Force from 1952 onwards. On the 15th November 1950, VX916 was completed and this machine represented the 7,781st and last Mosquito to be manufactured.

42 Chapter 8

Civil Mosquitoes

The first civil registered Mossie was a B Mk 35, TK655, which became G-AOSS and was registered to Derby Aviation Ltd. The type was intended for an attempt at the South Atlantic record by a Miss Roberta Cowell and although some work was done to it no suitable engines could be found and the aircraft was eventually broken up at Burnaston in 1960. B Mk 35 TK652 was also modified for civil use by Derby Aviation Ltd. and was used by Capt. Rudolfo Bay Wright as EC-WKH for radio emission and reception trials for the Spanish government. This machine later became EC-AKH and was eventually sold to the United States. US registered B Mk 35s included N9919F (ex-VR801), N9912F, N9913F and N9911F (ex-N6867C and TA717).

Canadian Civil Mosquitos

The first two Mosquitoes on the Canadian civil register were FB Mk 26s KA202 and KA244, and they became CF-GKK and CF-GKL respectively. These machines were registered to Kenting Aviation Ltd and were later acquired by Spartan Air Services Ltd, although CF-GKL was no longer active by 1957.

One of the biggest civil users of the Mosquito was Spartan Air Services Ltd. of Ottawa. Initial investigations into the purchase of Mosquitoes was undertaken in 1954 by Weldy Phipps of Spartan and in the end he arranged the purchase of ten machines for a unit price of Can$1,500 each. All those selected were at No.22 MU, RAF Silloth. The ten machines were overhauled and modified by Derby Aviation Ltd. from March 1955. Most of these machines were brand new, taken out of RAF storage, and they were allocated Canadian civil registrations; CF-HMK (ex-VR794), CF-HML (ex-VR796), CF-HMM (ex-TK623), CF-HMN (ex-TA713), CF-HMO (ex-TA696), CF-HMP (ex-TK648), CF-HMQ (ex-VP189), CF-HMR (ex-TA661), CF-HMS (ex-RS700, a PR Mk 35) and CF-HMT (ex-RS711). The first machine delivered was CF-HML which departed from Prestwick for Spartan's Uplands base on the 26th April 1946 and was followed by the other nine during the May 1955 to July 1956 period. All of these delivery flights were undertaken by Peter Nock of London Air Charter Ltd. Five B Mk 35s (registered CF-IMA to CF-IME) was also purchased by Spartan in July 1955 and although initially it was intended to fly these to Canada, in the end they were flown from RAF Shawbury (No.27 MU) to Hurn Airport by Marian Ozubski. On the 10th October 1957 their Canadian registrations were cancelled and the airframes were cannibalised for spares, being eventually scrapped in the 1960s. All of the Spartan machines were highly modified with the fitment of a blown nose-glazing, a forward-hinged upper-canopy panel, the replacement of the bomb doors with simple wooden covers and the fitment of Swiss RC-5 (later RC-5a and RC-8) cameras in the fuselage forward and aft of the bomb-bay. The types also had the rear lower-fuselage access panel enlarged and glazed and the instrumentation was supplemented by Collins radio equipment, a large DF loop and a number of antenna and radio leads. One of the most radical modifications undertaken by Spartan was the provision for the camera operator in the rear fuselage. The type also had a modified pilot's seat for better comfort during the long flights and an oxygen system, as the type was not used in its pressurised configuration due to the modifications to the fuselage. By 1963 Spartan only had four operational Mosquitoes.

Spartan Air Services B.35 Mosquitoes

(Shown in registration order)

- **CF-HMK.** Delivered 21-23 May 1955 via Keflavik and Goose Bay. Damaged at Barranquilla Airport, Columbia on the 8th January 1957 due to a heavy landing. Passed to Servicios Aéroes Spartan SA, Argentina in December 1960 as LV-HHN and written off at Rio Cuarto, Cordoba Province on the 22nd November 1964.
- **CF-HML.** Delivered 2-3 May 1955 via Keflavik and Goose Bay. Last flight 15th June 1963 from Lakehead to Ottawa. This machine was purchased by Don Cambel and partially restored. Moved to Mission, British Columbia in 1979 and further restoration work was carried out. The incompletely restored machine was sold to Ed & Rose Zalesky in 1986 and is currently up for sale.
- **CF-HMM.** Delivered 17-18 August 1955 via Keflavik and Goose Bay. This machine was lost at Cuidad Trujillo Airport, Dominican Republic on the 27th March 1960.
- **CF-HMN.** Delivered 11-14 September 1955 via Keflavik, Sondestromfjord and Goose Bay. Lost in Bogotá, Columbia on the 22nd January 1956.
- **CF-HMO.** Delivered 25-27 June 1955 via Keflavik, Blue West One and Moncton. Lost near Churchill, Manitoba on 9th August 1955.
- **CF-HMP.** Delivered 25th September - 29th October 1955 via Keflavik, Sondestromfjord and Goose Bay. Suffered an engine

One of the five B Mk 35s purchased by Spartan Air Services in July 1955 is seen here at RAF Shawbury prior to their delivery to Hurn Airport. None of these machines went to Canada and they were all cannibalised for spares and later scrapped (via S.Howe)

One of the Spartan Air Services' B Mk 35s is seen at their Upland base in the late 1950s (via S.Howe)

This sketch illustrates the revised 'blown' nose-glazing and hinged upper-canopy panel which were fitted to the B Mk 35s operated by Spartan Air Services (© A.Oliver)

CH-HMP of Spartan Air Services is seen here at Derby in April 1955. This machine is still in its RAF camouflage scheme and even carries the unit badge of the last squadron which operated it (via S.Howe)

A view of TA288 in flight prior to delivery (©P.Kempe)

Ex-TA288 is shown here prior to delivery to the Swedish Air Force. This machine later became 'Blue D' and was destroyed in a collision with another Mosquito on the 3rd March 1949 (via S.Howe)

One of the TT Mk 35s operated during the filming of 'Mosquito Squadron' in 1966. It is seen here taxying out at RAF Henlow towards the end of filming

A very atmospheric scene of two NF Mk 36s running up, with RL176 in the foreground (via S.Howe)

failure during the delivery flight and was grounded at Keflavik from 25th September to 27th October. Eventually lost near Neepawa, Manitoba on 10th September 1957.
• **CF-HMQ.** Delivered 9-10 June 1955 via Keflavik and Goose Bay. Damaged at Timmins Airport, Ontario on the 10th June 1956 when it was blown into a parked Stinson. Repaired and last flight Grand Prairie to Ottawa on the 7th October 1963.

Presented to No.418 Sqn. in September 1967 and restored to represent an FB Mk VI 'VA114' (TH•F). To City of Edmonton in 1975 and restored by the Alberta Aviation Museum as an FB Mk VI 'HR147 (TH•Z)' during 1993-5 period.
• **CF-HMR.** Delivered 2-4th November 1955 via Keflavik, Blue West One and Goose Bay. This machine was damaged during a landing on ice at Mont Joli Airport, Quebec on 19th April 1956. Eventually lost after a runaway propeller and crash landing at Pelly Lake, 10th July 1956. The remains of this machine were recovered by the Mosquito Bomber Group of the Canadian Aviation Historical Society in 1996.
• **CF-HMS.** Delivered 16-17 July 1956 via Keflavik, Blue West One and Goose Bay. This machine was purchased from Spartan in 1964 and in 1972 was donated by the owner to the Centennial Planetarium Museum, Calgary. Airframe moved into long-term store with the Aero Space Museum Association of Calgary in 1990.
• **CF-HMT.** Delivered 10-14 April 1956 via Keflavik, Blue West One and Goose Bay. This machine was non-operational and was stripped for spares before being passed to Uplands Airport fire department for rescue training.

Film Stars

By the summer of 1963 the Mosquito TT Mk 35's service had come to an end and three machines with No.3 CAACU were given civil registrations; G-ASKA (ex-RS709), G-ASKB (RS712) & G-ASKH (ex-TA719). These machines plus all of the unit's other Mosquitoes were used in the filming of *633 Squadron*, having all been modified to represent FB Mk VIs. In 1966 another film, *Mosquito Squadron*, was started and RR299, RS709, RS712 and TA634 were all used again.

Foreign Operators of the Mosquito

Swedish Hunter

Sixty surplus RAF NF Mk XIXs were supplied to the Flygvapnet (Swedish Air Force), where they were given the designation J 30. These machines were all refurbished and modified by Fairey Aviation Co. Ltd at Ringway. The modifications included the fitment of the non-feathering four-blade propellers as per the TR Mk 33 and TF Mk 37, the installation of the landing lights in the starboard wing leading-edge and the fitment of the revised fighter canopy with the bulged side-panel on the starboard side. Other detailed changes were also made but the type retained its A.I. Mk X (SCR 720/729) radar equipment. The first refurbished machine was test flown in July 1948, and the last in October 1949, before they were all flown to Hatfield for collection by Flygvapnet pilots. The first two machines supplied (Ex TA286 and TA275) were delivered on the 16th July and 19th August respectively and these machines were painted overall aluminium. The remaining machines retained their RAF scheme of Medium Sea Grey and Dark Green. The type was flown by the first, second and third squadrons of F1 wing. Each squadron devised a special unit badge which was applied to the access door in the side of the nose on the J 30 and each unit had colour coded serial number and propeller spinners. Therefore No.1 Sqn. had white spinners, No.2 had blue and No.3 had

yellow. It should be noted however that No.1 Sqn. later used red spinners and number in place of white. A number of these machines were lost during operational use and there were also a number of structural failures. One machine had the torque link for the radar scanner break which resulted in the scanner smashing the side of the perspex radome and a couple of others were lost in flight when the counter-weight of the rudder broke and the resulting flutter of the unit broke the tail off. Investigations were carried out by the Swedish authorities and one machine was tested to destruction to see where any stress faults lay. The most common reason for loss however was undercarriage failure of either one or both main legs. The last operational flight of a J 30 was flown by 30021 ('Red R') of No.1 Sqn. on the 19th March 1955 and the honour for the highest number of flight hours goes to 30058 ('Yellow M') of No.2 Sqn. which clocked up 1122 hours from November 1949 to March 1954. The J 30 was finally replaced in Flygvapnet service by the De Havilland Vampire in 1954 and much of the radar equipment was stripped from the J 30s for fitment into the Vampire (J 22 in Flygvapnet service) and all the J 30s had been scrapped by 1955.

French Air Force

The French Air Force operated the FB Mk VI, PR Mk XVI and the NF Mk 30. The FB Mk VIs were ex-RAF machines and the F.A.F. had about fifty-seven in total. These machines were used in Indo-China against the Viet-Minh. Fifteen FB Mk VIs of 10/Groupe de Chasse 1/3 'Corse' (Corsican) were sent in January 1947 to Saigon via Rabat in French Morocco. These machines flew their first operational mission on the 23rd January 1947

A PR Mk XVI (RF973) of 10/Groupe de Chasse 1/3 'Corse' in the company of another PR Mk XVI off the Algerian Coast in the late 1940s *(F.Bergesé)*

and by May they had amassed 345 sorties. The unit returned to Rabat to be renumbered as 10/Groupe de Chasse 1/6 'Corse' (Corsican) and they remained there until July 1949.

Twenty-nine ex-RAF PR Mk XVIs were also supplied to the French Air Force after the war and these were operated in French Morocco. Once their operation career had ended, many of these machines were sold to the Israeli Air Force. Twenty-three surplus NF Mk 30s were also supplied from ex-RAF surplus stocks.

Belgian Air Force

The Belgian Air Force acquired three ex-RAF FB Mk VIs between 1947 and 1953 and these were converted to target

An FB Mk VI converted to a target tug (MC-2) is seen here at Ringway on the 7th March 1954 *(R.A.Scholefield)*

tugs, designated TT.6 and given serial numbers from MC-1 to MC-3. These were supplemented by seven T Mk III trainers which were also converted to target tugs and designated TT.3. These machines were given serial numbers in the MC-4 to MC-11 range and operated alongside the Miles Martinet target tugs at the Towing Flight based at Koksijde. They were painted silver overall with yellow bands around the wings and aft fuselage.

The J 30 in Flygvapnet Service

S/NO	MARKING	RAF	DELIVERED	STRUCK OFF	FLYING HOURS	NOTES
30001	'Red A'	Ex-TA286	16/7/48	29/8/52	119	Struck off charge to reserve holdings
30002	'Red B'	Ex-TA275	19/8/48	29/8/52	96	Struck off charge to reserve holdings
30003	'Red C'	Ex-TA281	4/9/48	6/8/49	142	Crashed nr Valskog 12/5/49 due to failure of counterbalance weight on elevators - tail ripped off
30004	'Red D' & 'White A'	Ex-TA283	1/10/48	13/11/53	700	Taxied into 30031 24/1/52
30005	'Red E'	Ex-TA285	1/10/48	13/11/53	545	
30006	'Red F'	Ex-TA294	11/12/48	5/5/49	59.5	Crash landed at F1 base 14/3/49
30007	'Red G'		11/12/48	13/11/53	N/K	
30008	'Red H' & 'White A'	Ex-TA284	11/12/48	17/4/50	112.5	Crashed at Ystad 8/7/49
30009	'Red I'		11/12/48	13/11/53	384	
30010	'Red J' & 'Yellow R'		11/12/48	27/11/54	610	Used for trials
30011	'Blue A' & 'Red A'	Ex-TA357	19/12/48	19/3/53	503	Struck by vehicle whilst parked 20/1/53
30012	'Blue B'	Ex-TA276	19/12/48	31/3/49	32.05	Destroyed in collision with 30014 3/3/49
30013	'Blue C'		4/2/49	13/11/53	N/K	
30014	'Blue D'	Ex-TA288	4/2/49	31/3/49	22.3	Destroyed in collision with 30012 3/3/49
30015	'Blue E'		4/2/49	13/11/53	N/K	
30016	'Blue F'		11/2/49	13/11/53	N/K	
30017	'Blue G'		11/2/49	16/2/53	364	Wheels-up crash landing 25/8/52
30018	'Blue B'	Ex-TA242	28/2/49	29/10/51	495	Crashed 3/10/51
30019	'Blue H'		28/2/49	13/11/53	N/K	
30020	'Blue D'	Ex-TA353	28/2/49	14/12/49	143.1	Crashed at Svartklubben 5/10/49
30021	'Red B' & 'Red R'	Ex-TA193	28/2/49	19/2/55	585	Longest serving J 30
30022	'Red K'	Ex-TA239	28/2/49	12/8/50	296	Ground looped at F21 base 5/7/50
30023	'Red L'		28/2/49	13/11/53	N/K	
30024	'Red F'		28/3/49	23/2/54	697	
30025			28/3/49	13/11/53	N/K	
30026	'Blue I'		28/3/49	19/3/53	523	Crashed nr Lindesberg 26/1/53
30027	'Blue J'	Ex-TA265	28/3/49	27/11/54	607	
30028	'Blue K'		5/4/49	13/11/53	N/K	
30029	'Blue F', 'Blue K' & 'Blue L'	Ex-MM635	5/4/49	28/8/50	135	Crashed nr Junkön 10/7/50
30030	'Blue L' & 'Red N'		5/4/49	27/11/54	690	Tail sliced off when 30004 taxied into it 24/1/52 - repaired
30031	'Red H', 'Red N' & 'Blue A'		5/4/49	23/3/54	695	
30032	'Red K' & 'Yellow A'	Ex-TA291	7/5/49	23/3/54	694	
30033	'Red L' & 'Red I'		7/5/49	23/3/54	700	
30034	'Yellow B' & 'Red C'		7/5/49	13/11/53	N/K	Taxied into hanger 11/1/52 and damaged props - repaired
30035	'Blue P'		7/5/49	21/3/52	490	Undercarriage failure, Luleå 10/3/52
30036	'Red O' & 'Yellow H'	Ex-MM651	7/5/49	19/31/54	536	
30037	'Red C' & 'White A'		27/5/49	13/11/53	697	Crashed 2/9/53
30038	'Red A'		27/5/49	13/11/53	N/K	
30039			27/5/49	23/3/54	697	
30040			27/5/49	30/9/50	199	Tested to destruction by FFA
30041	'Red H' & 'Red N'		22/6/49	13/11/53	N/K	This a/c suffered damage to radome due to scanner torque link failure
30042	'Yellow D'		22/6/49	13/11/53	511	
30043	'Yellow E'		22/6/49	13/11/53	729	Crashed at Anjeskutan 7/1/53
30044	'White A'	Ex-MM624	17/7/49	19/9/50	97	Crashed 7/9/50
30045	'White B' & 'Blue B'		17/7/49	19/3/53	1005	Crashed nr Strömsholms 5/2/53
30046	'Yellow I'		17/7/49	13/11/53	N/K	
30047	'Yellow F'		17/7/49	23/3/54	984	
30048			18/8/49	23/3/54	1117	
30049	'Yellow H'		18/8/49	17/5/52	473	Crash landed at F1 base 20/6/51
30050			1/10/49	23/3/54	750	
30051	'Yellow K'		1/10/49	4/3/52	523	Crashed nr. Tärna 31/1/52
30052			1/10/49	23/3/54	803	
30053	'Blue O'		1/10/49	7/8/53	545	Wheels-up crash landing 3/6/53
30054	'D'		1/10/49	23/3/54	954	
30055	'Blue P'		15/11/49	4/3/52	596	Crash landed 21/1/52
30056	'Yellow N'		15/11/49	16/2/53	579	Crash landed at F9 base 14/6/52
30057			15/11/49	13/11/53	N/K	
30058	'Yellow M'		15/11/49	23/3/54	1122	Highest operational hours for a J 30
30059	'Blue L'		15/11/49	13/11/53	N/K	
30060	'Yellow O'		15/11/49	16/2/53	814	Port undercarriage failure on landing 10/7/52

NF Mk 30 (MB-11 KT•O) of No.10 Squadron, Belgian Air Force is seen in flight during the early 1950s *(via S.Howe)*

A total of twenty-four surplus NF Mk 30s were purchased in 1947 and these were allocated serials in the MB-1 to MB-24 range. They were operated by No.10 Sqn. of the 1st Wing from 1947 and by No.11 Sqn. (1st Wing) from 1951. Machines operated by No.10 Sqn. were coded ND, while those of No.11 Sqn. were KT. These machines retained their RAF camouflage of Medium Sea Grey and Dark Green. With the arrival of the Meteor NF 11 in 1952, all of No.11 Squadron's NF Mk 30s were transferred to No.10 Sqn. and in 1953 they were all grounded temporarily for fatigue checks. The last operational use of a Mosquito by the Belgian Air Force was in August 1955 and in

A close-up of the nose of NF Mk 30 ND•A (MB-19) operated by No.10 Squadron in 1951 *(R.Binnemans)*

Post War Operations   45

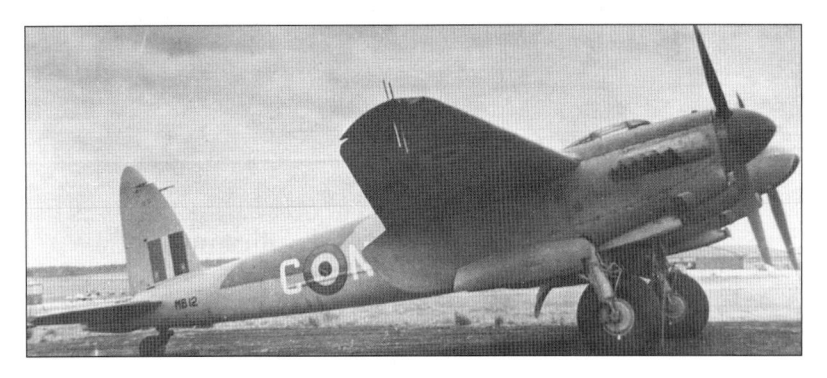

Another NF Mk 30 (MB-12) operated by No.10 Squadron is seen here at their base in 1952 (R.Binnemans)

A standard FB Mk VI (O•AP) (rear) and an APS-4 ASH equipped version (O•AG) of the Norwegian Air Force (Real Photos)

Another ex-Royal Navy PR Mk XVI (G-AOCL) is seen here at Thruxton. This machine also was purchased by the Israeli Air Force, although it was never to leave the UK (J.Brown)

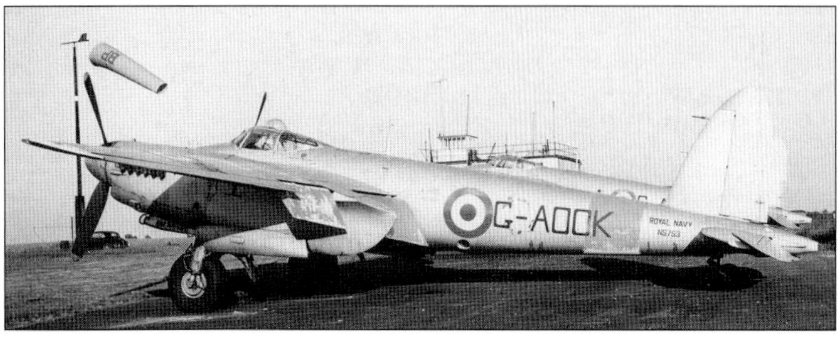

PR Mk XVI G-AOCK is seen here at Thruxton in 1957. This machine had only been at Thruxton for a year but is already showing signs of wear. This machine, although purchased by the Israeli Air Force, was never to leave Thruxton (via S.Howe)

early 1956 the Mosquitoes of No.10 Sqn. were officially replaced by the Meteor NF 11.

Today the world's only surviving NF Mk 30 Mosquito resides in the Belgian Air Force Museum.

South African Air Force

The SAAF had operated the Mosquito PR Mk XVI as No.60 Sqn. within the RAF in the war, and after the end of hostilities they took fourteen of these machines back to South Africa, which equipped No.60 Sqn. as a photo survey unit for a number of years.

Norwegian Air Force

After the war, eighteen FB Mk VIs were acquired by the Norwegian Air Force and were operated by No.334 Sqn. These machines featured the revised fighter canopy of the J 30 along with the landing lights in the starboard wing leading edge. In 1950 three were converted to night fighters with the installation of an ASH radar pod in a thimble nose radome, replacing the machine-guns.

Dominican Air Force

The El Cuerpo de Aviacion Militar acquired six FB Mk VIs in 1949, which had been refurbished by Fairey Aviation Co. Ltd. at Ringway. These machines featured the revised fighter canopy and four-blade non-featherable propellers and they were painted aluminium overall. They were test flown during July to September 1948 and were eventually flown by Airwork Ltd pilots to Dominica via Iceland, Canada and America later that year.

In Dominican service they were allocated a three figure serial; 301 (ex-TE612), 302 (Ex-TE909), 303 (Ex-TE822), 304 (Ex-TE874), 305 (Ex-RF939) and 306 (N/K). These serials however were later converted to four numbers with the addition of '21' in place of the '3', therefore 301 became 2101 and so on.

Turkish Air Force

The Turkish Air Force obtained ninety-six FB Mk VIs in 1949, and again these were all refurbished by Fairey Aviation Co. Ltd. at Ringway. They featured the revised fighter canopy and four-blade non-featherable propellers, along with the landing light in the starboard wing leading-edge. All were flight tested between November 1946 and June 1948 and they were ferried by British Aviation Services Ltd crews to Turkey.

Israeli Air Force

The Israeli Air Force acquired a number of different marks of the Mosquito during the late 1940s and early 1950s. They operated about sixty FB Mk VIs, and they also produced examples from various wrecks and components they acquired. The French Air Force supplied both FB Mk VIs and PR Mk XVIs to Israel and in 1952 they were being supplied at a rate of about two per week.

During the late 1940s there was an arms embargo in force which stopped the UK from supplying aircraft etc to Israel. However in 1948 two PR Mk XVIs (NS811 and NS812) were registered as G-AIRU and G-AIRT to a company calling itself VIP Associations Ltd. A Certificate of Airworthiness was refused for these machines, but on the 5th July 1948 G-AIRT was flown away from Cambridge aerodrome to an unspecified destination. Eventually it became apparent that this machine had gone to Israel. G-AIRU also flew out of Abingdon at the same time and made its way to France, where it was acquired by a buyer acting on behalf of the Israel Air Force. In 1956 the arms embargo was lifted and the Israeli Air Force acquired three ex-Royal Navy PR Mk XVIs. A batch of seventeen machines was registered to R.A.Short Aviation and flown from storage at Lossiemouth to Thruxton. Seven of this batch actually had the registrations applied (G-AOCI to G-AOCO), while the rest remained unmarked. Within the batch was TW246, a TR Mk 33 Sea Mosquito. Three machines were overhauled by Independent Air Travel Ltd at Hurn and these were; G-AOCM (Ex-RG174) which became 4XFDH-90 and departed on the 12th October 1956, G-AOCJ (Ex-NS742) which became 4XFDH-91 and left for Israel on the 20th October 1956, and G-AOCN (Ex-TA614) which became 4XFL-92 and departed on the 1st December 1956.

In 1954-5 about fourteen surplus TR Mk 33s were refurbished by Eagle Aviation Ltd at Blackbushe for sale to Israel. All of these had previously been in store at RAF Colerne, and during refurbishment all of the naval equipment, including the arrestor hooks, was removed. Some of these machines included early types without the wing-fold mechanism and the wing brought back to the UK by the Mosquito Museum for their FB Mk VI (TA122) was found to be one of this type.

Yugoslavian Air Force

The Yugoslavian Air Force acquired FB Mk VIs, NF Mk 38s and T Mk IIIs from ex-RAF stock. These machines were supplied from late 1951 and comprised at least seventy-four FB Mk VIs, fifty-seven NF Mk 38s and three T Mk IIIs. These machines were all supplied in their RAF camouflage and by 1953 were being used to patrol the Hungarian borders. By October 1953 trials were undertaken with a TR-45/A torpedo under the FB Mk VI, as per the TR Mk 33, and in 1954 four machines were equipped with this torpedo and were operated by the 32nd Bomber Division at Zegrab. During 1957 the Yugoslavian Letar-2 torpedo was tested in the same installation.

The first unit to operate the FB Mk VI was the 103rd Reconnaissance Regiment at Pancevo, near Belgrade. This unit also acted as a training and conversion centre for all the other units which later used the Mosquito.

NF Mk 38s were operated by the 97th Air Regiment and the 184th and 103rd Reconnaissance Regiments from 1952 to 1960. Some of these machines were fitted with German Rb-50 and Rb-57 cameras in the aft bomb bay and the 184th Reconnaissance Regiment was the last to operate the Mosquito in this role.

Nine of the FB Mk VIs were converted to target tugs in the late 1950s and these continued in service, alongside two T Mk IIIs, until 1963 at the Anti-Aircraft Gunnery School at Zadar.

Royal Australian Air Force

The RAAF had operated the Mosquito during the war and at the end of hostilities they imported thirty-eight British-built FB Mk VIs to supplement their FB Mk 40s.

It was not until after the end of the war that a two-stage conversion of any Australian Mosquitoes was achieved. The first type to have the two-stage units was the FB Mk 42 and only one was ever converted. This was basically an FB Mk 40 with the two-stage Packard Merlin 69 engines and it was based on an FB Mk 40 (A52-90), although it was later used as the basis for the PR Mk 41 conversion. The PR Mk 41 was basically similar to the PR Mk 40; twenty-eight were converted from FB Mk 40s in 1947-8 and were allocated serial numbers in the A52-300 to A52-327 range. The first of the PR Mk 41s was delivered on the 29th May 1947 and a number of PR Mk 41s joined the existing ex-RAF PR Mk XVIs in an aerial survey of the whole of Australia during the period 1946 to 1953. This survey was undertaken in conjunction with the Australian Survey Corp. and the Mosquitoes joined this company's Ansons and Hudsons from May 1948. The Flight became a Squadron in 1951 and was disbanded in 1953 after 2/3rds of the continent had been mapped. The rest of the task was passed out to civil firms and they took a further ten years to complete the remaining 1/3rd!

The Australian-built T Mk III trainer was the T Mk 43 and this was powered by the Packard Merlin 33s. The type retained its machine–guns but the cannon was deleted and it also featured dual trim–tabs on the elevators. Twenty-two T Mk 43s were converted from FB Mk 40s and were renumbered A52-1050 to A52-1071. Four of these were later passed to the RNZAF.

Australian Civil Mosquitoes

In 1953 an air race from London to Christchurch in New Zealand was set up. This race started at Heathrow and two Australian-built PR Mk 41s were entered. These machines were given civil registrations, becoming VH-KLG (ex-A52-62 (FB Mk 40) and A52-324 (PR Mk 41)) and VH-WAD (ex-A52-210 (FB Mk 40) and A52-319 (PR Mk 41)). These machines were to be flown by Sqn. Ldr. A.J.R.Oates DFC and Flt. Lt.H.Swain DFC (VH-KLG), and Capt. J.Woods (VH-WAD). The last named, later had to cancel his entry, however, due to lack of financial support. Both machines had had their camera, guns, radio equipment etc removed and although VH-WAD had retained its Packard Merlin 69 engines, VH-KLG was modified by De Havilland to have two Rolls Royce Merlin 77 engines installed with three-stage superchargers. To increase the fuel load the type had long-range tanks fitted in the bomb–bay and also had 100–gallon drop–tanks fitted. In the end the aircraft never got any further than Mergui, as it got off course during a second attempt and was crash-landed on a mud flat. The machine was badly damaged and looted, and as it could not be recovered, it was written off. VH-WAD however remained at Perth Airport until 1968, slowly decaying.

The only other Mosquitoes on the civil register were VH-WWS a PR Mk 41, ex-A52-197 (FB Mk 40) and A52-306 (PR Mk 41) and N1597V (ex-A52-313).

Royal New Zealand Air Force

The RNZAF acquired a number of ex-RAAF T Mk IIIs and T Mk 43s along with some FB Mk 40s. The main bulk of the RNZAFs force was made up of ex-RAF FB Mk VIs and the first ten of these were ferried from RAF Pershore to New Zealand on the 10th December 1946. The multi-stop flight took 10 to 12 days and covered 11,800 miles. Initially the intention was to equip No.75 Sqn. with the type but due to a severe lack of trained ground crews and spares, very few ever flew again after delivery and although serial numbers in the NZ2321 to NZ2396 batch were allocated to them, most were scrapped during 1955 and 1956.

Six machines were allocated civil markings (ZK-BCT to ZK-BCY) in 1953 and although ZK-BCV became N9909F and Z-BCT became N4935V in the USA the rest were eventually scrapped at Palmerston North in 1955.

Four T Mk 43 trainers had been supplied from Australia in 1947 and these were given serials NZ2305 to NZ2308. The T.43

One of the ex-Royal Navy PR Mk XVIs is seen here in Israeli Air Force service in the 1950s (J-J.Petit)

An FB Mk VI of the Israeli Air Force is seen here warming up its engines with the aft bomb bay doors open (via S.Howe)

A T Mk III refurbished by Fairey Aviation at Ringway is seen here at Hatfield prior to its delivery to Turkey in 1949 (BAe)

George Stewart, a Canadian instructor, is seen here leaning against the rudder of an FB Mk 26 (FB•24) of the Chinese Nationalist Air Force at Hankow. In the background can be seen a T Mk III (T•87) *(via S.Howe)*

supplemented the British-built T Mk IIIs and these Australian versions were fitted with Marconi radio equipment and navigational aids.

Chinese Air Force

With the cessation of hostilities between China and Japan at the end of the war, the old Civil War re-started in China between the Communist forces of Mao Tse-tung and the Nationalist forces of General Chiang Kai-shek. The nationalist forces soon found themselves under extreme pressure and they were in urgent need of more weapons. A total of 250 surplus Mosquito FB Mk 26s were purchased for a unit price of $10,000, taken out of storage and sent to China. The Chinese Government had already purchased some 1,000 ex-USAAF machines which were left in the theatre after the end of the war and these Mosquitoes joined them. An assembly plant was set up in Shanghai and Eddy Jacks of D.H. Canada came in as a supervisor. By the 18th November 1948 some 180 of the 250 machines had been assembled and test flown, the last being KA440. By this date however the Communist forces' advance meant the plant had to close and many incomplete FB Mk 26s were captured there. The precise number of Mosquitoes which saw action is not known, although serial numbers were allocated from 001 to 180 and 038, 044-105, 109-122, 124-144, 146-175 and 178 are all known to have been used. Training of crews was undertaken in Canada, where nine FB Mk 26s were retained in the markings of the China National Aviation Corp. (one of the nation's airlines) at Toronto.

American Civil Mosquitoes

A number of Canadian-built Mosquitoes ended up in the American civil register. A number of these machines were used for racing. In 1948 fifth place in the Bendix Trophy Race was taken by a B Mk 25, N66313 (Ex-KA984), flown by Jesse Stallings the president of Capitol Airways Inc.. Another example was a B Mk 25 (N37878) named *The Wooden Wonder*. This machine was modified with a solid nose, 50–gallon drop–tanks and a huge fuel cell in the bulged bomb–bay area. It took fourth place at an average speed of 343.757 mph at the 1949 Bendix Trophy Race held at Cleveland, Ohio. Other Mosquitoes on the US civil register in the late 1940s included an Ex-RAF FB Mk XVIII (PZ467) which was registered as NX66422 and a number of others including N1596V, N4928V, N60648 and N98691.

A very famous Mosquito was B Mk 35 N9919F (Ex-VR801). This machine was involved in a murder case in the USA in 1960. The aircraft was purchased for £2,850 by Richard E.Loomis, who in turn insured it for £17,850 and tried to get James K.Gibbs to crash it. The idea was to split the insurance money, but unfortunately it was alleged that Loomis sabotaged the machine's undercarriage before take-off, so Gibbs could not back-out of the deal and Gibbs was killed in the resulting crash on the 1st July 1957. On the 22nd June 1960, Loomis was charged with the murder of Gibbs and although acquitted of this charge on the 16th December, he was found guilty of conspiracy, destroying insured property and making out a false accident report.

RG314 holds a place in Mosquito history as it was the machine which carried out the last RAF operational sortie with the type on the 15th December 1955. The aircraft was operated by No.81 Squadron at Tengah and it was finally struck off charge on the 29th February 1956 *(via C.Foulds)*

N66313 'Miss Marta' was an ex-RCAF B Mk 25 (KA984) and was purchased by Don McVicar in June 1948. The machine is shown here in the colour scheme applied by its new owner, Jessie Stallings, for the 1948 Bendix Trophy Air Race *(R.T.O'Deu)*

N37878, a B Mk 25 (ex-KB377), was purchased by Don McVicar in 1948 and entered for the Bendix Trophy Air Race (as CF-FZG). It is shown here in its overall blue scheme for the 1949 race, when it was owned by Don Bussart *(R.T.O'Deu)*

Record Attempts

Two round-the-world record attempts were made in Mosquitoes. The first was by Mr and Mrs Bixby in a converted B Mk 25 (N1203V), and this machine left San Fransico on the 1st April 1950 and refuelled at Cairo. The attempt came to nothing however as engine trouble stopped them getting much further. This machine was later used by Dianna Bixby for a solo around-the-world attempt in 1954. This too came to nought as unfavourable weather and technical problems led her to cancel the attempt on the 6th April that year. This machine had been sponsored by the Flying *Tiger* Line and was later used by this all-freight airline to do high-altitude survey work. The type was fitted with metal skinning around the cockpit to allow it to be pressurised and had vertically mounted cameras in the longer nose. It is not known if this machine was even used in this guise, as the standard engines would have limited the operational altitude.

Colour Side-views • Plate 1

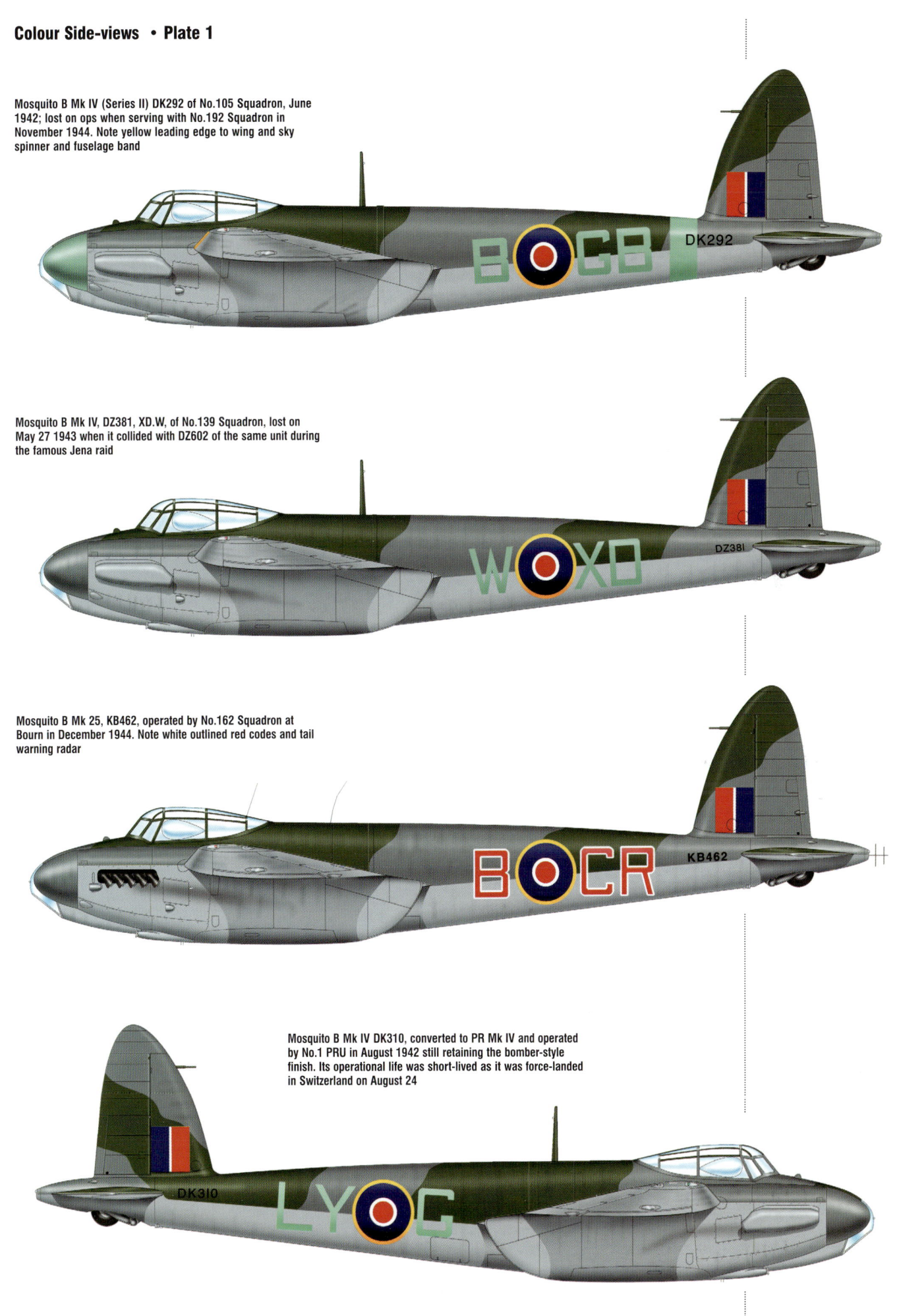

Mosquito B Mk IV (Series II) DK292 of No.105 Squadron, June 1942; lost on ops when serving with No.192 Squadron in November 1944. Note yellow leading edge to wing and sky spinner and fuselage band

Mosquito B Mk IV, DZ381, XD.W, of No.139 Squadron, lost on May 27 1943 when it collided with DZ602 of the same unit during the famous Jena raid

Mosquito B Mk 25, KB462, operated by No.162 Squadron at Bourn in December 1944. Note white outlined red codes and tail warning radar

Mosquito B Mk IV DK310, converted to PR Mk IV and operated by No.1 PRU in August 1942 still retaining the bomber-style finish. Its operational life was short-lived as it was force-landed in Switzerland on August 24

Scale 1:72   Colour Art © Richard J. Caruana

Colour Side-views • Plate 2

Mosquito FB Mk VI, MC2, converted for target-towing duties during the '50s and assigned to the Escadrille de Remorqueurs of the Belgian Air Force (Towing Flight) based at Coxyde

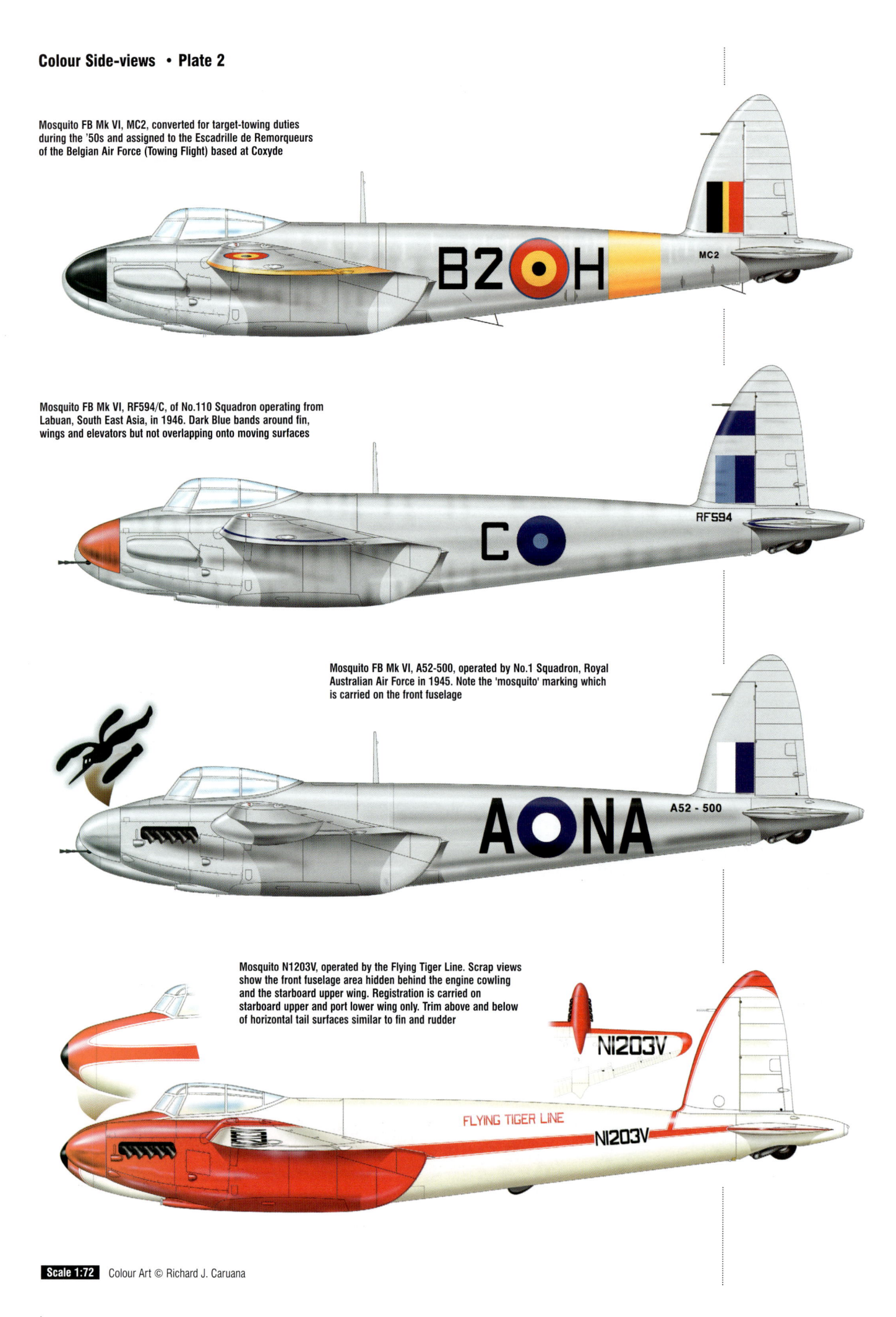

Mosquito FB Mk VI, RF594/C, of No.110 Squadron operating from Labuan, South East Asia, in 1946. Dark Blue bands around fin, wings and elevators but not overlapping onto moving surfaces

Mosquito FB Mk VI, A52-500, operated by No.1 Squadron, Royal Australian Air Force in 1945. Note the 'mosquito' marking which is carried on the front fuselage

Mosquito N1203V, operated by the Flying Tiger Line. Scrap views show the front fuselage area hidden behind the engine cowling and the starboard upper wing. Registration is carried on starboard upper and port lower wing only. Trim above and below of horizontal tail surfaces similar to fin and rudder

Scale 1:72   Colour Art © Richard J. Caruana

Colour Side-views • Plate 3

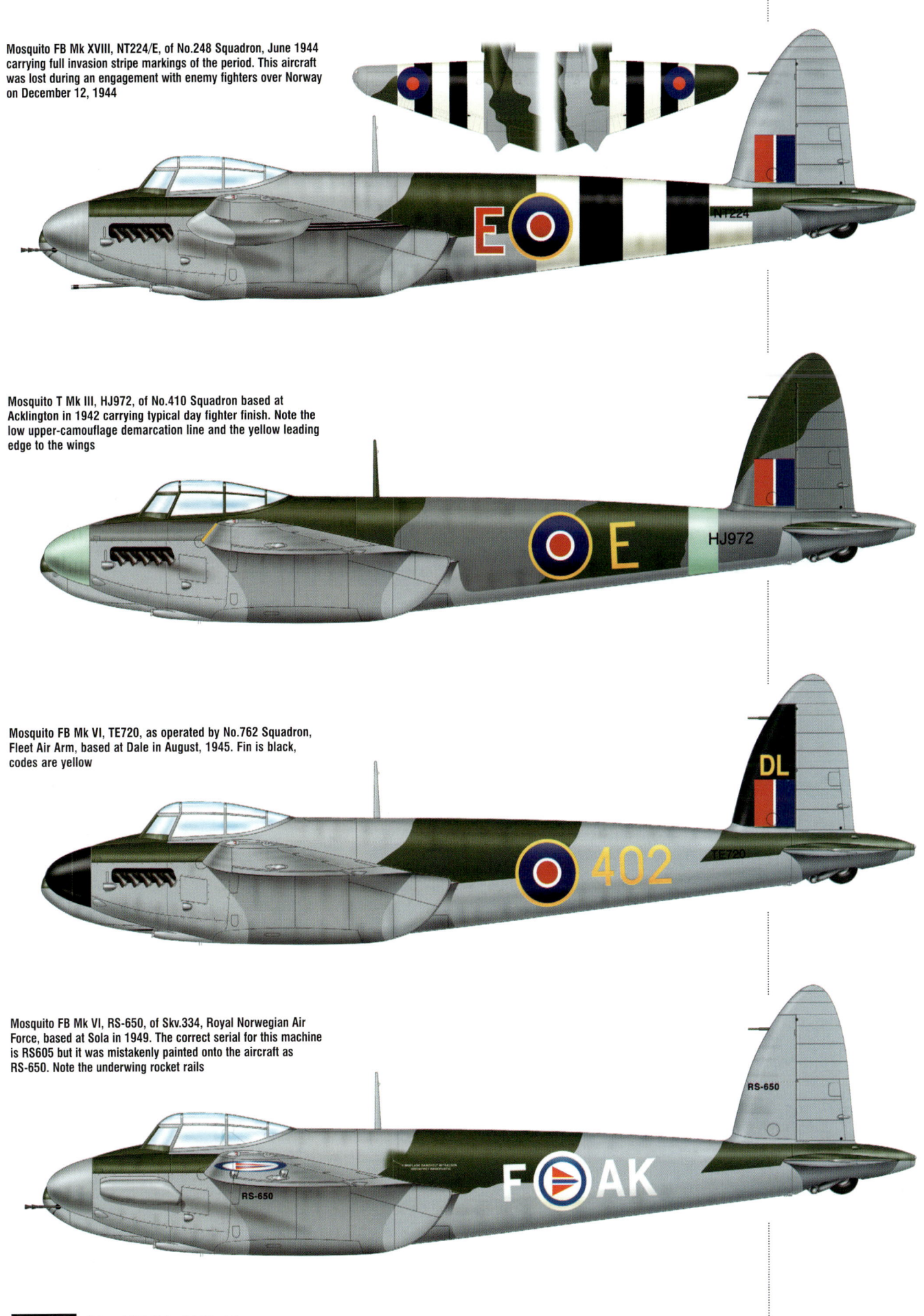

Mosquito FB Mk XVIII, NT224/E, of No.248 Squadron, June 1944 carrying full invasion stripe markings of the period. This aircraft was lost during an engagement with enemy fighters over Norway on December 12, 1944

Mosquito T Mk III, HJ972, of No.410 Squadron based at Acklington in 1942 carrying typical day fighter finish. Note the low upper-camouflage demarcation line and the yellow leading edge to the wings

Mosquito FB Mk VI, TE720, as operated by No.762 Squadron, Fleet Air Arm, based at Dale in August, 1945. Fin is black, codes are yellow

Mosquito FB Mk VI, RS-650, of Skv.334, Royal Norwegian Air Force, based at Sola in 1949. The correct serial for this machine is RS605 but it was mistakenly painted onto the aircraft as RS-650. Note the underwing rocket rails

Scale 1:72 Colour Art © Richard J. Caruana

Colour Side-views • Plate 4

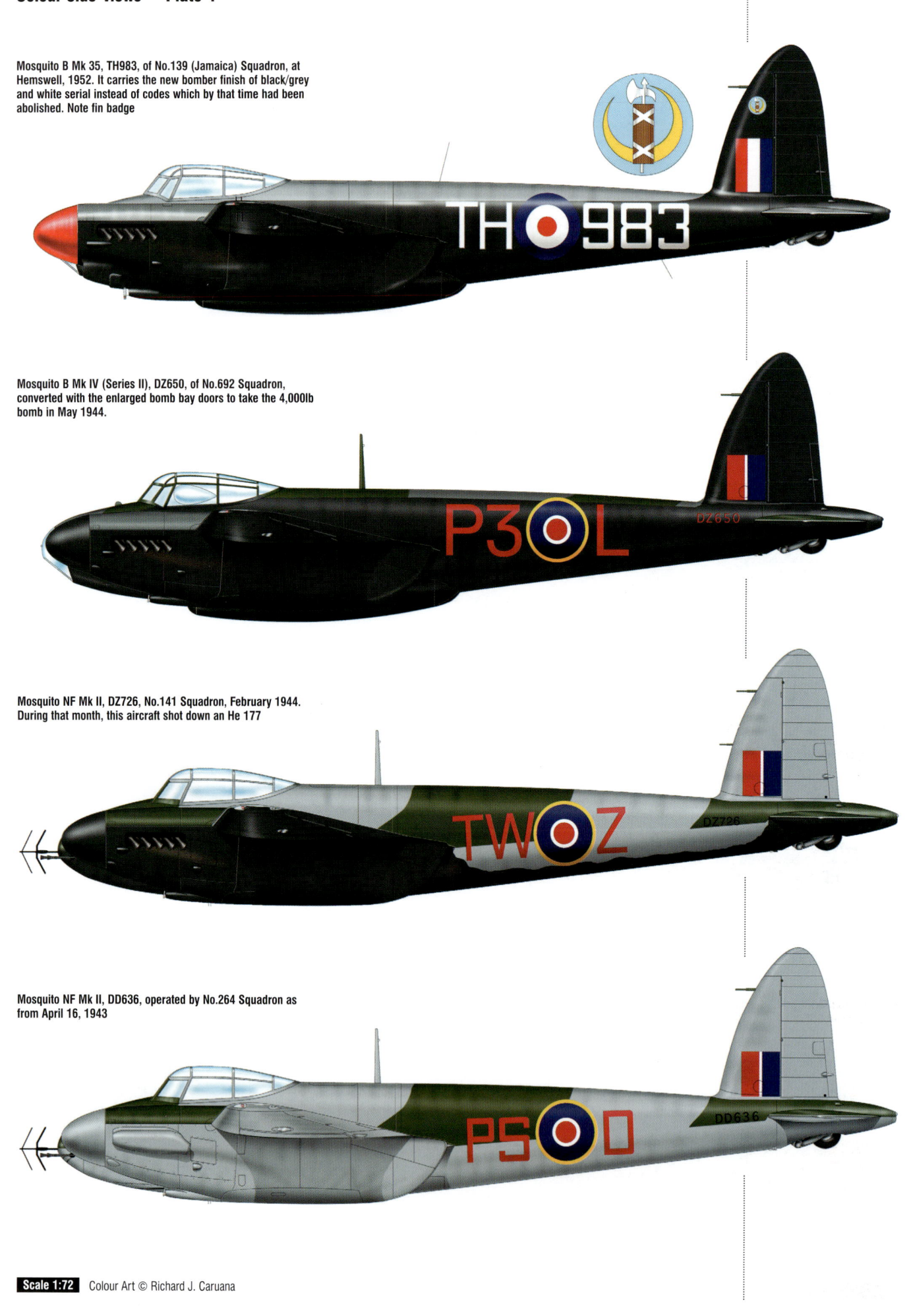

Mosquito B Mk 35, TH983, of No.139 (Jamaica) Squadron, at Hemswell, 1952. It carries the new bomber finish of black/grey and white serial instead of codes which by that time had been abolished. Note fin badge

Mosquito B Mk IV (Series II), DZ650, of No.692 Squadron, converted with the enlarged bomb bay doors to take the 4,000lb bomb in May 1944.

Mosquito NF Mk II, DZ726, No.141 Squadron, February 1944. During that month, this aircraft shot down an He 177

Mosquito NF Mk II, DD636, operated by No.264 Squadron as from April 16, 1943

Scale 1:72 Colour Art © Richard J. Caruana

52 Colour Side-views

Colour Side-views • Plate 5

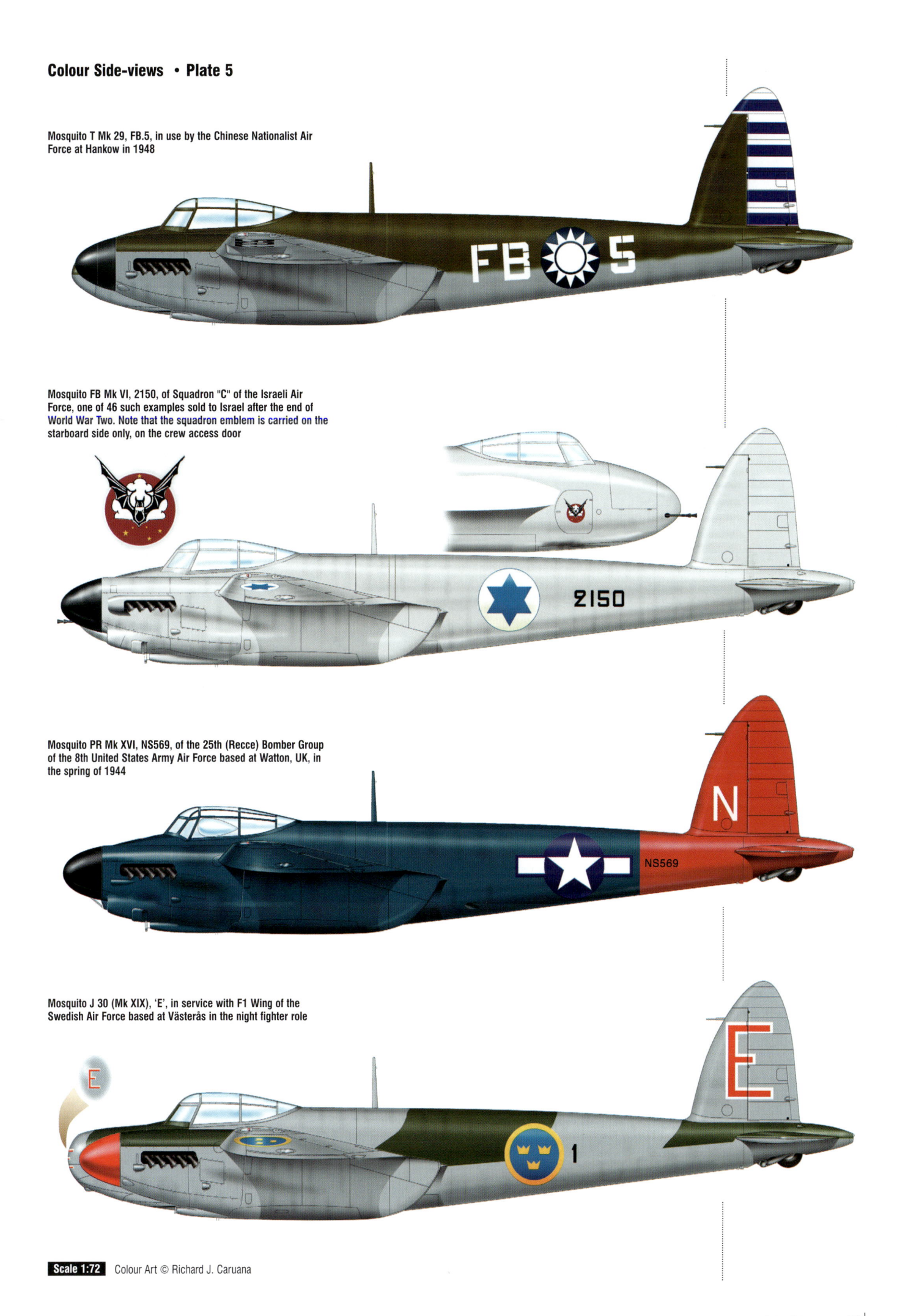

Mosquito T Mk 29, FB.5, in use by the Chinese Nationalist Air Force at Hankow in 1948

Mosquito FB Mk VI, 2150, of Squadron "C" of the Israeli Air Force, one of 46 such examples sold to Israel after the end of World War Two. Note that the squadron emblem is carried on the starboard side only, on the crew access door

Mosquito PR Mk XVI, NS569, of the 25th (Recce) Bomber Group of the 8th United States Army Air Force based at Watton, UK, in the spring of 1944

Mosquito J 30 (Mk XIX), 'E', in service with F1 Wing of the Swedish Air Force based at Västerås in the night fighter role

Scale 1:72   Colour Art © Richard J. Caruana

Colour Side-views • Plate 6

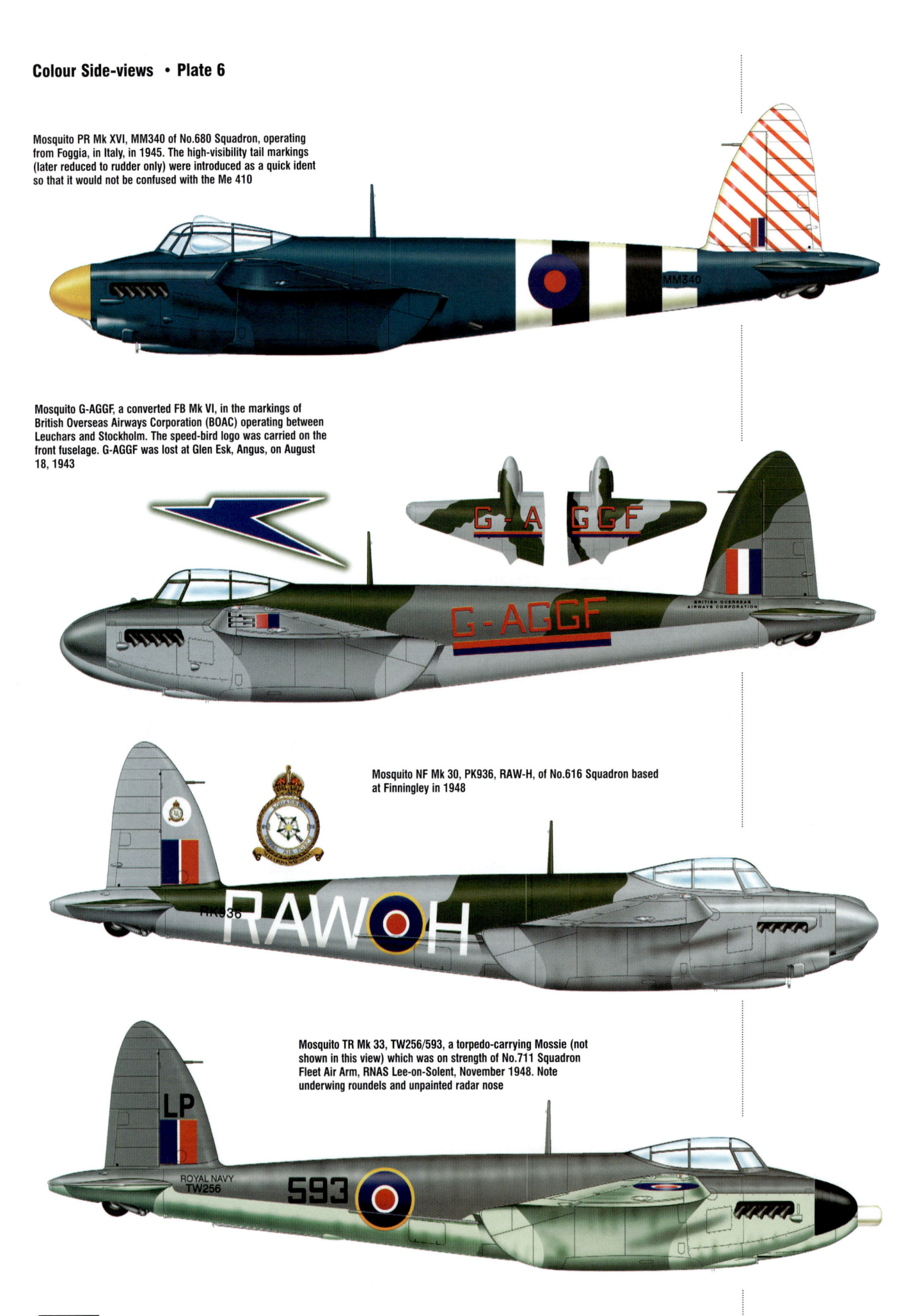

Mosquito PR Mk XVI, MM340 of No.680 Squadron, operating from Foggia, in Italy, in 1945. The high-visibility tail markings (later reduced to rudder only) were introduced as a quick ident so that it would not be confused with the Me 410

Mosquito G-AGGF, a converted FB Mk VI, in the markings of British Overseas Airways Corporation (BOAC) operating between Leuchars and Stockholm. The speed-bird logo was carried on the front fuselage. G-AGGF was lost at Glen Esk, Angus, on August 18, 1943

Mosquito NF Mk 30, PK936, RAW-H, of No.616 Squadron based at Finningley in 1948

Mosquito TR Mk 33, TW256/593, a torpedo-carrying Mossie (not shown in this view) which was on strength of No.711 Squadron Fleet Air Arm, RNAS Lee-on-Solent, November 1948. Note underwing roundels and unpainted radar nose

Scale 1:72 Colour Art © Richard J. Caruana

Colour Interior Views • 1

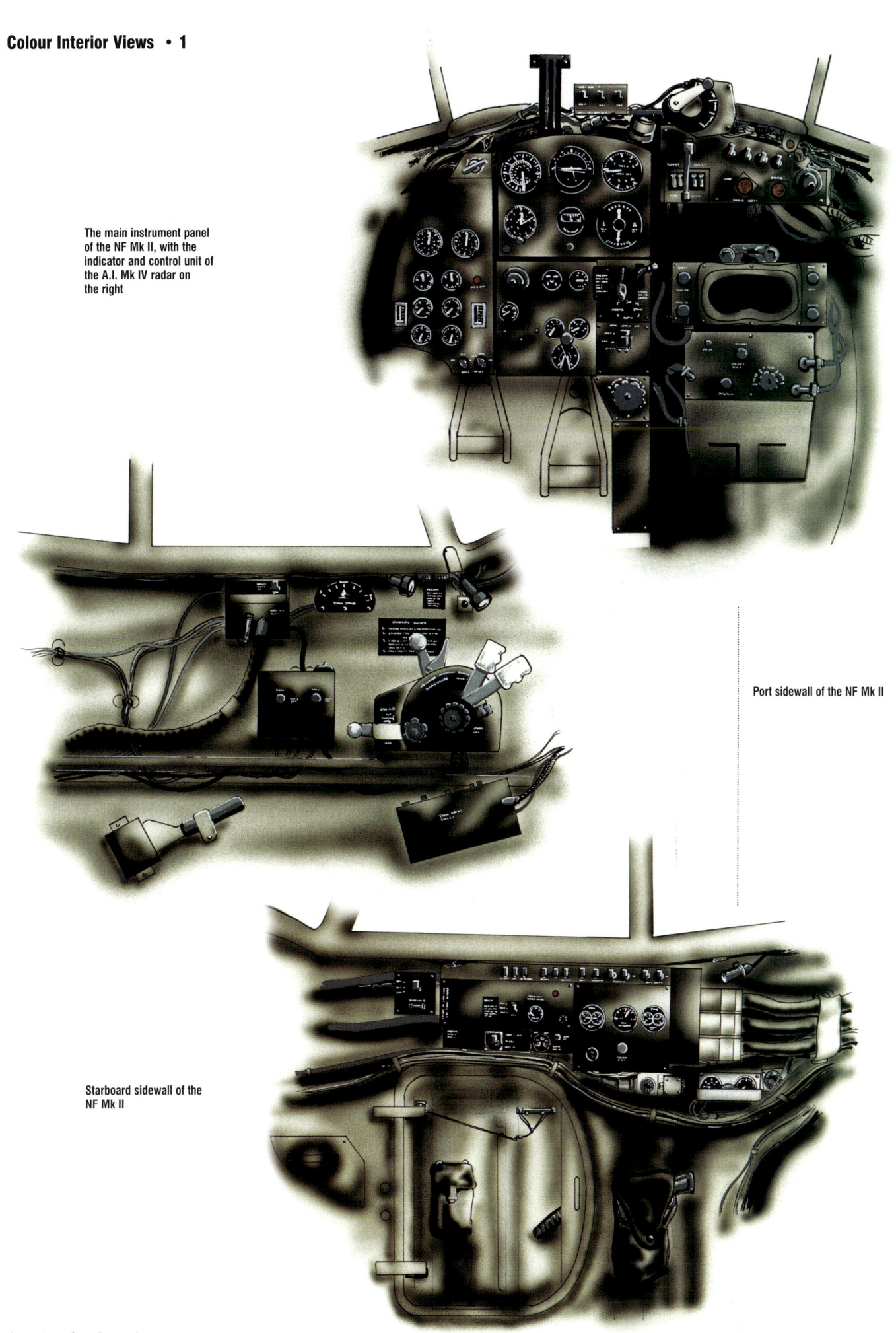

The main instrument panel of the NF Mk II, with the indicator and control unit of the A.I. Mk IV radar on the right

Port sidewall of the NF Mk II

Starboard sidewall of the NF Mk II

Colour Art © Steve Benstead

Colour Interior Views • 2

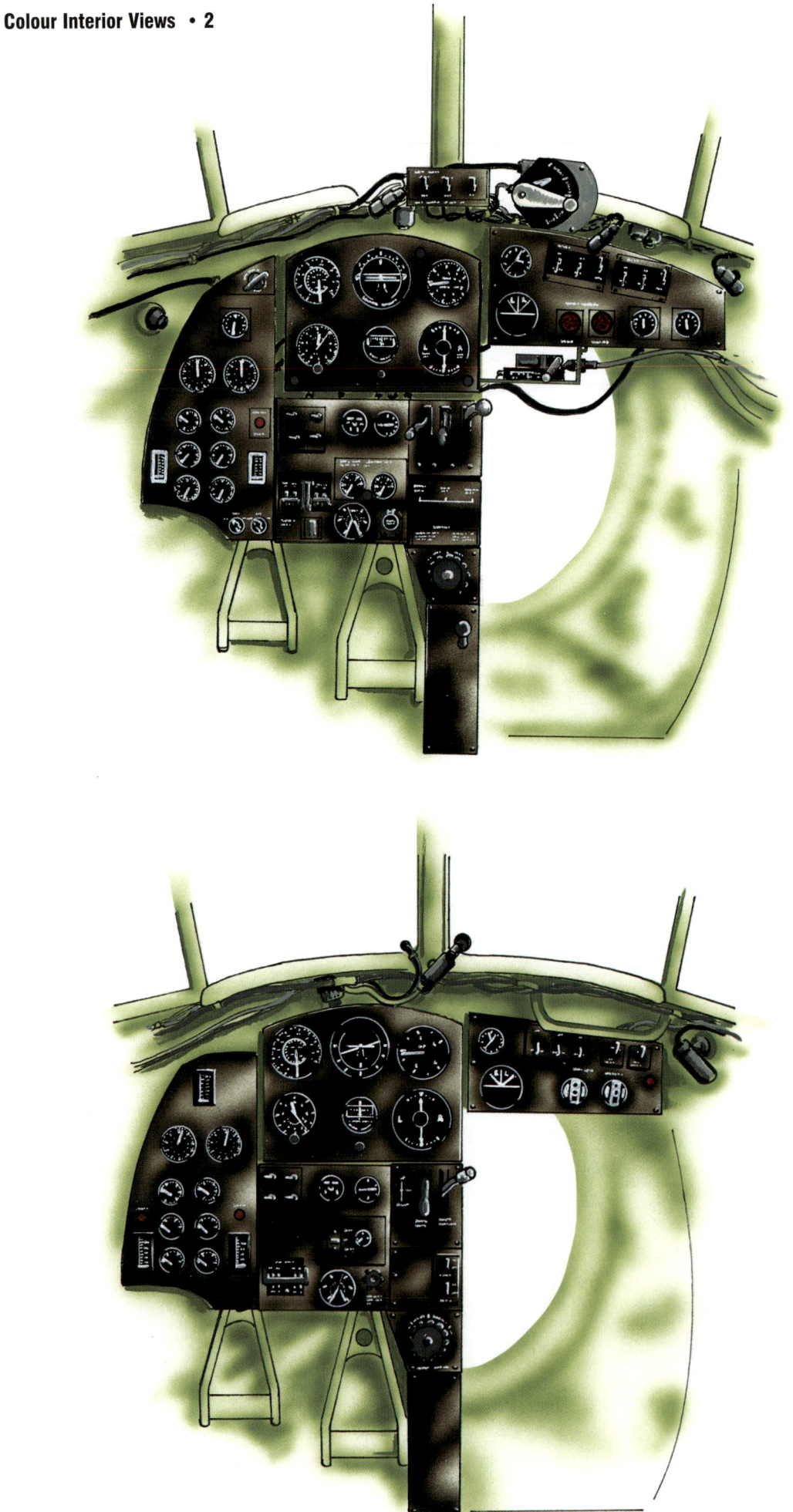

The main instrument panel of the B Mk XVI, although this is applicable to most early bomber variants

The main instrument panel of the PR Mk 34 illustrates how little the overall layout of the area changed throughout the Mosquito's evolution

Colour Art © Steve Benstead

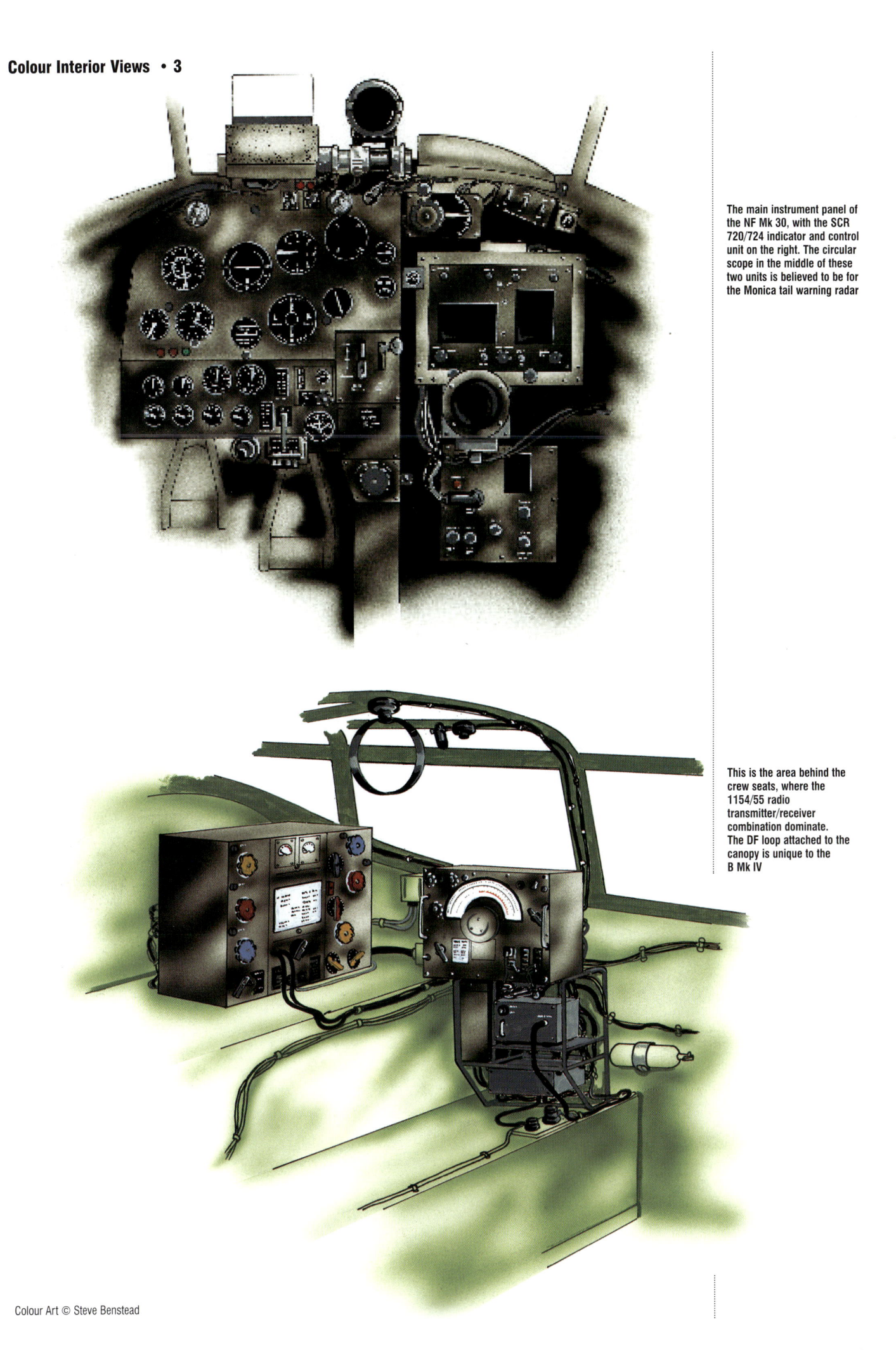

Colour Interior Views • 3

The main instrument panel of the NF Mk 30, with the SCR 720/724 indicator and control unit on the right. The circular scope in the middle of these two units is believed to be for the Monica tail warning radar

This is the area behind the crew seats, where the 1154/55 radio transmitter/receiver combination dominate. The DF loop attached to the canopy is unique to the B Mk IV

Colour Art © Steve Benstead

Colour Interior Views • 4

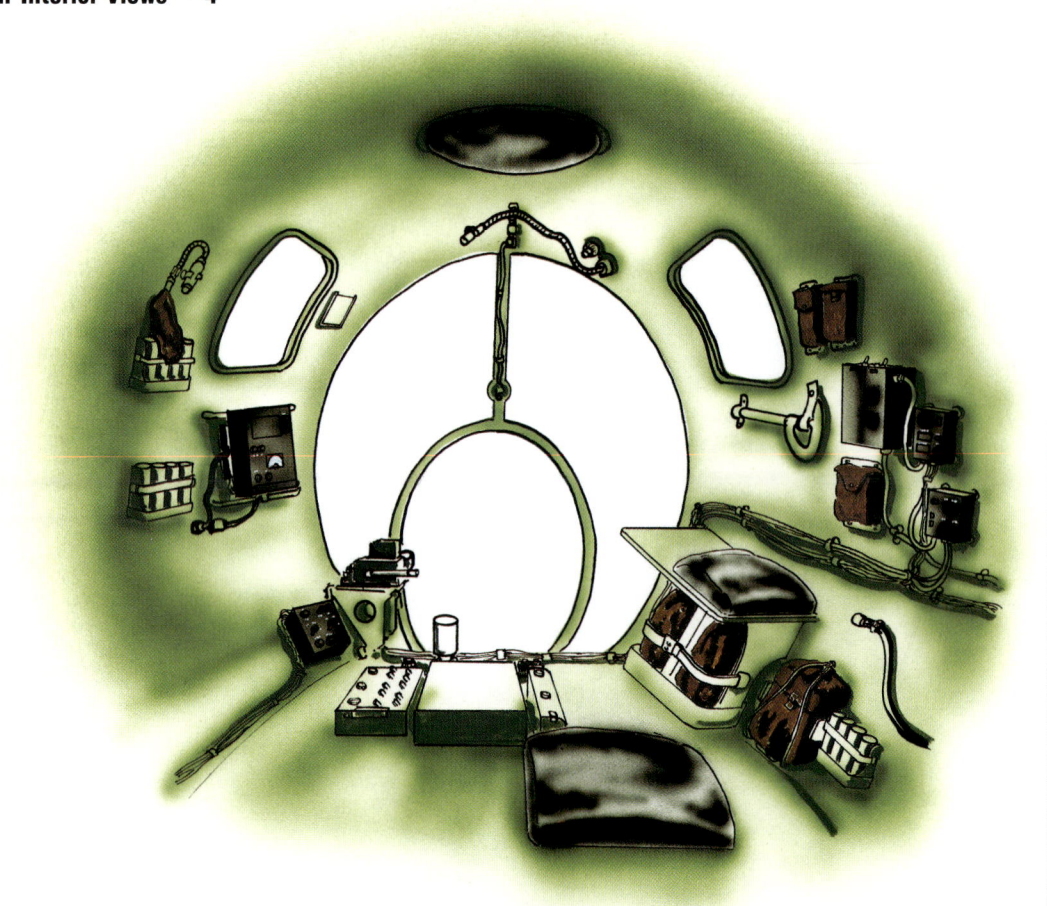

This is the nose of a B Mk XVI variant, but it is quite representative of all bomber variants

The slight differences in this, a PR variant, can be seen when compared to the bomber variant above

Colour Art © Steve Benstead

The Basics

Modelling the Mosquito

Chapter **9**

Considering the long and distinguished service of the Mosquito, not that many kits of it have been produced. At the time this book is being written there are currently available three in 1/72nd scale, two in 1/48th and one in 1/32nd and all of these kits, plus any others which have been made over the years, are listed at Appendix I. Now I do say that there are currently only two kits in 1/48th scale, but as with all things, just as this title was being finalised an announcement was made by Tamiya in Japan that Tamiya were going to create a brand-new kit of the Mosquito in this scale. So far only the B Mk IV Series II and FB Mk VI have been listed, but this does mean that they have the basis for all single-stage versions of the Mosquito. Once the kits arrive, further study of the breakdown of parts will tell if the kit is going to be used as the basis of a two-stage version, by having the engine cowlings separate (or 'gaps' in the sprues which indicate additional parts). With the obvious appeal of the type I cannot see this being the last new kit of this machine and although we have utilised the Airfix 1/48th scale kit to illustrate the various versions that can be built in this title, the concept of the Datafile is such that this title will offer you the background knowledge and details you require to make all (well, nearly all) versions of the Mosquito from any kit that is available. The subject can only be approached in a certain number of ways in kit form and therefore the information within this title will serve you well from whatever basis you start.

The Mosquito in 1/72nd Scale

Airfix: Mk II/VI/XVIII

This is the 'newer' Series 3 version of the Mosquito from this source and it dates back to 1972.

There are three decal options in the example we had and they are:

- Mk II (NF.II) YP•R, DD712 of No.23 Sqn.
- FB Mk VI NA•B, A52-520 of No.1 Sqn. RAAF.
- FB Mk XVIII QM•D, PZ468 of Nos.248/254 Sqn.

Even after twenty-six years this kit is still good and it has a good basic outline, which allows you to make a number of single-stage Merlin powered fighter options. The 57mm Molins armed FB Mk XVII does require you to undertake a bit of surgery on the kit parts, but nothing most modellers cannot deal with. There are a number of optional parts included with this kit, namely both narrow- and 'paddle'-blade propellers and the 'bow & arrow' antenna of the A.I Mk IV radar carried by the NF Mk II. Both shrouded and exposed exhaust stacks are included, although being a single-stage Merlin powered example, the exposed examples are the five-stack type. The cockpit interior is only basic, with two seats, bulkhead and floor, control column, instrument panel and radio equipment. You have two options to overcome this problem; firstly you could detail the interior from scratch using the information given in Chapter 11 of this title, or you can install one of the stunning resin cockpits from Hi-Tech. This French company currently have two such inserts in their range, being for either fighter or bomber configuration, and they are most heartily recommended if you want to save time. The canopy is also a bit thick and if you are going to fit the Hi-Tech interior I would recommend replacing the kit part with a vac-formed example from the Squadron or Falcon 'Clear-Vax' ranges. See Appendix II for a complete listing of all the accessories produced for the Mosquito. The undercarriage is very well produced and although only plain-style wheel hubs are included, these can now be replaced with both types from the Paragon range. The Paragon examples will also be better as the kit examples have no tread-pattern and the Mosquito's tyres had either square or diamond patterns, so it's a little difficult to cut them in with a razor saw. The Paragon examples are also 'weighted' to better represent the real thing and this is very much the vogue at present. The kit's tailwheel is well done with the twin-contact style of tyre included, although if you wish to convert to any of the earlier versions, this will have to be filled and reshaped. Underwing stores consist of the of the correct style 'T'-section rocket rails and good representations of 3" rocket projectiles with 60lb SAP heads. Of course if you want to depict an anti-shipping example more accurately you will have to make up the 25lb AP heads for these rockets. Two 500lb General Purpose (GP), High Explosive (HE) bombs are included along with 50 gallon drop tanks and

The decal sheet with three options

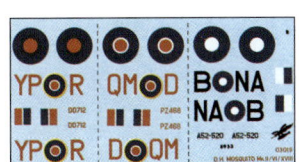

Kit Parts: Airfix Mk II/VI/XVIII

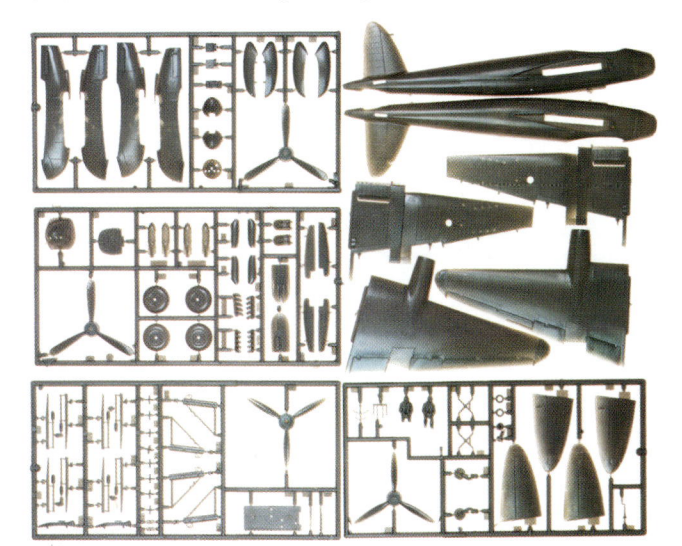

Clear parts

Modelling the Mosquito • The Basics   59

the correct location for each of these items is marked on the inside of each lower wing panel. Ensure the correct holes are opened up before the wing is assembled and remember that the NF Mk II didn't carry anything under its wings.

As far as accuracy goes, it has been said in the past that the profile of the lower surface of the rear fuselage towards the tail is too tapered. To be truthful, correcting this will be both complex and unnecessary, as it is hardly noticeable. Being a product of Airfix and being originally tooled in the 1970s, this kit's surface detail is all raised lines and I am sure that many modellers will want to remove and rescribe these. The kit also features raised rivets at the back of the engine nacelles and on the upper wing surface; these should be reduced slightly, as they are too prominent for this smaller scale.

Verdict
Overall, this is the 'pick of the bunch' for 1/72nd scale at present. I am sure in the future that another manufacturer will do this type, but for the meantime this kit from Airfix can form the basis of nearly all the variants produced, thanks to Paragon Designs.

Airfix: NF Mk XIX/J 30
This is a revised version of the Series 3 kit and it was released by Airfix in 1995. The reasoning behind the kit was that Airfix's Swedish importer said that a J 30 version of the kit would be a nice idea, so Airfix obliged! The only modifications to the old Series 3 kit are the scribing of a cut line inside the nose of the fuselage halves and the provision of additional parts such as the four-blade non-featherable propellers and spinners and the 'Universal' radome.

There are three decal options in the example we had and they are:

- NF Mk XIX RS•J, MM650 of No.157 Sqn.
- J 30 'Blue B' of the 2nd Squadron, F1 Wing, Swedish Air Force
- J 30 'Yellow H' of the 3rd Squadron, F1 Wing, Swedish Air Force

Kit Parts:
Airfix NF Mk XIX/J.30

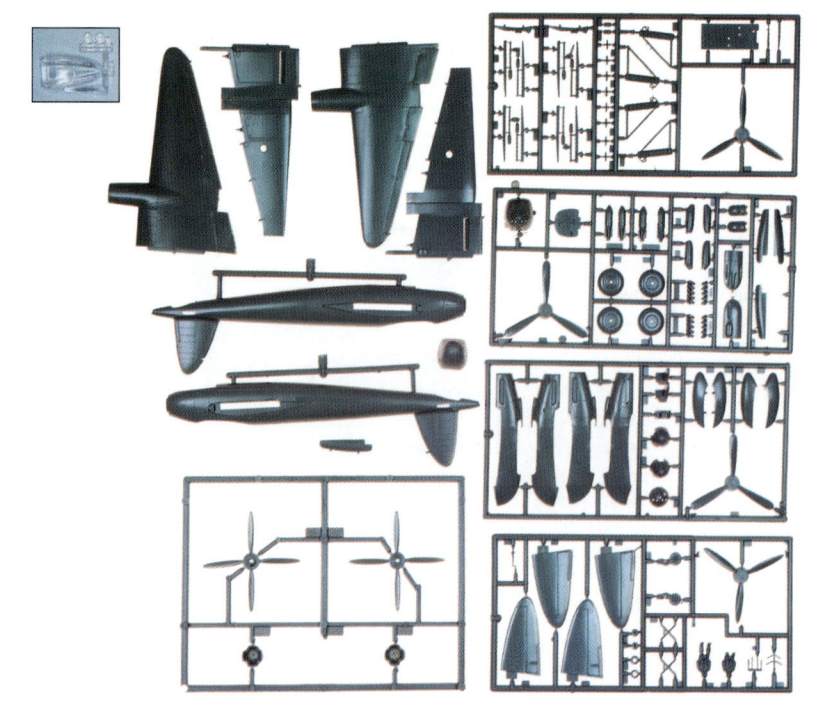

All of the points discussed above on its parent version apply to this kit and no amendments have been made to the kit, nor has any additional detail been added to the interior. The main problem with the kit is the new nose, which is the wrong shape for a true 'Universal' radome. It is something akin to a cross between that and the 'thimble' type fitted to the NF Mk XII. This is a shame, as the kit could so easily be converted into a two-stage powered NF Mk 30. The way to overcome this is to ignore it, or to purchase the replacement nose which is currently marketed by a UK based firm, Airparts. The only other problem with the kit is probably one that no-one else considered (and one we discovered only by chance), that all refurbished Mosquitos operated by foreign air forces had the glazed side-window on the starboard side blown, not flat as depicted in this kit. The only current way around this is to graft this section of a vac-formed example into either the kit's canopy (which is too thick anyway) or into another vac-formed replacement. Which ever way you choose, it will be a difficult task and I can only hope that some manufacturer issues an example to save our sanity. In relation to this point, all Australian and Canadian-built machines had that style of canopy as standard too!

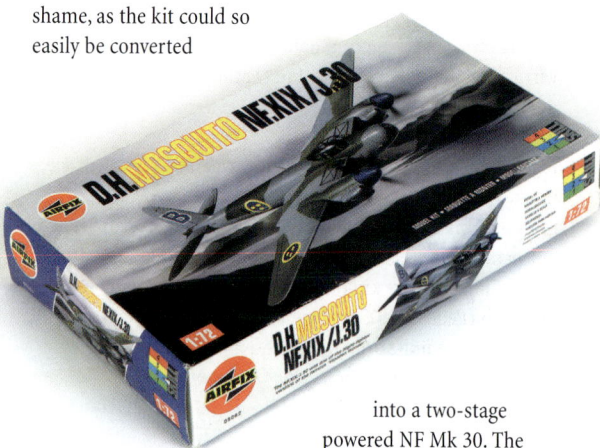

Verdict
All of the comments made about the original issue apply here also, although the inclusion of the four-blade propellers is a real treat and the decal sheet even has the semi-official squadron emblem that was sometimes carried on the access doors of each squadron's machines, which is something I could really have done with in 1/48th scale!

Matchbox: NF Mk 30 & B Mk IX
This kit was first issued by Matchbox in 1975 and it is produced in their 'standard' format. What I mean by this is that it was released as a kit which did not need to be painted and therefore is injected in three colours of plastic. This has always been a trademark for Matchbox, although now that all the toolings belong to Revell®, they will be injected in just one colour.

The colour options in the example we had were:

- NF 30 VY*Y, NT252 of No.85 Sqn.
- B Mk IX GB*E, ML913 of No.105 Sqn.

The kit itself is not that bad and it does offer the two-stage engine nacelles which are not included in the Airfix kits. Fitting these to the Airfix kit is not straightforward though, as each has been engineered in a different manner. The kit does have drop tanks and 500lb bombs, although the latter are incorrect and do not look right.

Accuracy-wise the kit is about 0.75mm too long, but it is simply not worth correcting in this scale. The radio-equipment access hatch on the starboard side of the fuselage is included, but there are no panel lines for the access-hatch under the nose or the dinghy-stowage bay behind the cockpit. The strengthening strake on the rear fuselage needs to be shortened by 4mm at its leading edge as well as being sanded down, as it is far too prominent. The fairing over the elevator actuator on the port side of the vertical fin/rudder is identical to that on the starboard side and this is incorrect. Increase this area to correspond with the photographs included in Chapter 11. There is no representation of the radiator matrix in either radiator intake, so pieces of fine mesh should be added to better represent this. The propellers in this kit are neither narrow nor paddle types, so they are best left off. Use examples left over from the Airfix kit, or get them from the UK firm, Aeroclub (Paddle: P075 Spinners: V1116). The undercarriage units are unfortunately over-simplified and they are therefore best replaced with examples from Aeroclub (V074). Cockpit detail is once again very limited, although you can use the cockpit update from Hi-Tech to correct this now. If you decided to just scratchbuild an interior you should note that the floor in this kit is located too high. To get around this I would recommend that you make a new one 1mm wider than the original and then locate it about 2mm lower down in the fuselage. The kit only comes with the bomber-style control yoke and this is not applicable to the NF.30, as that had the fighter-style control column. To get around this you will have to scratchbuild a new one. The canopy in the kit is too flat and therefore it should be replaced with the example available in Paragon set number 7229. The bulges at mid-chord of the undersurface of each wing, adjacent to the fuselage, are missing and these will have to be made from Milliput or similar. The kit also features the twin tip lights which were only fitted to the early marks and the back ones will have to be filled, as they are not applicable to the options offered in this kit. If however you are converting the kit to the earlier version, they will act as a guide for you when you replace these areas with clear stock.

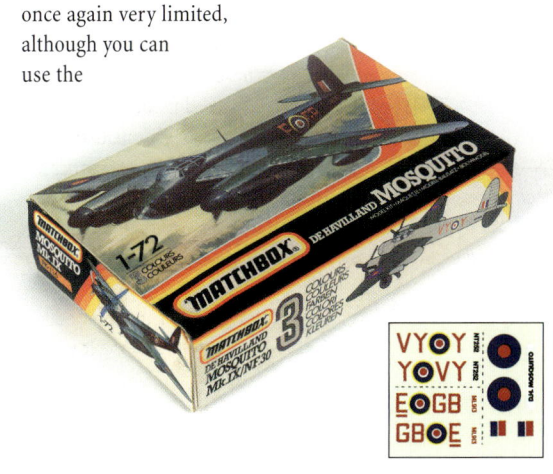

Verdict

This kit was never designed as a high price competitor for the Airfix kit. It was always designed as a basic, simple kit, which would attract younger modellers and although it is as expensive as the Airfix model today, it is still well worth tracking down, as it is the only two-stage option available. Secondhand examples are currently reasonably priced as the kit has been re-issued by the new owners of the Matchbox label, Revell®.

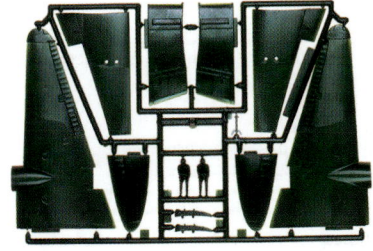

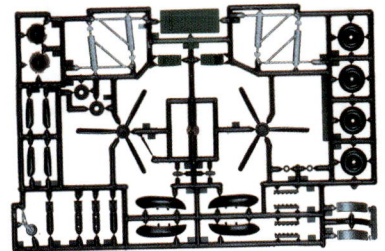

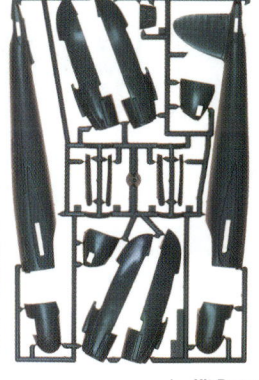

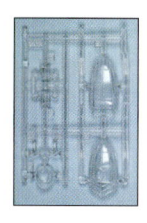

Kit Parts: Matchbox NF 30 & B Mk IX

Far left: The decal sheet for the Matchbox NF 30 & B Mk IX

FROG: B Mk IV & FB Mk VI

This kit was first released in 1968 and it remained under the FROG label until 1977. It was planned for release by NOVO in 1978, but this never happened.

The colour options in the kit we have are:

- B Mk IV flown by Wg. Cdr. J.Wooldridge, CO of No.105 Sqn.
- FB Mk VI of No.1 Sqn., RAAF.

The kit is a bit basic, being newer than the original Airfix offering, but not as good as their more recent example. The first area you will need to deal with is the cockpit interior. This is completely bare and a lot of scratchbuilding will be required, once you have decided on which variant you are building. Unfortunately the excellent cockpit updates from Hi-Tech are not designed for this kit and I suspect that they would not fit without major modification, so scratchbuilding the interior is the only real option. As both a fighter and bomber version are offered; the nose section in this kit is provided as a separate piece for each. The join line that will result from this is annoying and may well cause problems if you are not careful. Remove the fuselage stiffener from the starboard rear fuselage side, as it is too long and too far up the fuselage side. Replace it with a length of plastic rod 35mm long. Positioning this rod is relatively easy as 8mm of it should go under the wing and it should be about 1.5 mm below the wing's trailing edge. The drift sight panel in the crew-access door of the bomber version is not present, so drill this area out and glaze it with Krystal Klear or similar.

The biggest problems with this kit though are the vertical tail and the position of the wings in relation to the fuselage. The wings are too far up on the fuselage and correcting this fault is difficult and time consuming. Also, as there are better kits more readily available, you may not feel it is worth the bother anyway. The tail is the wrong shape and unless you have gone through with correcting the wings I doubt if it is worth correcting. If you do wish to do some remedial correction work, then the tail from the Airfix Series 3 kit could be grafted on, or you can use it as a template to make one from plastic card.

Modelling the Mosquito • The Basics 61

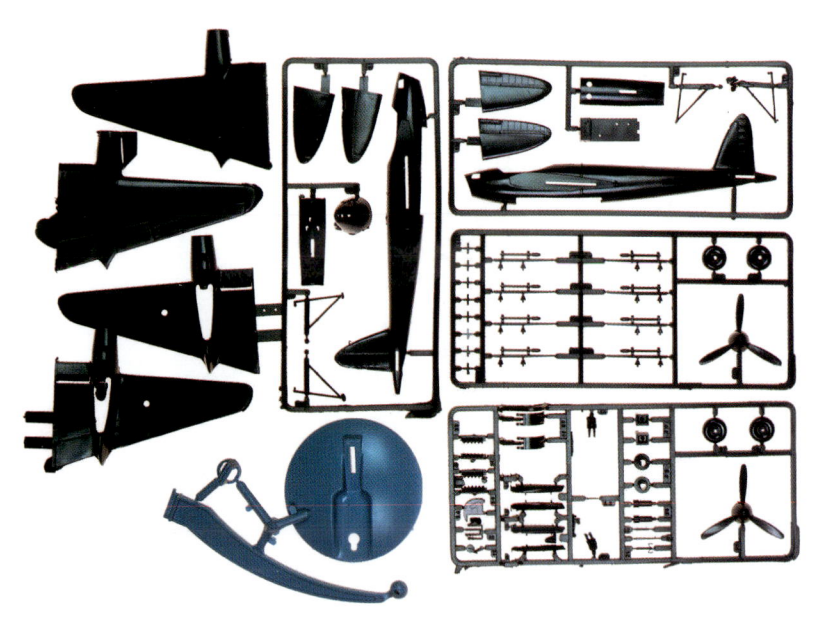

Kit Parts:
FROG B Mk IV & FB Mk VI

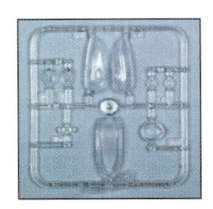

The Decal Sheet for the FROG

The rockets supplied in this kit have very thick overscale fins and the rails are the incorrect type for a Mosquito. The tailwheel has a ridge in the middle instead of the groove for the TC (twin-contact) type and the undercarriage and mudguards are very crude and heavy. These later parts can of course be replaced by the excellent Aeroclub examples mentioned earlier.

Verdict
Overall this kit is not really up to scratch, although it can be a source of a lot of useful parts for conversion of the Matchbox and Airfix kits. Being a Frog product this kit is worth far more to the collector than the modeller and I think it is best left that way!

The Mosquito in 1/48th Scale

Monogram: Mk II, NF Mk II, B Mk IV & FB Mk VI
This kit was released in 1965 and has been available off and on for the last 33 years. The kit itself is not too bad, although it does have a number of inaccuracies which I will mention in a moment.

The colour options in the example we had were:

- Mk II YP·A, DZ230 of No.23 Sqn.
- NF Mk II DD609 of an unidentified unit.
- B Mk IV GB·K, DZ378 of No.105 Sqn.
- FB Mk VI EG·T, MM417 of No.487 Sqn. RNZAF.

This kit was great when it was first released, but today it is overshadowed by the Airfix example and also has some serious problems in regard to accuracy. The vertical fin is nearly one scale foot too tall. To rectify this you have to remove the tail, cut 5mm off the base and then glue it back on. This however does mean that the lower hinge line is lost and has to be rescribed and the rudder actuator and fairing are now too low down. Remove these and build replacement ones from scrap in the middle of the rudder. Having done all that to the tail you then have to deal with the fuselage, which is too thin in plan view. Correcting this is a very involved task and it will be well outside the skills of all but the best modellers. To be honest a completely new fuselage would be better here, but you have the superior Airfix kit in any case and if you felt like a lot of conversion and grafting work I am sure the two could be joined. You may well wish to undertake this work, but all of the bomber versions are available using a combination of the Airfix kit and the Paragon conversion sets. The real problem with the Monogram fuselage is that it is basically too flat on the sides and needs to be built up with Milliput. This will however result in the wings being pushed out, making them the incorrect span. Shortening each by 5mm will cure this, but you will also have to re-profile the wing tips. The aileron lines now have to be filled and rescribed 3mm inboard. If you do all this work you will probably not be too happy to find that the engine nacelles forward of the front of the undercarriage bay are too tapered and have to be padded with filler and reshaped. Finally (there is more!), the propeller blades are too short, due to the closeness of the engines in the original layout of the kit, and you will have to recreate each from plasticard.

Verdict
With the Airfix kit available and conversions for all the bomber versions available in the Paragon range, there is no real need for you to build this kit. It is true that it was, and still is, a good seller and many modellers will still enjoy making it. However it will not form the basis of an accurate Mosquito in this scale without a lot of additional corrective work.

Airfix: FB Mk VI
This kit was originally announced by Airfix in 1977, however it did not appear until 1980. Many have said that this kit was originally proposed as a 1/24th scale version, and that the 1/48th scale kit is just reduced down by 50% from that example. Currently this is the best 1/48th scale Mosquito kit around, although it may well be surpassed by the forthcoming Tamiya examples. The kit is currently the basis of all of the Paragon conversions in this scale and it is also the basis of all the versions we have constructed for this title.

There are two colour options in this kit and they are:

- TH·M, N5850 of No.418 (City of Edmonton) Sqn., RCAF
- NE·A, NR405 of No.143 Sqn., Banff Strike Wing, RAF, 1945.

Overall the kit is excellent and I do not think that its accuracy

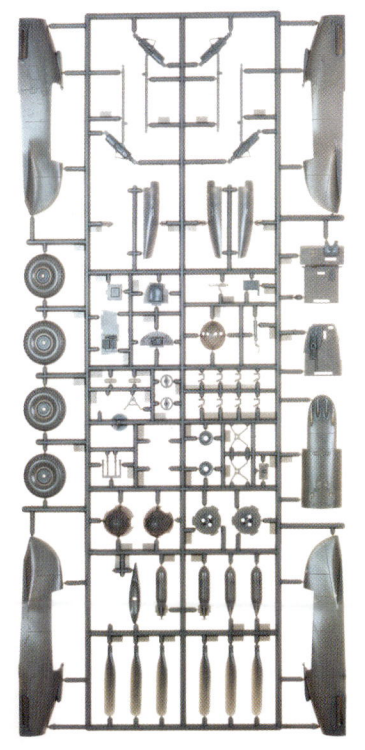

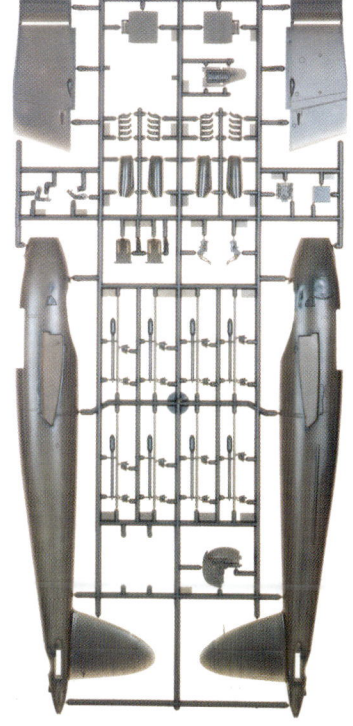

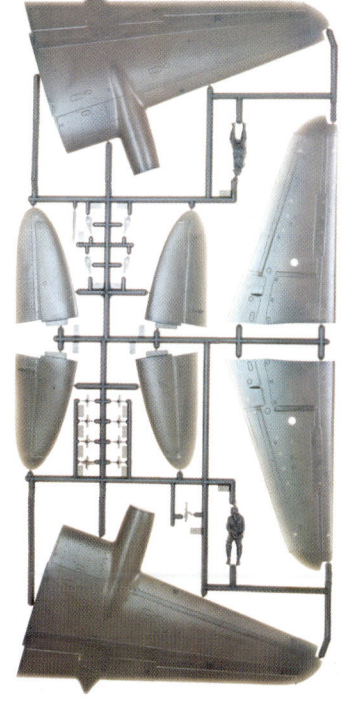

**Kit Parts:
AIRFIX FB Mk VI**

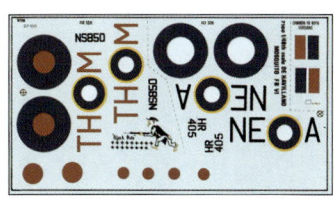

Far left: The decal sheet for the AIRFIX FB Mk VI

has ever been in doubt. The cockpit is well detailed, although the sidewalls are completely bare. To overcome this you can now utilise the excellent cockpit interior update set from Kendall Model Company (KMC). When I looked at this kit in 1996 I said that the crew-access door was impossible to remove intact and I am therefore glad to say that KMC have overcome this by including the door as a separate resin piece in their set.

The support stays for the mudguards (Kit part Nos.32, 33, 35 & 36) should be drilled out and the kit only offers the radial tread-pattern and plain hubs for each mainwheel. Luckily the Paragon and True Detail ranges include excellent resin wheels with both styles of hub. Only paddle-blade propellers are included in this kit, although once again Paragon offer a set of narrow-blade propellers in their range. Both shrouded and unshrouded exhaust stacks are included, although being a single-stage example, the unshrouded ones are of the five-stack type. One of the major shortcomings of this kit has always been that although an excellent set of 3" rocket projectiles and 500lb bombs are included, there were never any drop tanks. This has been solved, as both 50- and 100-gallon versions are available from Paragon. Hopefully before too long this firm will add the 200-gallon examples to their range, as these are extremely difficult to modify from their 100-gallon ones. The only other failings with the kit include the shrinkage around the starboard upper cockpit sidewall and the spar caps, which are too prominent.

Verdict

This kit is currently the best example available. With the announcement of a new B Mk IV and FB Mk VI from Tamiya in this scale, I am sure that this kit will be considered by many to have had its day. However it currently forms the basis of a long line of conversions and with the combination of the KMC and Paragon sets you will get a product equally as good as any other. The Mosquito is a subject which I am sure other manufacturers

will not leave for much longer in this scale, which is a shame as I am sure that Airfix would have soon converted this example to a two-stage bomber version.

The Mosquito in 1/32nd Scale

Revell: B Mk IV

This kit was first released in 1972 and it has only just recently been taken off the current stock lists by Revell®. For those who have examples stashed away however there is a mass of resin conversions based upon this kit which have been produced by UK manufacturer, Paragon. The kit has so far been offered with two different set of markings, which included:

- GB•E, DZ353 of No.105 Sqn.
- XD•G, DZ421 of No.139 Sqn. based at Horsham St. Faith
- 43-34926, an F-8-DH of the 3rd Photo Group (Recon) based in Italy in November 1943

This is a good kit, although the fuselage is slightly incorrect in

Modelling the Mosquito • The Basics **63**

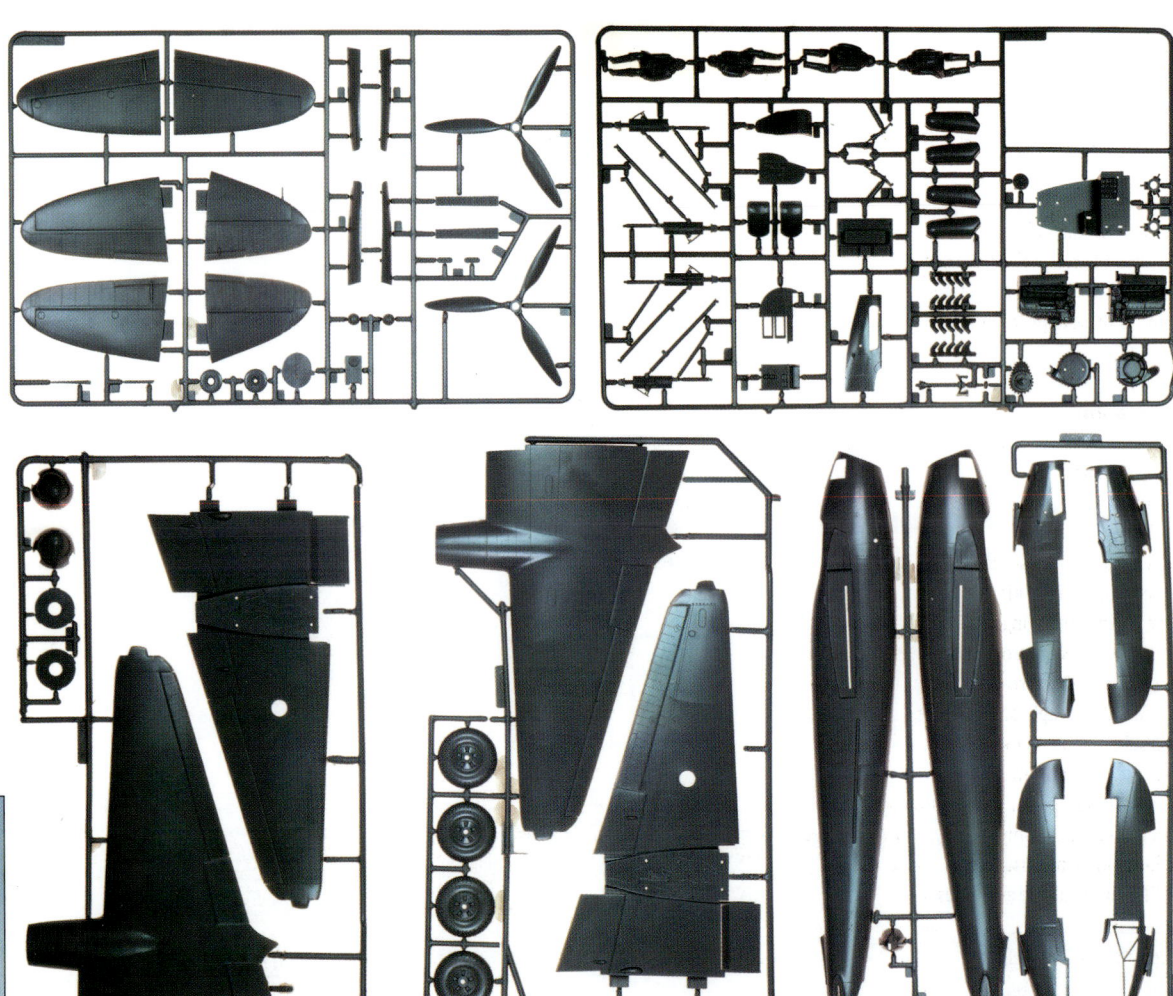

**Kit Parts:
Revell B Mk IV**

Far right: the decal sheet of the Revell B Mk IV, with two options

cross section; a little sanding on the upper fuselage joint will ensure the correct elliptical profile is achieved. The floor of the cockpit area needs to have a section cut out, otherwise the crew would never have been able to get into the aircraft. The major fault with the kit concerns the rear of each engine nacelle. Here the kit is completely incorrect as the nacelle sides are depicted as being parallel, where a complex bi-concave shape is really required in this area (look at the Airfix kit). The only way to overcome this is to pad the area with filler and slowly sand it to the correct shape. You should also shorten each undercarriage leg by 3mm, otherwise your model will sit too high.

The canopy, although very well moulded and clear, is made of two parts and split down the middle. It will also sit too high once in position so it is therefore best replaced by the new vac-formed example in the Paragon range. The annoying thing about the F-8-DH version offered in one boxing is that this type carried cameras in the nose and bomb-bay and no attempt to depict this or alert the modeller has been made by Revell. The cockpit interior of this kit is very basic but does include both crew members, however this entire area has recently been updated thanks to the excellent sets from Paragon, so you do not have to scratch-build it all. Neat renditions of the Merlin engines are included, although in this scale a lot of additional work and detailing will be required to make them acceptable. The inclusion of such details is a nice touch by Revell®, but it was one of their trademark features from the 1970s. Only shrouded exhausts are included in this kit, although the uncovered examples are now in one of the Paragon Fighter-bomber conversions. The spar caps and all other details in this kit are depicted by raised panel lines and I am sure many will want to rescribe these. Don't do this with the spar caps however, as it is

best to depict this area in this larger scale by overlaying very thin plastic card, or using clear decal strips.

Verdict

Overall this is a very sound kit and with the recent release of a large number of accessories and conversion sets for it by Paragon, there are very few examples of the type that you cannot make. The removal of the kit from the current stock list is a real shame, although I am sure it will be back before too long and that there are a great number stashed away in modeller's 'pending' piles for a rainy day.

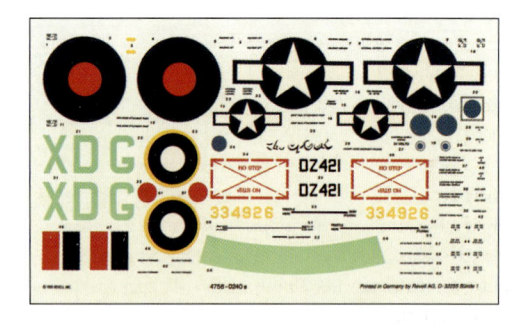

The above tells you what is currently available (or not!) in 1/72nd, 1/48th and 1/32nd scales. I have not included details of the lovely little 1/144th scale example from Aeroclub, as this B Mk 35 can only really be converted to the late series two-stage example and the small scale and total lack of accessories and decals would make that a daunting task.

Now that we have a starting point it is time to get a better understanding of the actual aircraft, so read on...

Addendum

Since the initial publication of this book a number of kits, decals, and accessories have appeared in various scales. The following is a brief digest of newer items. Further details of some of these appear in Chapter 12.

1/72 Scale

Hasegawa:
B. Mk. IV, B. Mk.VI & NF Mk. II, FB. Mk.18
Hasegawa released several boxings of the Frog kit prior to a new tooling appearing in 1996, after the first edition of this title. Initially a B.IV, this reappeared as a B. Mk. VI a couple of years later, and subsequent boxings as such have included new markings or new additional parts. The kit also appeared as a NF Mk. II, and an FB.Mk.18 an ti-ship variant, and was also reboxed by Revell as kit #04625 in 2001.

The kit has all the attributes of a modern Hasegawa tooling, and is designed – as one might expect – to accommodate a number of different variants. This makes for a more complex assembly, with a separate nose, and also the canopy is split down the middle, but the overall fit of parts is good. Full cockpit and bomb bay details are included, as well as a choice of propellers.

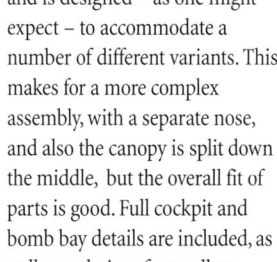

Verdict
A good tooling, possibly complicated by the engineering to allow multiple variants, and by no means the cheapest option. Nonetheless a good detailed model. No doubt Hasegawa will continue their usual practice with this kit of regular 'limited edition' reissues with minor variations or decal options.

Tamiya:
B. Mk.IV, PR. Mk.IV, B. Mk.VI, NF. Mk.II, NF. Mk.XIII, NF. Mk.XVII
Tamiya commenced what is likely to be the definitive range of 1/72 Mosquitoes in this scale with an initial boxing of the B. Mk.VI and NF. Mk.II. First appearing in 1999 it was followed by two subsequent boxings, offering both PR and Nightfighter variants.

Tamiya's Mosquitoes are finely engineered, highly detailed, and give every appearance of being scaled-down versions of the 1/48 toolings. With excellent fit of parts and plenty of options.

Decals include stencilling, instrument panels, and the usual seatbelts, which are not to everyone's taste, but are at least an acknowledgement of the need for some representation in this area.

Verdict
Currently the best kits of the Mosquito available in 1/72, Tamiya's prices are not cheap, but the quality of the tooling and the fit of parts is exceptional.

1/48 Scale

Tamiya:
B. Mk.IV, PR. Mk.IV, B. Mk.VI, NF. Mk.II, NF. Mk.XIII, NF. Mk.XVII
Following the first edition of this Datafile, Tamiya's 1/48 kits appeared and changed the face of Mosquito modelling. Highly detailed and superbly engineered, the kit has appeared in four boxings to date – three with revisions to allow for the different variants, and a fourth offering the NF Mk.II together with a Standard Tilly light utility vehicle.

These kits are widely regarded as among Tamiys's best. Surface detail is delicate and refined, mouldings are crisp and flash free and leave nothing to be desired.

Verdict
As with the 1/72 kits, Tamiya have set the benchmark with this tooling, and the current availability of aftermarket products is very much geared towards these kits.

Revell:
B. Mk.IV
Revell's new kit in 1/48 came as something as a surprise to many. Released in 2008 it offers a cheaper option than the Tamiya kit, whilst still offering a very high level of detail, along with the fine surface engraving and tooling that has made Revell's recent releases such superb value. The kit includes many excellent features and options, but has received some criticism over the length of the main undercarriage struts, which are too short, affecting the sit of the finished aircraft. Given the quality and value of the rest of the package this may not be regarded as insurmountable by many…

Verdict
Excellent value, and builds into a fine model, although the undercarriage problem will need to be tackled.

1/24 Scale

Heritage Aviation:
B. Mk. IV
Astonishing to think that two new 1/24 kits have appeared in recent years, but at time of writing no 1/32 – clearly a gap waiting for someone to exploit. No doubt the Far East will have discovered it before long…

Modelling the Mosquito • The Basics   i

Heritage release the Mosquito as a vacform – they also did a Lancaster, for those who have the time and space! The kit comprises basic sheets of vacform parts, along with metal and resin components. Decals provided offered a 487 Sqn machine.

Verdict

Now out of production, this is not a beginner's kit but can be built into an excellent replica by anyone with a little experience of vacform kits.

Airfix:

FB. Mk. VI

Airfix's new kit was rolled out to great fanfare at the end of 2009.

Comprising over 600 pieces, the kit is a strange mixture on the one hand, of impressive size and detail, but at the same time one can't quite help wondering if the tooling couldn't have been a little sharper in this large scale.

Verdict

An impressive-looking model when finished, and if 1/24 is your niche then guaranteed not to disappoint – you will certainly need to think about where you are going to keep it when it is finished though!

KITS:

Airfix #07111 1/48 NF 30 2003
Airfix #97111 1/48 B Mk XVI / PR XVI 2003
Airfix #25001 1/24 FB Mk VI 2009 New Tool
Hasegawa #51217 1/72 B Mk IV 1996 New Tool
Hasegawa #51218 1/72 FB Mk II 1998 Revision of above kit
Hasegawa #00050 1/72 NF Mk II 2005 Revision of above kit
Hasegawa #02024 1/72 FB Mk 18 2013 Revision of above kit
Heritage Aviation 1/24 FB Mk VI 2008 New Tool
Revell #04265 1/72 B Mk IV 2001 Ex-Hasegawa (1996 Tooling)
Revell #04555 1/48 B Mk IV   2008 New Tool
Tamiya 1/48 FB Mk VI/NF Mk II 1998
Tamiya 1/48 B.MkIV/PR.Mk IV 1999
Tamiya 1/48 NF Mk XIII/Mk XVII 2000
Tamiya 1/48 NF Mk II & British Light Utility Car 2009
Tamiya #60747 1/72 FB Mk VI/NF Mk II 1999
Tamiya #60753 1/72 B.MkIV/PR.Mk IV 2000
Tamiya #60765 1/72 NF Mk XIII/Mk XVII 2001

CONVERSIONS AND ACCESSORIES:

Alley Cat #24001C 1/24 FB Mk VI ASH Radar Nose & Radar Equipment for Airfix kits
Alley Cat #24002C 1/24 NF Mk XII / Mk XIII Nose & Radar Equipment for Airfix kits
Alley Cat #24003C 1/24 NF Mk XVII/XIX Nose & Radar for Airfix kits
Alley Cat #24004C 1/24 J.30 NF MK XIX nose radar for Airfix kits Aircraft
Alley Cat #24005C 1/24 TR Mk 33 Sea Mosquito conversion
Alley Cat #24006C 1/24 FB Mk XVIII Tse-tse for Airfix kits
Airwaves #72166 1/72 etched details for Airfix and Matchbox kits
Airwaves #72057 1/72 plain wheels
Aires #4086 1/48 Mk VI/NF.II cockpit for Tamiya kits
Aires #4152 1/48 Mk VI bomb bay for Tamiya kits
Aires #4177 1/48 Mk VI gun bay for Tamiya kits
Aires #4200 1/48 Mk VI engine set for Tamiya kits
Aires #4208 1/48 Mk VI/NF.II wheel bay for Tamiya kits
Aires #4463 1/48 Mk IV cockpit set for Tamiya kits
Aires #7067 1/72 Mk VI/NF.II cockpit for Tamiya kits
Aires #7077 1/72 Mk VI/NF.II detail set for Tamiya kits
Aires #7091 1/72 Mk VI gun bay for Tamiya kits
Aires #7099 1/72 Mk VI bomb bay for Tamiya kits
CMK #4036 1/48 Mk VI interior for Tamiya kits
CMK #4038 1/48 Rolls-Royce Merlin engine for Tamiya kits
CMK #4106M 1/48 Mk IV/Mk VI exterior set for Tamiya kits
CMK #4108 1/48 PR Mk XVI twin stage Merlin engine for Tamiya kits
CMK #4241 1/48 Wing mounted coolers for Tamiya kits
CMK #4260 1/48 Mk II/Mk IV/Mk VI Control Surfaces Set for Tamiya kits
CMK #7036 1/72 Mk IV engine for Hasegawa kits
CMK #7037 1/72 interior for Hasegawa kits
CMK #7038 1/72 separate control surfaces for Hasegawa kits
CMK #7047 1/72 Mk IV/Mk VI detail set for Hasegawa kits
CMK #7105 1/72 PR Mk XV for Hasegawa or Tamiya kits
CMK #7116 1/72 Mk IV armament set for Hasegawa kits
CMK #7227 1/72 FB Mk VI - Bomb bay for Tamiya kits
CMK #7228 1/72 Exterior set for Tamiya kits
CMK #7229 1/72 Control surfaces set for Tamiya kits
CMK #48114 1/48 Tail wheel for Tamiya kits
CMK #72024 1/72 Mk IV/Mk VI oil coolers
Eduard #48617 1/48 Mk IV exterior for Revell kits
Eduard #49239 1/48 Mk VI/NF.II details for Tamiya kits
Eduard #49242 1/48 Mk IV/PR Mk IV details for Tamiya kits
Eduard #49438 1/48 Mk IV interior for Revell kits
Eduard #72314 1/72 Mk IV details for Hasegawa kits
Eduard #CX119 1/72 fighter masks for Tamiya kits
Eduard #CX121 1/72 bomber masks for Tamiya kits
Eduard #EX028 1/48 Mk IV masks for Tamiya kits
Eduard #EX029 1/48 Mk VI/NF.II masks for Tamiya kits
Eduard #EX268 1/48 Mk IV masks for Revell kits

Paragon Designs #24001 1/24 NF.II / FB.VI early style '5-Spoke' wheels
Paragon Designs #24003 1/24 NF.II / FB.VI 50 Gallon drop tanks
Paragon Designs #24004 1/24 NF.II / FB.VI 100 gallon drop tanks detail
Paragon Designs #48151 1/48 Extended Tropical intakes for single-stage Merlins
Paragon Designs #72072 1/72 ASH 'Thimble' Radome for Tamiya kits
Paragon Designs #72074 1/72 4-blade alternate props
Pavla Models #C72038 1/72 T.III cockpit, seats, solid nose for Tamiya kits
Pavla Models #C72046 1/72 B.Mk IV cockpit for Tamiya kits
Pavla Models #U72060 1/72 B.Mk IV bomb bay and bombs for Tamiya kits
Quickboost #32066 1/32 exhaust for Revell kits
Quickboost #48030 1/48 de Havilland Sea Mosquito conversion for Tamiya kits
Quickboost #48140 1/48 undercarriage doors for Tamiya kits
Quickboost #48252 1/48 Mk VI Nose for Tamiya kits
Quickboost #48306 1/48 exhaust for Tamiya kits
Quickboost #48325 1/48 wheel fenders for Tamiya kits
Quickboost #72121 1/72 undercarriage doors for Tamiya kits
Quickboost #72204 1/72 Mk VI Nose for Tamiya kits
Quickboost #72301 1/72 exhaust for Tamiya kits
Rob Taurus #72071 1/72 Mk II/VI vacform canopy for Tamiya kits
Rob Taurus #72072 1/72 B/PR Mk IV vacform canopy for Tamiya kits
Scale Aircraft Conversions #24002 1/24 NF.II / FB.VI Landing Gear for Airfix kits
Scale Aircraft Conversions #48038 1/48 Landing Gear for Tamiya kits
Squadron #9156 1/72 Mk VI canopies for Airfix kits
Squadron #9532 1/48 Mk VI canopy for Airfix and Tamiya kits
Squadron #9600 1/48 Mk VI canopy for Tamiya kits
Valom #DSV02 1/48 Mk IX/Mk XVI and PR.34 conversion
Verlinden Productions #1460 1/48 cockpit for Tamiya kits
Verlinden Productions #1465 1/48 Sea Mosquito conversion for Tamiya kits
Verlinden Productions #1474 1/48 Gun Bay and moving surfaces for Tamiya kits

DECALS:

AeroMaster #48303 1/48 Post War Mosquito B 35s
Aviaeology #24005M 1/24 RCAF Mosquitoes
Aviaeology #24011 1/24 RCAF Mosquitoes - Canadians in Coastal Command
Aviaeology #32005M 1/32 RCAF Mosquitoes
Aviaeology #48011 1/48 RCAF Mosquitoes - Canadians in Coastal Command
Aviaeology #72005M 1/72 RCAF Mosquitoes
Aviaeology #72011 RCAF Mosquitoes - Canadians in Coastal Command
Airscale #S24MOSA 1/24 Mosquito NF.II / FB.VI Mk.VI Full Instrument Panel
Barracuda Studios #48010 1/48 Mosquito stencil data for all marks
Barracuda Studios #72008 1/72 Mosquito Stencil data for all marks
Colorado #48022 1/48 Mosquitoes Part 1 Armee de L'Air/USAAF
Colorado #48096 1/48 Mosquito Mk.VI Part 2 RAAF/Czech/Israeli /Armee de L'air;
Colorado #48097 1/48 Mosquito NF.30 Part 3 Belgian/RAF/Fleet Air Arm
Colorado #72030 1/72 Mosquito NF II/ NF 30/Mk.VI/ PR Mk.XVI
Colorado #72031 1/72 Mosquito RAAF/Norway/SAAF/RAF
Colorado #72053 1/72 Mosquito Mk.VI Normandie-Niemen
Freightdog #48005 1/48 Post War Mosquitoes
Freightdog #72007 1/72 Post War Mosquitoes
Iliad Design #48023 1/48 Canadian-built Mosquitoes (
IsraDecal #72 1/48 Israeli Air Force Mosquitoes T3; NF.30; FB 6; TR 33, PR 16
LF Models #4838 1/48 Mosquito over Switzerland - Part I
LF Models #4839 1/48 Mosquito over Switzerland - Part II
LF Models #4840 1/48 Mosquito over Dominican Republic
LF Models #7281 1/72 Mosquito over Switzerland Part I
LF Models #7282 1/72 Mosquito over Switzerland Part II
LF Models #7283 1/72 Mosquito over Switzerland Part III
LF Models #7293 1/72 Mosquito over Dominican Republic
MPD/Mini Print MPD72505 1/72 Mosquito NF.XIX
Ventura #3265 1/32 Israeli Mosquitoes
Vingtor #48106 1/48 Mosquito Mk.IV British Overseas Airways Corporation
Vingtor #48107 1/48 Mosquito Mk.VI British Overseas Airways Corporation
Vingtor #72106 1/72 Mosquito Mk.IV British Overseas Airways Corporation
Vingtor #72107 1/72 Mosquito Mk.VI, British Overseas Airways Corporation
Xtradecal #24001 1/24 Mosquito FB.VI

Understanding the Subject

Modelling the Mosquito

Chapter 10

In this chapter I hope that we can clear up most of your questions about each mark of the Mosquito, as well as those which were operated, and manufactured, in other nations. The following review of all of the Mosquitoes has been based on a detailed study of over 5,000 photographs and close reference to the official publications for each type. This has been backed up with the information carried in a great number of the titles listed in Appendix X of this title, along with both myself and Steve Benstead spending many a pleasant hour inside preserved examples here in the UK (its research honest!). We appreciate that there are many areas of the Mosquito which we will highlight in a different manner to that which has been accepted so far, and we also know that we will still miss things, so if anyone reading this has points they would like to raise and has evidence to back them up, we would love to hear from you as reprinted examples of this title in the future can incorporate any new information that may be brought to light.

Note:
All accessories listed are 1/72nd scale, 1/48th scale in brackets (), and 1/32nd in square brackets [ ].

Prototype (W4050)
Kit: M or A* (A) [R]
Use Paragon Designs conversion sets No.72028 (No.48068) to achieve this type.

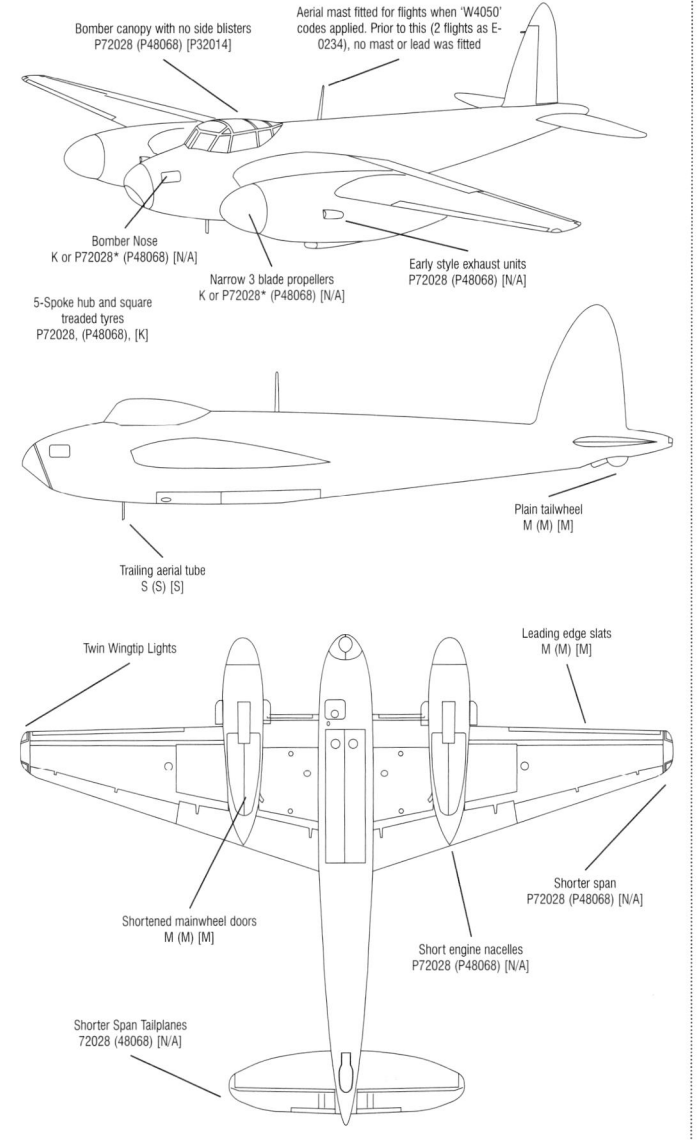

- Bomber canopy with no side blisters — P72028 (P48068) [P32014]
- Aerial mast fitted for flights when 'W4050' codes applied. Prior to this (2 flights as E-0234), no mast or lead was fitted
- Bomber Nose — K or P72028* (P48068) [N/A]
- Narrow 3 blade propellers — K or P72028* (P48068) [N/A]
- Early style exhaust units — P72028 (P48068) [N/A]
- 5-Spoke hub and square treaded tyres — P72028, (P48068), [K]
- Plain tailwheel — M (M) [M]
- Trailing aerial tube — S (S) [S]
- Twin Wingtip Lights
- Leading edge slats — M (M) [M]
- Shortened mainwheel doors — M (M) [M]
- Shorter span — P72028 (P48068) [N/A]
- Short engine nacelles — P72028 (P48068) [N/A]
- Shorter Span Tailplanes — 72028 (48068) [N/A]

Bomber • B Mk IV Series I
Kit: A (A) [R]

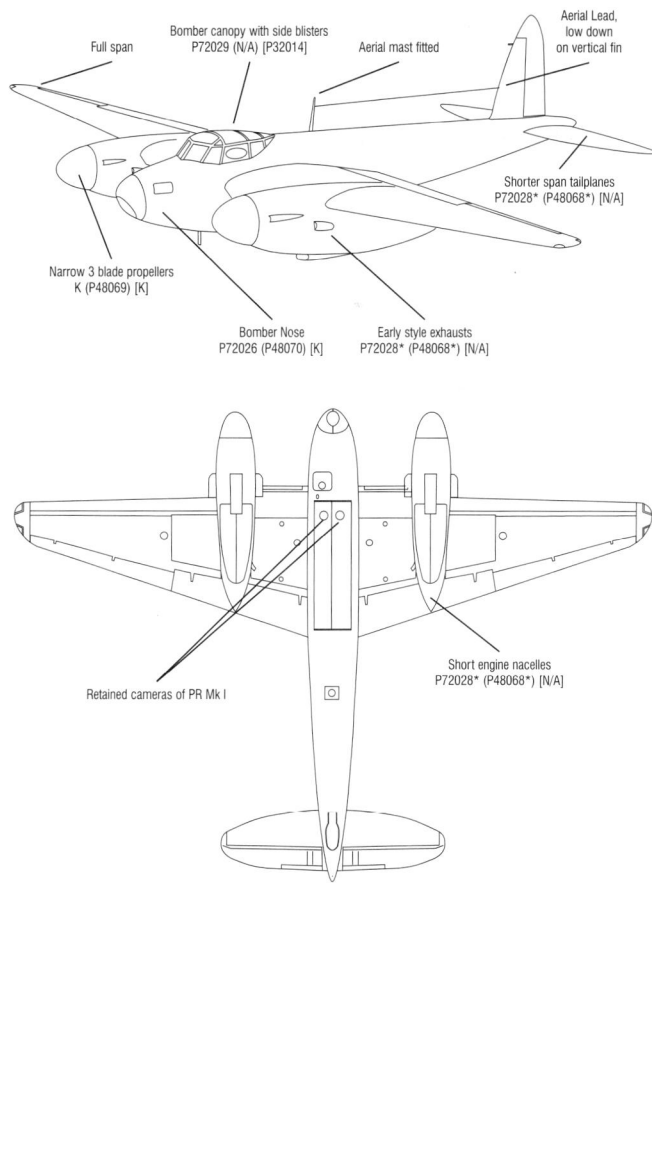

- Full span
- Bomber canopy with side blisters — P72029 (N/A) [P32014]
- Aerial mast fitted
- Aerial Lead, low down on vertical fin
- Shorter span tailplanes — P72028* (P48068*) [N/A]
- Narrow 3 blade propellers — K (P48069) [K]
- Bomber Nose — P72026 (P48070) [K]
- Early style exhausts — P72028* (P48068*) [N/A]
- Retained cameras of PR Mk I
- Short engine nacelles — P72028* (P48068*) [N/A]

Bomber • B Mk IV Series II
Kit: A (A) [R]

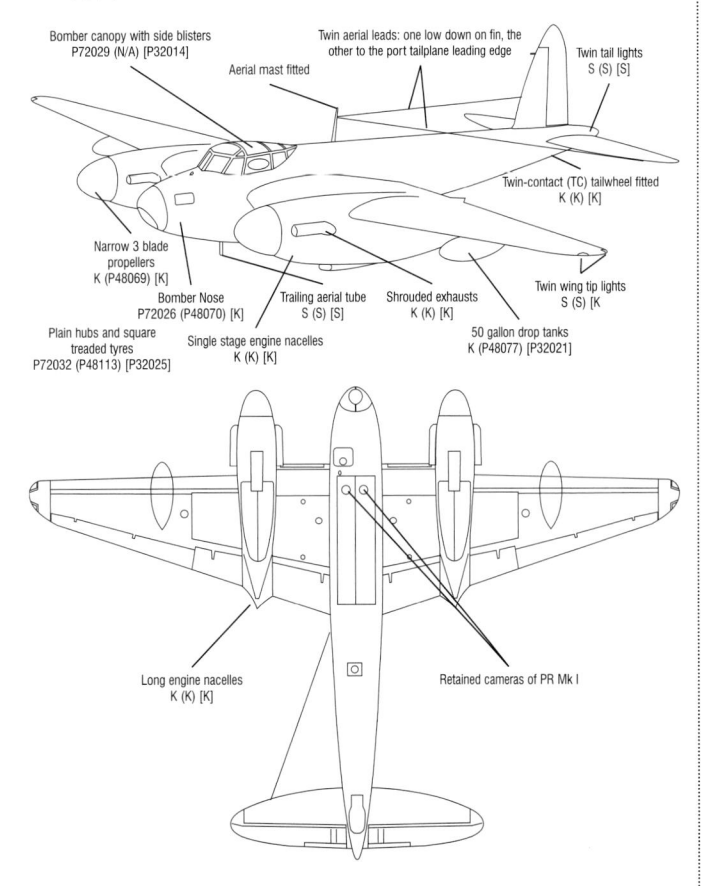

- Bomber canopy with side blisters P72029 (N/A) [P32014]
- Aerial mast fitted
- Twin aerial leads: one low down on fin, the other to the port tailplane leading edge
- Twin tail lights S (S) [S]
- Twin-contact (TC) tailwheel fitted K (K) [K]
- Narrow 3 blade propellers K (P48069) [K]
- Bomber Nose P72026 (P48070) [K]
- Trailing aerial tube S (S) [S]
- Shrouded exhausts K (K) [K]
- Twin wing tip lights S (S) [K
- Plain hubs and square treaded tyres P72032 (P48113) [P32025]
- Single stage engine nacelles K (K) [K]
- 50 gallon drop tanks K (P48077) [P32021]
- Long engine nacelles K (K) [K]
- Retained cameras of PR Mk I

Bomber • B Mk IV Series II 'Bulged Bomb Bay'
Kit: A (A) [R]

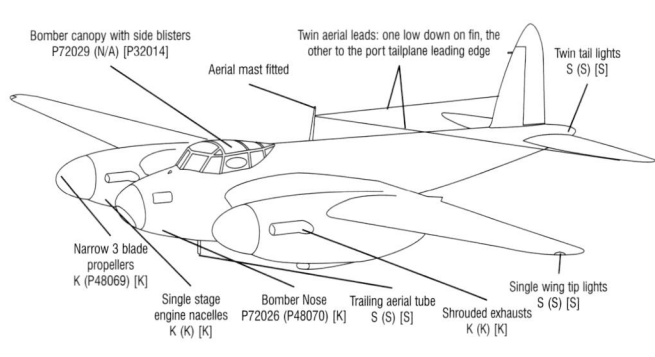

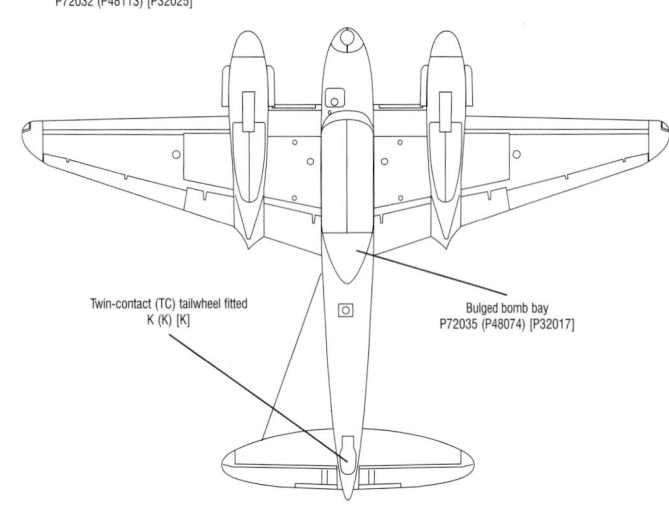

- Bomber canopy with side blisters P72029 (N/A) [P32014]
- Aerial mast fitted
- Twin aerial leads: one low down on fin, the other to the port tailplane leading edge
- Twin tail lights S (S) [S]
- Narrow 3 blade propellers K (P48069) [K]
- Single stage engine nacelles K (K) [K]
- Bomber Nose P72026 (P48070) [K]
- Trailing aerial tube S (S) [S]
- Shrouded exhausts K (K) [K]
- Single wing tip lights S (S) [S]
- Plain hubs and square treaded tyres. P72032 (P48113) [P32025]
- Twin-contact (TC) tailwheel fitted K (K) [K]
- Bulged bomb bay P72035 (P48074) [P32017]

Bomber • B Mk IV Series II 'Highball'
Kit: A (A) [R]

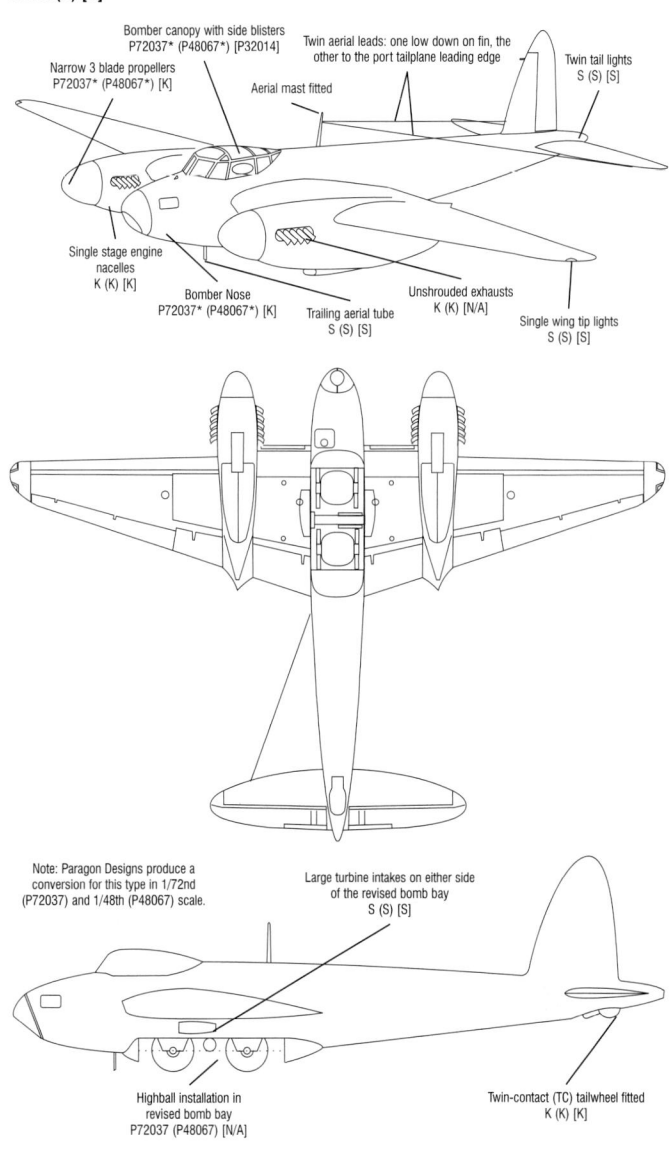

- Bomber canopy with side blisters P72037* (P48067*) [P32014]
- Aerial mast fitted
- Twin aerial leads: one low down on fin, the other to the port tailplane leading edge
- Twin tail lights S (S) [S]
- Narrow 3 blade propellers P72037* (P48067*) [K]
- Single stage engine nacelles K (K) [K]
- Bomber Nose P72037* (P48067*) [K]
- Trailing aerial tube S (S) [S]
- Unshrouded exhausts K (K) [N/A]
- Single wing tip lights S (S) [S]

Note: Paragon Designs produce a conversion for this type in 1/72nd (P72037) and 1/48th (P48067) scale.

- Large turbine intakes on either side of the revised bomb bay S (S) [S]
- Highball installation in revised bomb bay P72037 (P48067) [N/A]
- Twin-contact (TC) tailwheel fitted K (K) [K]

Bomber • B Mk V
The B Mk V is the same as the B Mk IV Series II but only one was built.

Bomber • B Mk VII (Canadian)
Kit: A (A) [R]

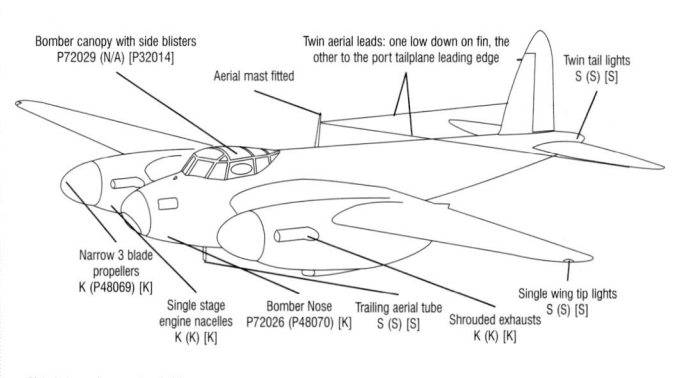

- Bomber canopy with side blisters P72029 (N/A) [P32014]
- Aerial mast fitted
- Twin aerial leads: one low down on fin, the other to the port tailplane leading edge
- Twin tail lights S (S) [S]
- Narrow 3 blade propellers K (P48069) [K]
- Single stage engine nacelles K (K) [K]
- Bomber Nose P72026 (P48070) [K]
- Trailing aerial tube S (S) [S]
- Shrouded exhausts K (K) [K]
- Single wing tip lights S (S) [S]
- Plain hubs and square treaded tyres. P72032 (P48113) [P32025]

Bomber • B Mk IX
Kit: M or A*(A) [R]

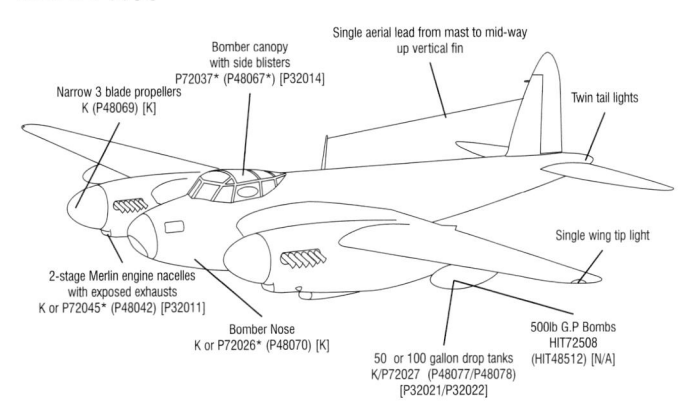

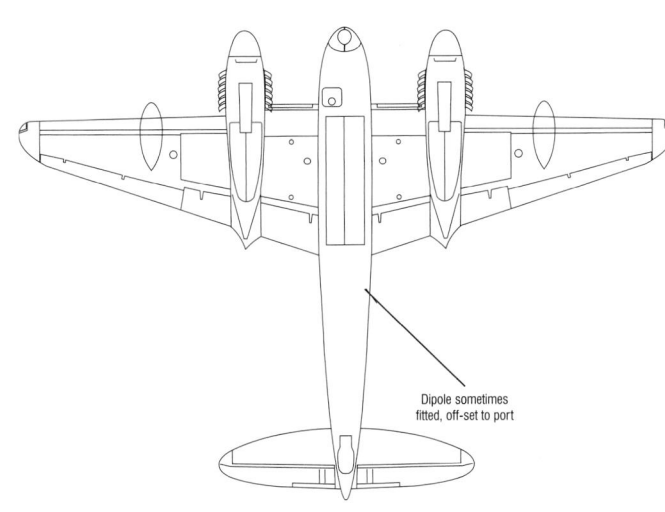

- Bomber canopy with side blisters P72037* (P48067*) [P32014]
- Narrow 3 blade propellers K (P48069) [K]
- Single aerial lead from mast to mid-way up vertical fin
- Twin tail lights
- 2-stage Merlin engine nacelles with exposed exhausts K or P72045* (P48042) [P32011]
- Bomber Nose K or P72026* (P48070) [K]
- 50 or 100 gallon drop tanks K/P72027 (P48077/P48078) [P32021/P32022]
- 500lb G.P Bombs HIT72508 (HIT48512) [N/A]
- Single wing tip light

Dipole sometimes fitted, off-set to port

Bomber • B Mk IX 'Special Operations'
Kit: M or A*(A) [R]

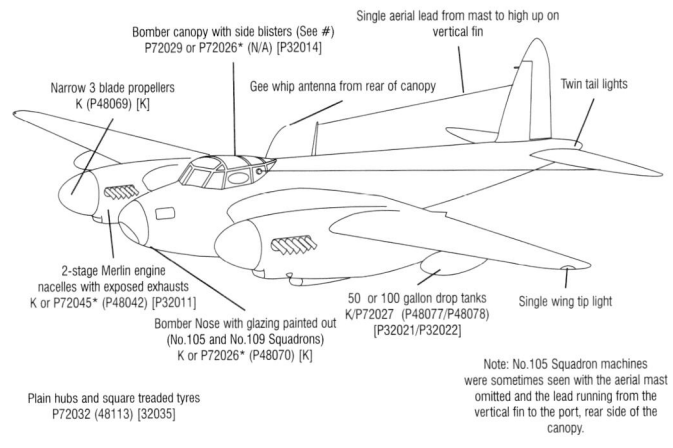

- Bomber canopy with side blisters (See #) P72029 or P72026* (N/A) [P32014]
- Narrow 3 blade propellers K (P48069) [K]
- Single aerial lead from mast to high up on vertical fin
- Gee whip antenna from rear of canopy
- Twin tail lights
- 2-stage Merlin engine nacelles with exposed exhausts K or P72045* (P48042) [P32011]
- Bomber Nose with glazing painted out (No.105 and No.109 Squadrons) K or P72026* (P48070) [K]
- 50 or 100 gallon drop tanks K/P72027 (P48077/P48078) [P32021/P32022]
- Single wing tip light
- Plain hubs and square treaded tyres P72032 (48113) [32035]

Note: No.105 Squadron machines were sometimes seen with the aerial mast omitted and the lead running from the vertical fin to the port, rear side of the canopy.

Bomber • B Mk IX Bulged Bomb Bay conversion
Kit: M or A*(A) [R]

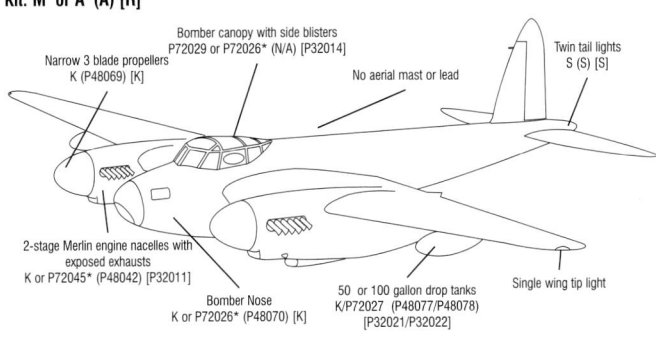

- Bomber canopy with side blisters P72029 or P72026* (N/A) [P32014]
- Narrow 3 blade propellers K (P48069) [K]
- No aerial mast or lead
- Twin tail lights S (S) [S]
- 2-stage Merlin engine nacelles with exposed exhausts K or P72045* (P48042) [P32011]
- Bomber Nose K or P72026* (P48070) [K]
- 50 or 100 gallon drop tanks K/P72027 (P48077/P48078) [P32021/P32022]
- Single wing tip light
- Plain hubs and square treaded tyres P72032 (P48113) [32035]

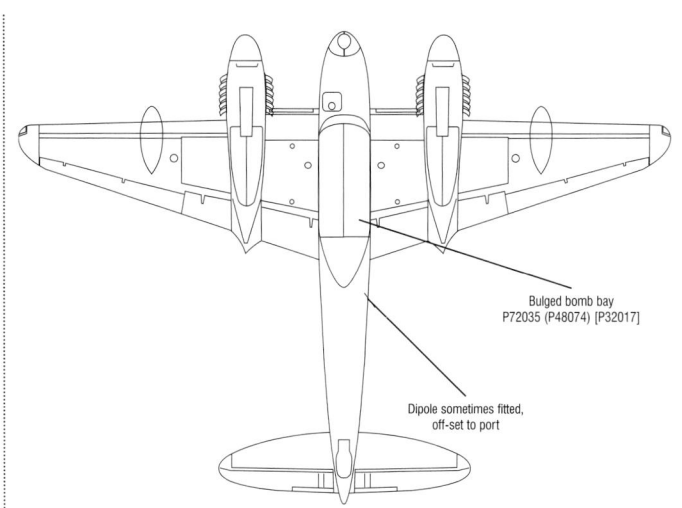

- Bulged bomb bay P72035 (P48074) [P32017]
- Dipole sometimes fitted, off-set to port

Bomber • B Mk XVI
Kit: M or A* (A) [R]

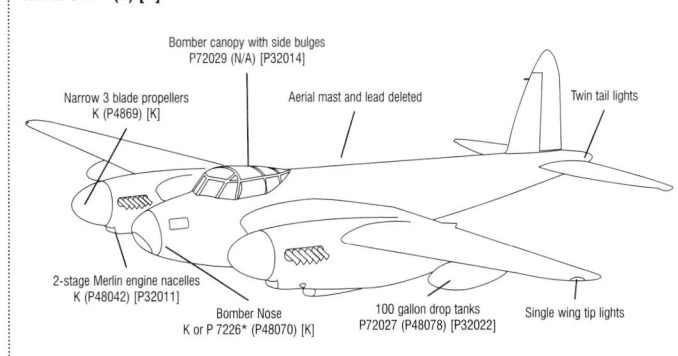

- Bomber canopy with side bulges P72029 (N/A) [P32014]
- Narrow 3 blade propellers K (P4869) [K]
- Aerial mast and lead deleted
- Twin tail lights
- 2-stage Merlin engine nacelles K (P48042) [P32011]
- Bomber Nose K or P 7226* (P48070) [K]
- 100 gallon drop tanks P72027 (P48078) [P32022]
- Single wing tip lights
- Plain hubs and square treaded tyres P72032 (P48113) [P32035]

- Bulged bomb bay P72035 (P48074) [32017]
- Enlarged elevator balance weights to compensate for enlarged bomb bay S (S) [S]

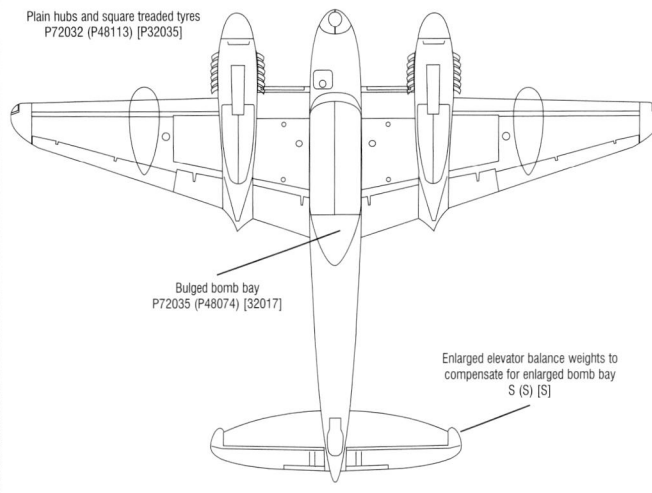

Bomber • B Mk XVI with H2S (Ventral)
Kit: M or A* (A) [R]

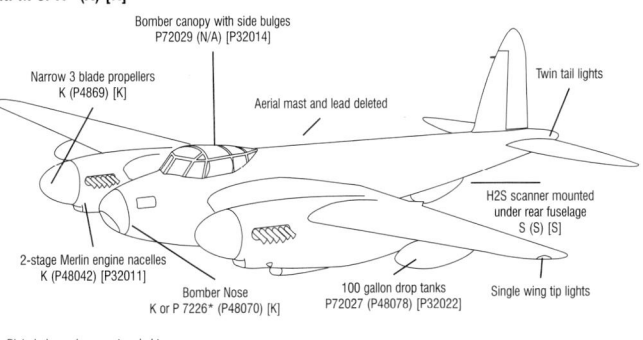

- Bomber canopy with side bulges P72029 (N/A) [P32014]
- Narrow 3 blade propellers K (P4869) [K]
- Aerial mast and lead deleted
- Twin tail lights
- 2-stage Merlin engine nacelles K (P48042) [P32011]
- Bomber Nose K or P 7226* (P48070) [K]
- 100 gallon drop tanks P72027 (P48078) [P32022]
- H2S scanner mounted under rear fuselage S (S) [S]
- Single wing tip lights
- Plain hubs and square treaded tyres P72032 (P48113) [P32035]

Modelling the Mosquito • Understanding the Subject

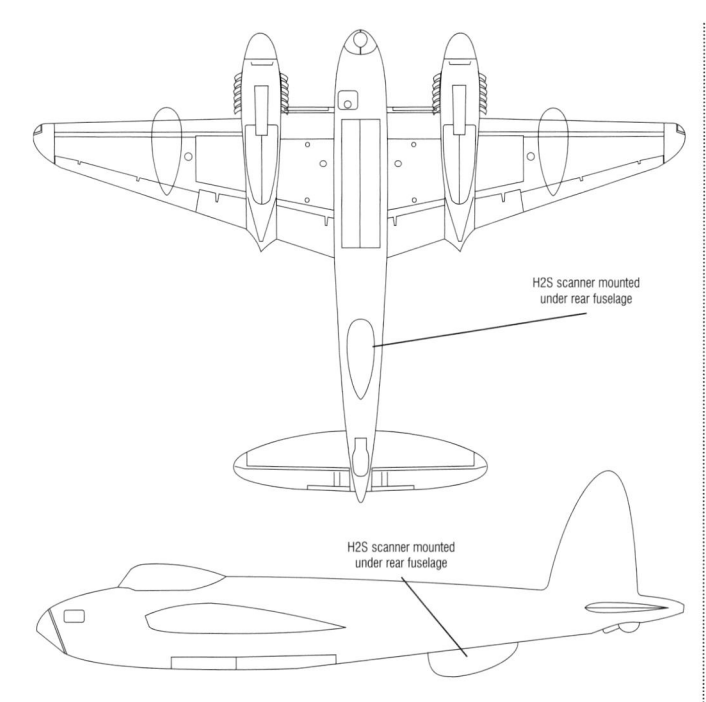

H2S scanner mounted under rear fuselage

H2S scanner mounted under rear fuselage

Bomber • B Mk XX (Canadian) #1
Kit: A (A) [R]

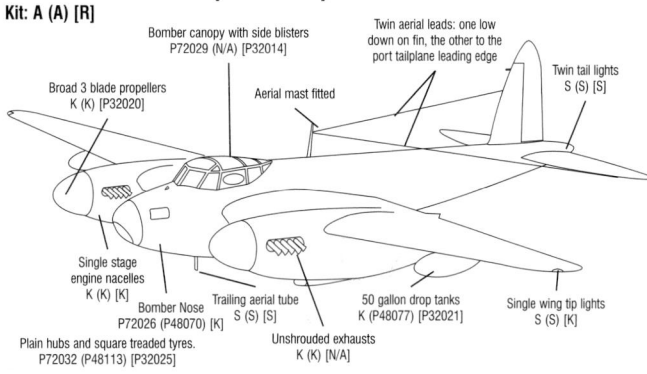

- Broad 3 blade propellers K (K) [P32020]
- Bomber canopy with side blisters P72029 (N/A) [P32014]
- Aerial mast fitted
- Twin aerial leads: one low down on fin, the other to the port tailplane leading edge
- Twin tail lights S (S) [S]
- Single stage engine nacelles K (K) [K]
- Bomber Nose P72026 (P48070) [K]
- Trailing aerial tube S (S) [S]
- 50 gallon drop tanks K (P48077) [P32021]
- Single wing tip lights S (S) [K]
- Unshrouded exhausts K (K) [N/A]
- Plain hubs and square treaded tyres. P72032 (P48113) [P32025]

Bomber • B Mk XX (Canadian) #2
Kit: A (A) [R]

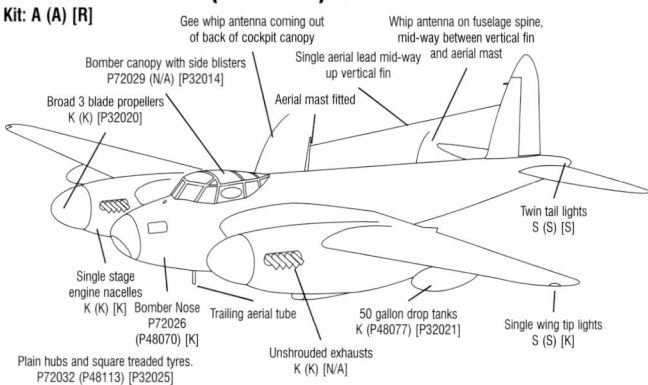

- Bomber canopy with side blisters P72029 (N/A) [P32014]
- Broad 3 blade propellers K (K) [P32020]
- Gee whip antenna coming out of back of cockpit canopy
- Single aerial lead mid-way up vertical fin
- Aerial mast fitted
- Whip antenna on fuselage spine, mid-way between vertical fin and aerial mast
- Twin tail lights S (S) [S]
- Single stage engine nacelles K (K) [K]
- Bomber Nose P72026 (P48070) [K]
- Trailing aerial tube
- 50 gallon drop tanks K (P48077) [P32021]
- Single wing tip lights S (S) [K]
- Unshrouded exhausts K (K) [N/A]
- Plain hubs and square treaded tyres. P72032 (P48113) [P32025]

Bomber • B Mk 25 (Canadian) #1
Kit: M (A) [R] Standard kit except;

- Bomber canopy with side blisters P72029 (N/A) [32014]
- 3 blade 'paddle' propellers... K (K) [P32020]
- ... or 3 blade narrow propellers K (P48069) [K]
- De-icer jet
- Aerial lead fitted from mid-way down fin to just in front of the whip antenna on the fuselage spine.
- Gee antenna coming out of rear of cockpit canopy
- Aerial mast deleted
- Tail mounted Monica radar antenna S (S) [S]
- 2-stage Merlin engine nacelles K (P48042) [P32011]
- Bomber Nose K (P48070) [K]
- 100 gallon drop tanks P72027 (P48078) [P32022]
- Plain hubs and square treaded tyres P72032 (P48113) [P32035]

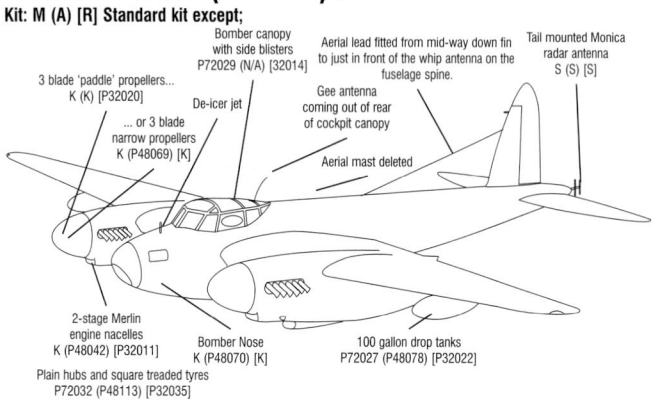

Bomber • B Mk 25 (Canadian) #2
Kit: M (A) [R] Standard kit except;

- Bomber canopy with side blisters P72029 (N/A) [32014]
- 3 blade 'paddle' propellers... K (K) [P32020]
- ... or 3 blade narrow propellers K (P48069) [K]
- De-icer jet
- Gee antenna coming out of rear of cockpit canopy
- Aerial mast
- Lead running from mast to mid-way up vertical fin
- Whip antenna mid-way along fuselage spine
- 2-stage Merlin engine nacelles K (P48042) [P32011]
- Bomber Nose K (P48070) [K]
- Trailing aerial tube
- 100 gallon drop tanks P72027 (P48078) [P32022]
- Plain hubs and square treaded tyres P72032 (P48113) [P32035]

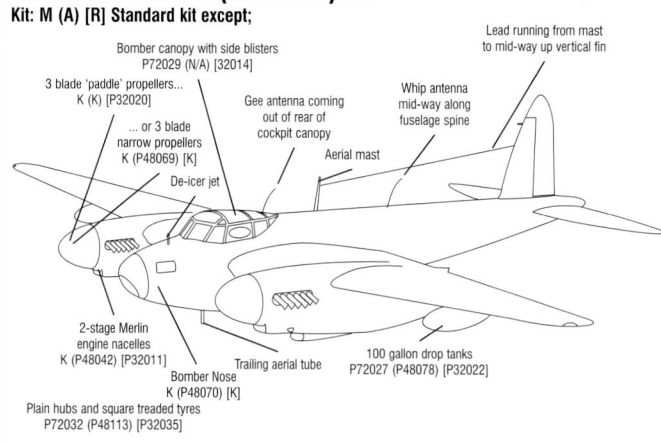

Bomber • B Mk 25 Bulged bomb bay version

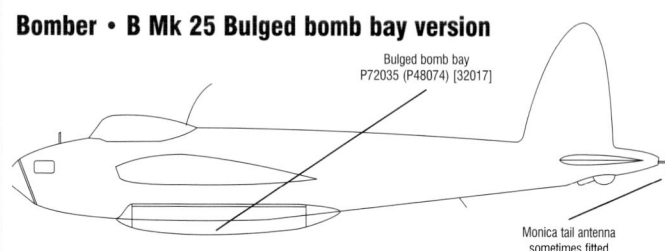

- Bulged bomb bay P72035 (P48074) [32017]
- Monica tail antenna sometimes fitted

Bomber • B Mk 35 #1
Kit: M (A) [R] Standard kit except;

- Three or four dipoles above and below each wing tip.
- Landing light (twin) in starboard wing leading edge
- PR canopy with side bulges P72029 (P48073) [P32016]
- Air intake below canopy on port side
- Aerial mast deleted
- Two whip antenna on top of rear fuselage
- Twin tail lights
- Boozer III dipole on lower port fuselage side
- 3 blade 'paddle' propellers K (K) [P32020]
- 2-stage Merlin engine nacelles K (P48042) [P32011]
- Bomber Nose K (P48070) [K]
- Single wing tip lights
- Plain hubs and square treaded tyres P72032 (P48113) [P32035]

- Landing light
- Boozer III dipole off-set to port
- Twin whip antenna on fuselage spine
- Bulged bomb bay
- Boozer III dipole

68 Chapter 10

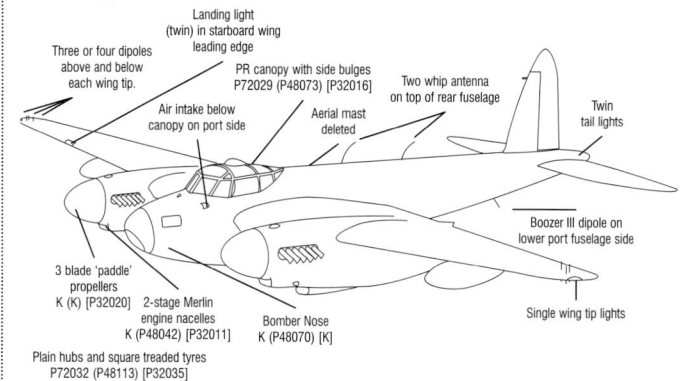

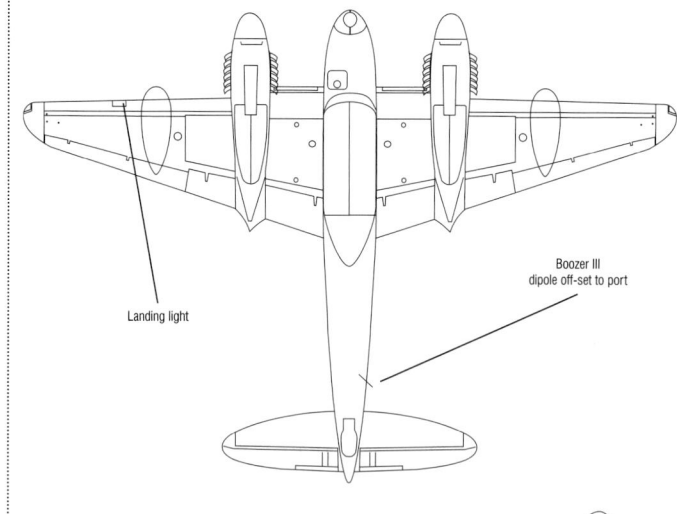

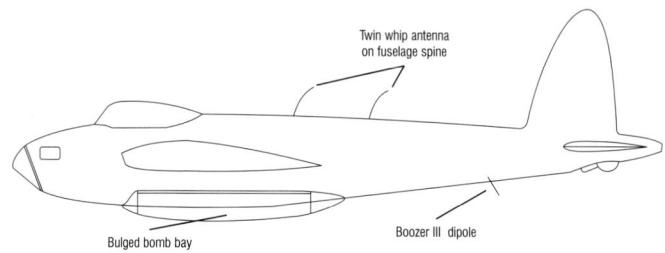

Bomber • B Mk 35 #2
Kit: M (A) [R] Same as version #1 except;

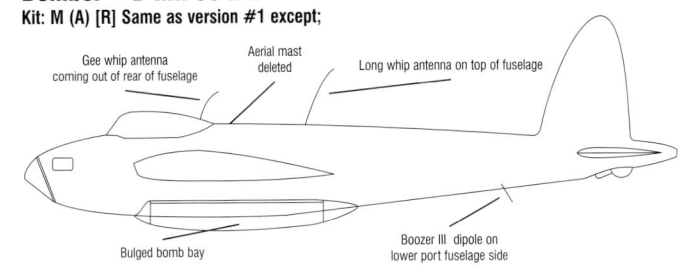

- Gee whip antenna coming out of rear of fuselage
- Aerial mast deleted
- Long whip antenna on top of fuselage
- Bulged bomb bay
- Boozer III dipole on lower port fuselage side

Bomber • B Mk 35 #3

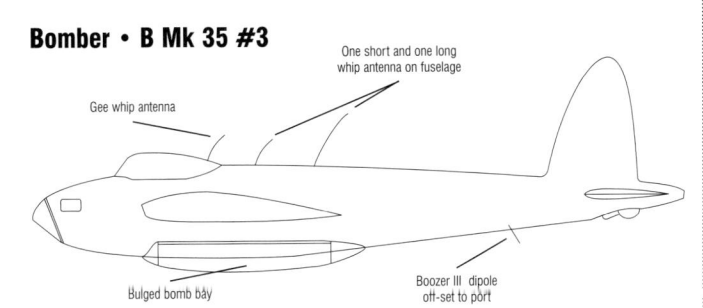

- Gee whip antenna
- One short and one long whip antenna on fuselage
- Bulged bomb bay
- Boozer III dipole off-set to port

Bomber • B Mk 35 #4

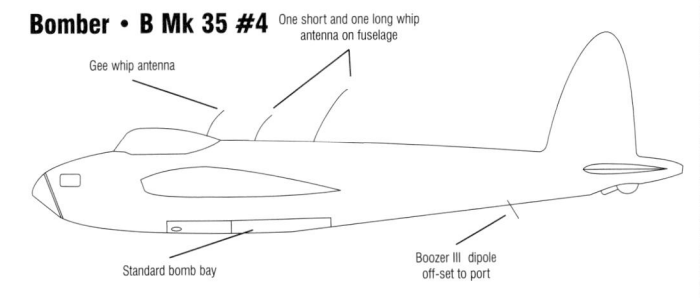

- Gee whip antenna
- One short and one long whip antenna on fuselage
- Standard bomb bay
- Boozer III dipole off-set to port

Bomber • B Mk 35 #5

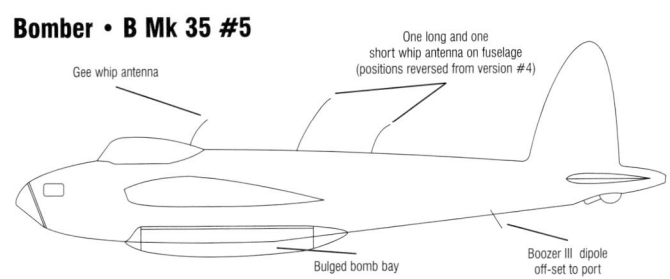

- Gee whip antenna
- One long and one short whip antenna on fuselage (positions reversed from version #4)
- Bulged bomb bay
- Boozer III dipole off-set to port

Bomber • B Mk 35 #6 (Central Bomber Establishment)

- Gee whip antenna
- One long and one short whip antenna on fuselage (same as version #5)
- Trailing aerial tube
- Bulged bomb bay
- Two dipoles off-set to starboard on lower fuselage
- Boozer III dipole off-set to port

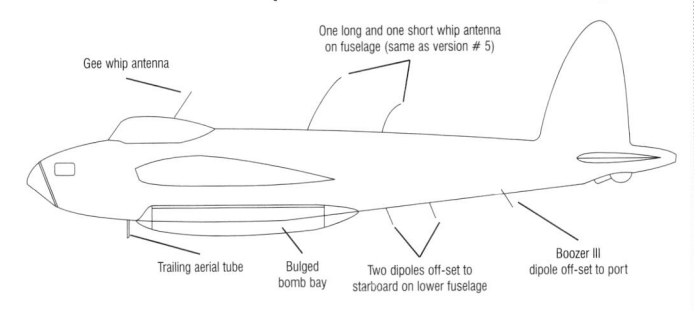

Bomber • B Mk 35 #7 (Central Bomber Establishment)

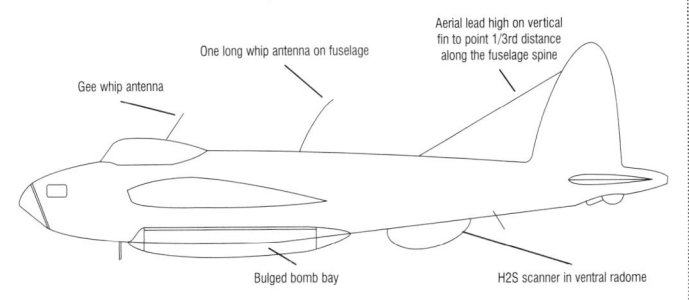

- Gee whip antenna
- One long whip antenna on fuselage
- Aerial lead high on vertical fin to point 1/3rd distance along the fuselage spine
- Bulged bomb bay
- H2S scanner in ventral radome

Bomber • B Mk 35 #8

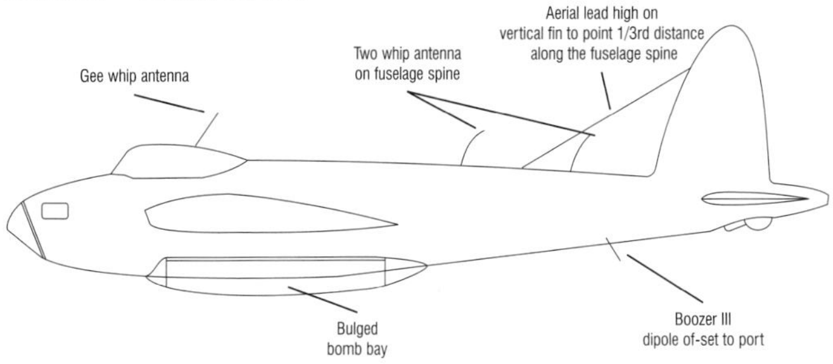

- Gee whip antenna
- Two whip antenna on fuselage spine
- Aerial lead high on vertical fin to point 1/3rd distance along the fuselage spine
- Bulged bomb bay
- Boozer III dipole of-set to port

Bomber • B Mk 35 'Spartan Air Services'
Kit: M (A) [R] Standard kit except;

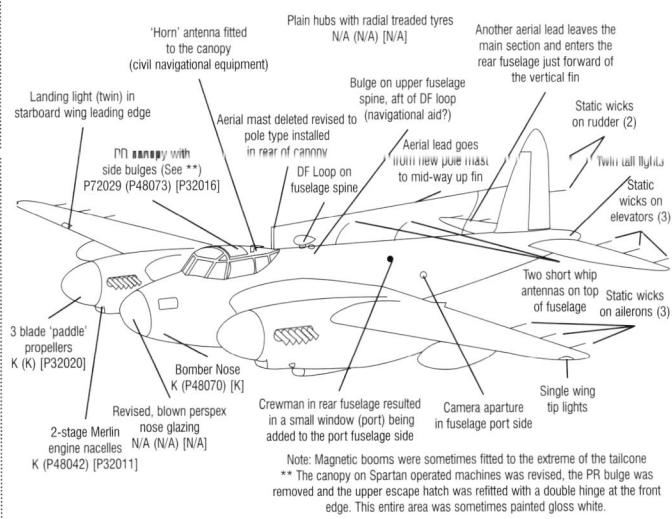

- 'Horn' antenna fitted to the canopy (civil navigational equipment)
- Plain hubs with radial treaded tyres N/A (N/A) [N/A]
- Another aerial lead leaves the main section and enters the rear fuselage just forward of the vertical fin
- Landing light (twin) in starboard wing leading edge
- Aerial mast deleted revised to pole type installed in rear of canopy
- Bulge on upper fuselage spine, aft of DF loop (navigational aid?)
- Static wicks on rudder (2)
- PR canopy with side bulges (See **) P72029 (P48073) [P32016]
- DF Loop on fuselage spine
- Aerial lead goes from new pole mast to mid-way up fin
- Twin tail lights
- Static wicks on elevators (3)
- 3 blade 'paddle' propellers K (K) [P32020]
- Bomber Nose K (P48070) [K]
- Two short whip antennas on top of fuselage
- Static wicks on ailerons (3)
- 2-stage Merlin engine nacelles K (P48042) [P32011]
- Revised, blown perspex nose glazing N/A (N/A) [N/A]
- Crewman in rear fuselage resulted in a small window (port) being added to the port fuselage side
- Camera aperture in fuselage port side
- Single wing tip lights

Note: Magnetic booms were sometimes fitted to the extreme of the tailcone
** The canopy on Spartan operated machines was revised, the PR bulge was removed and the upper escape hatch was refitted with a double hinge at the front edge. This entire area was sometimes painted gloss white.

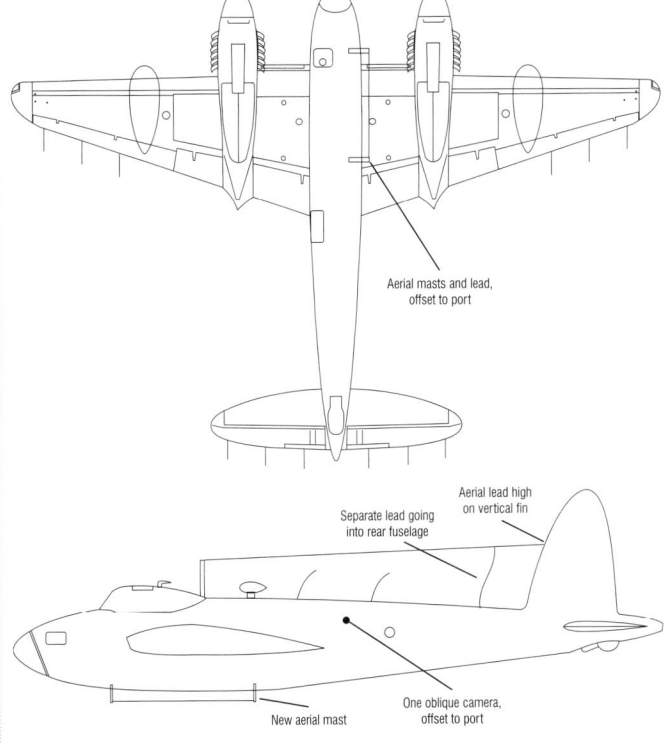

- Aerial masts and lead, offset to port
- Separate lead going into rear fuselage
- Aerial lead high on vertical fin
- New aerial mast
- One oblique camera, offset to port

Modelling the Mosquito • Understanding the Subject

Photo Reconnaissnce (PR) • PR Mk I
Kit: M (A) [R] Standard kit except;

- Short span
- Bomber canopy with side blisters P72029 (M) [P32014]
- Aerial mast and lead low on vertical fin
- Twin tail lights
- Narrow 3 blade propellers K (P48069) [K]
- Bomber Nose K (P48070) [K]
- Trailing aerial
- Early style exhausts & short engine nacelles P72028* (P48068*) [N/A]
- Twin tip lights
- Plain hub and square treaded tyres P72032 (TD48017 or P48113) [P32035]

NOTE: Some components of the PR Mk I can be obtained from the prototype conversion available from Paragon Designs (72028 & 48068).

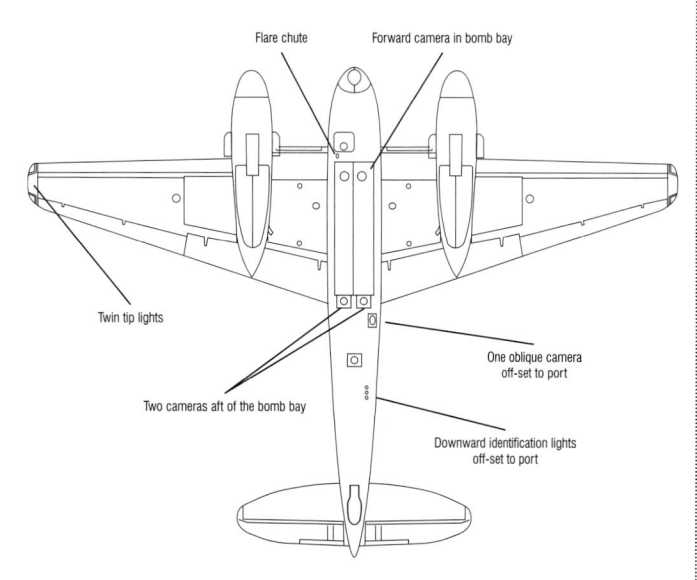

- Flare chute
- Forward camera in bomb bay
- Twin tip lights
- Two cameras aft of the bomb bay
- One oblique camera off-set to port
- Downward identification lights off-set to port

Photo Reconnaissnce (PR) • PR Mk II
This type was converted from F Mk IIs Kit: A (A) [R]

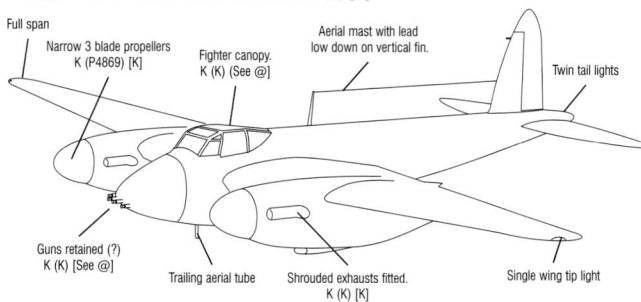

- Full span
- Narrow 3 blade propellers K (P4869) [K]
- Fighter canopy. K (K) (See @)
- Aerial mast with lead low down on vertical fin.
- Twin tail lights
- Guns retained (?) K (K) [See @]
- Trailing aerial tube
- Shrouded exhausts fitted. K (K) [K]
- Single wing tip light
- 5-Spoke hubs and square treaded tyres N/A (P48112) [P32034]

NOTE @ To obtain the fighter configuration on the Revell kit in 1/32nd scale the FB Mk VI conversion from Paragon Designs (32012) will be of use

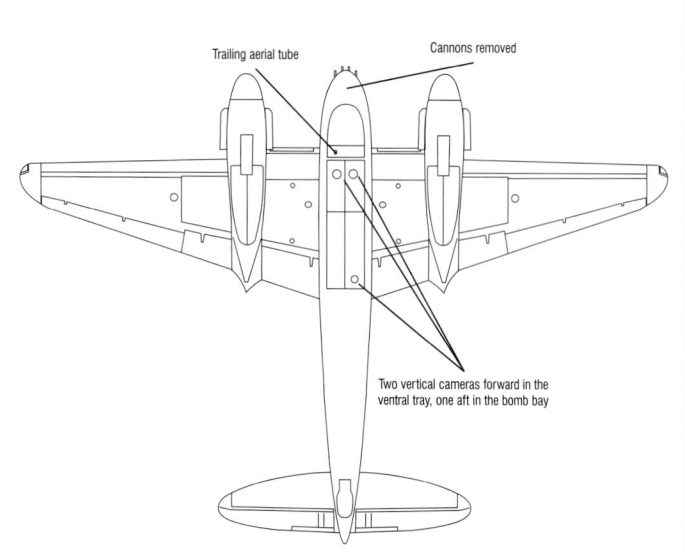

- Trailing aerial tube
- Cannons removed
- Two vertical cameras forward in the ventral tray, one aft in the bomb bay

Photo Reconnaissnce (PR) • PR Mk IV
This type was converted from the B Mk VI Series II Kit: A (A) [R]

- Narrow 3 blade propellers K (P48069) [K]
- Aerial mast fitted with aerial lead mid-way up vertical fin
- Bomber canopy with side blisters P72029 (N/A) [P32014]
- Twin tail lights S (S) [S]
- Bomber Nose P72026 (P48070) [K]
- Single stage engine nacelles K (K) [K]
- Trailing aerial tube S (S) [S]
- Shrouded exhausts fitted. K (K) [K]
- Twin-contact (TC) tailwheel fitted K (K) [K]
- Twin wing tip lights S (S) [K]
- 5-Spoke hubs and square treaded tyres N/A (P48112) [P32034]

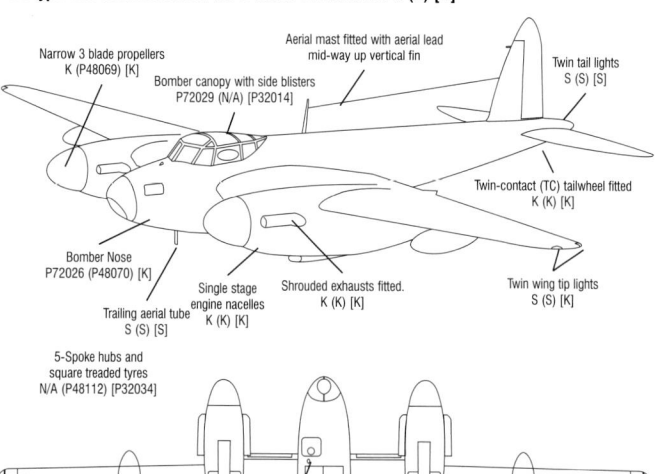

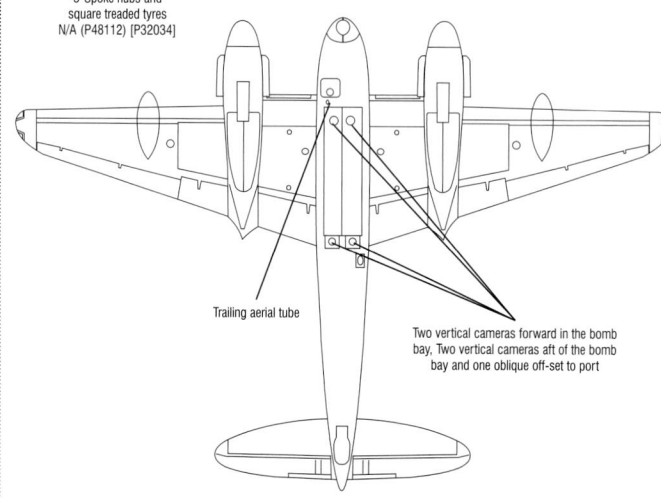

- Trailing aerial tube
- Two vertical cameras forward in the bomb bay, Two vertical cameras aft of the bomb bay and one oblique off-set to port

Photo Reconnaissnce (PR) • PR Mk VIII
This type was converted from the B Mk VI Series II Kit: M (A) [R]

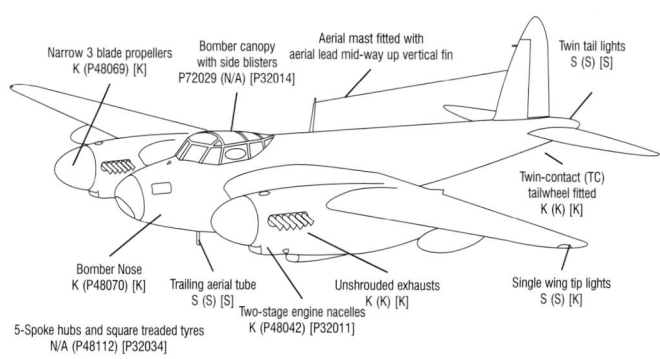

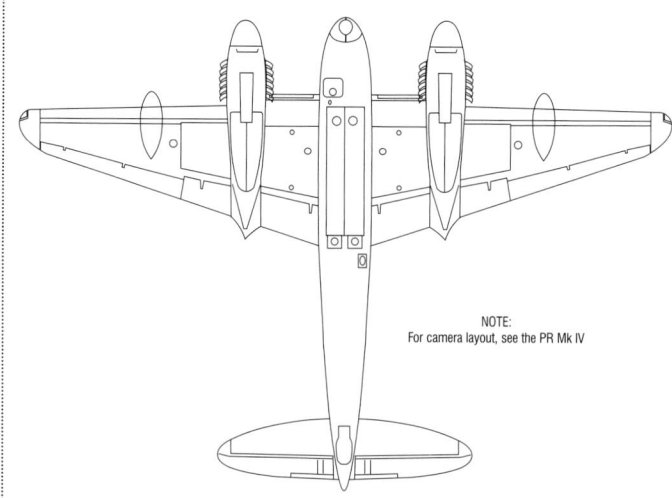

- Narrow 3 blade propellers K (P48069) [K]
- Bomber canopy with side blisters P72029 (N/A) [P32014]
- Aerial mast fitted with aerial lead mid-way up vertical fin
- Twin tail lights S (S) [S]
- Bomber Nose K (P48070) [K]
- Trailing aerial tube S (S) [S]
- Unshrouded exhausts K (K) [K]
- Two-stage engine nacelles K (P48042) [P32011]
- Twin-contact (TC) tailwheel fitted K (K) [K]
- Single wing tip lights S (S) [K]
- 5-Spoke hubs and square treaded tyres N/A (P48112) [P32034]

NOTE: For camera layout, see the PR Mk IV

70 Chapter 10

Photo Reconnaissnce (PR) • PR Mk IX
Kit: M or A* (A) [R]

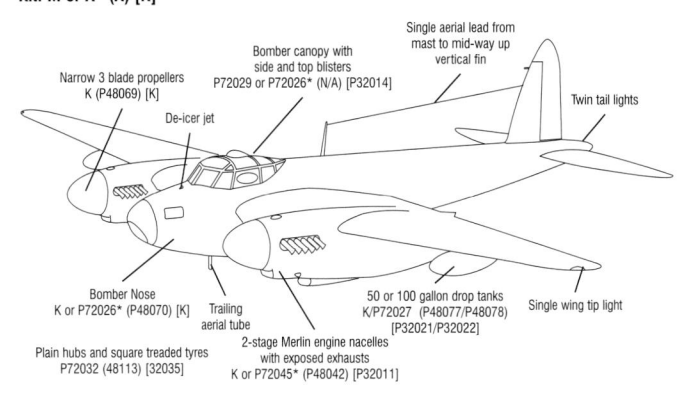

- Narrow 3 blade propellers
  K (P48069) [K]
- De-icer jet
- Bomber canopy with side and top blisters
  P72029 or P72026* (N/A) [P32014]
- Single aerial lead from mast to mid-way up vertical fin
- Twin tail lights
- Bomber Nose
  K or P72026* (P48070) [K]
- Trailing aerial tube
- 50 or 100 gallon drop tanks
  K/P72027 (P48077/P48078) [P32021/P32022]
- Single wing tip light
- Plain hubs and square treaded tyres
  P72032 (48113) [32035]
- 2-stage Merlin engine nacelles with exposed exhausts
  K or P72045* (P48042) [P32011]

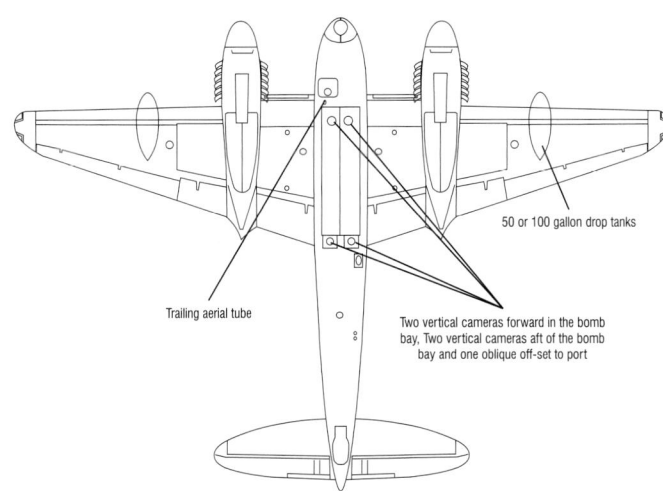

- 50 or 100 gallon drop tanks
- Trailing aerial tube
- Two vertical cameras forward in the bomb bay, Two vertical cameras aft of the bomb bay and one oblique off-set to port

Photo Reconnaissnce (PR) • PR Mk XVI
Kit: M or A* (A) [R]

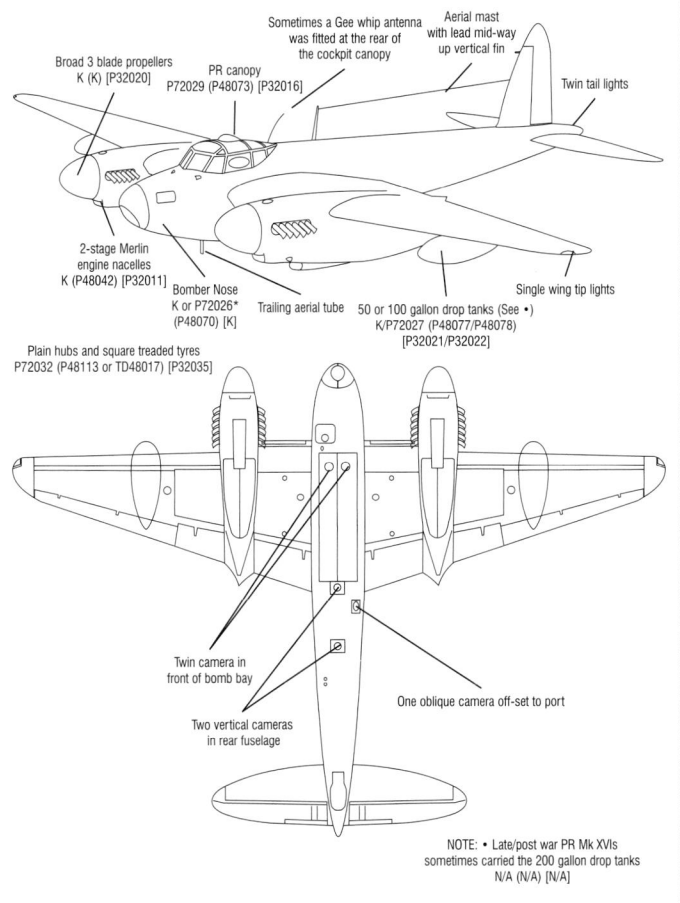

- Broad 3 blade propellers
  K (K) [P32020]
- Sometimes a Gee whip antenna was fitted at the rear of the cockpit canopy
- PR canopy
  P72029 (P48073) [P32016]
- Aerial mast with lead mid-way up vertical fin
- Twin tail lights
- 2-stage Merlin engine nacelles
  K (P48042) [P32011]
- Bomber Nose
  K or P72026* (P48070) [K]
- Trailing aerial tube
- 50 or 100 gallon drop tanks (See •)
  K/P72027 (P48077/P48078) [P32021/P32022]
- Single wing tip lights
- Plain hubs and square treaded tyres
  P72032 (P48113 or TD48017) [P32035]

- Twin camera in front of bomb bay
- Two vertical cameras in rear fuselage
- One oblique camera off-set to port

NOTE: • Late/post war PR Mk XVIs sometimes carried the 200 gallon drop tanks N/A (N/A) [N/A]

Photo Reconnaissnce (PR) • PR Mk XVI (Australian)
Same as PR Mk XVI except

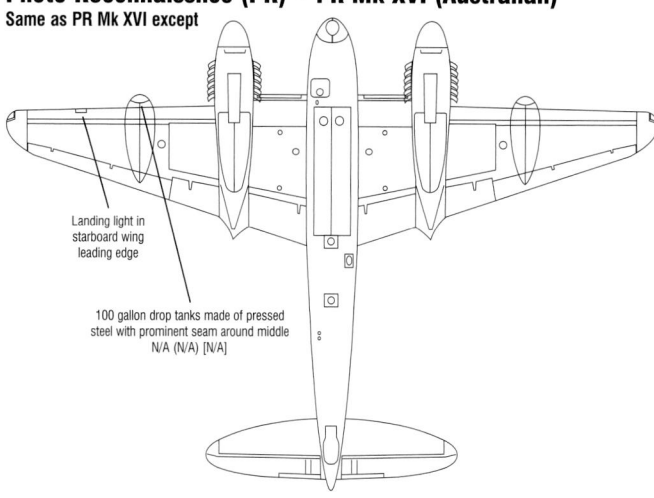

- Landing light in starboard wing leading edge
- 100 gallon drop tanks made of pressed steel with prominent seam around middle
  N/A (N/A) [N/A]

Photo Reconnaissnce (PR) • PR Mk XVI (Israel)
Same as PR Mk XVI except

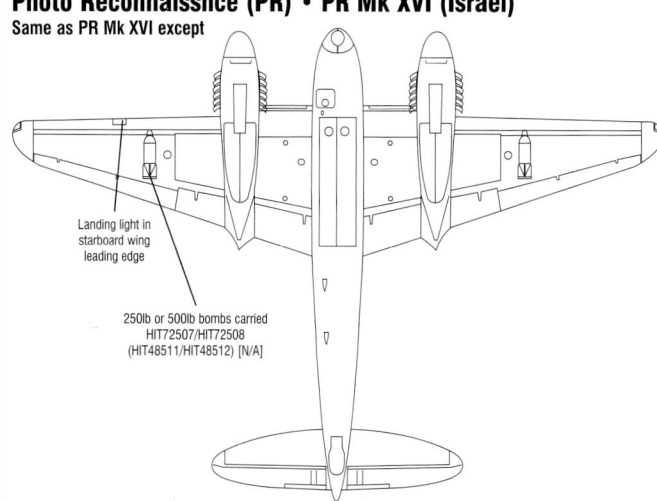

- Landing light in starboard wing leading edge
- 250lb or 500lb bombs carried
  HIT72507/HIT72508 (HIT48511/HIT48512) [N/A]

Photo Reconnaissnce (PR) • PR Mk XVI (H2X)
Kit: M or A* (A) [R]
NOTE: $ These machines had an H2X scanner fitted in a revised nose. The profile of this nose was unlike any other night fighter type radome

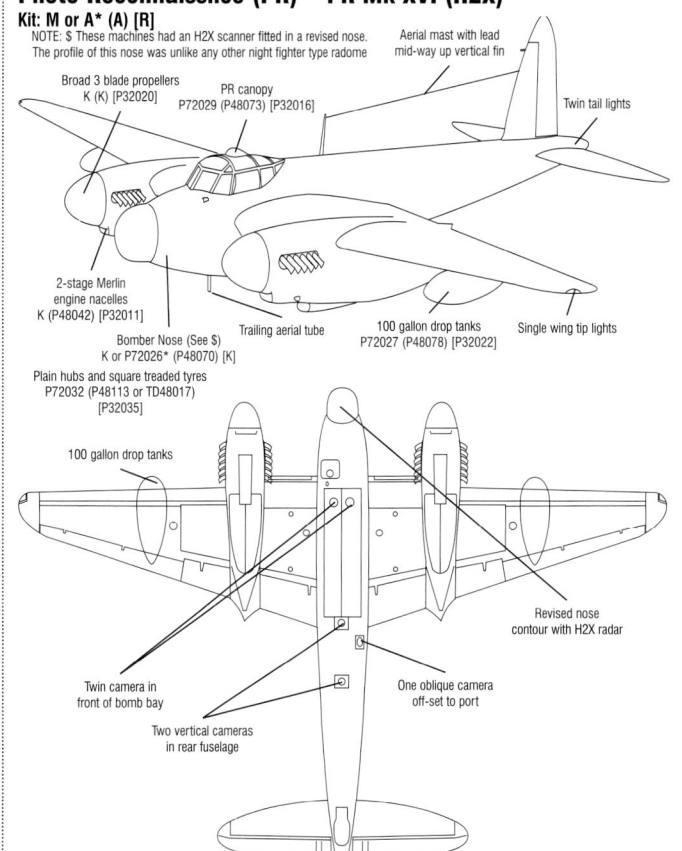

- Broad 3 blade propellers
  K (K) [P32020]
- PR canopy
  P72029 (P48073) [P32016]
- Aerial mast with lead mid-way up vertical fin
- Twin tail lights
- 2-stage Merlin engine nacelles
  K (P48042) [P32011]
- Bomber Nose (See $)
  K or P72026* (P48070) [K]
- Trailing aerial tube
- 100 gallon drop tanks
  P72027 (P48078) [P32022]
- Single wing tip lights
- Plain hubs and square treaded tyres
  P72032 (P48113 or TD48017) [P32035]

- 100 gallon drop tanks
- Twin camera in front of bomb bay
- Two vertical cameras in rear fuselage
- Revised nose contour with H2X radar
- One oblique camera off-set to port

Modelling the Mosquito • Understanding the Subject

Photo Reconnaissnce (PR) • PR Mk 32
Kit: M or A* (A) [R]

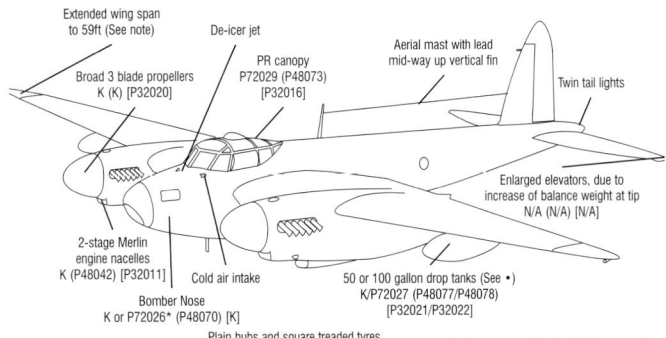

- Extended wing span to 59ft (See note)
- De-icer jet
- Broad 3 blade propellers K (K) [P32020]
- PR canopy P72029 (P48073) [P32016]
- Aerial mast with lead mid-way up vertical fin
- Twin tail lights
- Enlarged elevators, due to increase of balance weight at tip N/A (N/A) [N/A]
- 2-stage Merlin engine nacelles K (P48042) [P32011]
- Cold air intake
- 50 or 100 gallon drop tanks (See •) K/P72027 (P48077/P48078) [P32021/P32022]
- Bomber Nose K or P72026* (P48070) [K]
- Plain hubs and square treaded tyres P72032 (P48113 or TD48017) [P32035]

Note: Obtain the extended wing tips by contacting Paragon Designs, as they are included in their NF Mk XV conversion P72033 (P48071) [N/A]

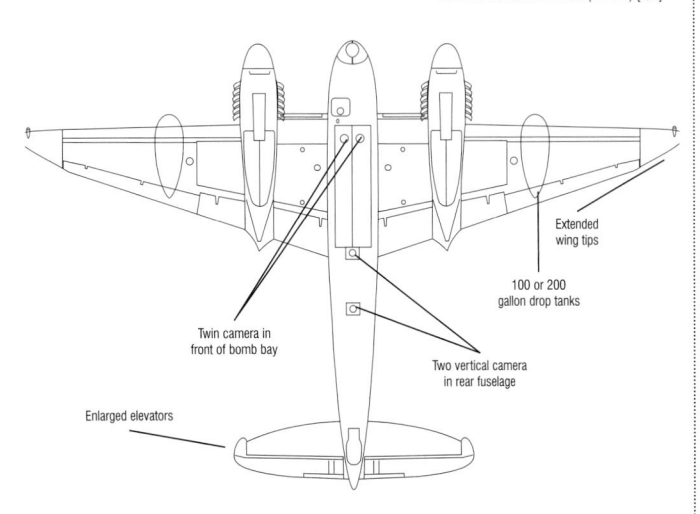

- Extended wing tips
- 100 or 200 gallon drop tanks
- Twin camera in front of bomb bay
- Two vertical camera in rear fuselage
- Enlarged elevators

Photo Reconnaissnce (PR) • PR Mk 34A
Kit: M or A* (A) [R]

- Landing light in starboard wing leading edge
- Broad 3 blade propellers K (K) [P32020]
- De-icer jet
- PR canopy P72029 (P48073) [P32016]
- Aerial mast with lead mid-way up vertical fin
- Gee whip antenna from rear of cockpit canopy
- Two whip antenna on fuselage spine
- Enlarged elevators, due to increase of balance weight at tip N/A (N/A) [N/A]
- Twin tail lights
- One oblique camera in fuselage (port) side
- 2-stage Merlin engine nacelles K (P48042) [P32011]
- Bomber Nose K or P72026* (P48070) [K]
- Cold air scoops on either side of nose
- 100 or 200 gallon drop tanks (See ~) P72027 (P48077/ N/K) [P32021/ N/K]
- Single wing tip light
- Three dipoles mounted above and below each wing tip (in 'L' shape)
- Plain hubs and square treaded tyres P72032 (P48113 or TD48017) [P32035]

Note: ~ Some post war PR Mk 34As had the 100 gallon drop tanks converted to hold F.52 cameras.
% The bulged bomb bay of this type was far more bulbous than the usual sort seen previously, as per the PR Mk 34
N/A (N/A) [N/A]

- Three dipoles mounted above and below each wing tip in 'L' shaped layout
- Landing light in starboard wing leading edge
- Petrol cooler intake on the fuselage just under the starboard wing on the centreline.
- Bulged bomb bay with four cameras in main section and two in the rear (%). Single camera mounted under fuselage, aft of bomb bay (with shutter rail)
- Enlarged elevators, due to increase of balance weight at tip

Photo Reconnaissnce (PR) • PR Mk 34
Kit: M or A* (A) [R]

- Landing light in starboard wing leading edge
- Broad 3 blade propellers K (K) [P32020]
- PR canopy P72029 (P48073) [P32016]
- Gee whip antenna from rear of cockpit canopy
- No aerial mast or lead
- Two whip antenna on fuselage spine
- Enlarged elevators, due to increase of balance weight at tip N/A (N/A) [N/A]
- Twin tail lights
- 2-stage Merlin engine nacelles K (P48042) [P32011]
- Bomber Nose K or P72026* (P48070) [K]
- Cold air scoops on either side of nose
- 100 or 200 gallon drop tanks P72027/ N/K (P48077/ N/K) [P32021/ N/K]
- Dipole on port lower fuselage side
- One oblique camera in fuselage (port) side
- Plain hubs and square treaded tyres P72032 (P48113 or TD48017) [P32035]

Note: % The bulged bomb bay of this type was far more bulbous than the usual sort seen previously N/A (N/A) [N/A]

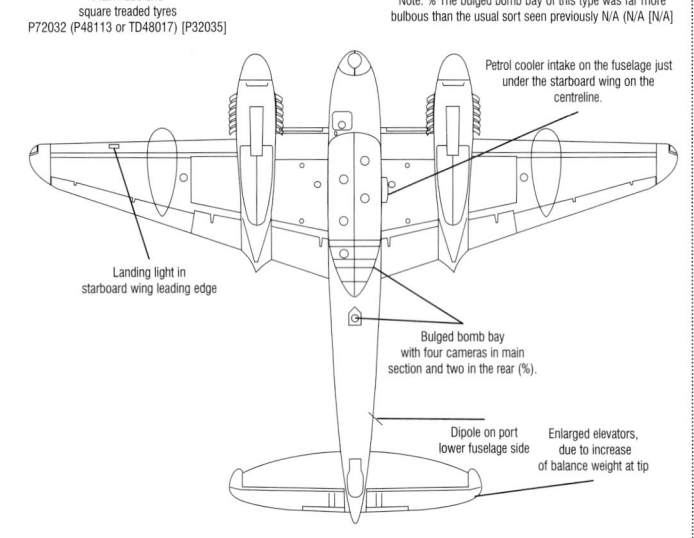

- Landing light in starboard wing leading edge
- Petrol cooler intake on the fuselage just under the starboard wing on the centreline.
- Bulged bomb bay with four cameras in main section and two in the rear (%).
- Dipole on port lower fuselage side
- Enlarged elevators, due to increase of balance weight at tip

Photo Reconnaissnce (PR) • PR Mk 34A
(No.22 Squadron navigational lead ship)
Kit: M or A* (A) [R]

- Landing light in starboard wing leading edge
- Broad 3 blade propellers K (K) [P32020]
- De-icer jet
- PR canopy P72029 (P48073) [P32016]
- Gee whip antenna from rear of cockpit canopy
- Aerial mast with lead high up on vertical fin
- Enlarged elevators, due to increase of balance weight at tip N/A (N/A) [N/A]
- One whip antenna aft of the DF loop and off-set to starboard
- DF Loop
- Twin tail lights
- 2-stage Merlin engine nacelles K (P48042) [P32011]
- Bomber Nose K or P72026* (P48070) [K]
- Cold air scoops on either side of nose
- 100 or 200 gallon drop tanks (See ~) P72027/ N/K (P48077/ N/K) [P32021/ N/K]
- One oblique camera in fuselage (port) side
- Single wing tip light
- Plain hubs and square treaded tyres P72032 (P48113 or TD48017) [P32035]

Note: The bulged bomb bay of this type was far more bulbous than the usual type seen previously, as per the PR Mk 34
N/A (N/A) [N/A]

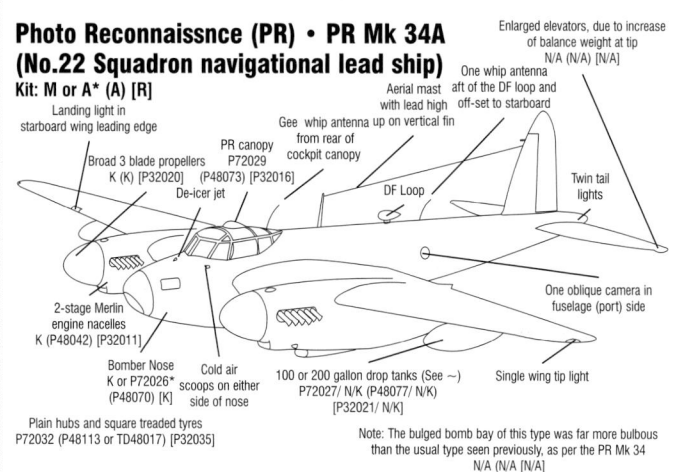

Photo Reconnaissnce (PR) • PR Mk 34A
(BOAC Gust Research Unit, Typical Layout)
Kit: M or A* (A) [R]

- Landing light in starboard wing leading edge
- Broad 3 blade propellers K (K) [P32020]
- De-icer jet
- PR canopy P72029 (P48073) [P32016]
- Gee whip antenna from rear of cockpit canopy
- Aerial mast deleted and lead runs from high up on vertical fin to the rear of the cockpit canopy
- Two whip antenna on the rear fuselage decking
- Enlarged elevators, due to increase of balance weight at tip N/A (N/A) [N/A]
- Twin tail lights
- 2-stage Merlin engine nacelles K (P48042) [P32011]
- Bomber Nose K or P72026* (P48070) [K]
- Cold air scoops on either side of nose
- Trailing aerial tube
- 100 gallon drop tanks P72027 (P48077) [P32021]
- One oblique camera in fuselage (port) side
- Single wing tip light
- Plain hubs and square treaded tyres P72032 (P48113 or TD48017) [P32035]

Note: % The bulged bomb bay of this type was far more bulbous than the usual kind seen previously, as per the PR Mk 34.
N/A (N/A) [N/A]

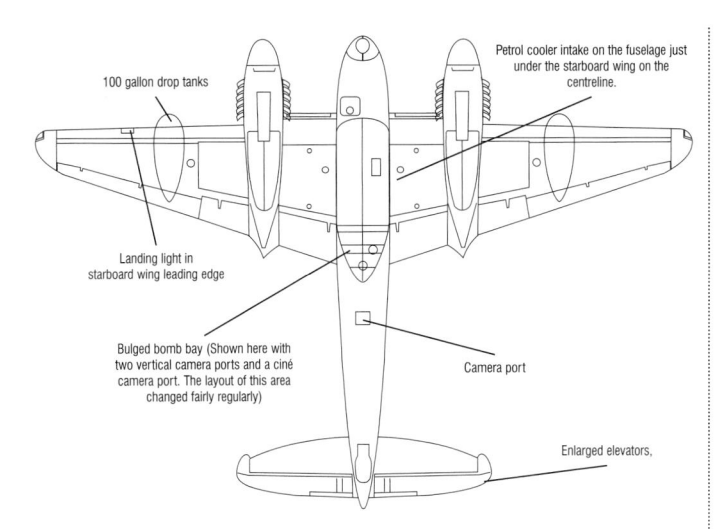

100 gallon drop tanks

Petrol cooler intake on the fuselage just under the starboard wing on the centreline.

Landing light in starboard wing leading edge

Bulged bomb bay (Shown here with two vertical camera ports and a ciné camera port. The layout of this area changed fairly regularly)

Camera port

Enlarged elevators,

Front view of camera fairing shape

Close-up of camera port in fairing under nose

Single camera port in fairing under nose

100 gallon drop tanks

Twin camera in ventral tray

Photo Reconnaissnce (PR) • PR Mk 40 (Australia)
Converted from an FB Mk 40 Kit: A (A) [R]

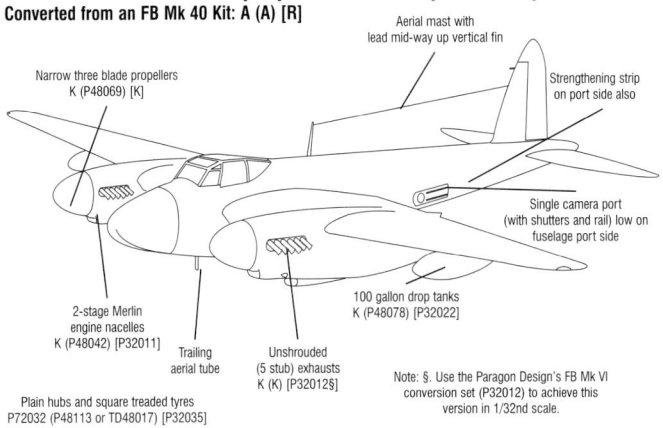

Narrow three blade propellers K (P48069) [K]

Aerial mast with lead mid-way up vertical fin

Strengthening strip on port side also

Single camera port (with shutters and rail) low on fuselage port side

2-stage Merlin engine nacelles K (P48042) [P32011]

Trailing aerial tube

100 gallon drop tanks K (P48078) [P32022]

Unshrouded (5 stub) exhausts K (K) [P32012§]

Plain hubs and square treaded tyres P72032 (P48113 or TD48017) [P32035]

Note: §. Use the Paragon Design's FB Mk VI conversion set (P32012) to achieve this version in 1/32nd scale.

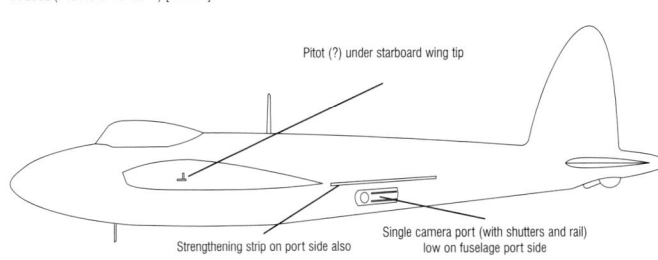

Pitot (?) under starboard wing tip

Strengthening strip on port side also

Single camera port (with shutters and rail) low on fuselage port side

Photo Reconnaissnce (PR) • PR Mk 41 (Australia)
Converted from an FB Mk 40 Kit: A (A) [R]

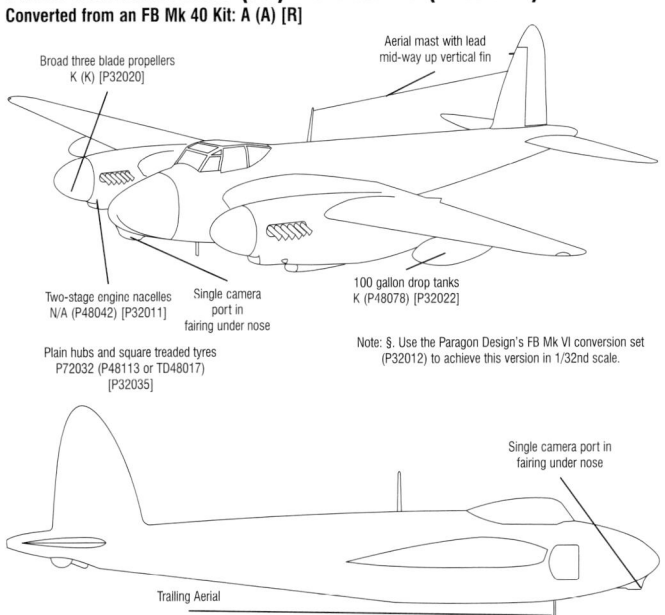

Broad three blade propellers K (K) [P32020]

Aerial mast with lead mid-way up vertical fin

Two-stage engine nacelles N/A (P48042) [P32011]

Single camera port in fairing under nose

100 gallon drop tanks K (P48078) [P32022]

Plain hubs and square treaded tyres P72032 (P48113 or TD48017) [P32035]

Note: §. Use the Paragon Design's FB Mk VI conversion set (P32012) to achieve this version in 1/32nd scale.

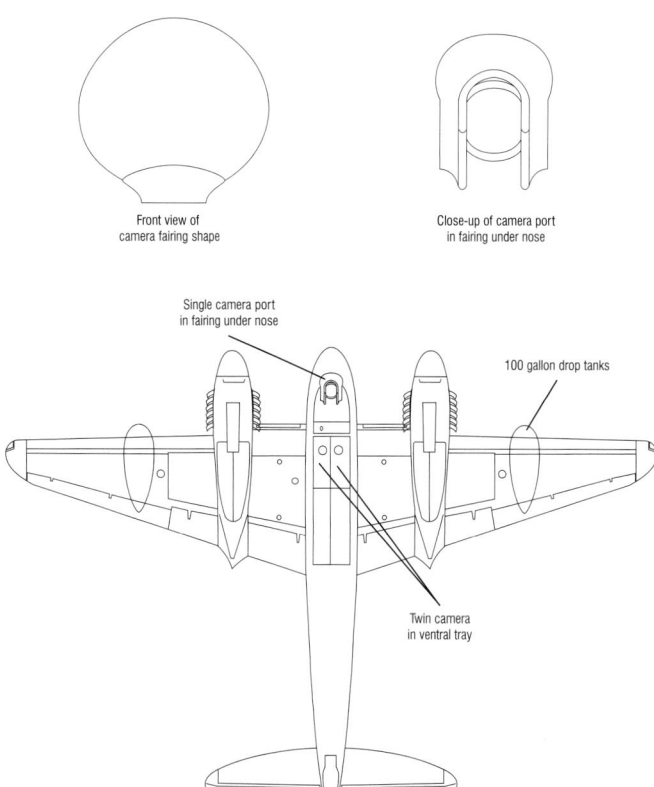

Single camera port in fairing under nose

Trailing Aerial

Meteorological Flights (Met) • Met Mk IX
Converted from PR Mk IX Kit: M or A* (A) [R]

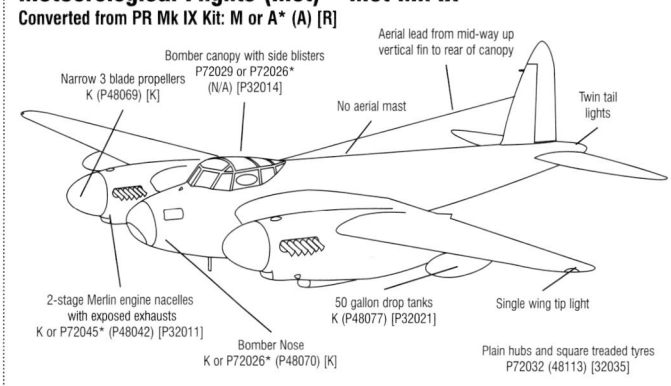

Bomber canopy with side blisters P72029 or P72026* (N/A) [P32014]

Narrow 3 blade propellers K (P48069) [K]

Aerial lead from mid-way up vertical fin to rear of canopy

No aerial mast

Twin tail lights

2-stage Merlin engine nacelles with exposed exhausts K or P72045* (P48042) [P32011]

50 gallon drop tanks K (P48077) [P32021]

Bomber Nose K or P72026* (P48070) [K]

Single wing tip light

Plain hubs and square treaded tyres P72032 (48113) [32035]

Meteorological Flights (Met) • Met Mk 38
Same as NF Mk 38 except

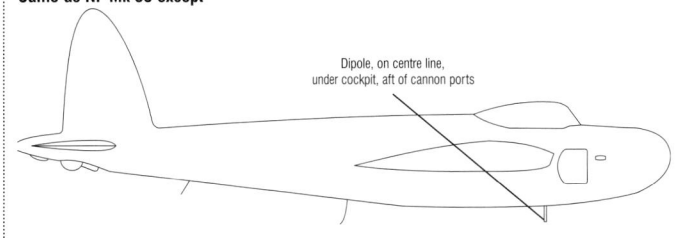

Dipole, on centre line, under cockpit, aft of cannon ports

Night Fighter • NF Mk II with A.I. Mk IV radar
Kit: A (A) [R]

Note: §. Use the Paragon Design's FB Mk VI conversion set (P32012) to achieve the basis of this version in 1/32nd scale.

Two swept back dipoles on the upper and lower surface of starboard wing. Approx halfway between wing tip and engine nacelle.

Two dipole antenna above & below each wing tip

Fighter canopy. K (K) [P32012§]

Aerial mast, but no lead

Twin tail lights

Narrow 3 blade propellers K (P4869) [K]

'Bow & Arrow' Antenna

Shrouded exhausts. K (K) [K]

Twin wing tip lights

Single-stage engine nacelles K (K) [K]

Modelling the Mosquito • Understanding the Subject   73

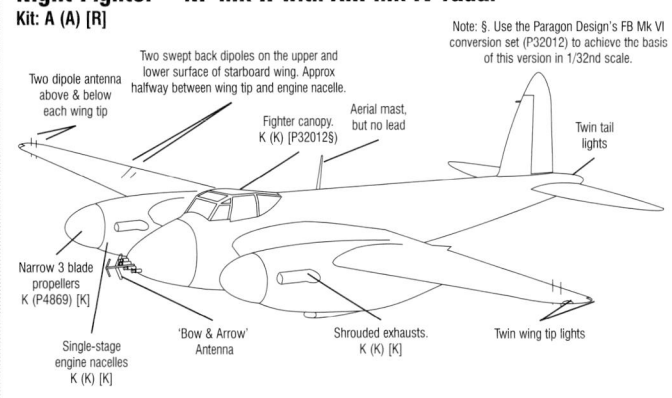

Night Fighter • NF Mk II (Intruder)
Kit: A (A) [R]

Note: §. Use the Paragon Design's FB Mk VI conversion set (P32012) to achieve the basis of this version in 1/32nd scale.

- Twin dipoles deleted
- Swept back dipoles on starboard wing deleted.
- Fighter canopy. K (K) [P32012§]
- Aerial mast and twin leads. One going mid-way up the vertical fin and the other to the leading edge of the port tailplane
- Twin tail lights
- Narrow 3 blade propellers K (P4869) [K]
- Single-stage engine nacelles K (K) [K]
- 'Bow & Arrow' antenna deleted
- Shrouded exhausts. K (K) [K]
- Twin wing tip lights
- 5-spoke hubs and square treaded tyres P72025 (48112) [32034]

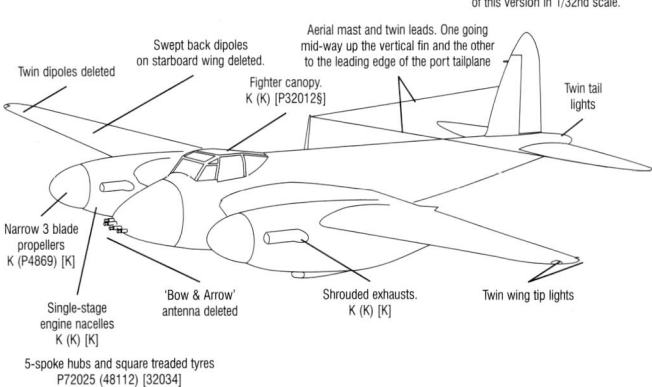

Night Fighter • NF Mk XII
Kit: A (A) [R]

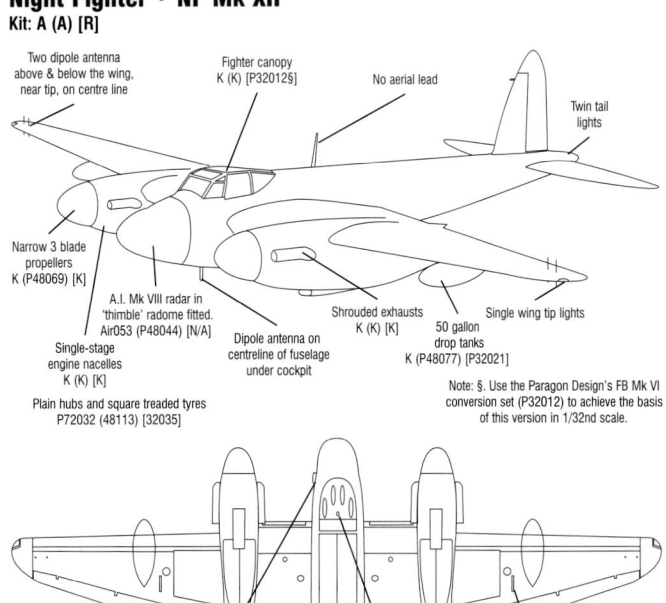

- Two dipole antenna above & below the wing, near tip, on centre line
- Fighter canopy K (K) [P32012§]
- No aerial lead
- Twin tail lights
- Narrow 3 blade propellers K (P48069) [K]
- A.I. Mk VIII radar in 'thimble' radome fitted. Air053 (P48044) [N/A]
- Single-stage engine nacelles K (K) [K]
- Shrouded exhausts K (K) [K]
- Dipole antenna on centreline of fuselage under cockpit
- Single wing tip lights
- 50 gallon drop tanks K (P48077) [P32021]
- Plain hubs and square treaded tyres P72032 (48113) [32035]

Note: §. Use the Paragon Design's FB Mk VI conversion set (P32012) to achieve the basis of this version in 1/32nd scale.

- Camera gun
- Dipole antenna
- Radio altimeter 'T' antenna (both sides)

- Dipole antenna
- Radio altimeter 'T' antenna (both sides)

- Radio altimeter 'T' antenna (both sides)
- Camera gun
- Dipole antenna

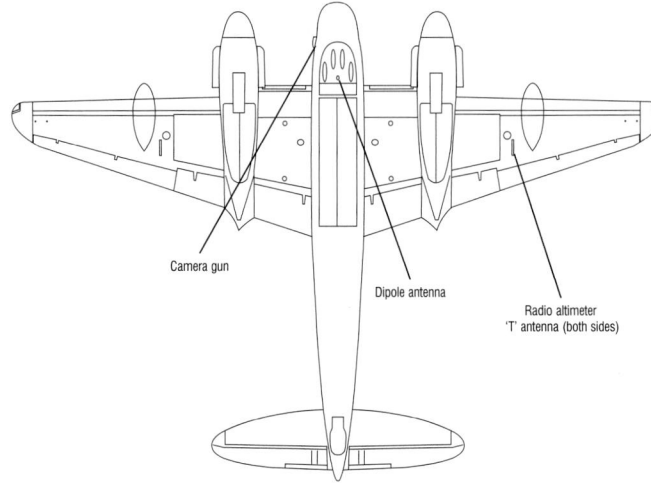

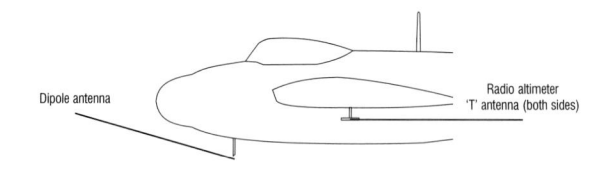

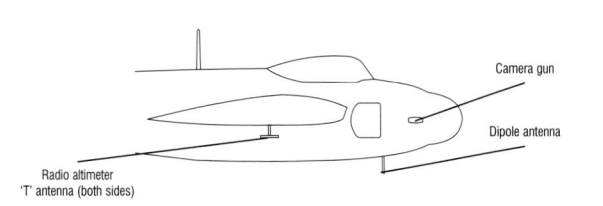

Night Fighter • NF Mk XIII
Kit: A (A) [R]

Note: §. Use the Paragon Design's FB Mk VI conversion set (P32012) to achieve the basis of this version in 1/32nd scale.

- Two dipole antenna above & below the wing, near tip, on centre line
- Gee antenna sometimes fitted to rear of cockpit canopy
- Fighter canopy. K (K) [P32012§]
- Aerial mast, but no aerial lead
- Twin tail lights
- Narrow 3 blade propellers K (P48069) [K]
- Single-stage engine nacelles K (K) [K]
- Universal ('Bullnose') radome Air052 (P48043) [N/A]
- Shrouded exhausts K (K) [K]
- Single wing tip lights
- 50 gallon drop tanks K (P4877) [P32021]
- Plain hubs and square treaded tyres P72032 (48113) [32035]

- Camera gun
- Radio altimeter 'T' antenna (both sides)

- Aerial mast
- Gee antenna
- Radio altimeter 'T' antenna (both sides)
- Camera gun

74 Chapter 10

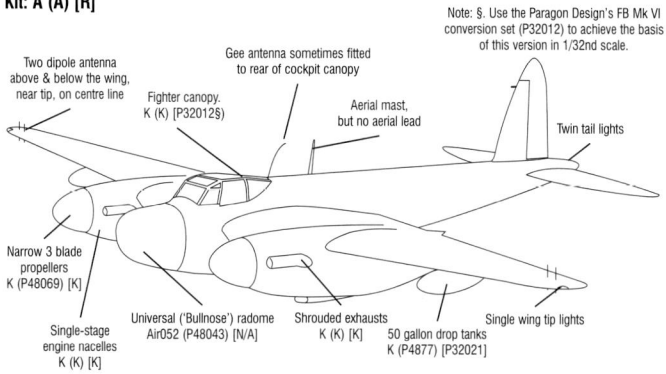

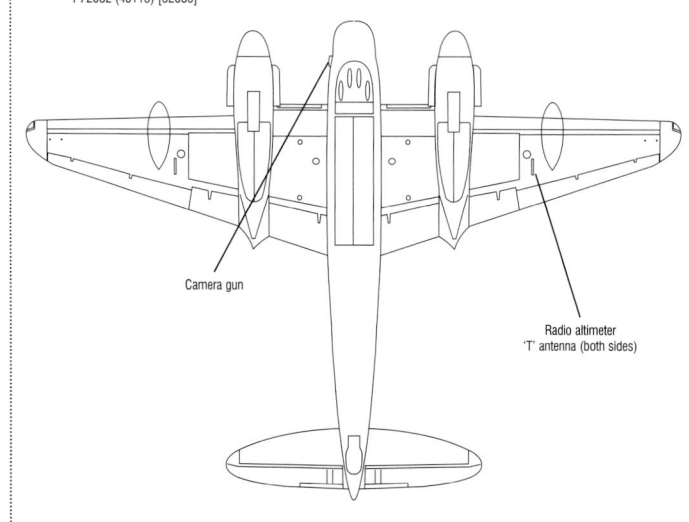

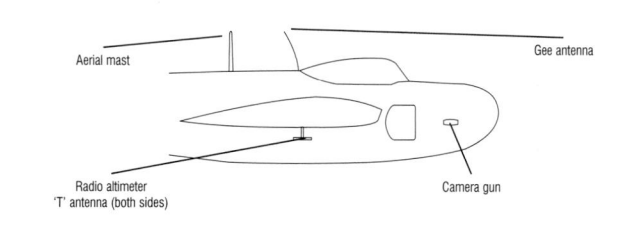

Night Fighter • NF XV (Production)
Kit: A (A) [R]

Note: All items sourced as P72033 (P48071) are included in those conversion sets.
* The prototype (MP469) had the 62ft 2in span, while production versions had a span of only 59ft. The extended tips in the current Paragon sets are the former and need to be modified for production versions.

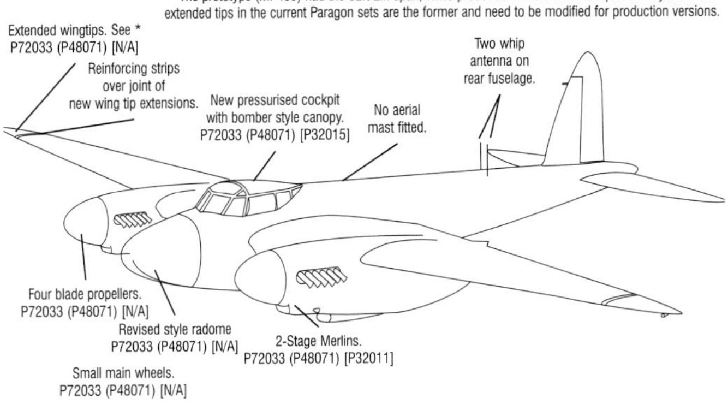

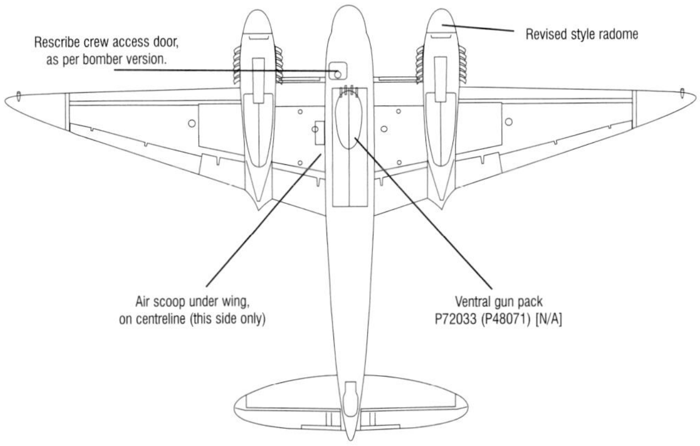

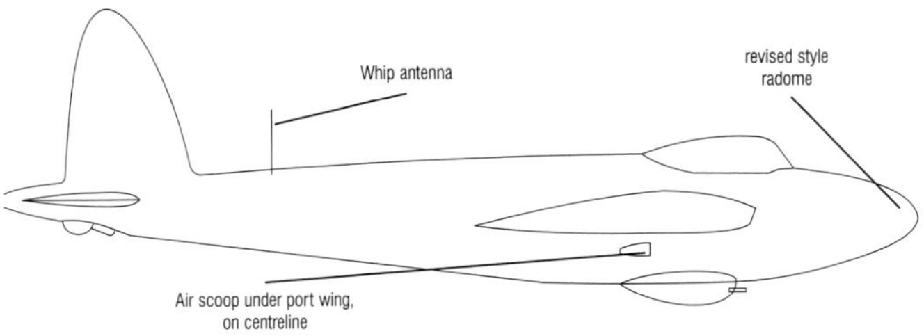

- Extended wingtips. See * P72033 (P48071) [N/A]
- Reinforcing strips over joint of new wing tip extensions. P72033 (P48071) [P32015]
- New pressurised cockpit with bomber style canopy. P72033 (P48071) [P32015]
- Two whip antenna on rear fuselage.
- No aerial mast fitted.
- Four blade propellers. P72033 (P48071) [N/A]
- Revised style radome P72033 (P48071) [N/A]
- 2-Stage Merlins. P72033 (P48071) [P32011]
- Small main wheels. P72033 (P48071) [N/A]
- Rescribe crew access door, as per bomber version.
- Revised style radome
- Air scoop under wing, on centreline (this side only)
- Ventral gun pack P72033 (P48071) [N/A]
- Whip antenna
- revised style radome
- Air scoop under port wing, on centreline

Night Fighter • NF Mk XVII
Kit: A (J.30/Mk XIX) (A) [R]

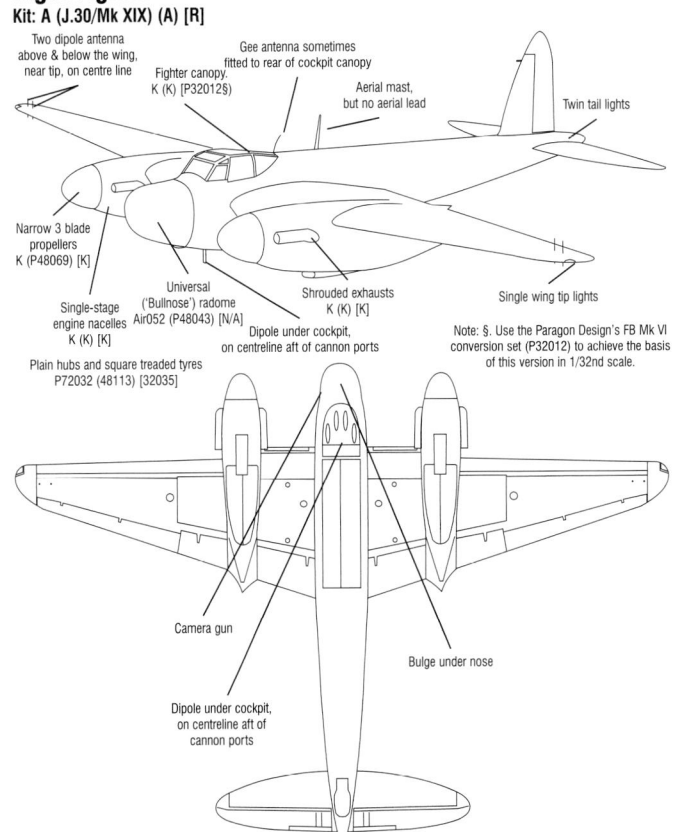

- Two dipole antenna above & below the wing, near tip, on centre line
- Gee antenna sometimes fitted to rear of cockpit canopy
- Fighter canopy. K (K) [P32012§]
- Aerial mast, but no aerial lead
- Twin tail lights
- Narrow 3 blade propellers K (P48069) [K]
- Universal ('Bullnose') radome Air052 (P48043) [N/A]
- Shrouded exhausts
- Single wing tip lights
- Single-stage engine nacelles K (K) [K]
- Plain hubs and square treaded tyres P72032 (48113) [32035]
- Dipole under cockpit, on centreline aft of cannon ports

Note: §. Use the Paragon Design's FB Mk VI conversion set (P32012) to achieve the basis of this version in 1/32nd scale.

- Camera gun
- Bulge under nose
- Dipole under cockpit, on centreline aft of cannon ports

Night Fighter • NF Mk XIX
Kit: A (J.30/Mk XIX) (A) [R]

- Two dipoles above and below each wing tip on centreline
- Fighter canopy K (K) [P3012§]
- Note: §. Use the Paragon Design's FB Mk VI conversion set (P32012) to achieve the basis of this version in 1/32 scale.
- Twin tail lights
- Broad 3 blade propellers K (K) [P32020]
- Bullnose radome Air052 (P48043) [N/A]
- 50 or 100 gallon drop tanks K/P72027 (P48077/P48078) [P32021/P32022]
- Single wing tip lights
- Single-stage engine nacelles K (K) [K]
- Plain hubs and square treaded tyres P72032 (48113) [32035]
- Bulge under nose
- Camera gun

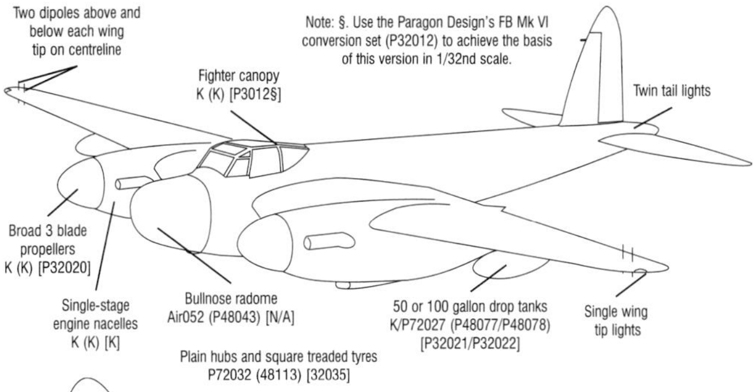

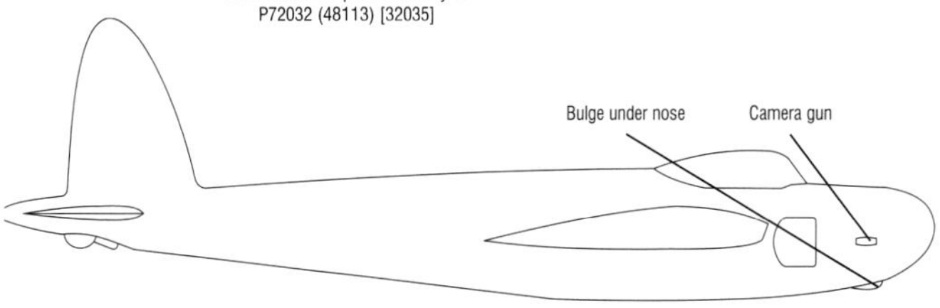

Night Fighter • J 30 'Hunter' (NF Mk XIX)
Kit: A (J.30/Mk XIX) (A) [R]

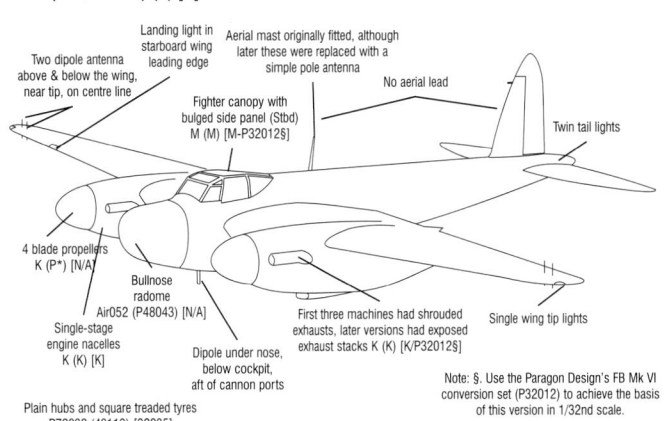

- Landing light in starboard wing leading edge
- Aerial mast originally fitted, although later these were replaced with a simple pole antenna
- Two dipole antenna above & below the wing, near tip, on centre line
- Fighter canopy with bulged side panel (Stbd) M (M) [M-P32012§]
- No aerial lead
- Twin tail lights
- 4 blade propellers K (P*) [N/A]
- Bullnose radome Air052 (P48043) [N/A]
- First three machines had shrouded exhausts, later versions had exposed exhaust stacks K (K) [K/P32012§]
- Single wing tip lights
- Single-stage engine nacelles K (K) [K]
- Dipole under nose, below cockpit, aft of cannon ports
- Plain hubs and square treaded tyres P72032 (48113) [32035]

Note: §. Use the Paragon Design's FB Mk VI conversion set (P32012) to achieve the basis of this version in 1/32nd scale.

- Bullnose radome
- Bulge under nose
- Dipole under nose, below cockpit, aft of cannon ports
- Camera gun
- Landing light in starboard wing leading edge
- Radio altimeter 'T' antenna on centreline, below each wing. Positioned between engine nacelle and drop tank
- Universal shackle for bombs or drop tanks
- Radio altimeter 'T' antenna on centreline, below each wing. Positioned between engine nacelle and drop tank

Modelling the Mosquito • Understanding the Subject

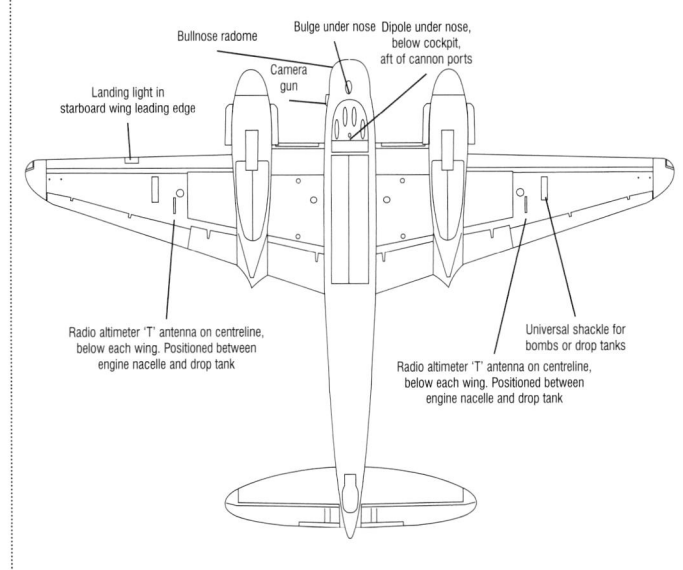

Night Fighter • NF Mk 30
Kit: M (A) [R]

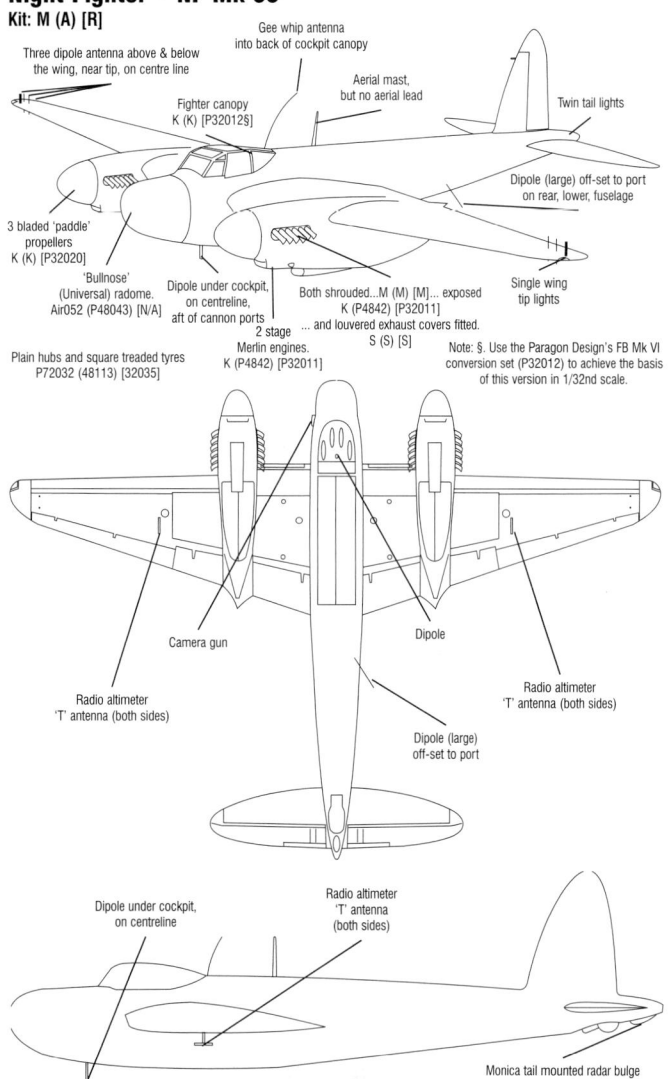

- Three dipole antenna above & below the wing, near tip, on centre line
- Gee whip antenna into back of cockpit canopy
- Fighter canopy K (K) [P32012§]
- Aerial mast, but no aerial lead
- Twin tail lights
- Dipole (large) off-set to port on rear, lower, fuselage
- 3 bladed 'paddle' propellers K (K) [P32020]
- 'Bullnose' (Universal) radome. Air052 (P48043) [N/A]
- Dipole under cockpit, on centreline, aft of cannon ports
- Both shrouded...M (M) [M] exposed K (P4842) [P32011] ... and louvered exhaust covers fitted. S (S) [S]
- Single wing tip lights
- 2 stage Merlin engines. K (P4842) [P32011]
- Plain hubs and square treaded tyres P72032 (48113) [32035]

- Camera gun
- Dipole
- Radio altimeter 'T' antenna (both sides)
- Radio altimeter 'T' antenna (both sides)
- Dipole (large) off-set to port

- Dipole under cockpit, on centreline
- Radio altimeter 'T' antenna (both sides)
- Monica tail mounted radar bulge

Note: §. Use the Paragon Design's FB Mk VI conversion set (P32012) to achieve the basis of this version in 1/32nd scale.

Night Fighter • NF Mk 36 (with A.I. Mk X)
Kit: M (A) [R]

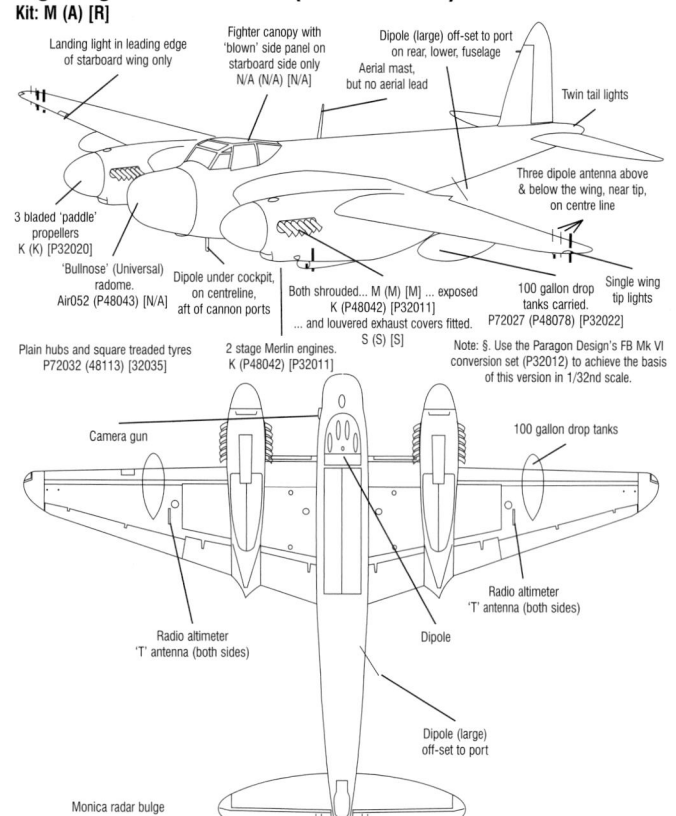

- Landing light in leading edge of starboard wing only
- Fighter canopy with 'blown' side panel on starboard side only N/A (N/A) [N/A]
- Dipole (large) off-set to port on rear, lower, fuselage
- Aerial mast, but no aerial lead
- Twin tail lights
- Three dipole antenna above & below the wing, near tip, on centre line
- 3 bladed 'paddle' propellers K (K) [P32020]
- 'Bullnose' (Universal) radome. Air052 (P48043) [N/A]
- Dipole under cockpit, on centreline, aft of cannon ports
- Both shrouded... M (M) [M] ... exposed K (P48042) [P32011] ... and louvered exhaust covers fitted. S (S) [S]
- 100 gallon drop tanks carried. P72027 (P48078) [P32022]
- Single wing tip lights
- 2 stage Merlin engines. K (P48042) [P32011]
- Plain hubs and square treaded tyres P72032 (48113) [32035]

Note: §. Use the Paragon Design's FB Mk VI conversion set (P32012) to achieve the basis of this version in 1/32nd scale.

- Camera gun
- 100 gallon drop tanks
- Radio altimeter 'T' antenna (both sides)
- Dipole
- Radio altimeter 'T' antenna (both sides)
- Dipole (large) off-set to port
- Monica radar bulge

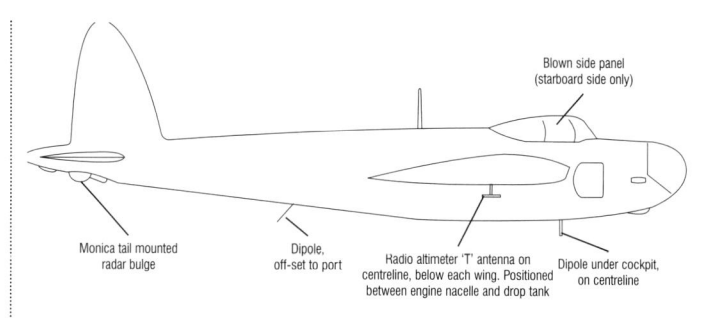

Night Fighter • NF Mk 36 #2
Kit: M (A) [R]

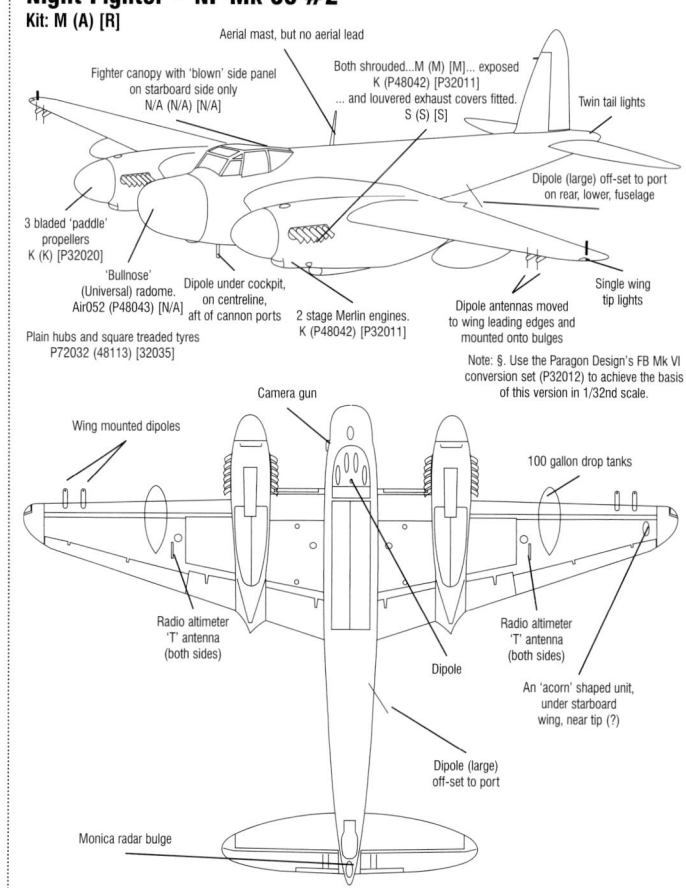

- Monica tail mounted radar bulge
- Dipole, off-set to port
- Blown side panel (starboard side only)
- Radio altimeter 'T' antenna on centreline, below each wing. Positioned between engine nacelle and drop tank
- Dipole under cockpit, on centreline

- Aerial mast, but no aerial lead
- Fighter canopy with 'blown' side panel on starboard side only N/A (N/A) [N/A]
- Both shrouded...M (M) [M] ... exposed K (P48042) [P32011] ... and louvered exhaust covers fitted. S (S) [S]
- Twin tail lights
- Dipole (large) off-set to port on rear, lower, fuselage
- 3 bladed 'paddle' propellers K (K) [P32020]
- 'Bullnose' (Universal) radome. Air052 (P48043) [N/A]
- Dipole under cockpit, on centreline, aft of cannon ports
- 2 stage Merlin engines. K (P48042) [P32011]
- Dipole antennas moved to wing leading edges and mounted onto bulges
- Single wing tip lights
- Plain hubs and square treaded tyres P72032 (48113) [32035]

Note: §. Use the Paragon Design's FB Mk VI conversion set (P32012) to achieve the basis of this version in 1/32nd scale.

- Camera gun
- 100 gallon drop tanks
- Wing mounted dipoles
- Radio altimeter 'T' antenna (both sides)
- Dipole
- Radio altimeter 'T' antenna (both sides)
- An 'acorn' shaped unit, under starboard wing, near tip (?)
- Dipole (large) off-set to port
- Monica radar bulge

Night Fighter • NF Mk 38
Kit: M (A) [R]

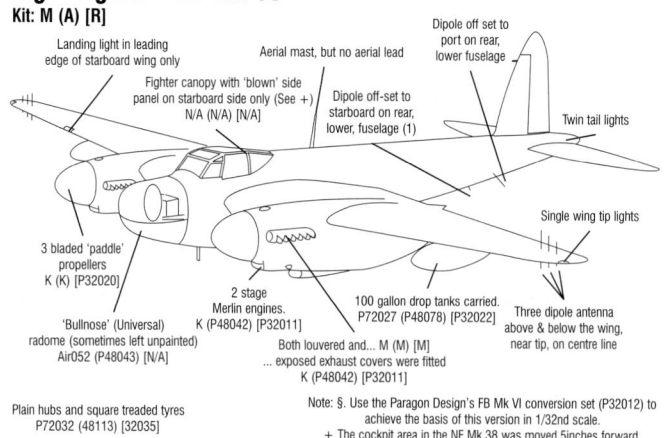

- Landing light in leading edge of starboard wing only
- Fighter canopy with 'blown' side panel on starboard side only (See +) N/A (N/A) [N/A]
- Aerial mast, but no aerial lead
- Dipole off set to port on rear, lower fuselage
- Dipole off-set to starboard on rear, lower, fuselage (1)
- Twin tail lights
- Single wing tip lights
- 3 bladed 'paddle' propellers K (K) [P32020]
- 2 stage Merlin engines. K (P48042) [P32011]
- 'Bullnose' (Universal) radome (sometimes left unpainted) Air052 (P48043) [N/A]
- 100 gallon drop tanks carried. P72027 (P48078) [P32022]
- Both louvered and... M (M) [M] ... exposed exhaust covers were fitted K (P48042) [P32011]
- Three dipole antenna above & below the wing, near tip, on centre line
- Plain hubs and square treaded tyres P72032 (48113) [32035]

Note: §. Use the Paragon Design's FB Mk VI conversion set (P32012) to achieve the basis of this version in 1/32nd scale.
+ The cockpit area in the NF Mk 38 was moved 5inches forward.
(1) Yugoslavian A.F. operated NF Mk 38s did not have this dipole

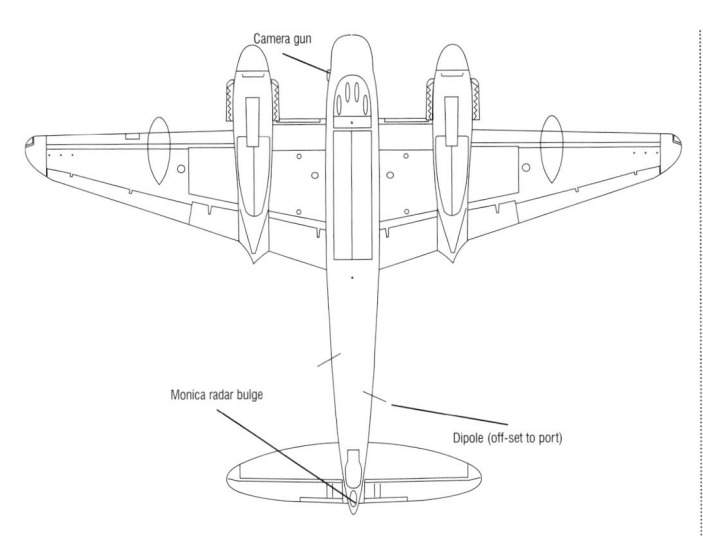

Camera gun

Monica radar bulge

Dipole (off-set to port)

Plan View #3

Universal carrier for 50 or 100 gallon drop tank (FB Mk VI Series II only)

Universal carrier for 50 or 100 gallon drop tank (FB Mk VI Series II only)

Fighter Bomber • FB Mk VI
Kit: A (A) [R]

Note: Use the Paragon conversion set (P32012) to achieve this version in 1/32nd scale.
(2) Some FB MK VIs did not have a mast or aerial lead
(4) This was only fitted late/post war and to machines operated in Israel

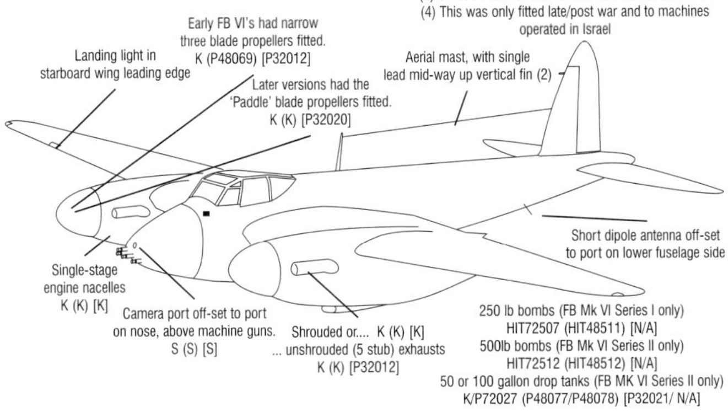

Early FB VI's had narrow three blade propellers fitted. K (P48069) [P32012]

Landing light in starboard wing leading edge

Later versions had the 'Paddle' blade propellers fitted. K (K) [P32020]

Aerial mast, with single lead mid-way up vertical fin (2)

Short dipole antenna off-set to port on lower fuselage side

Single-stage engine nacelles K (K) [K]

Camera port off-set to port on nose, above machine guns.

Shrouded or.... K (K) [K] ... unshrouded (5 stub) exhausts K (K) [P32012]
S (S) [S]

250 lb bombs (FB Mk VI Series I only) HIT72507 (HIT48511) [N/A]
500lb bombs (FB Mk VI Series II only) HIT72512 (HIT48512) [N/A]
50 or 100 gallon drop tanks (FB MK VI Series II only) K/P72027 (P48077/P48078) [P32021/ N/A]

Plan View #1

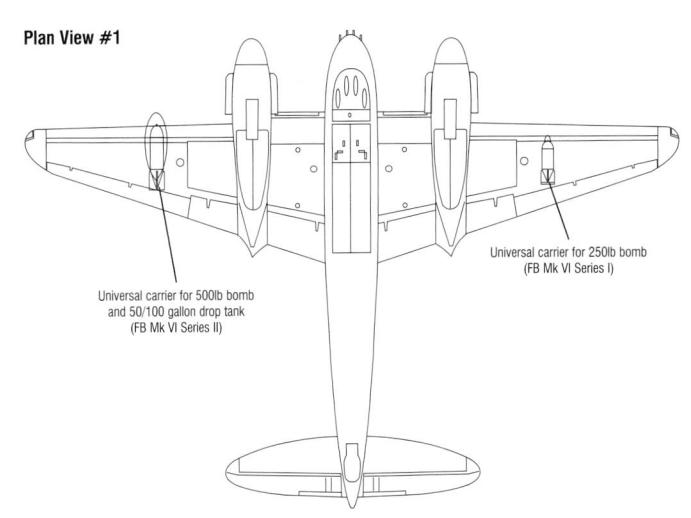

Universal carrier for 500lb bomb and 50/100 gallon drop tank (FB Mk VI Series II)

Universal carrier for 250lb bomb (FB Mk VI Series I)

Plan View #2

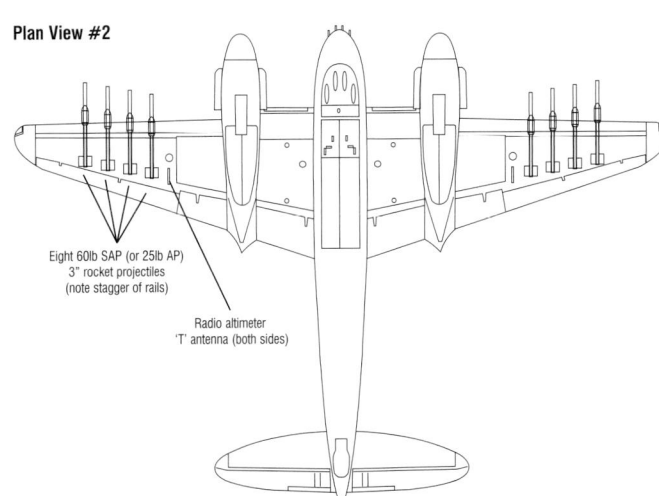

Eight 60lb SAP (or 25lb AP) 3" rocket projectiles (note stagger of rails)

Radio altimeter 'T' antenna (both sides)

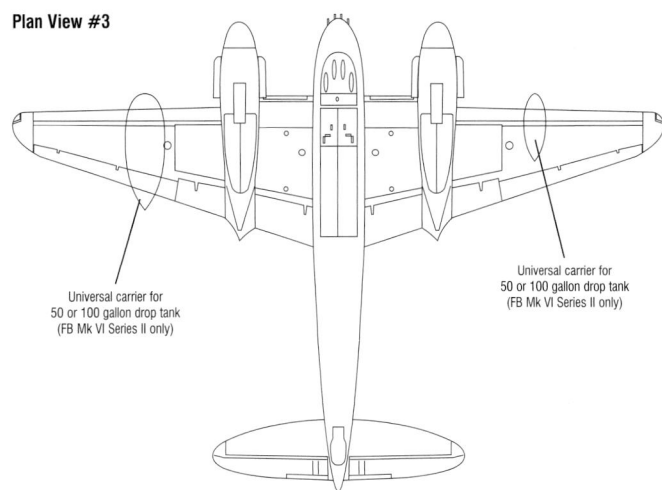

Fighter Bomber • FB Mk VI (Turkish Air Force)
Plan View #3

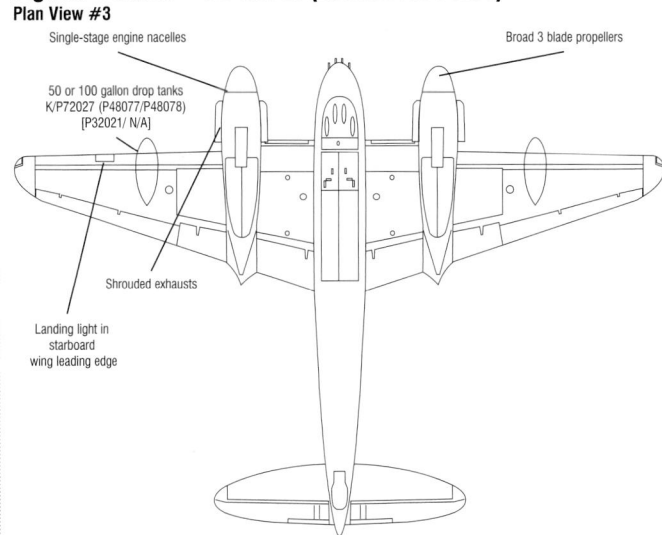

Single-stage engine nacelles

Broad 3 blade propellers

50 or 100 gallon drop tanks K/P72027 (P48077/P48078) [P32021/ N/A]

Shrouded exhausts

Landing light in starboard wing leading edge

Fighter Bomber • FB Mk VI (Norwegian Air Force)
Plan View #3

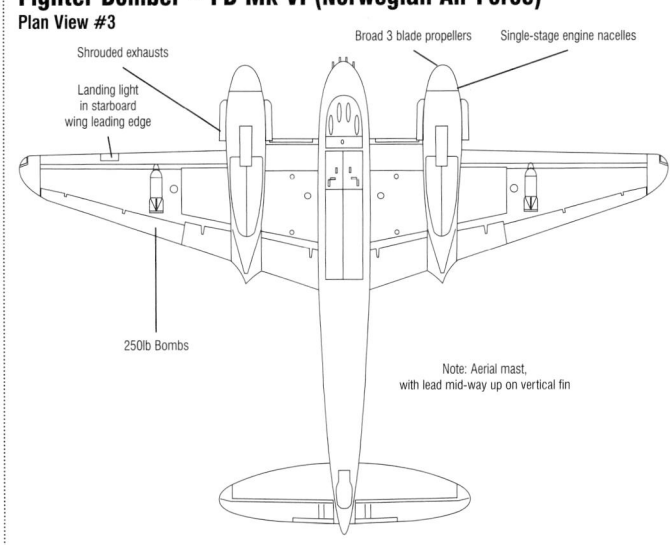

Broad 3 blade propellers   *Single-stage engine nacelles*

Shrouded exhausts

Landing light in starboard wing leading edge

250lb Bombs

Note: Aerial mast, with lead mid-way up on vertical fin

Modelling the Mosquito • Understanding the Subject

Fighter Bomber • FB Mk VI (Dominican Republic)
Plan View #3

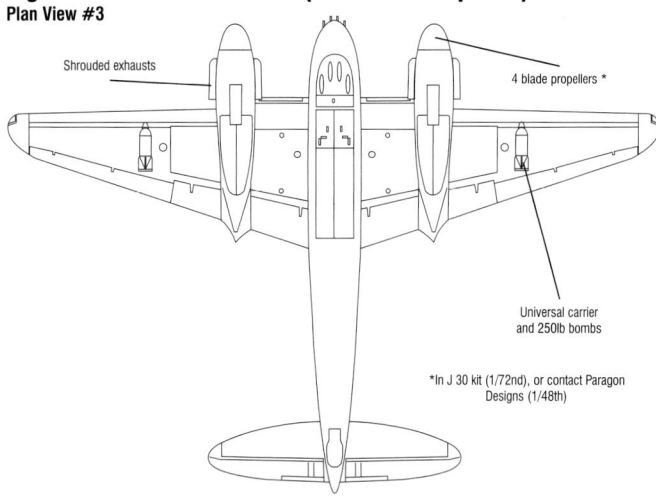

- Shrouded exhausts
- 4 blade propellers *
- Universal carrier and 250lb bombs

*In J 30 kit (1/72nd), or contact Paragon Designs (1/48th)

Fighter Bomber • FB Mk VI (Banff)
Kit: A (A) [R]

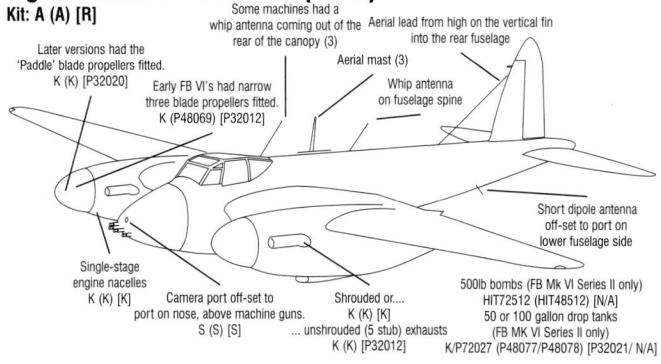

- Later versions had the 'Paddle' blade propellers fitted. K (K) [P32020]
- Some machines had a whip antenna coming out of the rear of the canopy (3)
- Aerial lead from high on the vertical fin into the rear fuselage
- Early FB VI's had narrow three blade propellers fitted. K (P48069) [P32012]
- Aerial mast (3)
- Whip antenna on fuselage spine
- Short dipole antenna off-set to port on lower fuselage side
- Single-stage engine nacelles K (K) [K]
- Camera port off-set to port on nose, above machine guns. S (S) [S]
- Shrouded or.... K (K) [K]
- ... unshrouded (5 stub) exhausts K (K) [P32012]
- 500lb bombs (FB Mk VI Series II only) HIT72512 (HIT48512) [N/A]
- 50 or 100 gallon drop tanks (FB MK VI Series II only) K/P72027 (P48077/P48078) [P32021/ N/A]

Note: Use the Paragon conversion set (P32012) to achieve this version in 1/32nd scale.
(3) When the whip antennas (canopy and spine) were fitted, the aerial mast and lead was not

Fighter Bomber • FB Mk XVIII (Early)
Kit: A (A) [R]

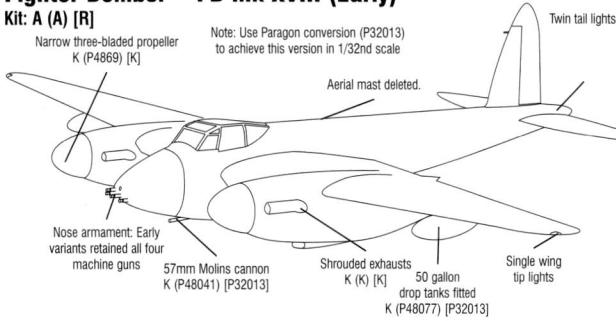

- Narrow three-bladed propeller K (P4869) [K]
- Note: Use Paragon conversion (P32013) to achieve this version in 1/32nd scale
- Twin tail lights
- Aerial mast deleted.
- Nose armament: Early variants retained all four machine guns
- 57mm Molins cannon K (P48041) [P32013]
- Shrouded exhausts K (K) [K]
- 50 gallon drop tanks fitted K (P48077) [P32013]
- Single wing tip lights

Fighter Bomber • FB Mk XVIII (Early)
Plan View

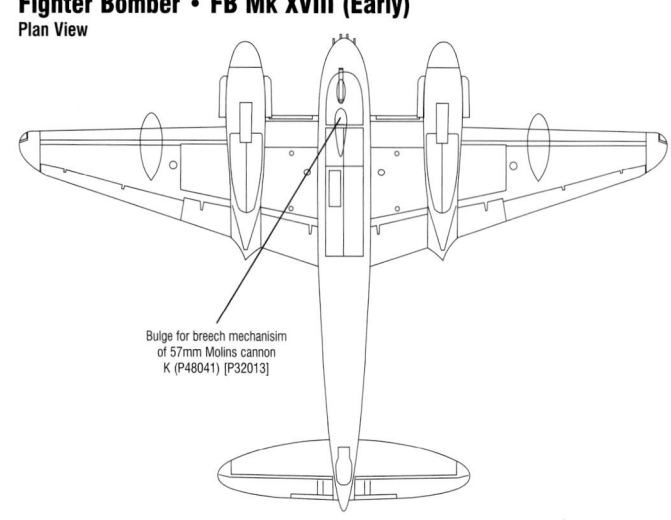

- Bulge for breech mechanisim of 57mm Molins cannon K (P48041) [P32013]

Fighter Bomber • FB Mk XVIII (Late)

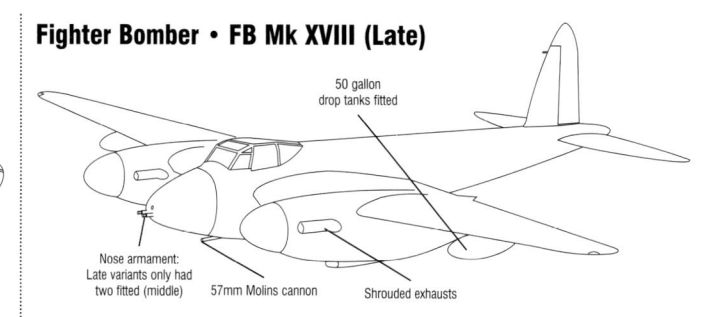

- 50 gallon drop tanks fitted
- Nose armament: Late variants only had two fitted (middle)
- 57mm Molins cannon
- Shrouded exhausts

Fighter Bomber • FB Mk 21 (Canadian)
Kit: A (A) [R]

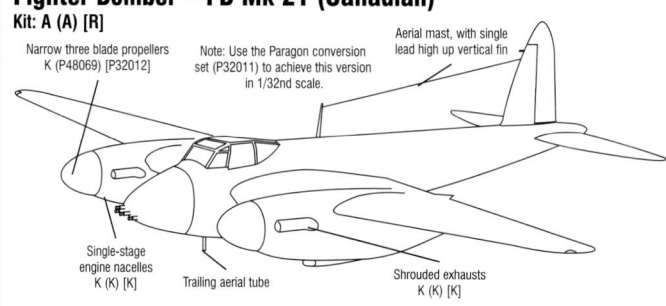

- Narrow three blade propellers K (P48069) [P32012]
- Note: Use the Paragon conversion set (P32011) to achieve this version in 1/32nd scale.
- Aerial mast, with single lead high up vertical fin
- Single-stage engine nacelles K (K) [K]
- Trailing aerial tube
- Shrouded exhausts K (K) [K]

Fighter Bomber • FB Mk 26 (Canadian. Inc Chinese operated examples)
Kit: A (A) [R]

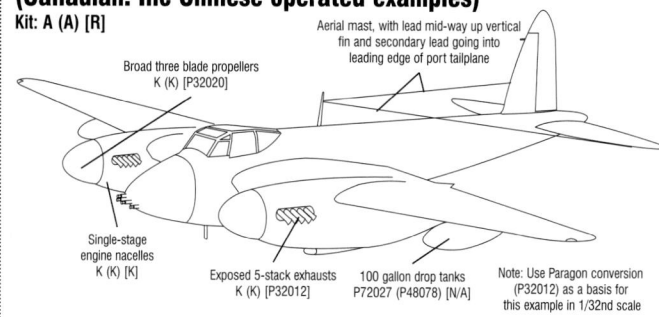

- Broad three blade propellers K (K) [P32020]
- Aerial mast, with lead mid-way up vertical fin and secondary lead going into leading edge of port tailplane
- Single-stage engine nacelles K (K) [K]
- Exposed 5-stack exhausts K (K) [P32012]
- 100 gallon drop tanks P72027 (P48078) [N/A]
- Note: Use Paragon conversion (P32012) as a basis for this example in 1/32nd scale

Fighter Bomber • FB Mk 40 (Australia)
Kit: A (A) [R]

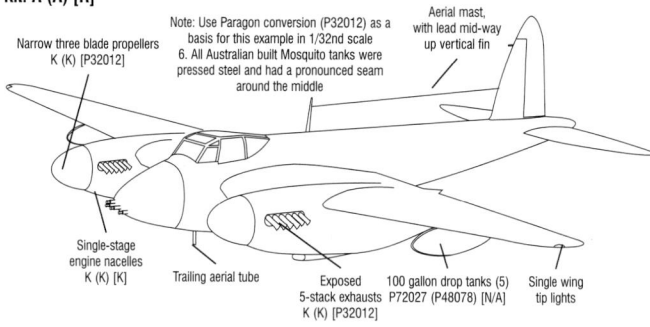

- Narrow three blade propellers K (K) [P32012]
- Note: Use Paragon conversion (P32012) as a basis for this example in 1/32nd scale 6. All Australian built Mosquito tanks were pressed steel and had a pronounced seam around the middle
- Aerial mast, with lead mid-way up vertical fin
- Single-stage engine nacelles K (K) [K]
- Trailing aerial tube
- Exposed 5-stack exhausts K (K) [P32012]
- 100 gallon drop tanks (5) P72027 (P48078) [N/A]
- Single wing tip lights

78 Chapter 10

Sea Mosquito • TR Mk 33
Kit: A (A) [R]

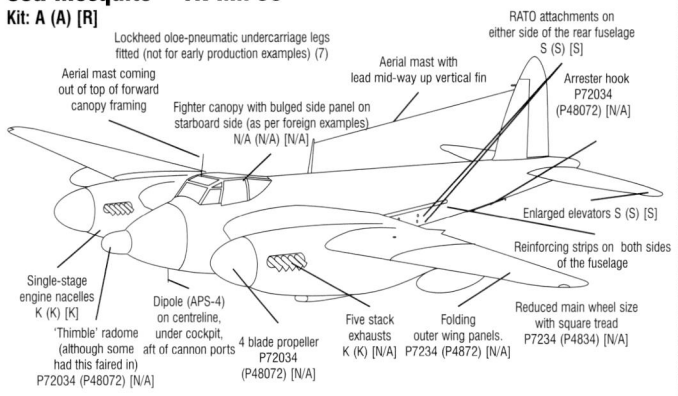

- Lockheed oleo-pneumatic undercarriage legs fitted (not for early production examples) (7)
- Aerial mast coming out of top of forward canopy framing
- Fighter canopy with bulged side panel on starboard side (as per foreign examples) N/A (N/A) [N/A]
- RATO attachments on either side of the rear fuselage S (S) [S]
- Aerial mast with lead mid-way up vertical fin
- Arrester hook P72034 (P48072) [N/A]
- Enlarged elevators S (S) [S]
- Reinforcing strips on both sides of the fuselage
- Single-stage engine nacelles K (K) [K]
- 'Thimble' radome (although some had this faired in) P72034 (P48072) [N/A]
- Dipole (APS-4) on centreline, under cockpit, aft of cannon ports
- 4 blade propeller P72034 (P48072) [N/A]
- Five stack exhausts K (K) [N/A]
- Folding outer wing panels. P7234 (P4872) [N/A]
- Reduced main wheel size with square tread P7234 (P4834) [N/A]

Note: Use Paragon conversion set P7234 (P4834), N/A in 1/32nd scale
(7). Usually the Sea Mosquito had standard rubber-in-compression undercarriage units. However Lockheed oleo-pneumatic units were fitted and this resulted in the oleo legs being round in cross-section. You will have to effectively rebuild the kits oleo legs to replicate this. The type also had the enlarged elevator horn balances and these too will have to be created by modifying the kit parts.

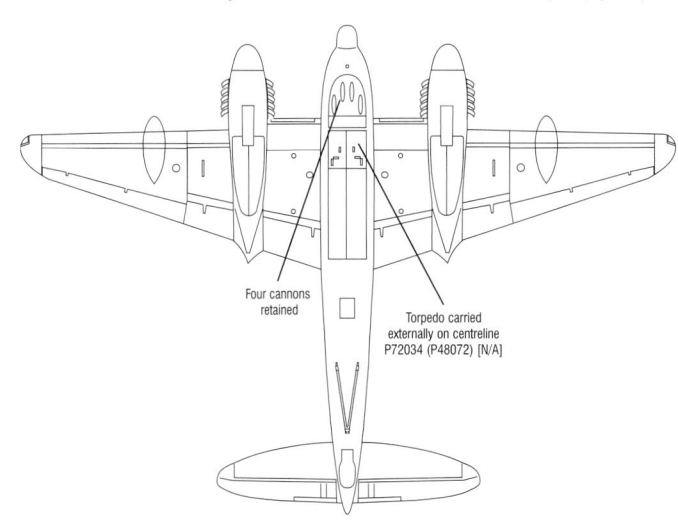

- Four cannons retained
- Torpedo carried externally on centreline P72034 (P48072) [N/A]

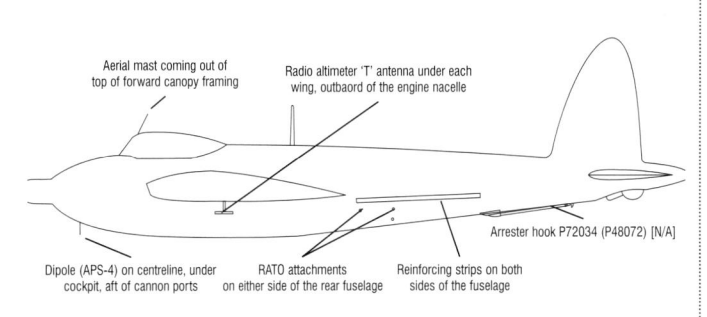

- Aerial mast coming out of top of forward canopy framing
- Radio altimeter 'T' antenna under each wing, outboard of the engine nacelle
- Arrester hook P72034 (P48072) [N/A]
- Dipole (APS-4) on centreline, under cockpit, aft of cannon ports
- RATO attachments on either side of the rear fuselage
- Reinforcing strips on both sides of the fuselage

Sea Mosquito • TR Mk 33 (#2)
Kit: A (A) [R] Same as TR Mk 33 except;

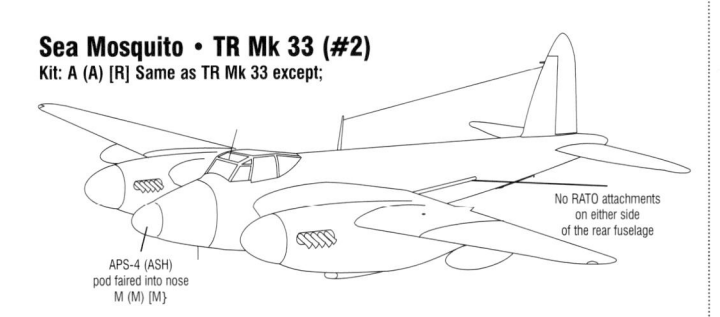

- APS-4 (ASH) pod faired into nose M (M) [M]
- No RATO attachments on either side of the rear fuselage

Sea Mosquito • TF Mk 37
Kit: A (A) [R]

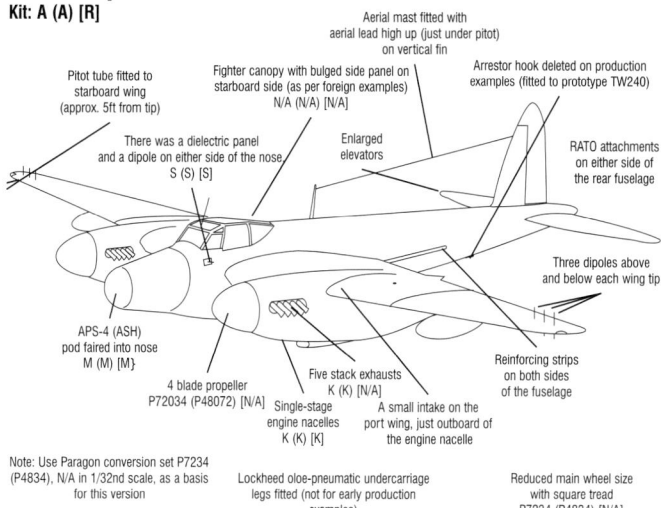

- Pitot tube fitted to starboard wing (approx. 5ft from tip)
- Aerial mast fitted with aerial lead high up (just under pitot) on vertical fin
- Fighter canopy with bulged side panel on starboard side (as per foreign examples) N/A (N/A) [N/A]
- Arrestor hook deleted on production examples (fitted to prototype TW240)
- There was a dielectric panel and a dipole on either side of the nose. S (S) [S]
- Enlarged elevators
- RATO attachments on either side of the rear fuselage
- Three dipoles above and below each wing tip
- APS-4 (ASH) pod faired into nose M (M) [M]
- Five stack exhausts
- Reinforcing strips on both sides of the fuselage
- 4 blade propeller P72034 (P48072) [N/A]
- Single-stage engine nacelles K (K) [K]
- A small intake on the port wing, just outboard of the engine nacelle

Note: Use Paragon conversion set P7234 (P4834), N/A in 1/32nd scale, as a basis for this version

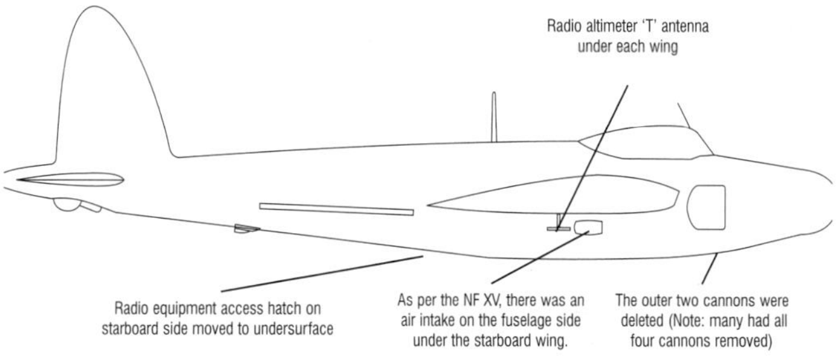

- Lockheed oleo-pneumatic undercarriage legs fitted (not for early production examples)
- Reduced main wheel size with square tread P7234 (P4834) [N/A]
- Radio altimeter 'T' antenna under each wing
- Radio equipment access hatch on starboard side moved to undersurface
- As per the NF XV, there was an air intake on the fuselage side under the starboard wing.
- The outer two cannons were deleted (Note: many had all four cannons removed)

Target Tug • TT Mk 35
Kit: M (A) [R] Standard kit except;

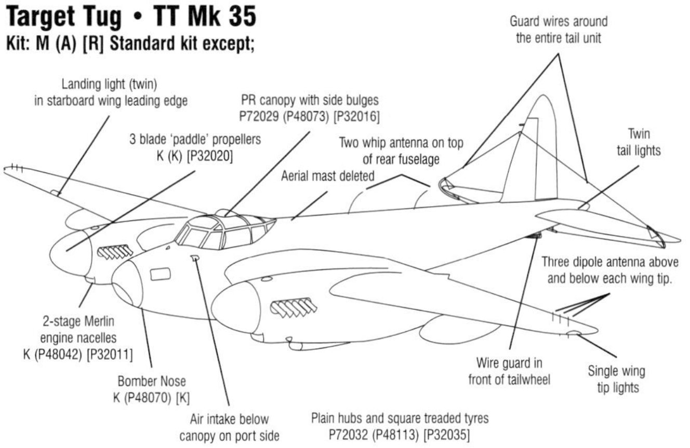

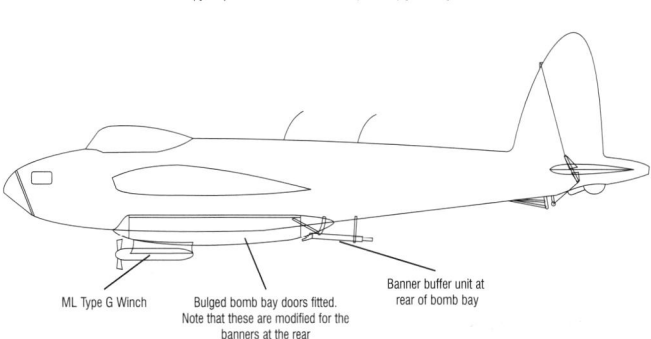

- Landing light (twin) in starboard wing leading edge
- PR canopy with side bulges P72029 (P48073) [P32016]
- 3 blade 'paddle' propellers K (K) [P32020]
- Guard wires around the entire tail unit
- Two whip antenna on top of rear fuselage
- Aerial mast deleted
- Twin tail lights
- 2-stage Merlin engine nacelles K (P48042) [P32011]
- Bomber Nose K (P48070) [K]
- Three dipole antenna above and below each wing tip.
- Air intake below canopy on port side
- Plain hubs and square treaded tyres P72032 (P48113) [P32035]
- Wire guard in front of tailwheel
- Single wing tip lights
- ML Type G Winch
- Bulged bomb bay doors fitted. Note that these are modified for the banners at the rear
- Banner buffer unit at rear of bomb bay

Modelling the Mosquito • Understanding the Subject

Target Tug • TT Mk 39
Kit: M or A (A) [R] Standard kit except;

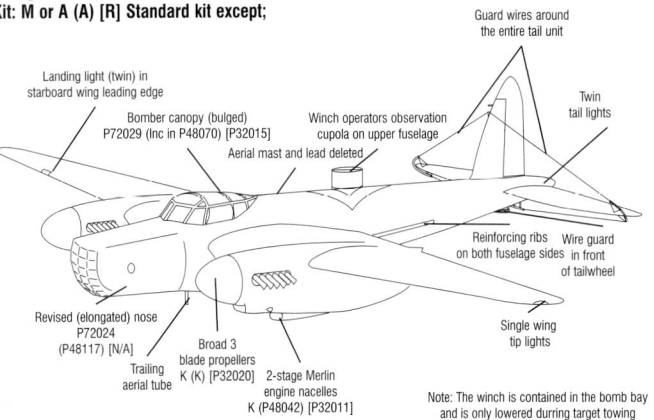

- Landing light (twin) in starboard wing leading edge
- Bomber canopy (bulged) P72029 (Inc in P48070) [P32015]
- Winch operators observation cupola on upper fuselage
- Aerial mast and lead deleted
- Guard wires around the entire tail unit
- Twin tail lights
- Reinforcing ribs on both fuselage sides
- Wire guard in front of tailwheel
- Single wing tip lights
- Revised (elongated) nose P72024 (P48117) [N/A]
- Trailing aerial tube
- Broad 3 blade propellers K (K) [P32020]
- 2-stage Merlin engine nacelles K (P48042) [P32011]
- Note: The winch is contained in the bomb bay and is only lowered durring target towing
- Plain hubs and square treaded tyres P72032 (P48113 or TD48017) [P32035]

Trainer • T Mk III
Kit: A (A) [R] Single-stage engine nacelles

- Twin landing light unit in starboard wing leading edge
- Fighter canopy
- Two whip antennas on spine
- Dual controls in cockpit. Tutor had a sliding seat fitted in original engineers position.
- Aerial mast deleted
- 3 blade 'paddle' propellers K (K) [P32020]
- Single-stage engine nacelles K (K) [K]
- Machine gun armament deleted (Note some versions retained it for gunnery training)
- Unshrouded 5 stack exhausts K (K) [N/A]
- Universal carrier on each wing allowed drop tanks or bombs to be carried. Drop tank K (P4877) [P32021] Bombs K (K) [N/A]
- Single wing tip lights
- Plain hubs and square treaded tyres P72032 (P48113) [P32035]
- Cannons deleted

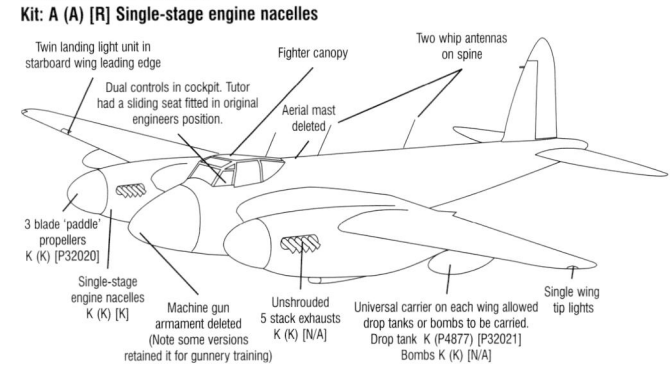

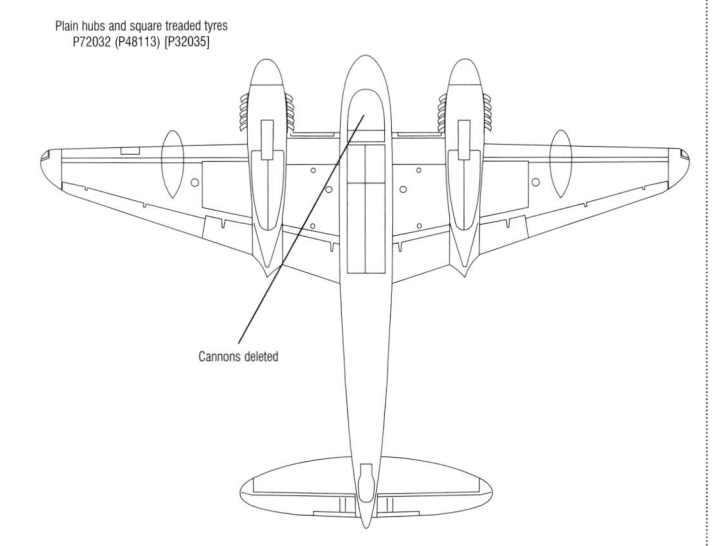

Trainer • T Mk 22/27 (Canada)
Kit: A (A) [R]

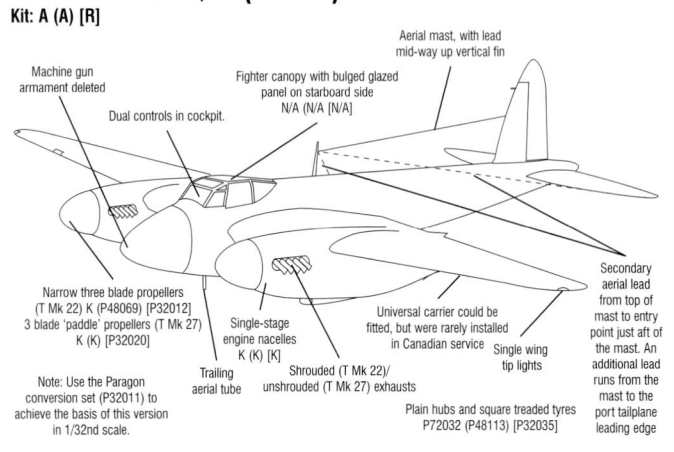

- Machine gun armament deleted
- Dual controls in cockpit.
- Fighter canopy with bulged glazed panel on starboard side N/A (N/A [N/A]
- Aerial mast, with lead mid-way up vertical fin
- Narrow three blade propellers (T Mk 22) K (P48069) [P32012] 3 blade 'paddle' propellers (T Mk 27) K (K) [P32020]
- Single-stage engine nacelles K (K) [K]
- Trailing aerial tube
- Universal carrier could be fitted, but were rarely installed in Canadian service
- Shrouded (T Mk 22)/ unshrouded (T Mk 27) exhausts
- Single wing tip lights
- Secondary aerial lead from top of mast to entry point just aft of the mast. An additional lead runs from the mast to the port tailplane leading edge
- Plain hubs and square treaded tyres P72032 (P48113) [P32035]
- Note: Use the Paragon conversion set (P32011) to achieve the basis of this version in 1/32nd scale.

Trainer • T Mk 29 (Canada)
Kit: A (A) [R]

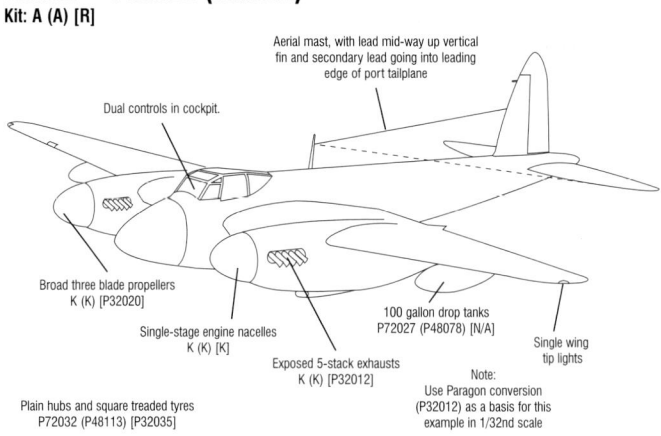

- Dual controls in cockpit.
- Aerial mast, with lead mid-way up vertical fin and secondary lead going into leading edge of port tailplane
- Broad three blade propellers K (K) [P32020]
- Single-stage engine nacelles K (K) [K]
- Exposed 5-stack exhausts K (K) [P32012]
- 100 gallon drop tanks P72027 (P48078) [N/A]
- Single wing tip lights
- Plain hubs and square treaded tyres P72032 (P48113) [P32035]
- Note: Use Paragon conversion (P32012) as a basis for this example in 1/32nd scale

Trainer • T Mk 43 (Australia)
Kit: A (A) [R]

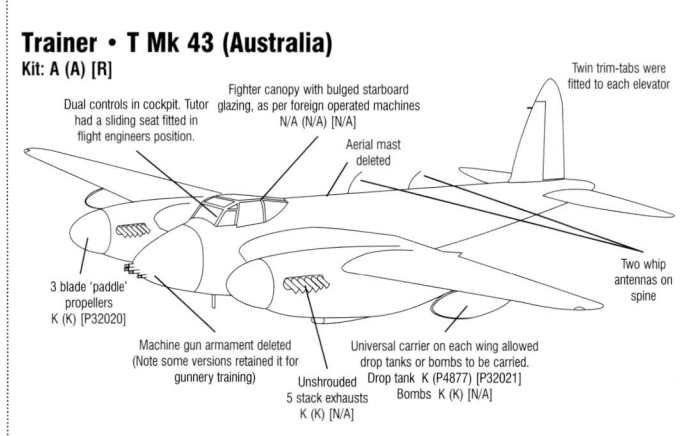

- Dual controls in cockpit. Tutor had a sliding seat fitted in flight engineers position.
- Fighter canopy with bulged starboard glazing, as per foreign operated machines N/A (N/A) [N/A]
- Twin trim-tabs were fitted to each elevator
- Aerial mast deleted
- 3 blade 'paddle' propellers K (K) [P32020]
- Machine gun armament deleted (Note some versions retained it for gunnery training)
- Unshrouded 5 stack exhausts K (K) [N/A]
- Universal carrier on each wing allowed drop tanks or bombs to be carried. Drop tank K (P4877) [P32021] Bombs K (K) [N/A]
- Two whip antennas on spine

Chapter 10

Detailing

Modelling the Mosquito

Chapter 11

One of the most difficult areas to deal with in any modelling project is the details. What precisely is in the cockpit? What do the interior of the wheel wells look like? etc are all questions which make modellers as must researchers as historians. It can be a long drawn out process gathering all the information you need to attempt detailing any subject. What we will offer in the Datafile series is a concise (ish!) section dealing with all those areas of the subject that you will be wanting to know about.

Cockpit Interior • 1

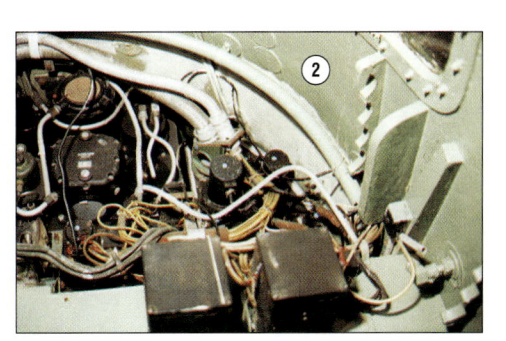

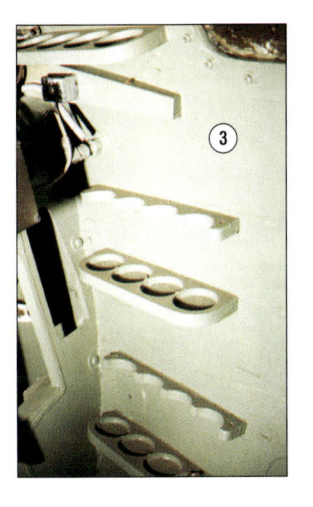

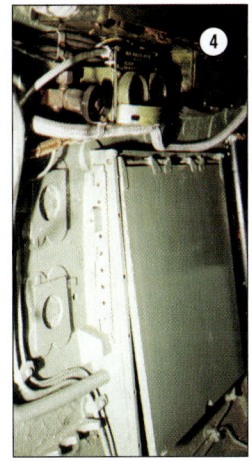

The Prototype: W4050

The prototype as it stands today has undergone a massive numbers of changes and in many ways it no longer represents itself, as first flown! The prototype is housed in the Mosquito Museum, London Colney.

• **1** This is the view from the back of the instrument panel. The mass of piping and electrical cable is common for all bomber versions and it is an area which most modellers miss (or choose to!)

• **2** Moving round to the starboard side of the nose area. Here you can see the instrument panel and the bulkhead and flare racks on the fuselage side.

• **3** These are the three sets of flare racks on the starboard side of the nose. This is not common to the bomber variants, as in later versions this area was covered in electrical equipment or the bombing computer.

• **4** Looking through the crawl-way into the main cockpit area, this is the foldaway chart table on the port sidewall.

• **5** Looking up above the crawl-through, this is the back of the instrument panels and their associated pipework.

• **6** Above the chart table on the port sidewall is this little set of dials. This is the oxygen control panel and it comprises the oxygen tank level and a delivery gauge.

• **7** An overall look at the instrument panel and control column. The plastic wrapping on the control yoke has broken up and parts have fallen off, but the overall shape is indicative of most of the early bomber versions.

• **8** On the port sidewall, alongside the control column is the compass and throttle box. The throttle box is missing the plastic knobs on all of the levers and the unit would have originally been black.

Modelling the Mosquito • Detailing   81

Cockpit Interior • 2

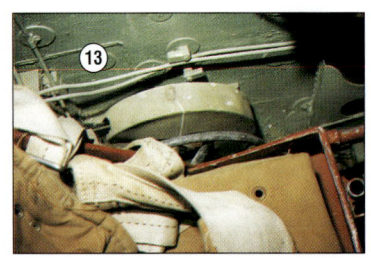

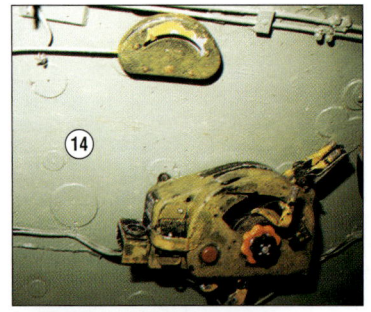

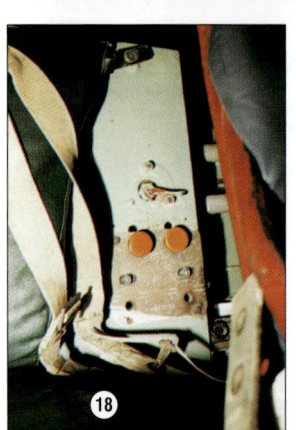

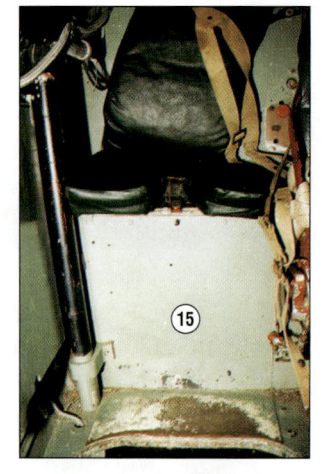

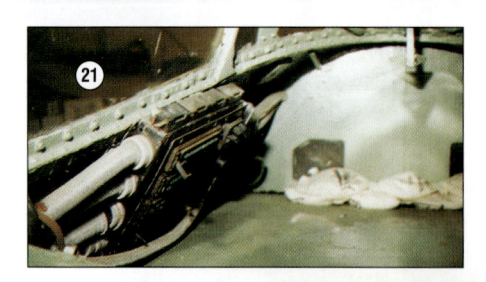

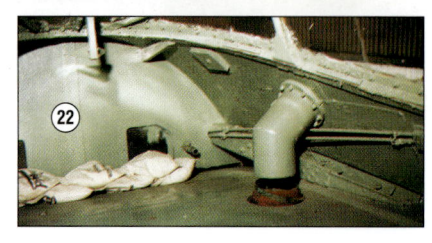

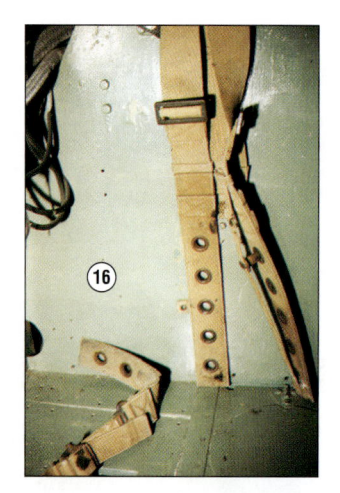

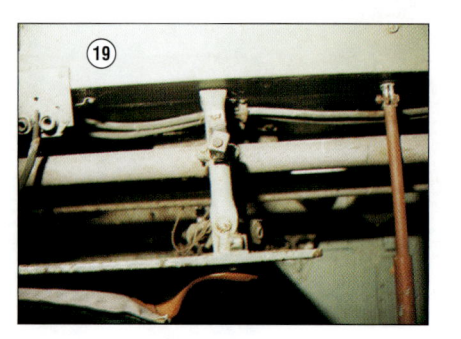

The Prototype continued...

• **9** A close-up of the P.4 compass fitted just below the instrument panel.

• **10** The rudder pedals.

• **11** Looking back from the rudder pedals, under the pilot's seat. Here you can see the control column linkage, the trim tab control (at the back) and the emergency hydraulic pump unit (left).

• **12** A look under the pilot's seat shows the elevator linkage from the control column, which runs from right to left.

• **13** Looking down alongside the pilot's seat, here can be seen the trim wheel and the seat height adjustment lever at the front of the seat pan.

• **14** Right alongside the pilot, on the sidewall, is the throttle box and above this is the trim position indicator.

• **15** Looking back from the access door, here is the bulkhead (front wing spar) on which the navigator sits. The tube to the left is for the trailing aerial wire.

• **16** This is the navigators 'seat' and harness. The simple Sutton harness is common for aircraft of this era and it comprises four straps with just a post and clip to secure them together.

• **17** To the left of the navigator is a small control panel which is for the fuel cocks.

• **18** A close-up view of the fuel cock control panel. The padded seat cushion for the navigator is in position in this shot, although we are unsure if this was never an 'official' fitment.

• **19** This is the view looking directly down on the back of the armour plate behind the navigator. The supporting strut is visible, as is the one for the pilot's seat to the right.

• **20** Looking behind the pilot's seat, here you can see the support strut for the armoured plate, as well as the control linkage and rods for the ailerons and flaps.

• **21** A look back into the rear of the cockpit. This is in fact the roof of the bomb bay area and it is devoid of all equipment in the prototype. Note the two clear panels in the rear bulkhead. This is with regard to the trials when other members of the D.H. team were carried during flights to look into the tailwheel problems etc. The large black panel to the left is the fuse box, an item which in production versions moved to the starboard sidewall alongside the navigator.

• **22** This is the port side of the rear of the cockpit. The pipe is the filler port for the fuel tank, although the lower section is not connected now.

Cockpit Interior • 3

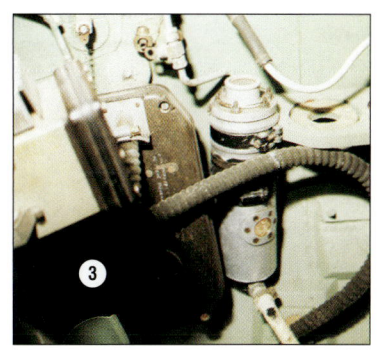

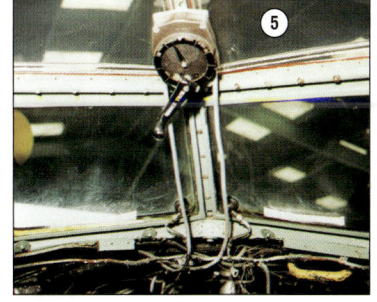

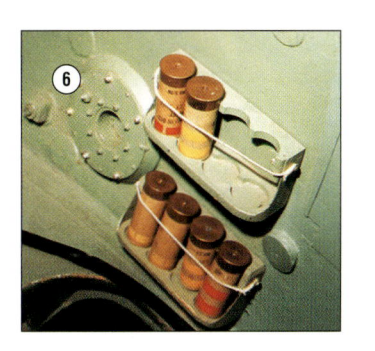

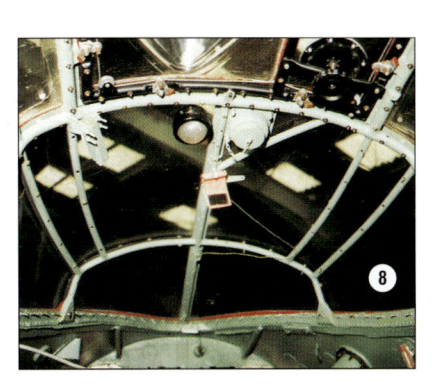

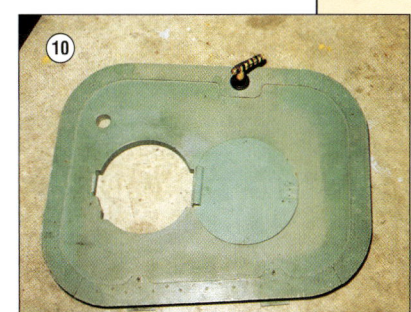

B Mk 35: (TA634)
Housed at Salisbury Hall.

• **1** This is the crew access door on the bomber version. Note the normal opening handle on the lower edge, and the foot operated emergency release lever on the top edge. The glazed port in this door is for the navigator to use the drift sight through.

• **2** Looking forward into the nose area, on the starboard side, is this rack. It is designed to hold oxygen bottles and the padded cushion on the top is for the navigator to lean against while he is kneeling in the nose.

• **3** Looking into the nose, on the port side, just forward of the instrument panel. Here you can see an oxygen economiser (far left) and the dry air filter unit.

• **4** On the opposite side of the nose area, above the oxygen storage rack, is another oxygen economiser.

• **5** Looking directly up onto the cockpit. Here you can see the rudder trim control in the centre of the windscreen. Note the pipes connected to each glazed panel, this is for the 'dry-air' units fitted throughout.

• **6** Just inside the access door, on the starboard sidewall is this rack for flares.

• **7** This view with the pilot's seat removed, shows the control surface linkage.

• **8** A view right up into the canopy. Note the light on the centreline and the little tab hanging down to the right of it. This is the release toggle for the dinghy which is stowed in the upper decking behind the cockpit.

• **9** This is the emergency escape panel in the upper canopy. Note the yellow release lever strapped in place on the front edge and the 'PR' bulge in the centre

• **10** The inside of the crew access door is usually covered with this wooden panel. The hinged circular panel to the left is to use the drift sight through, or to release the door from the outside.

• **11** Looking up into the crew access door, you can see the vacuum control panel on the front spar. The pilot's seat is not fitted in this shot.

Modelling the Mosquito • Detailing 83

Cockpit Interior • 4

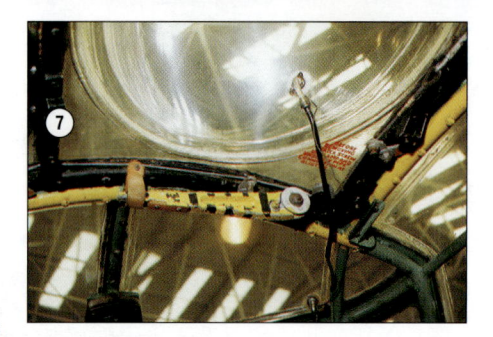

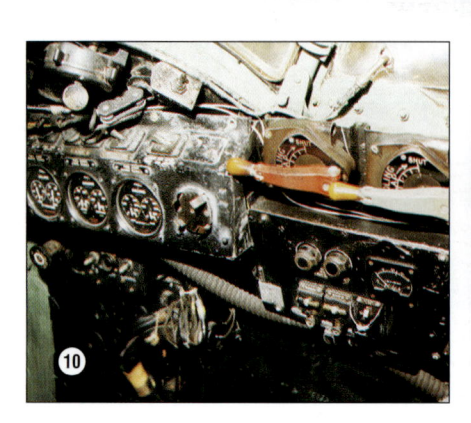

B Mk 35: (TJ138)
Housed at the Aerospace Museum, Cosford.

• **1** The control yoke.

• **2** This view shows the throttle box and the P series compass on the port sidewall.

• **3** This is the edge of the main instrument panel, here you can see the air filter switch in the middle, just below the undercarriage levers.

• **4** The starboard side of the nose in this version is still very much in TT Mk 35 configuration (to which this machine was converted in the 1950s). The storage rack for the oxygen bottles and the oxygen economiser can be clearly seen and below it are the emergency axe and the stowage straps which held the winch operators parachute in position.

• **5** On the edge of the crew access hatch, to the starboard side, is this Methyl-Bromide fire extinguisher.

• **6** Looking up into the canopy, you can see the cockpit lamp and dimmer switch. The larger circular panel, with a screw-on cover, is for the flare pistol.

• **7** This is the forward edge of the emergency escape panel in the top of the canopy. Here you can see the release handle held in position with a leather strap. Of note is the pipe fitted to the 'dry-air' PR bulge.

• **8** An overall view of the main instrument panel. Note the lamps fitted to the top edge of the canopy frame and the colour coded dials on the far left. (blue for coolant, yellow for oil and red for boost).

• **9** The cluttered starboard sidewall. Note the large distribution panel on the far right.

• **10** A closer view of the starboard sidewall. The three dials to the left are for the fuel tanks and the two folded handles to their right are for opening the coolant flaps. Below these are the electrical fusing panel.

• **11** A look at the port side of the nose. Here can be seen the dry-air filter unit to the left and the rack for oxygen bottles.

• **12** This is a view directly down on the area under the pilot's seat. The seat itself is not fitted at this time so you can see the pilot's relief funnel and pipe leading into the relief bottle.

Cockpit Interior • 5

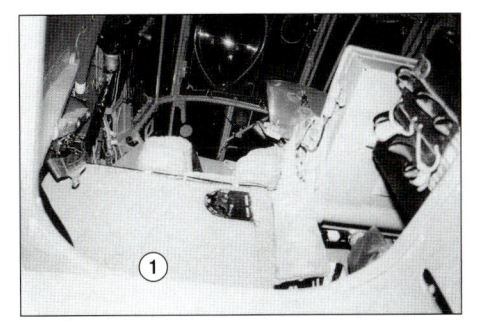

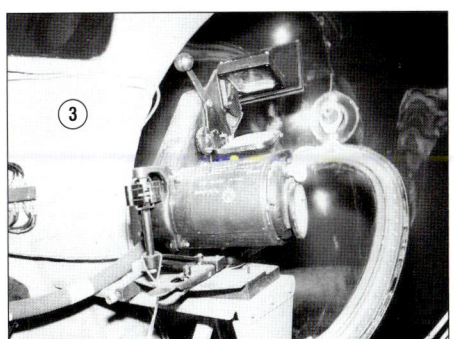

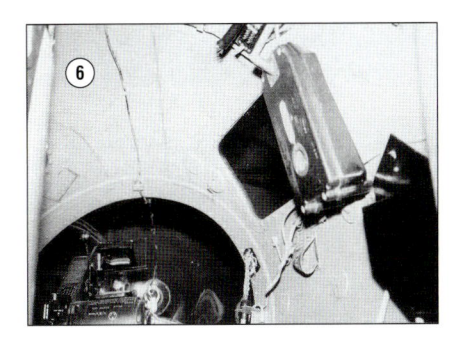

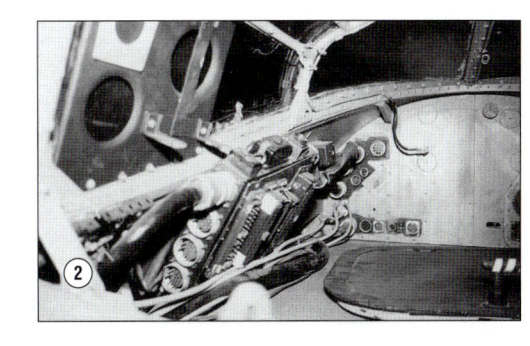

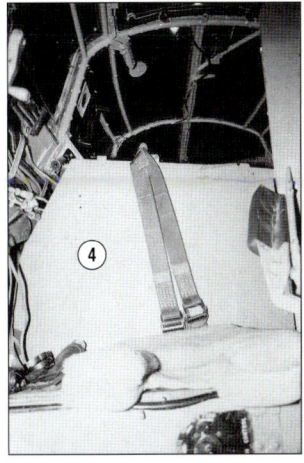

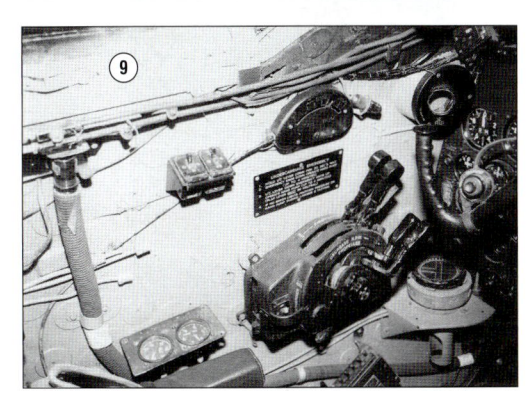

B Mk 35 (TA634)
Housed at the Royal Air Force Museum, Hendon.

- **1** This is the view up into the crew access hatch.
- **2** A look back along the starboard side. This area is dominated by a large electrical fusing box and a mass of electrical cabling. The panel laying on the rear floor is that from the inside of the access hatch.
- **3** This is the T-1 bomb sighting head fitted in the nose of the machine.
- **4** This is an overall view of the navigator's position. The straps and the furry seat are not original, these being modern examples from an ejector seat!
- **5** A overall view of the armour plate on the pilot's seat. The folding arm rest can be clearly seen along with the seat harness attached to the top of the armour.
- **6** This is the upper section of the starboard side of the nose. The oxygen economiser dominates this area.
- **7** This is a view of the small auxiliary panel in between the main panel and the starboard sidewall. This unit contains a beam approach indicator (left) and an outside air temperature gauge (right).
- **8** This view of the panel on the starboard side. This comprises three fuel gauges. On the top are the IFF destruction switches and above the unit is the morse key. The odd circular panel with projecting clips to the far right is a watch holder.
- **9** An overall view of the port sidewall. Here you can see the throttle box, tail trim indicator and the pilot's oxygen pipe clipped to the sidewall.
- **10** This is the top corner of the port sidewall. Here you can see the instrument panel and control yoke, and to the left is the cold air punkha-louvre.
- **11** A look back to the rear of cockpit area. Here you can see a mass of electrical connectors on the rear bulkhead, although none of the radio equipment is fitted.

Radio & Radar Equipment • 1

T.1154 Transmitter

• **1** This is a top view of a T.1154 transmitter. Note the stencil which warns that the item is made of steel.

• **2** This is the back of the T.1154. Note the louvres and the pressed shape which increases the strength of the panel. The frames on either side are not applicable for the Mosquito, as similar mounting rails are carried on the bottom.

• **3** This is the right side of the T.1154.

• **4** This is the left side of the T.1154. Note the plug-in points.

• **5** This is the front of the T.1154. Note the colour of the tuning knobs. The gaps on the lower right corner would usually have blocks and leads plugged into them when the unit was installed.

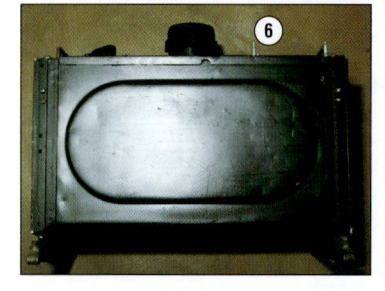

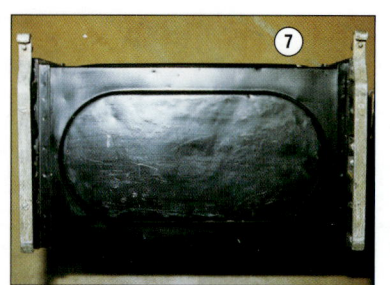

R.1155 Receiver

• **6** This is the top of the R.1155.

• **7** This is the back of the R.1155. The support frames on either side are not applicable to the Mosquito. The bottom face is identical to this.

• **8** This is the right side of the R.1155. Note the installation handle on the front edge.

• **9** This is the left side of the R.1155.

• **10** This is the front of the R.1155 receiver. The large scale dominates the unit and the plugs down in the bottom right corner would also have block connectors fitted into them once the unit was installed.

A.I. Mk X

• **11** This is the indicator unit for the SCR 720/729 (A.I. Mk X) which was fitted in the NF Mk XIX amongst others.

• **12** This is the side view of the indicator unit for the SCR 720/729 system.

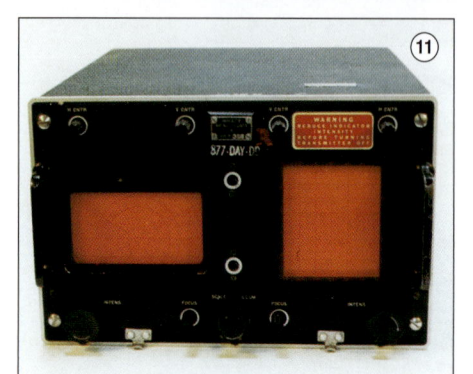

(All K.Real Collection)

Cameras • 1

F.24 Camera

• **1** This is the front view of a Williamson F.24 camera, as carried by the Mosquito, and it is fitted here with a 5" lens and 4" cone.

• **2** Left side view of the F.24 camera.

• **3** The back view of the F.24 shows the magazine and drive motor (top).

• **4** The right hand side view of the F.24. Here you can see the f-stop lever on the cone.

• **5** A top view of the F.24 camera showing the motor unit on the top and the electrical socket on its front edge.

• **6** The underside of the F.24. Note the wire locks on the main assembly bolts.

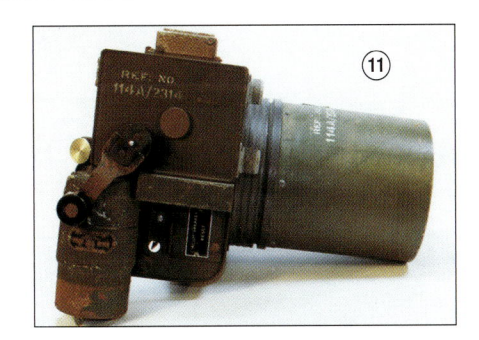

K-24 Camera

• **7** The Fairchild K-24 camera could be installed in the Mosquito in lieu of the Williamson F.24.

• **8** The left hand side of the K-24, without the film cassette attached. This unit is basically similar in shape to the one on the F.24. Note the manual winding handle on the top.

• **9** A shot of the back of the K-24. With the film cassette removed you can see the large film format on which these aerial camera worked.

• **10** The right hand side of the K-24. Note the motor unit on the top edge.

• **11** Top view of the K-24.

• **12** The undersurface of the K-24. Note the f-stop setting lever on the cone, allowing f2.5 to f5.6 to be achieved.

(All K.Real Collection)

Modelling the Mosquito • Detailing 87

Cameras • 2

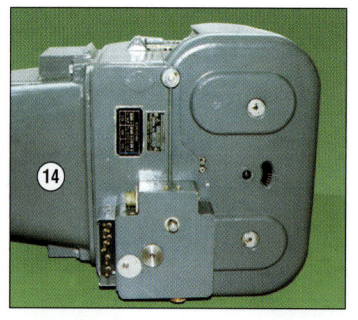

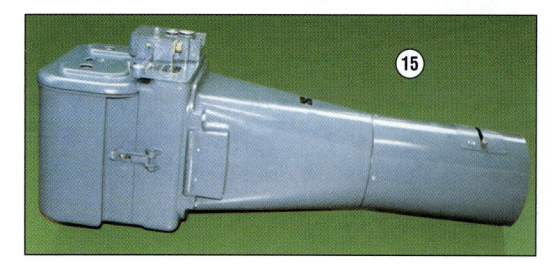

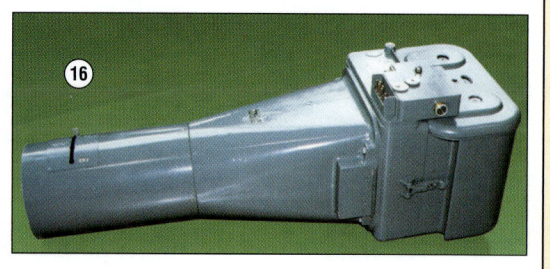

F.52 Camera

• **13** This is a view of the film cassette (right) and camera body (left) of an F.52 separated.

• **14** The top edge of the F.52 camera with the film cassette installed.

• **15** An F.52 camera with an 18" cone attached. It is unlikely that a Mosquito would accommodate this size of lens, but the camera body was identical to the type used and the lens cone would just be a smaller version of the one shown.

• **16** The left side of the F.52.

• **17** The back face of the F.52.

(All K.Real Collection)

Bomb Sights • 1

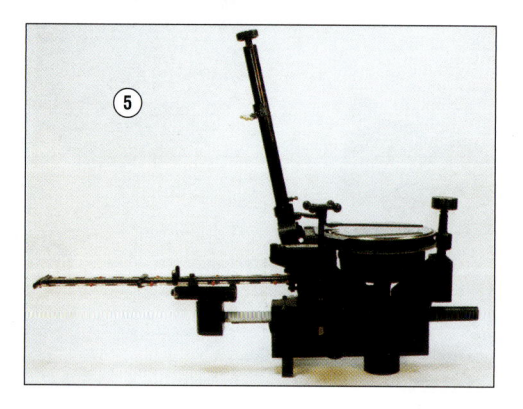

• **1** Top view of the early style of bomb sight as fitted to the Mosquito.

• **2** Side view of the early bomb sight.

• **3** Side view of the early bomb sight.

• **4** The later style of bomb sight fitted to the Mosquito. It is shown here with the vertical scale in the stowed position.

• **5** The left side of the later style of bomb sight, with the vertical scale in the operational position.

• **6** The right side of the later bomb sight.

• **7** Underside of the later bomb sight.

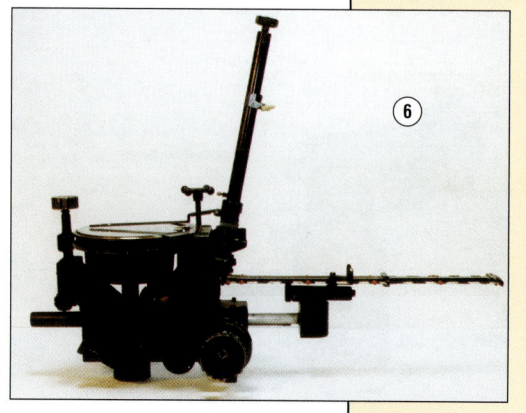

(All K.Real Collection)

Bomb Sights • 2

• **8** Later versions of the Mosquito used the T-1 bomb computer and this is the sighting head associated with that system.

• **9** The front of the T-1 sighting head.

• **10** The left side of the sighting head.

• **11** The rear of the sighting head.

• **12** A top view of the sighting head, with the shield removed from the reflecting glass.

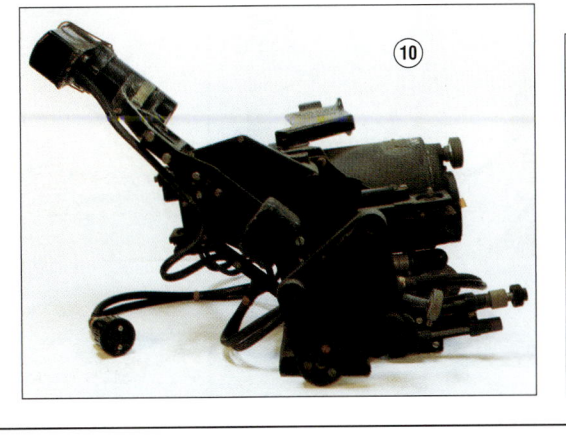

(All K.Real Collection)

Throttle Box • 1

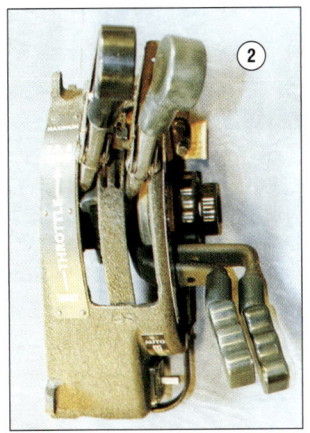

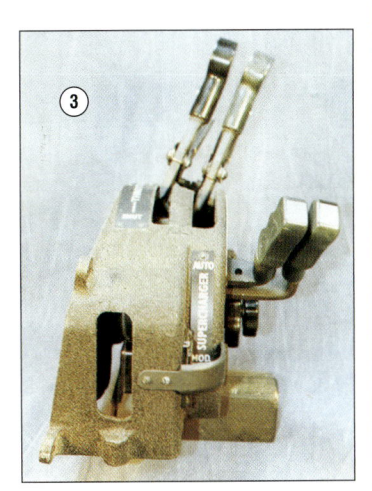

• **1** The throttle box fitted to the two-stage powered Mosquitos.

• **2** The top of the throttle box

• **3** The rear of the throttle box.

• **4** A close-up of the propeller control levers on the side of the throttle box.

• **5** Close-up detail of the throttle levers and emergency catches and stops.

(All K.Real Collection)

Modelling the Mosquito • DETAILING | 89

Undercarriage • 1

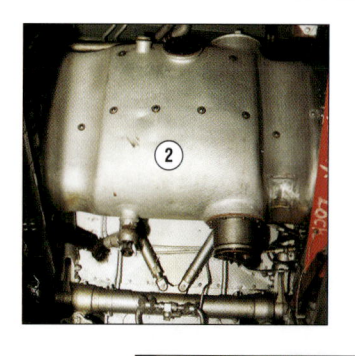

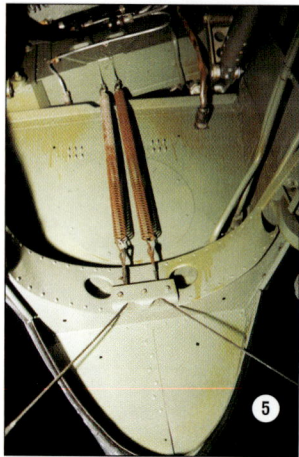

Details - B Mk 35

- **1** Detail of the fender over the main wheel.
- **2** The hydraulic header tank fitted to the front bulkhead in the undercarriage well.
- **3** The electrical distribution box installed above the hydraulic header tank.
- **4** The door tension springs attached to the rear bulkhead in the wheel well.
- **5** The tension springs and rear wires.
- **6** The rear strut (top) and radius rod (foreground).
- **7** The bakelite rubbing plates inside each door.
- **8** The undercarriage cross-bracing struts and door operating wires.
- **9** The roller, for the undercarriage door operating wire, fitted to the front of each undercarriage leg.
- **10** The door operating wires pulley, built into the front edge of the door, just aft of the undercarriage leg.
- **11** Wheel hub and brake line.

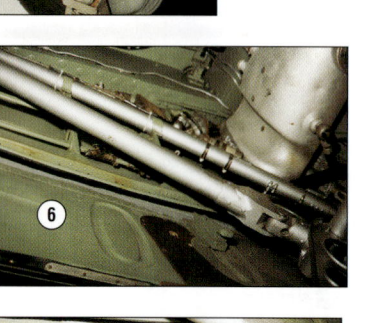

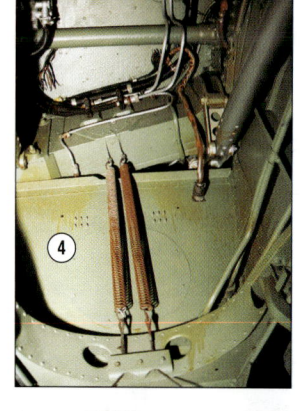

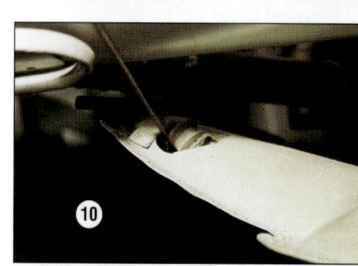

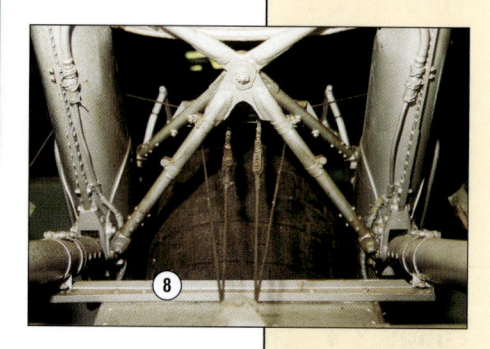

Fuel Tanks • 1

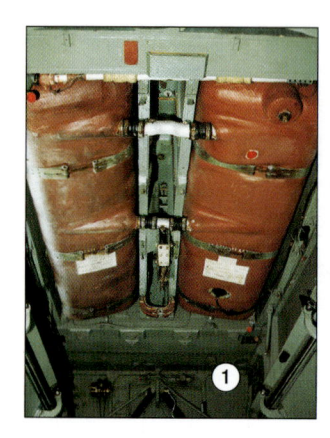

- **1** The standard fuel cells fitted in the bomb bay of a B Mk 35. Note that No.11 and 12 tanks would fit below these on long-range variants.
- **2** The interconnecting pipes between the two fuel cells.
- **3** The petrol cooler fitted to the starboard side of the bomb bay in all late (and high-altitude) Mosquitoes.

Chapter 11

Tail

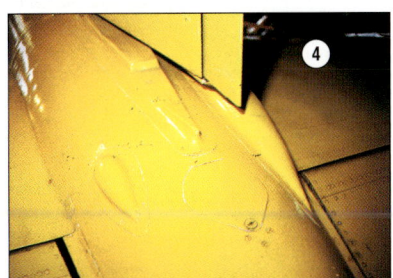

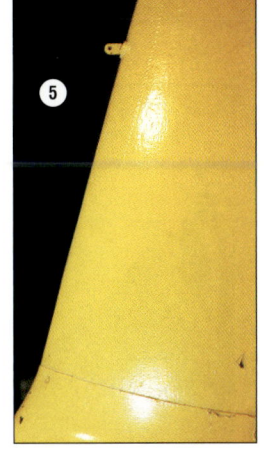

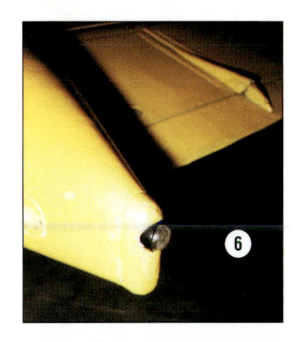

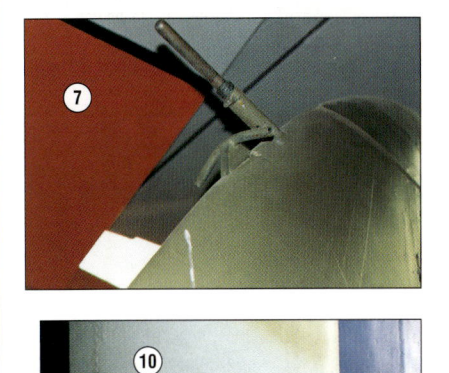

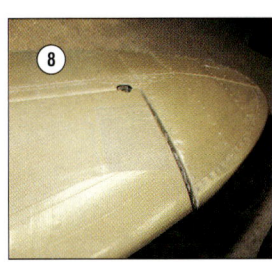

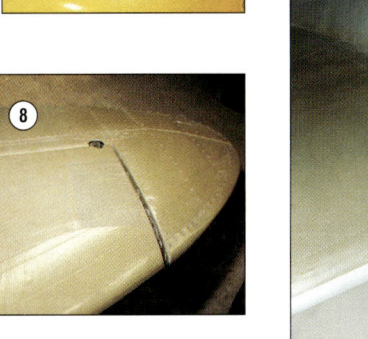

Prototype

• **1** The trim tab linkage on the starboard (upper) tail plane of the prototype.

• **2** The trim tab linkage on the port (lower) tail plane of the prototype.

• **3** The pitot static head on the leading edge of the vertical fin.

• **4** Viewed from the back, the tail cone can be seen to have bulges of different sizes on each side of the rudder. This is common to all Mosquitoes and they cover the elevator linkage levers.

• **5** The leading edge of the vertical fin, showing the location of the aerial lead pick-up mid-way up it.

• **6** The single tail light fitted to the prototype. Production versions had two lights (one above the other), one being formation (clear) and the other anti-collision (red).

TT Mk 35

• **7** The leading edge of the vertical fin of a TT Mk 35. Note the position and shape of the anti-fouling wire retainer just below the pitot static tube.

• **8** The upper surface of the tail plane on a TT Mk 35. Just visible is the patch applied to convert the type back to a B Mk 35, which was the location of the anti-fouling wire supports near the tip of the tail plane.

• **9** This gap in the leading edge of the tail planes is usually covered with doped fabric, however in this shot it is not and it gives you a good idea of the size of the gap involved.

• **10** A close-up of the gap under the rudder.

Wings • 1

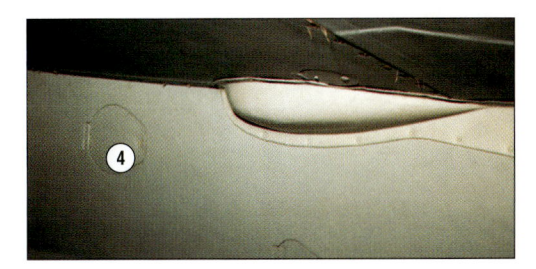

B Mk 35

• **1** This shot shows the raised spar caps applied to the wings of the Mosquito, a point which the Airfix kit over accentuates.

• **2** The metal access panel at the rear of the engine nacelle. This gives access to the flap linkage and control rods and as you can see the fit of this panel is not very flush.

• **3** The twin landing lamp installation in the leading edge of the starboard wing. This was installed in many late war and all post-war Mosquitoes, along with all those refurbished for sale abroad.

• **4** This bulge, under the centre line of each main plane has been referred to throughout the book, so here is a shot of it so you know what we are talking about. The bulge covered the main plane aft spar bolts.

Modelling the Mosquito • Detailing

Fuselage • 1

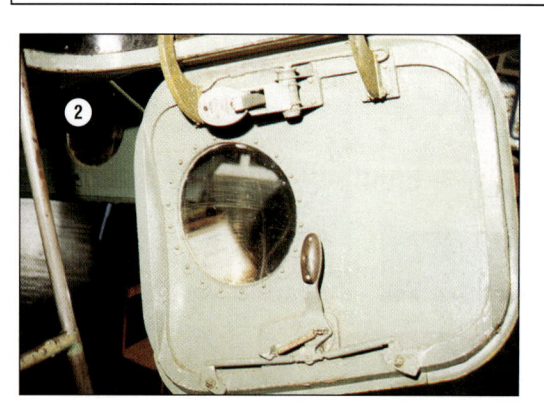

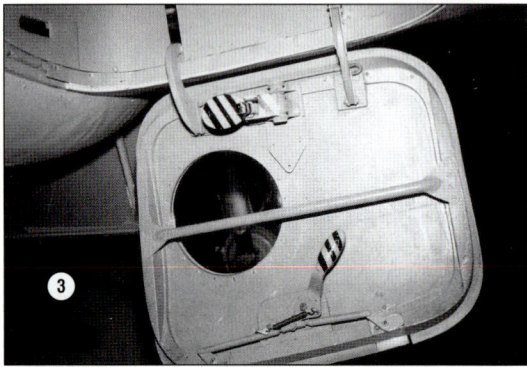

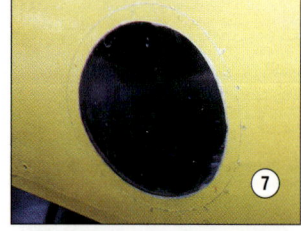

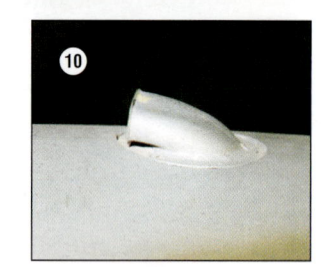

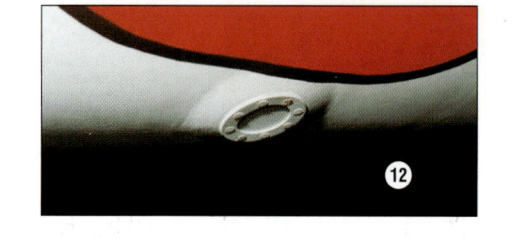

• **1** This is the outside of the crew access hatch on the prototype.

• **2** This is the inside of the crew access hatch of the prototype.

• **3** This is the access hatch interior in a production bomber variant.

• **4** This is all that remains of the trailing aerial tube on the prototype. This tube would extend about four feet longer than this, but you get an idea of the aerofoil section used and its position in relation to the crew hatch (right).

• **5** This is the fuel filler cover on the port lower fuselage side, about mid-chord.

• **6** On the port side of the fuselage, under the leading edge of the wing, are these two sockets on the prototype. I suspect they are ground electric and oxygen charging points.

• **7** This is the glazed port in the front edge of the bomb-bay doors.

• **8** This is the camera window which is now fitted to the underneath of the prototypes fuselage on the centreline, aft of the radio hatch.

• **9** This is the static vent on each side of the nose on bomber variants.

• **10** This is the cold air intake which is fitted to either side of the cockpit.

• **11** This is the radio hatch on the prototype, which has a glazed panel in it for a camera installation.

• **12** This is the dipole mount for the IFF aerial on the lower edge of the port fuselage side.

• **13** This is the radio equipment access hatch.

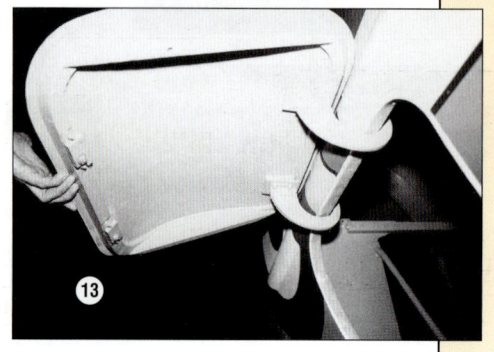

92 Chapter 11

Fuselage • 2

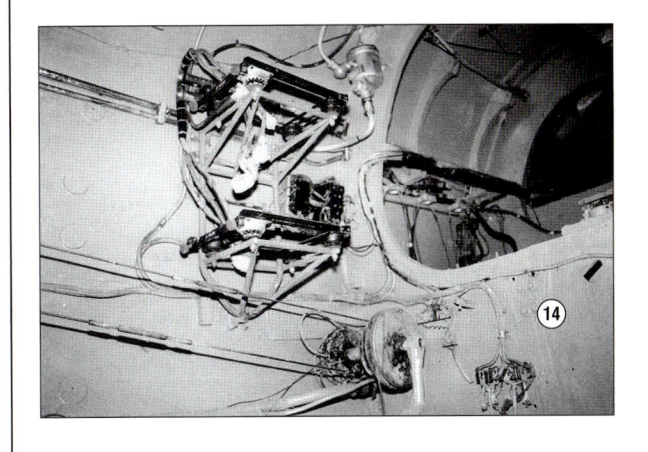

- **14** This is the view inside the radio compartment of a B Mk 35, looking forward. Although the radio equipment is not installed, the racks etc are all still in place.

- **15** This is the camera port in the front edge of the bomb doors on the prototype.

- **16** This is the petrol cooler air intake on the fuselage side of the prototype, below the wing (mid-chord). This unit is similar to the type fitted to later variants and high-altitude version, although the intake is usually screened.

Control Surfaces

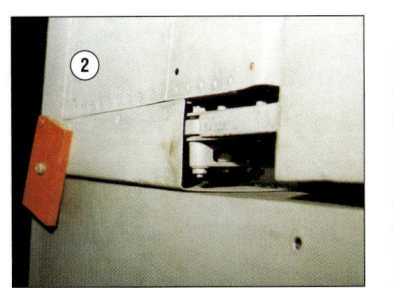

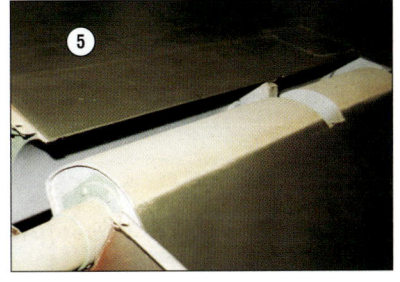

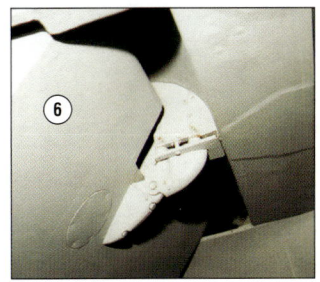

- **1** This is the aileron hinge just outboard of the flaps (viewed from underneath).

- **2** The outer hinge on the aileron.

- **3** The outer hinge of the inboard flap.

- **4** This view shows the inner flap in the down position and gives you some idea of the huge gap that is visible.

- **5** A look along the outboard flap, with it down, illustrates the large gap (and colour demarcation).

- **6** This is the outboard flaps hinge, with the flap down. As you can see the resultant gap is very prominent.

Engine Nacelles • 1

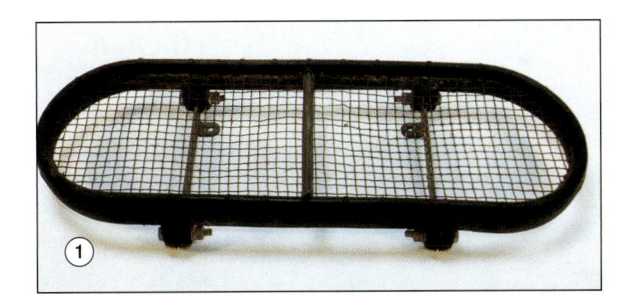

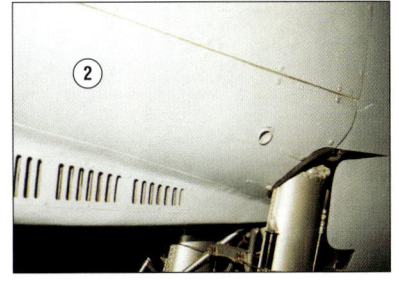

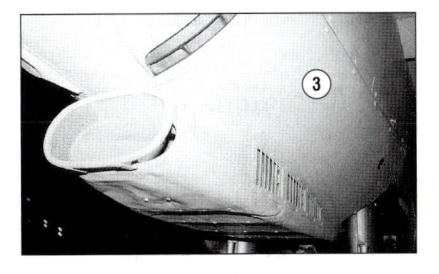

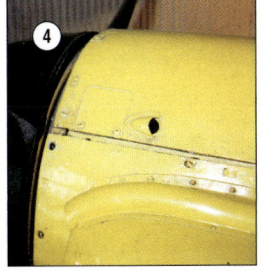

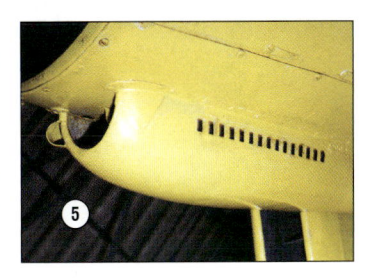

- **1** Detailed view of a 'snow guard' as fitted to the two-stage Merlin air intakes. This is a different shape from those fitted to the single-stage versions.

- **2** Details of the lower section of a two-stage nacelle. Note the louvers on the lower intake and the fuel dump pipe coming out to the right.

- **3** Overall view of the front of the two-stage nacelles intake (B Mk 35 illustrated).

- **4** On the upper panel of the prototypes engine nacelle there is this vent. It is inboard on both sides and it is just above the exhaust stacks.

- **5** A view up underneath the exhaust shrouds currently fitted to the Mosquito prototype. These are not applicable to the prototype, but are for all variants fitted with single-stage engines and shrouded exhausts.

Modelling the Mosquito • Detailing 93

Engine & Propeller

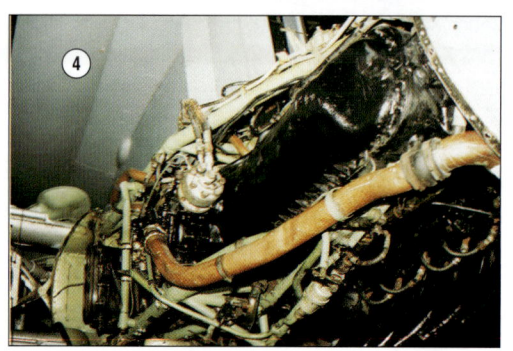

- **1** This shows the cut-out in the spinner for the broad style of propeller fitted to the Mosquito (B Mk 35 illustrated).

- **2** Starboard engine (outer side) of the Merlin 113 fitted to the B Mk 35.

- **3** Starboard engine (inner side) of the Merlin 113 fitted to the B Mk 35.

- **4** Starboard engine (underside) of the Merlin 113 fitted to the B Mk 35.

Bomb-bay & Bomb Carriers • 1

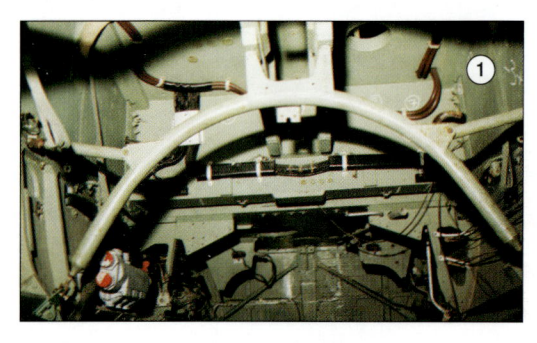

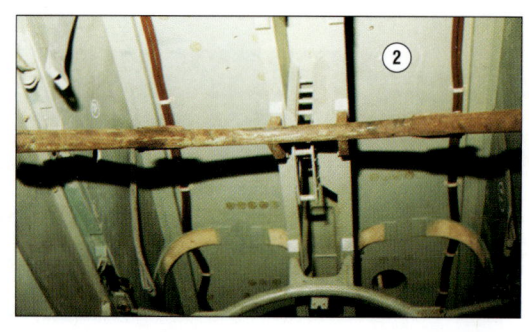

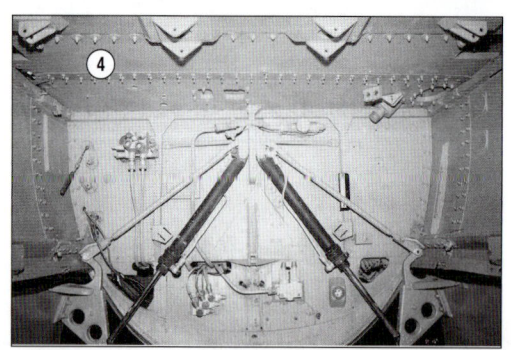

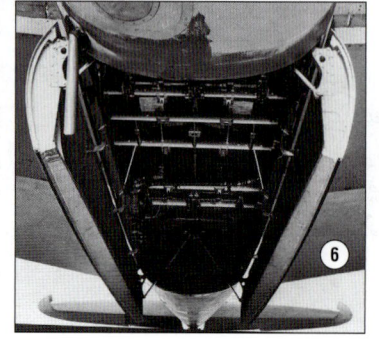

- **1** View inside the bulged bomb bay of a B Mk 35, looking aft. The large hoop in the foreground is the sway brace for the 4,000lb bomb.

- **2** A look up into the forward section of the bulged bomb bay.

- **3** The aft bulkhead of the bomb bay.

- **4** The forward bulkhead of the bomb bay.

- **5** A nice shot of armourers loading a 500lb bomb into the bomb bay of a B Mk IV. *(C.E.Brown)*

- **6** A view inside the open bomb bay of a B Mk IV. Note the trailing aerial tube in front of the left hand bomb door.

- **7** Armourers doing the final adjustments to the bomb load in a B Mk IV. *(C.E.Brown)*

Target Tug Equipment • 1

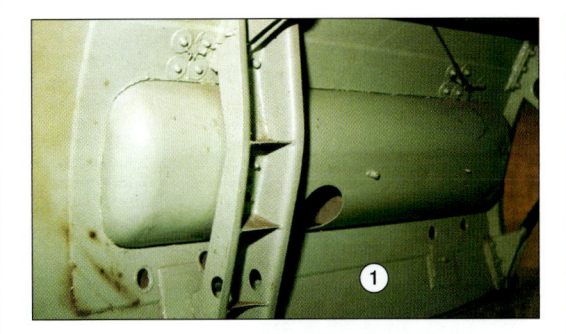

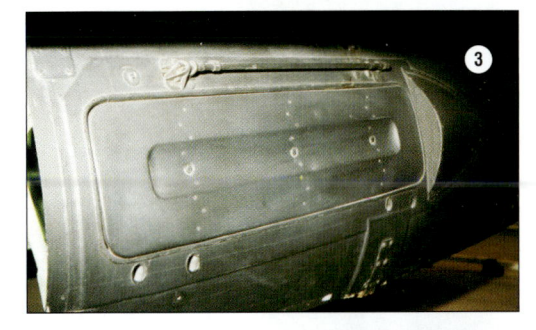

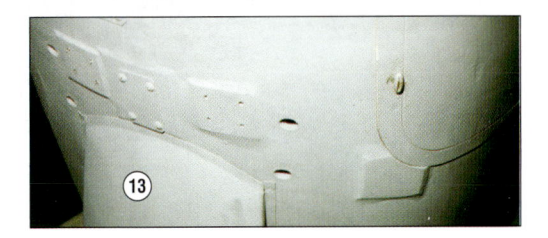

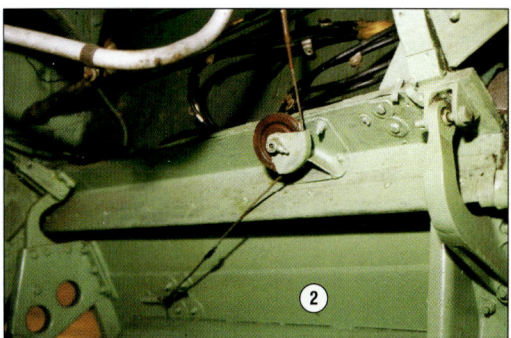

- **1** The banner pockets built into the aft section of the bulged bomb-bay doors.
- **2** The release control cable running from the cockpit to the banner pocket.
- **3** The banner pocket on the outside of the door. The centre section is under tension from internal springs and once the banner retaining straps are released, the banner is pushed out into the slipstream and drawn away from the aircraft.
- **4** The flattened section for the pylon of the ML winch, as viewed from inside the bomb bay. The cut-outs (now covered over with fabric) would have been for the supporting brackets for the winch, which was suspended from the usual bomb shackles in the top of the bomb-bay.
- **5** This is the outside of the bomb bay at the point at which the winch was fitted. This area has had all the holes for the winches support frames covered with fabric. The large bracket is actually to lock the bomb bay doors shut and it is repeated at the back of the doors.
- **6** The aft fairing of the bulged bomb bay in the target tugs is cut down as shown here and the rod you can see is the bar which retains the wire hoops fitted to hold the banner in place. This rod is sprung tensioned and pivots around its axis, when the retaining clip at the end is pulled back. This results in the strops slipping off and the banner falling away. The two projections at either end of the rod hold the loops in the end of the retaining strops.
- **7** These wire guides are fitted aft of the rear cut-outs.
- **8** The banner pockets on the doors operate in the same manner as described for the rear pockets and here you can see the holes through which the retaining strops come. They go around the banner and into the retaining rod which runs along the top edge of this area.
- **9** This is the mounting point, on the centreline, aft of the bomb-bay, where the buffer unit fits.
- **10** This is the prominent warning plate carried on the crew access door of all target tug Mosquitoes.
- **11** This is the wire guide on the undersurface of the tail. The wire simply passes through the tub and it is situated about 6" aft of the back of the tail wheel well.
- **12** This view (looking aft) shows the rear mounting bracket positions and the switch unit mount (left) which have all been plated over. The circle to the right is the cover for the tactical camera carried in the rear fuselage.
- **13** This is the view of the same area as previously shown, but looking forward now. The switch mounting as seen in the previous picture is on the top left and the other three blocks are for the buffer unit truss bar (either side) and the manual operating lever (central).

Modelling the Mosquito • Detailing 95

Miscellaneous • 1

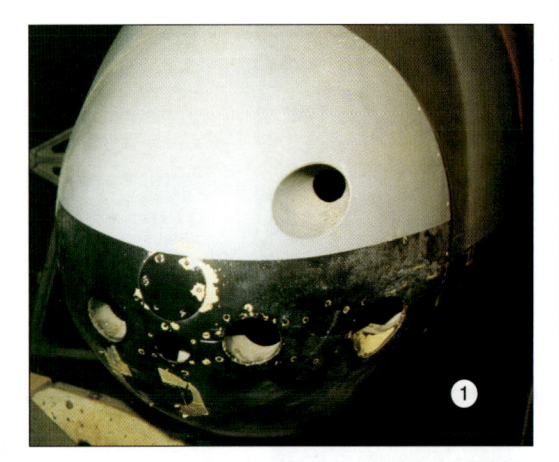

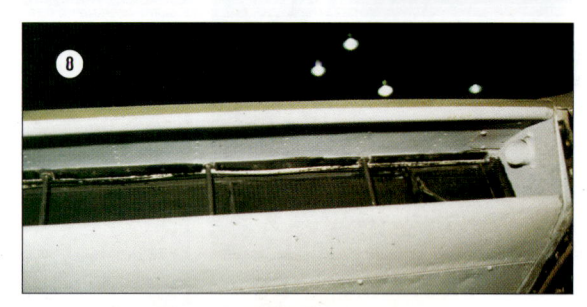

• **1** This is the forward nose of an FB Mk VI. The four gun ports run along the middle, while the small circular plate in the middle is the aerial mounting point for the A.I. Mk IV (and V) radar. The larger opening off-set to port is for the camera gun.

• **2** The inside structure of the doors which cover the machine gun bay in the nose. Note the simple hinge and clip attachments.

• **3** An unusual view inside the nose compartment of an FB Mk VI. With all the equipment removed you get an excellent idea of what the actual structure inside this area was like.

• **4** Nice clear shot of the standard tail wheel unit fitted to the Mosquito.

• **5** This is the door which covered the stowage location of the folding access ladder inside the forward edge of the entrance hatch of bomber Mosquitos.

• **6** This is the ladder stowage area with the door open.

• **7** A detailed view inside the radiator of the prototype.

• **8** A view into the leading edge radiator unit of a B Mk 35

• **9** This is the fuel dump outlet which is fitted at the back of each engine nacelle (outer face) of the prototype.

96 Chapter 11

Miscellaneous • 2

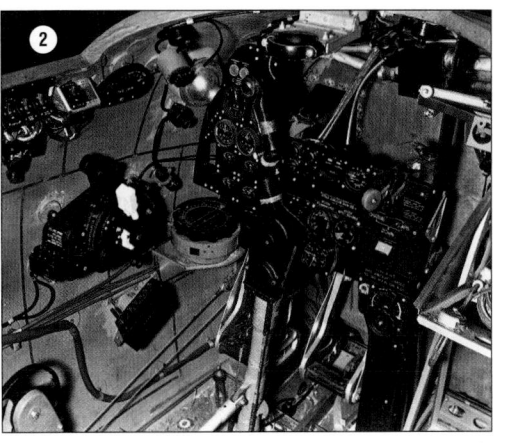

•1 A excellent shot of the cockpit area of a night fighter Mosquito during assembly. *(BAe)*

•2 Another good shot of the cockpit interior of a night fighter Mosquito during construction. *(BAe)*

•3 NS993 was later put into use by the KTA for development work with the new SM-1, a turbofan development of the Armstrong-Siddeley Mamba, which had been chosen for the new Swiss N-20 jet fighter-bomber project. In this shot the aircraft is shown fitted with an aerodynamic shape to test the effect on the aircraft in flight.

•4 This shows NS993 (B-3) with the SM-1 engine slung under the bomb bay for ground running trials.

•5 A close-up of the SM-1 under NS993. The engine unit is not fitted with the front section of the aerodynamic fairing.

•6 Although of poor quality this shot shows NT220 with the Uncle Tom rockets suspended underneath it at Boscombe Down for trials.

•7 A nice clear shot of the Merlin 114 installed in the Mosquito B Mk 35.

•8 During Firestreak missile trials De Havilland used this Mosquito B Mk 35 (TH988). The radar transmitter was carried in the ventral pod suspended under the bomb bay and the nose was modified to carry a large camera or IR emitter(?). *(D.Skeggs)*

•9 TH998 is seen here in flight at the RAeS garden Party held at Astwick Manor, Hatfield in 1953. *(D.Skeggs)*

Modelling the Mosquito • Detailing 97

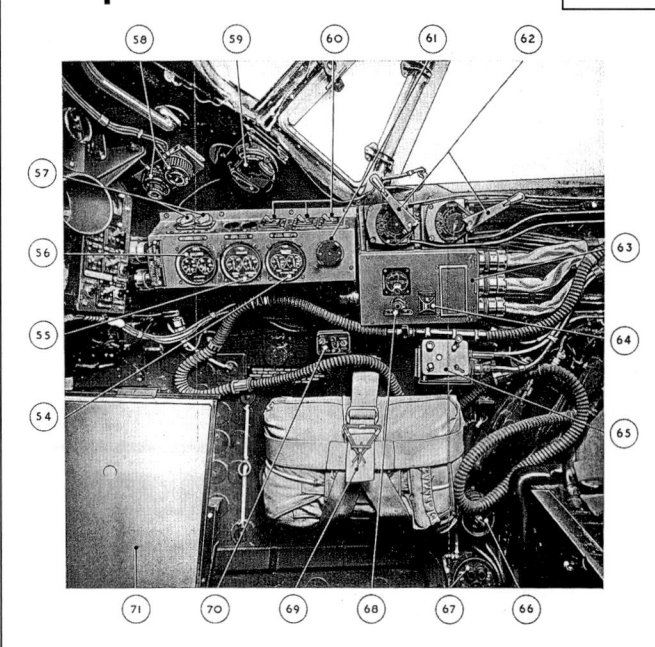

Cockpit Interior • 6

TT Mk 39
The starboard sidewall (Crown Copyright)
54. Fuel contents gauges, inner tanks
55. Fuel contents gauges, centre tanks
56. Fuel contents gauges, outer tanks
57. Port and starboard engine fire extinguisher push buttons
58. Dimmer switches (auxiliary)
59. Morse key
60. Identification lamp switch, navigation and IFF switches
61. Watch holder
62. Radiator shutter controls
63. Master junction box
64. Light switch
65. Z.B.X controller
66. 'WINDOW' launcher control switch
67. 'WINDOW' launcher master control
68. Generator warning light
69. Observer's parachute
70. A.P.X switch, G band control box
71. Chart board

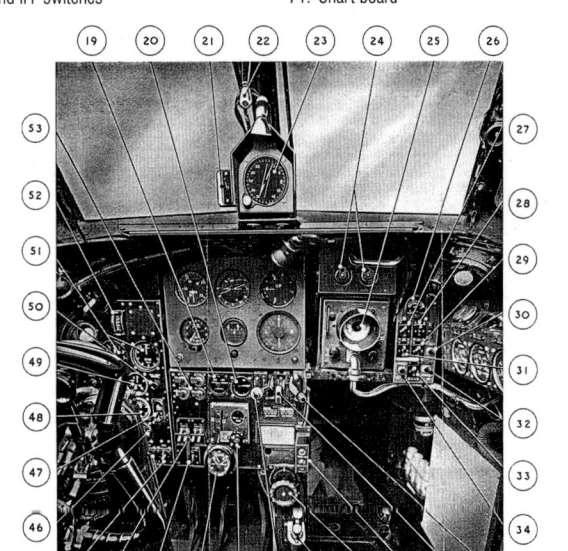

TT Mk 39
Starboard sidewall (Crown Copyright)
1. Beacon switch
2. I.F.F. switch
3. Intercommunication socket
4. VHF 1520 radio control unit
5. Cockpit lights master switch
6. Ultra-violet dimmer switches and cockpit flood lights
7. 'WINDOW' master switch
8. Elevator trimming tab position indicator
9. Press-to-mute and wing drop tank jettison switches
10. Emergency light switches
11. Cabin ventilator
12. Intercommunication receiver and call light box
13. Propeller control levers
14. Compass
15. Propeller and throttle levers friction controls
16. Seat adjusting lever
17. Throttle levers
18. Superchargers gear change switch

TT Mk 39
The main instrument panel (Crown Copyright)
19. Undercarriage position indicator
20. Flap position indicator
21. 'On-Off' switch for D.R. compass
22. Rudder trim tab control
23. D.R. compass repeater
24. Propeller feathering push buttons
25. Radio altimeter indicator S.C.R.718
26. Air temperature gauge
27. Pitot heat heater switch
28. Navigation lights switch
29. Starboard booster pump switch
30. VHF emergency switch
31. Port booster pump switch
32. VHF emergency switch
33. S.C.R.718 switch
34. Master switch for power unit
35. Flap selector lever
36. Undercarriage selector lever
37. Air-intake filter push buttons
38. Aileron trimming tab control and indicator
39. Windscreen de-icer pump
40. Bomb door and windmill arm control lever
41. Oxygen control panel
42. Triple pressure gauge
43. Master electrical services switch
44. Ignition switches
45. Port and starboard landing lamp switches
46. Starboard radiator coolant temperature gauges
47. Starboard oil pressure gauges
48. Starboard oil temperature gauges
49. Starboard boost pressure gauges
50. Fuel pressure warning gauges
51. R.P.M indicators
52. Pressure venting suction gauge
53. Engine starting push buttons and booster coil switches

B Mk XVI
Main instrument panel (Crown Copyright)
13. Press-to-transmit switch
14. Brake control
16. Bomb release button
17. Landing lamp switch
18. Radiator coolant temperature gauges
19. Oil temperature gauges
20. Oil pressure gauges
21. Fuel pressure warning lights
22. Boost pressure gauges
23. R.P.M. indicators
24. Instrument flying panel
25. Undercarriage position indicator
26. Flaps position indicator
27. Spare switches
28. Pitot-head heater switch
29. Immersed fuel pump switch
30. Navigation lights switch
31. Immersed fuel pump warning light
32. Rheostat for chart table floodlight
33. Air temperature gauge
34. Feathering buttons
35. DF visual indicator
36. Flaps selector lever
37. Undercarriage selector lever
38. Bomb door selector lever
39. Aileron trimming tab control and indicator
40. Windscreen de-icing pump
41. Bomb jettison control
42. Bomb containers jettison control
43. Pilot's oxygen regulator
44. Triple pressure gauge

Cockpit Interior • 7

NF Mk II
Port sidewall *(Crown Copyright)*

1. Elevator trimming tab control
2. Brake control
3. Control column
4. Cannon trigger
5. Camera gun button
6. Radio normal/special switch
7. Intercommunication switch
8. Beam approach switch
9. Elevator trim indicator
10. Mixture control lever
11. Supercharger gear change switch
12. Throttle levers
13. Mixture control friction adjuster
14. Throttle control friction adjuster
15. Propeller speed control levers
16. Compass light switch
17. Port instrument panel light switch
18. Engine instrument panel
19. Radio control box
20. Seat adjusting lever

NF Mk II
Main instrument panel *(Crown Copyright)*

21. Radiator temperature gauges
22. Oil temperature gauges
23. Oil pressure gauges
24. Boost pressure gauges
25. Fuel pressure warning lights
26. Engine R.P.M. indicator
27. Ventilator
28. Port instrument panel light
29. Boost control cut-out
30. Instrument flying panel
31. Centre instrument panel light
32. Rudder trimming tab control and indicator
33. Main services switches
34. Magneto switches
35. Engine starter switches
36. Booster coil switches
37. Propeller feathering switches
38. Undercarriage position indicator
39. Undercarriage selector lever
40. Flap selector lever
41. Flap position indicator
42. Gun master switch
43. Aileron trimming tab control and indicator
44. Triple pressure gauge
45. Oxygen regulator
46. Remote contractor switch
47. Machine gun firing control

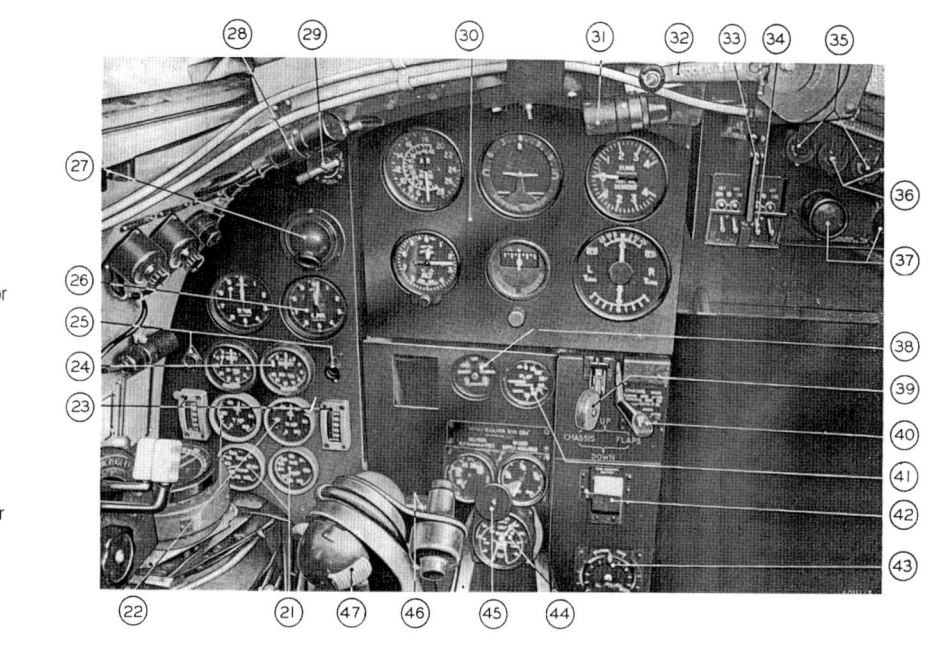

NF Mk II
Starboard Sidewall *(Crown Copyright)*

48. Radiator shutter switches
49. Navigation lamps switch
50. Camera gun switch
51. Contractor supply switch
52. Ultra-violet light switch
53. Pressure head heater switch
54. Generator switch
55. Navigation headlamp switch
56. R.3078 switch
57. R.3078 destruction switches
58. Fire extinguisher
59. Fuel contents gauges
60. Air temperature gauge
61. High pressure oxygen control valve
62. Oxygen regulator
63. Observer's intercommunication switch
64. Collapsible ladder
65. Cold air ventilating control
66. Windscreen wiper switch (replaced by rheostat on later aircraft)
67. Voltmeter
68. Identification switchbox
69. Formation lights switch
70. Emergency door release handle

Modelling the Mosquito • Detailing

Cockpit Interior • 8

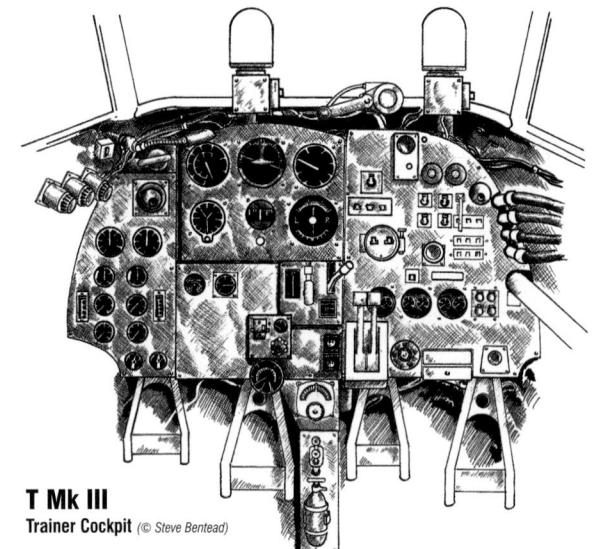

T Mk III
Trainer Cockpit (© Steve Bentead)

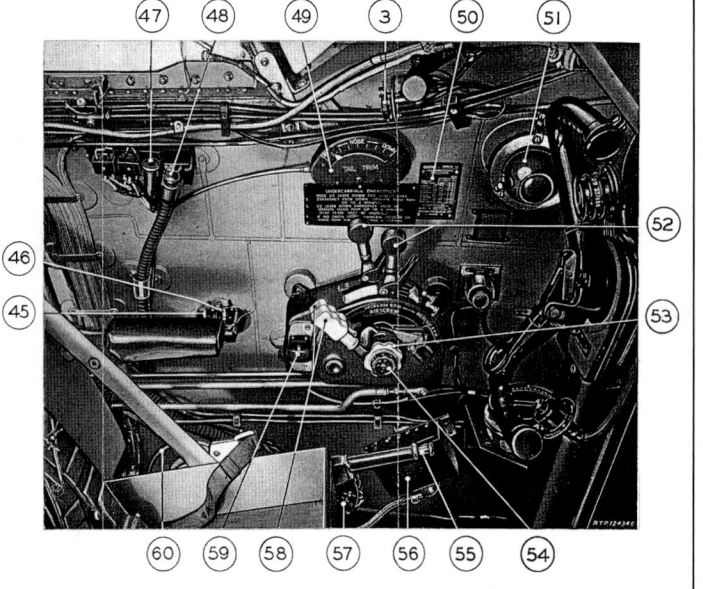

B Mk XVI
Main instrument panel (Crown Copyright)
1. Electrical services switch
2. Magneto switches
3. Drop tank jettison control
4. Left-hand floodlight
5. Booster coil switches
6. Electric starter switches
7. Rheostat for left-hand floodlight
8. Rheostat for right-hand floodlight
9. Rudder trim tab control and indicator
10. Right-hand floodlight
11. Chart table floodlight
12. Junction box B
13. Press-to-transmit switch
14. Brake control
15. Parking brake catch
16. Bomb release button

B Mk XVI
Starboard sidewall (Crown Copyright)
11. Chart table floodlight
12. Junction box B
32. Rheostat for chart table floodlight
61. Pressure cabin warning light
62. Pressure cabin altimeter
63. Cabin air pressure gauge
64. Oxygen line valve
65. Observer's oxygen regulator
66. Fuel contents gauges
67. Engine fire-extinguisher switches
68. Rheostat for DF visual indicator
69. I.F.F. detonator switches
70. I.F.F. master switch
71. Identification switchbox and key
72. Navigation headlamp switch
73. Identification colour selector switch
74. Radiator shutter controls and indicators
75. Voltmeter
76. Generator warning light
77. Rear lights switch
78. Switch and warning light for transmitter Type F
79. GP/VHF change-over switch
80. Trailing aerial winch
81. Stowage for signal cartridges

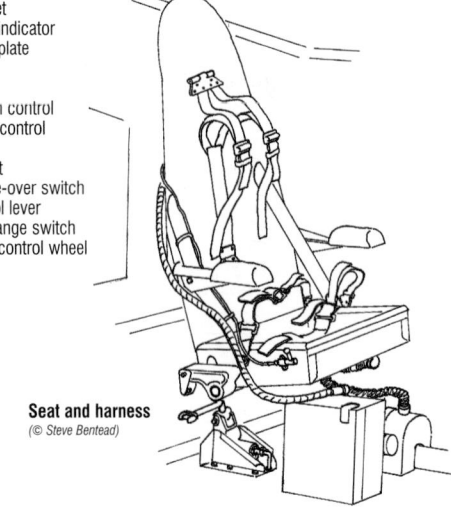

B Mk XVI
Port Sidewall (Crown Copyright)
3. Drop tank jettison control
45. I.F.F. 'D' switch
46. Beam approach switch
47. Intercommunication socket
48. Oxygen bayonet socket
49. Elevator trimming tab indicator
50. Engine limitation data plate
51. Ventilator
52. Throttles
53. Propeller levers friction control
54. Throttle levers friction control
55. Seat adjustment lever
56. Radio push-button unit
57. Pilot's GP/VHF change-over switch
58. Propeller speed control lever
59. Supercharger gear change switch
60. Elevator trimming tab control wheel

Seat and harness
(© Steve Bentead)

100 Chapter 11

Cockpit Interior • 9

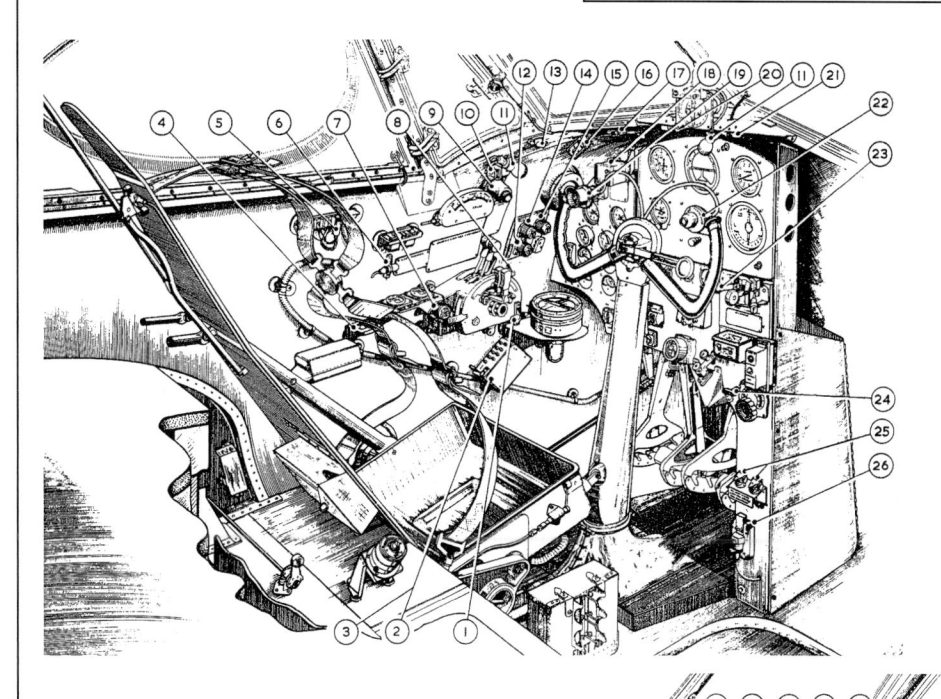

B Mk 35
Port sidewall and instrument panel (Crown Copyright)
1. Flood light for controller
2. Controller for VHF
3. Controller for VHF (Mod. 1446)
4. Distress switch
5. Pilot's intercommunication socket
6. Floodlamp for temperature gauges
7. Dimmer switch for floodlamp
8. Compass floodlight
9. Volume control (pre-Mod 1446)
10. Drop tank jettison switch
11. Ultra-violet floodlamps
12. Dimmer switch for items (1) and (8)
13. Port floodlamp
14. Dimmer switch for U.V. floodlamps
15. Dimmer switch for port floodlamp
16. Emergency floodlamp switch
17. Mechanical bomb release for 4,000lb bomb
18. Indicator unit, Type 237
19. Pilot's push switch for camera operation
20. Emergency floodlamp
21. Starboard floodlamp
22. Pilot's press-to-transmit switch
23. Bomb door selector lever
24. Mechanical bomb jettison toggle
25. Sockets for firing switch plug
26. Firing switch (locked in interlock firing position)

B Mk 35
Starboard sidewall (Crown Copyright)
1. Drift sight cover
2. Camera control unit
3. Camera heater switch
4. Air temperature gauge
5. Stowage for camera control unit leads
6. Bomb angle computer stowage
7. Stowage for inspection lamp
8. Stowage for inspection lamp extension lead
9. Indicating unit for A.R.I. 5610
10. Chronometer stowage
11. Pressure-head heater switch
12. Navigation lamps switch
13. Dimmer switch for instrument panel starboard floodlamp
14. Dimmer switch for chartboard lamp
15. Identification lamps switchbox
16. Navigator's transmit switch
17. Switch for I.F.F.
18. Selector switch (navigation head lamp-off-on-morse)
19. Selector switch, downward identification
20. Connecting socket for lead from wind finding attachment
21. Lamp for chartboard
22. Resin light
23. Transmitter Type F switch and indicating lamp
24. Chart board in stowage

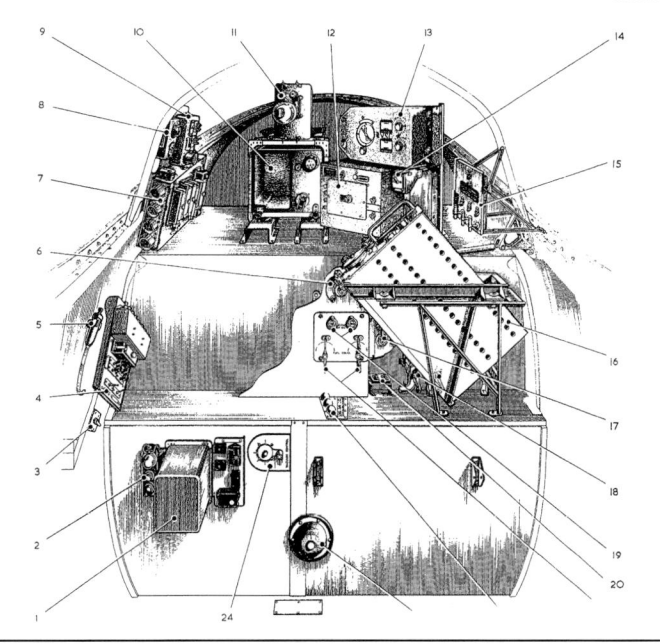

TT Mk 35
Rear of crew station (Crown Copyright)
1. Flasher unit Type F
2. Morse key
3. VHF and intercommunication switch
4. Power supply switch panel
5. Computer release switch
6. Pressure venting cock
7. Junction box 'C'
8. Control unit Type 89
9. Control unit Type 90
10. Receiver Type R.3582 (alternative to R.1355)
11. R.F. Unit Type 25
12. Control Unit Type 522
13. Air position indicator
14. A.P.I. transmission switch
15. Target control panel
16. Indicator Type 62 (alternative to Indicator type 166)
17. Wing drop tanks transfer cock
18. Long-range oil transfer cock
19. Engine slow-running cut-out controls
20. Oil dilution push-switches
21. Fuel cock controls
22. Target tow release toggles
23. Undercarriage emergency lowering selector (under removable cover)
24. Vacuum control cock

Throttle Box • 2

The Merlin 76 Throttle box

Throttle box for Merlin 72 engines

Throttle box for single-stage Merlins

(Crown Copyright)

Rudder Pedals

Details of the rudder pedal installation which was common to all Mosquitos

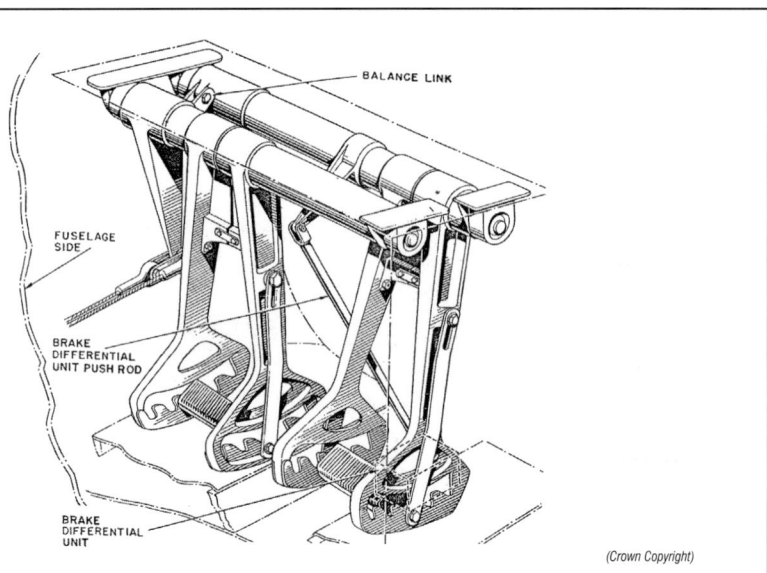

(Crown Copyright)

Chapter 11

Bomber Equipment

Cockpit equipment diagram B Mk XX
1. Dimmer switch
2. Intercommunication box and plug
3. Fireman's axe
4. Distributor stowage
5. Extension lead satchel
6. Inspection lamp
7. Stowage for plugs (distribution box)
8. Camera wedge plates
9. Observer's oxygen regulator
10. Flood lamp
11. Identification light switch
12. Identification switch box
13. Watch pocket
14. Folding navigation table
15. Pencil box
16. Compass
17. Roof lamp
18. Sandwich window drying apparatus (bomb aimer's window)
19. Emergency oxygen bottles
20. Telescopic ladder
21. Stowage for Syko instrument
22. Verey cartridge holder
23. Drift sight mount
24. Immersion switch
25. Navigation computer
26. Drift sight control
27. Folding seat
28. Aerial winch
29. Fire extinguisher
30. Verey signal pistol
31. Navigation charts etc.
32. Pocket for pilot's misc. articles
33. Pilot's oxygen regulator
34. Bomb firing switch
35. Undercarriage warning label
36. Engine data plate
37. Instrument panel
38. Sandwich window drying apparatus (windscreen)
39. Glycol spray
40. Head cushion
41. Impact and gravity switches
42. Card holder
43. Bomb firing switch pocket
44. Sanitary funnel
45. Torch
46. Urinary container
47. First aid box
48. Map case
49. Compass
50. Anti-icer pump
51. Punkha louvre
52. Observer's parachute stowage
53. Bomb sight bracket
54. Vacuum flasks

Cockpit equipment diagram NF Mk II
1. A.I. Mk IV tuning unit
2. A.I. Mk IV indicator
3. Dimmer switch for right hand flood lamp
4. Right hand flood lamp
5. Telescopic steps
6. Cold air ventilation controls
7. Intercommunication switch
8. Observer's oxygen regulator
9. Observer's oxygen control
10. Observer's intercommunication jack
11. Observer's oxygen pipe clip
12. Gun heater control
13. Observer's parachute
14. Inspection lamp
15. Extension lead
16. Electrical box 'B'
17. Film footage indicator
18. Pocket for navigational equipment
19. Fire extinguisher
20. Signal cartridges
21. Hydraulic hand pump handle
22. Cockpit heating control
23. Upward identification lamp
24. Fireman's axe
25. Map case
26. Cockpit roof lamp
27. Signal pistol
28. Pilot's intercommunication jack
29. TR.1133 radio switch
30. Intercommunication switch
31. Blind approach switch
32. Pilot's oxygen pipe clip
33. Reflector sight
34. Windscreen wiper
35. Compass lamp dimmer switch
36. Left hand flood lamp
37. Left hand flood lamp dimmer switch
38. Reflector sight plug
39. Instrument panel
40. Engine and undercarriage data plates
41. Pilot's harness release catch
42. Sanitary tank and funnel
43. First aid box and electric torch
44. TR.1133 radio controls
45. Compass
46. De-icer pump
47. Compass deviation card
48. Compass flood lamp

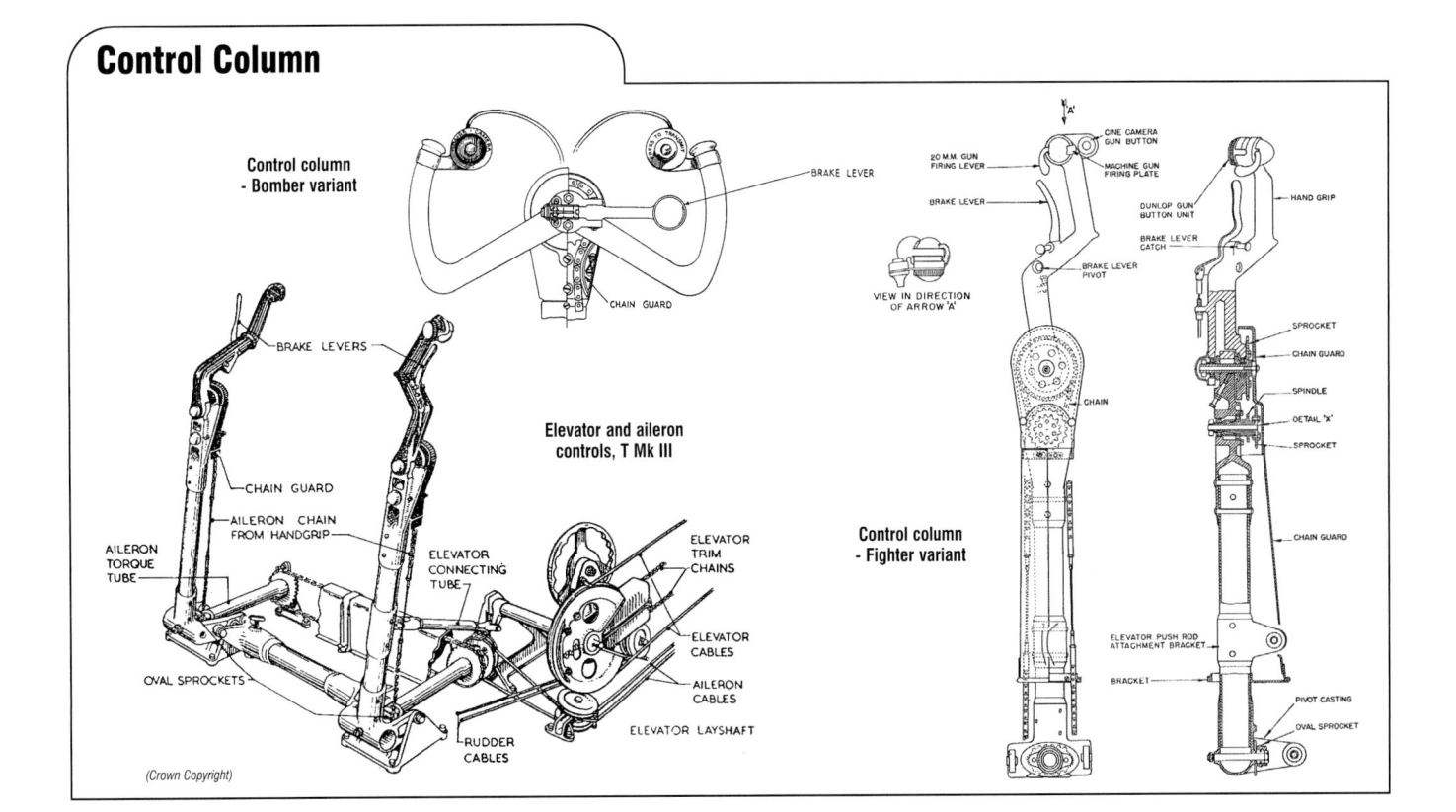

Control Column

Control column - Bomber variant

Elevator and aileron controls, T Mk III

Control column - Fighter variant

(Crown Copyright)

Undercarriage • 2

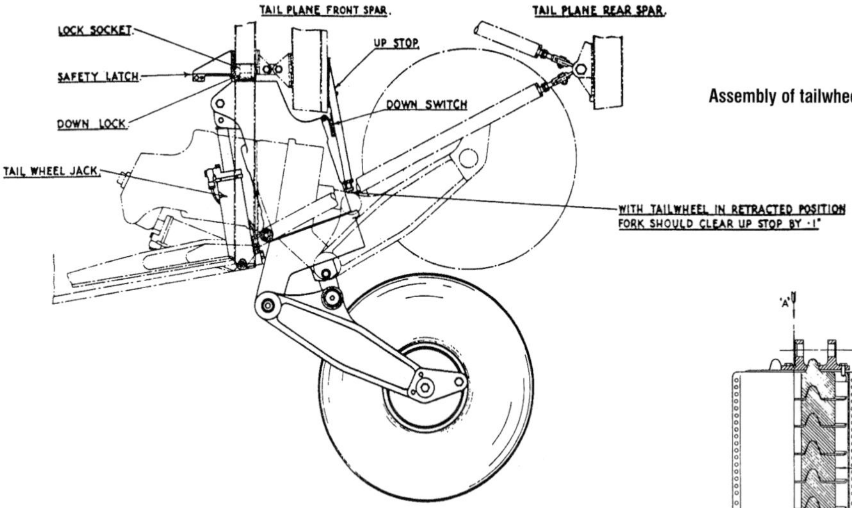

Assembly of tailwheel

LOCK SOCKET
SAFETY LATCH
DOWN LOCK
TAIL WHEEL JACK
TAIL PLANE FRONT SPAR
UP STOP
DOWN SWITCH
TAIL PLANE REAR SPAR

WITH TAILWHEEL IN RETRACTED POSITION FORK SHOULD CLEAR UP STOP BY ·1"

Shock-absorber strut

ASSEMBLY ROD 26 BY/5041 INSERT HERE
VIEW IN DIRECTION OF ARROW 'A'
11 RUBBER BLOCKS
11 SEPARATOR PLATES
½ RUBBER BLOCK
BAKELITE PISTON
BOTTOM BEARING SECURING BOLTS
REBOUND RUBBER
TELESCOPING TUBE
GAITER
AXLE ATTACHMENT BRACKET

SECTION 'XX'

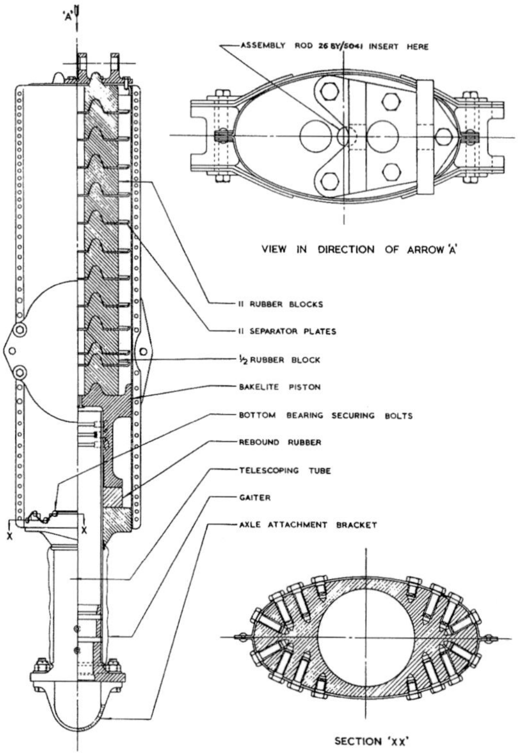

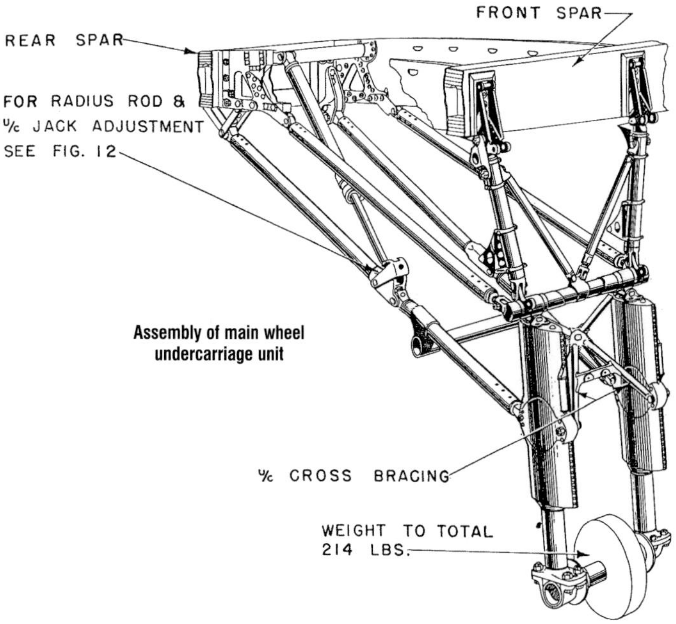

Assembly of main wheel undercarriage unit

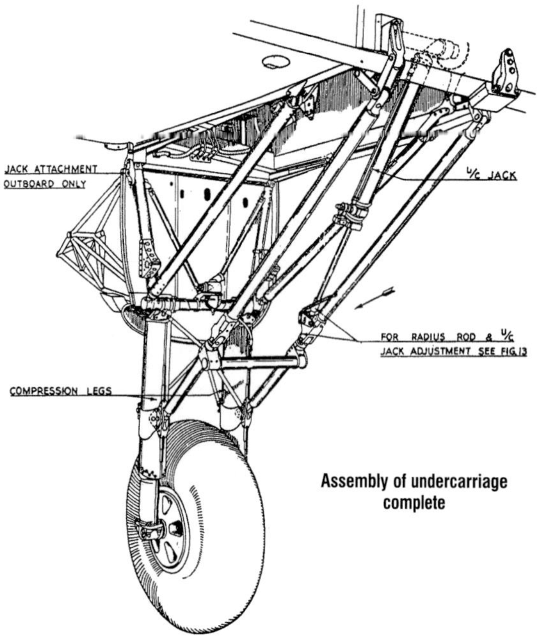

REAR SPAR
FRONT SPAR
FOR RADIUS ROD & U/C JACK ADJUSTMENT SEE FIG. 12
U/C CROSS BRACING
WEIGHT TO TOTAL 214 LBS.

Assembly of undercarriage complete

JACK ATTACHMENT OUTBOARD ONLY
U/C JACK
FOR RADIUS ROD & U/C JACK ADJUSTMENT SEE FIG.13
COMPRESSION LEGS

Assembly of undercarriage complete (Lockheed type)

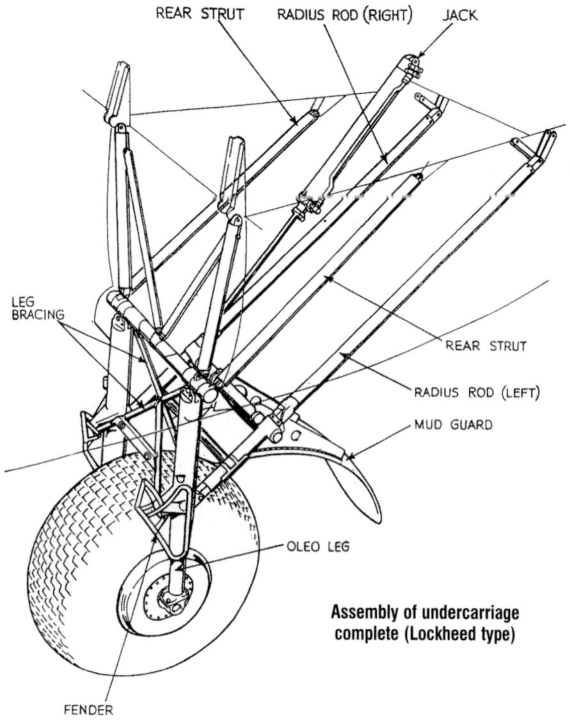

REAR STRUT
RADIUS ROD (RIGHT)
JACK
LEG BRACING
REAR STRUT
RADIUS ROD (LEFT)
MUD GUARD
OLEO LEG
FENDER

(Crown Copyright)

Undercarriage • 3

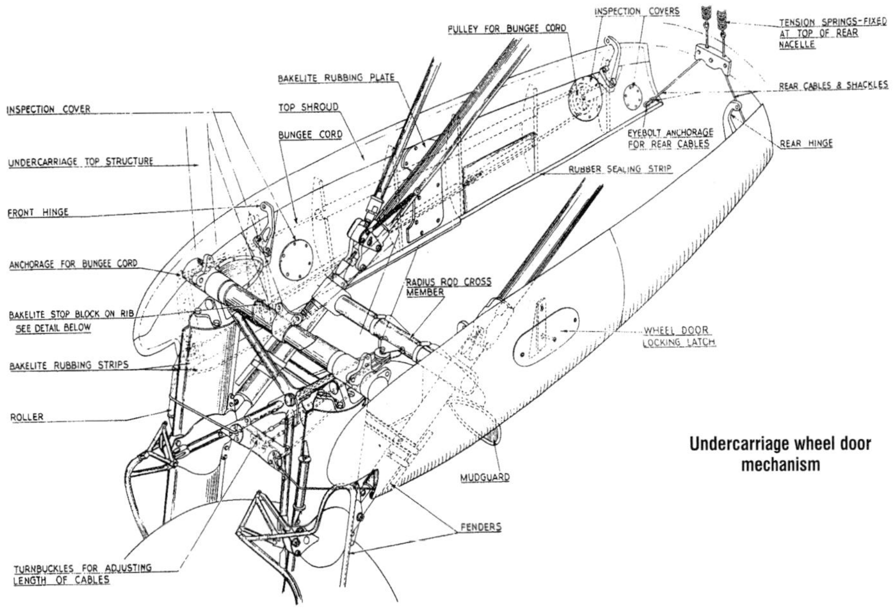

Undercarriage wheel door mechanism

(Crown Copyright)

Radio & Radar Equipment • 2

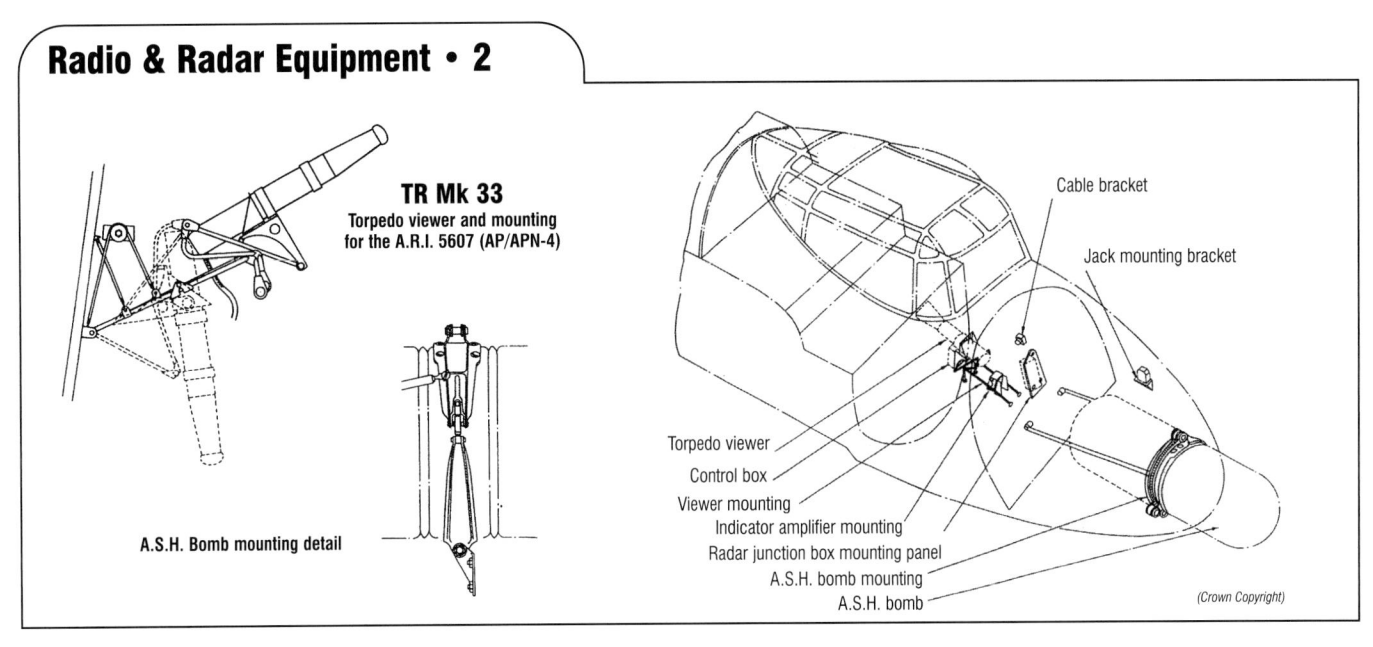

TR Mk 33
Torpedo viewer and mounting for the A.R.I. 5607 (AP/APN-4)

A.S.H. Bomb mounting detail

- Cable bracket
- Jack mounting bracket
- Torpedo viewer
- Control box
- Viewer mounting
- Indicator amplifier mounting
- Radar junction box mounting panel
- A.S.H. bomb mounting
- A.S.H. bomb

(Crown Copyright)

Bomber Nose

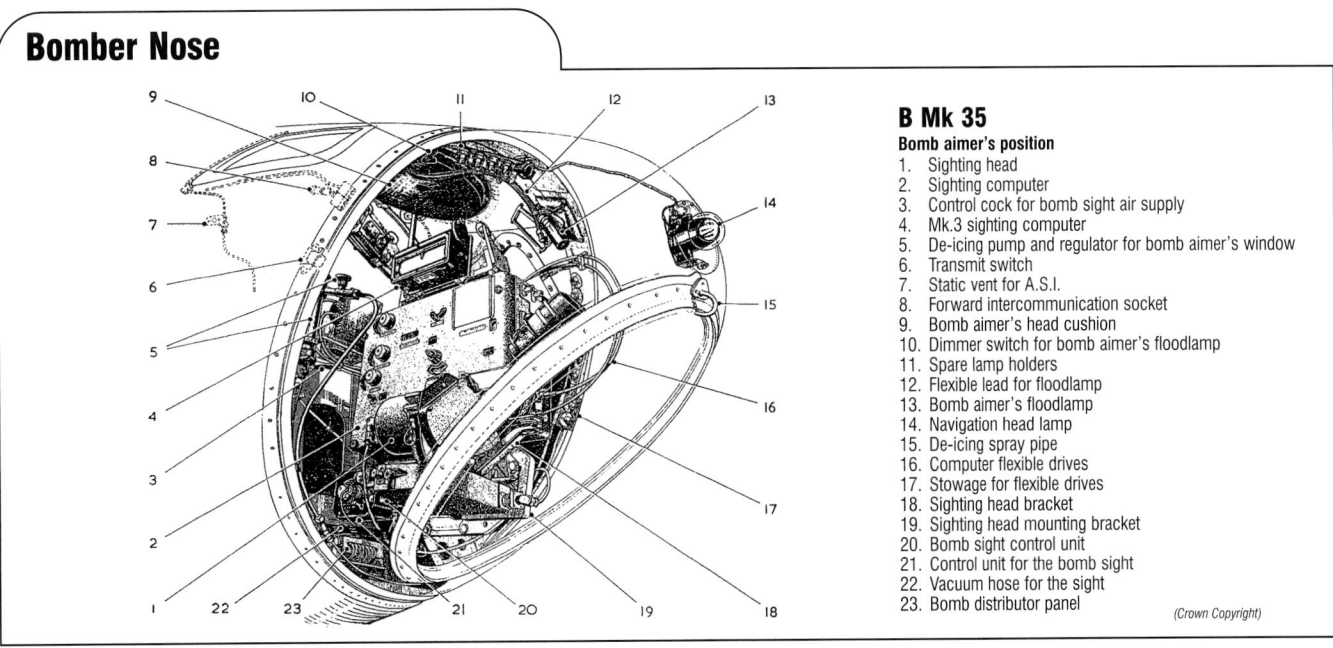

B Mk 35
Bomb aimer's position
1. Sighting head
2. Sighting computer
3. Control cock for bomb sight air supply
4. Mk.3 sighting computer
5. De-icing pump and regulator for bomb aimer's window
6. Transmit switch
7. Static vent for A.S.I.
8. Forward intercommunication socket
9. Bomb aimer's head cushion
10. Dimmer switch for bomb aimer's floodlamp
11. Spare lamp holders
12. Flexible lead for floodlamp
13. Bomb aimer's floodlamp
14. Navigation head lamp
15. De-icing spray pipe
16. Computer flexible drives
17. Stowage for flexible drives
18. Sighting head bracket
19. Sighting head mounting bracket
20. Bomb sight control unit
21. Control unit for the bomb sight
22. Vacuum hose for the sight
23. Bomb distributor panel

(Crown Copyright)

Modelling the Mosquito • Detailing **105**

Canopy • 1

Cockpit canopy - fighter

Cockpit canopy - bomber (teardrop) side blister & PR top bulge

Cockpit canopy - bomber ('blown') side bulges and flat top panel e.g B Mk XVI & TT Mk 39

Cockpit canopy - Details of bulged side panel on starboard side e.g. Australian and Canadian built plus Sea Mosquitoes and foreign service machines refurbished in the UK

Cockpit canopy - fighter (foreign production and operation)

(BAe)

Drop Tanks

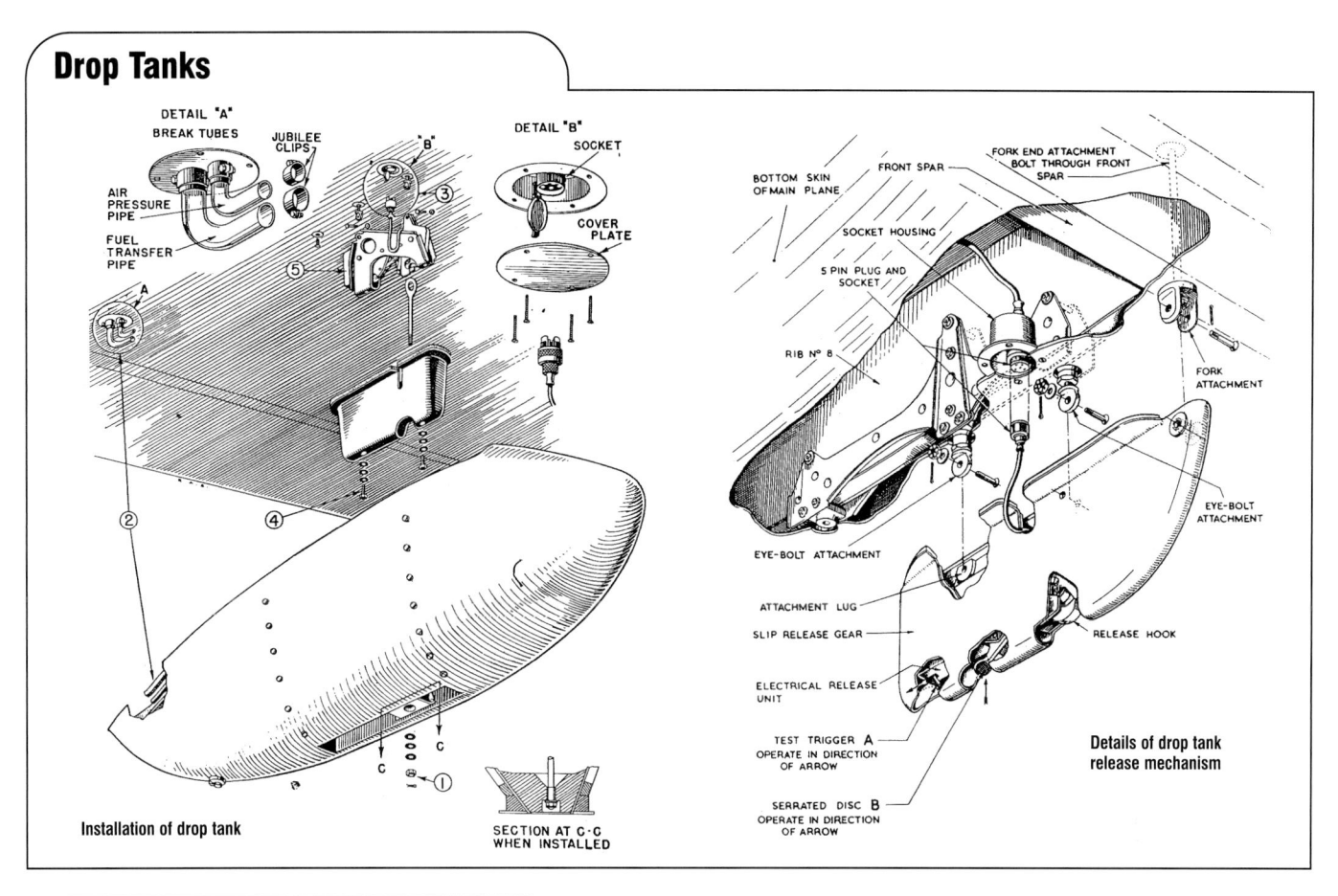

Installation of drop tank

Details of drop tank release mechanism

Bomb Bay Doors

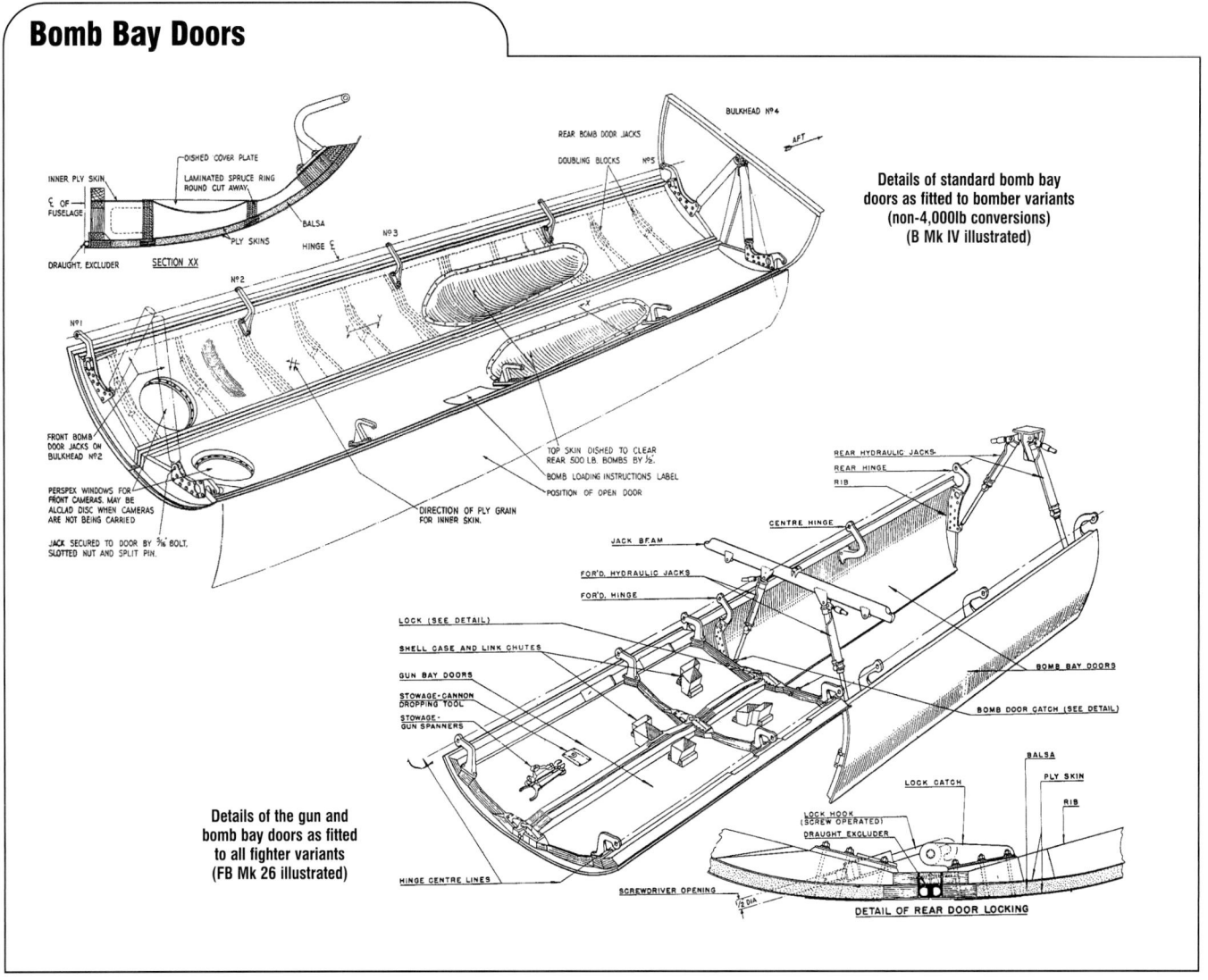

Details of standard bomb bay doors as fitted to bomber variants (non-4,000lb conversions) (B Mk IV illustrated)

Details of the gun and bomb bay doors as fitted to all fighter variants (FB Mk 26 illustrated)

Modelling the Mosquito • Detailing   107

Fuel Tanks • 2

Installation of main tanks (No.11 & 12) in the bomb bay

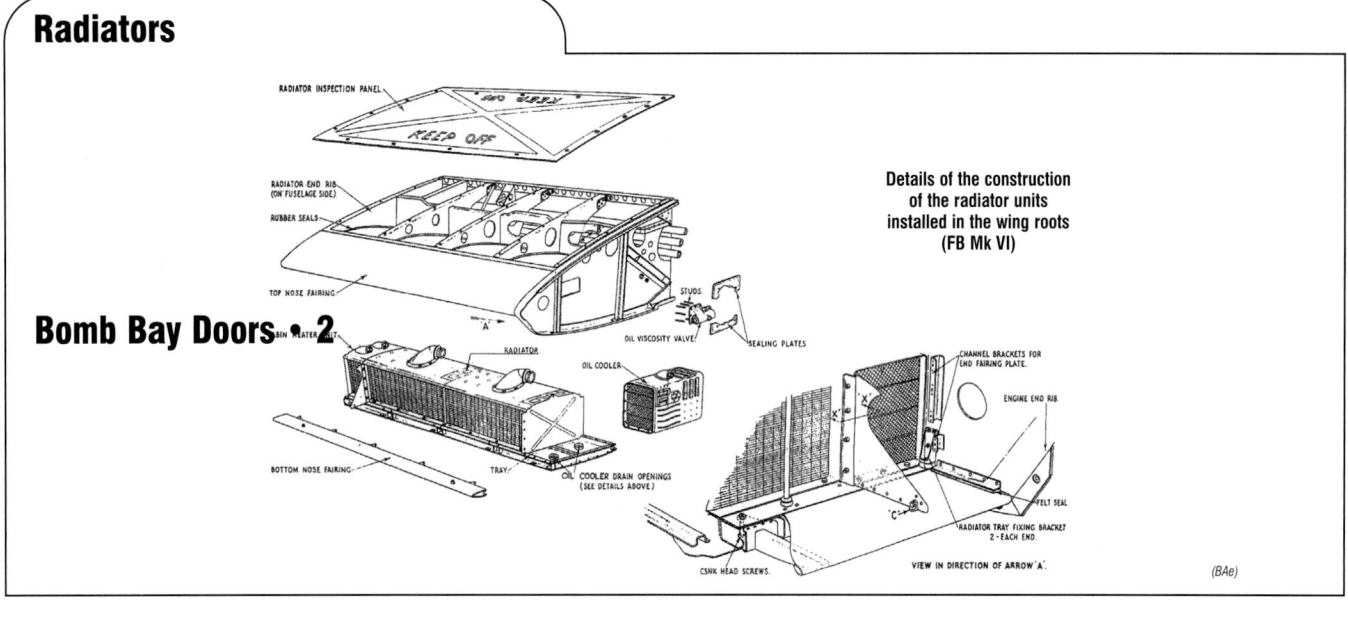

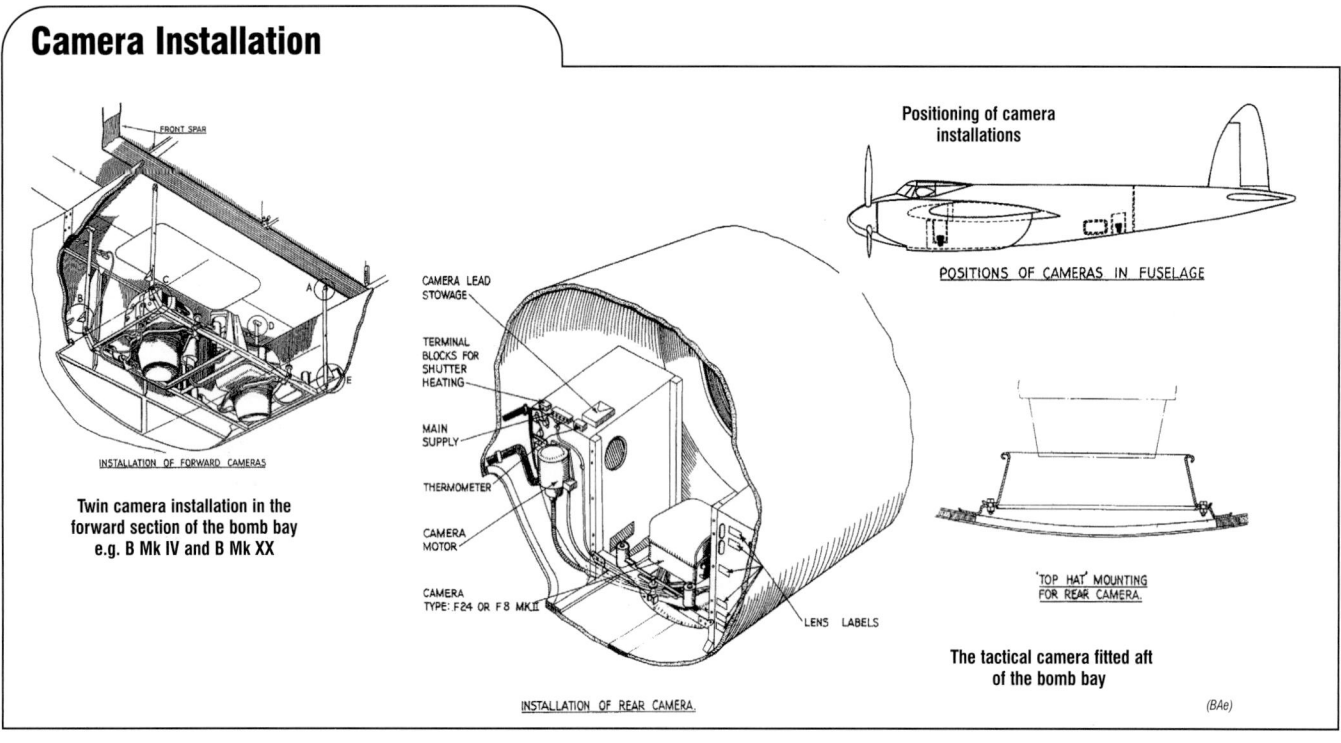

1 FRONT BOMB MOUNTING FRAME
2 BRACING STRUTS
3 TANK STRAPS
4 TANK BEARERS
5 BRACING STRUTS
6 TANK STRAPS
7 BRACING STRUTS
8 CENTRE TANK BEARER
9 TANK STRAPS
10 TANK BEARERS
11 TANK STRAPS
12 TANK BEARERS BOTTOM PORTION
13 VENT PIPES
14 LEAD TO IMMERSED PUMP
15 TANK STRAPS
16 FLEXIBLE HOSE
17 IMMERSED PUMP
18 REAR BOMB MOUNTING FRAME
19 VENT CONNECTIONS
20 BALANCE PIPES
21 FILLER CAP

Radiators

Details of the construction of the radiator units installed in the wing roots (FB Mk VI)

Bomb Bay Doors • 2

(BAe)

Camera Installation

Positioning of camera installations

POSITIONS OF CAMERAS IN FUSELAGE

INSTALLATION OF FORWARD CAMERAS

Twin camera installation in the forward section of the bomb bay e.g. B Mk IV and B Mk XX

INSTALLATION OF REAR CAMERA.

'TOP HAT' MOUNTING FOR REAR CAMERA.

The tactical camera fitted aft of the bomb bay

(BAe)

Chapter 11

Wings • 2

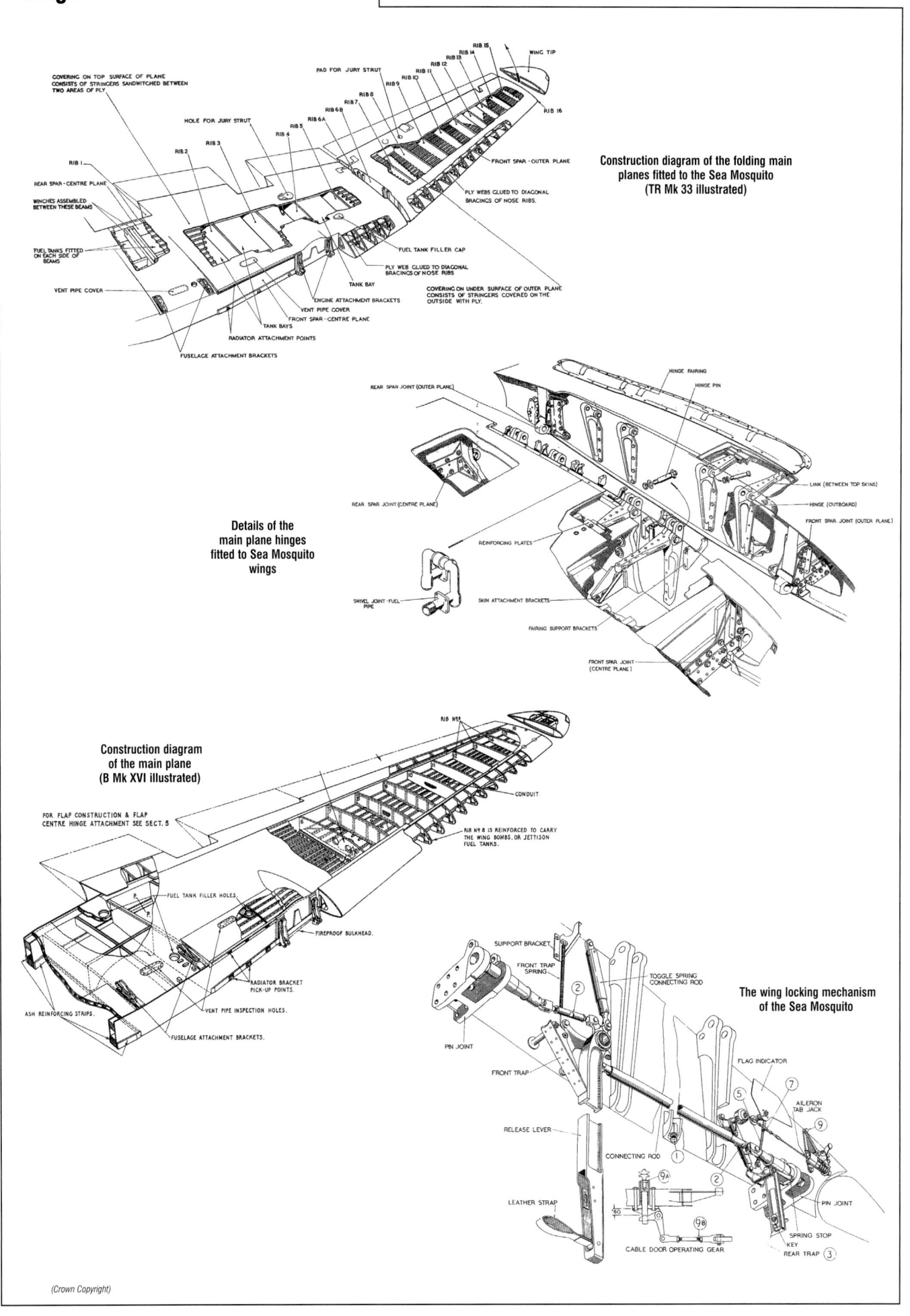

Construction diagram of the folding main planes fitted to the Sea Mosquito (TR Mk 33 illustrated)

Details of the main plane hinges fitted to Sea Mosquito wings

Construction diagram of the main plane (B Mk XVI illustrated)

The wing locking mechanism of the Sea Mosquito

(Crown Copyright)

Engine Nacelles • 2

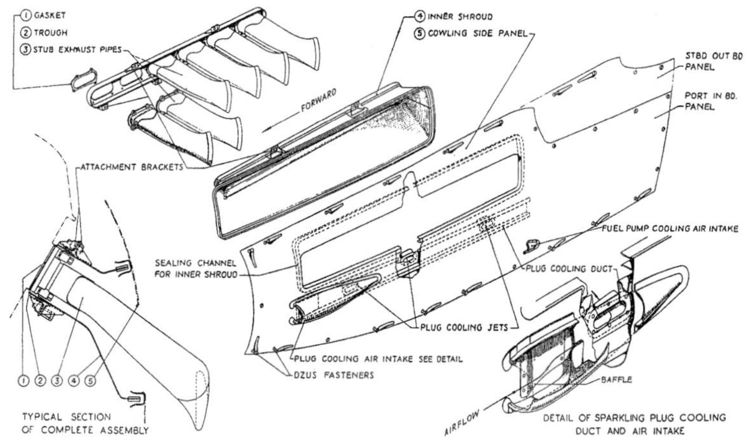

Details of the exhaust system
('6-stack, two-stage')
(B Mk 35 illustrated)

Details of the exhaust system
('5-stack')
(FB Mk 26 illustrated)

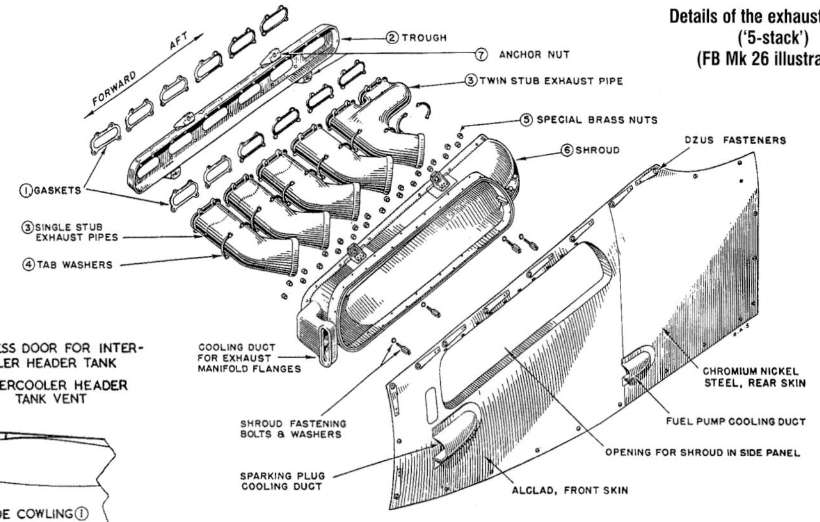

Side view of
two-stage Merlin nacelle
(B. Mk 35 illustrated)

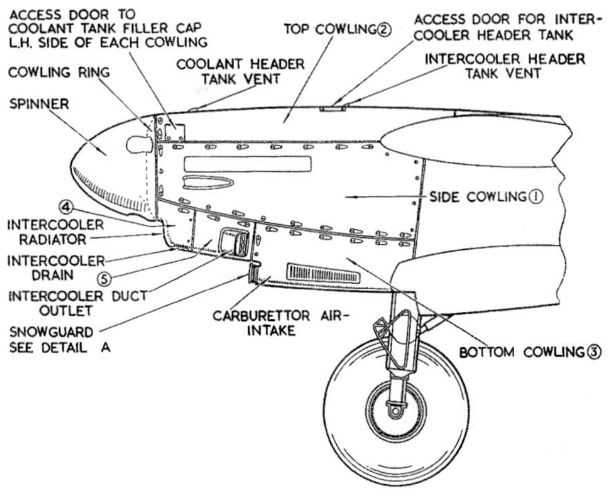

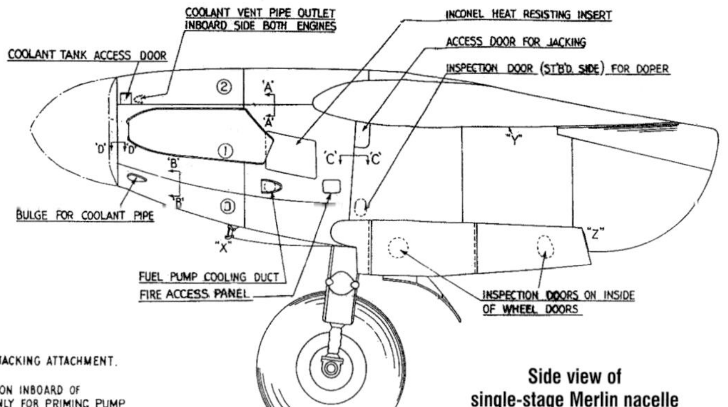

Side view of
two-stage Merlin nacelle
(B Mk XVI illustrated)

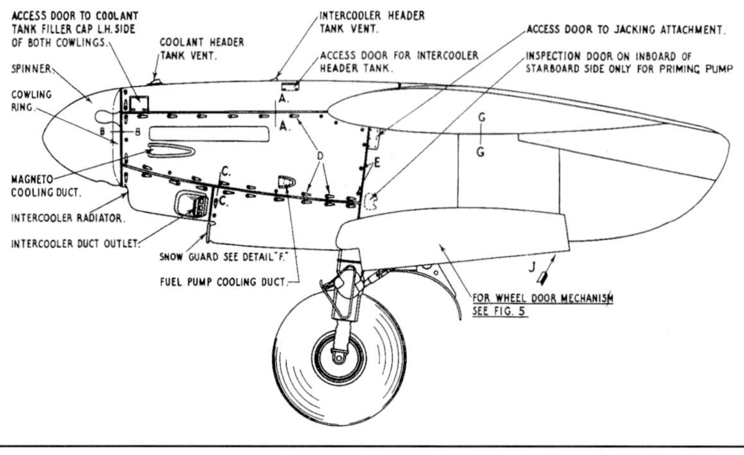

Side view of
single-stage Merlin nacelle
(TR Mk 33 illustrated)

(Crown Copyright)

Engine Nacelles • 3

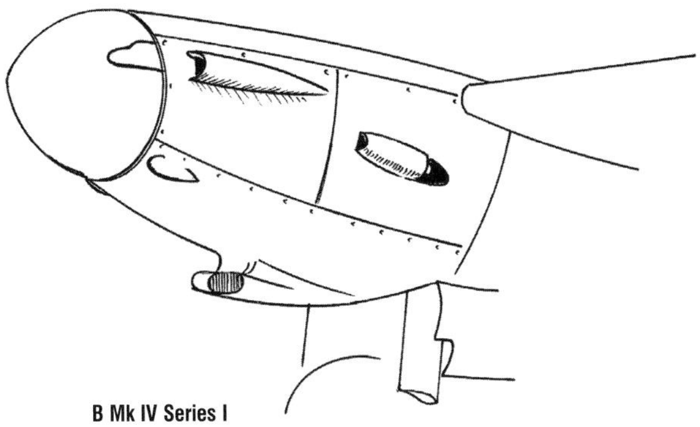

B Mk IV Series I

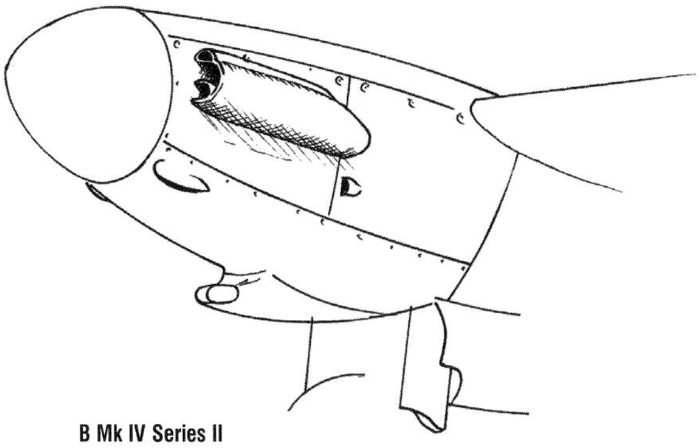

B Mk IV Series II

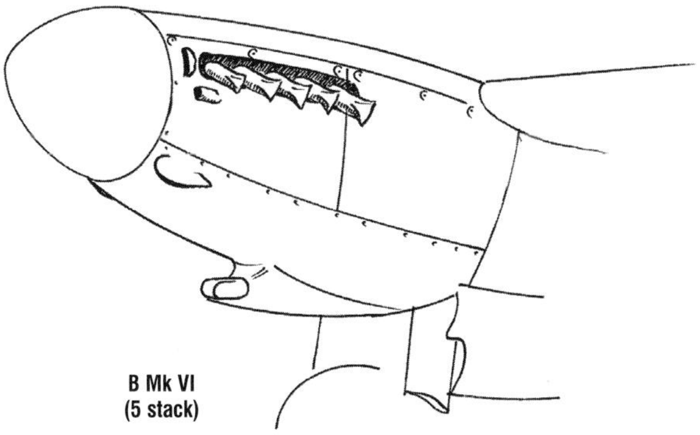

B Mk VI
(5 stack)

(© A.Oliver)

Armament

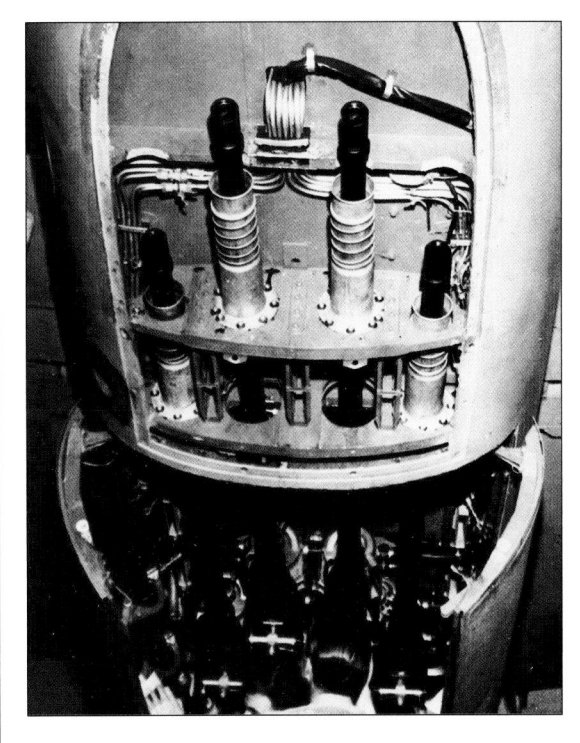

The 20mm cannon installation in the
ventral tray of a Mosquito
(National Museum of Science and Technology)

This is the back section of the cannon bay, without the weapons in place.

The oxygen economizers for the crew can be seen fixed to the roof of this area
(BAe)

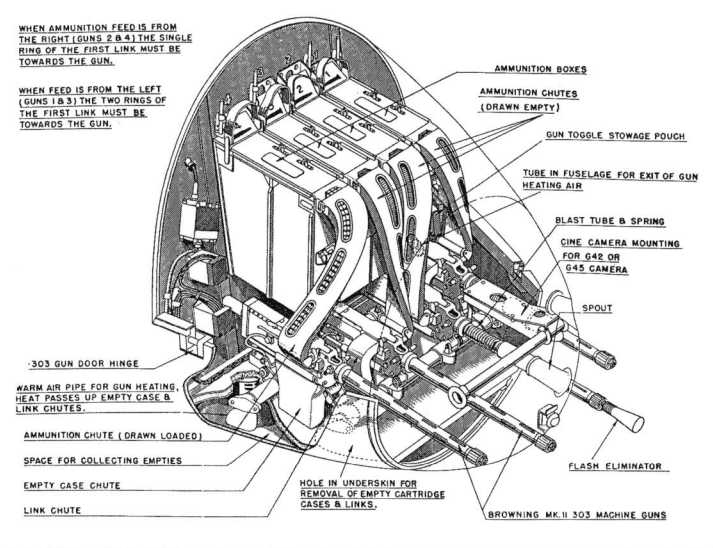

The basic dimensions
of the machine gun locations
in the nose of the
fighter Mosquitoes
(Crown Copyright)

WHEN AMMUNITION FEED IS FROM THE RIGHT (GUNS 2 & 4) THE SINGLE RING OF THE FIRST LINK MUST BE TOWARDS THE GUN.

WHEN FEED IS FROM THE LEFT (GUNS 1 & 3) THE TWO RINGS OF THE FIRST LINK MUST BE TOWARDS THE GUN.

- AMMUNITION BOXES
- AMMUNITION CHUTES (DRAWN EMPTY)
- GUN TOGGLE STOWAGE POUCH
- TUBE IN FUSELAGE FOR EXIT OF GUN HEATING AIR
- BLAST TUBE & SPRING
- CINE CAMERA MOUNTING FOR G42 OR G45 CAMERA
- SPOUT
- FLASH ELIMINATOR
- BROWNING MK.II 303 MACHINE GUNS
- HOLE IN UNDERSKIN FOR REMOVAL OF EMPTY CARTRIDGE CASES & LINKS.
- LINK CHUTE
- EMPTY CASE CHUTE
- SPACE FOR COLLECTING EMPTIES
- AMMUNITION CHUTE (DRAWN LOADED)
- WARM AIR PIPE FOR GUN HEATING, HEAT PASSES UP EMPTY CASE & LINK CHUTES.
- .303 GUN DOOR HINGE

Modelling the Mosquito • Detailing

Bomb Bay & Bomb Carriers • 2

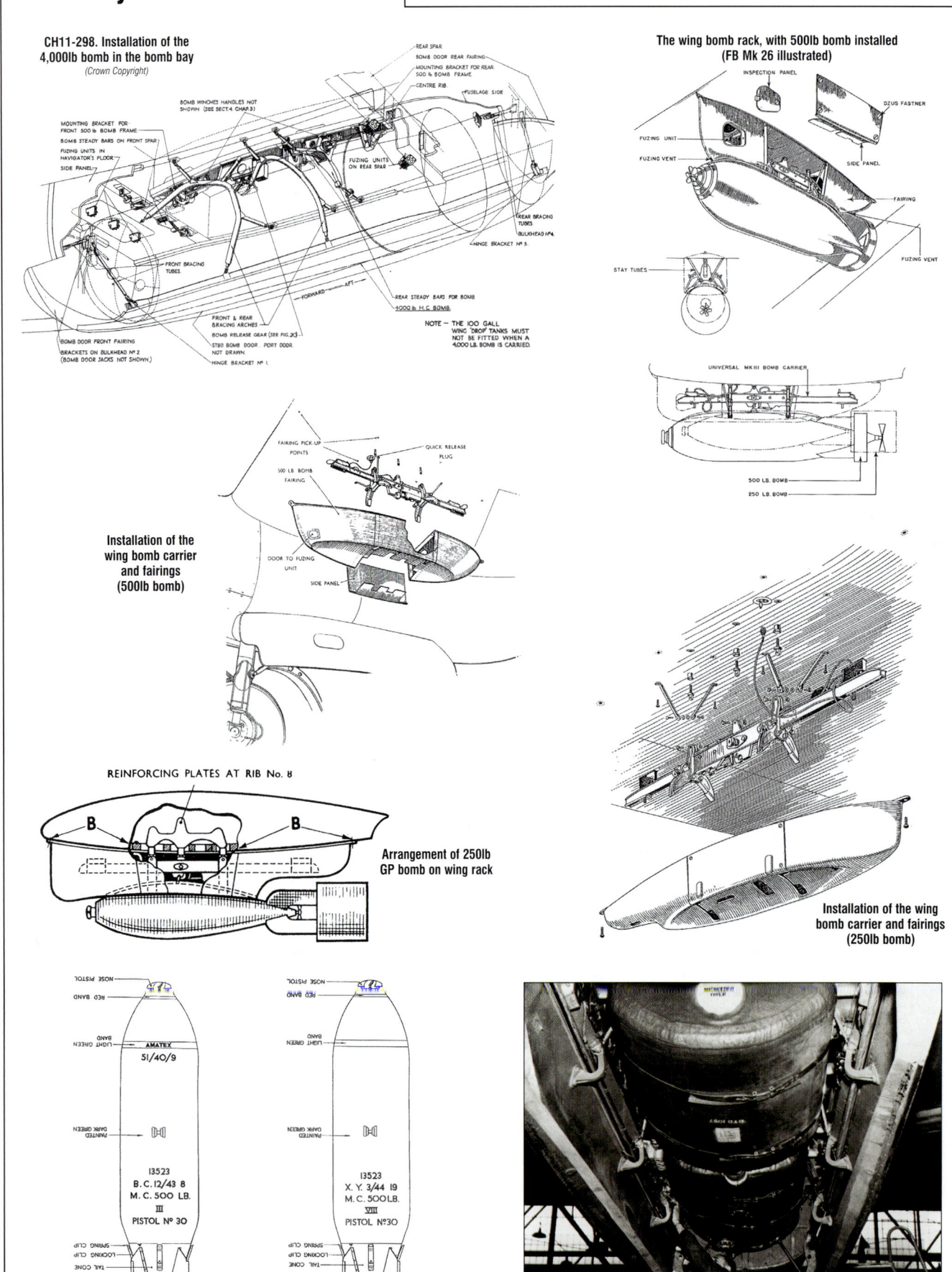

CH11-298. Installation of the 4,000lb bomb in the bomb bay
(Crown Copyright)

The wing bomb rack, with 500lb bomb installed (FB Mk 26 illustrated)

Installation of the wing bomb carrier and fairings (500lb bomb)

Arrangement of 250lb GP bomb on wing rack

Installation of the wing bomb carrier and fairings (250lb bomb)

500lb Mk III bomb fitted with the No.28 Mk II tail unit

500lb Mk VIII bomb fitted with the No.28 Mk II tail unit

A view of the large tanks (No.11 & 12) in the bomb bay of a Canadian produced Mosquito
(National Museum of Science & Technology)

112   Chapter 11

Target Tug Equipment • 2

The installation of target towed banners in a three-crate system within the bomb bay of a TT Mk 35

* See rocket projectile section

ML Type G winch, as installed under the TT Mk 35 (1/72nd scale)

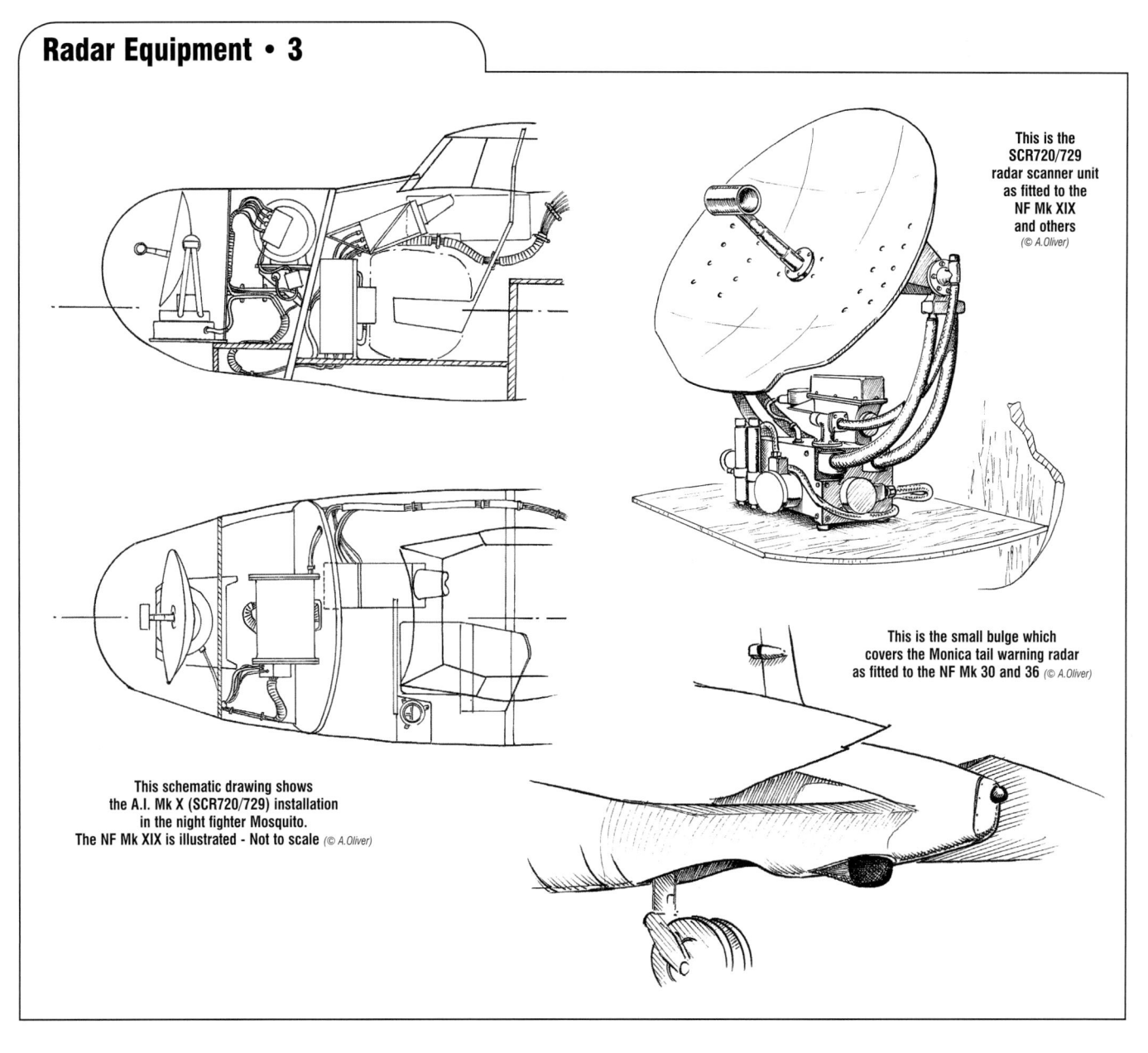

(© A.Oliver)

Radar Equipment • 3

This is the SCR720/729 radar scanner unit as fitted to the NF Mk XIX and others (© A.Oliver)

This schematic drawing shows the A.I. Mk X (SCR720/729) installation in the night fighter Mosquito. The NF Mk XIX is illustrated - Not to scale (© A.Oliver)

This is the small bulge which covers the Monica tail warning radar as fitted to the NF Mk 30 and 36 (© A.Oliver)

Modelling the Mosquito • Detailing 113

Miscellaneous • 3

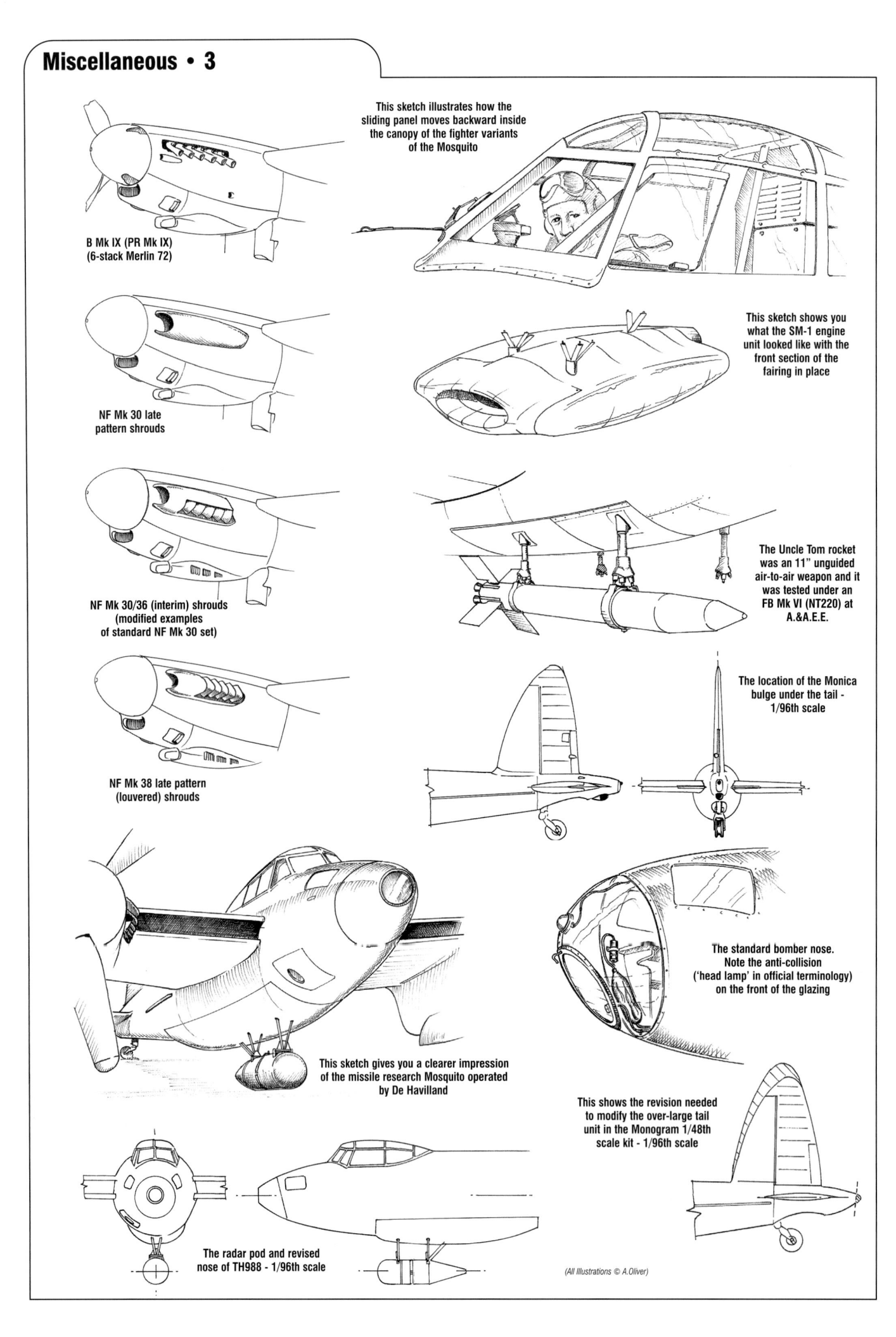

B Mk IX (PR Mk IX)
(6-stack Merlin 72)

NF Mk 30 late
pattern shrouds

NF Mk 30/36 (interim) shrouds
(modified examples
of standard NF Mk 30 set)

NF Mk 38 late pattern
(louvered) shrouds

This sketch illustrates how the sliding panel moves backward inside the canopy of the fighter variants of the Mosquito

This sketch shows you what the SM-1 engine unit looked like with the front section of the fairing in place

The Uncle Tom rocket was an 11" unguided air-to-air weapon and it was tested under an FB Mk VI (NT220) at A.&A.E.E.

The location of the Monica bulge under the tail - 1/96th scale

This sketch gives you a clearer impression of the missile research Mosquito operated by De Havilland

The standard bomber nose. Note the anti-collision ('head lamp' in official terminology) on the front of the glazing

This shows the revision needed to modify the over-large tail unit in the Monogram 1/48th scale kit - 1/96th scale

The radar pod and revised nose of TH988 - 1/96th scale

(All Illustrations © A.Oliver)

114   Chapter 11

Building the Mosquito

Modelling the Mosquito

Chapter 12

When I originally built a number of Mosquitoes in 1/48th scale for my articles in *Scale Aviation Modeller International,* 1996, I decided on a number of types, but once completed I still had a few I fancied making. From this, and an improved understanding of the subject, came the basis of the Datafile series. Therefore for this first title I have made nine more Mosquitoes, to illustrate the large spectrum of tasks that the Mosquito undertook during its service. Of these, only the NF Mk XV is a type I have built before, however this time I have decided to build it as it was in its initial form. All of the examples I have made are to 1/48th scale and they utilise the Airfix kit (Kit No.07100). The reason for this is to allow me to work in my preferred scale but also to be of a better size to photograph for illustrative purposes. The versions which are covered are as follows:

- 1 The prototype (W4050)
- 2 NF Mk II
- 3 NF Mk XV prototype (MP469) in its initial form
- 4 J 30 (NF Mk XIX)
- 5 B Mk IV Series II
- 6 FB Mk VI in Dominican Air Force markings
- 7 PR Mk XVI in French Air Force markings
- 8 PR Mk 34A
- 9 TT Mk 35

• 1 The Prototype (W4050)

Making this version is very simple now as a conversion set is available for it in 1/48th scale (and 1/72nd) from UK firm, Paragon Designs. This set, 4868, consists of all the resin and vac-form components necessary to convert the Airfix kit and the only additional work you will need to undertake is the scribing of the leading-edge slats.

All of the versions I built utilised the resin cockpit-detail set which is currently available from American company, Kendall Model Company Inc. (KMC). This set (No.48-4014) is based on a standard FB Mk VI interior, as it is designed for the Airfix kit, but for the various versions built here it was simply modified to better suit each role. Really, if I had invested a lot more time on each, I could have modified each to accurately represent its variant. However for this book I contented myself with some simple modifications which resulted in a 'bomber' and 'fighter' style interior. The details included in Chapter 11 of this title will help you to accurately detail the interior of most variants, although the KMC set will still form an excellent basis. As I will deal with a bomber first, I will note the changes I made to the KMC set now, and refer back to them in subsequent versions.

The fighter Mosquito had the forward bulkhead made of armour plate, but in a bomber this area was open, so the navigator could move forward into his bomb-aiming position. Therefore, with the KMC set, I removed the armoured bulkhead from the new instrument panel unit with a razor saw. The same can be done to the Airfix component (Part No. 19) if you choose not to use the KMC set. The new rudder-pedal cover included in the Paragon conversion can now be affixed to the KMC (or Airfix) instrument panel and if you feel like adding all the pipework to the back of the panel it would be a good idea to do it at this time. Once again Chapter 11 will assist you with the details that are visible in this area, and their inclusion in your kit will be a good idea as they can be seen through the new glazed nose. The fighter style control column in the KMC set (Airfix Part No. 15) can be replaced with the 'yoke' bomber style unit included in the Paragon set. The main changes you will have to make to the KMC sidewalls, when utilising them in a bomber, is to remove certain areas so they will fit and also to carry some of the pipework further forward into the bomb aimer's position. You will also have to sand off all the moulded

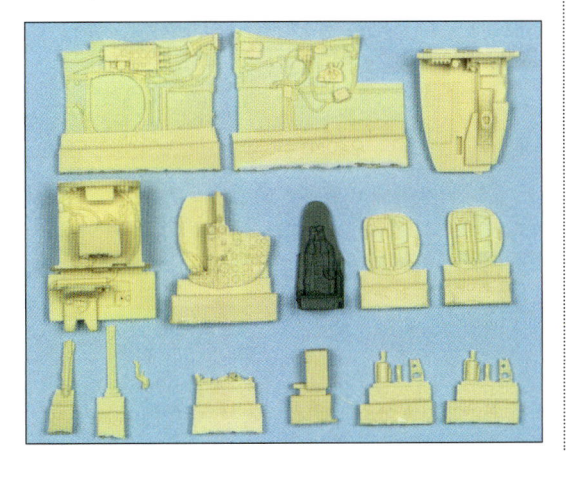

The excellent cockpit update set for the Airfix FB Mk VI kit in 1/48th scale is offered by Kendall Model Company Inc. (48-4014)

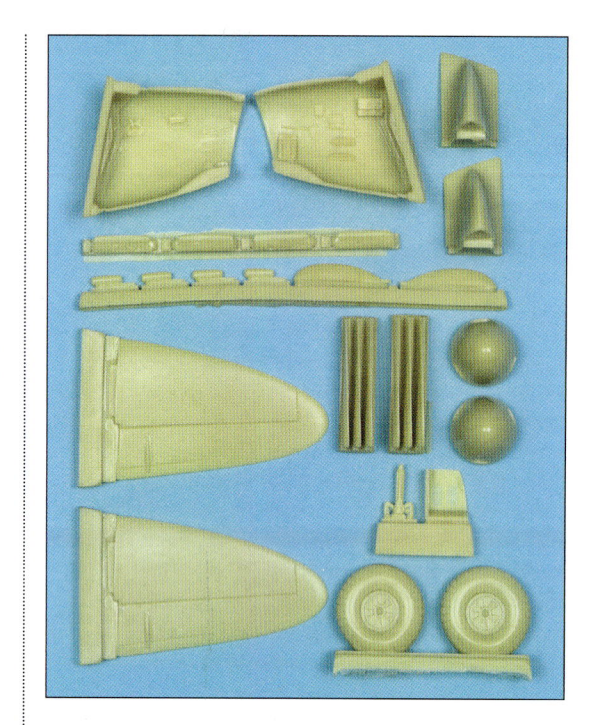

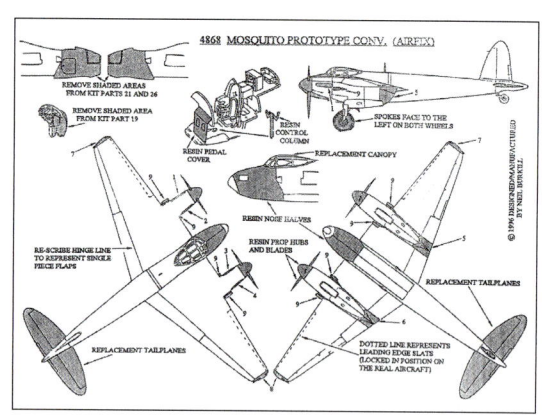

Far right: The instructions for the prototype conversion give an idea of the level of work involved

The Protoype conversion in 1/48th scale (P48068)

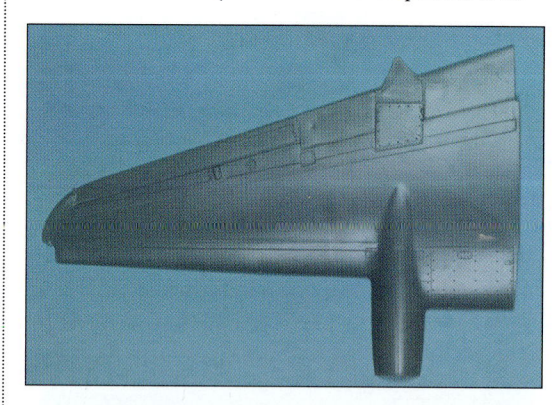

The standard upper wing half from the Airfix kit, before the raised spar caps and flpas were removed.

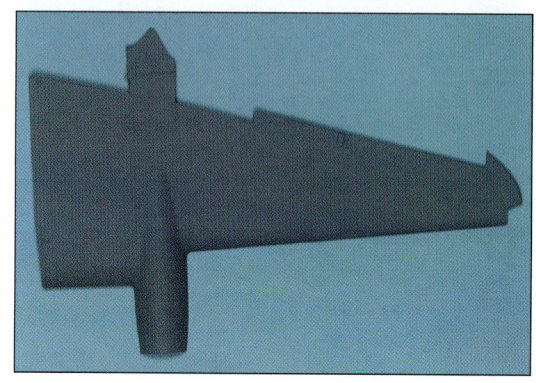

The port upper wing half with the spar caps removed and the flaps cut out

details from the Airfix kit parts, so the new KMC pieces can be installed. Once again the information in Chapter 11 should assist you with details for this area. The remainder of the KMC interior set can be used as supplied, although the crew-access door moulded into the starboard side will have to be covered with a square piece of plastic card (to represent the chart table and to cover the 'hole') and the new access hatch cover will have to be made from a piece of plastic card and cemented to the floor, just to the right of the pilot's seat.

As the Airfix kit is a fighter, the first major task is to convert it into the bomber style. This is achieved by removing areas of the front of each fuselage half (Kit Part Nos. 21 and 26), as indicated on the Paragon instruction sheet. These areas just butt-joint to the new resin sections and I must admit that I have never liked that, as it seems a very weak joint. However, the inclusion in the KMC set of separate sidewalls will help to secure the new nose sections. To ensure that you remove the correct portions of the nose from the kit fuselage, use the new resin pieces as a template. I marked off each area on the kit parts and then cut them off with a razor saw. The interior was then stripped of all raised detail with a router bit in a power tool, ensuring that you have one with a speed control, otherwise the plastic will melt! The revised KMC interior was now offered up to check its fit. When this was satisfactory, I moved on to installing the KMC sidewalls and once these were secured I test fitted the new resin nose sections. I tacked each piece on with tape and then taped the fuselage halves together. With the fuselage as one piece, I was able to align the nose sections and then cement them in position. This whole assembly is left to dry and once it is set you can untape the fuselage halves and add the interior. If you do not align the nose sections, you may well end up with them being splayed out at the front when you try to join the two fuselage halves! Also keep checking the fit of the new vac-formed canopy, to ensure that you have removed enough of the fuselage halves, otherwise the canopy will not cover the resulting hole. With the interior installed, it was painted, given a couple of colour washes and then detail painted and left to dry. Once that was completed the fuselage halves were joined and the tailwheel yoke installed, before the whole unit was put aside to dry.

I now turned my attention to the wings and engines. Something which I have never been happy with on the Airfix kit is the representation of the spar caps on the upper and lower wing panels (Part Nos. 80, 81, 86 & 87). To get around this I removed the raised details from each. This was a time consuming task and required careful scraping off of all of the details, without damage being inflicted to the adjacent areas. I masked off the area near the spar caps with tape, to help me define the boundaries whilst I worked. Once this detail was removed I considered a number of ways of better replicating the spar caps. Eventually I decided that strips of decal film would best fit the bill and these were applied once all the assembly and preparations were completed.

Returning to the construction of the prototype, this machine had the short nacelles and the single-piece flaps which were peculiar to it and the B Mk IV Series Is. Paragon Designs have approached this area be supplying new resin rear sections for each nacelle. Each unit (Part Nos. 51, 55, 59 & 63) has to have the rear section removed on a panel line, after which this area is replaced with the new resin component. This new resin piece will fill the gap in the upper wing section as well and after the join line in that area is filled and sanded smooth, the new flap hinge-line will have to be scribed. With the wings thus far assembled, the wing span could now be decreased and the new tips installed. Only the prototype had the shorter span, so you have to cut the entire tip off each wing along a panel line adjacent to the outer aileron line. The new resin tips are now installed and some of you may well want to cut out each tip light (two per side), so at a later point they can be replaced with clear plastic. The final details that now have to be added are the exhaust-stack fillers and the new shorter-span tailplanes. The exhaust fillers are simple resin plugs which fit into the holes in each side of the engine nacelles, and to the rear and slightly below them the new single exhaust ports are installed. The resin tailplanes are simple replacements for the kit parts (Nos. 92, 93, 94 & 95).

At this stage the model can be prepared for painting. An amount of filler was required for nearly all of the main joints and once these were sanded smooth the entire model was primed with acrylic grey primer. Once I was satisfied with the finish of the model I removed the masking from the cockpit area and attached the vac-formed canopy. The joints around this area in the real aircraft were covered with tape, which was doped on, and on this model I applied strips of decal film over the joint to better replicate the real thing. The same system was also utilised for the wing and tailplane joints, as these too were like that on the real aircraft. As I had decided to make the prototype with the RAF serial (W4050), it had the radio equipment and mast installed. If you choose to make the aircraft with its E-0234 registration, you will have to omit the radio equipment from the cockpit interior and the mast (Part No. 30) from the upper-fuselage decking. No radio lead was installed on the prototype during its initial test career. The tailwheel on the prototype was not the twin-contact type installed on the FB Mk VI, so the kit parts (No.22 & 23) will have to have the centre filled. Once set the whole unit will have to be reprofiled before installation. Painting the prototype could not be easier, as it is yellow overall. Many have debated the colour used, but as De Havilland were building Tiger Moths at that time, it is most likely that it was painted a standard 'Trainer Yellow' overall. I therefore selected this colour from the Xtracolor range of paints and applied it overall with an airbrush. The interiors of the cockpit and wheel wells were painted in accordance with the painting note given in Chapter 12 of this title. Decals were applied once the overall colour scheme had dried. The prototype had A type roundels applied to the fuselage sides and lower wings, plus B types on the upper wings. As I did not have A type roundels of the correct proportions in this scale I just utilised an RAAF roundel in 1/72nd scale with the small red centres from another. If you study pictures of the prototype you will see that the red dot in the centre of each roundel is not in proportion with the rest of the roundel and I found that the method I adopted resulted in quite acceptable representations. The serial number was made from characters from a rub-down transfer sheet, which were applied to a piece of clear decal film. These were then applied in the usual manner and they looked very much the part. The fin flash was obtained from an AeroMaster sheet, although any suitable B type flash will be acceptable.

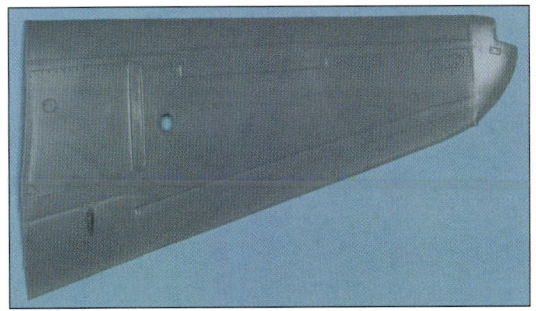

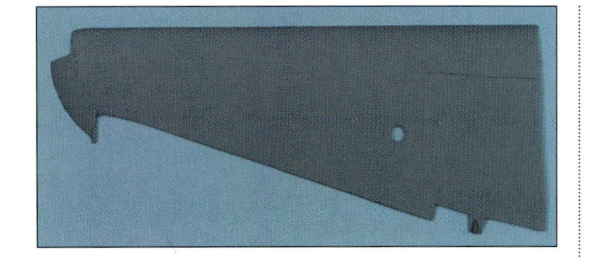

With everything in place the entire model was over-sprayed with gloss varnish and left to dry, while the detail parts were prepared. The propellers on the prototype were the narrow style and these are supplied as resin replacements in the Paragon set. I did not feel like using these, as they have a rather weak joint at the base of each blade, so I just used one of them as a template and then reprofiled the existing kit parts. Both the propeller blades and spinners are painted black, with the tips of each blade in yellow. The entire undercarriage was built up at this stage. The wheels need to be replaced with the 5-spoke hub style, which are supplied as resin pieces in the Paragon set, and the only amendments I made to the kit's undercarriage was to drill out the holes in the mudguard supports (Pt. Nos. 32, 33, 35 & 36). Each unit was painted a bright aluminium overall, while the wheel hubs were painted dull aluminium, and the tyres a very dark grey.

With the whole model now dry, the detail parts were added and then the model was sprayed overall with a semi-gloss varnish, as that better represents the finish of the prototype. Now for a fighter...

•2 NF Mk II

Building this example is very easy, as it is basically the standard Airfix kit with a few amendments and a new colour scheme. The KMC interior can be installed directly as supplied, although a scratchbuilt A.I. Mk IV radar unit will have to be made. Use the details given in Chapter 11 of this title to assist you in this. If you do not use the KMC set, you can use the kit's interior with a little extra detailing and the addition of the radar unit. One of the good options offered when using the KMC set is that you can display the crew-access door open, as this area is supplied as a separate item. I chose not to do this with the NF Mk II, as I wanted to do it with the J 30, however the choice is there. The rest of the model is built up as per the kit instructions and the only things you need to change are the

The starboard lower wing half with the spar caps removed and the flaps cut out

The port lower wing half from the Airfix kit, before the raised spar caps and flaps were removed

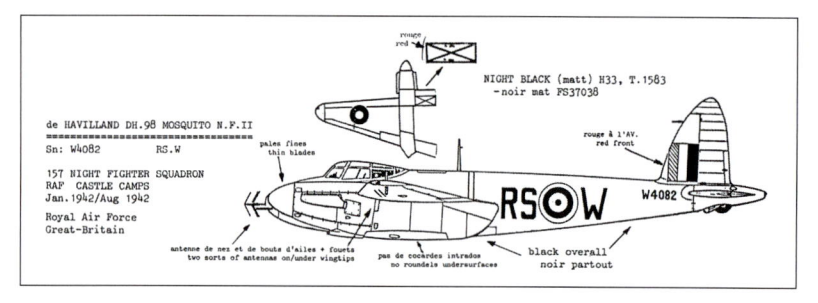

W4082, RS•W of No.157 Sqn. is one of the options on Carpena sheet 48-22

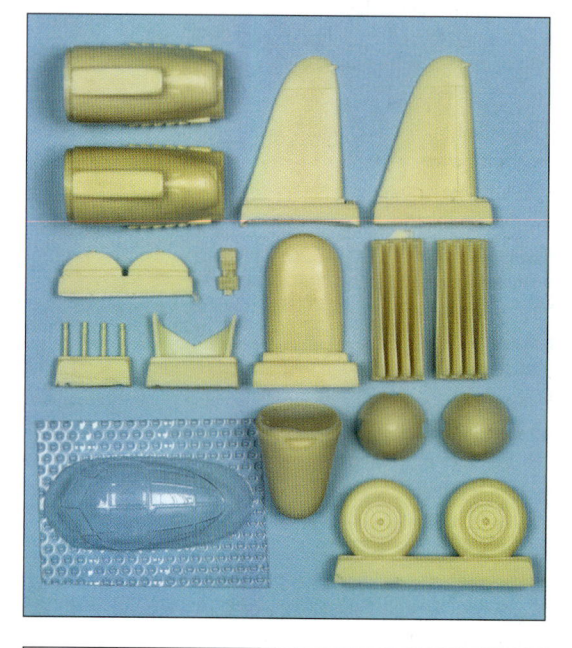

The NF Mk XV conversion in 1/48th scale (P48071)

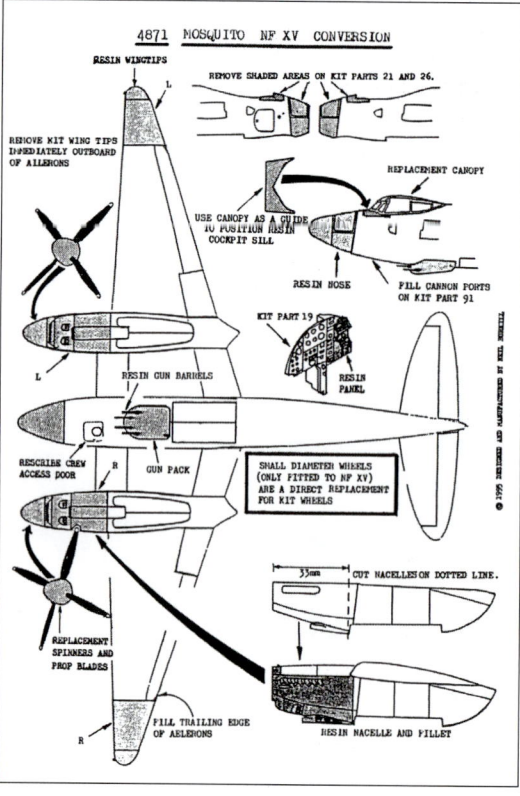

The instructions for the NF Mk XV conversion (P48071)

propeller blades. These are the narrow style, which can be replaced with the Paragon examples, or the kit blades can be reprofiled.

Very quickly the model was completed and at a stage where it could be primed. The cockpit area was masked off and then the entire model was sprayed with grey primer. Once this was dry the cockpit was unmasked and the canopy installed. The canopy was later masked with Parafilm M (or tape) and then sprayed with Interior Green, so as to be visible through the canopy once completed. Once this had all dried the model was sprayed black overall and left to dry. Decalling was very easy, as an NF Mk II was one of the options on the old Carpena decal sheet (No. 48-22). This example is W4082, coded RS•W of No.157 Squadron and is black overall with the unit codes and serial number in dull red. An A1 roundel is applied to the fuselage with B type on the upper wings.

Once all of these were applied and dry, the model was detailed with the undercarriage, which had been prepared in the same way as that in the prototype. The completed model could then be sprayed overall with a good matt varnish, as the NF Mk II was very, very matt and it wore very quickly, so weathering is a definite option with this version. Once all this had dried, the detailed radar antennas could be created from plastic rod and wire. The 'bow and arrow' antenna on the nose was a bit tricky to make and in the end it was created by making the main sections in plastic rod and each V of the unit in copper wire. Because the rear section of this antenna is flat in profile, I used a loop of wire and then filled this in with PVA glue. With hindsight I suspect that an easier option to this is to make this section out of plastic card and just secure it to the central rod, with wire for the front 'V' section. The style and positioning of all of the antennas were achieved by using the excellent 1/48th scale plans by Richard J. Caruana which are included in this title.

•3 NF Mk XV Prototype (MP469) in its initial form

Now, I originally made this variant in my articles in *Scale Aviation Modeller International* in 1996, so initially I did not intend to do it again. However, whilst doing the initial research for this title I came across a picture of MP469 in its initial form and decided that this was what I wanted to build. The reason behind this is that MP469 was converted (in 7 days!) from the high-altitude development airframe into the forerunner of the NF Mk XV series. In this state the aircraft was quite different from the version I had originally built; it had the full extended span (64ft 2in), a fighter nose grafted onto a bomber fuselage, two-stage engines, standard undercarriage and wheels and four machine-guns in the nose. The type was also finished in an odd mix of colours, being Ocean Grey and Dark Green on top and a colour called 'Deep Sky' underneath. This lower surface colour was applied late in the day and was sprayed up onto the top colours on the fuselage side, resulting in a soft demarcation which is very unusual for any Mosquito. The type also retained Medium Sea Grey spinners, but four-blade propellers. All in all a stunning machine.

Making this machine was quite straightforward and the main fuselage is built up as per the kit instructions, although you do have to correct the forward windscreen join, as the type featured the bomber style of canopy and the kit depicts the flat fighter style. I got around this by not installing the separate new section for this area supplied by Paragon (Conversion No.4871), but by using the new vac-formed canopy to act as a template on the kit's fuselage, and then simply cut the excess out of this area. The new nose, ventral gun pack and radar unit for the interior included in the Paragon conversion can be consigned to the spares box, as they were not used on MP469 initially. The two stage Merlin engines need to be used however and each kit nacelle should be built up and left to dry. Include the undercarriage mounting plate (Pt. Nos. 44 and 49) in each nacelle at this point, as it acts as a bulkhead to keep the unit aligned when you cut off the front. Removing the front of each nacelle will require your measuring, exactly, 33mm from the

118 Chapter 12

front of the unit, at which point you cut off this area. Now you can join the new front end of the nacelle and the upper insert, as the two-stage units are slightly longer than the single-stage examples. Now the tips of each wing need to be removed and replaced with the extended tips included in the conversion. These depict the maximum-span version fitted to MP469, although they are too long for the subsequent five NF Mk XV conversions, which only had a span of 59ft. The kit's wings have the tips cut off immediately outboard of the ailerons, and some plastic card and filler will be needed to reprofile the ailerons, as the new wing tips also extend the trailing-edge. Ensure that you get a good parallel joint with each tip, otherwise when viewed from above, the new tips will bend forward (or back) and the leading-edge will no longer be straight. I ensure a good bond at these joints by drilling each tip with a couple of holes and adding reinforcing pins. When the new tips are slipped into position the pins go inside the existing wing halves, thereby ensuring a strong joint. The actual joints on the real aircraft were covered with a ply skin and to reproduce this strips of decal film were applied over these joints once the model was primed and prior to final painting.

Since I last built this conversion, Paragon have replaced their metal propeller blades with resin ones and this now means that assembling each unit into the resin spinner is nowhere near as much of a problem. Once again I drilled holes into the hub at the root joint and at the base of each blade, and inserted a wire pin into it before I cemented each blade in position. This ensures a good strong joint, and also means that the blades are far less likely to 'sag' whilst the cement sets. The cockpit area was masked and the model primed. Once all the problem areas were dealt with further, the model was primed again and then it was time to removing the masking and fit the vac-formed canopy. With this style of canopy I now adopt a system I learned from expert French model maker Jacque Niot, namely I secure strips of plastic rod or card all along the edge of the canopy opening. These are then painted the interior colour and once dry the vac-formed canopy is secured to them. The strips act as a lip, onto which the canopy will catch. This ensures a good joint, while also making the whole assembly far more rigid and therefore less prone to cracking if you have to do any filling and sanding near it. Once the canopy was secure, it was masked and sprayed Interior Green. The canopy join was covered with strips of decal film, as per the previous example and then the whole model was sprayed with the final colour scheme. The upper colours are applied, Ocean Grey, then Dark Green. The camouflage pattern is achieved through using simple masks made of paper which are loosely held in position with tape or Blu-tak. This ensures you get a nice soft edge to the demarcation without running the risk of overspray onto the other colour. The lower surface is a bit of a mystery still, as 'Deep Sky' was never an official colour and when you see Federal Standard numbers quoted for the colour, it is obviously based on the fact that many assume it is PR Blue. I have seen every colour from light blue to PR Blue, so I simply lightened PR Blue from the Xtracolor range with 30% white and applied that. This colour has to be free-hand sprayed onto the fuselage sides as that was how it was done on the real aircraft. With all this dry, the decals were

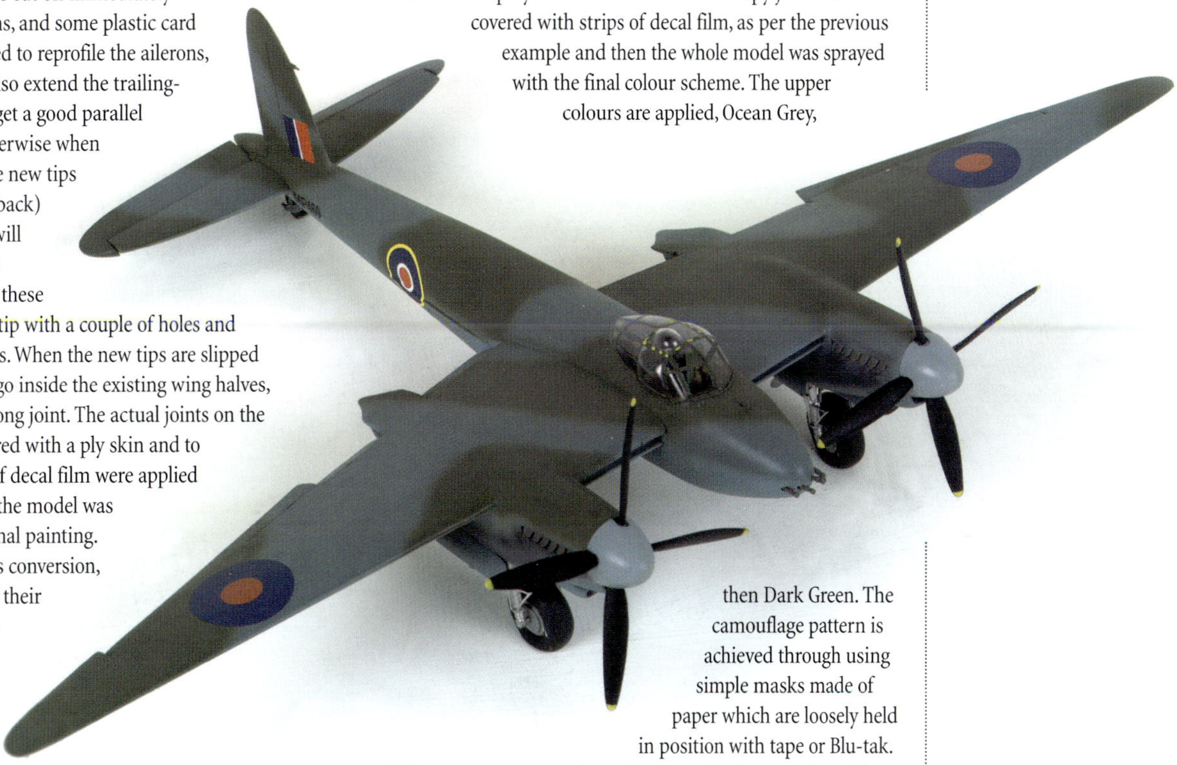

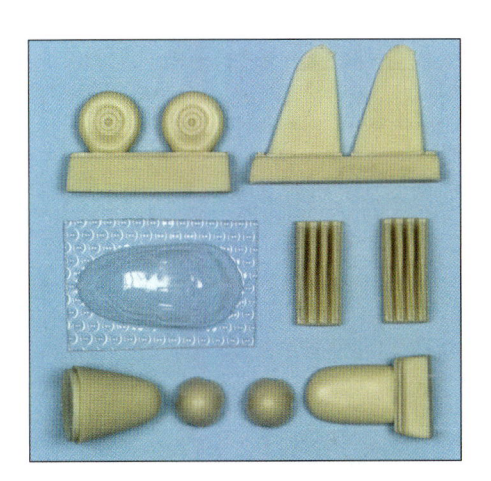

The NF Mk XV conversion in 1/72nd scale (P72033) is for the Matchbox kit

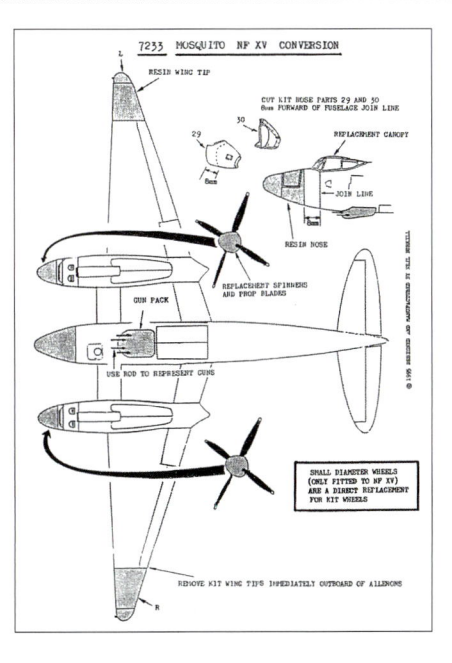

The instructions for conversion P72033

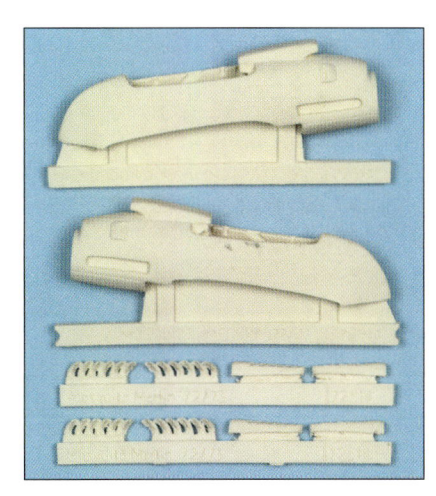

The two-stage Merlin (72/73) engine nacelles are offered in 1/72nd scale (72514) by Hi-Tech

Modelling the Mosquito • Building the Mosquito   **119**

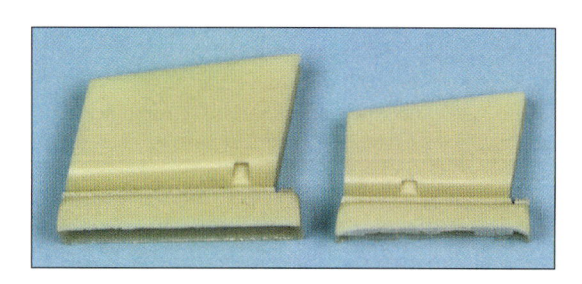

The separate flaps for the Airfix kit in 1/48th scale (P48040)

applied. These came from a combination of Xtradecal and AeroMaster sheets. The upper wings have B type roundels on them, in the usual position and size as applied to all Mosquitoes. I have seen the upper surface of the production versions and the roundel remained the same, so there is no reason to assume the prototype was any different. The lower wings carried no roundels or serials and the fuselage roundel is an A2 style. The fin flash is the B type and this machine carried no prototype 'P', just its serial number in black.

Once the decals were dry the model was sprayed with a semi-gloss varnish and then the detail parts were fitted. These include the undercarriage, doors and tailwheel. The undercarriage is made up in the same way as in the previous examples, although the prototype in its initial form retained standard wheels with the plain hubs. Later on this machine, and all subsequent production versions, had reduced diameter mainwheels of a lower pressure. This later style of wheel is included in the Paragon conversion, but in this example I used their 'weighted' standard wheels (48113). No aerial mast was installed and in this very early scheme, the twin whip antennae on the upper, rear fuselage were not installed either.

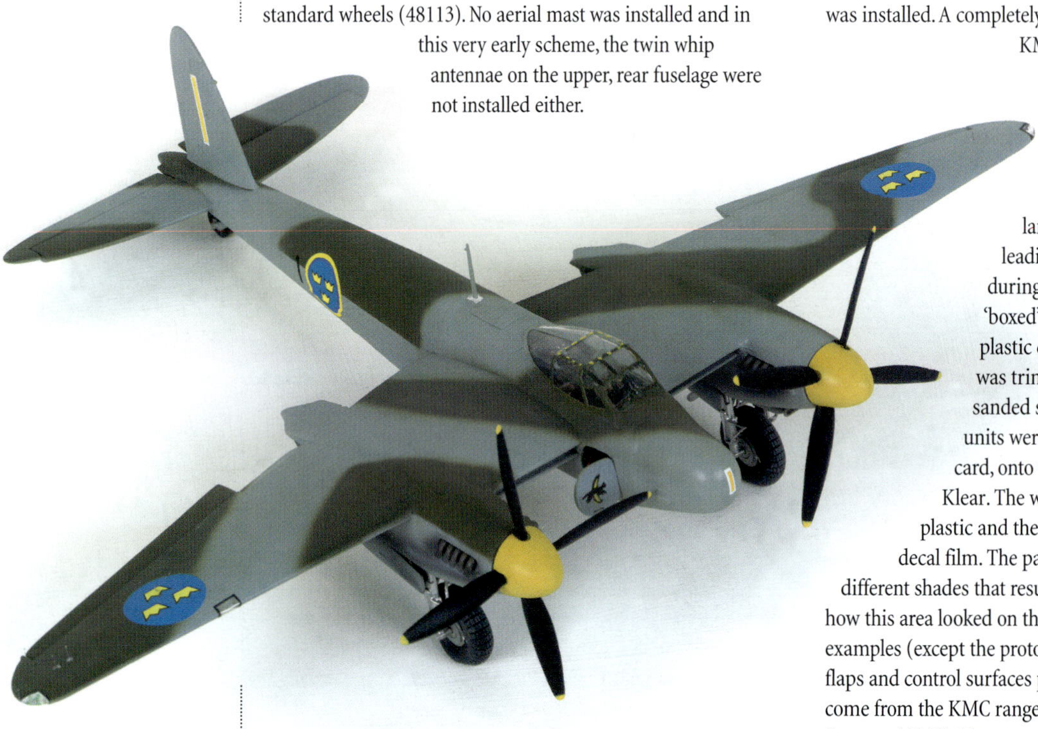

• 4 J 30 (NF Mk XIX)

This conversion is basically the standard Airfix kit with the addition of the 'Universal' (Bullnose) radome and four-blade propellers. The four-blade props are not marketed separately, however if you contact Paragon directly they will supply them. The Bullnose radome (4843) is fitted to the fighter nose once this area is cut away from the kit fuselage halves, and the four-blade propellers simply replace the three-blade examples. The cockpit interior was detailed with the KMC update set, although as this machine is a night fighter, an additional resin unit is supplied in the Bullnose set by Paragon which represents the A.I. Mk X radar equipment. This unit just fits into the recess by the armour bulkhead to the right of the main instrument panel and I did find that it was a little too narrow. This resulted in the unit being too far in once in position. To get over this I added a 3mm wedge of plastic card to the back of the unit before it was finally cemented in position. It was with this variant that I decided to pose the crew-access door open and therefore I cut the area away from the fuselage half before the KMC sidewall was installed. A completely new resin door is supplied in the KMC set, so this was painted separately and added after all painting and assembly was completed. Many foreign operated Mosquitoes, along with a number of post-war RAF examples, had a twin set of landing lights in the starboard wing leading-edge. I cut the area out of the wing during the initial assembly stage and then 'boxed' the resulting hole in with strips of plastic card. Once these had dried the excess was trimmed off and the joins were filled and sanded smooth. After painting the twin light units were replicated from small discs of plastic card, onto which was added a blob of Krystal Klear. The whole unit was then glazed with clear plastic and the joins sealed with narrow strips of decal film. The paintwork was touched up, as the different shades that resulted from this did not matter, it was how this area looked on the real aircraft. As with all the other examples (except the prototype), this kit was built to have the flaps and control surfaces posed separately. The control surfaces come from the KMC range (48-5065) and the flaps from Paragon (4840). The corresponding areas were carefully cut away from the kit parts, with a little final tidying up being achieved with some gentle sanding. There is no need to box in the open areas at the side of each engine nacelle, as this area is wide open on the real aircraft. Both the flaps and control surfaces were added just prior to the final priming and painting stage. The only thing that I did not choose to add was the bulged panel in the starboard side of the cockpit canopy. This was because it would have involved some major surgery to the kit's canopy, or the modification of a vac-formed example. Hopefully before too much longer a correct style canopy will be released by an accessory manufacturer (hint!).

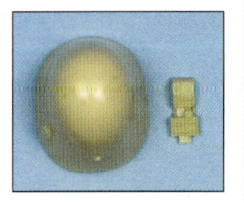

The 'Universal' radome and SCR 720/729 indicator unit (P48043)

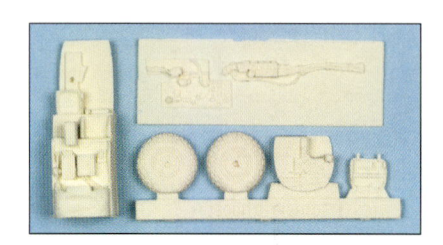

An update set for any fighter version of the Mosquito is offered in 1/72nd scale (72018) by Hi-Tech. Once again this is designed for both the Matchbox and Airfix kits

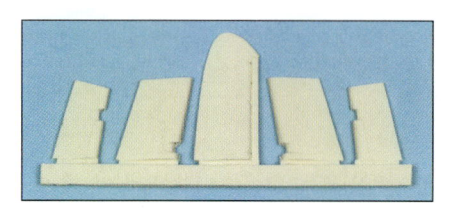

Hi-Tech offer a set of flaps and a rudder in 1/72nd scale (72513)

The Airfix NF Mk XIX has an inaccurate radome, so Air Kit Enterprises have included a new one (as in set Air053) and these two 100 gallon drop tanks

Chapter 12

The model was, at this stage, ready for priming and painting and this was achieved in the same manner as the previous examples. The cockpit was masked, the model primed and then the masking was removed from the canopy so that the canopy could be installed, masked and sprayed Interior Green. Any flaws in the finish were corrected and then the model was sprayed Medium Sea Grey overall. The Swedish Air Force J 30s were finished in RAF colours, although the camouflage pattern was applied in a different manner (See Chapter 13). The upper areas, less the vertical fin, had a camouflaged pattern of Dark Green applied over the Medium Sea Grey and this was achieved in the same manner as the previous example, namely basic paper masks taped loosely in position. The spinners were painted yellow with the blades in black with yellow tips, and the undercarriage and wheels were painted in the manner described for the previous examples. Applying the decals was a bit complex, as I did not have the correct style of Swedish roundel. To get around this I used the yellow ring from an RAF Type C1 roundel and applied the Swedish roundel over it. I am sure that the Specialtryck range of decals from Sweden do offer the correct style of roundel and squadron codes in this scale, but unfortunately I did not have them. The option I had gone for was 'Yellow I' (S/No.30046) and this letter was applied on the vertical fin and on the front of the nose. To make these up I used decal film, sprayed both yellow and white, and cut out strips of the correct length and width. The white strips had to be wider than the yellow sections, so they could be applied first to form the border of the letter. Using white as a base had the added bonus of ensuring that the yellow was not affected by the colours underneath. The squadron motif on the crew-access door was a bit of a problem, as there were no decals I know of that offer it (unless Specialtryck do). I therefore hand painted a representation of it on the separate resin door from the KMC set before it was secured to the model. The small serial number in line with the tailplanes on the fuselage sides were obtained from a sheet of Letraset rub-down transfers and these were applied onto clear decal film, so that they could be applied as a decal onto the model.

Once all of the above was applied and dry, the model was sprayed with semi-gloss varnish and the detail parts added. An aerial mast was installed, but no lead, and the dipoles on each wing tip were made from lengths of copper wire which were secured through holes drilled in each wing. The final detail painting included clear aluminium patches below the aerial mast and dipoles on each wing, as these dielectric panels were never painted on the real aircraft. An alternative to painting these is to use aluminium foil (shiny side down), cut to shape and attached to the model after painting is completed.

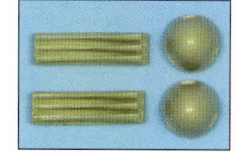

The three blade narrow propellers in 1/48th scale (P48069)

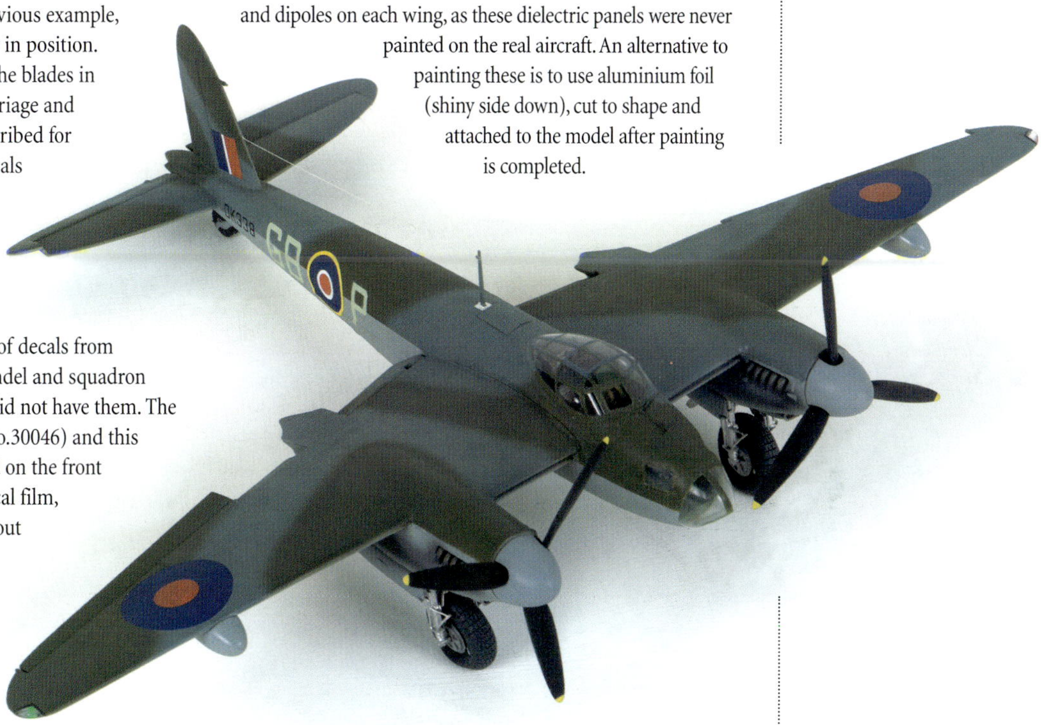

5 B Mk IV Series II

This version utilises the bomber nose conversion (Paragon 4870) which was used in the prototype conversion. The KMC interior set was again used and, as with the prototype, modifications were made to it to ensure that it better represented the bomber style of interior. Once again care must be taken in ensuring that the new resin nose halves are correctly

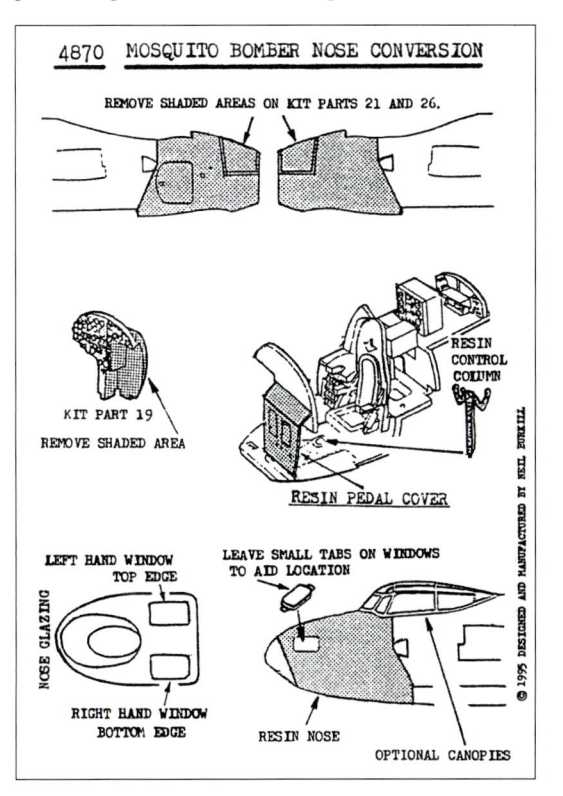

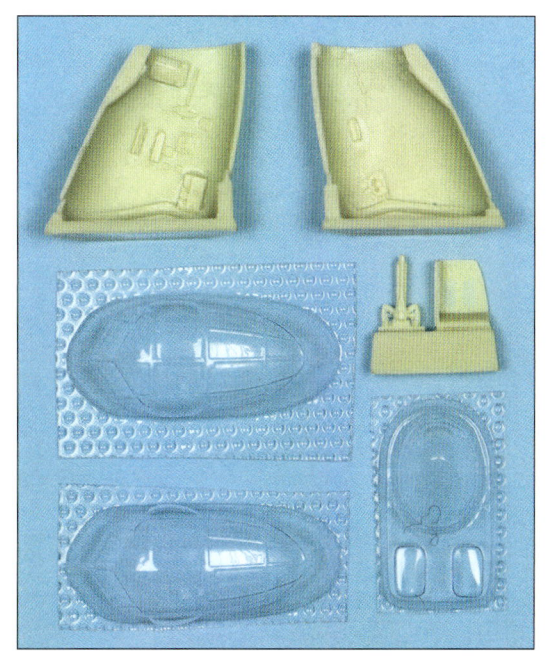

Left: The bomber nose conversion (P48070) is used in a number of the variants, if you use the Airfix kit as a basis

Far left: The instructions for conversion set P48070 show how the Airfix kit parts have to be cut to fit the new nose

Modelling the Mosquito • Building the Mosquito

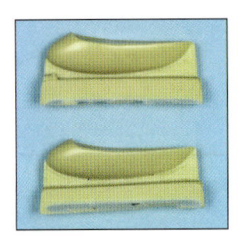

aligned. The fuselage halves were taped together, so that the resin nose halves could be tacked into position before they were finally cemented onto each kit section. The revised instrument panel and 'yoke' style of control column were installed as per the prototype and once again the back of the instrument panel should be detailed, as it is going to be visible through the glazed nose. The only other modifications required with this example were the addition of the 50-gallon drop-tanks (Paragon 4877) under each wing and the fitment of a bomber canopy with 'teardrop' side blisters which is included in the bomber nose conversion set (Paragon 4870). This version of the Mosquito also requires the narrow style of propellers, so these can either be achieved by modifying the kit parts, or installing the resin examples from Paragon (4869).

With all of the above work completed, the cockpit was masked off and the model was primed. All of the flaws were dealt with and then the model was reprimed so that the overall camouflage scheme could be applied. The cockpit masking was removed and the canopy installed. The edges were sealed with strips of decal film and it was then masked and sprayed Interior Green. The option I was going for was GB•P (DK338) of No.105 Squadron which is offered on AeroMaster sheet 48-299, so the overall scheme was Ocean Grey and Dark Green over Medium Sea Grey. The lower surface was applied first, then it was masked off so the Ocean Grey could be applied to the entire upper surface. Once this had dried the camouflage pattern was masked with paper and the Dark Green sprayed on. The decals for this option came directly from the AeroMaster sheet and these consisted of the squadron codes in Sky, the serial in black, Type A2 roundels on the fuselage sides and Type Bs on the upper wings.

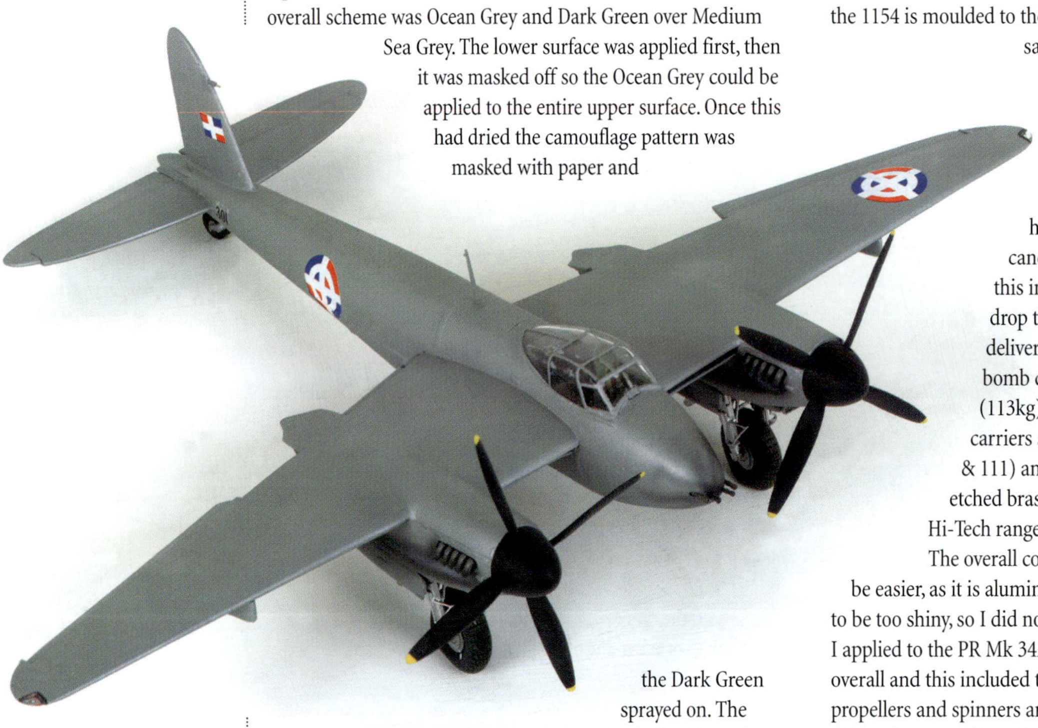

With all the painting and decals applied, the model was sprayed with semi-gloss varnish and the detail parts added.

The 50 gallon drop tanks (P48077)

The five-spoke hubs and the square tread tyres are offered in 1/72nd (P72025) and 1/48th (P48112)

This machine has the exposed exhaust stacks, unlike the other machines of the squadron at that time, and these are of course supplied in the Airfix kit. An aerial mast was fitted, so this is installed at the painting stage and later on the aerial leads can be attached to it. The early style of wheel hubs with five spokes were used and these were obtained from the Paragon range (48112).

•6 FB Mk VI in Dominican Air Force markings

This was the easiest of the options made, as it is just the Airfix kit with the addition of the KMC interior set and the fitment of four-blade propellers. The landing light unit in the starboard leading edge of the wing is created as per the J 30 and apart from the replacement of the kit's mainwheels with the Paragon 'weighted' examples (48113), that was it. It is very unlikely that the FB Mk VIs supplied to Dominica had British radio equipment still installed (although I could be wrong), so the 1155/1154 combination depicted in the KMC update needs to be removed. This is fine with the 1154 unit, as this is separate, but the 1155 is moulded to the rear decking and will need to be sawn off. Great care is needed here to ensure you do not damage the decking and you will also have to ensure that only the wiring relating to the radio is cut away. As with the J 30, this option should have the bulged side panel in the fighter canopy, although I was unable to represent this in the example I built. The type had drop tanks (100-gallon) fitted only for the delivery flights and in service a universal bomb carrier was fitted and American 250lb (113kg) bombs were installed. I used the carriers supplied in the Airfix kit (Pt. Nos 110 & 111) and plan to install the excellent resin and etched brass 250lb (113kg) bombs from the Hi-Tech range (48511) at a later date.

The overall colour scheme for this option could not be easier, as it is aluminium overall. I did not want this colour to be too shiny, so I did not use the acrylic aluminium spray that I applied to the PR Mk 34A. Instead I sprayed Humbrol 56 overall and this included the undercarriage bays as well. The propellers and spinners are black and that's that. The decals for this option came from the AeroMaster sheet number 48-298 (*International Mosquito Collection*). This sheet includes '2108' in a later scheme with the entire rudder in the national colours. The option I wanted was '301' in the initial delivery scheme and therefore I used the national markings from this option. The tail was marked with a small flash of the national colours and this

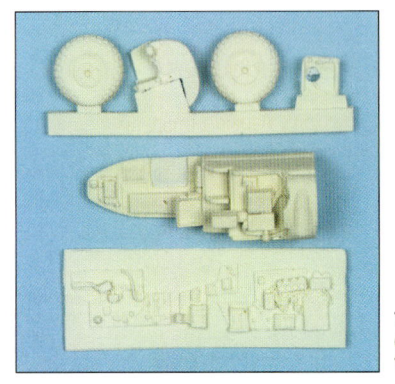

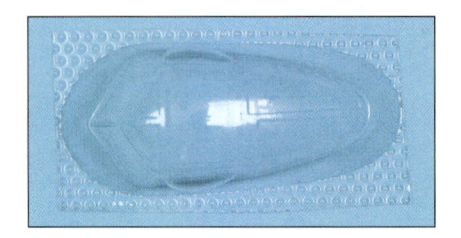

The bomber canopy with 'teardrop' side panels in 1/32nd scale (P32014)

The update set for the bomber versions of the Mosquito which is offered in 1/72nd scale (P72019) by Hi-Tech. This set is designed for both the Matchbox and Airfix kits

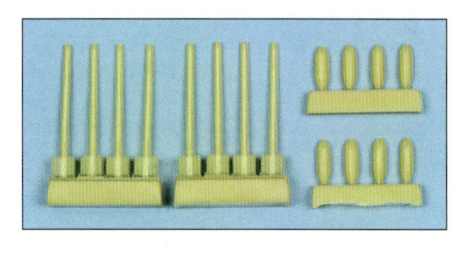

The 60lb SAP rockets which can be used instead of the Airfix kit examples (48055)

was achieved by simply cutting down the large rudder markings on the AeroMaster sheet. The codes offered on this sheet are not usable with my chosen option however, as they are too big, so these came from the good old Letraset range once again.

With all the markings etc applied, the model was sprayed with varnish and the detail parts such as the undercarriage added. This option has exposed exhaust stacks and an aerial mast and lead, and these are all applied in this final stage.

•7 PR Mk XVI in French Air Force markings

This option was one of the more involved conversions, as it required the bomber nose (4870), two-stage Merlins (4842), PR canopy (4873), 100-gallon drop tanks (4878), flaps (4840) and plain hub main wheels (48113) from Paragon and the separate control surfaces (48-5065) and cockpit update set (48-4014) from KMC. The fitment of these was as in the previous examples and the cockpit interior was modified slightly to better represent the bomber configuration, although the complex PR equipment fit in the nose area was not represented. Study of the information given in Chapter 11 should assist all those who wish to better replicate this area.

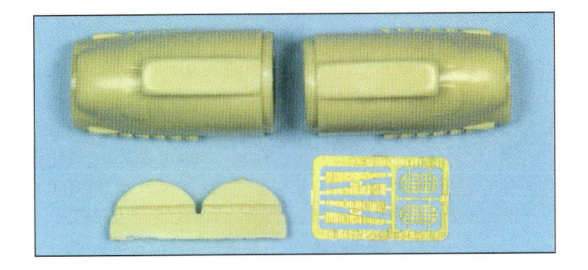

Initially I had thought about doing the lovely USAAF version of this mark, as I had done in my original feature in *Scale Aviation Modeller International,* but AeroMaster sheet 48-298 took a hand! This sheet includes an option for a machine operated by 'Lorraine' squadron of the French Air Force. This machine is PR Blue overall (very faded), with yellow spinners and the entire rudder in the French tricolour. It was certainly a stunning option and one I could not help but make. Everything bar the detail parts was fitted to the model and it was primed and prepared as per the previous examples. Spraying the model could not be easier as it was one colour overall. I did however decide, after a study of pictures of this machine, that this colour was very faded so after the initial application of PR Blue, I gradually lightened it and then applied batches of these revised shades over the top. The end result was quite effective, although it needs fine tuning! Application of the AeroMaster decals caused no problems and the colour density of the rudder tricolour was good even over the dark PR Blue. The fit of this decal was also excellent, and once a decal softener (MicroSol) had been used, it snuggled down onto all the rib details very nicely. The fuselage and wing roundels are supplied in three sections. The first is the white base and yellow edge, onto which is applied the next red ring and finally you apply the blue dot for the centre. The only other decals required on this option were the white 'R' and the black serial number (NS517), all of which were applied with little fuss.

After all the decals were dry the model had to be varnished. Now as this option was very faded I felt that a very matt finish was in order, so the completed model was sprayed with a matt varnish. Detail parts included the camera ports on the underside, which can either be represented with plastic card discs or, like me, you can use the resin ports which are included in the Paragon bulged camera bay (4875). The main wheels have the plain hubs and an aerial mast is fitted, but no leads.

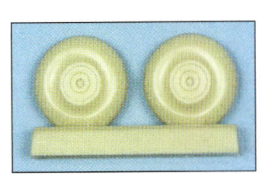

•8 PR Mk 34A

This model was to become the heaviest I had made, as it included all of the items fitted to the PR Mk XVI, plus the use of a bulged camera bay (4875). Construction and detailing of the type is identical to the previous example except for one very interesting detail. You cannot use the elevators out of the KMC set (48-5065), as the PR Mk 34 (and 34A) had enlarged balance horns and this makes the ends of each elevator larger. To overcome this I used the elevators off the kit and modified them according to the scale drawings I had. The easiest way to do this is to trap a piece of plastic card between each section, and once the unit is dry cut the new profile from the card. To increase the thickness and blend the whole area in you will have to add filler and sand the area smooth, but in doing so you will remove all the detail from the kit part. I did not worry too much about this, but if you wish to re-apply the raised details I suspect that dabs of PVA or similar would fit the bill, albeit the task would be a bit tedious and time consuming. The bulged camera bay is a simple 'add-on' item which is secured over that area of the kit and I also added the camera ports at this early stage, as I wanted to deal with the small gaps around each before the overall colour scheme was applied

There was only one real option I could go for with a PR Mk 34A and that was RG314, the example which flew the last RAF operational sortie in 1955. The whole model was sprayed

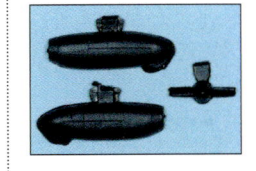

The plain hub main wheels with square tread tyres (P48113)

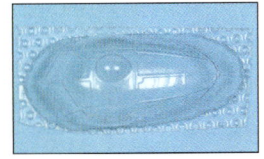

The PR style of canopy in 1/48th scale (P48073)

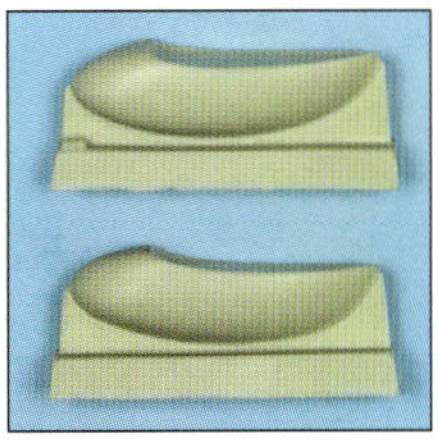

The 100 gallon drop tanks (P48078)

The two-stage Merlin engine nacelles (P48042) are designed for the Airfix kit

The ML Type G winch that is offered in 1/72nd scale by Aeroclub (V079)

with a shiny aluminium acrylic car paint and once this was dry (about 30 minutes!) the nose area was masked and the anti-dazzle panel was applied in black. Markings for this machine were simple, being the bright post-war D Type roundels in four positions and the code in black on each side of the rear fuselage and in bigger letters under each outer wing panel.

The roundels came off AeroMaster sheet 48-303 (Post War Mosquitoes) and the serial from those Letraset sheets again. No other markings were required and once all of them were applied and had dried the model was lightly sprayed with a semi-gloss varnish to take the edge of the sheen of the decals and the shiny aluminium colour scheme. Once this had dried the anti-dazzle panel was masked out and this area was sprayed with matt varnish.

Detail parts included the undercarriage, the plain style of mainwheels, the aerial mast and lead, painting the camera ports black and then glazing them with Krystal Klear (or gloss varnish) and the fitment of the 'paddle-blade' propellers and the glossy red spinners. With all that resin, this kit is very heavy once completed and I am sure that undercarriage is going to have its work cut-out in the long run!

•9 TT Mk 35

This model is basically identical in component usage as the PR Mk 34A, but it does require some complex modification work and scratch building. The model is completed as per the PR Mk 34A, but the drop-tanks are omitted as this type did not carry them. The bulged bomb-bay (4874) is used in place of the camera version (4875) and modifications will have to be made to the back of it. The TT Mk 35 was modified from a B Mk 35 and the rear fairing of the bomb-bay had two cutouts in it, one on either side. These were for the stowage of the forward section of the banner and the example also had the banner stowage units built into each bomb-bay door. A detailed study of preserved examples and documentation never quite explained how the system, especially the buffer unit, actually worked, so much of what I have built is speculation. A detailed study of the information on the type contained within Chapter 11 of this title may help the reader make his own decisions about this variant. At a very early stage one has to decide which machine one is going to make as a number of different equipment fits are applicable to this mark. I opted for VP181 flown by the commander of No.3 CAACU at Exeter and I wanted to make this machine as it was in the latter stages of its operational use. This meant that I had to fit the ML Type G winch and apply day-glo

The FB Mk VI conversion in 1/32nd scale (P32012) is for the Revell kit and even includes a complete cockpit interior

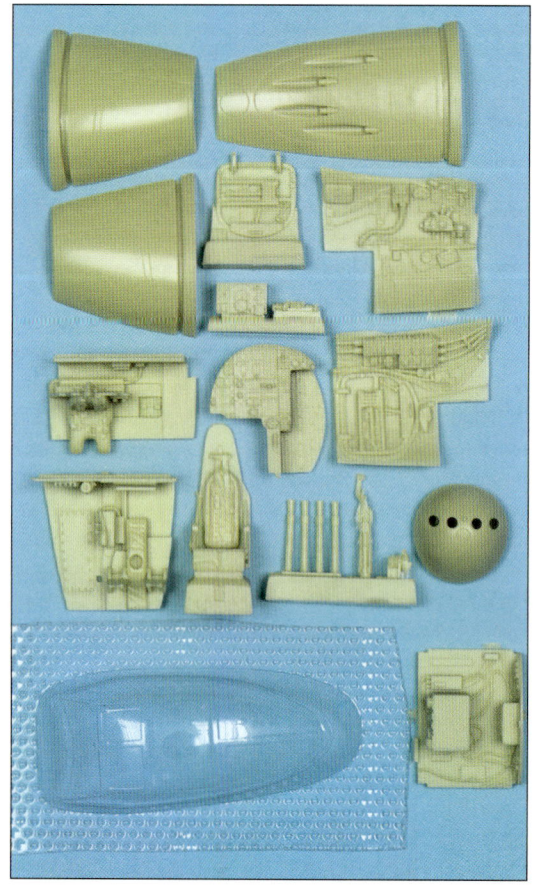

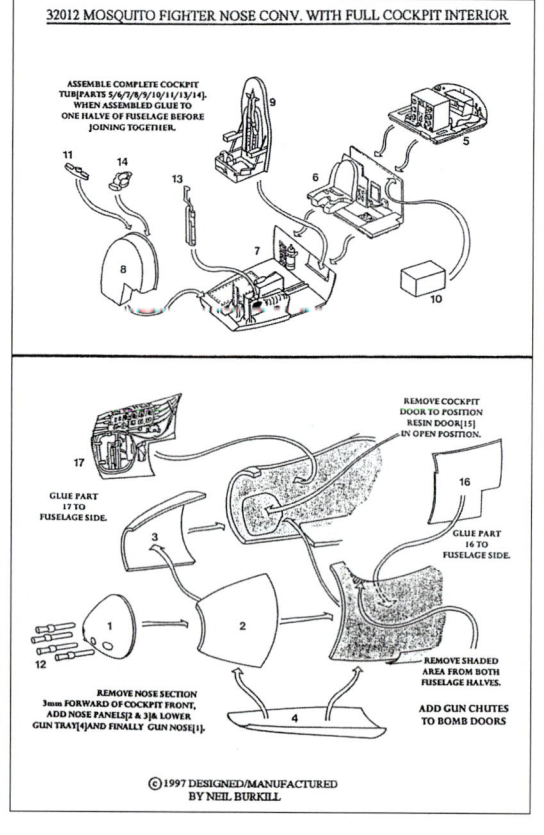

The instructions for set P32012

panels in lieu of the usual trainer yellow bands. Having made up the model as per the previous example and having fitted the modified bomb-bay it was time to paint the model. Now this machine has a complex overall scheme. It is silver on top and yellow with black stripes on the under surface. Now, when I say that the upper surface is silver this in fact does extend down under the wings on the fuselage sides and each engine nacelle. I therefore just sprayed the entire model with aluminium acrylic spray and once this was dry masked these areas off so that the yellow could be applied. I opted for Trainer Yellow from the Xtracolor range, but with hindsight I feel that it is too dark going by the colour pictures of the type which I have seen, so maybe Humbrol 24 would be a better option. Once this is dry the black stripes are masked off, so that they can be applied. One thing to note is that the serial numbers on the under surface of each wing are on yellow and that includes those areas which go into the black. This means that you either have to work all this out in the initial masking stage, or, like me, spray it all up then remask and spray yellow onto the appropriate areas of the black stripes! The other thing, and one which is common with target tugs, is that the tailplanes are not striped with black and yellow and therefore on the Mosquito the elevator is yellow and the fixed portion of the tailplane is black. As I was not going to apply the wide trainer yellow bands of the type I did not have to mask these out during the earlier stages, if however you wish to do that type of scheme, these areas need to be masked prior to the overall yellow being applied. Because I wanted VP181 in a late scheme, this meant it had stripes of day-glo orange on the inner flaps, upper wing tips and wing leading-edges and around the entire rear fuselage. Now you can either buy day-glo decals, or, like me, get the same colour in the 'odds'n'ends' paint range (enamel) and spray that onto clear decal stock. My reason for using the latter was to see if it was really day-glo and although it is not massively bright, it is very good for use with models. My only advice with this colour however is do not try to mask and spray it directly onto your model as the colour pigment is a bit temperamental and you will not get a good result first of all. I had to spray my decal film three times to get a good finish and if this was done on a masked model the resulting 'step' in the paint at the masked edge would be quite pronounced. Strips of the decal were now cut and I used photographs of the real aircraft to guide their dimensions as there is no official regulations for this type of marking (remember the aircraft were operated by civilian contractors, so RAF rules do not strictly apply). Once again the D type post war roundels are carried in four positions and luckily with my chosen option the fuselage code is included on AeroMaster sheet 48-303, as this sheet includes an option for VP181 when it was serving as a B Mk 35 with No.98 Squadron in Germany. The serials under each wing are once again Letraset rub-down transfers, although I am sure that there are after-market decal manufacturers that include black serials of a suitable size in their range. The final marking was the large black '54' applied aft of the fuselage roundel and this also came from the Letraset range. With all of these markings applied the model was lightly sprayed with semi-gloss varnish and allowed to dry.

Now the real work began as the winch had to be constructed. This was achieved by converting a drop-tank from a 1/72nd scale F/A-18 kit. I used the scale plans included elsewhere in this

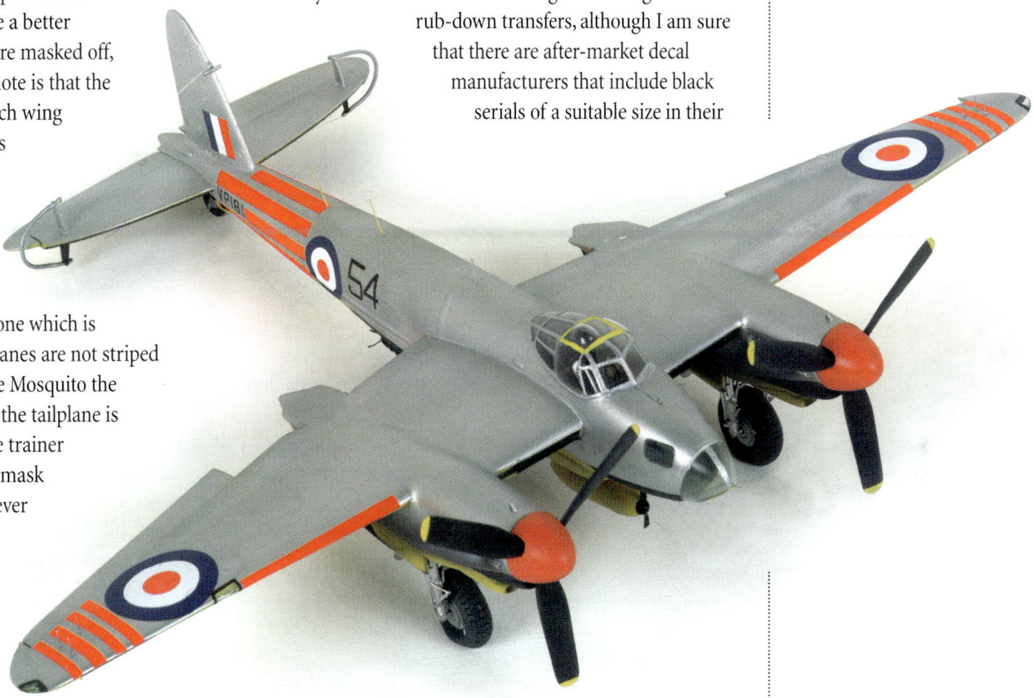

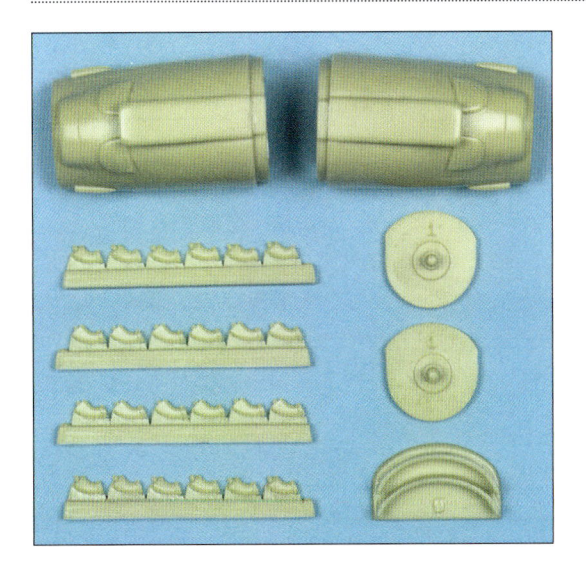

The huge two-stage Merlins in 1/32nd scale (P32011) include separate exhaust stacks

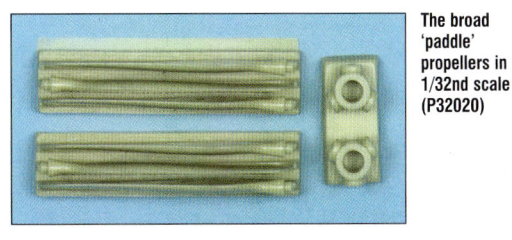

The broad 'paddle' propellers in 1/32nd scale (P32020)

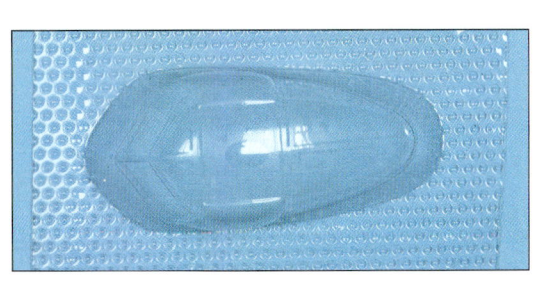

The bomber canopy with 'blown' side panels in 1/32nd scale (P32015)

The bulged bomb bay for the 4,000lb 'Cookie'-carrying Mosquito variants (P48074)

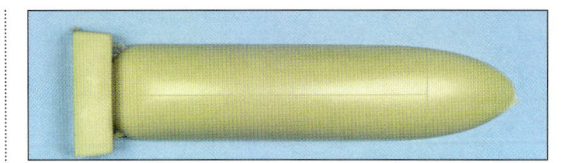

title to get the dimensions correct and once completed it was sprayed the same yellow overall and left to dry. Using the numerous pictures of the type I have, I hand painted all the black markings onto the winch and then built a simple support pylon from a 1/32nd scale pylon I found in the spares box. The whole unit was then cemented to the bomb-bay, on the centre-line, in the correct position. The small propeller and spinner for the unit were made from plastic card for the blades which were secured either side of the pointed nose of the winch unit, and the separating line was just drawn on with a graphic pen. The buffer unit at the rear of the bomb-bay was made of copper wire and plastic rod and once again I studied a number of photographs to get some idea of what this should look like. This was also painted yellow and secured in position on the underneath of the fuselage aft of the bomb-bay. The next task was the wire guard around the tail. First of all the support struts were added above and below the fixed tailplane, towards the tips. These items were made of plastic card and were approximations going by a study of a number of pictures. Once dry they were painted and the fact that they are a slightly different colour to the rest of the model is no problem as they seem to be so on the real aircraft anyway. The wire guide under the tail was made of plastic tube, as was the guide on the front edge of the vertical fin. The wire hoop around the tip of each tailplane was made of thick wire and once this was secured on position the gaps in between each guide were filled with lengths of the fibre filament available from Aeroclub. This filament is very flexible and its use ensures that the model has a far greater durability (I hope!). The next additions were the banners, which were made of rolled up white tissue paper soaked in thinned PVA glue, and these were secured to the bomb-bay doors and into the recesses cut in the rear fairing. The fibre filament was again used to make the straps that secured these banners and to make it black it was first dipped in ink. The final detail for this target equipment was the banner-towing cable, and this was made from elastic cut to length and secured from the pulley unit under the rear fuselage, and then looped back around the buffer unit and connected to the banners. With all of this secure the final items such as the 'paddle' propellers, undercarriage units and plain-hub wheels were all added and the model was complete - lovely!

Well, there you have it, nine Mosquito variants from the first (prototype) to the last (operational variant). All of the conversions I have made can be also done in 1/72nd scale using the information listed in Chapter 10 of this title. At present there are not sufficient accessories to make all of the types in 1/32nd scale, but I am sure that will change in the not too distant future. Once new kits of this type are released the amount of conversion work needed to make each type will of course decrease, but all of the factors mentioned here and elsewhere in this title will ensure that you get a good representation of the Mosquito, whatever kit you start with.

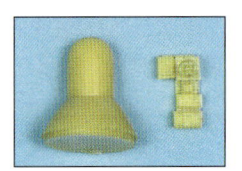

The 'Thimble' radome of the APS-4 (ASH) pod (P48044)

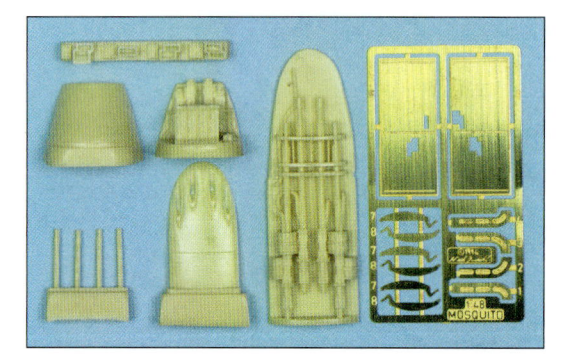

The open 20mm ventral cannon and .303" machine gun bays (P48039)

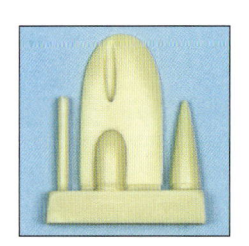

The FB Mk XVIII conversion for the 1/48th scale Airfix kit is offered as set P48041

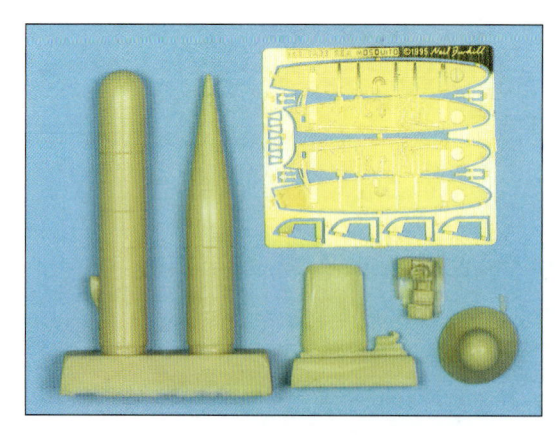

The TR Mk 33 Sea Mosquito conversion is for the Airfix kit in 1/48th (P48072)

The FB Mk XVIII conversion in 1/32nd scale (P32013)

126 Chapter 12

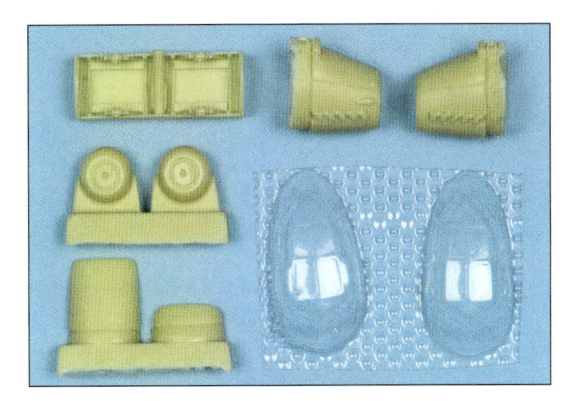

The 'Highball' conversion in 1/72nd scale (P72037) is designed for the Matchbox kit

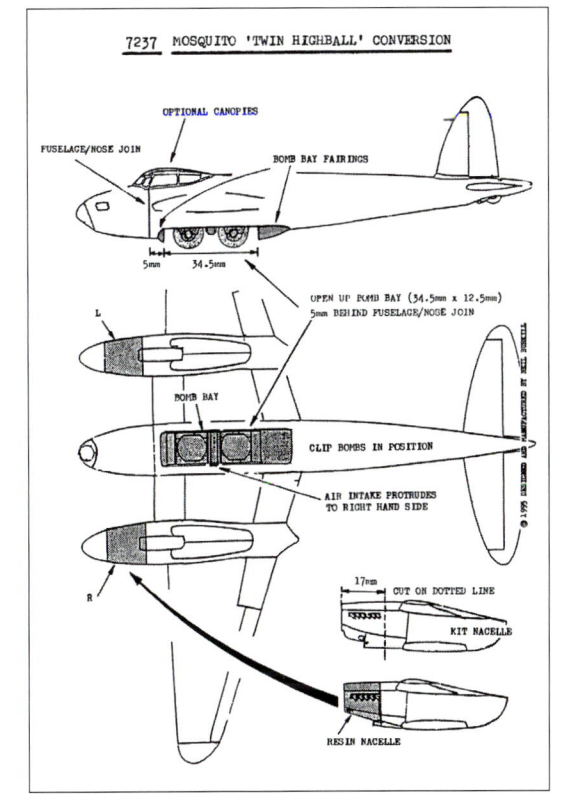

The 'Highball' conversion in 1/48th scale (P48076) is designed for the Airfix kit

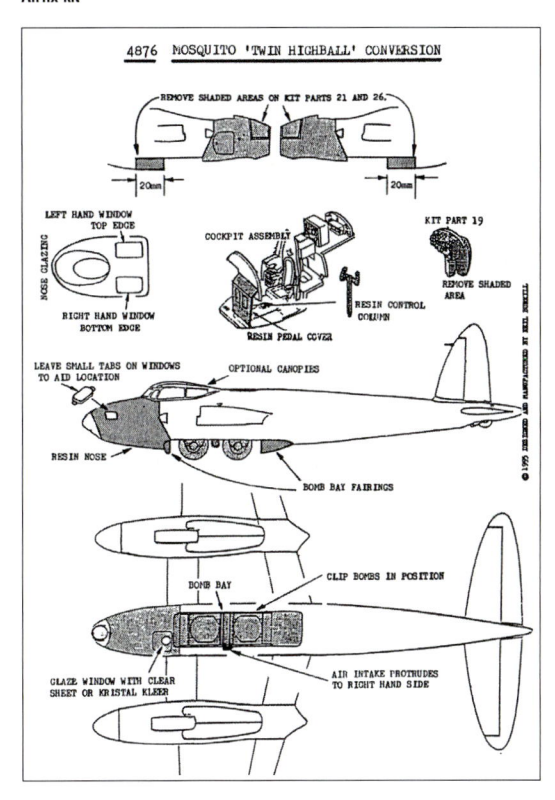

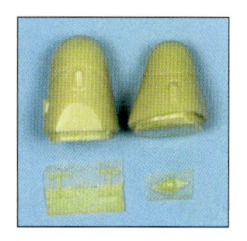

The components of the NF Mk XIII (early) and (late) conversions for the Airfix kit in 1/72nd scale (Air052 and Air053) by Air Kit Enterprises

The instructions for conversion P72037

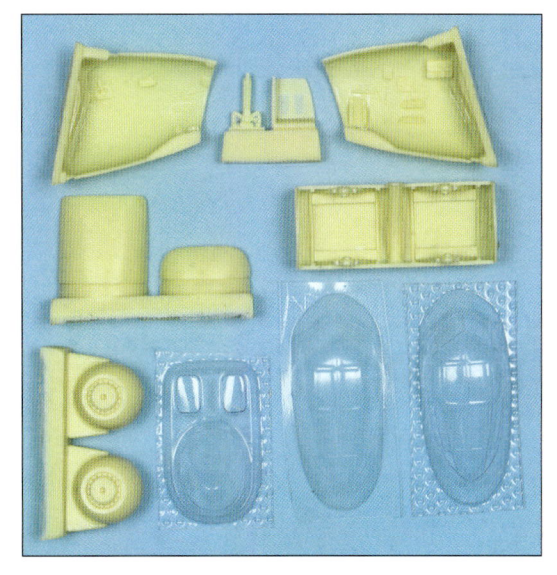

The instructions for conversion P48076

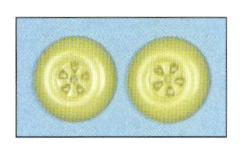

The 5-spoke hubs for the NF Mk XVII which are offered along with the Universal radome of set Air053 by Air Kit Enterprises

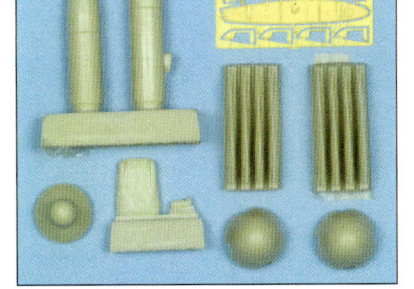

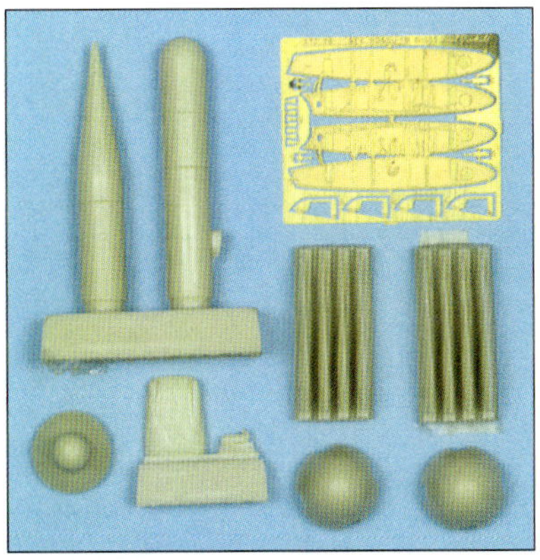

The TR Mk 33 Sea Mosquito conversion in 1/72nd scale is for the Matchbox kit (P72034)

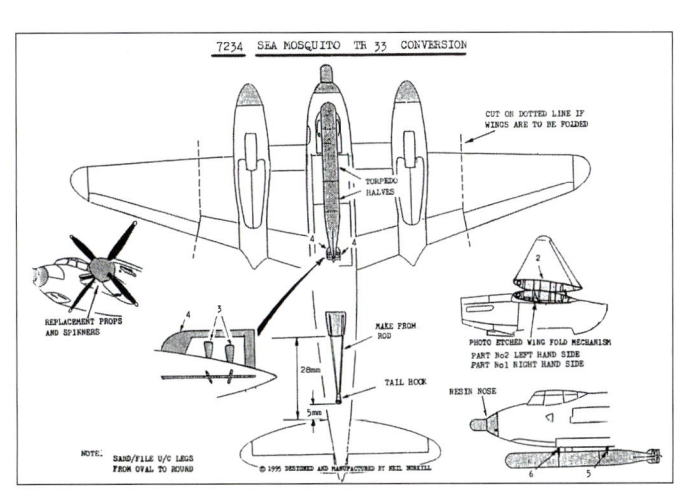

The instructions for P72034

Modelling the Mosquito • Building the Mosquito   127

Addendum

Modelling Mosquitoes

Tamiya's Tooling in 1/72
By Alec Smith

For many years modellers wishing to build a Mosquito in 1/72 were restricted to three basic kits in various boxings: those of Airfix, Frog and Matchbox. Then at the end of the 1990s both Hasegawa and Tamiya weighed in with editions of both fighter and bomber-nosed models, albeit they were only of the single-stage Merlin airframes. This then gave the 1/72 model maker choices that were much better detailed, and generally better builds (if not necessarily quicker).

Of the two Hasegawa did their usual trick of releasing many different editions in terms of markings, whereas Tamiya released the basic kits and stopped there. At the time I remember getting several different Hasegawa releases, these being the cheaper kits compared to the couple of Tamiya ones I bought. Things have moved the other way these days. What was also apparent was that the Tamiya kits contained much more detail than the Hasegawa.

The overall engineering of the Tamiya kit is excellent with very good detail, matched to a great fit of parts. (Something that trumps the Hasegawa kits I built). The cockpit interior has a very good amount of moulded-on detail that can be easily be picked out with careful painting. All of this fits together very smoothly, and is helped along by having colour callouts for the various detail parts. Also thoughtfully included for the interior in this boxing are the cameras for the PR.IV option to go behind the various windows/ports, which is something that is often overlooked. What could be seen as problem areas in fit are the separate nose for the various editions, and the wings to fuselage. However these have both been thoughtfully engineered, with spars for the wings and an assortment of plates and

Chapter 12

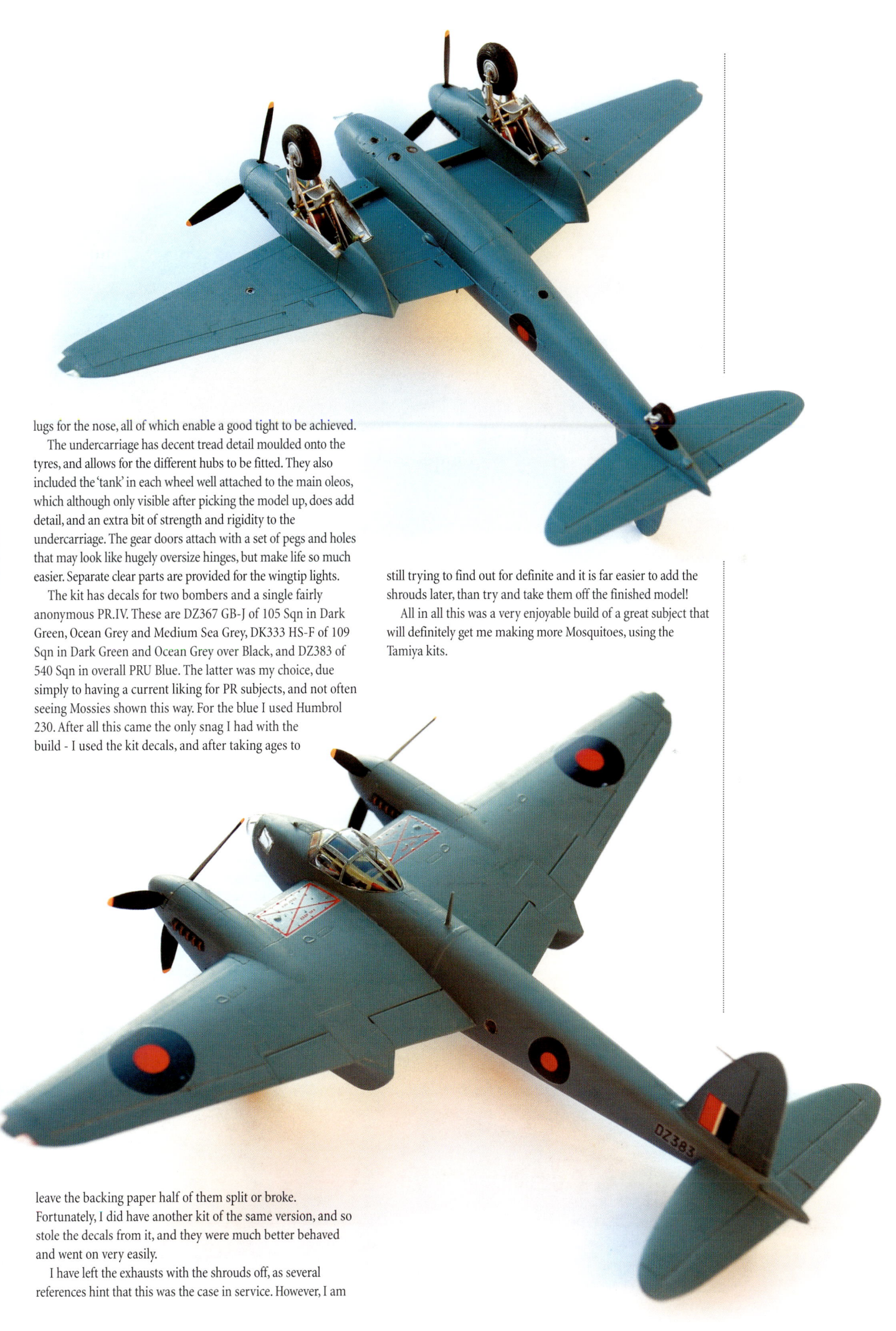

lugs for the nose, all of which enable a good tight to be achieved.

The undercarriage has decent tread detail moulded onto the tyres, and allows for the different hubs to be fitted. They also included the 'tank' in each wheel well attached to the main oleos, which although only visible after picking the model up, does add detail, and an extra bit of strength and rigidity to the undercarriage. The gear doors attach with a set of pegs and holes that may look like hugely oversize hinges, but make life so much easier. Separate clear parts are provided for the wingtip lights.

The kit has decals for two bombers and a single fairly anonymous PR.IV. These are DZ367 GB-J of 105 Sqn in Dark Green, Ocean Grey and Medium Sea Grey, DK333 HS-F of 109 Sqn in Dark Green and Ocean Grey over Black, and DZ383 of 540 Sqn in overall PRU Blue. The latter was my choice, due simply to having a current liking for PR subjects, and not often seeing Mossies shown this way. For the blue I used Humbrol 230. After all this came the only snag I had with the build - I used the kit decals, and after taking ages to still trying to find out for definite and it is far easier to add the shrouds later, than try and take them off the finished model!

All in all this was a very enjoyable build of a great subject that will definitely get me making more Mosquitoes, using the Tamiya kits.

leave the backing paper half of them split or broke. Fortunately, I did have another kit of the same version, and so stole the decals from it, and they were much better behaved and went on very easily.

I have left the exhausts with the shrouds off, as several references hint that this was the case in service. However, I am

The tale of two Mossies

A pair of Tamiya 1/48 scale Mosquito FB VIs
By Nick Greenall

In the lucky position of having two of Tamiya's superb 1/48 scale FB.VI kits to make, the hardest decision was their colour schemes. I wanted something different from the kit options, but one had to be a Banff Strike Wing 'Mossie' – as I have long admired the bravery of the crews and the work they did off the coast of Norway and Denmark.

The Banff Strike Wing

The Banff Strike Wing was formed in early September 1944 with three Mosquito-equipped squadrons - Nos 235, 248 and 333 (Norwegian), plus Nos 144 and 404 (RCAF) Beaufighter squadrons. At the time No 248 was partially equipped with the FB.XVIII 'Tsetse', equipped with the Molins 'six pounder' 57mm gun and just two Browning .303-in machine guns. Later in the month, the two Beaufighter squadrons left to form the Dallachy Wing with Nos 455 and 489 Beaufighter squadrons, being replaced by No 143 Sqn which converted from the Beau to the Mossie at Banff.

In late 1944, the two Strike Wings flew several joint operations escorted by RAF Mustang Mk IIIs and IVs, which saw up to 75 Beaus and Mossies plus a dozen escorts set out from northern Scotland for the Norwegian coast - where the local knowledge of the No 333 Sqn crews proved invaluable.

To ensure surprise, the Wings and their escorts flew out at very low level to stay below the German radar screen. Ditching in the North Sea in winter was a real possibility for the Mosquito crews if a problem, such as a bird-strike, occurred en route. Climbing to bale out was not an option as that would be picked up by the enemy's radar. For the Mustang pilots ditching was not practical due to the Mustang's under fuselage intake.

The reliability of the Packard-built licensed version of the RR Merlin meant that no crews were lost in this way, as far as I am aware. On some missions Vickers Warwicks of No 279 Sqn dropped survival gear to ditched Mosquito crews.

On 15 January 1945, as the 25lb armour piercing rocket projectile (RP) was proving more effective than the heavy cannon, despite the weight and drag of the RP installation, No 248's 'Tsetses' were withdrawn to be used later by No 254 Sqn at North Coates. To extend the range of the RP armed FB.VIs, it was decided to fit drop tanks. The inboard pair of rocket rails were removed to allow the tanks to be carried and the rockets were mounted in pairs on the outer rails.

When going into attack, the tanks had to be jettisoned and they sometimes broke away sideways, the falling tanks fouling or wiping off the rockets - not good! To prevent this happening, the Banff squadrons' engineers developed, made and fitted steel guard rails. Attached to the rocket rail hard-points, they did the job they were designed to do, but were heavy and caused extra drag.

Modelling a Banff Wing Mossie

The biggest problem I faced was working out the layout of the rocket guard rails. A fellow IPMS(UK) member, Terry Campion, helped by pointing me in the direction of the photo in the centre of page 143 of the International Air Power Review's Mosquito article. By blowing the photo up and using a ruler and pencil like a pantograph I was able to produce a 3-D drawing of the guard rails. Then, by measuring known dimensions in side views of RS625 in the Osprey book, I was able to produce scale drawings of the guard rails and so create the scale replicas.

As DM•H was to be displayed on a base, as 'just returned from a mission', with empty rocket rails and no drop tanks, the areas of the kit I set out to improve were:
1) The cockpit detail - using the Pilot's Notes and photos as references.
2) The undercarriage legs and bays - referring to photos in the SAM Publications Modellers' Datafile 1.
3) To give the model some 'personality' - I 'drooped' the elevators, and...
4) Fitted Ultracast exhausts and scratch-built the carburettor snow guards.
5) Made and fitted the rocket guard rails and drop tank attachment points.
6) Undertook some limited structural tidying-up to the fuselage and nacelles.

Rather than following the kit instructions, I first detailed the cockpit before adding it to the fuselage. Next I assembled the wings and fitted the nacelles before adding the wings and tailplanes to the fuselage. Lastly I added the undercarriage and propellers.

So, onto the detail work…

Cockpit detailing

I removed and filled the NF.II radar mount on part H7 and the pad in front of it on the floor of part H6. I then removed the existing sidewall detail and inside cockpit door detail and replaced it with scratch-built items made from plastic rod, fuse-wire and scrap plasticard, using the Pilot's Notes and other photos as references. 10 thou plastic card was used for the fittings between the instrument panel and the door, and the tops of the ladder fixing hoops were removed. A small disc was engraved on the starboard fuselage between the door opening and machine gun cover, in line with the latter's hinges.

The T1154 radio transmitter had rear vents and reinforcing panels added from 10 thou card whilst the R1155 receiver had similar reinforcing panels added and a frame made from rod for the scratch-built components it required underneath it. These are not supplied in the kit - presumably as the navigator figure would obscure them. Reference to the photos and drawings on pp 57 and 86 of the Modellers' Datafile helped with these items. Cable runs for the radio sets were added from thin rod.

Modifications to the navigator's seat included adding the arm rest on the right side of the seat and filing some creases into the upholstery. The harness was made from Tamiya masking tape cut to width, with buckles from 5amp fuse wire. The masking tape was easy to work with, just needing final securing with a dab of superglue at each end. Additional laminations of tape were used to depict the passing of straps through buckles. A similar harness was added to the pilot's seat. An escape axe was made from scrap and fitted behind the pilot's seat. The rudder pedals were canted to port and the control column pushed forward - to match up with the 'slightly deflected over to port' rudder and the 'drooped' elevators - the model was to be finished with.

A hole was drilled in the canopy for the flare pistol, fashioned from scrap card and rod. The cockpit light and dimmer switch near the pistol were also from rod. Fine rod and scrap were used for the upper and lower runners for the sliding side panel windows and the emergency panel release handle.

Undercarriage legs and wheel bays

Brake cables were made from very thin plastic rod and were added to the rear of all the main undercarriage legs. Plastic rod was also used for the front roller for the undercarriage door operating wires and then fitted to the main legs. The more complex wheel guards carried by many Mosquitoes were fashioned from plastic rod too.

The kit's lower location holes for the cross braces, (parts E4 and E5), were filled and sanded to shape, new holes being drilled within the triangular mounting points on the leading and trailing edges of the legs. Microstrip was used for the bar across the lower part of E4 that is missing from the kit. Frame detail came from 5 and 10 thou plastic card and was fitted in the rear of both wheel wells with the spring door closing mechanism made from fine rod added to the rear bulkhead. The photos on p90 of the Modellers' Datafile helped with all these changes.

To detail the mudguard mounts, I drilled two holes in the wedges and cut off the front portion along a vertical line from the bottom of attachment U to the guard itself. Flats were cut into the main wheels and brake cable attachments added to the hubs from scrap. Once the wheels were fitted and secured, the cables were bent, cut and attached to the hubs.

The tailwheel is one of the weak points in the Tamiya kit. To improve its appearance I scribed a more defined line between the wheel and leg. As part of adding 'personality', I also swivelled the tailwheel to starboard.

I fitted the doors after painting them and the model, completing their attachment by using fine rod for the door closing cables front and back. Again, the Modellers Datafile photos and drawings helped here. Note that the cut-out on the front of the lower portion of the kit doors is too shallow and needs a further 2mm taking off its front.

Adding 'personality'

The rudder was set slightly over to port, the elevators drooped and the cockpit door fitted in the 'open' position. I further detailed the door by adding the triangular emergency door release handle and cable, and the hydraulic handpump handle, from scrap and rod. Both the aerial mast part A23 and dipole trailing aerial tube part A8 were fitted. Part A23 needs the aerial attachment point attaching to its rear from scrap, with the aerial wire from Aeroclub's lycra.

Part A8 was mounted vertically downwards in the circular

panel near the lower edge of the cockpit door in front of the bomb-bay and was faired into that panel with filler. All machine gun and cannon barrels were drilled out. Oh, and before anyone asks, there are many photos of Mossies with the tailwheel swivelled in the opposite direction to the rudder! The later paddled-bladed props were carried by RF610.

Exhausts and snow-guards

The kit exhausts, shrouded or unshrouded, are either inaccurate (shrouded) or way too small (unshrouded). Whilst normally happy to detail my cockpits in the 'traditional' way, I drew the line at building four sets of exhaust stacks from scratch, so I replaced them with the excellent Ultracast items!

For the snow guards, I etched the mesh lines into a piece of thin acetate then defined them with a black wash. I cut the mesh portion of the guards to shape using the kit item as a template. Then, using superglue - carefully - I attached the 'mesh' to a microstrip outerframe wound around it. Two vertical strips at the back of the guards attached it to the carburettor intakes. I painted the frames and mountings Humbrol 53 Gunmetal and matt varnished both sides of the acetate before fixing the guards in place.

Rocket guard rails and drop tank attachments

Holes were opened for the outer two rocket rails and part E31 radio altimeter 'T' antennas fitted. The drop tank mounting points were made from 20 thou plastic card with 5 thou flanges and were placed over the two small engraved mounting points on the tank centre-line just behind the spar. The J-shaped fuel and air pipes were fashioned from bent thin rod and were fitted into a hole drilled in the small engraved circular panel ahead of the ailerons, also on the tank centre line. The drawings on p107 of the Datafile were helpful here.

The tank guard rails are scratchbuilt from rod as four vertical frames with horizontal arms to attach them to the rocket rail hardpoints. Two of the frames are then attached to the chordwise parts of the set-up and the whole lot attached to the rocket rails. With reference to photos, the guard rails were painted with Humbrol 27002 Metalcote Polished Aluminium, whilst 27001 Metalcote Matt Aluminium was used for the rocket rails, the detail on the latter being highlighted with Metallic gunmetal 53.

Structural tidying-up

The camera hatch, part F2, was covered by a piece of 10thou plastic card and sanded flush as this hatch was not fitted to the FB.VI. Filler was needed to smooth out the underside of the carburettor intakes, the upper-surface nacelle/wing joints and around the wing mounting pegs parts B4 and B5. The electrical point on the fuselage above the port inner flap needed moving up 3 scale inches and back 6 scale inches and the contact point partially drilling out. The lower rear light was removed.

Chordwise aileron and all trim tabs lines were cut; the ends of the inner flaps were sanded down a fraction before the wings were fitted so they did not quite touch the fuselage.

Painting and decals

Looking at the Charles E Brown colour photos of Banff Wing Mossies, Humbrol 90 Matt Beige Green, their equivalent for Sky, looks much too 'green', so I made a mix of 80% 90 Matt Beige Green and 20% 28 Matt Camouflage Grey for the Sky undersurfaces, thinned by 10% and applied with a flat 1/4" brush. Tonally it looks perfect - the only problem was that 4 coats were needed to get a decent finish! Two coats of Humbrol Authentic HB7 Extra Dark Sea Grey provided the top surface colour, thinned by 10% and slightly whitened, again applied with a flat 1/4" brush.

Johnson's Klear was applied before decalling. The fuselage roundels and fin markings came from Xtradecal sheet X030-48 - Tamiya's roundel red looks too red. Note that the Tamiya kit fin flashes are 27 inches x 24inches and should be cut down to 24inch x 24inch square, for all but the earliest NF.IIs - this smaller size being used from 30 April 1942. The upper wing roundels were from Xtradecal sheet X029-48. For the serial number, the Rs and 6s came from the kit decal sheet, the Fs and 1s from Xtradecal's DH Hornet sheet and the 0s from the spares box!

Having looked at the photos of DM·H and other photos of 248 Sqn aircraft, I'm sure the DM·H was black and not red, as shown in the Osprey book. The letters look too dark to be red. I made the DM·H by 'cutting and pasting' elements taken from the underwing serials in the Hornet sheet. All the decals settled well using Micro Set, although several applications of Micro Sol were needed on the upper wing roundels over the aileron control points.

As RF610's standard Medium Sea Grey and Dark Green scheme would have been overpainted with the Special Coastal Duties Scheme A - comprising Extra Dark Sea Grey upper surfaces and Sky undersides - on the squadron, the only stencils I applied were two 22s from the kit's decals over the port fin flash, partially trimming these to depict overpainting. Dark Green and Medium Sea Grey were applied around the port serial numbers and Medium Sea Grey around the starboard serials to depict the fact that these areas were not overpainted Extra Dark Sea Grey.

Careful examination of the photo of DM·H showed some darker, (new?), areas of paint covering the parts of a letter 'R' that the 'H' doesn't cover and around the machine gun access panel. Other photos of Banff Wing Mossies show various access panels on the wings to have been repainted too. I mixed a wash of Extra Dark Sea Grey and black and carefully applied it using a 00 brush held quite flat.

Conclusion

As a bonus, when test fitting the canopy I found out that Tamiya have engineered this kit so well that the canopy can be just snapped into place with no gaps, (unless one really looks hard for them), so all that cockpit detail is not distorted or lost from view for ever. However, I did paint the underside rims of the canopy that fit flush with the fuselage in the fuselage colours to stop light defracting.

Mosquito FB.VI, LR355, SY•H of No 613 (City of Manchester) Sqn, April 1944, Lasham, Hampshire

This Mossie was flown by Acting Wing Commander, Robert Norman Bateson DFC with Fg Off. Standish as navigator in the low-level daylight attack on the five-storey Kunstzall Kleizkamp Art Gallery in The Hague on 11 April 1944. The building had been occupied by the Gestapo and was being used to house the Dutch Central Population Registry, as well as duplicates of all legally issued Dutch personal identity papers. As a key installation, it was strongly defended by light flak batteries and a difficult target to hit without damaging neighbouring buildings.

Having already outlined the detail work needed to Tamiya's 1/48 scale FB.VI kit to produce a Banff Strike Wing aircraft, I'll simply highlight the differences between the two aircraft here.

Spring 1944 photos of 613 Sqn aircraft show them predominantly without exhaust shrouds, presumably for the extra few knots airspeed this would gain them, so again I used the excellent Ultracast resin replacements. The only difference needed for the undercarriage is that LR355 had the earlier style wheel guards, just needing one small piece of rod adding to the kit parts.

Neither the aerial mast nor dipole trailing aerial tube are fitted. The Guidelines 'Combat Colours' profile of LR366 shows the aircraft with the aerial mast, although no contemporary photos of 613 Sqn aircraft I've looked at confirm this fit, nor the fitting of any whip aerials through the canopy and on the fuselage spine. Indeed, the photo of LR263 being towed out of the factory at Hatfield in the Combat Legends book has no fuselage aerials visible at all. Under the wings I fitted the empty bomb carriers, having detailed them with sway braces from plastic rod. The 'T' aerials are not fitted. The structural tidying-up follows the Banff aircraft model list in full. Lastly, the pointed props were used for LR355.

Painting and decals

Several photos in the references are captioned as being of LR355, although from studying them I have my doubts…

'Mosquito at War' - p63 - shows a very battered looking machine in the EG codes of 487 Sqn, RAAF, at Swanton Morley on 8 April 1944, just three days before the attack on The Hague. Whilst aircraft were moved around the squadrons, from Bateson's log book he had been with 613 Sqn since 19 October 1943 and had been regularly flying LR355 since 14 January 1944. (This photo also appears on p19 of the Squadron/Signal book.)

'Osprey Combat Aircraft' - p57 - this close-up, bombing-up, photo only shows the serial and last code letter on the port side, an 'H'. This would make this a 21 Sqn aircraft with the 'H' being from their 'YH' squadron codes? To me the serial appears to be LR356 or LR358 and not LR355. A photo on p40 of 'Mosquito at War' appears to confirm this, showing the 250lb bomb in place under the port wing and the 'YH' codes. The caption credits the aircraft as being LR356 of 21 Sqn at Hunsdon in 1944. The 'step' of the green camouflage caused by the 'H' seems to confirm that these are two photos of the same aircraft.

So, no photos appear to exist of LR355 in the markings it carried on the raid. However, several do exist of 613 Sqn aircraft at that time, including a few in 'experimental' schemes detailed in the Combat Colours book. However, I opted for the usual Night Fighter scheme of Medium Sea Grey and Dark Green. The two photos I made most use of are on page 89 of Philip Birtles' book, 'Mosquito - A Pictorial History', showing LR297 and LR366 at Lasham in January and February 1944 respectively; the profile of LR366 SY•L on p29 of the Guidelines Combat Colours book was also referred to.

Getting Down to the Wood

First Build – A Test Shot of Revell's 1/48 Mosquito built and appraised
By Ted Taylor

Cockpit assembly with spars in place. Note moulded seatbelts

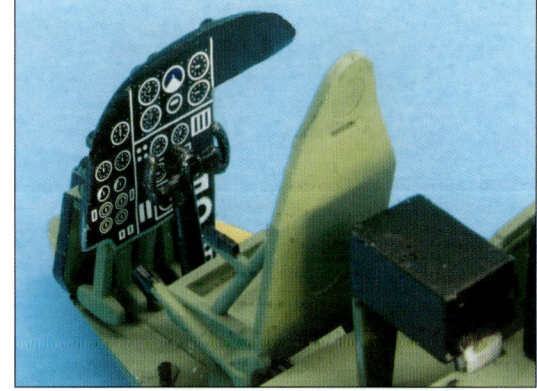

The instruction sheets for this unexpected release follow the usual Revell pattern with pictures of the sprue frames included and paint colour references in the standard mix of Revell Paints, with no hint of the actual colour names which are Dark Green, Ocean Grey and Medium Sea Grey for the undersides on the 105 Squadron machine or Black on the two remaining options. Quite a number of parts supplied are not for

The assembled cockpit with decal used for the instrument panel

use on this model so I guess they are meant for further releases in the fullness of time.

The decal sheet covers full markings for three squadrons and is nicely printed, with separate red dots for the roundels, and even has markings for the bombs, a nice touch.

A lot of painting can be done before assembly starts. All the interior surfaces are cockpit green, and careful detail painting of the parts in the front office and the bomb bay will pay dividends.

Some Construction Notes
The following notes were made during the build and may be of use to readers making the kit from the box. Bear in mind this

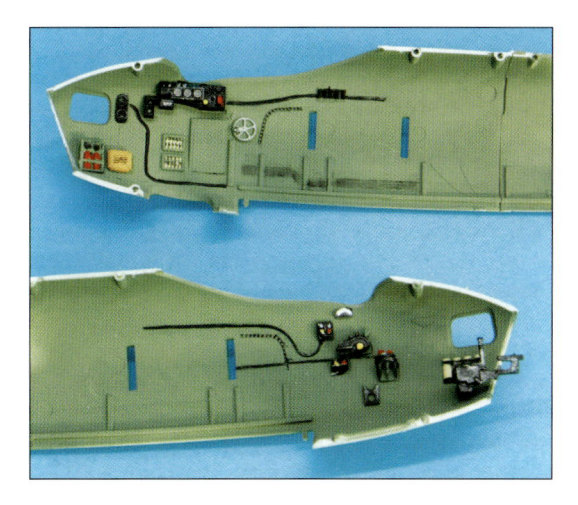

All the small detail parts are in place and look good once painted

build was made from various sprues taken from two test shots, and while they will more or less reflect the production kit, some minor differences in fit cannot be ruled out.

Step 3:
I found some of the locating pins did not match up with parts 6 and 7 so be aware.

Step 4:
Part 8 needs the gap that fits over part 7 widening slightly; a few strokes with a sanding board is all that is needed.

Step 8:
There are straps moulded on the two seats but these are unconvincing so I would remove them before assembly and use the decal straps provided after painting.

Step 13:
I departed from the instructions here and joined the two parts of each fuselage half together, leaving them to harden before inserting the cockpit and tailwheel structure. I had a dry run first and found it a tight fit around the cockpit so a little sanding around the formers etc. was required to get a snug fit.

Step 16:
Do make sure you fit the tailwheel in the desired position before you close the fuselage around it as it will not go in later.

Step 20/25:
Remember that the tailplanes on the Mosquito are not built handed, just one type, which means that the actuator for the trim tab will be above on one side and below on the other, so don't think you have made a mistake.

Step 26:
I found the spars for the tailplanes were a little tight and the planes would not seat properly, so I trimmed the edges slightly and sanded the surfaces to make them a little thinner.

Two types of props are provided

Modelling the Mosquito • Building the Mosquito

One side panel has been removed from the starboard nacelle to show one of the engines

The first camouflage colour is sprayed on freehand and then the outlines for the second colour are pencilled in

Step 30:
I would suggest that you do not fit the wings to the fuselage here, wait until the engine nacelles are fitted as this will make it easier to clean up any joins.

Step 32/34:
I again strayed from the instruction sheets here and assembled the engines and mounted them on the firewalls (parts 78) between the bearers (parts 79/80).

Step 36:
I found it better to mount the engines then add the rear bulkheads (Parts 82) to the nacelle halves before closing up and adding the completed nacelle to the wings. The exhausts can be slipped in from the outside later. I did cut one of the side panels out to expose one engine using the thin cut-lines on the inside.

Step 40/45:
The undercarriage legs are very delicate and the cross braces will need careful removal from the sprues. If all the parts are assembled as a separate unit the whole structure can be wiggled into the nacelle and cemented in position ignoring the Revell construction sequence. There are two types of wheel centres but no indication as to which version each goes on or which way round they go. One other point - the front edges of the struts normally carry the curved wheelguard frameworks, a very prominent feature on a Mosquito but they are totally missing on these legs. There is a problem with the undercarriage legs and wheels, as the compression parts of the legs are much shorter than those in the Tamiya kit, in itself not a problem, but also the wheels are a bit larger than Tamiya's offering and the result is that the wheels, when fitted, rub on the cross braces and in the final model the nose is much too low for the crew entry ladder to hang down properly. The angle that the fuselage sits at will not line up with any drawings I have.

Step 48/49:
One thing I do like are the one-piece undercarriage and bomb bay doors, which are very welcome for those who like their models all closed up, and are easy to separate for those who don't.

Step 50:
The exhaust shrouds are supposed to be fitted here but another problem arises. There is a tiny intake at the front of the nacelle and it should be inside the shroud when fitted, but is too low on the cowling so the shroud will not seat properly unless it is modified or the intake cut off and moved upwards.

Step 54:
It is advisable to load the bombs here as they can be awkward to load when the doors are in place. Remember also that if you have chosen the wing-mounted bomb racks you will need two of the four for them.

The completed bomb bay, with full load decalled and painted, is particularly impressive

water from the decal, using a small brush I put a tiny amount of Klear under the film and levelled it out with a dry finger, which tends to get rid of any air beneath and eliminates silvering. A couple of thin coats of Klear were followed by a light dusting with a mix of Klear and Tamiya flat base X21 in four-to-one proportions, which just takes the shine off the Klear to give a nice sheen and looks most realistic, I think.

Summary

Having seen and built some of Revell's modern kits such as the Lancaster, with some nice detail and excellent fit, I am a little disappointed with some aspects of the Mosquito, notably the undercarriage, although there are some very nice touches here like movable flaps that work quite realistically. The cockpit details are nice but as with so many injected kits, the instrument panel and seatbelts will require either some work or replacement.

Step 58/59:
The main canopy does not depict the complete framework towards the rear end but this can be replaced with thin strips of painted decal if you so wish. There are three types of side window provided for the pilot but two of them are not used on this model, yet step 59 shows a flat window being used.

Step 64:
This step shows dipole aerials (parts 148) being fitted to the wingtips but these should not be used on this kit at all.

With all the construction done the painting was next on the list. I have sprayed my colours on but as the edges should be sharp there is no reason why you can't use a good quality flat brush, with slightly thinned paint, to make an excellent job, but you really must mask off the top surfaces to get that sharp line for the underside colour.

When my paint had hardened overnight I sprayed a couple of coats of Johnsons Klear before placing the decals, to prevent any silvering wherever there was any decal film that showed such as the red 'No Walk' area over the radiators. After dabbing away the

Mosquito FB Mk VI

Heritage 1/24
By Graham Marsh

Heritage's kit comes in a huge box containing four white sturdy plastic vacform sheets, white-metal parts, a large bag of resin, clear vacform canopy, main wheel rubber tyres, 3-page instruction booklet and a decal sheet for 1 aircraft. There is no surface detail on the vacformed parts; the white-metal and resin will need the usual cleaning up and casting blocks removed.

Plans used were from the SAM Datafile book and the colour template from the Tamiya kit, both scaled up from 1/48, and I also used the Tamiya kit as a guide.

Construction

After outlining the vacform parts with a marker, they were carefully cut from the sheet using a scalpel and after taping some rough sandpaper to a sturdy surface the parts were sanded back to the marker line. Using a finer grade of sandpaper the parts were sanded down until the line disappeared, as when you get this far the lip of plastic around the part lifts off.

Once all the sub-assemblies are sanded, any remedial work needed to get them flush fitting can be carried out. The enlarged

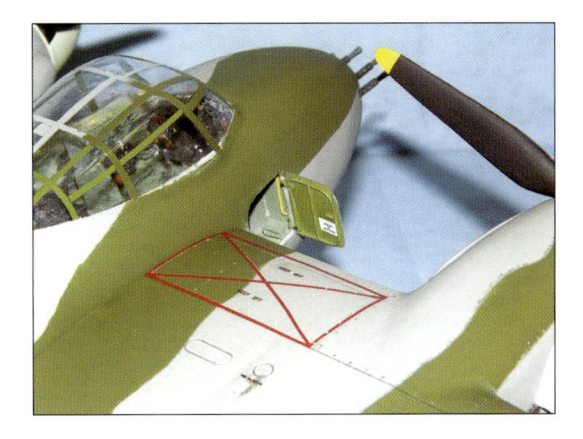

Tamiya plan showed the kit's canopy was very close to the real thing in its overall shape so this was cut out and stuck onto the taped fuselage, at which point the outline was chain drilled. Using a scalpel, I cut through the holes leaving a gap that was sanded to shape, then did the same with the crew door and the bomb bay.

Most of the necessary detail for the cockpit is provided, including the seats, instrument panel and radios all cast in resin and white metal, although a template is provided to make up the actual structure from 60 thou styrene sheet. Should one wish to do so, the ample detail provided can be further enhanced using fuse wire, Milliput and Microstrip. Instrument dials came from the spares box and MDC, and RAF 1/32 Sutton Harnesses also came from this source.

Using a contour gauge I built the bulkheads for the open bomb bay and the roof from 60 thou card. The fuel tanks were made from Milliput and detail copied from the Tamiya kit.

A hole was cut into the rear of the fuselage for the tailwheel and a 5mm plastic tube was fitted to support the strut. Thin plastic tabs were fitted along the length of the fuselage and it was glued together and left to dry.

Removing the rudder, this was improved by copying the rib detail from the Tamiya plan onto 5 thou plastic sheet and glued on. It was covered in thin tissue paper soaked with liquid glue for a fabric effect and left to dry; the excess was removed with a scalpel and reattached.

Using a 0.3mm drill, rivet detail was added to the elevators by twisting the drill part way into the plastic and, along with the tail, they were attached to the fuselage.

Smaller components such as the mainwheels and propellers were completed and painted.

Holes were cut into the nacelles where the exhausts would be and the stacks from the 1/32nd Revell Mosquito were added. Undercarriage doors were removed, the wells boxed in and detailed. The nacelles were glued together and the resin intakes added.

One upper and two lower parts make up the wing, and these were detailed and assembled with the engines.

Work commenced on the undercarriage. The oil tank was made from Milliput and plastic rod was used for the crossbeams. Holes were drilled into the bottom of the gear legs and the wheels held in place with brass rod.

Holes were drilled into the nose for the machine guns and gun camera, and blast ports sanded into the bottom of the nose with plastic tube added for the 20mm cannons. Chunks cut from a sheet of 5mm Perspex, detailed by drilling a small hole in each for the bulbs and colouring with Tamiya clear red/green, were superglued to the wing and sanded to shape. This concluded the bulk of the construction work, save for some details and elements of the final assembley.

Colour Options

One option is provided, FB Mk VI HX917/E of 487 Squadron in the standard day fighter scheme of disruptive Dark Green over Medium Sea Grey. Tamiya spray cans AS-9 and AS-11 were used. I also sprayed these onto clear decal sheet above interior green, as this would be used for the cockpit framing. Once the model was coated with Klear the decals were applied. They are very thin and settled down without any help.

A final coat of Klear to seal the decals and the final assemblies were added. Machine guns were from the Trumpeter Spitfire kit, 500lb bombs came from Ultracast and MV lenses were used for the landing lights. Panel lines were highlighted using a wash of thinned black enamel and the entire model was matted down using Testors dullcoat.

Conclusion

This was a very enjoyable build but not for the novice builder, and some experience with mixed media and vacform parts is essential. This was my first completed vacform kit, after a few false starts, and it was well worth the effort involved. The completed model captures the look of the aircraft and it certainly suits the scale, in addition, it will stretch the modelling skills you possess and open doors to new techniques.

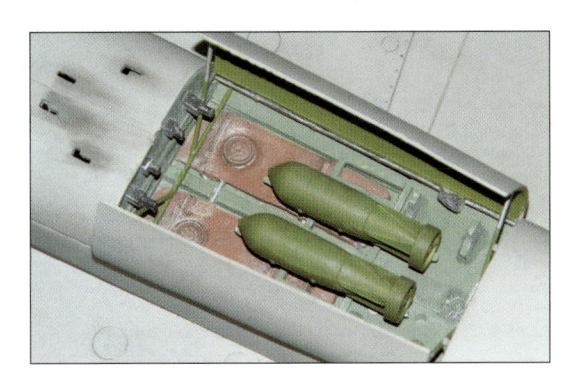

Colour Photographs • Plate 1

A rare colour shot of PR Mk 34 RG314, which flew the last operational RAF Mosquito mission in December 1955 *(via S.Howe)*

This J 30 ('Red E') was originally TA285 in RAF service and is seen here being refuelled at the F1 Wing base in the early 1950s *(P.Kempe)*

TA686 of the CAACU is shown alongside the groups main hanger in the early 1960s
(via S.Howe)

TA669, a TT Mk 35 of the CAACU is seen here in flight with the ML winch in position
(via S.Howe)

128 Chapter 12

Colour and Marking Notes

Modelling the Mosquito

Chapter **13**

Many of you may feel that this subject in regard to the Mosquito is a very simple one, as the type only had a limited number of colour schemes, and one style of camouflage pattern. To some extent this is true, but the type served with Bomber and Fighter Command from 1941 to 1955, in the UK, Europe, the Middle East and Far East. It was flown in Australia, Canada and many other nations post war and it was also operated by civilian companies from 1952 to 1963.

As you can see the subject is by no means limited and what we will try to do in this section is give you a baseline from which to work. There is no way we can cover all areas and eventualities, as the subject of colour and markings is a hotly debated one and therefore we could easily fill this entire book with it. What follows therefore is a basic guide that has been created from the official RAF and RAAF regulations, coupled with the study of a number of articles and features on the subject over the past thirty years and a detailed study of a huge number of photographs.

RAF Operations

Now the first thing to remember about the Mosquito's camouflage scheme is that at no time was this pattern ever 'mirrored' from one aircraft to the next, as per Hurricanes and Spitfires. The pattern remained the same throughout the war and was only replaced when the type took on post war schemes in its later life.

The Prototype

When the prototype undertook test flying in late 1940, the regulations stated that all "prototype and experimental aircraft, including private venture aircraft" were to be yellow overall. As already noted, at the time the Mosquito was built De Havilland Ltd was making Tiger Moths and these machines were painted Trainer Yellow on the under surface. It is fairly safe to assume that the colour applied to the prototype Mosquito was of that type also. The aircraft carried the class B registration 'E-0234' in black on either side of the fuselage, just forward of the tailplane, for just two flights. After this the official serial number 'W4050' was applied in its place, also in black. At no time when the aircraft was yellow overall did the aircraft carry a prototype 'P' marking. An A1 roundel was applied under each wing and on the fuselage sides and the proportions of the red dot in the centre looks to be smaller than standard. Upper wing roundels were the B Type of 54" diameter and the spinners and propellers were matt black with the tips (6") painted yellow.

When the machine was repainted in January 1941, the yellow undersurface was retained, but the top surface was now painted in Dark Green and Dark Earth disruptive camouflage. These colours covered all the upper surface and extended mid-way down each fuselage side, ending in a hard demarcation. The machine now carried a prototype 'P' and because it was partially on the yellow lower surfaces, it was bordered in Dark Green on those areas affected, to offer some contrast. The propellers and spinners remained black as did the serial number, although no serials were applied under the wings. A 24" wide, 27" high flash was carried either side of the vertical fin, with the red section leading and the remaining segments being of equal proportions.

When the prototype was fitted with two-stage Merlin 61 engines the camouflage scheme was still Dark Green and Dark Earth over Yellow but the demarcation line had now become soft and the line towards the nose now swooped down from mid-way up the sides by the cockpit, to encircle the whole nose by the glazed section. The prototype 'P' was still applied and by this time the serial on the fuselage was also in yellow. Studying photographs of the machine at this time it is easy to see that the entire front set of engine cowls was a different colour, but what colour is debatable. It certainly looks quite dark, so I suspect it is

Scrap view showing the typical upper camouflage pattern of the Mosquito, which is applicable to both bomber and fighter versions
Colour Art © Richard J. Caruana

When T Mk II RR299 was originally flown by Hawker Siddeley, the aircraft was painted silver overall, with post war D Type roundels and fin flashes (M.J.Hooks)

The company logo for British European Airways (BEA) was often called the 'flying key'. This motif was carried on the nose and vertical fin of the Gust Research Unit's PR Mk 34s based at Cranfield
(© A.Oliver)

Although depicting the prototype as it is today, this view of W4050 at Salisbury Hall does illustrate the correct style of fuselage roundel, fin flash and serial applied to the type

Modelling the Mosquito • Colour and Marking Notes 129

RR299, the T Mk III operated by BAe until its tragic loss in 1996, carries a typical day fighter scheme. The serial numbers are in dull red, although the squadron codes seem a little high on the fuselage (S.Howe)

This diagram shows the method used to determine the position of the fuselage roundel

The D Type fin flash

A diagram showing the style and dimensions of fuselage serial numbers

This chart shows the standard style of identification characters applied by the RAF
- The thickness of the strokes for all letters and numerals is H x 1/8
- The width of all letters and numerals is H x 5/8 excepting letter 'S', the width of which is H x 9/16

not likely to be Zinc Chromate primer, although it may well be the more usual grey-green primer referred to as Interior Green by most modellers. This latter colour would certainly look quite dark in a black and white photograph, but I think that the entire set of cowlings are in fact a glossy blue colour, similar to PR Blue, as there is obviously some glossy effect to the paint around the chin intakes on all the photographs I have seen

Bombers

When the Mosquito entered service in 1941 the current regulations dictated that the overall scheme applied was Dark Green and Earth Brown over Sky. This is the scheme in which the type therefore began operations with No.105 Sqn. The national markings consisted of the B Type roundel (54" Dia.) on the upper surface and a C1 Type (36" Dia.) on the fuselage sides. All versions of the Mosquito were supposed to have the fuselage roundel (centre) positioned 54" aft of the wing trailing edge. The squadron codes were in Medium Sea Grey and were 36" high and the serial number was black (8") and applied parallel with the demarcation of the upper camouflage colours, not overlapping into the lower surface colours. The standard red, white and blue fin flash (24") was carried on either side of the vertical fin, with the red segment always leading, although by this time the C1 Type fin flash was in use, which had a narrow white band in the middle.

When the first B Mk IV Series I bombers entered service, this was the scheme they carried; however these early machines had an odd demarcation on the engine nacelles. Usually the upper and lower colour demarcation followed the panel line high on the engine cowls side; however with the early versions the camouflage demarcation applied by the manufacturer curved down, back towards the wing slightly and then back towards the front, following a straight line, slightly downhill, until it reached

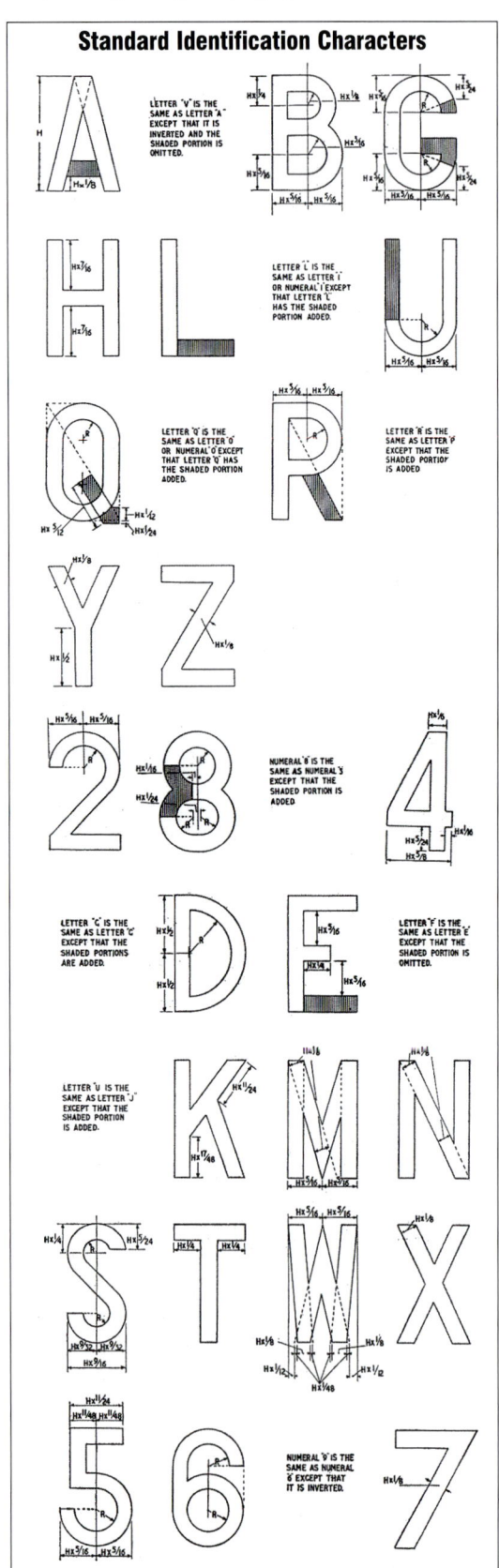

Standard Identification Characters

130 Chapter 13

the front of the nacelle at a point approximately four inches above the lower engine cowl joint. Spinners remained black, as did the propellers.

In July 1942 the markings applied to the bomber Mosquito were radically changed. The upper surfaces were camouflaged in Dark Green and Ocean Grey, whilst the under surfaces were now Medium Sea Grey. Examples were also seen during this

This shot of B Mk 35 (TA539) at Celle in Germany post-war, shows the black and grey scheme applied to Bomber Command machines of this era. The high demarcation of the upper and lower colours are of note, as is the fact that the wheel hubs have been painted gloss black. On the black under surface the lower wing codes have been applied in white, although they are still 30" high (via S.Howe)

changeover period with a grey shade equivalent to Slate Grey on the upper surfaces in lieu of Ocean Grey, although this was rare. The spinners were usually Ocean Grey and the serial numbers remained black (8"). The squadron codes however were now Sky and for a short period in the summer of 1942 Bomber Command Mosquitos had a Sky band applied around the rear fuselage, plus Sky spinners. This was to make the enemy aircraft think they were armed fighters, but in the end it made the Mosquito too conspicuous, so these elements of the markings were removed in the late autumn. This new overall scheme was to remain with the Mosquito until post-war, although *Oboe* Mosquitos were often painted with the lower surfaces in Night Black. The demarcation for this colour was on the centre line datum from the tailplanes and the demarcation itself was usually soft. The first examples of this scheme were seen on No.109 machines in late 1942. To identify these *Oboe* aircraft, some were marked with two thin (2") white lines around the aft fuselage (basically in the position where the Sky bands had been applied). This seems to have been quite common after late 1943.

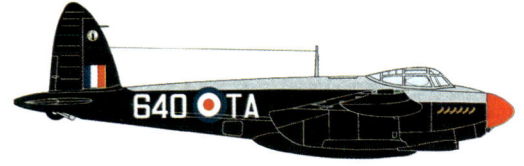

This B Mk 35 illustrates the post-war scheme of black and grey carried by Bomber Command machines. The application of the serial number in white, in lieu of a squadron code, was commonplace (© AeroMaster Products)

No.105 Squadron machines were also listed as having dark blue serials at this stage.

One scheme considered at the end of the war in Europe was for *Tiger Force* Mosquitoes in Japan. These machines were going to be Night Black on the under surfaces, with a demarcation high on the fuselage sides. The upper fuselage decking and upper wings were then to be in white, although the end of the war in Japan stopped this scheme from ever being necessary.

By the 1950s most of the remaining (night) bomber Mosquitoes were in two schemes. The first was glossy (anti-searchlight) black on the lower surfaces and high up the fuselage sides, and Dark Sea Grey on the upper fuselage decking and upper wing surfaces. The demarcation line was hard edged and

This nice shot of B Mk IV Series II (DZ313) illustrates the overall camouflage scheme of these bombers. Note the unpainted area at the base of the aerial mast and the roundel position on the upper wings (De Havilland)

it ran basically parallel to the centre line of the aircraft, but just 1/4 of the depth from the top of the fuselage top. This demarcation swept up to the base of the vertical fin in the last few inches. Squadron codes were initially carried, although later these were replaced with just the serial number in their place.

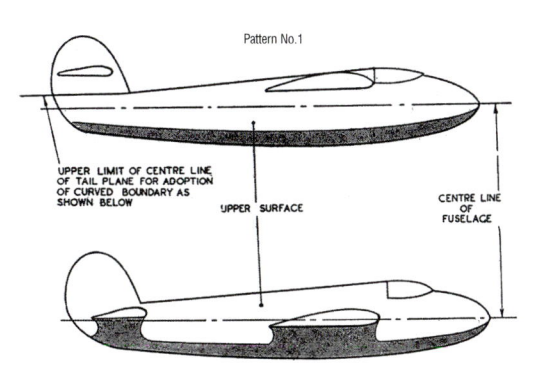

Pattern No.1: These two plans show the different styles of fuselage demarcation as applied to mid or high wing aircraft. The lower scheme was applied to RAAF Mosquitoes

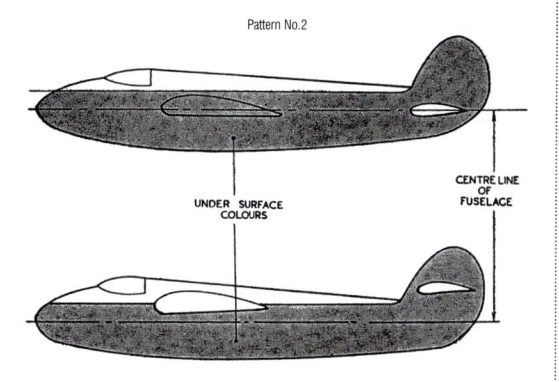

Pattern No.2: Two other methods of determining the fuselage demarcation n RAF aircraft, as applied post war. The lower option was usually applied to Mosquitoes

These were originally red, but later became white. They were positioned mid-way between the top and bottom of the fuselage. These serials were also carried under each wing and they were usually 30" high and 18.75" wide with 3.75" gaps between each letter. The underwing serial was usually broken up by the drop tanks, which sat on Rib 8, and the serials commenced 18" either side of the centreline of the tank. It was not usual for these serials to be reversed and they could be read on both sides from the rear of the mainplane. National insignia had reverted to the post war 'bright' D type roundels and fin flashes and the roundels were carried on the fuselage sides and upper wing

Pattern No.2: The formula applied to fuselage colour demarcation post-war (doesn't the outline look suspiciously like a Mossie?)

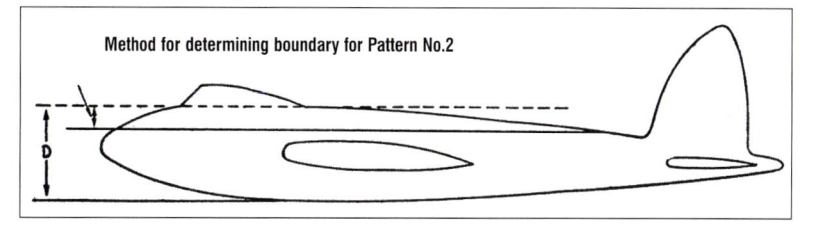

Modelling the Mosquito • Colour and Marking Notes   131

Figure captions (left column):

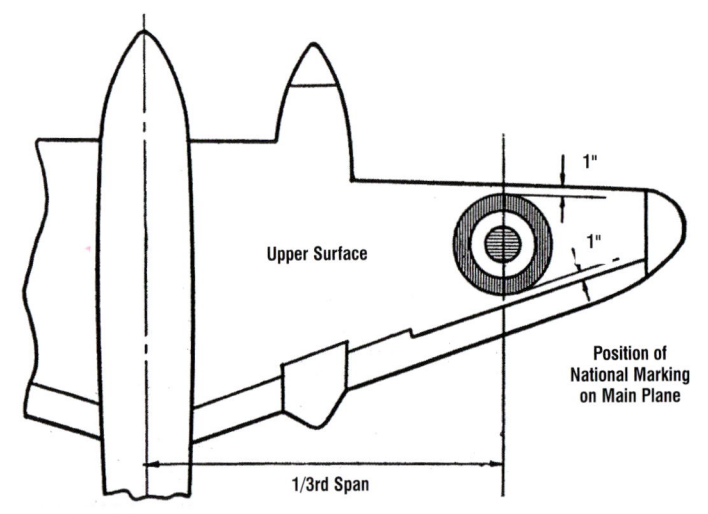

The position of the D Type roundel on the upper wings. Note that this is standard even for the B Type roundel on wartime Mosquitos

The D Type post war roundel

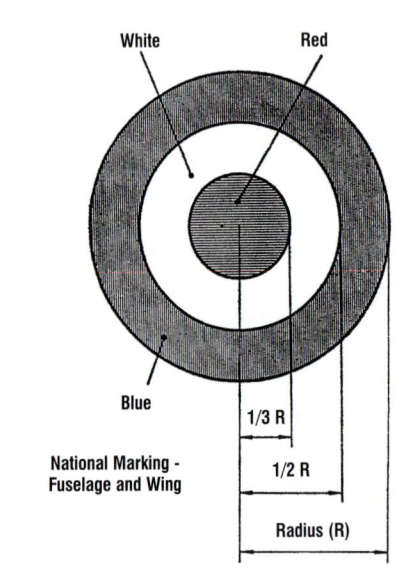

National Marking - Fuselage and Wing

This clear shot of T Mk III (TW117) shows the 30" codes carried under each wing. Note how they can be read from both directions. Note also the 'bright' post war roundels on the under surface (no war time Mosquitoes carried any in this position) (R.Bouser)

---

surfaces only. Once again the dimensions of these roundels remained the same, with 36" diameter examples on the fuselage and 54" examples on the upper wings. Serial numbers were 1" wide, 8" tall and in black, although their location seems to be higher up on the fuselage, as if the centreline of the tailplane has been used as the baseline for their application. The other option applied to post war bombers was aluminium overall. This scheme dictated that black codes and serials were applied, but other than that their markings were identical to the previous example styles.

Night Fighters

When the NF Mk II came into service it was painted in very matt black called 'Black (Special Night)' or RDM2A to the official spec. This paint was very thick and it resulted in not only a considerable speed penalty on the Mosquito, but it also had a high wear rate. The national markings consisted of the 54" Type B roundels on the upper wing surfaces and the 36" C1 Type on the fuselage sides. At this stage the 24" C1 Type fin flash was also applied and the 8" serial numbers were Dull Red. Squadron codes on night fighters of this period were also Dull Red and to the same proportions of those on the bombers.

By the Autumn of 1942 the RDM2A scheme was replaced and all night fighter Mosquitoes adopted an overall scheme of Medium Sea Grey with a disruptive pattern of Dark Green on the upper surfaces. This disruptive scheme did not get applied to the vertical fin, which remained in Medium Sea Grey overall. The squadron codes and serials remained Dull Red and the roundels and fin flashes also remained of the same type and style as previously applied. This scheme was applied to all night fighters until they were withdrawn from service in the 1950s. During the D-Day landings all night fighters of the ADGB had the invasion stripes applied to their Mosquitoes. Initially these were carried around the wings and fuselage, but later they were confined to the fuselage and finally, just to the lower section of the fuselage.

A good shot of an NF Mk 30 in the standard RAF scheme of Medium Sea Grey overall with a disruptive camouflage of Dark Green on top. Note the lack of camouflage on the vertical fin and the style and type of roundels and serials applied to this type (via S.Howe)

The only deviations from the 1942 scheme were carried by the aircraft operated by 100 Group. These machines retained the overall scheme listed above but the lower surfaces were oversprayed with Night Black. The demarcation of this colour on the fuselage sides was quite low and soft. The black did not usually cover the squadron codes and roundels, so that these did not need to be re-applied, but the radomes in the NF Mk XII, XIII and XVII were often finished in black overall. The revised demarcation did swoop down from the wing trailing edge, go along under the codes and roundel and then move back up to a point on the centre line of the tailplane. This did of course mean that the hard demarcation of the original scheme was still visible behind the squadron codes and roundels. This style of demarcation was by no means a 'golden rule' for 100 Group aircraft and careful study of photographs will highlight many variations.

This side view of a Mosquito bomber illustrates the 'night' under surface applied to many Bomber Support machines during the war (© AeroMaster Products)

The intruders of No.23 Squadron with their NF Mk II (Intruder) had a scheme identical to the night fighters of 100 Group, although they had this scheme applied from 1942 and it was still on their aircraft when they operated from Malta. Usually the individual aircraft's letter was repeated in Medium Sea Grey on the nose cone.

Fighter Bomber

From the arrival of the FB Mk VI this element of the Mosquito's use always carried the same style of camouflage. By this time the overall scheme of Medium Sea Grey with a disruptive pattern of Dark Green on the upper surfaces was standard and the fighter-bomber Mosquito squadrons had this scheme applied to their aircraft. The spinners were also painted Medium Sea Grey, while the propellers remained black with yellow tips. The demarcation on the fuselage was hard and on the centreline from the tailplane. The 8" black serial number

132 Chapter 13

was centred on this demarcation and 36" squadron codes in Medium Sea Grey were applied. The C1 Type (36") roundel was carried on the fuselage side and the B Type (54") remained in use for the upper wings.

During D-Day all fighter-bombers acquired the AEAF invasion stripes and as with the night fighters these were initially carried around each wing and the fuselage. By September 1944 they were carried around the fuselage only and finally, by December 1944, they were just on the lower section of the fuselage.

Coastal Strike

Initially all Mosquitoes operating on coastal strike operations were fighter-bombers and therefore had the scheme listed for the type. The FB Mk XVIIIs used for this task also had that scheme applied. Towards the end of the war however No.143 Squadron had their aircraft painted Dark Slate Grey and Ocean Grey over Sky with the spinners in yellow with a Medium Sea Grey ring near the tip. It is interesting to note that these machines had squadron codes in yellow outlined black (e.g. NE•A and NE•D), but other example in the squadron had the serial in Sky high up on the fuselage, above the wing, applied thus; NE-B. The demarcation on all coastal strike Mosquitoes was low down on the fuselage, basically parallel to the centre line but at 3/4 of the depth of the fuselage.

Again after the D-Day landing of June 1944, all coastal strike Mosquitoes carried the AEAF invasion stripes around the wings and fuselage. Like all other units though, these had been reduced to just around the fuselage by September and just on the lower fuselage by December. It is interesting to speculate on the famous pictures of NE•D (RS625) which show that the upper surfaces have been oversprayed (you can see that the serial still has traces of the old colours behind it) and we wonder if this indicated that the aircraft was painted Extra Dark Sea Grey overall?

Codes, roundels and fin flashes of these coastal strike machines were the same as with the fighter-bombers, although the notes about the revised colours applied to some of No.143 Squadron's machines should be taken into consideration

Target Tugs

The Mosquito was only operated post-war as a target tug and therefore it was painted aluminium on the upper surfaces and with yellow and black stripes underneath. The aluminium areas had a hard demarcation which was parallel to the centre line, but only 2/3 of the depth of the fuselage. This demarcation was carried onto the engine nacelles, although the line at the rear of the nacelle followed the panel line up at a curve. The under surface was yellow with 3' wide black stripes placed 6' apart. Now the problem with applying this to a model is in how it was applied to the real aircraft. In reality the lines were not applied straight to the aircraft at the distances mentioned. What happened was a box was drawn on the floor of the maximum dimensions of the aircraft. Onto this were applied the 3' bands, 6' apart, and then a plumb line was used to carry these up onto the aircraft. This does mean that many of the lines distorted as they move around the complex curvature of the airframe. This is almost impossible for a modeller to reproduce, so applying the stripes to the dimensions given is the only way. It should also be considered that the demarcation line was not decided as a simple '2/3rd of the depth of the fuselage', usually two 60° lines were drawn up from the ground, using the centreline of the aircraft as their starting point, and where they touched the fuselage sides was the demarcation point. Once again this is a bit involved for a modeller to achieve, so careful study of photographs should illustrate the correct demarcation points.

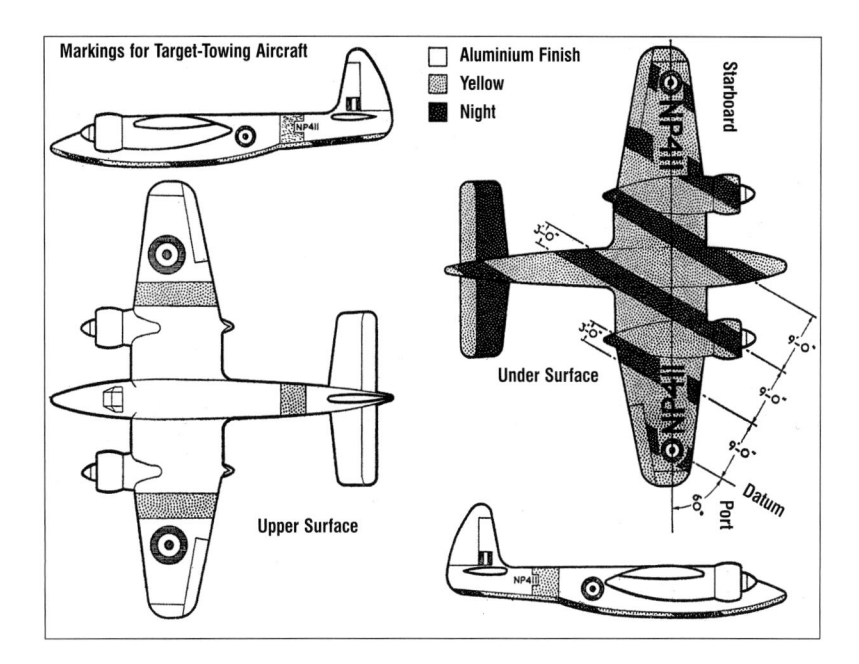

Although not for the TT Mk 35, this scheme does show the standard method for applying the black and yellow stripes to a target tug

Photo-reconnaissance

The prototype PR Mosquito (W4051) was originally painted Dark Earth and Dark Green over Sky, with B Type roundels on the upper wings and a 36" A1 roundel on the fuselage sides. The fin flash was the wide banded C Type and was 27" high. When this machine entered service with No.1 PRU it carried this scheme, but it later carried the overall PRU Blue scheme of the rest of the PR Mk 1s.

When the first production PR Mk 1s entered service they were painted PR Blue overall with the LY code of No.1 PRU in Medium Sea Grey either side of the fuselage. The 54" B Type roundel was applied to the upper wings and a C1 Type roundel was carried on the fuselage sides. The C1 style of fin flash (24") was carried on the vertical fin. By the time the PR Mk IX arrived the bright fuselage roundel had been replaced with a B type (36"). Squadron codes were rarely applied and in many examples a small aircraft letter was applied in Medium Sea Grey forward of the roundel in about 8" high letters. Other examples carried this identifying mark as an 8" high black letter below the serial number.

D-Day invasion stripes were carried by PR Mosquitoes for quite a while and unlike their fighter-bomber cousins, there are examples of all sorts of variations in how they were applied on or around the roundels and serial numbers. By mid-1944 the PR types operated by No.680 Sqn. at Foggia in Italy had had a number of close calls with Allied pilots who thought their Mosquitoes were Messerschmitt Me 210/410s. To overcome this the aircraft had the entire vertical fin painted in red and white

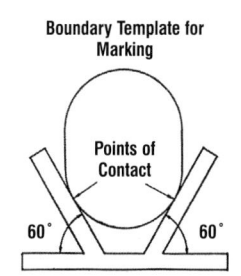

This diagram shows the official method used to determine the demarcation line on the fuselage of aircraft by the RAF painters
Caption: Boundary Template for Marking

This odd view from the back of an NF Mk XIX in the Far East allows you to see the SEAC theatre bands carried by the Mosquito. Note that the bands have been applied over the ailerons and rudder, but not the elevators. This is by no means odd, as examples were without them on the ailerons and elevators, or even all three surfaces!
(via S.Howe)

diagonal stripes. The aircraft also had the spinners painted yellow and the backs of each propeller blade had the tip marking moved down the blade to create a yellow band about 6" wide approximately 8" from the tip. Most Mosquitoes of this squadron also painted the invasion stripes around the aircraft serial number and the individual aircraft number was in red (24"), outlined in black and positioned aft of the fuselage roundel on both sides of the fuselage.

SEAC operations of PR Mosquitoes initially saw them in the above listed PR Blue scheme, however the intense heat in this theatre did result in their eventually being painted a dull aluminium colour overall. Some trials with the PR colour in the Middle East had been undertaken as early as 1942, but it was not until 1944 that the aluminium overall scheme became standard. SEAC machines carried the SEAC roundels in four positions and had the wide black recognition bands of this theatre applied to the wings, tailplane and rudder. Many variations of this marking on Mosquitoes can be found and it was not uncommon for them to not extend over the control surfaces. Serial numbers were in black (8") and were carried above the tailplane centreline on each fuselage side. The individual aircraft letter was usually carried aft of the fuselage roundel.

It should be noted that when No.60 Sqn. (RSAAF) retained a number of PR Mk XVIs post war, these machines retained their RAF camouflage of aluminium overall, but the upper and inner engine cowls were painted black (anti-dazzle) and the upper, back section of the cockpit canopy was painted gloss white. This included the glazing and frames.

Post-war, both the overall aluminium and PR Blue Mosquitoes were still about and these were joined by other examples which operated in Egypt that were painted Silver on top and PR Blue underneath! The demarcation for this scheme seems to have been a line running from the centreline of the tailplane to the wing trailing edge and the types also retained the B Type roundels in four positions. Once wartime operations were over the roundels applied to the Mosquito changed to the bright D type and most PR versions which operated into the 1950s had these, a 54" example being applied to the wing upper surface and a 36" example on the fuselage sides. The serial numbers remained in black (8"), although the 30" high black serials under the wings were also applied as per the post-war bomber and target tug versions. Some examples of the late PR Mk 34A series were seen with the upper surfaces finished in either white or Medium Sea Grey, although this was very rare and the version we can bring to mind is RG248 which was with the Met Flight at RAE Farnborough. Post war codes on the PR types were applied in white and were 36" high. Many units in the late 40s and early 50s applied unit badges to either side of the vertical fin and this was also practiced by the bomber squadrons.

Sea Mosquitoes

The prototype Sea Mosquito (FB Mk VI) was actually painted Dark Slate Grey and Extra Dark Sea Grey over yellow. The demarcation on the fuselage was basically half way down and the lower loop of the prototype 'P' marking was outlined in black. The serial was carried in 8" black figures, which used the demarcation as a baseline. Below this on the yellow was the 'ROYAL NAVY' title which was also in black but the letters were only 4" high, 2.5" wide and had a stroke of 0.5" and a gap between each character of just 0.5". Type C roundels (32") were applied under the wings, with a similar sized C1 roundel on the fuselage side. Note that due to the yellow under surface of this type and the yellow ring on the fuselage roundel, the roundel was outlined in the Dark Slate Grey of the upper surface. A standard 54" B Type roundel was applied to the upper surface of the wings and the four blade propellers were black with yellow tips.

Production FB Mk VIs operated by the Navy were finished in the Medium Sea Grey and Dark Green scheme. National markings at this time were as per the fighter-bomber versions.

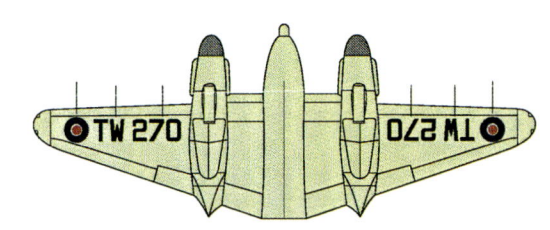

Post war many of these machines carried bands of squadron and flight colours on the spinners and a number also had the squadron codes on the fuselage outlined in yellow. The 'ROYAL NAVY' title was usually carried above the serial number in 4" high black numbers. The TR Mk 33 was initially supplied in Slate Grey and Ocean Grey over Sky, although it was not long before most of these machines were aluminium overall. The radome on many Royal Navy TR Mk 33s was painted in squadron and flight colours and the operating unit's code was carried in black on either side of the vertical fin, above the fin flash (e.g. LP = Lee-on-Solent). The serial number was repeated in black (30") figures under each wing and an aircraft number in black was also carried aft of the fuselage roundel. The size and style of this number varied quite considerably however.

Foreign Production

Canada

The Canadian-built examples adopted the camouflage schemes laid down by the RAF, although the shades of the colours used may well not have been an exact match. It is interesting to note that many of the Mosquitoes pictured in Canada awaiting delivery have the wing leading edges (half span) painted yellow. All roundels, fin flashes and serial numbers were applied as per the RAF machines and this also applied to the examples retained in Canada.

Australia

The first locally produced Mosquito did not appear in Australia until 1944 and by the end of the war only 104 Mosquitoes had been produced by De Havilland Australia. Initially the RAAF received a number of Mosquitoes from the RAF and these were supplied in the standard RAF schemes. The FB Mk VIs were therefore Medium Sea Grey and Dark Green and these were operated by No.1 and No.92 Squadrons. Squadron codes and

This under surface view of a TR Mk 33 shows the positioning and orientation of the serial number under each wing. This was identical to those applied to fighters and bombers post-war (© AeroMaster Products)

A Canadian-built B Mk XX (KB144:F) of C Flight, 36 OTU at Greenland, Novia Scotia in June 1944. Note the standard RAF scheme of Medium Sea Grey underneath and Ocean Grey and Dark Green on top. The spinners and fuselage bands are Sky and the wing leading edges are yellow. This was a common feature on Mosquitoes used in the OTUs in Canada (R.H.Dargue)

A52-413 was one of the FB Mk VIs supplied to Australia. This machine carries the overall aluminium scheme applied once the Foliage Green scheme had been found to be unsuitable. The position and style of the roundel, fin flash and squadron codes are a fair representation of those applied to most RAAF Mosquitos (F.Smith)

134 Chapter 13

serial numbers were applied in Sky Blue. When the RAAF received a number of T Mk IIIs these were painted Dark Green and Ocean Grey over Sky with an 18" wide Sky band on the rear fuselage and each spinner was painted in that colour. The PR Mk XVIs supplied to the RAAF were painted PR Blue overall with the B Type roundels in four positions. Those that survived into 1946 were soon repainted aluminium overall with a black anti-dazzle panel on the upper nose and inner engine cowlings. The spinners of these machines were also black.

When the first Australian-built example was envisaged to arrive in service the scheme applied to RAAF types at that time was Foliage Green and Earth Brown over Sky Blue. The camouflage pattern applied was identical to that used on British-built examples, but the demarcation line on the fuselage ran parallel to the tailplanes' centreline, high on the fuselage, before curving down onto the wing trailing edge. The RAAF style of roundel was in the same size and position as those used in RAF machines, and the serial numbers were applied in Medium Sea Grey. The provision of roundels on these machines omitted those on the wing lower surface, as per RAF machines. A number of the very first batch of Mosquitoes built actually flew in this scheme, although it was soon changed. By the time the Mosquitoes actually built in Australia arrived with the squadrons the official scheme was Foliage Green overall and a large number of Mosquitoes flew in the scheme. The dark colour absorbed the heat very quickly and with a wooden airframe that was not good, so by March 1945 Foliage Green was giving way to Aluminium overall. By this stage the RAAF roundels were 48" on the upper wings and 32" on the fuselage sides and the serials and squadron codes were applied in black.

After 1948 the RAAF roundel returned to the red, white and blue style and they were of the same proportions as post war RAF examples. Each new roundel was positioned in the same location as the marking it replaced and they were also of the same diameter. Therefore these post war markings were 48" on the wings and 32" on the fuselage.

Finally, and to quell any thought of it, the Kangaroo style of RAAF roundel did not appear until 1955 and there is no evidence to support the fact that any RAAF Mosquito ever carried them, as the type had been withdrawn by this time. Pity that!

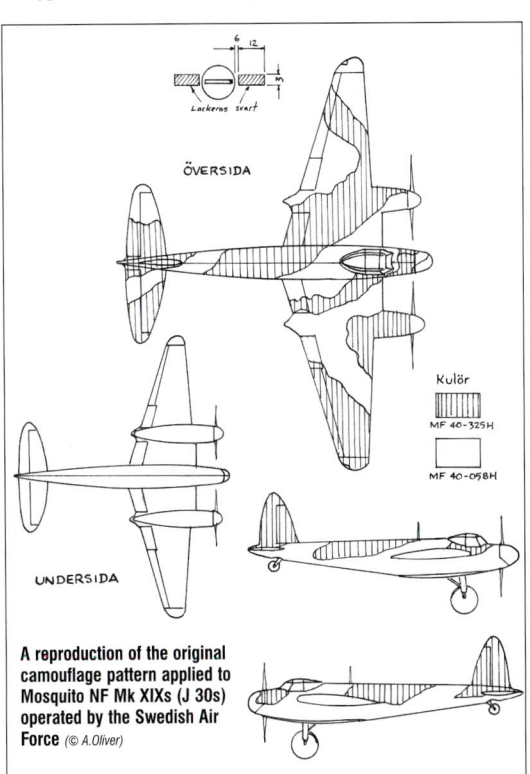

The (originally) unofficial squadron badge of No.1 Sqn. F1 Wing, Swedish Air Force. This motif was officially accepted and was carried on the entrance door on many of the squadron's J 30s (NF Mk XIXs) (© A Oliver)

This is the unofficial/official badge of No.2 Sqn. F1 Wing (© A Oliver)

This is the badge of No.3 Sqn. F1 Wing (© A Oliver)

Swedish Air Force

The NF Mk XIXs supplied to Sweden in 1948/9 were painted in the standard RAF scheme of Medium Sea Grey overall with a disruptive pattern of Dark Green on the upper surfaces. The vertical tail remained in grey and the spinners were usually

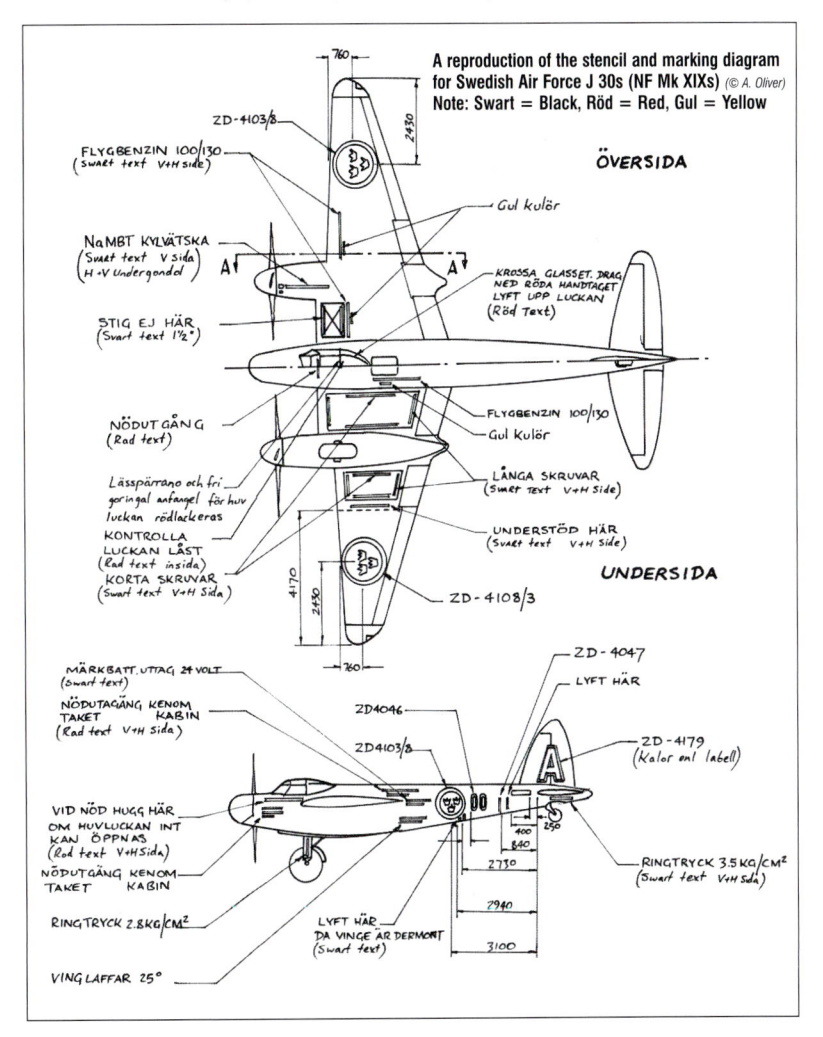

A reproduction of the original camouflage pattern applied to Mosquito NF Mk XIXs (J 30s) operated by the Swedish Air Force (© A.Oliver)

A reproduction of the stencil and marking diagram for Swedish Air Force J 30s (NF Mk XIXs) (© A. Oliver) *Note: Swart = Black, Röd = Red, Gul = Yellow*

Modelling the Mosquito • Colour and Marking Notes 135

By the time T Mk III TW117 had made its way into the Royal Air Force Museum at Hendon, it carried the standard RAF trainer scheme of silver overall with 18" wide Trainer Yellow bands around the wings and fuselage (S.Howe)

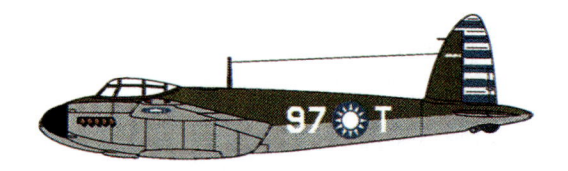

This trainer (T Mk 27) of the Chinese Nationalist Air Force is shown with the Olive Green and Neutral Grey scheme applied by this nation. The fuselage codes are white and will read T•97 on the other side, the 'T' denotes a trainer (all FB Mk 26s were prefixed 'FB') (© AeroMaster Products)

The emblem of No.3 Squadron, Chinese Nationalist Air Force, as seen applied to the nose of FB Mk 26s at Hankow (© A.Oliver)

The 'aluminium bronze' painted FB Mk VI (TE603) flown by the squadron commander while this machine was operated by the Czech Air Force (S.Spurny)

painted in the squadron colour. National markings were carried in six locations and were the yellow-rimmed style of roundel. A black '1' was applied just aft of the fuselage roundel and the serial number of each machine was applied in small black figures just in front of the tailplane. A squadron letter was applied to each side of the vertical fin and this was outlined in white, with the exception of those letters in white, which were outlined in black. This individual aircraft letter was also carried in a much smaller size on the nose. Stencilling was in black and was initially in English. When each aircraft went for a major service or was repaired these gave way to new stencils applied in Swedish. A final small detail with the J 30 was that the dipole fitted on the centreline, aft of the cannon ports, was painted in red and white stripes, although this does not seem to be a universal occurrence.

Turkey

The FB Mk VIs supplied to Turkey were painted silver dope overall and carried the national marking in six locations. The national flag was also carried on the vertical fin, about mid-way up. These machines had four blade propellers, painted black, as were the spinners. The RAF serial number was retained in 8" high black figures just forward of the tailplane.

The T Mk IIIs supplied to Turkey were painted yellow overall, with yellow spinners and black propeller blades. The national insignia was carried in six positions and the national flag was again on the vertical fin.

Belgian Air Force

The NF Mk 30s, FB Mk VIs and T Mk IIIs operated post-war by this Air Force were initially retained in their standard RAF camouflage. The RAF roundels were soon replaced with Belgium examples and these seem to have been of similar sizes. Unlike RAF machines the NF Mk 30s and FB Mk VIs (converted to TT Mk VIs) had roundels applied under the wings. The NF Mk 30s also had the aircraft serial number repeated in white inboard of the roundel under each wing. These serials seem to be approximately 12" (30cm) high. The serial number was also repeated in black on the fuselage, forward of the tailplane, and these seem to be about the same size as RAF serials (8"). Operational NF Mk 30s had the squadron code and aircraft letter applied in white on the fuselage side and they also seem to be the same size as RAF codes. Once the FB Mk VIs and T Mk IIIs were converted to target tug duties, they were painted silver overall and had 18" wide yellow bands applied around the rear fuselage and each wing. The roundels were retained in six positions and the serial number was applied in black under the wings and on the rear fuselage. Squadron codes and aircraft numbers were now black and these were applied as per RAF machines e.g. B2•H. Propellers and spinners on these target tugs were black.

Chinese Nationalist Air Force

All of the machines supplied to China in 1947 were ex-Canadian-built and therefore when they were delivered they must have been in standard RAF camouflage. Most were FB Mk 26s, although some T Mk 22s and T Mk 27s were also supplied. Each aircraft was shipped to China and then assembled; the camouflage initially looks quite standard with the serial number retained in black on the rear fuselage and Chinese National roundels applied in six positions. The Chinese national flag was also carried either side of the vertical fin. Looking at later photographs of these machines they have obviously gained a new colour scheme and it looks like Olive Green over Neutral Grey (or similar). The National roundels are retained in six positions and the flag is still on the vertical fin. The entire rudder on these latter machines is striped in white and light blue and each machine carries a white identification number either side of the fuselage, T•85 being an example of a trainer version (the 'T' stood for trainer).

Czechoslovakian Air Force

Twenty-four FB Mk VIs and two T Mk IIIs were operated by this nation. The FB Mk VIs were designated B-36 (and later LB-36 when they were fitted with ex-German armament) and the T Mk IIIs were CB-36s. They were allocated to the No.24 Bomber Regiment (coded IY and JX) and to the 47th Air Regiment (coded PU and US). Study of photographs shows that a number of these machines seem to be Ocean Grey and Dark Green over Medium Sea Grey, while others are Medium Sea Grey and Dark Green. One machine (KP-1, ex-TE603) is listed as being sprayed 'Aluminium Bronze' overall and it is also assumed

136 Chapter 13

that the trainers were yellow overall. The nose cones on the fighter-bombers were all painted Dark Grey and the spinners were red (Marker Red). Unit codes were white, with black outlines, and the RAF serial number was retained in black (8") on the rear fuselage. There was no roundel on the fuselage sides, so the squadron codes were applied thus: IY-12. Once the fighter-bombers were overhauled they were painted a dark grey colour overall, although they retained the red spinners. National markings were carried above and below the wings and on either side of the vertical fin, the roundels on the wings being approximately 36" diameter, those on the tail being 18", and the fuselage codes about 30" high.

A head-on view of IY-1 of the Czech Air Force in the late 1940s (S.Spurny)

Far left: A Czech Air Force FB Mk IV (IY-12 ex-RF838) is shown wearing a standard RAF scheme of Ocean Grey and Dark Green over Medium Sea Grey. The squadron codes are in white outlined in black and they are also carried on the undersurfaces as well (S.Spurny)

USAAF

The USAAF operated a number of PR Mosquitoes in the war and these machines were painted RAF PR Blue overall. The British roundels were painted out with a close match to this colour and then American stars'n'bars were applied alongside them. The serial number was retained in 8" high black figures near the tail and the entire tail unit of the machines operated by the 653rd and 654th BS (Light), 25th Bomb Group at Watton was red overall. The individual aircraft letter was applied in white in a blue disc on the vertical fin. The PR Mk XVIs operated by the 482nd Bomb Group at Alconbury (and modified to carry the H2X in the nose), were also in the same overall scheme as the previous examples, although the vertical tail was not red. The only USAAF fighter squadron to equip with the Mosquito was No.416 Sqn at Pisa, Italy and this squadron flew the NF Mk 30, left in the RAF camouflage scheme. The stars'n'bars on these machines were carried on the fuselage side and below the starboard and above the port wings. The squadron painted the spinners of its machines red and it retained the RAF style C1 Type fin flashes.

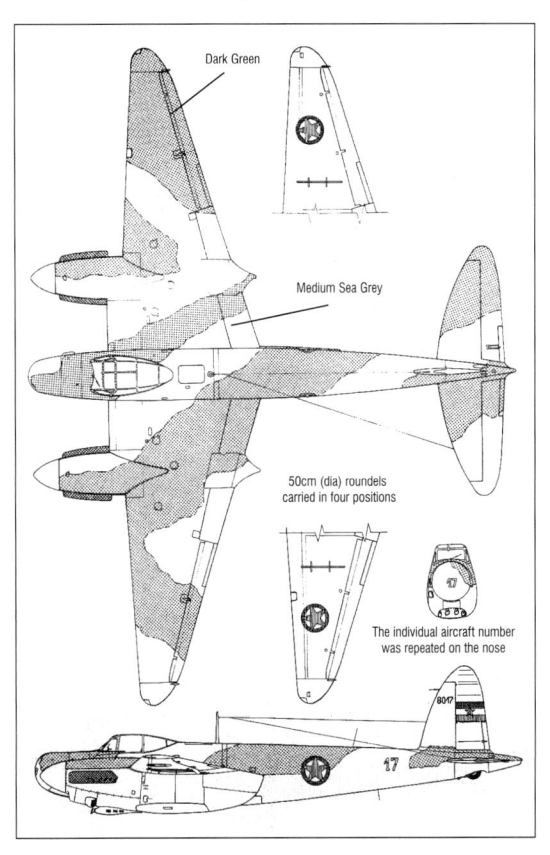

Canadian-built examples (F-8-DH) supplied to the USAAF were Ocean Grey and Dark Green over Medium Sea Grey and the RAF roundels were painted out. The USAAF insignia was applied on either side of the fuselage and on the lower starboard and upper port wing. The serial number was applied in yellow on the vertical fin (e.g. 334934) in a stencil style of numeral and all these machines had the Hamilton Standard manufacturer's logo on each propeller blade.

Norwegian Air Force

This country retained a number of FB Mk VIs after the war. After a period of inactivity ten more FB Mk VIs were obtained along with three trainers, and operational service was resumed. The machines retained their RAF camouflage of Medium Sea Grey and Dark Green and roundels were carried in six positions. The aircraft serial number was moved onto the vertical fin and applied in 4" high figures thus; RS-650. The squadron codes were applied in white either side of the roundel (e.g. F•AK).

Late in 1949 two FB Mk VIs were fitted with airborne radar in the ASH style of pod (as per the TR Mk 33) and these machines had a different style of squadron code on the fuselage, and the serial was relocated in larger figures just aft of the squadron codes. The radome on these machines was painted white.

Yugoslavian Air Force

About 140 Mosquitoes were supplied to this nation in the 1950s and these included T Mk IIIs, FB Mk VIs and fifty NF Mk 38s.

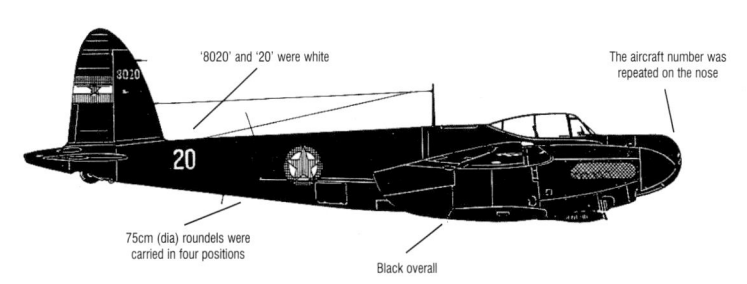

Far left: De Havilland Mosquito NF Mk 38, 8017/17 of the Yugoslavian Air Force based at Polovinom in the 1950s

All of these machines were supplied in RAF camouflage and all the roundels just had a red star superimposed onto them. The national flag was red, white and blue with a red star superimposed over the middle (white) section, and this was carried mid-way up the rudder. The RAF fin flashes and serials were all painted out prior to delivery, although these areas are distinguishable by the fresher paint. The upper wing roundels

Above: De Havilland Mosquito NF Mk 38, 8020/20 of the Yugoslavian Air Force (JRV) in 1953

De Havilland Mosquito NF Mk 38, 8056/56 of the Yugoslavian Air Force (JRV) in 1951/2

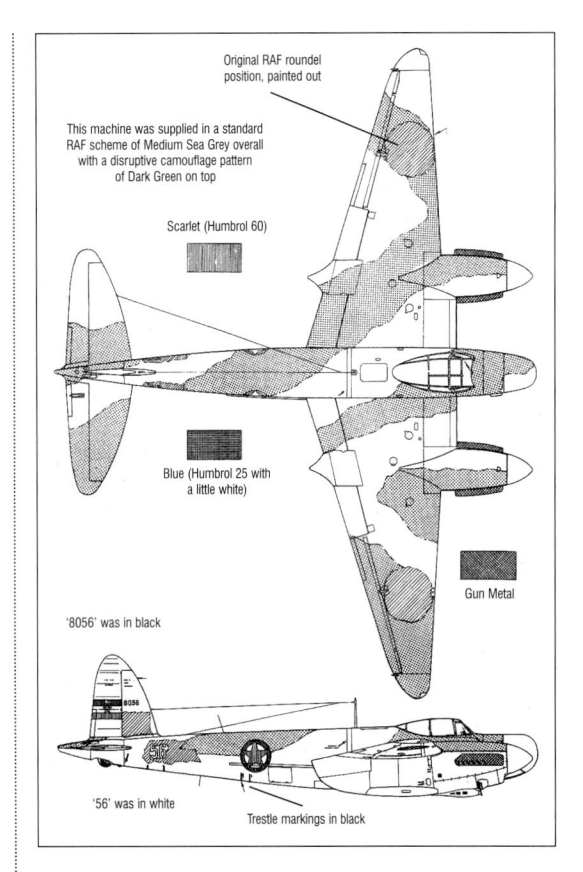

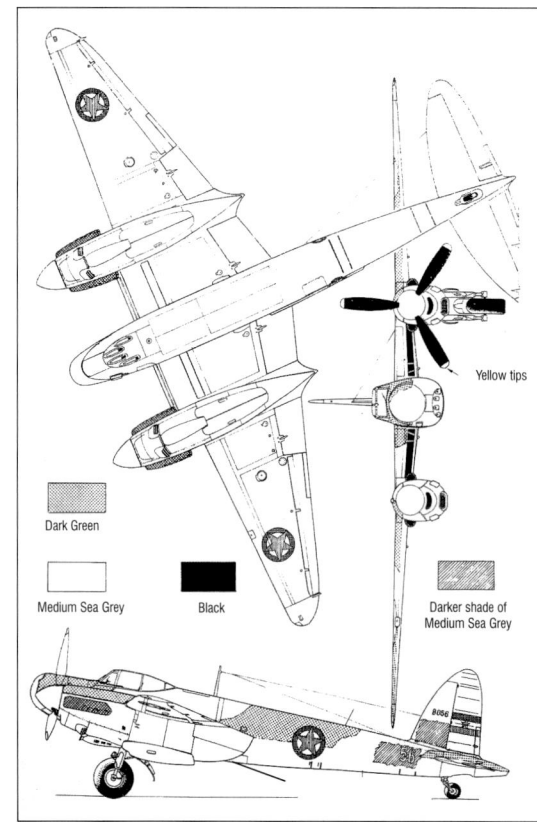

Original RAF roundel position, painted out

This machine was supplied in a standard RAF scheme of Medium Sea Grey overall with a disruptive camouflage pattern of Dark Green on top

Scarlet (Humbrol 60)

Blue (Humbrol 25 with a little white)

Gun Metal

'8056' was in black

'56' was in white

Trestle markings in black

Yellow tips

Dark Green

Medium Sea Grey

Black

Darker shade of Medium Sea Grey

were also painted out, usually in Medium Sea Grey, regardless of the fact that they are on Dark Green camouflage! No upper wing roundels were re-applied and the dimensions of the versions on the lower wings and fuselage were quite small, being

approximately 24" diameter. Each aircraft was allocated a four figure serial number, which did not relate to the RAF serial number and this was applied half way up the vertical fin in 8" black characters. An individual aircraft serial number was

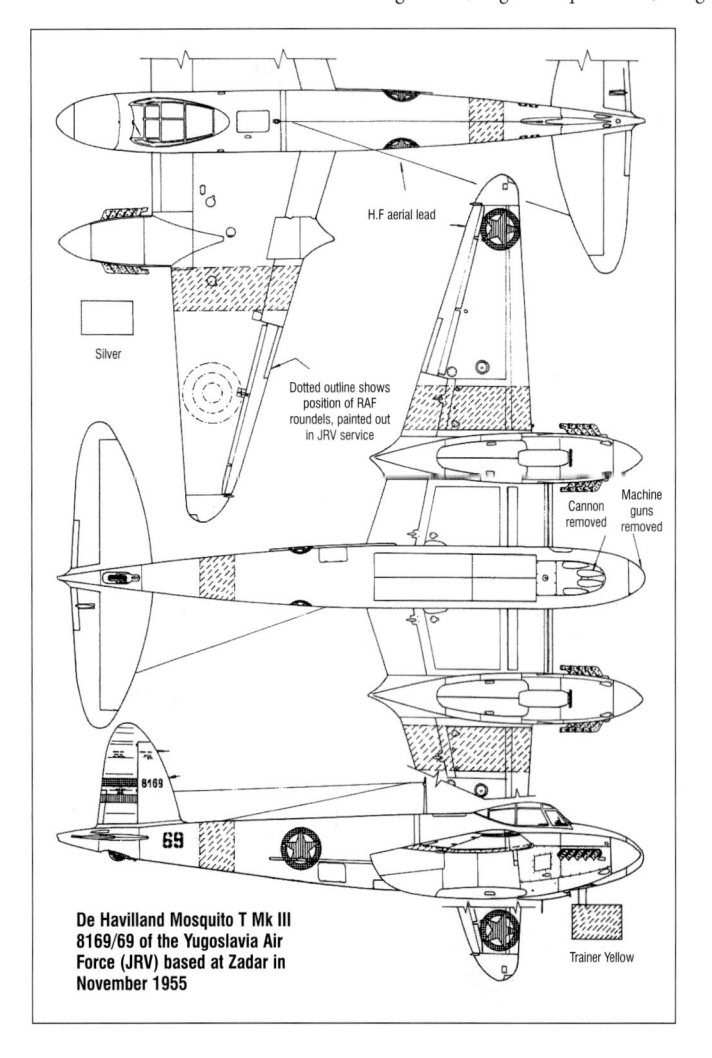

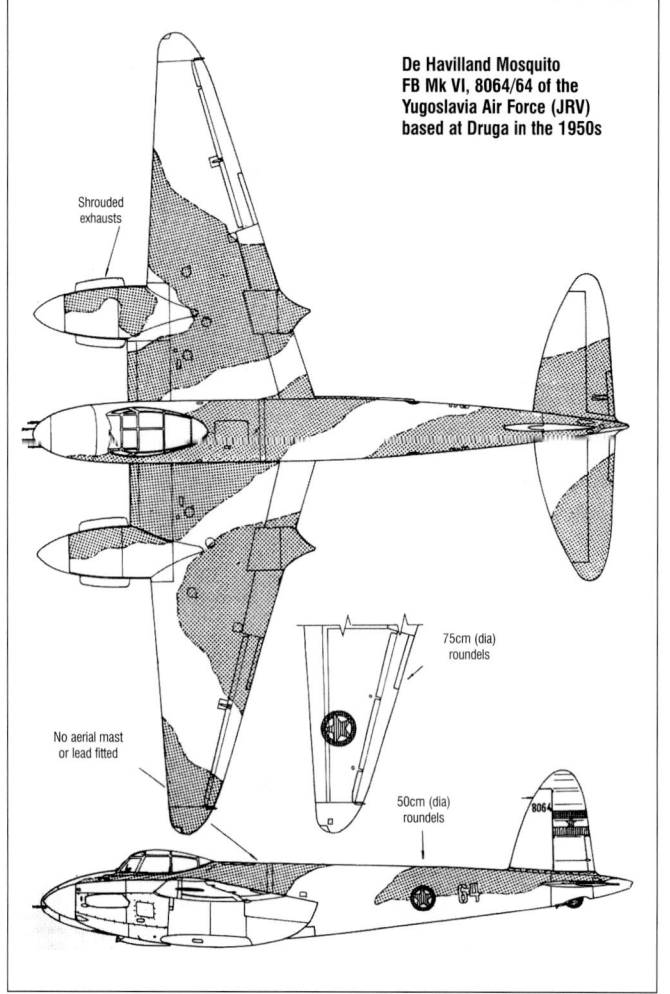

Silver

Dotted outline shows position of RAF roundels, painted out in JRV service

H.F aerial lead

Cannon removed

Machine guns removed

Trainer Yellow

De Havilland Mosquito T Mk III 8169/69 of the Yugoslavia Air Force (JRV) based at Zadar in November 1955

De Havilland Mosquito FB Mk VI, 8064/64 of the Yugoslavia Air Force (JRV) based at Druga in the 1950s

Shrouded exhausts

75cm (dia) roundels

No aerial mast or lead fitted

50cm (dia) roundels

138   Chapter 13

Modeller's Cross-reference Colour Chart

COLOUR	FS595A	BS or RAL	USE	AVAILABLE PAINTS
ROYAL AIR FORCE				
Dark Earth			Topside camouflage with Dark Green	AeroMaster Warbird Enamel: 9110 Dark Earth
				AeroMaster Warbird Acrylic: 1110 Dark Earth
	~0118			Floquil M189: Field Drab 30118
	~0118			Floquil 145: Dark Earth 30118
				Gunze Sangyo: H072 Dark Earth
				Humbrol Authentic: HU02, Dark Earth
				Humbrol Authentic: HF03, Terre Fonce
	~0118			Humbrol Authentic: HU18, Brown 30118
		450		Humbrol Super Enamel: No.29 Dark Earth
				ModelMaster: 1702 Field Drab
	~0118			Pactra Acrylics: A24, Brown Drab FS 30118
				Polly-S 830: Field Drab
	~0118			Polly-S Acrylic 5252: British Dark Earth 30118
		450		Xtracolor: X2 Dark Earth BS450
	~0118			Xtracolor: X101 Earth 30118
Dark Green	~4079		Topside camouflage with Dark Earth	AeroMaster Warbird Enamel: 9111 Dark Green
				AeroMaster Warbird Acrylic: 1111 Dark Green
				Compucolor: CAC2, Forest Green
	~4079			Floquil: M196, Dark Green 34079
	~4079			Floquil: 3143, British Dark Green (34079)
				Humbrol Authentic: HG02, Dark Green RLM71
	~4079			Humbrol Authentic: HU07, Green 34079
				ModelMaster: 1710, Dark Green
	~4079			Mr Color: 309, Dark Green FS34079
				Pactra: M5
	~4079			Pactra Acrylics: A29, Jungle Green FS34079
				Polly-S: 835, Forest Green
				Polly-S: 814 Dark Green
	~4079			Polly-S Acrylic: Dark Green (34079)
	~4079			Polly-S Enamel: Dark Green 34079
				Tamiya: XF58, Olive Green
	~4079			Xtracolor: X110, Forest Green FS14079
		451		Xtracolor: X1 Dark Green (BS451)
Sky			Undersurface until 1942	AeroMaster Warbird Enamel: 9114
				AeroMaster Warbird Acrylic: 1114
	~4424			Compucolor: CAS10, Light Grey Green
	~4424			Gunze Sangyo Acrylic: H074, Sky
		210		Humbrol Authentic: HB05, Sky Type S
	~4454			Tamiya: XF21, Sky
		210		Xtracolor: X7, Sky
Medium Sea Grey			Early code letters, Under surface colour Overall for night fighters	AeroMaster Warbird Enamel: 9113
				AeroMaster Warbird Acrylic: 1113
	~6270			Compucolor: CAC28, Neutral Grey
	~6270			Floquil: M206, Neutral Grey
	~6270			Floquil Enamel: 3151, Sea Grey, Medium
		640		Gunze Sangyo Acrylic: Medium Sea Grey
	~6270			Gunze Sangyo Acrylic: Grey
	~6270			Humbrol Authentic: HF04 Gris Bleu Clair
	~6440			Humbrol Authentic: HB06 Sea Grey Medium
	~6270			Humbrol Authentic: USN2, Medium Gray
		637		Humbrol Super Enamel: No.165
				ModelMaster: 1725, Neutral Grey
	~6293			Polly-S: 5258, Sea Grey, Medium
	~6293			Polly-S Acrylic: British Sea Grey, Medium
	~6270			Replicolor: Grey
	~6424			Tamiya: XF20 Medium Grey
	~6270			Xtracolor: X133, Neutral Gray (FS 16270)
		637		Xtracolor: X3, Medium Sea Grey
Ocean Grey			Upper surface camouflage with Dark Green from 9/41	AeroMaster Warbird Enamel: 9112, Ocean Grey
				AeroMaster Warbird Acrylic: 1112, Ocean Grey
	~6152			Floquil: 3149, Ocean Grey
	~6152			Humbrol Authentics: HN02 Dark Grey
				Humbrol Super Enamels: No.106 Ocean Grey
	~6187			Polly-S: 823, Ocean Grey
	~5237			Polly-S: 5256, Ocean Grey
	~5237			Polly-S: 5256, Ocean Grey
				Xtracolor: X6, Ocean Grey
Dark Slate Grey			Upper surface camouflage with Ocean Grey on FAA TR Mk 33s	AeroMaster Warbird Acrylic: 1119, Slate Grey
	~4096			Floquil Classic: 3159, Dark Slate Grey
	~4091			Gunze Sangyo Acrylic: H036, Dark Green
	~4091			Gunze Sangyo Acrylic: H052, Olive Drab
	~4096			Gunze Sangyo Acrylic: H320, Dark Green
	~4096			Humbrol Authentics: HB01, Dark Green
	~4091			Humbrol Authentics: HI03, Overall Green
	~4096			Humbrol Authentics: HG17, Dark Green
	~4096			Humbrol Authentics: HJ01, Green N1
	~4127			Humbrol Authentics: HI01, Mottle Green
	~4127			Humbrol Authentics: HM07, Khaki Drab
				Humbrol Super Enamel: No.102 Dark Slate Grey
	~4127			Humbrol Super Enamel: No.150 Forest Green
	~4096			Pactra: MG54, Sherwood Green
	~4127			Pactra Acrylic: A34, Artillery Olive
	~4096			Polly-S Acrylic: 5266, Dark Slate Grey
	~4127			Floquil: M200, Forest Green
	~4127			ModelMaster: 1714, Forest Green
				Xtracolor: X25, Dark Slate Grey
Extra Dark Sea Grey			FAA Sea Mosquitoes	AeroMaster Warbird Acrylic: 1118
	~6118			Compucolor: CAC16, Gunship Grey
	~6118			Floquil: M204, Sea Grey
	~6118			Floquil Classic: 3157, Extra Dark Sea Grey
	~6118			Gunze Sangyo Acrylic: H032, Field Grey
	~6118			Gunze Sangyo Acrylic: H072, Dark Sea Grey
	~6118			Gunze Sangyo Acrylic: H305, Grey
	~6118	638		Gunze Sangyo Acrylic: H331, Dark Sea Grey
	~6118			Humbrol Authentics: HF02, Gris Blue Fonce
	~6118			Humbrol Authentics: HM04, German Panzer Grey
	~6118			Humbrol Authentics: HU03, Neutral Grey
	~6118			Humbrol Authentics: HU22, Blue Grey ANA 603
	~6118			Humbrol Authentics: USN1, Dark Grey
		638		Humbrol Super Enamel: No.123, Extra Dark Sea Grey
	~6118			ModelMaster: 1723, Gunship Gray
	~6118			Mr Color: 305, Grey
	~6118			Polly-S, 822, Sea Grey
	~6118			Poly-S Acrylic: 5264, Extra Dark Sea Grey
	~6118			Xtracolor: X130, Gunship Gray
Night	~7038		Night fighters Under surfaces	AeroMaster Warbird Enamel: 9001, Black
	~7038			Floquil Classic: 3010, Black
	~7038			Gunze Sangyo Acrylic: H002, Black
	~7038			Gunze Sangyo Acrylic; H012, Flat Black
	~7038			Humbrol Authentics: HB1, Night Black
	~7038			Humbrol Authentics: HU12, Night Black
		624		Humbrol Super Enamels: No.33, Black
	~7038			ModelMaster: 1747, Gloss Black
	~7038			ModelMaster: 1749, Flat Black
	~7038			Pactra: MG61, Ebony Black
	~7038			Pactra Acrylic: A46, Black
	~7038			Polly-S: PF-10, Black
	~7038			Polly-S: 5214, Night Black
		RAL 9005		Revell: 07, Black
		RAL 9011		Revell: 08, Black
	~7038			Tamiya: X01, Black
	~7038			Tamiya: X18, Semigloss Black
	~7038			Tamiya: XF01, Flat Black
	~7038			Testors: 1749, Black
	~7038			Testors: 1747, Black
		624		Xtracolor: X12, Night Black
Identification Blue (Dull)	~5044		Roundels	Gunze Sangyo Acrylic: H326, Blue
	~5044			ModelMaster: 1719, Insignia Blue
	~5044			Mr Color: 326, Blue
	~5044			Tamiya: XF17, Sea Blue
	~5044			Xtracolor: X122, Insignia Blue
		110		Xtracolor: X30, RAF Roundel Blue
Identification Blue (Bright)	~5056		Post-war Roundels	Compucolour: CIS7, Insignia Blue
Identification Red (Dull)	~0109		Roundel centre & codes	N/A
Identification White	~7875		Roundels Post-war codes	AeroMaster Warbird Enamel: 9002, White
	~7875			Compucolor: CAC12, White
	~7875			Humbrol Super Enamel: No.22, White
	~7875			Humbrol Super Enamel: No.34, Matt White
	~7778			Gunze Sangyo Acrylic: H021, Off White
	~7875			Gunze Sangyo Acrylic: H001, White
	~7875			Gunze Sangyo Acrylic: H011, Flat White
	~7875			Humbrol Authentics: USN6, White
	~7875			ModelMaster: 1745, Insignia White
	~7875			ModelMaster: 1768, Flat White
	~7875			Mr Color: 316, White
	~7875			Pactra: MG52, Alpine White
	~7875			Pactra Acrylic: A47, White
	~7875			Polly-S: PG-10, White
	~7875			Polly-S: II-33, White
	~7875			Polly-S: PF-11, White
	~7875			Tamiya: X02, White
	~7875			Tamiya: XF02, Flat White
	~7875			Testors: 1168, White
	~7875			Xtracolor: X141, White
Aluminium	~7178		Overall Post-war	Compucolor: CIS12, Aluminium
				Halford Acrylic: Aluminium
				Halford Acrylic: Nissan Silver (Met)
				Humbrol Super Enamel: No.11, Silver
				Humbrol Super Enamel: No.191, Chrome Silver
	~7178			ModelMaster: 1790, Chrome Silver
				ModelMaster Metalizer: 1401 Aluminium Plate
	~7178			Polly-S, IJ-17
	~7178			Tamiya: XF16, Flat Aluminium
	~7178			Testors: 1146 Aluminium
	~7178			Xtracolor: X142, Aluminium
Identification Yellow			Trainers Target Tugs	AeroMaster Warbird Enamel: 9003, Yellow
	~3538			Gunze Sangyo Acrylic: H024, Orange Yellow
	~3538			Gunze Sangyo Acrylic: H329, Yellow
				Humbrol Super Enamel: No.24, Trainer Yellow
				Humbrol Super Enamel: No.154, Insignia Yellow
	~3538			ModelMaster: 1707, Chrome Yellow
	~3538			ModelMaster: 1708, Insignia Yellow
	~3538			Pactra Acrylics: A27, Flat Yellow
	~3538			Polly-S, F-3, Yellow
	~3538			Polly-S: PF-40, Yellow
	~3538			Testors: 1169, Yellow
				Xtracolor: X11, Trainer Yellow
	~3538			Xtracolor: X106, Insignia Yellow
PR Blue			Overall -PR a/c	AeroMaster Warbird Acrylic: 1117, PR Blue
		636		Xtracolor: X8, PR Blue
USAAF				
Note: For PR Blue, Medium Sea Grey and Dark Green, see entry under 'RAF' section. Also, RAF roundels on PR machines were possibly painted out with 'Insignia Blue' (FS~5044)				
Insignia Blue	~5044		See above	Gunze Sangyo Acrylic: H326, Blue
	~5044			ModelMaster: 1719, Insignia Blue
	~5044			Mr Color: Blue
	~5044			Tamiya: XF17, Sea Blue
	~5044			Xtracolor: X122, Insignia Blue
Insignia Red	~1136		Tail on PR machines	Gunze Sangyo Acrylic: H327, Red
	~1136			Humbrol Authentics: HT06, Marker Red
				Humbrol Super Enamel: No.153, Matt Insignia Red
	~1136			ModelMaster: 1705, Insignia Red
	~1136			Mr Color: 327, Red
	~1136			Pactra Acrylics: A26, Insignia Red
	~1136			Polly-S, IR-45, Red
	~1136			Polly-S, PF-20, Red
	~1136			Tamiya, XF07, Flat Red
	~1136			Testors: 1150, Flat Red
	~1136			Xtracolor: X103, Insignia Red
ROYAL AUSTRALIAN AIR FORCE				
Note: For 'Sky', 'Medium Sea Grey', 'Dark Earth', 'Dark Green', Insignia Red (Dull)', see the entries under the 'RAF' section. Note also that the aluminium applied overall to RAAF Mosquitoes was far brighter than that applied to RAF machines (FS ~7178 still applies).				
Sky	~4504		Lower surface	See entry in 'RAF' section
Medium Sea Grey	~6270		Camouflage colour	See entry in 'RAF' section
Dark Earth	~0118		Camouflage colour	See entry in 'RAF' section
Dark Green	~4096		Topside camouflage	See entry in 'RAF' section
Insignia Yellow	~3538		Trainers	See entry in 'RAF' section
Identification White	~7778		Identification markings	See entry in 'RAF' section
Foliage Green	~4092		Overall	Compucolor: CAC32, Green
	~4092			Gunze Sangyo Acrylic: H320, Green
	~4092			Humbrol Authentic: HU01, Medium Green 42
	~4092			ModelMaster: 1764, Euro Dark Green
	~4092			Mr Color: 302, Green
	~4092			Pactra Acrylic: A31, Dark Green
	~4092			Tamiya: XF61, Dark Green

Modeller's Cross-reference Colour Chart continued

COLOUR	FS595A	BS or RAL	USE	AVAILABLE PAINTS
	~4092			Xtracolor: X114, Medium Green
Sky Blue	~5622		Under surface	Compucolor: CAC21, Pale Blue
	~5622			Floquil: M203, Pale Blue
	~5622			Gunze Sangyo Acrylic: H314, Blue
	~5622			Humbrol Authentics: IAF4, Pale Blue
	~5622			ModelMaster: 1722, Duck Egg Blue
	~5622			Mr Color: 314, Blue
	~5622			Pactra: M4, Artillery Olive
	~5622			Polly-S: 877, Blue
Earth Brown	~0099		Top surface camouflage	Floquil: M187, Earth Brown
	~0099		for early production	Humbrol Authentics: HF06, Chocolate
			Mosquitoes	Humbrol Super Enamel: No.93, Chocolate
	~0099			Polly-S: 831, Earth Brown
	~0099			Polly-S Acrylic: 5244, Earth Brown
				Tamiya: XF 10, Flat Brown
Dull Blue	~5050		Roundels	Compucolor: CAC26, Blue Angels Blue
	~5050			Gunze Sangyo Acrylic: H328, Blue
	~5050			ModelMaster: 1772, Blue Angels Blue
	~5050			Mr Color: 328, Blue
	~5050			Pactra: MG53, Imperial Blue
	~5050			Xtracolor: X123, Blue Angels Blue
Bright Blue	~5056		Roundels	Compucolor: CIS7, Insignia Blue
Red (Dull)	~0166		Identification colour	Humbrol Authentics: HP02, Camouflage Red-Brown

SWEDISH AIR FORCE
All J 30s were delivered in Medium Sea Grey and Dark Green. For these colours see the relevant entry in the 'Royal Air Force' section. No specific shades have been listed for the squadron colours (red, white, blue and yellow), but we would assume that the blue, white and yellow matches that of the Swedish roundel and the red would be similar to 'Insignia Red' (See 'USAAF' section).

TURKISH AIR FORCE
The FB Mk VIs delivered to this country were aluminium overall (~7178) and the T Mk IIIs were also this colour, with yellow (~3538) bands. See the entries for these colour in the 'Royal Air Force' section.

BELGIAN AIR FORCE
The FB Mk VIs and NF 30s were delivered to this country in standard RAF schemes. Therefore see the entries for Medium Sea Grey (~6270) and Dark Green (~4079) under the 'Royal Air Force' section. The T Mk IIIs were aluminium (~7178) overall with yellow (~3538) bands and when the FB Mk VIs were converted to target towing duties (TT Mk 6), they too carried this scheme.

COLOUR	FS595A	BS or RAL	USE	AVAILABLE PAINTS
Red	~1105		Roundels	Gunze Sangyo Acrylic: H003, Red
	~1105			Gunze Sangyo Acrylic: H013, Flat Red
	~1105			Humbrol: HM09, Scarlet
		RAL 3000		Humbrol Super Enamel: No.19, Bright Red
	~1105			Revell: No.31, Fiery Red
				Tamiya: X07, Red
				Testors: 1503, Red

COLOUR	FS595A	BS or RAL	USE	AVAILABLE PAINTS
Yellow	~3655		Roundels	Gunze Sangyo Acrylic: H004, Yellow
				Humbrol Authentics: HT06, Insignia Yellow
		RAL 1026		Humbrol Super Enamel: No.69, Lemon Yellow
				Revell: Luminous Yellow
	~3655			Tamiya: XF08, Lemon Yellow
	~3655			Tamiya: XF03, Flat Yellow
				Testors: 1514, Yellow
	~3655			Xtracolor, Blue Angels Yellow
Black	~7038			See entry in 'Royal Air Force' section

CHINESE NATIONALIST AIR FORCE

Olive Green			Upper Surface	AeroMaster Warbird Enamel: 9092, Dark Army Green
	~4098			Humbrol Authentics: HJ03, Green A3
				Xtracolor: X351, Japanese Army Green
Neutral Grey 43			Lower Surface	AeroMaster Warbird Enamel: 9043, Neutral Grey 43
	~6173			AeroMaster Warbird Acrylic: 1043, Neutral Grey 43
				Gunze Sangyo Acrylic: H063, Neutral Grey
	~6118			Humbrol Authentics: HU03, Neutral Grey 43

CZECHOSLOVAKIAN AIR FORCE
The Mosquitoes operated by this nation were supplied in RAF camouflage. Therefore see entries for Ocean Grey (~6152), Medium Sea Grey (~6270) and Dark Green (~4079) under the 'Royal Air Force' section. The T Mk IIIs were supplied painted yellow (~3538); see the entry for this in the 'Royal Air Force' section also.

| Grey | ~6595* | | Overall after overhaul | N/A |

*Note: The colour reference used here is only an approximation

ROYAL NORWEGIAN AIR FORCE
The Mosquitoes operated by this nation were supplied in RAF camouflage. Therefore see entries for Medium Sea Grey (~6270) and Dark Green (~4079) under the 'Royal Air Force' section.

YUGOSLAVIAN AIR FORCE
The Mosquitoes supplied to this nation were painted in RAF camouflage. Therefore see entries for Medium Sea Grey (~6270) and Dark Green (~4079) under the 'Royal Air Force' section. The T Mk IIIs were aluminium (~7178) and had yellow bands (~3538); these too can be found under the 'Royal Air Force' section

ISRAELI AIR FORCE
All Mosquitoes supplied to this nation were aluminium (~7178) overall. See the entry in the 'Royal Air Force' section for this colour.

NOTE:
The above list's reference to Federal Standard (FS 595A) reference numbers do not include the prefix number. This just denotes the sheen of the colour e.g. 1 = Gloss, 2=Semi-gloss and 3 =Matt.
The above list has been compiled using manufacturer's paint lists and in conjunction with the 'IPMS Color Cross-Reference Guide' by David Klaus. Although every care has been taken to offer modellers the broadest spectrum of appropriate colours, further research for each scheme is advisable.

---

applied to either side of the fuselage where the RAF serial would be, and this was in white stencilled characters of approximately 15" high. This serial was also repeated on the nose, sometimes in black, but usually white.

The FB Mk VIs operated by this nation were again supplied in the usual RAF scheme and the roundels on the upper wings, serials and fin flashes were all painted out with Medium Sea Grey before delivery. The same style and type of markings applied to the NF Mk 38s were also used on the fighter-bombers and the type carried American bombs which were painted Olive Drab 66.

The T Mk III trainers operated were silver overall with the 18" wide RAF trainer bands in yellow around the wings and rear fuselage. No upper wing roundels were applied and those on the lower wing were right out at the tip. The individual number on the rear fuselage was again stencilled, but this time in black. None of the trainers operated had any guns fitted.

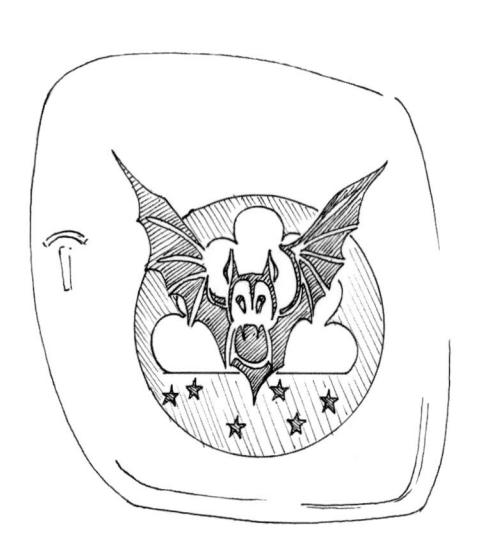

The emblem carried on the entrance door of a number of FB Mk VIs operated by the Israeli Air Force in April 1956. Possible colours are:
Disk = red
Bat = black
Stars = gold
Cloud = white

Israeli Air Force
During the 1948 War of Independence a number of Mosquitoes were clandestinely obtained, or made out of parts. These machines were sprayed silver and carried roundels in six positions plus an individual aircraft serial number, in black, on the rear fuselage. After the arms embargo was lifted, the Israeli Air Force obtained a number of TR Mk 33s and PR Mk XVIs. These were overhauled in the UK by Eagle Aviation and were sprayed silver and given Israeli roundels in six locations. For delivery flights the aircraft carried large serial numbers on the fuselage (e.g. IDFSF 4x3186). These were removed once the aircraft arrived and were replaced with the individual aircraft number. Some of the machines had the propellers and spinners painted black, while all the TR Mk 33s had the ASH radar pod (empty) faired smoothly into the nose contours.

Kit Listing

Appendix I

MANUFACTURER	SCALE	TYPE	SUBJECT	RELEASED	NOTES
Aeroclub	1/144	Ltd IM/V	PR.34/B.35	1992	
Airfix	1/72	IM	FB Mk VI	1957	
Airfix	1/72	IM	FB Mk VI	1967	'Dogfight Doubles' with Me 262
Airfix	1/72	IM	Mk II/VI/XVIII	1972	See also NF.XIX/J 30
Airfix	1/72	IM	Mk XIX/J 30	1995	Revision of above kit
Airfix	1/48	IM	FB Mk VI	1980	
Airfix Corporation	1/72	IM	Mk II/VI	1963	Ex-Airfix
Airfix Craftmaster	1/72	IM	Mk II/VI	1965	Ex-Airfix
USAirfix	1/72	IM	Mk II/VI/XVIII	1980	Ex-Airfix
AMT	1/72	IM	B Mk VI/FB Mk IV	1968	Ex-Frog
Bandai	1/48	IM	B Mk IV	1976-78	Ex-Monogram
Crown	1/144	IM	–	1976	Announced but never issued
Frog Penguin	1/72	Plastic	B Mk VI	1946-9	
Frog	1/72	IM	B Mk IV/FB Mk VI	1968	
Hasegawa	1/72	IM	B Mk IV/FB Mk VI	1967	Ex-Frog
Hasegawa	1/48	IM	B Mk IV	1992	Ex-Monogram
Hi-Tech	1/72	IM/R/M/V	Mk II/VI/XVIII	1992	Upgrade including Airfix kit
Lodela	1/32	IM	B Mk IV	1990's	Ex-Revell
Maquettes Dauzie	1/72	R	B Mk IV	1988	
Matchbox	1/72	IM	B Mk IX/NF 30	1975	
Monogram	1/48	IM	B Mk IV	1965	
MPC	1/72	IM	FB Mk VI	1970	Ex-Airfix
Necomisa	1/48	IM	B Mk IV	1980	Ex-Monogram
Novo	1/72	IM	B Mk IV/FB Mk VI	1978	Ex-Frog. Planned but never issued
Revell	1/32	IM	B Mk IV	1972	
Sanwa/Tokoyo Plamo	N/K	N/K	N/K	1950's	Never issued
Tamiya	1/48	IM	B Mk IV	1998	Due for release late 1998
Tamiya	1/48	IM	FB Mk VI	1998	Due for release late 1998
Toltoys	N/K	N/K	N/K	1957	Announced but never issued

B Mk IV DZ637 was one of a small number converted to carry a 4,000lb bomb and it was to be the first to drop a 'Cookie' operationally when it was flown by Flt. Lt. McKeard of No.692 Sqn. on a mission to Düsseldorf on the 23rd February 1944 (via S.Howe)

English-built FB Mk VI A52-518 of No.1 Squadron based at Amerley in 1945 (F.F.Smith)

Conversions & Accessories

Appendix II

MANUFACTURER	SCALE	TYPE	PRODUCT NO	ITEM	DESIGNED FOR/NOTES
Accurate Aircraft	1/32nd	R		2-stage Merlin Engines	
Accurate Aircraft	1/32nd	R/VF		Conversion	2-stage PR/Bomber Variants
Aeroclub	1/72nd	VF	No.C004	Canopies	Matchbox kit
Aeroclub	1/72nd	VF	No.C005	Fighter Canopy	
Aeroclub	1/72nd	VF	No.C006	Radome	
Aeroclub	1/72nd	M	No.V116	3 Blade Propeller & Spinner	
Aeroclub	1/72nd	VF	No.VA60	PR.34 Deep Belly	
Aeroclub	1/72nd	VF/I		Conversion	B Mk 35, PR Mk 34, PR Mk XVI, B Mk XVI, PR Mk IX & B Mk VI
Air Conversions	1/72nd	VF		Radome	Released 1972-4 Ex-Airframe
Airframe	1/72nd	VF		Radome	Released early 1970's
Airkit	1/72nd	A	C.59	Instrument Panel	B Mk VI
Airparts	1/72nd	R	050	100 Gallon tanks	
Airparts	1/72nd	R	051	Conversion	NF Mk XII - Airfix kit
Airparts	1/72nd	R	052	Conversion	NF Mk XIII (Early) - Airfix kit
Airparts	1/72nd	R	053	Conversion	NF Mk XIII (Late) - Airfix kit
Airparts	1/72nd	R	054	Conversion	NF Mk XVII - Airfix kit
Airparts	1/72nd	R	055	Conversion	NF Mk XIX - Airfix kit
Airwaves	1/72nd	R	72056	Merlin (2 stage) engines	
Airwaves	1/72nd	R	72057	Wheels - Plain Hub	
Airwaves	1/72nd	R	72058	Wheels - Spoked Hub	
DB	1/72nd	R		Two-stage engines	Released 1991
Eduard	1/72nd	EB	72072	Detail Set	For Airfix kit
Falcon	1/72nd	VF	Set 2	Fighter Canopy	'RAF Fighter' set
Falcon	1/72nd	VF	Set 8	Bomber Canopy	'RAF Bombers' set
Falcon	1/72nd	VF	Set 17	B Mk XVI Canopy	'RAF WWII Pt.3'
Falcon	1/48th	VF	Set 31	B Mk IV Canopy x2	'RAF WWII' set
Hi-Tech	1/72nd	R	72018	Fighter Update	Airfix/Matchbox kits
Hi-Tech	1/72nd	R	72019	Bomber Update	Airfix/Matchbox kits
Hi-Tech	1/72nd	R	72513	Flaps & Rudder	
Hi-Tech	1/72nd	R	72514	Merlin 72/73 Nacelles	Airfix/Matchbox kits
Hi-Tech	1/48th	R	48031	Fighter Update Set	
Hi-Tech	1/48th	R	48032	Mosquito Update Set	
Hi-Tech	1/48th	R	48014	Flaps, Wheels & Rudder	For Airfix kit
Hi-Tech	1/48th	R	48515	Merlin 72/73 Nacelles	
Horizon	1/32nd	I		Drop Tanks	Released late 1970's
KMC	1/48th	R	48-4014	Cockpit Detail Set	For Airfix kit
KMC	1/48th	R	48-5065	Control Surfaces	For Airfix kit
Koster	1/48th	VF		Conversion	Mk IV/XIII/XVI & XVII
Marine Air Products	1/32nd	R		Cockpit Detail Set	For Revell (B Mk IV) kit
Missing Link	1/48th	VF		Conversion	Mk XII/XIII & XIX. Released 1987
Magna	1/72nd	R/M/VF		Conversion	TT Mk 39 Due 1996 - Cancelled
Paragon Designs	1/72nd	R/VF	7224	Conversion	TT Mk 39 - Due 1998
Paragon Designs	1/72nd	R	7225	Wheels - Spoked Hub	
Paragon Designs	1/72nd	R/VF	7226	Conversion	Bomber Nose - Airfix kit
Paragon Designs	1/72nd	R	7227	100 Gallon Drop Tanks	
Paragon Designs	1/72nd	R/VF	7228	Conversion	Prototype
Paragon Designs	1/72nd	VF	7229	PR/Bomber Canopies	For Matchbox kit
Paragon Designs	1/72nd	R/EB	7230	Open .303" & 20mm bays	For Airfix kit
Paragon Designs	1/72nd	R	7231	Flaps	
Paragon Designs	1/72nd	R	7232	Wheels - Plain Hubs	
Paragon Designs	1/72nd	R	7233	Conversion	NF XV - Matchbox kit
Paragon Designs	1/72nd	R/EB	7234	Conversion	Sea Mosquito TR.33 - Airfix kit
Paragon Designs	1/72nd	R	7235	Bulged Bomb Bay	
Paragon Designs	1/72nd	R	7236	Bulged Camera Bay	
Paragon Designs	1/72nd	R	7237	Conversion	'Highball' - Matchbox kit
Paragon Designs	1/72nd	R	7245	2-Stage Merlin Engines	Due 1998
Paragon Designs	1/48th	R/EB	4839	Open .303" & 20mm bays	For Airfix kit
Paragon Designs	1/48th	R	4840	Flaps	For Airfix kit
Paragon Designs	1/48th	R	4841	Conversion	FB Mk XVIII 'Molins' - Airfix kit
Paragon Designs	1/48th	R	4842	2-Stage Merlin engines	For Airfix kit
Paragon Designs	1/48th	R	4843	'Universal' Radome	
Paragon Designs	1/48th	R	4844	'Thimble' Radome	
Paragon Designs	1/48th	R/VF	4868	Conversion	Prototype
Paragon Designs	1/48th	R	4869	Narrow Blade Props/Spinners	
Paragon Designs	1/48th	R	4870	Conversion	Bomber Nose - Airfix kit
Paragon Designs	1/48th	R/VF	4871	Conversion	NF XV - Airfix kit
Paragon Designs	1/48th	R/VF/EB	4872	Conversion	Sea Mosquito TR.33 - Airfix kit
Paragon Designs	1/48th	VF	4873	PR Canopy	
Paragon Designs	1/48th	R	4874	Bulged Bomb Bay	
Paragon Designs	1/48th	R	4875	Bulged Camera Bay	
Paragon Designs	1/48th	R	4876	Conversion	'Highball' - Airfix kit
Paragon Designs	1/48th	R	4877	50 Gallon Drop Tanks	
Paragon Designs	1/48th	R	4878	100 Gallon Drop Tanks	
Paragon Designs	1/48th	R/VF	48117	Conversion	TT Mk 39 - Due 1998
Paragon Designs	1/32nd	R	32011	2-Stage Merlin Engines	
Paragon Designs	1/32nd	R/VF	32012	Conversion	FB Mk VI inc interior
Paragon Designs	1/32nd	R/VF	32013	Conversion	FB Mk XVIII inc interior
Paragon Designs	1/32nd	VF	32014	Bomber Canopy	'Blister'
Paragon Designs	1/32nd	VF	32015	Bomber Canopy	'Bulged'
Paragon Designs	1/32nd	VF	32016	PR Canopy	
Paragon Designs	1/32nd	R	32017	Bulged Bomb Bay	
Paragon Designs	1/32nd	R	32018	Bulged Camera Bay	
Paragon Designs	1/32nd	R	32019	Flaps	
Paragon Designs	1/32nd	R	32020	'Paddle' Propellers x2	
Paragon Designs	1/32nd	R	32021	50 Gallon Drop Tanks x2	
Paragon Designs	1/32nd	R	32022	100 Gallon Drop Tanks x2	
Paragon Designs	1/32nd	R	32023	3" 60lb Rockets & Rails x8	
Paragon Designs	1/32nd	R	32034	Wheels - Spoked Hub	
Paragon Designs	1/32nd	R	32035	Wheels - Plain Hub	
Reyhex	1/72nd	VF		Radome	NF Mk XII - Ex-Airframe
Squadron	1/48th	VF	9532	Canopy	FB Mk VI - Airfix kit
True Details	1/48th	EB	26023	Detail Set	B Mk IV - Monogram kit
True Details	1/48th	R	48017	Wheels - Plain Hub	
True Details	1/48th	R	48093	Wheels - Spoked Hub	
True Details	1/72nd	R	72033	Wheels - Plain Hub	

KEY
A = Acetate
EB = Etched Brass
I = Injection Moulded Plastic
M = Metal or Pewter
R = Resin
VF = Vac-form (inc clear)
KMC = Kendall Model Company Inc.

Decals

Appendix III

MANUFACTURER	SCALE	SHEET NO.	TITLE	SUBJECTS	NOTE
AeroMaster	1/72nd	72032	'Recon Birds'	PR Mk XVI NS644 'G', No. 680 Sqn., Foggia, Italy, 1944 PR Mk XVI M345 'Z', 653rd BS, 25th BG, Watton, 1944	
AeroMaster	1/48th	48043	Mosquito FB Mk VI Collection	G-AGE/HJ718, BOAC, 1943 HR241, TH•M, No.418 Sqn., 1944 HR549 '3', No.1672 OCU, 1944 RS625 NE•D, No.143 Sqn., Banff Strike Wing, April 1945	
AeroMaster	1/48th	48082	'Recon Birds'	PR Mk XVI NS644 'G', No. 680 Sqn., Foggia, Italy, 1944 PR Mk XVI M345 'Z', 653rd BS, 25th BG, Watton, 1944	
AeroMaster	1/48th	48298	International Mosquito Collection	T Mk 29, 97•T of the Nationalist Chinese Air Force, Hankow, 1948 T Mk 29, '2108' of the Dominican Air Force, 1952. PR Mk XVI, NS517 'R', French Air Force, 'Lorraine' Sqn., North Africa. PR Mk IV after internment in Switzerland	
AeroMaster	1/48th	48299	'Mossey Collection'	B Mk IV Sr I, DK338, GB•P, No.105 Sqn.RAF Marham, 1942 B Mk IV, DZ637, P3•C, Sqn.692 Sqn., 1944 B Mk XX, KB288, V1•46, No.7 OTU, Canada, 1944 TR Mk 33, TW270 '413' of No.790 Sqn., FAA, RNAS Culdrose, 1948-9 T Mk III, TV969, FMO•A of No.204 ATS.	
AeroMaster	1/48th	48303	Post War Mosquitoes	B Mk 35, VP181, VO•B, No.98 Sqn., Germany 1949 B Mk 35, TA695, CX•W, No.4 Sqn., Celle, Germany 1949 B Mk 35, TA640, No.139 (Jamaica) Sqn., Hemswell, July 1950	
Almark	1/48th	4826	RAF PRU Aircraft	PR Mk XVI	
Blue Rider	1/72nd	CD-003	Hergé's Tintin	FB Mk VI Khemedi Air Force flown by Estonian mercenary Piotr Skut FR Mk VI flown by Col. Achmed Both of these featured in Tintin title 'The Red Sea Sharks'	
Carpena	1/72nd	72-30	D.H. Mosquito	NF.II W4082 RS-W, No. 157 (NF) Sqn NF.II Belgium, KT-O, No. 11 Night Fighter Sqn FB Mk IV Czech Air Force, RF838, IY-12, 311 Sqn FB Mk IV Israeli Air Force, 2110 PR Mk XVI French Air Force, 1/31 Lorraine Sqn., NS517 'R'	
Carpena	1/72nd	72-31	D.H. Mosquito	FB Mk VI, French Air Force, TE605, No.31 Sqn FB Mk VI, RAAF, NA-E, No.1 Sqn FB Mk VI, Norwegian Air Force,HR910 KK•4, 333 Sqn FB Mk VI, FAA, TE711 FD•4L, 811 Sqn PR Mk XVI USAAF, NS594 'LL' PR Mk XVI USAAF, NS502 'M', 544th Photo Sqn (Recon.)	
Carpena	1/72nd	72-53	Normandie-Niemen	FB Mk VI PZ381 '5', 1949	
Carpena	1/48th	48-22	D.H. Mosquito Pt 1	FB Mk VI French Air Force, TE605 '31', G de C 2/6, Rabat, Morocco, 1947-9 NF.II W4082 RS•W, No.157 Sqn., Castle Camps, Jan 1942/Aug 1942 PR Mk XVI USAAF, NS594 'U', 653rd BS, 25th BG, Watton, April-July 1944 PR Mk XVI USAAF, NS502 'M', No.544 PR Sqn., June 1944	
Cloud Master	1/72nd	72/2	BOAC at war	FB Mk VI, HJ681/G-AGGD, BOAC, 1943-4	
Dutch Decals	1/72nd	72014		Either Dutch Sqns or Dutch RAF Pilots	
Esci	1/72nd	37		PR Mk XVI, No. 680 Sqn	
Microscale	1/72nd	72-105	Israeli A.F	Israeli A.F Mosquito	See also Superscale
Microscale	1/48th	48-13	D.H. Mosquito	FB Mk VI TH•X, No.418 Sqn FB MK VI No.143 Sqn. Banff Strike Wing FB MK VI NA•M No.1(Bomber) Sqn., RAAF FB MK VI NA•S, No.1(Bomber) Sqn., RAAF	See also Superscale
Modeldecal	1/72nd	017		FB Mk VI, 4 Sqn., RAF Celle, Germany, 1946	
PD Decals	1/72nd	72001	Mosquito Bombers	Mk II DZ269 RX•V, 456 Sqn., 1943 NF Mk XVII HK290/G RX•J, No. 456 Sqn., 1944 NF.30 NT264/G RX•R, No.456 Sqn., 1945 B Mk IV MM403 SB•U, No.464 Sqn., 1944 B Mk IV HR715 SB•4, No.464 Sqn., 1944 B Mk IV NS994 SB•F, No.464 Sqn., 1944	
PD Decals	1/72nd	72004	Mosquito Bombers	B Mk IV Sr I W4072 GD•D, No.105 Sqn., 1942 B Mk IV DZ464 XD•C, No.139 Sqn., 1942 B Mk IV DZ548 GB•D, No.105 Sqn., 1943 B Mk IV DZ319 HS•S, No.109 Sqn., 1944 B Mk IV DK333 HS•F, No.109 Sqn., 1944 B Mk IX LR503 GB•F, No.105 Sqn., 1945	
PD Decals	1/48th	48001	Mosquito Bombers		Same as 72001
PD Decals	1/48th	48004	Mosquito Bombers		Same as 72004
PD Decals	1/32nd	32001	Mosquito Bombers		Same as 72004
Superscale	1/72nd	72-105		Israeli A.F Mosquito	
Superscale	1/72nd	72-303		NF.30 VY•Y, RAAF	
Superscale	1/72nd	72-718	Mosquito FB Mk VI	HJ338, OM•B, No.107 Sqn., Germany 1947 TF711, FD•4L, No.811 Sqn., Royal Navy RS679, UP•A, No.4 Sqn., RAF Celle, Germany 1949 RS625, NE•D, No.143 Sqn., Banff Strike Wing, 1945 A52-525, NA•J, No.1 Sqn., RAAF Israeli Defence Force, 1950	
Superscale	1/48th	48-13	D.H. Mosquito	TH•X, No.418 Sqn YP•P, No.23 Sqn NA•M No.1(Bomber) Sqn., RAAF. NA•S, No.1(Bomber) Sqn., RAAF.	
Superscale	1/48th	48-542	D.H. Mosquito FB.VI	HR338 OM•B, No.107 Sqn., Germany, 1947 RS625 NE•D, No.143 Sqn., Banff Strike Wing, 1945 RS679 UP•A, No.4 Sqn., RAF Celle, Germany, 1949 TF711 FD•4L, No.811 Sqn. Royal Navy	
Ventura	1/72nd	7256	Mosquito PR Mk XVI	NS594 'U', 653rd BS, USAAF NS569 'R', 653rd BS, USAAF NS753 'Y', 653rd BS, USAAF NS519 'P', 653rd BS, USAAF	
Ventura	1/72nd	7265	Mosquito, Israeli	FB Mk VI ,2109 FB Mk VI, 2114 TR Mk 33, No.78	
Ventura	1/48th	4857			Same as 7256
Ventura	1/48th	4867			Same as 7265
Ventura	1/32nd	3265	Mosquito, Israeli		Same as 7265
Xtradecal	1/72nd	X039-72	Normandy Invasion	FB Mk VI HR241 TH•M, No.418 Sqn	

Mosquito Powerplants

Appendix **IV**

The Rolls Royce Merlin
The Parentage

Merlin X
This, 1,145 hp engine was the first two-speed engine. It featured a 42:1 reduction gear, suitable for long-distance cruising (à la bombers) and was pressure water-glycol cooled.
Production: 312 (Derby), 4,589 (Crewe).
Total Production: 4, 901
Production Period: 1938-1942

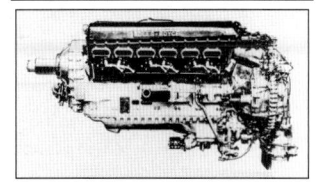

Rolls-Royce Merlin X (Rolls-Royce Ltd)

Merlin XX
A 1,390 hp version designed to replace the Merlin X. This engine featured a two-speed supercharger and was 70/30 ethylene-glycol pressure cooled. The reduction gear remained at 42:1.
Production: 2,592 (Derby), 3,391 (Crewe), 9,500 (Glasgow) and 12.538 (by Ford Ltd)
Total Production: 28,021
Production Period: 1940-1944

The Rolls Royce Merlin
Mosquito Usage

Merlin 21
Designed in 1940, this engine gave 1,390 hp and was similar to the Merlin XX. The engine featured a type of 'reversed-flow cooling'. Because the Mosquito featured wing mounted radiators and not the more usual 'chin' mounted units, the coolant went from the header tank, via the pump, to the coolant pump outlets (which usually feed the cylinder blocks) to the radiator. Then the coolant travels back to the cylinder blocks via a splitter pipe. This engine was only suitable for the Mosquito because of this coolant system.
Fitted to: Mosquito Prototype, PR Mk I, F Mk II, NF Mk II, T Mk III (early), B Mk IV Sr I & II, PR Mk VI, B Mk V (Project), NF Mk VI, NF Mk XII, NF Mk XIII, NF Mk XVII, NF Mk XIX
Production: 3 (Derby), 2,026 (Crewe)
Total Production: 2,029
Production Period: 1941-1943

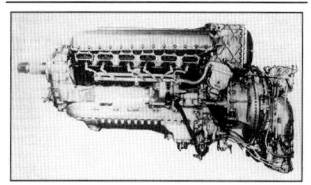

The basic single stage engine for the Mosquito, the Merlin 21 (Rolls-Royce Ltd)

Merlin 22
A 1.390hp two-speed supercharged engine modified from the Mk XX and Mk 21.
Fitted to: Mosquito F Mk II, FB Mk VI
Production: 1,484 (Derby inc 8 Mk 22Ys), 1,387 (Crewe), 2,164 (Glasgow), 5,590 (Ford -USA)
Total Production: 10,627
Production Period: 1942-1943

The Merlin 38, which was a Packard built version of the Merlin 22 (Rolls-Royce Ltd)

Merlin 23
This was a 1,390hp development of the Mk 22 with a two-speed supercharger and 'reverse-flow coolant'. Once again this type was only suitable for the Mosquito.
Fitted to: Mosquito PR Mk I, F Mk II, NF Mk II, T Mk III, B Mk IV Sr II, PR Mk VI, FB Mk VI, NF Mk XII, NF Mk XIII, NF Mk XVII, NF Mk XIX
Production: 758 (Crewe), 836 (Glasgow)
Total Production: 1,694
Production Period: 1942-1943

Merlin 25
A 1,610hp development of the Mk 24, but with the 'reverse-flow coolant' system suitable for the Mosquito.
Fitted to: Mosquito T Mk III, FB Mk VI, NF Mk XII, NF Mk XIII, NF Mk XVII, FB Mk XVIII, NF Mk XIX, TR Mk 33 & TR Mk 37
Production: 176 (Derby), 3,274 (Glasgow) and 2,900 (by Ford)
Total Production: 6,350
Production Period: 1943-1947

Merlin 61
This 1,280hp engine had the two-stage, two-speed supercharger for the first time and it was similar to the Mk 60. It featured a cabin supercharger and the first two-piece cylinder blocks.
Fitted to: Mosquito PR Mk VIII, NF Mk X (Project), FB Mk XI (Project), NF Mk XV
Production: 734 (Derby)
Total Production: 734
Production Period: 1942-1942

Merlin 67
This 1,315hp engine was the first of the 60 series to feature reverse coolant-flow.
Fitted to: Mosquito NF Mk XIV (Project)
Production: 2 (Derby), 35 (Crewe), 34 (Glasgow)
Total Production: 71
Production Period: 1943-1944

Merlin 72
This was a 1,280hp engine with a two-stage, two-speed supercharger and was similar to the Mk 63 and 70, but had the 'reverse-flow coolant' system for the Mosquito.
Fitted to: Mosquito B Mk IX, PR Mk IX, NF Mk XIV (Project), B Mk XVI, PR Mk XVI, NF Mk 30 and TT Mk 39
Production: 500 (Derby), 500 (Crewe)
Total Production: 1,000
Production Period: 1943-1944

Merlin 73
This engine was similar to the Mk 72 and the Mk 63, but had a cabin supercharger and an SU carburettor.
Fitted to: Mosquito B Mk IX, PR Mk IX, NF XV, B Mk XVI, PR Mk XVI and TT Mk 39
Production: 700 (Derby)
Total Production: 700
Production Period: 1942-1944

The two-stage engine, with the cabin-supercharger drive taken off the reduction gear. This type would be the Merlin 73 in the Mosquito (Rolls-Royce Ltd)

Merlin 76
This 1,280hp engine was basically similar to the Mk 66 but had better high altitude performance due to a higher supercharger gear ratio. It was fitted with a Bendix carburettor and also had the cabin supercharger as per the Mk 73.
Fitted to: Mosquito B Mk IX, PR Mk IX, B Mk XVI, PR Mk XVI, NF Mk 30 and TT Mk 39
Production: 600 (Crewe), 1,200 (Derby)
Total Production: 1,800
Production Period: 1944-1945

The Bendix carburettor equipped Merlin 76/77 series

Merlin 77
This 1,250hp engine was similar to the Mk 66 but had better high altitude performance due to a higher supercharger gear ratio. It was fitted with a Bendix carburettor and also had the cabin supercharger as per the Mk 73.
Fitted to: Mosquito NF Mk XV, PR Mk XVI, B Mk XVI & TT Mk 39
Production: 584 (Derby)
Total Production: 584
Production Period: 1944-1945

Merlin 113/113A
Producing 1,535 hp this engine featured the two-stage two-speed supercharger of the Mk 110 and Mk 112 with the 'reverse-flow coolant' system for the Mosquito. An anti-surge diffuser was fitted for the supercharger, and being of the 110 series, this engine featured the overhung first-stage impeller, end-feed lubrication and single-point fuel injection
Fitted to: Mosquito PR Mk 32, B Mk 35 & NF Mk 36
Production: 650 (Glasgow)
Total Production: 650
Production Period: 1944-1945

The final Merlin powerplant series for the Mosquito, the 113/114 (Rolls-Royce Ltd)

Merlin 114/114A
Producing 1,535 hp this engine was similar to the Mk 113 series, but also had a cabin supercharger fitted.
Fitted to: Mosquito PR Mk 32, PR Mk 34, PR Mk 34A, B Mk 35, NF Mk 36, NF Mk 38
Production: 1 (Derby) 1,198 (Glasgow)
Total Production: 1,199
Production Period: 1944-1945

The Rolls Royce Merlin
The American Connection

Merlin 22
See entry under 'Mosquito Usage'
Fitted to: Mosquito NF Mk II
Production: 5,590 (Ford)
Total Production: 10,627 (inc 5,037 in the UK)
Production Period: 1942-1943

Merlin 25
See entry under 'Mosquito Usage'
Fitted to: Mosquito FB Mk VI, NF Mk XII, NF MK XIII, NF Mk XVII, NF Mk XIX, TR Mk 33 & TR Mk 37
Production: 2,900 (by Ford)
Total Production: 6,350 (inc UK production)
Production Period: 1943-1947

Packard Merlin 31
A 1,390 two-speed, single-speed supercharged version of the Merlin 21, used in Canadian and Australian produced Mosquitoes.
Fitted to: B Mk VIII, B Mk XX, FB Mk 21 (Canada), FB Mk 40 (Australia)
Manufactured by: Packard

Rolls-Royce Merlin 30 Series (Rolls-Royce Ltd)

Packard Merlin 33
A 1,390hp two-speed, single-speed supercharged version of the Merlin 23, used in Canadian and Australian produced Mosquitoes.
Fitted to: Mosquito B Mk XX, T Mk 22 (Canada), FB Mk 40, T Mk 43 (Australia)
Manufactured by: Packard

Packard Merlin 69
A 1,315hp two-stage engine identical to the Merlin 67 and built in the USA. This engine was similar to the Allison V-1650-7 and the Merlin 65, 66 & 68 and was used in Australian produced Mosquitoes and projected for use in some UK and Canadian versions.
Fitted to: Mosquito B Mk 23 (Canadian project), NF 31 (project), PR Mk 41, PR Mk 42 (one only built)
Manufactured by: Packard

Packard Merlin 225
A 1,610hp two-speed, single-stage supercharged engine equivalent to the Merlin 25 and similar to the Merlin 224, although built specifically for Mosquito use. Used in Canadian produced Mosquitoes.
Fitted to: Mosquito B Mk 25, FB Mk 26, T Mk 27 & T Mk 29
Manufactured by: Packard

Packard Merlin 301
A 1,660hp two-stage two-speed supercharged engine designed to replace the Merlin 69. Also known as the V-1650-7.
Fitted to: Mosquito FB Mk 24 (Canadian project)
Manufactured by: Packard

Mosquito Variants

Appendix V

Designation: Prototype
(E-0234 for two flights, then W4050)
First Flight: 25th November 1940
Span: 52ft 6in (15.75m)
Length: 40ft 6in (12.35m)
Height: 12ft 6in (3.75m)
Engines: Two 1,460hp Merlin 21 (short nacelles)

Designation: PR Mk I
First Flight: 10th June 1941 (W4051 prototype)
Type: Unarmed photo-reconnaissance aircraft
Span: 54ft 2in (16.5m)
Length: 40ft 6in (12.35m)
Height: 12ft 6in (3.75m)
Engines: Two 1,460hp Merlin 21 (short nacelles)
Weight: 12,824lb (5,817kg) empty, 19,670lb (8,922kg) maximum
Speed: 382 mph (614km/h) maximum, 255mph (410km/h) cruising
Range: 2,180 miles (3,508km)
Ceiling: 35,000ft (10,668m)

Designation: PR/Bomber Conversion
(in service B Mk IV Sr I)
First Flight: March 1942
Type: Unarmed day & night bomber
Span: 54ft 2in (16.5m)
Length: 40ft 9.5in (12.41m)
Height: 12ft 6in (3.75m)
Engines: Two 1,460hp Merlin 21 (short nacelles)
Weight: 13,400b (6,351kg) empty, 21,462lb (9,734kg) maximum
Speed: 380mph (611km/h) maximum, 265mph (426km/h) cruising
Range: 2,040 miles (3,283km)
Bomb load: 2,000lb

Designation: NF Mk II
First Flight: 15th May 1941 (W4052 Prototype)
Type: Long-range night fighter
Span: 54ft 2in (16.5m)
Length: 42ft 11in (13.07m)
Height: 12ft 6in (3.75m)
Engines: Two 1,460hp Merlin 21, 22 or 23 (long nacelles)
Weight: 13,431lb (6,092kg) empty, 18,547lb (8,413kg) maximum
Speed: 370mph (595km/h) max, 255mph (410mk/h) cruising
Range: 1,560 miles (2,508km)
Ceiling: 36,000 (10,972m)
Bomb load: 1,000lb
Armament: 4x20mm Hispano Mk III cannon in ventral tray and 4x Browning .303" machine-guns in nose
Radar: A.I. Mk IV (100 Group = A.I. Mk IV & V)
Notes: Turbinlite & Turret armed configurations achieved with this variant

Designation: NF Mk II (Special)
First Flight: See NF Mk II
Type: Long-range day fighter and night intruder
Span: 54ft 2in (16.5m)
Length: 41ft 2in (12.54m)
Height: 12ft 6in (3.75m)
Engines: Two 1,460hp Merlin 21, 22 or 23 (long nacelles)
Weight: 13,431lb (6,092kg) empty, 18,547lb (8,413kg) maximum
Speed: 370mph (595km/h) max, 255mph (410km/h) cruising
Range: 1,705 miles (2,744km)
Ceiling: 36,000 (10,972m)
Bomb load: 1,000lb
Armament: 4x20mm Hispano Mk III cannon in ventral tray and 4x Browning .303" machine-guns in nose
Radar: None

Designation: T Mk III
First Flight: January 1942
Type: Dual-control trainer
Span: 54ft 2in (16.5m)
Length: 40ft 6in (12.3m)
Height: 12ft 6in (3.75m)
Engines: Two 1,460hp Merlin 21, 22 or 23 (long nacelles)
Weight: 13,1041b (5,944kg) empty, 16,833lb (7,637kg) maximum
Speed: 384mph (618km/h) max, 260mph (418km/h) cruising
Range: 1,560 miles (2,510km)
Ceiling: 37,500ft (11,430m)
Bomb load: N/A
Armament: None
Radar: None

Designation: B Mk IV Sr II
First Flight: March 1942
Type: Unarmed day & night bomber
Span: 54ft 2in (16.5m)
Length: 40ft 9.5in (12.41m)
Height: 12ft 6in (3.75m)
Engines: Two 1,460hp Merlin 21 (long nacelles) - few Merlin 23
Weight: 13,400lb (6,531kg) empty, 21,462lb (9,734kg) maximum
Speed: 380mph (611km/h) max, 265mph (426km/h) cruising
Range: 2,040 miles (3,283km)
Ceiling: 34,000ft (10,363m)
Bomb load: 2,000lb
Armament: None
Radar: None

Designation: B Mk IV Sr II (4,000lb conversion)
Type: Unarmed day & night bomber
Span: 54ft 2in (16.5m)
Length: 40ft 9.5in (12.41m)
Height: 12ft 6in (3.75m)
Engines: Two 1,460hp Merlin 21 (long nacelles) - few Merlin 23
Weight: 13,400lb (6,531kg) empty, 22,570lb (11,000kg) maximum
Speed: 380mph (611km/h) max, 265mph (426km/h) cruising
Range: 2,040 miles (3,283km)
Ceiling: 34,000ft (10,363m)
Bomb load: 4,000lb
Armament: None
Radar: None

Designation: PR Mk IV
First Flight: April 1942
Type: Unarmed day & night photo-reconnaissance
Span: 54ft 2in (16.5m)
Length: 40ft 9.5in (12.41m)
Height: 12ft 6in (3.75m)
Engines: Two 1,460hp Merlin 21 or 23 (long nacelles)
Weight: 13,400lb (6,531kg) empty, 18,000lb (8,165kg) maximum
Speed: 380mph (611km/h) max, 265mph (426km/h) cruising
Range: 2,040 miles (3,283km)
Bomb load: None
Armament: None
Radar: None
Other: One oblique and three vertical cameras

The prototype W4050, as she is displayed today in her own hanger at Salisbury Hall, the place of her birth (S.Howe)

Designation: B Mk V
First Flight: B Mk IV prototype (W4057) known as B Mk V
Type: Unarmed day & night bomber
Span: 54ft 2in (16.5m)
Length: 40ft 9.5in (12.41m)
Height: 12ft 6in (3.75m)
Engines: Two 1,460hp Merlin 21 (long nacelles)
Weight: 12,881lb (5,842.5kg) empty, 18,994lb (8,616kg) maximum
Speed: 380mph (611km/h) max, 265mph (426km/h) cruising
Range: 2,040 miles (3,283km)
Bomb load: 3,000lb (2,000lb internal, 1,000 under wings)
Armament: None
Radar: None
Note: Project only

Designation: FB Mk VI
First Flight: 1st June 1942 (Prototype), February 1943 (Production)
Type: Day & night fighter, bomber, intruder and long-range fighter
Span: 54ft 2in (16.5m)
Length: 41ft 2in (12.54m)
Height: 12ft 6in (3.75m)
Engines: Two 1,460hp Merlin 21, 22, 23 or 25 (long nacelles)
Weight: 14,344lb (6,508kg) empty, 22,258lb (10,099kg) maximum
Speed: 378mph (608km/h) max, 255mph (410km/h) cruising
Range: 1,855 miles (2,985km)
Ceiling: 33,000ft (10,058m)
Bomb load: 500lb (226kg) internally, 500lb (226kg) under wings. Later aircraft could carry 1,000lb (454kg) under wings or eight 60lb (27kg) 3" rocket projectiles. Depth charges and mines could also be carried
Armament: 4x 20mm Hispano cannon in ventral tray and 4x 0.303" Browning machine-guns in the nose
Radar: None

Designation: B Mk VIII
First Flight: 24th September 1942
Type: Unarmed day & night bomber
Span: 54ft 2in (16.5m)
Length: 40ft 9.5in (12.41m)
Height: 12ft 6in (3.75m)
Engines: Two Packard Merlin 31 (long nacelles)
Weight: 13,400lb (6,531kg) empty, 21,462lb (9,734kg) maximum
Speed: 380mph (611km/h) max, 265mph (426km/h) cruising
Range: 2,040 miles (3,283km)
Bomb load: 2,000lb
Armament: None
Radar: None
Note: Canadian production and use only

Designation: PR Mk VIII
First Flight: 20th October 1942
Type: Unarmed photo-reconnaissance
Span: 54ft 2in (16.5m)
Length: 40ft 9.5in (12.41m)
Height: 12ft 6in (3.75m)
Engines: Two Merlin 61 (long nacelles)
Weight: 14,800lb (6,713kg) empty, 21,395lb (9,704kg) maximum
Speed: 436mph (702km/h) max, 258mph (459km/h) cruising
Ceiling: 38,000ft (11,582m)
Range: 2,550 miles (4,104km)
Bomb load: None
Armament: None
Radar: None
Note: One oblique and four vertical cameras

Designation: B Mk IX
First Flight: 24th March 1943
Type: Unarmed bomber
Span: 54ft 2in (16.5m)
Length: 44ft 6in (13.5m)
Height: 12ft 6in (3.75m)
Engines: Two 1,680hp Merlin 72/73 or 76/77 (long nacelles, 2-stage)
Weight: 14,644lb (7,137kg) empty, 23,745lb (11,573kg) maximum
Speed: 408mph (656km/h) max, 250mph (402km/h) cruising
Range: 2,450 miles (3,943km)
Bomb load: 2,000lb (Small number converted to carry 4,000lb bomb)
Armament: None
Radar: None
Note: Oboe and H2S could be fitted

Designation: PR Mk IX
First Flight: April 1943
Type: Unarmed photo-reconnaissance
Span: 54ft 2in (16.5m)
Length: 44ft 6in (13.5m)
Height: 12ft 6in (3.75m)
Engines: Two 1,680hp Merlin 72/73 or 76/77 (long nacelles, 2-stage)
Weight: 14,569lb (6,610kg) empty, 22,000lb (9,982kg) maximum
Speed: 408mph (656km/h) max, 250mph (402km/h) cruising
Range: 2,450 miles (3,943km)
Ceiling: 38,000ft (11,582m)
Bomb load: None
Armament: None
Radar: None
Note: One oblique and four vertical cameras. *Rebecca* and *Boozer* systems could be installed

Designation: NF Mk X
First Flight: N/A
Type: Night fighter
Span: 54ft 2in (16.5m)
Length: 41ft 2in (12.54m)
Height: 12ft 6in (3.75m)
Engines: Two Merlin 61 (long nacelles, 2-stage)
Weight: N/K
Speed: N/K
Range: N/K
Bomb load: None
Armament: 4x 20mm cannon in ventral tray and 4x .303" Browning machine-guns in the nose
Radar: A.I. Mk V(?)
Note: Project only, although originally ordered in quantity

B Mk IV DK296 was operated by both No.139 and No.105 Squadrons. This machine was the lead aircraft on the low-level attack on the Gestapo Headquarters in Oslo on the 25th September 1942. The aircraft was sent to No.10 MU and is pictured here in September 1943 awaiting collection. It left for Russia on the 25th March 1944, although nothing further is known of its use by the Russia Air Force (BAe)

Appendix 5 • Mosquito Variants 145

T Mk III VT592 is seen in the static park at an air show held at RAF Hendon on the 19th July 1951 (P.Clifton)

Designation: FB Mk XI
First Flight: N/A
Type: Day & night fighter, bomber, intruder and long-range fighter
Span: 54ft 2in (16.5m)
Length: 41ft 2in (12.54m)
Height: 12ft 6in (3.75m)
Engines: Two Merlin 61 (long nacelles, 2-stage)
Weight: N/K
Speed: N/K
Range: N/K
Bomb load: 500lb (226kg) internally, 500lb (226kg) under wings. Later aircraft could carry 1,000lb (454kg) under wings or eight 60lb (27kg) 3" rocket projectiles. Depth charges and mines could also be carried
Armament: 4x 20mm Hispano cannon in ventral tray and 4x 0.303" Browning machine-guns in the nose
Radar: None
Note: Project only

Designation: NF Mk XII
First Flight: August 1942
Type: Long-range night fighter
Span: 54ft 2in (16.5m)
Length: 40ft 5in (12.3m)
Height: 12ft 6in (3.75m)
Engines: Two 1,460hp Merlin 21 or 23 (long nacelles)
Weight: 13,696lb (6,213kg) empty, 19,700lb (8,938kg) maximum
Speed: 370mph (595km/h) max, 255mph (410km/h) cruising
Range: 1,705 miles (2,744km)
Ceiling: 36,000ft (10,972m)
Bomb load: 1,000lb
Armament: 4x20mm Hispano Mk III cannon in ventral tray
Radar: A.I. Mk VIII
Notes: Conversion of NF Mk II with A.I. Mk VIII in 'thimble' radome

Designation: NF Mk XIII
First Flight: August 1943
Type: Long-range night fighter
Span: 54ft 2in (16.5m)
Length: 40ft 6in (12.34m)
Height: 12ft 6in (3.75m)
Engines: Two 1,460hp Merlin 21 or 23 (long nacelles)
Weight: 15,300lb (6,942kg) empty, 20,000lb (9,074kg) maximum
Speed: 370mph (595km/h) max, 255mph (410km/h) cruising
Range: 1,860 miles (2,993km)
Ceiling: 34,500ft (10,515m)
Bomb load: 1,000lb
Armament: 4x20mm Hispano Mk III cannon in ventral tray
Radar: A.I. Mk VIII
Notes: Conversion of NF Mk II with A.I. Mk VIII in 'universal' (Bullnose) radome

Designation: NF Mk XIV
First Flight: N/A
Type: Long-range night fighter
Span: 54ft 2in (16.5m)
Length: 40ft 6in (12.34m)
Height: 12ft 6in (3.75m)
Engines: Two Merlin 67 or 72 (long nacelles, 2-stage)
Weight: N/K
Speed: N/K
Range: N/K
Armament: 4x20mm Hispano Mk III cannon in ventral tray
Radar: A.I. Mk VIII or X
Notes: Projected conversion of NF Mk XIII, not proceeded with and superseded by the NF Mk XIX

Designation: NF Mk XV
First Flight: September 1942
Type: High-altitude night fighter
Span: 62ft 6in (19m) prototype, 59ft (17.97m) for production versions
Length: 44ft 6in (13.5m)
Height: 12ft 6in (3.75m)
Engines: Two 1,680hp Merlin 72/73 or 1,710hp Merlin 76/77 (long nacelles, 2-stage)
Weight: 13,746lb (6,235kg) empty, 17,600lb (7,983kg) maximum
Speed: 412mph (663km/h) maximum, 230mph (370km/h) cruising
Range: 1,030 miles (1,657km)
Ceiling: 43,000ft (13,106m)
Bomb load: N/A
Armament: Prototype retained 4x .303" machine-guns in nose. Production versions had these guns in a separate ventral gun pack
Radar: A.I. Mk VIII

Designation: PR Mk XVI
First Flight: July 1943
Type: Unarmed pressurised high-altitude photo-reconnaissance
Span: 54ft 2in (16.5m)
Length: 44ft 6in (12.69m)
Height: 12ft 6in (3.75m)
Engines: Two 1,680hp Merlin 72/73 or 76/77 (long nacelles, 2-stage)
Weight: 14,635lb (6,638kg) empty, 23,350lb (10,141kg) maximum
Speed: 415mph (667km/h) max, 250mph (402km/h) cruising
Ceiling: 38,500ft (11,734m)
Range: 2,450 miles (3,941km)
Bomb load: None
Armament: None
Radar: None
Note: One oblique and four vertical cameras. *Rebecca*, *Boozer* and *H2X* systems could be installed

Designation: B Mk XVI
First Flight: 1st January 1944
Type: Unarmed pressurised high-altitude bomber
Span: 54ft 2in (16.5m)
Length: 44ft 6in (13.5m)
Height: 12ft 6in (3.75m)
Engines: Two 1,680hp Merlin 72/73 or 76/77 (long nacelles, 2-stage)
Weight: 14,635lb (6,638kg) empty, 23,000lb (10,436kg) maximum
Speed: 408mph (656km/h) max, 245mph (394km/h) cruising
Ceiling: 37,000ft (11,277m)
Range: 1,485 miles (2,389km)
Bomb load: 2,000lb, 3,000lb (Avro 6-store carrier) or 4,000lb 'Cookie' conversion
Armament: None
Radar: None
Note: *Boozer*, *Oboe*, *Album Leaf*, *Fishpond*, *Monica*, *Gee* and *H2X* systems could all be installed

Designation: NF Mk XVII
First Flight: March 1943
Type: Night fighter
Span: 54ft 2in (16.5m)
Length: 40ft 6in (12.34m)
Height: 12ft 6in (3.75m)
Engines: Two 1,460hp Merlin 21 or 23 (long nacelles)
Weight: 13,224lb (5,998kg) empty, 20,393lb (9,250kg) maximum
Speed: 370mph (595km/h) max, 255mph (410km/h) cruising
Range: 1,705 miles (2,774km)
Ceiling: 36,000ft (10,972m)
Bomb load: 1,000lb
Armament: 4x20mm Hispano Mk III cannon (500 rounds) in ventral tray
Radar: A.I. Mk X or SCR720/729
Notes: Also fitted with rearward-looking radar and a perspex tail cone.

Designation: FB Mk XVIII
First Flight: 8th June 1943
Type: Ground-attack and anti-shipping fighter-bomber
Span: 54ft 2in (16.5m)
Length: 41ft 2in (12.54m)
Height: 12ft 6in (3.75m)
Engines: Two 1,460hp Merlin 25 (long nacelles)
Weight: 14,756lb (6,693kg) empty, 23,274lb (10,557kg) maximum
Speed: 358mph (576km/h) max, 255mph (410km/h) cruising
Bomb load: None. 65 Gallon long-range tank could be carried in bomb bay
Armament: Ventrally mounted 57mm (6 pdr) Molins cannon with 25 rounds (weight 1,580lb (622.5kg))
Note: Some retained 4x .303" Browning machine-guns in the nose, although most just retained two to use as bore sights for the Molins

Designation: NF Mk XIX (J 30 in Swedish service)
First Flight: April 1944
Type: Night fighter
Span: 54ft 2in (16.5m)
Length: 40ft 6in (12.34m)
Height: 12ft 6in (3.75m)
Engines: Two Merlin 25 (long nacelles)
Weight: 14,471lb (6,563.5kg) empty, 21,750lb (9,865kg) maximum
Speed: 378mph (608km/h) max, 255mph (410km/h) cruising
Bomb load: 1,000lb
Armament: 4x20mm Hispano Mk III cannon (500 rounds) in ventral tray
Radar: SCR720/729/A.I. Mk X or A.I. Mk VIII in 'Universal' (Bullnose) radome

Designation: B Mk XX
Type: Unarmed day & night bomber
Span: 54ft 2in (16.5m)
Length: 40ft 9.5in (12.41m)
Height: 12ft 6in (3.75m)
Engines: Two Packard Merlin 31 or 33 (long nacelles)
Weight: 13,400lb (6,531kg) empty, 21,980lb (8,659kg) maximum
Speed: Similar to B Mk IV Sr II
Range: Similar to B Mk IV Sr II
Origin: Canada
Bomb load: 2,000lb
Armament: None
Radar: None

Designation: FB Mk 21
Type: Day & night fighter, bomber, intruder and long-range fighter
Span: 54ft 2in (16.5m)
Length: 41ft 2in (12.54m)
Height: 12ft 6in (3.75m)
Engines: Two Packard Merlin 31 (long nacelles)
Weight: 13,797lb (6,258kg) empty, 20,804lb (9,436kg) maximum
Speed: Similar to FB Mk VI
Range: Similar to FB Mk VI
Origin: Canada
Bomb load: 500lb (226kg) internally, 500lb (226kg) under wings. Later aircraft could carry 1,000lb (454kg) under wings or eight 60lb (27kg) 3" rocket projectiles. Depth charges and mines could also be carried
Armament: 4x 20mm Hispano cannon in ventral tray and 4x .303" Browning machine-guns in the nose
Radar: None

Designation: T Mk 22
Type: Dual-control trainer
Span: 54ft 2in (16.5m)
Length: 41ft 2in (12.54m)
Height: 12ft 6in (3.75m)
Engines: Two Packard Merlin 33 (long nacelles)
Weight: Similar to T Mk III
Speed: Similar to T Mk III
Range: 1,560 miles (2,510km)
Origin: Canada
Bomb load: N/A
Armament: None
Radar: None
Note: Canadian-built version of T Mk III, developed from FB Mk 21

Designation: B Mk 23
First Flight: N/A
Type: Unarmed bomber
Span: 54ft 2in (16.5m)
Length: 44ft 6in (13.5m)
Height: 12ft 6in (3.75m)
Engines: Two Packard Merlin 69 (long nacelles, 2-stage)
Weight: Similar to B Mk IX
Speed: Similar to B Mk IX
Range: 2,450 miles (3,943km)
Origin: Canada
Bomb load: 2,000lb
Armament: None
Radar: None
Note: Projected Canadian-built version of B Mk XI. Never built

Designation: FB Mk 24
Type: High-altitude fighter-bomber
Span: 54ft 2in (16.5m)
Length: 41ft 2in (12.54m)
Height: 12ft 6in (3.75m)
Engines: Two Packard Merlin 301 (long nacelles, 2-stage)
Weight: N/K
Speed: Similar to FB Mk 21
Range: Similar to FB Mk 21
Origin: Canada
Bomb load: 500lb (226kg) internally, 500lb (454kg) under wings
Armament: 4x 20mm Hispano cannon in ventral tray and 4x 0.303" Browning machine-guns in the nose
Radar: None
Note: Projected development of FB Mk 21, not proceeded with

Designation: B Mk 25
Type: Unarmed day & night bomber
Span: 54ft 2in (16.5m)
Length: 40ft 9.5in (12.41m)
Height: 12ft 6in (3.75m)
Engines: Two Packard Merlin 225 (long nacelles)
Weight: 13,400lb (6,531kg) empty, 21,980lb (8,659kg) maximum
Speed: Similar to B Mk XX
Range: Similar to B Mk XX
Origin: Canada
Bomb load: 2,000lb
Armament: None
Radar: None
Note: Improved version of B Mk XX

Designation: FB Mk 26
Type: Day & night fighter, bomber, intruder and long-range fighter
Span: 54ft 2in (16.5m)
Length: 41ft 2in (12.54m)
Height: 12ft 6in (3.75m)
Engines: Two Packard Merlin 225 (long nacelles)
Weight: 13,797lb (6,258kg) empty, 21,473lb (8,459kg) maximum
Speed: Similar to FB Mk 21
Range: Similar to FB Mk 21
Origin: Canada
Bomb load: 500lb (226kg) internally, 500lb (226kg) under wings. Later aircraft could carry 1,000lb (454kg) under wings or eight 60lb (27kg) 3" rocket projectiles. Depth charges and mines could also be carried
Armament: 4x 20mm Hispano cannon in ventral tray and 4x 0.303" Browning machine-guns in the nose
Radar: None
Note: Revised version of FB Mk 21

Designation: T Mk 27
First Flight: N/A
Type: Dual-control trainer
Span: 54ft 2in (16.5m)
Length: 41ft 2in (12.54m)
Height: 12ft 6in (3.75m)
Engines: Two Packard Merlin 225 (long nacelles)
Weight: Similar to T Mk 22
Speed: Similar to T Mk 22
Range: 1,560 miles (2,510km)
Origin: Canada
Bomb load: N/A
Armament: None
Radar: None
Note: Development of T Mk 22

Designation: Mk 28
Note: Allocated for Canadian production, not taken up

Designation: T Mk 29
Type: Dual-control trainer
Span: 54ft 2in (16.5m)
Length: 41ft 2in (12.54m)
Height: 12ft 6in (3.75m)
Engines: Two Packard Merlin 225 (long nacelles)
Weight: Similar to T Mk 22
Speed: Similar to FB Mk 26
Range: Similar to FB Mk 26
Origin: Canada
Bomb load: None
Armament: None
Radar: None
Note: Trainer version of FB Mk 26 brought about by lack of cannon and radio equipment for that type

Designation: NF Mk 30
First Flight: March 1944
Type: Night fighter
Span: 54ft 2in (16.5m)
Length: 44ft 6in (13.5m)
Height: 12ft 6in (3.75m)
Engines: Two 1,680hp Merlin 72 or 1,690hp 76 (long nacelles, 2-stage)
Weight: 13,400lb (6,078kg) empty, 21,600lb (9,797kg) maximum
Speed: 407mph (655km/h) max, 250mph (402km/h) cruising
Range: 1,300 miles (2,092km)
Ceiling: 38,000ft (11,582m)
Bomb load: 1,000lb
Armament: 4x20mm Hispano Mk III cannon (500 rounds) in ventral tray
Radar: SCR720/729/A.I. Mk X 'Universal' (Bullnose) radome
Note: 2-stage development of NF Mk XIX

Designation: NF Mk 31
First Flight: N/A
Type: Night fighter
Span: 54ft 2in (16.5m)
Length: 44ft 6in (13.5m)
Height: 12ft 6in (3.75m)
Engines: Two Packard Merlin 69 (long nacelles, 2-stage)
Weight: N/A
Speed: N/A
Range: N/A
Production: N/A, project only
Bomb load: N/A
Armament: 4x20mm Hispano Mk III cannon (500 rounds) in ventral tray (proposed)
Radar: SCR720/729/A.I. Mk X 'Universal' (Bullnose) radome
Note: 2-stage Packard powered version of NF Mk 30, not proceeded with

Designation: PR Mk 32
First Flight: August 1944
Type: Unarmed pressurised high-altitude photo-reconnaissance
Span: 59ft 2in (18m)
Length: 40ft 6in (12.3m)
Height: 12ft 6in (3.75m)
Engines: Two Merlin 113/114 (long nacelles, 2-stage)
Weight: 14,281lb (6,477kg) empty, 22,122lb (10,034kg) maximum
Speed: N/K
Ceiling: 43,000ft (13,106m)
Range: N/K
Bomb load: None
Armament: None
Radar: None
Note: One oblique and four vertical cameras. Merlin 2-stage development based on PR Mk XVI

Designation: TR Mk 33
Type: Torpedo-reconnaissance, fighter/fighter-bomber for carrier operations
Span: 54ft 2in (16.5m)
Length: 42ft 3in (12.8m)
Height: 12ft 6in (3.75m)
Engines: Two 1,460hp Merlin 25 (long nacelles)
Weight: 14,850lb (6,735.5kg) empty, 23,850lb (10,818.5kg) maximum
Speed: 376mph (605km/h) max, 262mph (421km/h) cruising
Range: 1,265 miles (2,036km)
Ceiling: 30,100ft (9,174m)
Bomb load: 2,000lb (907kg) Mk XV or Mk XVII torpedo under fuselage centreline
Armament: 4x 20mm Hispano cannons (500 rounds) in ventral tray
Radar: ASH (APS-4) radar in pod, mounted in nose. Some versions had the pod faired into the nose for a more streamline effect.
Note: First 13 machines did not have folding outer wing panels. Arrestor hook, RATO bottle fitment, oleo-pneumatic undercarriage, enlarged elevators and four blade non-featherable propellers fitted.

Designation: PR Mk 34 & PR Mk 34A
Type: Very long range, unarmed high-altitude photo-reconnaissance
Span: 54ft 2in (16.5m)
Length: 40ft 6in (12.3m)
Height: 12ft 6in (3.75m)
Engines: Two Merlin 114 (PR Mk 34), Merlin 114A (PR Mk 34A) (long nacelles, 2-stage)
Weight: 14,180lb (6,431kg) empty, 25,500lb (11,567kg) maximum
Speed: 425mph (684km/h) maximum, 300mph (483km/h) cruising
Ceiling: 43,000ft (13,106m)
Range: 3,340 miles (5,375km)
Bomb load: None
Armament: None
Radar: None
Note: One oblique and four vertical cameras.

Designation: B Mk 35
Type: Day and night bomber
Span: 54ft 2in (16.5m)
Length: 40ft 6in (12.3m)
Height: 12ft 6in (3.75m)
Engines: Two Merlin 113A or 114A (long nacelles, 2-stage)
Weight: 14,635lb (6,638kg) empty, 25,200lb (11,431kg) maximum
Speed: 415mph (668km/h) maximum, 276mph (444km/h) cruising
Ceiling: 42,000ft (12,801m)
Range: 1,955 miles (3,146km)
Bomb load: 4,000lb
Armament: None
Radar: None

Designation: PR Mk 35
Type: Photo-reconnaissance
Span: 54ft 2in (16.5m)
Length: 40ft 6in (12.3m)
Height: 12ft 6in (3.75m)
Engines: Two Merlin 113A or 114A (long nacelles, 2-stage)
Weight: Similar to B Mk 35
Speed: Similar to B Mk 35
Ceiling: Similar to B Mk 35
Range: N/K
Bomb load: None
Armament: None
Radar: None
Note: One oblique and three vertical cameras plus additional fuel tankage for special reconnaissance missions. All converted from B Mk 35s

Designation: TT Mk 35
Type: High-speed target tug
Span: 54ft 2in (16.5m)
Length: 40ft 6in (12.3m)
Height: 12ft 6in (3.75m)
Engines: Two Merlin 113A or 114A (long nacelles, 2-stage)
Weight: Similar to B Mk 35
Speed: Similar to B Mk 35
Ceiling: Similar to B Mk 35
Range: Similar to B Mk 35
Bomb load: None
Armament: None
Radar: None
Note: Three styles of banner stowage and towing used. ML Type G winch could be carried on centreline, under bomb bay.

Designation: NF Mk 36
Type: Night fighter
Span: 54ft 2in (16.5m)
Length: 41ft 6in (12.5m)
Height: 12ft 6in (3.75m)
Engines: Two Merlin 113/114 or 114A (long nacelles, 2-stage)
Weight: 18,229lb (8,269kg) empty, 21,400lb (9,706kg) maximum
Speed: 404mph (650km/h) maximum
Ceiling: 36,000ft (10,973m)
Bomb load: 1,000lb
Armament: 4x 20mm Hispano cannon (500 rounds) in ventral tray
Radar: A.I. Mk X

An interesting photograph, although the squadron codes and serials are obscured, this shot does illustrate a rather impressive piece of artwork on the entrance door of the Mosquito in the foreground

Designation: TF Mk 37
Type: Torpedo/fighter-bomber
Span: 54ft 2in (16.5m)
Length: 42ft 3in (12.8m)
Height: 12ft 6in (3.75m)
Engines: Two 1,460hp Merlin 25 (long nacelles)
Weight: 14,850lb (6,735.5kg) empty, 23,850lb (10,818.5kg) maximum
Speed: 383mph (616km/h) max
Range: 1,100 miles (1,770km)
Bomb load: None
Armament: 4x 20mm Hispano cannon (500 rounds) in ventral tray, although usually only the two outer ones were retained
Radar: ASV (Air-Surface Vessel) Mk XIII mounted in revised radome
Note: Folding outer wing panels, arrestor hook, RATO bottle fitment, oleo-pneumatic undercarriage, reduced mainwheel diameter, enlarged elevators and four-blade non-featherable propellers fitted.

Designation: NF Mk 38
Type: Night fighter
Span: 54ft 2in (16.5m)
Length: 41ft 5.5in (12.5m)
Height: 12ft 6in (3.75m)
Engines: Two Merlin 114A (long nacelles, 2-stage)
Weight: 16,000lb (7,260kg) empty, 21,400lb (9,706kg) maximum
Speed: 404mph (650km/h) maximum
Ceiling: 36,000ft (10,973m)
Range: N/K
Bomb load: 1,000lb
Armament: 4x 20mm Hispano cannon (500 rounds) in ventral tray
Radar: A.I. Mk X
Note: Not taken up in RAF service, a number supplied to Yugoslavian Air Force

Designation: TT Mk 39
Type: Target tug
Span: 54ft 2in (16.5m)
Length: 43ft 4in (13.1m)
Height: 12ft 6in (3.75m)
Engines: Two 1,680hp Merlin 72/73 (long nacelles, 2-stage)
Weight: 15,980lb (7,248.5kg) empty, 23,000lb (10,433kg) maximum
Speed: 299mph (481km/h) max
Bomb load: None
Armament: None
Radar: None
Note: Banners carried in bomb bay. All aircraft were converted from PR Mk XVIs by General Aircraft Ltd to RN Spec. Q.19/45

Designation: FB Mk 40
Type: Fighter-bomber
Span: 54ft 2in (16.5m)
Length: 40ft 6in (12.3m)
Height: 12ft 6in (3.75m)
Engines: Two Packard Merlin 31 or 33 (long nacelles)
Weight: 14,344lb (6,506kg) empty, 22,258lb (10,096kg) maximum
Speed: 378mph (608km/h) maximum, 255mph (410km/h) cruising
Range: 1,855 miles (2,985km)
Ceiling: 33,000ft (10,058m)
Origin: Australia
Bomb load: 500lb (226kg) internally, 1,000lb (454kg) under wings or eight 60lb (27kg) 3" rocket projectiles.
Armament: 4x 20mm Hispano cannon in ventral tray and 4x 0.303" Browning machine-guns in the nose
Radar: None
Note: Australian-built version of FB Mk VI

Designation: PR Mk 40
Type: Photo-reconnaissance
Span: 54ft 2in (16.5m)
Length: 41ft 2in (12.54m)
Height: 12ft 6in (3.75m)
Engines: Two Packard Merlin 31 or 33 (long nacelles)
Weight: Similar to FB Mk 40
Speed: Similar to FB Mk 40
Ceiling: 33,000ft (10,058m)
Origin: Australia
Bomb load: None
Armament: None
Radar: None
Note: Modified FB Mk 40 with vertical camera mounted in nose

Designation: PR Mk 41
Type: Photo-reconnaissance
Span: 54ft 2in (16.5m)
Length: 41ft 2in (12.54m)
Height: 12ft 6in (3.75m)
Engines: Two Packard Merlin 69 (long nacelles, 2-stage)
Weight: Similar to B Mk IX
Speed: Similar to B Mk IX
Ceiling: 33,000ft (10,058m)
Origin: Australia
Bomb load: None
Armament: None
Radar: None
Note: Australian 2-stage Merlin powered version of PR Mk 40, bearing close relationship to UK PR Mk IX. One oblique and three vertical cameras installed.

Designation: FB Mk 42
Type: Fighter-bomber
Span: 54ft 2in (16.5m)
Length: 41ft 2in (12.54m)
Height: 12ft 6in (3.75m)
Engines: Two Packard Merlin 69 (long nacelles, 2-stage)
Weight: Similar to FB Mk 40
Speed: Similar to FB Mk 40
Range: N/K
Ceiling: N/K
Origin: Australia
Bomb load: 500lb (226kg) internally, 1,000lb (454kg) under wings or eight 60lb (27kg) 3" rocket projectiles
Armament: 4x 20mm Hispano cannon in ventral tray and 4x 0.303" Browning machine-guns in the nose
Radar: None
Note: Prototype only constructed

Designation: T Mk 43
Type: Dual-control trainer
Span: 54ft 2in (16.5m)
Length: 41ft 2in (12.54m)
Height: 12ft 6in (3.75m)
Engines: Two Packard Merlin 33 (long nacelles)
Weight: Similar to T Mk III
Speed: Similar to T Mk III
Range: Similar to T Mk III
Origin: Australia
Bomb load: N/A
Armament: None
Radar: None

VT974 was a Leavesden-built T Mk III which was originally sent to the Middle East in 1946, but returned to storage in the UK in September. It was allocated to the Institute of Aviation Medicine at Farnborough in May 1947 and was sold for scrap in 1951 (via S.Howe)

Appendix 5 • Mosquito Variants   147

Mosquito Genealogy

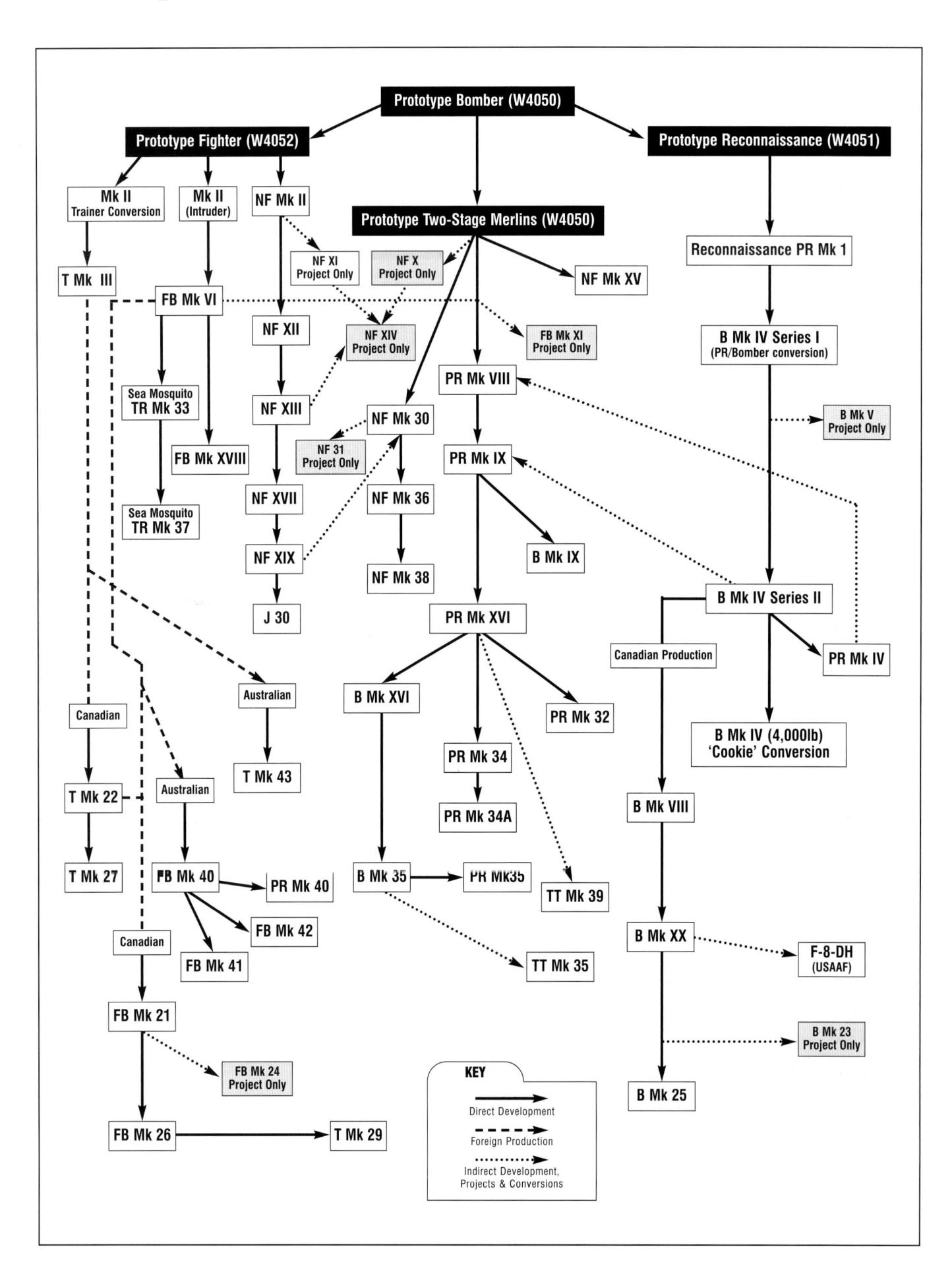

Appendix **VI**

Mosquito Squadrons

Appendix VII

No. 4 Squadron
Code: **NC** (WWII), **UP** (Post war)
Started Mosquito Operations: Sawbridgeworth 1/44
UK Based: 8/43 to 4/44
Foreign Based: Germany 31/8/44 to 7/50
Re-formed: Vokel 31/8/44 (No.605 Sqn.)
Disbanded: N/A
Re-equipped: 7/50 at Wunsdorf
Variants Operated: FB.VI (9/45 to 7/50). B Flight PR.XVI (8/43 to 5/44)

No. 8 Squadron
Code: **HV**
Started Mosquito Operations: Khormaksar (Aden) 1/9/46
UK Based: N/A
Foreign Based: Aden 9/46 to 5/47
Re-formed: N/A
Disbanded: N/A
Re-equipped: 5/47 at Khormaksar
Variants Operated: FB.VI (9/46 to 5/47).

No. 11 Squadron
Code: **OM**
Started Mosquito Operations: Formed at Wahn 4/10/48 from No.107 Sqn. renumbered
UK Based: N/A
Foreign Based: Wahn & Celle, Germany 4/10/48 to 9/50
Re-formed: N/A
Disbanded: N/A
Re-equipped: 9/50
Variants Operated: FB.VI (10/48 to 9/50).

No. 13 Squadron
Code: Nil
Started Mosquito Operations: Formed at Ein Shemer 1/9/46 from No.680 Sqn. re-numbered
UK Based: N/A
Foreign Based: Ein Shemer, Kabrit and Fayid, Middle East 9/46 to 2/52
Re-formed: N/A
Disbanded: N/A
Re-equipped: 2/52
Variants Operated: PR.XI, PR.XVI and PR.34 (9/46 to 2/52).

No. 14 Squadron
Code: **CX**
Started Mosquito Operations: Formed at Banff 1/6/45 from No.143 Sqn. re-numbered
UK Based: 6/45 to 1/4/46
Foreign Based: Wahn, Celle, Fassberg, Germany 4/46 to 2/51
Disbanded: Banff 1/4/46
Re-formed: Wahn 1/4/46 from No.128 Sqn. re-numbered
Re-equipped: 2/51
Variants Operated: FB.VI (6/45 to 4/46), B.XVI & B.35 (4/46 to 10/47) and B.35 (12/47 to 2/51).

No. 16 Squadron
Code: **EG**
Started Mosquito Operations: Celle 20/9/45
UK Based: N/A
Foreign Based: Celle, Germany 20/9/45 to 31/3/46
Disbanded: Celle 31/3/46
Re-formed: N/A
Re-equipped: N/A
Variants Operated: FB.VI (9/45 to 3/46)

No. 18 Squadron
Code: **QV**
Started Mosquito Operations: 3/47
UK Based: N/A
Foreign Based: Suez Canal Zone 3/47 to 11/47
Disbanded: N/A
Re-formed: N/A
Re-equipped: 11/47
Variants Operated: FB.VI (3/47 to 11/47)

No. 21 (City of Norwich) Squadron
Code: **YH**
Started Mosquito Operations: Sculthorpe 10/43
UK Based: Sculthorpe, Hunsdon, Gravesend & Thorney Island 10/43 to 6/44
Foreign Based: Rosieres & Melsbroek 2/45 to 4/45, Gutersloh & Munster/Handorf, Germany 11/45 to 11/47
Disbanded: Gutersloh 7/11/47
Re-formed: N/A
Re-equipped: N/A
Variants Operated: FB.VI (10/43 to 11/47)

No. 22 Squadron
Code: Nil
Started Mosquito Operations: Formed at Seletar 1/5/46 from No.89 Sqn. re-numbered
UK Based: N/A
Foreign Based: Seletar 5/46 to 8/46
Disbanded: Seletar 15/8/46
Re-formed: N/A
Re-equipped: N/A
Variants Operated: FB.VI (5/46 to 8/46)

No. 23 Squadron
Code: **YP**
Started Mosquito Operations: Ford 7/42
UK Based: Ford, Manston, Bradwell Bay 7/42 to 9/42. Back to UK (8/5/44 to 1/6/44), Little Snoring 6/44 to 9/45. Wittering, Coltishall, Church Fenton, Horsham St. Faith, West Malling 10/46 to 12/51
Foreign Based: Luqa, Malta, Pomigliano, Alghero 11/42 to 5/44
Disbanded: Little Snoring 9/45
Re-formed: Wittering 10/10/46
Re-equipped: West Malling 12/51
Variants Operated: NF.II (7/42 to 8/43), B.IV (6/43 to 9/45), NF.30 (8/45 to 2/47), NF.36 (10/46 to 12/51)

No. 25 Squadron
Code: **ZK**
Started Mosquito Operations: Church Fenton 17/5/42
UK Based: Church Fenton, Acklington, Coltishall, Castle Camps, Boxted, West Malling (5/42 to 9/51)
Foreign Based: N/A
Disbanded: N/A
Re-formed: N/A
Re-equipped: West Malling 9/51
Variants Operated: NF.II (5/42 to 3/44), FB.VI (8/43 to 9/43), NF.XVII (12/43 to 11/44), NF.30 (9/44 to 9/46), FB.VI (1/45 to 2/45), NF.36 (9/46 to 9/51)

No. 27 Squadron
Code: Nil
Started Mosquito Operations: Agartala, India 5/43
UK Based: N/A
Foreign Based: India 5/43 to 3/44
Disbanded: N/A
Re-formed: N/A
Re-equipped: N/A
Variants Operated: NF.II (5/43 to 6/43), FB.VI (12/43 to 4/44)

No. 29 Squadron
Code: **RO**
Started Mosquito Operations: West Malling 10/42
UK Based: West Malling, Bradwell Bay, Ford, Drem, West Malling, Hunsdon, Colerne, Manston, West Malling, Tangmere 10/42 to 1/51
Foreign Based: N/A
Disbanded: N/A
Re-formed: N/A
Re-equipped: Tangmere 1/51
Variants Operated: NF.II (5/43 to 4/44), NF.XIII (10/43 to 2/45), NF.30 (2/45 to 6/46), NF.36 (8/46 to 6/50), NF.30

No. 36 Squadron
Code: Nil
Started Mosquito Operations: Formed at Thorney Island 10/46 from No.248 Sqn. re-numbered
UK Based: Thorney Island 10/46 to 10/47
Foreign Based: N/A
Disbanded: Thorney Island 10/47
Re-formed: N/A
Re-equipped: N/A
Variants Operated: FB.VI (10/46 to 10/47)

No. 39 Squadron
Code: Nil
Started Mosquito Operations: Khartoum 25/9/45
UK Based: N/A
Foreign Based: Khartoum, Fayid, Kabrit 9/45 to 3/53
Disbanded: Khartoum 5/10/46
Re-formed: Fayid 9/49
Re-equipped: Kabrit 3/53
Variants Operated: FB.VI (9/45 to 10/46), NF.36 (9/49 to 3/53)

No. 45 Squadron
Code: **OB**
Started Mosquito Operations: Yelahanka (India) 12/2/44
UK Based: N/A
Foreign Based: Yelahanka (India), Dalbhumgarth (India), Ranchi (India), Kumbhirgram (India), Joari (India), Cholavaram, Madras, St Thomas's Mount (India) 2/44 to 5/46
Disbanded: N/A
Re-formed: N/A
Re-equipped: N/A
Variants Operated: FB.VI (2/44 to 5/46)

No. 47 Squadron
Code: **KU**
Started Mosquito Operations: Kumbhirgram (India) 10/44
UK Based: N/A
Foreign Based: Kumbhirgram (India), Kinmagan (Burma), Hmawbi (Burma), Butterworth (Malaya), 2/45 to 3/46
Disbanded: Butterworth (Malaya) 21/3/46
Re-formed: N/A
Re-equipped: N/A
Variants Operated: FB.VI (10/44 to 3/46)
Note: 11/44 to 2/45 period non-active due to structural failures with Mosquito in this theatre, aircraft grounded for checks

No. 55 Squadron
Code: Nil
Started Mosquito Operations: Hassani, Greece 7/46
UK Based: N/A
Foreign Based: Hassani, Greece 7/46 to 11/46
Disbanded: Hassani, Greece 1/11/46
Re-formed: N/A
Re-equipped: N/A
Variants Operated: FB.26

No. 58 Squadron
Code: **OT** (Post war)
Started Mosquito Operations: Benson 8/47
UK Based: Benson, Wyton 8/47 to 4/54
Foreign Based: N/A
Disbanded: N/A
Re-formed: N/A
Re-equipped: Wyton 4/54
Variants Operated: T.III, PR.34 (10/46 to 8/52), PR.34A (10/51 to 1/54), PR.35 (11/51 to 4/54)

No. 60 Squadron, SAAF
Code: Nil
Started Mosquito Operations: Western Desert 2/43
UK Based: N/A
Foreign Based: Western Desert & Italy 2/43 to 1945
Disbanded: N/A
Re-formed: N/A
Re-equipped: N/A
Variants Operated: F.II (2/43 to 11/43), B.IV, PR.IV and PR.IX (8/43 to 1945)
Note: This squadron returned to South Africa with some of its Mosquitoes after the end of the war and continued to use them for aerial mapping work.

No. 68 Squadron
Code: **WM**
Started Mosquito Operations: Castle Camps 7/44
UK Based: Castle Camps, Coltishall, Wittering, Coltishall, Church Fenton 7/44 to 4/45
Foreign Based: N/A
Disbanded: Church Fenton 20/4/45
Re-formed: N/A
Re-equipped: N/A
Variants Operated: NF.XVII (7/44 to 4/45), NF.XIX (7/44 to 2/45), NF.30 (6/44 to 4/45)

No. 69 Squadron
Code: **WI**
Started Mosquito Operations: Cambrai, France 8/45 from No.613 Sqn. re-numbered
UK Based: N/A
Foreign Based: Cambrai, France & Wahn, Germany
Disbanded: Cambrai, France 28/3/46. Wahn, Germany 6/11/47
Re-formed: Wahn, Germany 1/4/46 from No.180 Sqn. re-numbered
Re-equipped: N/A
Variants Operated: FB.VI (8/45 to 3/46), B.XVI (4/46 to 11/47)

VA890 was a T Mk III operated by the Armament Practice School (hence the 'APS' codes) based at Acklington from 1947 to 1950 (Angus Fraser)

No. 81 Squadron
Code: **FL**
Started Mosquito Operations: Bangkok 1/9/46 by renumbering No.684 Sqn.
UK Based: N/A
Foreign Based: Bangkok, Seletar, Changi, Tengah 9/46 to 12/55
Disbanded: N/A
Re-formed: N/A
Re-equipped: Tengah 12/55
Variants Operated: PR.XVI (9/46 to 9/47), PR.34 (9/46 to 5/53), PR.34A (9/52 to 12/55)
Note: This squadron flew the last RAF operational Mosquito sortie, with RG314, on the 15th December 1955

No. 82 (United Provinces) Squadron
Code: **UX**
Started Mosquito Operations: Kolar, India 4/7/44
UK Based: N/A
Foreign Based: Kolar (India), Ranchi (India), Chharra (India), Kumbhirgram (India), Cholavaram (India), Madras, St.Thomas' Mount (India) 7/44 to 3/46
Disbanded: Madras, St.Thomas' Mount (India) 15/3/46
Re-formed: N/A
Re-equipped: N/A
Variants Operated: FB.VI (7/44 to 3/46)

No. 84 Squadron
Code: **PY**
Started Mosquito Operations: Yelahanka (India) 2/45
UK Based: N/A
Foreign Based: Yelahanka (India), Chharra (India), Madras, St.Thomas' Mount (India), Guindy (India), Seletar (Singapore), Soerabaja, Batavia, Kuala Lumpur (Malaya), Seletar (Singapore) 2/45 to 12/46
Disbanded: N/A
Re-formed: N/A
Re-equipped: Seletar 12/46
Variants Operated: FB.VI 2/45 to 12/46

No. 85 Squadron
Code: **VY**
Started Mosquito Operations: Hunsdon 8/42
UK Based: Hunsdon, West Malling, Swannington, West Malling, Swannington, Castle Camps, Tangmere, West Malling 8/42 to 10/50
Foreign Based: N/A
Disbanded: N/A
Re-formed: N/A
Re-equipped: West Malling 11/51
Variants Operated: NF.II (8/42 to 5/43), NF XII (2/43 to 2/44), FB.VI (8/43 to 9/43), NF.XV (3/43 to 8/43), NF.XVII (11/43 to 10/44), NF.XIX (5/44 to 12/44), NF.30 (9/44 to 1/46), NF.36 (1/46 to 11/51)

No. 89 Squadron
Code: Nil
Started Mosquito Operations: Baigachi (India) 21/5/45
UK Based: N/A
Foreign Based: Baigachi (India), Seletar (Singapore) 5/45 to 4/46
Disbanded: Seletar (Singapore) 30/4/46
Re-formed: N/A
Re-equipped: N/A
Variants Operated: FB.VI and NF.XIX (5/45 to 4/46)

Appendix VII • Mosquito Squadrons 149

NF Mk 30, NT336, FW•G of No.307 (Polish) Squadron at Castle Camps in January 1945
(Polish Aircraft Archives)

No. 96 Squadron
Code: ZJ
Started Mosquito Operations: Drem 6/43
UK Based: Drem, West Malling, Ford, Odiham 6/43 to 12/44
Foreign Based: N/A
Disbanded: Odiham 12/12/44
Re-formed: N/A
Re-equipped: N/A
Variants Operated: NF.XII (6/43 to 11/43), NF.XIII (10/43 to 12/44)

No. 98 Squadron
Code: VO
Started Mosquito Operations: Melsbroek (Belgium) 9/45
UK Based: N/A
Foreign Based: Melsbroek (Belgium), Wahn (Germany), Celle (Germany) 9/45 to 2/50
Disbanded: N/A
Re-formed: N/A
Re-equipped: Cell (Germany) 2/50
Variants Operated: B.XVI (9/45 to 7/48), B.35 (8/48 to 2/50)

No. 105 Squadron
Code: GB
Started Mosquito Operations: Swanton Morley 11/41
UK Based: Swanton Morley, Horsham St. Faith, Marham, Bourn, Upwood 11/41 to 2/46
Foreign Based: N/A
Disbanded: Upwood 1/2/46
Re-formed: N/A
Re-equipped: N/A
Variants Operated: B.IV (11/41 to 3/44), B.IX (6/43 to 8/45), B.XVI (4/44 to 1/46)
Note: This was the first operational Mosquito squadron

No. 107 Squadron
Code: OM
Started Mosquito Operations: Lasham 2/44
UK Based: Lasham & Hartford Bridge 2/44 to 23/10/44
Foreign Based: Cambrai, Melsbroek (Belgium), Gutersloh (Germany), Wahn (Germany) 19/11/44 to 4/10/48
Disbanded: Re-numbered as No.11 Sqn. at Wahn 4/10/48
Re-formed: N/A
Re-equipped: N/A
Variants Operated: FB.VI 2/44 to 10/48

No. 108 Squadron
Code: Nil
Started Mosquito Operations: Luqa (Malta) 2/44
UK Based: N/A
Foreign Based: Luqa (Malta), Hal Far (Malta), Alghero, Catania 2/44 to 7/44
Disbanded: N/A
Re-formed: N/A
Re-equipped: Alghero 24/7/44
Variants Operated: NF.XII (2/44 to 7/44), NF.XIII (4/44 to 7/44)

No. 109 Squadron
Code: HS
Started Mosquito Operations: Wyton 8/42
UK Based: Wyton, Marham, Little Staughton, Woodhall Spa, Hemswell, Wickenby, Hemswell, Coningsby 8/42 to 7/52
Foreign Based: N/A
Disbanded: Little Staughton 30/9/45
Re-formed: Woodhall Spa (1/10/45) by renumbering No.627 Sqn.
Re-equipped: Coningsby 7/52
Variants Operated: B.VI (12/42 to 7/44), B.XI (4/43 to 12/45), B.XVI (10/45 to 12/48), B.35 (1948 to 7/52)

No. 110 (Hyderabad) Squadron
Code: Nil
Started Mosquito Operations: Yelahanka (India) 11/44
UK Based: N/A
Foreign Based: Yelahanka (India), Joari (India), Kinmagan (Burma), Hmawbi (Burma), Seletar (Singapore) 11/44 to 4/46
Disbanded: Seletar (Singapore) 15/4/46
Re-formed: N/A
Re-equipped: N/A
Variants Operated: FB Mk VI (11/44 to 4/46)

No. 114 (Hong Kong) Squadron
Code: RT
Started Mosquito Operations: Khormaksar (Aden) 11/45 by renumbering No.8 Sqn.
UK Based: N/A
Foreign Based: Khormaksar (Aden)
Disbanded: N/A
Re-formed: N/A
Re-equipped: Khormaksar 1/9/46
Variants Operated: B.VI (11/45 to 9/46)

No. 125 (Newfoundland) Squadron
Code: VA
Started Mosquito Operations: Valley 1/44
UK Based: Valley, Hurn, Middle Wallop, Coltishall, Church Fenton 1/44 to 11/45
Foreign Based: N/A
Disbanded: Church Fenton 20/11/45 re-numbered as No.264 Sqn.
Re-formed: N/A
Re-equipped: N/A
Variants Operated: NF.XVII (2/44 to 3/45), NF.30 (3/45 to 11/45)

No. 128 (Hyderabad) Squadron
Code: M5
Started Mosquito Operations: Wyton (re-formed) 15/9/44
UK Based: Wyton & Warboys 9/44 to 6/45
Foreign Based: Gilze Rijen (Holland), Melsbroek (Belgium), Wahn (Germany)
Disbanded: Gilze Rijen (Holland) 20/9/45 absorbed into No.226 Sqn. Wahn 1/4/46 re-numbered No.14 Sqn.
Re-formed: Melsbroek (Belgium) 8/10/45. Wahn (Germany) 3/46 re-established
Re-equipped: N/A
Variants Operated: B.XX (9/44 to 12/45), B.XVI/25 (10/44 to 3/45)

No. 139 (Jamaica) Squadron
Code: XD
Started Mosquito Operations: Horsham 6/42
UK Based: Horsham, Marham, Wyton, Upwood, Hemswell, Coningsby, Hemswell 6/42 to 6/53
Foreign Based: N/A
Disbanded: N/A
Re-formed: N/A
Re-equipped: Hemswell 6/53
Variants Operated: B.VI (6/42 to 7/44), B.IX (9/43 to 9/44), B.XVI (11/44 to 11/48), B.XX (11/43 to 9/45), B.35 (7/48 to 6/53)

No. 140 Squadron
Code: Nil
Started Mosquito Operations: Hartford Bridge 11/43
UK Based: Hartford Bridge 11/43 to 9/44, Fersfield, Acklington, Fersfield 7/45 to 11/45
Foreign Based: A.12/Balleroy (Normandy), Amiens, Melsbroek (Belgium), Eindhoven 9/44 to 4/45
Disbanded: Fersfield 10/11/45
Re-formed: N/A
Re-equipped: N/A
Variants Operated: PR.IX (11/43 to 7/44), PR.XVI (12/43 to 11/45)

No. 141 Squadron
Code: TW
Started Mosquito Operations: Wittering 10/43
UK Based: Wittering, West Raynham, Little Snoring, Wittering, Coltishall, Church Fenton, Coltishall 10/43 to 3/52
Foreign Based: N/A
Disbanded: Little Snoring 7/9/45
Re-formed: Wittering 17/6/46
Re-equipped: N/A
Variants Operated: NF.II (10/43 to 8/44), FB.VI (8/44 to 4/45), NF.30 (3/45 to 9/45 and 6/46 to 8/47), NF.36 (8/47 to 1/52)

No. 142 Squadron
Code: 4H
Started Mosquito Operations: Gransden Lodge (re-formed) 25/10/44
UK Based: Gransden Lodge 10/44 to 9/45
Foreign Based: N/A
Disbanded: Gransden Lodge 28/9/45
Re-formed: N/A
Re-equipped: N/A
Variants Operated: B.25 (10/44 to 9/45)

No. 143 Squadron
Code: NE
Started Mosquito Operations: Banff 11/44
UK Based: Banff 11/44 to 6/45
Foreign Based: N/A
Disbanded: Banff 1/6/45 re-numbered No.14 Sqn.
Re-formed: N/A
Re-equipped: N/A
Variants Operated: NF.II (10/44 to 11/44) FB.VI (10/44 to 6/45)

No. 151 Squadron
Code: DZ
Started Mosquito Operations: Wittering 4/42
UK Based: Wittering, Colerne, Middle Wallop, Colerne, Predannack, Castle Camps, Hunsdon, Bradwell Bay, Predannack, Exeter, Weston Zoyland 4/42 to 10/46
Foreign Based: N/A
Disbanded: Weston Zoyland 10/10/46
Re-formed: N/A
Re-equipped: N/A
Variants Operated: NF.II (4/42 to 7/43) FB.VI (8/43 to 9/43), NF.XIII (11/43 to 9/44), NF.30 (8/44 to 10/46)

No. 157 Squadron
Code: RS
Started Mosquito Operations: Debden 12/41
UK Based: Debden, Castle Camps, Bradwell Bay, Hunsdon, Predannack, Valley, Swannington, West Malling, Swannington 12/41 to 8/45
Foreign Based: N/A
Disbanded: Swannington 16/8/45
Re-formed: N/A
Re-equipped: N/A
Variants Operated: NF.II (1/42 to 6/44) FB.VI (7/43 to 4/44), NF.XIX (5/44 to 4/45), NF.30 (2/45 to 8/45)

No. 162 Squadron
Code: CR
Started Mosquito Operations: L.G.91 (Amriya S.) 1/44
UK Based: Bourn & Blackbushe 12/44 to 7/46
Foreign Based: LG 91(Amriya S.) & Idku 1/44 to 9/44
Disbanded: Idku 25/9/44, Blackbushe 14/7/46
Re-formed: Bourn 18/12/44
Re-equipped: N/A
Variants Operated: B.25 (12/44 to 7/46), N.XX (1945)

No. 163 Squadron
Code: Nil
Started Mosquito Operations: Re-formed at Wyton 1/45
UK Based: Wyton 1/45 to 8/45
Foreign Based: N/A
Disbanded: Wyton 10/8/45
Re-formed: N/A
Re-equipped: N/A
Variants Operated: B.XVI & B.25 (1/45 to 8/45)

No. 169 Squadron
Code: VI
Started Mosquito Operations: Re-formed Ayr 10/43
UK Based: Ayr, Little Snoring, Great Massingham 10/43 to 8/45
Foreign Based: N/A
Disbanded: Great Massingham 10/8/45
Re-formed: N/A
Re-equipped: N/A
Variants Operated: NF.II (1/44 to 7/44) FB.VI (6/44 to 4/45), NF.XIX (1/45 to 8/45)

No. 176 Squadron
Code: Nil
Started Mosquito Operations: Baigachi (India) 7/45
UK Based: N/A
Foreign Based: Baigachi 7/45 to 5/46
Disbanded: Baigachi 31/5/46
Re-formed: N/A
Re-equipped: N/A
Variants Operated: FB.VI (6/45 to 8/45), NF.XIX (7/45 to 5/46)

No. 180 Squadron
Code: EV
Started Mosquito Operations: Melsbroek (Belgium) 9/45
UK Based: N/A
Foreign Based: Melsbroek (Belgium), Wahn (Germany) 9/45 to 4/46
Disbanded: Wahn (Germany) 1/4/46 re-numbered No.69 Sqn.
Re-formed: N/A
Re-equipped: N/A
Variants Operated: B.XVI (9/45 to 4/46)

No. 192 Squadron
Code: DT
Started Mosquito Operations: Gransden Lodge 11/42
UK Based: Gransden Lodge, Feltwell, Foulsham 9/42 to 8/45
Foreign Based: N/A
Disbanded: Foulsham 22/8/45
Re-formed: N/A
Re-equipped:
Variants Operated: B.IV (11/42 to 8/45) B.XVI (3/45 to 8/45)
Note: There were three B.XVIs operated by B Flight

No. 199 Squadron
Code: Nil
Started Mosquito Operations: Hemswell 1/52
UK Based: Hemswell 1/52 to 3/53
Foreign Based: N/A
Disbanded: N/A
Re-formed: N/A
Re-equipped: Hemswell 3/53
Variants Operated: NF.36 (12/51 to 3/53)

No. 211 Squadron
Code: Nil
Started Mosquito Operations: Yelahanka (India) 6/45
UK Based: N/A
Foreign Based: Yelahanka (India), St. Thomas' Mount (India), Daun Maung (Siam) 6/45 to 2/46
Disbanded: Duan Maung (Siam) 22/2/46
Re-formed: N/A
Re-equipped: N/A
Variants Operated: FB.VI (6/45 to 2/46)

No. 219 (Mysore) Squadron
Code: FK
Started Mosquito Operations: Woodvale 2/44
UK Based: Woodvale, Honiley, Colerne, Bradwell Bay, Hunsdon, Wittering, Acklington, Church Fenton 2/44 to 9/46
Foreign Based: Amiens, Gilze Rijen, Twente 10/44 to 7/45 & Kabrit 4/51 to 3/53
Disbanded: Church Fenton 1/9/46
Re-formed: Kabrit 4/51
Re-equipped: Kabrit 3/53
Variants Operated: NF.II & NF.XVII (2/44 to 11/44) NF.XIX (6/44 to 9/46), NF.36 (4/51 to 3/53)

No. 235 Squadron
Code: LA
Started Mosquito Operations: Portreath 6/44
UK Based: Portreath, Banff 6/44 to 7/45
Foreign Based: N/A
Disbanded: Banff 10/7/45
Re-formed: N/A
Re-equipped: N/A
Variants Operated: FB.VI (6/44 to 7/45)

No. 239 Squadron
Code: HB
Started Mosquito Operations: Ayr 12/43
UK Based: Ayr & West Raynham 12/43 to 7/45
Foreign Based: N/A
Disbanded: West Raynham 10/7/45
Re-formed: N/A
Re-equipped: N/A
Variants Operated: NF.II (12/43 to 9/44) FB.VI (12/43 to 2/45), NF.30 (1/45 to 7/45)

No. 248 Squadron
Code: DM (WR Post war)
Started Mosquito Operations: Predannack 10/43
UK Based: Predannack, Portreath, Banff, Chivenor, Ballykelly, Thorney Island 10/43 to 9/46
Foreign Based: N/A
Disbanded: Thorney Island 30/9/46
Re-formed: N/A
Re-equipped: N/A
Variants Operated: FB.VI (12/43 to 9/46), FB.XVIII (10/43 to 1/45)

No. 249 (Gold Coast) Squadron
Code: GN
Started Mosquito Operations: Eastleigh (Nairobi) 2/46
UK Based: N/A
Foreign Based: Eastleigh (Nairobi), Habbaniya (India) 2/46 to 12/46
Disbanded: N/A
Re-formed: N/A
Re-equipped: Habbaniya (India) 12/46
Variants Operated: FB.26 (2/46 to 12/46)

No. 254 Squadron
Code: **QM**
Started Mosquito Operations: North Coates 3/45
UK Based: North Coates 3/45 to 5/45
Foreign Based: N/A
Disbanded: N/A
Re-formed: N/A
Re-equipped: North Coates 5/45
Variants Operated: FB.XVIII (3/45 to 5/45)
Note: Five of the above machines were on detachment to this squadron from No.618 Sqn. at the times stated

No. 255 Squadron
Code: **YD**
Started Mosquito Operations: Rosignano (Italy) 2/45
UK Based: N/A
Foreign Based: Rosignano (Italy), Istres & Falconara (detachments), Hal Far (Malta), Gianaclis 2/45 to 3/46
Disbanded: Gianaclis 31/3/46
Re-formed: N/A
Re-equipped: N/A
Variants Operated: NF.XIX (1/45 to 3/46), NF.30 (4/45 to 3/46)

No. 256 Squadron
Code: **JT**
Started Mosquito Operations: Ford 4/43
UK Based: Ford, Woodvale 4/43 to 9/43
Foreign Based: Luqa (Malta), Catania, Alghero, Pomigliano, La Senia, Alghero, Foggia, Forli, Lecce, Aviano, El Ballah, Deversoir, Nicosia 10/43 to 9/46
Disbanded: Nicosia 12/9/46
Re-formed: N/A
Re-equipped: N/A
Variants Operated: NF.XII (4/43 to 8/43 & 2/45 to 5/45) NF.XIII (11/43 to 8/45), FB.VI (4/45 to 8/45), NF.XIX (9/45 to 9/46)

No. 264 (Madras Presidency) Squadron
Code: **PS**
Started Mosquito Operations: Colerne 5/42
UK Based: Colerne, Bradwell, Predannack, Fairwood, Predannack, Coleby Grange, Church Fenton, Hartford Bridge, Hunsdon, Predannack, Odiham, Church Fenton, Linton-on-Ouse, Wittering, Coltishall, Linton-on-Ouse 5/42 to 2/52
Foreign Based: A.8/Picauville, B.17/Carpiquet, B.51/Lille, B.77/Gilze Rijen, B.108/Rheine, B.77/Gilze Rijen, B.106/Twente 8/44 to 6/45
Disbanded: B.106/Twente 6/45
Re-formed: Church Fenton 20/11/45
Re-equipped: Linton-on-Ouse 2/52
Variants Operated: NF.II (5/42 to 3/43), FB.VI (8/43 to 12/43), NF.XIII (12/43 to 8/45), NF.30 (5/45 to 3/46), NF.36 (3/46 to 2/52)

No. 268 Squadron
Code: **EG**
Started Mosquito Operations: Cambrai 10/45 by renumbering No.487 Sqn.
UK Based: N/A
Foreign Based: Cambrai 10/45 to 4/46
Disbanded: Cambrai 31/3/46
Re-formed: N/A
Re-equipped: N/A
Variants Operated: FB.VI (10/45 to 4/46)

No. 305 (Polish) Squadron
(Ziemia Wielkopolska)
Code: **SM**
Started Mosquito Operations: Laham 12/43
UK Based: Lasham, Hartford Bridge, Lasham, Hartford Bridge 12/43 to 10/44
Foreign Based: Epinoy, Volkel, B.77/Gilze Rijen, Melsbroek, Wahn 11/44 to 10/46
Disbanded: Wahn 10/46
Re-formed: N/A
Re-equipped: N/A
Variants Operated: FB.VI (12/43 to 10/46)

No. 307 (Lwow) (Polish) Squadron
Code: **EW**
Started Mosquito Operations: Exeter 12/42
UK Based: Exeter, Fairwood Common, Predannack, Drem, Coleby Grange, Church Fenton, Castle Camps, Coltishall, Horsham St. Faith 12/42 to 1/47
Foreign Based: N/A
Disbanded: Horsham St. Faith 2/1/47
Re-formed: N/A
Re-equipped: N/A
Variants Operated: NF.II (1/43 to 3/44), FB.VI (9/43 to 1/44), NF.XII (1/44 to 4/44), NF.30 (10/44 to 1/47)

No. 333 (Norwegian) Squadron
Code: **KK** (B Flight Only)
Started Mosquito Operations: Formed at Leuchars 5/43
UK Based: Leuchars & Banff 5/43 to 5/45
Foreign Based: N/A
Disbanded: Banff 30/5/45 (B Flight) became No.334 Sqn.
Re-formed: N/A
Re-equipped: N/A
Variants Operated: NF.II (5/43 to 10/43), FB.VI (9/43 to 11/45)

No. 334 (Norwegian) Squadron
Code: **VB**
Started Mosquito Operations: Banff 30/5/45 ex B Flight of No.333 Sqn.
UK Based: Banff 5/45 to 11/45
Foreign Based: N/A
Disbanded: Banff 21/11/45
Re-formed: N/A
Re-equipped: N/A
Variants Operated: FB.VI (5/45 to 10/45)

No. 400 Squadron
Code: Nil
Started Mosquito Operations: Odiham 12/43
UK Based: Odiham 12/43 to 7/44
Foreign Based: N/A
Disbanded: N/A
Re-formed: N/A
Re-equipped: Odiham 7/44
Variants Operated: PR.XVI (12/43 to 7/44)

No. 404 (Buffalo) Squadron
Code: **EO**
Started Mosquito Operations: Banff 4/45
UK Based: Banff 4/45 to 5/45
Foreign Based: N/A
Disbanded: Banff 25/5/45
Re-formed: N/A
Re-equipped: N/A
Variants Operated: FB.VI (4/45 to 5/45)

No. 406 (Lynx) Squadron, RCAF
Code: **HU**
Started Mosquito Operations: Winkleigh 4/44
UK Based: Winkleigh, Colerne, Manston, Predannack 4/44 to 8/45
Foreign Based: N/A
Disbanded: Predannack 31/8/45
Re-formed: N/A
Re-equipped: N/A
Variants Operated: NF.XII (7/43 to 12/44), NF.30 (7/44 to 8/45)

No. 409 (Nighthawk) Squadron, RCAF
Code: **KP**
Started Mosquito Operations: Acklington 3/44
UK Based: Acklington, Hunsdon, West Malling 3/44 to 6/44
Foreign Based: B.17/Carpiquet, St. Andre, Le Culot, Lille, Rheine, Gilze Rijen, Twente 8/44 to 7/45
Disbanded: Twente 1/7/45
Re-formed: N/A
Re-equipped: N/A
Variants Operated: NF.XIII (3/44 to 7/45)

No. 410 (Cougar) Squadron, RCAF
Code: **RA**
Started Mosquito Operations: Acklington 12/42
UK Based: Acklington, Coleby Grange, West Malling, Hunsdon, Castle Camps, Hunsdon, Zeals, Colerne, Hunsdon 12/42 to 9/44
Foreign Based: Amiens, Lille, Amiens, Gilze Rijen 9/44 to 6/45
Disbanded: Gilze Rijen 7/9/45
Re-formed: N/A
Re-equipped: N/A
Variants Operated: NF.II (10/42 to 12/43), FB.VI (7/43 to 9/43), NF.XIII (12/43 to 8/44), NF.30 (8/44 to 9/45)

No. 418 (City of Edmonton) Squadron, RCAF
Code: **TH**
Started Mosquito Operations: Bradwell Bay 2/43
UK Based: Bradwell Bay, Ford, Holmsley South, Hurn, Middle Wallop, Hunsdon, Hartford Bridge 2/43 to 11/44
Foreign Based: Coxyde & Volkel 3/45 to 9/45
Disbanded: Volkel 7/9/45
Re-formed: N/A
Re-equipped: N/A
Variants Operated: FB.VI (5/43 to 9/45)

No. 456 Squadron, RAAF
Code: **RX**
Started Mosquito Operations: Valley 12/42
UK Based: Valley, Middle Wallop, Ford, Church Fenton, Bradwell Bay 12/42 to 5/45
Foreign Based: N/A
Disbanded: Bradwell Bay 31/5/45
Re-formed: N/A
Re-equipped: N/A
Variants Operated: NF.II (12/42 to 2/44), FB.VI (7/43 to 2/44), NF.XVII (1/44 to 12/44), NF.30 (12/44 to 5/45)

No.464 Squadron, RAAF
Code: **SB**
Started Mosquito Operations: Sculthorpe 9/43
UK Based: Sculthorpe, Hunsdon, Swanton Morley, Hunsdon, Gravesend, Thorney Island 9/43 to 6/44
Foreign Based: Rosieres & Melsbroek 2/45 to 9/45
Disbanded: Melsbroek 9/45
Re-formed: N/A
Re-equipped: N/A
Variants Operated: FB.VI (8/43 to 9/45)

No. 487 Squadron, RNZAF
Code: **EG**
Started Mosquito Operations: Sculthorpe 10/43
UK Based: Sculthorpe, Hunsdon, Swanton Morley, Gravesend, Thorney Island 10/43 to 6/44
Foreign Based: Rosieres, Melsbroek, Cambrai 2/45 to 9/45
Disbanded: Cambrai 20/9/45 became No.16 Sqn.
Re-formed: N/A
Re-equipped: N/A
Variants Operated: FB.VI (8/43 to 9/45)

No. 488 Squadron
Code: **ME**
Started Mosquito Operations: Heathfield 8/43
UK Based: Heathfield, Bradwell Bay, Colerne, Zeals, Colerne, Hunsdon 8/43 to 10/44
Foreign Based: Amiens & Gilze Rijen 11/44 to 4/45
Disbanded: Gilze Rijen 26/4/45
Re-formed: N/A
Re-equipped: N/A
Variants Operated: NF.XII (8/43 to 5/44), NF.XIII (10/43 to 10/44), NF.30 (10/44 to 4/45)

No. 489 Squadron, RNZAF
Code: **P6**
Started Mosquito Operations: Dallachy 5/45
UK Based: Dallachy 5/45 to 8/45
Foreign Based: N/K
Disbanded: Dallachy 1/8/45
Re-formed: N/A
Re-equipped: N/A
Variants Operated: FB.VI (8/45)

No. 500 (County of Kent) Squadron
Code: **RAA**
Started Mosquito Operations: West Malling 2/47
UK Based: West Malling 2/47 to 10/48
Foreign Based: N/A
Disbanded: N/A
Re-formed: N/A
Re-equipped: West Malling 10/48
Variants Operated: NF.XIX (3/47 to 7/48), NF.30 (2/47 to 11/49)

No. 502 (County of Ulster) Squadron
Code: **RAC**
Started Mosquito Operations: Aldergrove 8/47
UK Based: Aldergrove 8/47 to 6/49
Foreign Based: N/A
Disbanded: N/A
Re-formed: N/A
Re-equipped: Aldergrove 6/49
Variants Operated: B.25 (7/46 to 1/47), NF.30 (8/47 to 6/49

No. 504 (County of Nottingham) Squadron
Code: **RAD**
Started Mosquito Operations: Hucknall 3/48
UK Based: Hucknall 3/48 to 7/48
Foreign Based: N/A
Disbanded: N/A
Re-formed: N/A
Re-equipped: Hucknall 7/48
Variants Operated: NF.30 (5/47 to 8/48)

No. 515 Squadron
Code: **3P**
Started Mosquito Operations: Little Snoring 3/44
UK Based: Little Snoring 3/44 to 6/45
Foreign Based: N/A
Disbanded: Little Snoring 10/6/45
Re-formed: N/A
Re-equipped: N/A
Variants Operated: NF.II (2/44 to 5/44), FB.VI (73/44 to 6/45)

No. 521 Squadron
Code: Nil
Started Mosquito Operations: Bircham Newton 8/42
UK Based: Bircham Newton 8/42 to 3/43
Foreign Based: N/A
Disbanded: 31/3/43 became No.1409 Flt
Re-formed: N/A
Re-equipped: N/A
Variants Operated: B.IV (8/42 to 3/43)

No. 540 Squadron
Code: Nil (**DH** Post war)
Started Mosquito Operations: Benson 10/42
UK Based: Benson, Leuchars, Benson, Wyton 10/42 to 7/53
Foreign Based: Coulommiers, Trondheim 3/45 to 10/45
Re-formed: N/A
Re-equipped: Benson 7/53
Variants Operated: PR.IV (10/42 to 5/43), PR.IX (6/43 to 5/44), PR.XVI (6/44 to 9/46), PR.34 (12/47 to 12/52)

No. 544 Squadron
Code: Nil
Started Mosquito Operations: Benson 3/43
UK Based: Benson, Leuchars
Foreign Based: Gibraltar (B Flight detachment) 3/43
Disbanded: Leuchars 13/10/45
Re-formed: N/A
Re-equipped: N/A
Variants Operated: PR.IV (4/43 to 9/43), PR.IX (10/43 to 10/45)

No. 571 Squadron
Code: **8K**
Started Mosquito Operations: Downham Market 4/44
UK Based: Downham Market, Graveley, Oakington, Warboys 4/44 to 9/45
Foreign Based: N/A
Disbanded: Warboys 28/9/45
Re-formed: N/A
Re-equipped: N/A
Variants Operated: B.XVI (4/44 to 9/45), B.IX (6/44 to 7/44)

No. 578 Squadron
Code: Nil
Started Mosquito Operations: Burn 4/45
UK Based: Burn 4/45
Foreign Based: N/A
Disbanded: Burn 4/45
Re-formed: N/A
Re-equipped: N/A
Variants Operated: B.XX

No.600 (City of London) Squadron
Code: **BQ**
Started Mosquito Operations: Cesenatico (Italy) 1/45
UK Based: N/A
Foreign Based: Cesenatico, Campofordion, Aviano 1/45 to 8/45
Disbanded: Aviano 21/8/45
Re-formed: N/A
Re-equipped: N/A
Variants Operated: NF.XIX (12/44 to 8/45)

No. 604 (County of Middlesex) Squadron
Code: **NG**
Started Mosquito Operations: Scorton 4/44
UK Based: Scorton, Church Fenton, Hurn, Zeals, Colerne, Predannack, Odiham 4/44 to 12/44
Foreign Based: A.8/Picauville, B.17/Carpiquet, Lille 8/44 to 9/44 and 1/45 to 4/45
Disbanded: Lille 18/4/45
Re-formed: N/A
Re-equipped: N/A
Variants Operated: NF.XII & NF.XIII (2/44 to 4/45)

No. 605 (County of Warwick) Squadron
Code: **UP** (**RAL** Post war)
Started Mosquito Operations: Ford 2/43
UK Based: Ford, Castle Camps, Bradwell Bay, Manston, Hartford Bridge 2/43 to 11/44, Honiley 5/47 to 1/49
Foreign Based: Coxyde, Volkel 3/45 to 8/45
Disbanded: Volkel 31/8/45 became No.4 Sqn.
Re-formed: Honiley 5/47
Re-equipped: Honiley 1/49
Variants Operated: NF.II (2/43 to 7/43), FB.VI (7/43 to 8/45), NF.XIX (4/47 to 11/48), NF.30 (4/47 to 1/49)

DD739 was one of a batch of F Mk IIs built at Hatfield in 1941 and it is seen here in the markings of No.456 (RAAF) Squadron in 1943 (Crown Copyright)

A view of B Mk IV DZ637 being loaded with its 4,000lb 'Cookie' by armourers of No.692 Squadron (via S.Howe)

USAAF UNITS WHICH OPERATED THE MOSQUITO

25th Bomb Group, 653rd BS (Recon), 8th Air Force, Watton
25th Bomb Group, 654th BS (Recon), 8th Air Force, Watton
Each of the above operated the T Mk III and PR Mk XVI

NAVAL MOSQUITOES
The squadrons of the Royal navy which used the Mosquito & Sea Mosquito

No.728 Squadron, Fleet Requirement Unit (FRU), Hall Far, Malta, 1948-50
No.762 Squadron, Ford 1946-49
No.771 (Training) Squadron, Gosport 11/45
No.771 (Training) Squadron, Lee-on-Solent 1947-50
No.772 (Training) Squadron, Arbroath 1946-7
No.790 Squadron, Dale 10/45
No.790 Squadron, Culdrose 1948/9
No.811 (Training) Squadron, Ford 1945/46 (Code: **FD**)
No.811 (Training) Squadron, Brawdy 1946/47 (Code: **BY**)

OTHER UNITS WHICH HAVE USED THE MOSQUITO
(In alphabetical order)

Armament Practice School (APS), Acklington, 1947-50
Armament Practice School, Sylt, Germany
Air Torpedo Development Unit (ATDU), Gosport, 1944-50
Bomber Development Unit, Feltwell, 1943-45
Bomber Support Development Unit (BSDU), Foulsham 4/44
Bomber Support Development Unit, Swanton Morley 12/44
Bombing Trials Unit, West Freugh, 1945-51
Civilian Anti-Aircraft Co-operation Units
Central Bomber Establishment, 1946-9 (Code: **DF**)
Central Fighter Establishment
Central Flying School/Empire Central Flying School
Central Gunnery School, Leconfield, 1944-51
Central Signals Establishment (Code: **4S**)
Empire Test Pilots School, Boscombe Down, Cranfield, Farnborough
Empire Air Armament School, Manby
Fighter Interception Unit. Ford, Wittering
Fighter Interception Development Squadron
Fighter Experimental Flight
Night Fighter Development Wing (Code: **ZE**)
Pathfinder Navigational Training Unit, Upwood, Warboys
Photographic Development Unit, Benson
Ranger Flight
Special Installation Unit, Defford
Signals Flying Unit, Honiley
No.1 Photographic Reconnaissance Unit (PRU), Benson
No.8 Operational Training Unit (OTU), Fraserburgh, Dyce, Haverford West, Benson
No.13 OTU, Bicester/Finmere, Harwell/Finmere, Finmere, Middleton St. George
No.16 OTU, Upper Heyford/Barford, Cottesmore
No.51 OTU, Cranfield
No.54 OTU, Charter Hall, East Moor
No.60 OTU, High Ercall, (Code: **AT**)
No.132 OTU, East Fortune, Haverford West
No.204 Advanced Flying School, Cottesmore, Driffield, Brize Norton, Swinderby, Bassingbourn
No.228 Operational Conversion Unit (CU), Leeming
No.229 CU, Chivenor
No.230 OCU, (Code: **A3**) 1947
No.231 OCU, Bassingbourn
No.237 OCU, Leuchars & Benson
No.1300 Met Flight
No.1317 Met. Flight
No.1401 Flight, Bircham Newton
No.1409 Flight, Oakington
No.1655 Mosquito Training Unit, Horsham, Marham, Finmere, Warboys (became No.16 OTU)
No.1672 Mosquito Conversion Unit, Yellahanka, Kolar (India)
No.1692 Bomber Support Training Flight, Great Massingham (Code: **4X**)

RAAF SQUADRONS

No.1 Sqn. (Code: **NA**)
No.87 Sqn.
No.94 Sqn.
No.5 Operational Training Unit

RCAF SQUADRONS

No.13 Sqn.

FOREIGN SERVICE
The following nations operated the Mosquito. Note that many of these machines were surplus RAF and Canadian stock and they were refurbished before delivery. Therefore there are a number of changes in the equipment fitted to these types.
See Chapter 10 of this title for a more detailed guide

Belgium Air Force: FB Mk VI, NF Mk 30
Chinese Nationalist Air Force: FB Mk 26
Czechoslovakian Air Force: FB Mk VI (Code: **IY**)
Dominican Air Force: FB Mk VI
French Air Force: FB Mk VI, PR Mk XVI
Israeli Air Force: FB Mk VI, PR Mk XVI
Norwegian Air Force: T Mk III, FB Mk VI
Swedish Air Force: NF Mk 30
Turkish Air Force: FB Mk VI
Yugoslavian Air Force: FB Mk VI, NF Mk 38

No. 608 (North Riding) Squadron
Code: **6T** (**RAO** Post war)
Started Mosquito Operations: Downham Market 8/44
UK Based: Downham Market, Thornaby 8/44 to 8/45 & 8/47 to 10/48
Foreign Based: N/A
Disbanded: Downham Market 28/8/45
Re-formed: Thornaby 8/47
Re-equipped: Thornaby 10/48
Variants Operated: B.XX (8/4 to 8/45), B.XVI (3/45 to 8/45), T.III (7/46 to 1947), NF.30 (7/47 to 10/48)

No. 609 (West Riding) Squadron
Code: **RAP**
Started Mosquito Operations: Church Fenton 4/47
UK Based: Church Fenton (4/47 to 9/47), Yeadon (9/47 to 3/49)
Foreign Based: N/A
Disbanded: N/A
Re-formed: N/A
Re-equipped: Church Fenton 9/47, Yeadon 3/49
Variants Operated: NF.30 (7/46 to 3/49)

No. 613 (City of Manchester) Squadron
Code: **SY**
Started Mosquito Operations: Lasham 12/43
UK Based: Lasham, Swanton Morley, Lasham, Hartford Bridge, Epinoy, Fersfield, Epinoy
Foreign Based: N/A
Disbanded: Epinoy 8/8/45 became No.69 Sqn.
Re-formed: N/A
Re-equipped: N/A
Variants Operated: FB.VI (10/43 to 8/45)

No. 616 (South Yorkshire) Squadron
Code: **RAW**
Started Mosquito Operations: Finningley 11/46
UK Based: Finningley 11/46 to 12/48
Foreign Based: N/A
Disbanded: N/A
Re-formed: N/A
Re-equipped: Finningley 12/48
Variants Operated: NF.30 (11/46 to 12/48)

No. 617 (Dambusters) Squadron
Code: Nil
Started Mosquito Operations: Woodhall Spa 4/44
UK Based: Woodhall Spa 8/43 to 3/45
Foreign Based: N/A
Disbanded: N/A
Re-formed: N/A
Re-equipped: Woodhall Spa 3/45
Variants Operated: FB.VI & B.XVI (8/43 to 3/45)

No. 618 Squadron
Code: Nil
Started Mosquito Operations: Formed at Skitten 4/43
UK Based: Skitten, Turnberry, Predannack, Wick, Beccles, Turnberry 4/43 to 10/44
Foreign Based: (In transit 10/44 to 12/44) Australia 11/43, Narromine (Australia) 9/45
Disbanded: Narromine 25/6/45
Re-formed: N/A
Re-equipped: N/A
Variants Operated: B.IV (4/43 to 6/45), B.VI (7/44 to 9/44), PR.XVI (9/44 to 3/45)

No. 627 Squadron
Code: **AZ**
Started Mosquito Operations: Formed at Oakington 11/43
UK Based: Oakington, Woodhall Spa 11/43 to 9/45
Foreign Based: N/A
Disbanded: Woodhall Spa 30/9/45
Re-formed: N/A
Re-equipped: N/A
Variants Operated: B.IV (11/43 to 12/44), B.XVI (6/44 to 12/44), B.XX (8/44 to 9/45), B.IX (1/45 to 9/45)

No. 680 Squadron
Code: Nil
Started Mosquito Operations: H.Q. Matariah 2/44
UK Based: N/A
Foreign Based: H.Q. Matariah (Tocra, San Severo), H.Q. Deversoir (Habbaniya, Aqir, Teheran, Athens), H.Q Ein Shemer 2/44 to 9/46
Disbanded: Ein Shemer 1/9/46 became No.13 Sqn
Re-formed: N/A
Re-equipped: N/A
Variants Operated: PR.IX & PR.XVI (2/44 to 9/46)

No. 681 Squadron
Code: Nil
Started Mosquito Operations: Dum Dum (India) 8/43
UK Based: N/A
Foreign Based: Dum Dum 8/43 to 12/43
Disbanded: N/A
Re-formed: N/A
Re-equipped: Dum Dum 12/43
Variants Operated: F.II (8/43 to 10/43), B.VI (8/43 to 12/43), PR.IX (8/43 to 12/43)

No. 683 Squadron
Code: Nil
Started Mosquito Operations: Luqa (Malta) 5/43
UK Based: N/A
Foreign Based: Luqa (Malta) 5/43 to 7/43
Disbanded: N/A
Re-formed: N/A
Re-equipped: Luqa (Malta) 7/43
Variants Operated: F.II & B.VI (5/43 to 7/43)

No. 684 Squadron
Code: Nil
Started Mosquito Operations: Dum Dum (India) 10/43
UK Based: N/A
Foreign Based: Dum Dum, Comilla, Dum Dum, Alipore, China Bay, Saigon, Bangkok 10/43 to 9/46
Disbanded: Bangkok 1/9/46 became No.81 Sqn.
Re-formed: N/A
Re-equipped: N/A
Variants Operated: PR.II (11/43 to 12/43), PR.VI (11/43 to 8/44), PR.IX (10/43 to 7/45), PR.XVI (2/44 to 2/46), PR.34 (7/45 to 9/46)

No. 692 (Fellowship of the Bellows) Squadron
Code: **P3**
Started Mosquito Operations: Formed at Graveley 1/44
UK Based: Graveley, Gransden 1/44 to 9/45
Foreign Based: N/A
Disbanded: Gransden 20/9/45
Re-formed: N/A
Re-equipped: N/A
Variants Operated: B.IV (1/44 to 6/44), B.XVI (3/44 to 9/45)

Please note:
The abbreviated form of mark number (e.g. FB.IV) has been used in this appendix to save space.

152 Appendix VII • Mosquito Squadrons

Mosquito Chronology

Appendix VIII

1938

During this year the ideas which ultimately lead to the D.H.98 are considered. Initially the aim is to produce a two engined version of the D.H.91 Albatros and this machine is envisaged to be powered by the new Rolls Royce Merlin.

October
During this month the initial design concept is refused by the Air Ministry.

1939

December 29th
Finally the Air Ministry officially sanctions the D.H. design.

1940

March 1st
An official contract for 50 machines, serials W4050 to W4099 inclusive, is issued by the Air Ministry. This contract, to specification B.1/40, identifies the unit cost of each D.H.98 at £600,000.

Summer
Churchill orders because of the worsening war situation, to "stop work on the Mosquito".

July
It it during this month that Lord Beaverbrook relents and the Mosquito is once again 'on'.

August 7th
By this date the second Mosquito fuselage shell has been completed at Salisbury Hall.

September
Seven fuselage shells have been completed by the end of this month.

October 3rd
A Ju 88 of KG 77 sets out from Loan on a bomber run to a biscuit factory in Reading and, being unable to find the primary target due to bad weather, the pilot goes east and bombs Hatsfield. The raid leaves 80% of the machined parts for the Mosquito destroyed as well as resulting in the death of 21 and injury of 70 workers.

November 3rd
The first prototype, coded E0234, is sent by road from Salisbury Hall to Hatfield.

November 25th
The first prototype flies for the first time. The aircraft only undertakes two flights with the class B registration (E-0234), before the official serial W4050 is applied.

December
During this month the prototype flies most days at Hatfield and for the first time 'blistering' is encountered on the engine cowlings. By mid-month 14 fuselage shells have been completed.

1941

February
During the early part of this month the prototype is painted in a camouflage scheme of Dark Earth and Dark Green over Yellow.

February 19th
W4050 is handed over to the RAF to start a 3 month series of official acceptance trials.

February 24th
When the aircraft lands at Boscombe Down for the start of its acceptance trials, the tailwheel catches in a rut and the rear fuselage is fractured.

March 2nd
Just one week after the accident at Boscombe Down, W4050 receives the fuselage of the bomber prototype (W4051) and is repaired by D.H. technicians at Boscombe.

April 20th
W4050 is displayed at Hatfield in front of Lord Beaverbrook and General Arnold of the USAAF.

May 13th
SS Obersturmfuhrer Karl Richter parachutes into the fields near Salisbury Hall and, after laying low for a night, movs off towards London. He is captured at 11.45pm on May 14th and executed at Wandsworth Prison on December 10th 1941. If he had waited a few more hours he would have witnessed the first flight of the NF prototype from the meadow behind Salisbury Hall!

May 15th
The night fighter (NF) prototype (W4052) is flown out of the meadow behind Salisbury Hall. To allow the aircraft to cope with the soft ground, it is fitted with oversized wheels from a D.H. Flamingo.This aircraft also features an enlarged tailplane in comparison to W4050 and this is to become standard for the whole Mosquito range.

May 20th
W4052 is undertaking cannon firing trials in the firing butts at Hatfield.

May 24th
PR Prototype (W4051) enters the paint shop at Hatfield.

June
During this month the Canadian and British governments agrees on plans for Mosquito production at D.H. Canada's Downsview plant. The initial contract placed by the Ministry of Supply is for 400 aircraft.

June 10th
First flight of the prototype PR Mosquito (W4051).

June 21st
W4050 is fitted with the mock-up of a powered turret behind the cockpit canopy.

July
This is the date originally agreed by D.H. with the RAF for the delivery of the first 50 machines.
In this month D.H. also receives the official go-ahead to start building bombers. The first ten machines were converted from PR.Is which are coming off the production line and therefore they features the short engine nacelles of this type and are referred to initially as the 'PRU/Bomber Conversion', but this is revised before they enter service to become B Mk IV Series I.

July 10th
The PR prototype (W4051) lands at RAF Benson and is handed over to 1 Photo Reconnaissance Unit (PRU).

August 7-13th
During this period De Havilland deliver four production PR Mk 1s (W4055, W4056, W4058 and W4059) to No.1 PRU, Benson.

September
The first bomber prototype,W4057 (the eighth Mosquito), is completed at the beginning of this month.

September 8th
W4057, the B Mk IV Series I prototype, flew for the first time.

September 15th
W4053 flies with the dummy turret installed for the first time.

September 17/18th
The first operational flight of a Mosquito, when W4055 flown by S/Ldr. Clarke, sets off on a PR mission. The aircraft flies to Brest and then on to the Franco/Spanish border without incident.

27th September
W4057, the B Mk IV Series I prototype, is delivered to A&A.E.E Boscombe Down for acceptance trials.

October
W4050 is returned to De Havillands for fitment of new two-stage Merlin 61 engines.

18th October
The first of eighteen PRU/Bomber Conversions (later designated B Mk IV Sr I), is delivered.

November 15th
Geoffrey De Havilland Jnr flies W4064 to No.105 Sqn. at Swanton Morley. This unit is to become the first to operate the bomber version of the Mosquito.

November/December
During this period W4065 is flown against AFDU Duxford's Spitfires and it out-performs them!

December
During this month the first Mosquito loss is encountered, when W4055 is shot down by AA fire near Bergen, Norway.
No.105 Sqn., the first to operate the bomber Mosquito, moves to Horsham St. Faith.

December 5th
W4073 flies for the first time with a turret installed behind the cockpit.

1942

Australia
The only F Mk I day fighter is sent to Australia during this year and it becomes A52-1001. This year also sees the start of productionof the Mosquito in Australia.

January
Ten PR Mk 1s in use by No.1 PRU, Benson. W4073, the ex-turreted machine, is passed to No.157 Sqn. at Castle Camps. NF Mk IIs start to enter service with Fighter Command.

January 30th
The first flight of the T Mk III trainer version. This machine is a converted NF Mk II.

February
Bomber versions of the type enter the production line at Hatfield. W4050 is fitted with Merlin 61 (two-stage) engines.

March
No.157 Sqn. start flying training and later in the month NF Mk IIs with A.I. Mk V radar begin to be delivered.

April
Deliveries of the improved B Mk IV Series II begin during this month.

27/28th April
The first operational sortie by the NF Mk II is undertaken by No.23 Sqn. This squadron is based at Ford and is the first Home Defence Squadron operating the Mosquito. It is followed by No.157 Sqn. in August.

May
By this month both the bomber and fighter versions of the Mosquito are operational.
The third night fighter squadron (No. 264) forms at Colerne.
By mid-month the first B Mk IV Series II has been delivered to No.105 Sqn.

May 29th
Flt. Lt. Pennington of No.151 Sqn. shoots down a He 111 (or Do 217) off the coast.

May 31st
First daylight raid by B Mk IVs of No.105 Sqn. W4072 (GB*D) flown by Sqn.Ldr. Oakeshot and W5046 goes to Colerne. W5046 does not return as it is shot down by AA fire.

June
The first flight of W4050 fitted with Merlin 61 engines.

1st June
The FB Mk VI prototype (HJ662/G) flies for the first time. It has been converted from an NF Mk II on the production line.

July
The NF Mk II (Intruder), which is basically a machine without A.I. (Airbourne Interception) radar, becomes operational for the first time.
During this month W4050, fitted with Merlin 61s, reaches 432mph.

August
No.157 Sqn. at Castle Camps joins No.23 Sqn. to become operational with the NF Mk II. This is the second Home Defence Squadron operating the Mosquito.
The Pathfinder Force is formed.

8th August
A pressurised bomber prototype (MP469) flies for the first time. This machine has no specific mark, but is converted in September into the NF Mk XV prototype.

August 24th
During a PR mission to Italy, DK310 (PR Mk IV) has a glycol leak and has to land in Switzerland. The aircraft is interned, and fearing the Germans will get hold of it, the UK and Swiss government agree on a plan whereby the aircraft is passed to Swissair as 'B-4'. This does not happen however and the aircraft is returned to the Swiss A.F. and later becomes the N.20 engine test bed.

September
W4052, is still equipped with the turret at this time.
All NF Mosquitoes are repainted from RDM 2A overall to an improved (and smoother) black.
No.139 Sqn. at Marham becomes the second operational Mosquito bomber squadron during this month.
The first deliveries of the T Mk III trainer are made to the Mosquito Training Unit (later No.1655 MTU).

September 7-14th
MP469 is converted in this seven day period to become the high altitude test bed, which ultimately lead to the NF Mk XV.

19th September
No.105 Squadron makes a high-level bombing raid on Berlin.

September 24th
KB300, the first B Mk VIII built by D.H.Canada, flies for the first time.

September 26th
Low level raid by No.105 Sqn. results in the destruction of the Gestapo HQ at Oslo.

October
No.1 PRU divided into four squadrons, two of which use the Mosquito (No.540 and 544).

December
No.23 Sqn. takes its NF Mk II (Special) to Malta.

20/21st December
Mosquitoes of No.109 Sqn. use *Oboe* for the first time during a raid on a power-station at Lutterade, Holland.

30/31st December
No.23 Sqn. makes its first intruder mission from Luqa, Malta.
By the end of this year No.s 25, 307, 410 and 456 are all operational with bomber Mosquitoes.

1943

Early in the year HJ719 has a trial installation of 3" rocket projectiles tested.
During the latter half of this year an NF Mk II (DD723) is experimentally fitted with the 'power eggs' from a Lancaster by Rolls Royce.

January
The first NF Mk XII, converted from an NF Mk II, flies. This machine has been converted by Marshall's and includes the fitment of the new Centrimetric A.I. Mk VIII radar.

31st January
No.105 Sqn. Mosquitoes bomb Berlin for the first time. The attack is planned to coincide with a speech by Field-Marshal Goering. Later in the day Mosquitoes of No.139 Sqn. do the same thing while Goebbels is making another speech!

February
During this month No.683 (PR) Squadron is formed at Luqa, Malta.

4th February
BOAC begin their Leuchars to Bromma service with the Mosquito.

19th February
The first operational sortie by the PR Mk VIII.

February/March
The NF Mk XII goes into service with No.85 Sqn. based at Hunsdon.

23rd March
First flight of the production B Mk IX (LR495).

April
No.109 Sqn. at RAF Wyton receives the new B Mk IX. This is followed by deliveries to No.139 and No.105 Squadrons.
No.27 Sqn. starts to use the NF Mk II in the Far East.
The concept of enlarging the Mosquito's bomb capacity to 4,000lb is considered for the first time.

This is the way many Mosquitoes ended their days, as instructional airframes. The four examples that can be seen in this shot were at RAF Halton in the 1960s (via S.Howe)

Appendix VIII • Mosquito Chronology 153

No.618 Squadron forms to use the new *Highball* weapon.

May

PR Mk IX enters service with No.540 Squadron.

During this month Mosquitoes of No.2 (Light Bomber) Group ceased daylight operations.

The NF Mk XIII goes into service with No.256 Sqn. based at Ford.

The FB Mk VI enters service for the first time with No.418 Sqn. based at Ford. Deliveries of the NF Mk II cease.

6th May

The first PR Mk IX flies.

15th May

This is the original date set for the *Highball* attack on *Tirpitz*.

27th May

Last big raid by No.105 and No.139 Sqns takes place. The target is the Zeiss Optical factory and the Schott Glass Works at Jena.

June

During this month the NF Mk IIs of No.23 Sqn. are replaced with FB Mk VIs.

1st June

No.2 (Light Bomber) Group is assigned to the 2nd Tactical Air Force in readiness for D-Day.

8th June

An FB Mk VI (HJ732) fitted with 57mm Molins cannon flies for first time and in so doing becomes the FB Mk XVIII prototype.

July

During this month the B Mk XVI prototype (DZ540) flies for the first time.

The first B Mk IV converted to carry a 4,000lb bomb is test flown.

23rd July

The first Australian-built FB Mk 40 (based on the FB Mk VI), registered A52-1, flies for the first time.

October

The FB Mk XVIII starts to equip No.248 Sqn.

October 3rd

After a PR mission by Mosquitoes of No.540 Sqn. over Peenemünde, WAAF photographic interpreter Fg. Off. Babington-Smith discovers the first evidence of the new V-1 flying bomb.

No.139 Squadron take the B Mk XI into operational use.

November

No.540 and 544 Sqns (PR) are joined by a third, No.140 Sqn., at RAF Benson.

No.627 forms with Mosquito B Mk IVs.

The first Canadian-built B Mk XXs begin to be delivered to No.139 Sqn.

4th November

The FB Mk XVIII sees action for the first time with No.248 Sqn.

28th November

No.540 Sqn. returns to Peenemünde and obtains confirmation of the existence of the V-1 which they had first photographed on the 3rd October.

December

Mosquito PR missions begin in the Far East.

The FB Mk VI starts to equip Coastal Command squadrons.

The FB Mk VI starts operational use in the Far East.

2nd December

The first Canadian-built B Mk XX begins operational service with No.139 Sqn.

24rd December

No.605 Sqn. achieves its 100th kill.

1944

No.684 Sqn. take part in an aerial survey of the whole of Burma.

January

H2S equipped B Mk IVs begin operational use with No.139 Squadron. No.692 Squadron forms with Mosquito B Mk IVs.

1st January

Geoffrey de Havilland flies the first (production) B Mk XVI with bulged bomb bay.

February

The first NF Mk XII flies. This range are all converted from NF Mk IIs.

The NF Mk XIII starts into production.

The PR Mk XVI becomes operational.

1st February

H2S equipped B Mk IVs used to mark a target for the first time, when No.139 Squadron marks Berlin for a raid. The first B Mk XVI is passed to A&A.E.E for acceptance trials.

10/11th February

No.139 Squadron takes the B Mk XVI on its operational debut.

18th February

Nineteen FB Mk VIs of Nos. 21, 464 and 487 Squadrons attacks the Amiens Jail at low-level. The raid is led by Gp. Capt.P.C.Pickard and it results in the escape of 258 French Resistance workers.

23/24th February

A Mosquito of No.692 Sqn. drops the first 4,000lb 'Cookie', the target being Düsseldorf.

March

No.139 Squadron drops a 4,000lb 'Cookie' from a B Mk XVI for the first time at the beginning of this month during a raid on Mönchengladbach.

Also during this month the B Mk XVI is issued to two *Oboe* squadrons; No.105 and No.109.

25th March

The prototype TR Mk 33 (LR359 - A modified FB Mk VI) is landed on HMS Indefatigable by Ltn. Cmr. Eric 'Winkle' Brown MBE, DSC.

FB Mk XVIII attacks and sinks a U-boat near the French coast.

April

No.571 Squadron becomes operational with the B Mk XVI.

11th April

Six FB Mk VIs of No.613 Sqn. attacks and destroys the Gestapo records of Dutch Resistance workers, which are stored in the Kleizkamp Art Galleries in The Hague.

21st April

The NF Mk XIX with its A.I Mk X radar is cleared for operational use over enemy territory.

21/22nd April

The first four-engined enemy aircraft (He 177) is shot down by a Mosquito of No.151 Squadron.

24/25th April

Wg. Cmdr. G.L.Cheshire, the CO of No.617 A.I. borrows an FB Mk VI and uses it as a target marker for the heavy bombers during a raid on Augsburg.

May

The first flight of the NF Mk XIX takes place. This type equips No.s 157 and 85 Squadrons and is used in the bomber support role with 100 Group.

12-13th May

Mosquitoes lay mines for the first time, the target being the Kiel Canal.

26th May

The first PR Mk 41 conversion, based on the FB Mk 40, flies in Australia.

June

The NF Mk 30 goes into production.

6th June

An FB Mk VI of No.605 Sqn. is the first aircraft to shoot down an enemy after H-Hour on D-Day.

14/15th June

Flt. Lt. J.G.Musgrove of No.605 Sqn. shoots down the first V-1, whilst flying an FB Mk VI.

July

No.618 Squadron is detailed to trial for anti-shipping operations in the Pacific with the *Highball* weapon.

7th July

The first B Mk 25 is accepted at Downsview, Canada.

15th July

By this date Fighter Command Mosquitoes have shot down 428 V-1s.

25th July

A Mosquito of No.544 Sqn. encounters the new Messerschmitt Me 262 for the first time.

August

Five PR Mk 32s built.

September

The FB Mk VIs of the Banff Wing, Coastal Command start operations. This wing comprises Nos. 235, 248 and 333 Squadrons.

19th September

Wg. Cmdr. Guy Gibson VC, DSO, DFC is killed in a B Mk XX.

20th October

A Mosquito of No.45 Squadron suffers structural failure during a low-level pull-out and all Mosquitoes operating in Far East are grounded. All those built with formaldehyde glue are found to be unaffected and therefore all production changed to this type of glue.

December

The Mosquitoes grounded in the Far East are cleared and begin operations again.

4th December

The first production PR Mk 34 flies.

5th December

The first operational use of the PR Mk 32. Towards the end of this year No.618 Squadron take their 29 modified B Mk IVs to Australia on the escort carriers HMS Fencer and Striker.

1945

25 British-built FB Mk VIs are assembled in Australia for use by the RAAF. They are allocated serials in the A52-500 to 537 range. Twenty-three PR Mk XVIs are also sent (A52-600 to 622).

12th March

The prototype B Mk 35 flies for the first time.

21st March

Mosquito FB Mk VIs of No.464 Sqn. attacks and destroys the Gestapo records of Danish Resistance workers in the Shellhaus Building, Copenhagen.

April

Best delivery time from Canada (via Northern route) achieved, being 5 hours and 30 minutes.

May

The NF Mk 36 prototype (RK955) flies for the first time.

2nd May

The last operational sortie by Bomber Command of the war is flown by sixteen B Mk XVIs of No.608 Sqn. against Kiel.

3rd July

PR Mk 34s on the Cocos Islands undertake their first mission with RG185.

6th September

Wg. Cdr. J.R.H. Merrifeild DSO, DFC and Flt. Lt. J.H.Spires DFC, DFM flies a PR Mk 34 (RG241) on the east-west crossing of the Atlantic from St. Mawgan to Gander in 7 hours.

October

Canadian Mosquito production ceases after 1,134 have been made.

23rd October

Wg. Cdr. J.R.H. Merrifeild DSO, DFC and Flt. Lt. J.H.Spires DFC, DFM fly the west-east crossing (in RG241) of the Atlantic from Gander to St. Mawgan in 5 hours 10 minutes.

10th November

The first production TR Mk 33 (TW227) flies for the first time at Leavesden.

1946

During this year the new TR Mk 33s replace the aging FB Mk VIs in Royal Navy service.

27th June

The first T Mk 43 (A52-1050), an Australian-built conversion of the FB Mk 40 based on the T Mk III, flies for the first time.

August

The 122nd and last B Mk 35 flies.

1947

During this year trial drops with both powered and un-powered models of the Miles M.52 are carried out off the Scilly Isles from a B Mk XVI (OF604).

May

Sqn. Ldr. H.B.Martin DSO, DFC and Sqn. Ldr. E.Sismore fly the 6,717 miles from London to Cape Town in 21 hours and 31 minutes, at an average speed of 279 mph in PR Mk 34 (RG238).

27th May

The first PR Mk 41 conversion (A52-300) is delivered to a squadron in Australia.

18th November

The prototype NF Mk 38 flies at Leavesden.

1948

Sixty ex-RAF NF Mk XIXs are refurbished by Fairey Engineering Ltd and sold to the Swedish Air Force.

Another batch of T Mk IIIs are built at Chester during this year.

Trials with both the powered and un-powered models of the Miles M.52 continue off the Scilly Isles with B Mk XVI (PF604).

March

Two PR Mk 34A owned by the RAF are loaned to B.E.A.C. at Cranfield. These machines are registered G-AJZE and G-ALZF and are flown by the Gust Research Unit.

30th May

PF604, carrying the second Miles M.52 research model enters a spin in cloud and the model breaks away and is destroyed.

30th September

The first production NF Mk 38 flies at Hawarden.

9th October

The third and final launch of the Miles M.52 research model is achieved from B Mk XVI (PF604).

The trials are abandoned soon afterwards as the government feels manned supersonic flight is too dangerous.

1949

Post-war construction of the T Mk III continues at Leavesden.

1950

The two PR Mk 34A loaned to B.E.A.C. at Cranfield for gust research work stop flying during 1950.

November

The last NF Mk 38 (VX916) flies. This machine is the 7,781st and last Mosquito built.

1952

30th May

Possibly the last UK based RAF sortie by a Mosquito is the disposal flight of RL210 by No.23 Sqn. from RAF Coltishall to West Raynham.

1953

RAF PR Mk 34s used to assess damage during the floods along the east coast of England during the early part of this year. In total in excess of 40,000 miles are flown and 100,000 photographs are produced.

Two PR Mk 41s are registered VH-WAD and VH-KLG in Australia for entry in the London-Christchurch Air Race.

T Mk IIIs are in service with No.204 Advanced Flying School and Bomber Command Operational Conversion Units up until this year.

The aerial survey of Australia, undertaken by RAAF PR Mk 41s, is completed.

3rd October

VH-KLG flown by Sqn. Ldr. A.J.R. Oates DFC and Flt. Lt. D.H.Swain DFC, ditches off the south west coast of Burma during their second attempt in the London-Christchurch Air Race.

1954

Fifteen ex-RAF PR Mk 35s are obtained by Canadian-based firm Spartan Air Services Ltd.

1955

A number of PR Mk 34As are converted for civil use at Hatfield and sold to Fotogrametric Engineers Inc. in Los Angeles and IREX Survey Co.

15th December

The last operational RAF sortie by a Mosquito is undertaken by a PR Mk 34A (RG314) of No.81 Sqn. in Malaya.

1963

The last operator of the Mosquito, No.3 Civil Anti-Aircraft Co-operation Unit, based at Exeter, fly their TT Mk 35s for the last time during this year. After use they are sold to a film company and used in the film *Mosquito Squadron*.

1964

27th July

B Mk 35 TA719 crashes whilst flying on one engine at Staverton.

An FB Mk VI, in the form of TA122, is also housed at the Mosquito Museum and it is hoped that restoration work on this machine will someday result in a complete fighter-bomber on display in the UK *(S.Howe)*

Mosquito Production

Appendix IX

50 (Hatfield) Contract B.69990/40
Placed 1st March 1940, amended to 21 aircraft June 1941.
Remaining 29 aircraft produced against Contract B.1355522
16th November 1940.

W4050 (first two flights as E0234): Prototype
W4051: Photo Reconnaissance Prototype
W4052: F Mk II Prototype
W4053: Turret Fighter & later Trainer Prototype
W4054-56: Bomber Prototype Mk I
W4057: Bomber Prototype
W4058-9: PR Mk I
W4060-1: PR Mk I (Long Range)
W4062-3: PR Mk I (Long Range & Troplicalised)
W4064-72: PR/Bomber Conversion. later redesignated B Mk IV Series I
W4073: Turret Prototype (No.2), later modified to T Mk III
W4074: First Production Mk II
W4075, 77, 79, 81: Production T Mk III (or dual control Mk II)
W4076, 78, 80, 83, 84-99: Mk II delivered 27/12/41 to 1/3/42

150 ordered 9/2/41 (Hatfield)
F Mk II. DD600-644, DD659-691, DD712-759, DD777-800
Merlin 21/22. Delivered 25/2/42 to 15/10/42.

DD670-691 & DD712-4 converted to NF Mk II(Special) Intruder for No.23 Sqn.
DD715 the prototype NF Mk XII
DD759 converted to an NF Mk XII
DD613 used for Airborne Interception radar clearance (R.A.E)
DD735 Utilised for tailplane incidence and stick load tests (D.H)
DD664 Sent to Australia (6/9/42), renumbered A52-1001
DD668 used for A.I. Mk V trials at the Fighter Interception Unit, July 1942
DD723 Fitted with Lancaster power units with chin radiators by Rolls Royce

50 (Hatfield) Ordered 21/4/41
B Mk IV Series II DK284-303, DK308-33, DK-336-339
Merlin 21/23. Delivered 11/4/42 to 13/9/42

DK324 Converted to PR Mk VIII and later to a B Mk IX
DK287 Sent to Canada as 'pattern' aircraft on Oregon 9/9/42

400 (Hatfield)
F Mk II DZ228-272, DZ286-310 (70 a/c)
Merlin 21/22. Delivered 12/10/42 to 30/12/42

DZ302 Converted to an NF Mk XII (Marshall's Flying Services)
DZ294 Used on stability trial by D.H. and R.A.E
B Mk IV Series II DZ311-320, DZ338-340, DZ404-442, DZ458-497, DZ515-559, DZ575-618, DZ630-652 (250 a/c)
Merlin 21/23.
DZ342, 364, 404 & 424 Built as PR Mk VIII
DZ366, 385, 409 & 417 Built as NF Mk XV
27 aircraft converted to PR Mk IV 5/12/42-21/3/43
DZ411, 419, 431, 438, 459, 466, 473, 480, 487, 494, 517, 523, 527, 532, 538, 544, 549, 553, 557, 576, 580, 584, 588, 592, 596, 600, 604
20 aircraft converted to carry 4,000lb 'Cookie' (1944) :
By D.H. = DZ594 (prototype) & DZ534; by Vickers-Armstrong & Marshall's = DZ599, 606, 608, 630-4, 636-44, 646, 650 & by Vickers-Armstrong & D.H. = DZ647
DZ540 converted to the Mk XVI pressurised prototype (Merlin 73).Sent to A&A.E.E 5/11/43 & SOC 28/7/45
DZ471 (prototype), DZ531/G, DZ520, DZ524/G, DZ529, DZ530/G, DZ533, DZ534/G, DZ535/G, DZ537/G, DZ539, DZ541, DZ542, DZ543, DZ546, DZ547, DZ552, DZ554, DZ555, DZ556, DZ559, DZ575, DZ577, DZ578, DZ579, DZ581, DZ583 modified by Vickers-Armstrong & D.H to carry *Highball* weapon for 618 Sqn.
DZ520, 529, 531, 537, 539, 541, 542, 543, 546, 552, 554, 555, 556, 559, 575, 578, 579, 581, 582, 583, 585, 586, 618, 639, 646, 651, 652 modified by Vickers-Armstrong, Airspeed & Marshall's with Merlin 24s, arrestor hooks, new canopy, armour plate, power unit and four blade propellers for *Highball* operations by No.618 Sqn. Aug-Sept 1944
DZ411 (PR Mk IV) passed to B.O.A.C. Operated 10/1/43-6/1/45
DZ382 to M.A.C
NOTE - First DZ434 converted to FB Mk VI prototype and renumbered HJ662, replaced by a second DZ434 on production line
DZ350 to R.A.E
DZ345 & 412 to the TFU
DZ541 to Vickers (4/48)
B Mk IV Series II DZ653-661, DZ680-727, DZ739-761 (80 a/c)
Merlin 21/23. Delivered 31/12/42 to 22/3/43

Five to M.A.C 31/12/42-22/3/43 -
DZ659 fitted with Merlin 21 & SCR720/729 and sent to the Fighter Interception Unit 4/43-5/45 -
To Royal Navy - DZ700

150 (Hatfield)
Mk II HJ642-661, HJ699-715 (37 a/c)
Merlin 21. Delivered 12/3/43 to 20/5/44

HJ659 Used for bomb release trails with Target Indicators
FB Mk VI Series I HJ662-682, HJ716-743, HJ755-792, HJ808-833 (113 a/c)
Merlin 23/25. Delivered 12/3/43 to 20/5/44

DZ434 Converted to Mk VI prototype and renumbered HJ662/G after several flights. To A&A.E.E 13/6/42 written off 30/7/42
HJ666 to A.F.D.U for trials in 1943
HJ672 to No.60 Sqn. SAAF
HJ679 used for radar trial work by A&A.E.E, D.H. and A.S.W.D.U
HJ 732 converted into Mk XVIII prototype

450 (Leavesdon)
Mk III HJ851-899, HJ958-999 (91 a/c)
Merlin 21. Delivered 14/5/42 to 22/12/43
Mk II HJ911-944 (34 a/c)

Merlin 21/22. Delivered 9/9/42 to 9/1/43

HJ-945-6, HK107-141, HK159-204, HK222-235 to Marshall's for conversion to NF Mk XII 8/1/43 to 6/6/43
HK186 Originally sent to Southern Aircraft, however later passed to Marshall's and converted into an NF Mk XII 10/2/43 to 14/7/43
HK195 To Marshall's for conversion to NF Mk XVII 19/5/43
HK-236-265, HK278-327, HK344-362 (99 a/c) To Marshall's for conversion to NF Mk XVII 6/6/43 to 26/2/44
NF Mk XIII HK363-382, HK396-437, HK453-481, HK499-536 (129 a/c)
Merlin 23. Delivered 15/9/43 to 2/2/44
Some 'Universal 'nose, others 'Thimble'
NOTE HK535/536 renumbered SM700 and SM701 due to duplicate allocation with Lancaster production
HK364 Converted into the NF Mk XIX prototype
HK369 Used for A.I. Mk VIII trials at F.I.U. 12/43
HK472 Allocated to the Royal Navy

500 (Standard Motors)
FB Mk VI HP848-888, HP904-942, HP967-989, HR113-162, HR175-220, HR236-262, HR279-312, HR331-375, HR387-415, HR432-465, HR485-527, HR539-580, HR603-649 (500 a/c)
Merlin 23/25. Delivered 16/6/43 to 17/12/44

130 (Hatfield)
FB Mk VI HX802-835, HX849-869, HX896-922, HX937-984 (130 a/c)
Merlin 21/23. Delivered 14/7/43 to 11/11/43
NOTE HX902-904 delivered as FB Mk XVIII (Merlin 25) 5/9/43 and 6/10/43
HX809 to A&A.E.E for performance trials 12/43
HX918 to A&A.E.E for 3" rocket projectile trials 11/43
HX849 & 850 NOT DELIVERED
HX902/G To A&A.E.E 5/9/43. Later issued to No.248 Sqn. (23/10/43)

200 (Hatfield)
FB Mk VI LR248-276, LR289-313, LR327-340, LR343-389, LR402-404 (118 a/c)
Merlin 21/23/25. Delivered 17/10/43 to 8/1/44
LR367 converted to TR Mk 33 (fitted with folding wings and an arrestor hook) August 1945 and issued to the Royal navy in 1946
PR Mk IX LR405-446, LR459-474, LR478-481 (60 a/c)
Merlin 72. Delivered 20/5/43 to 21/10/43
LR410 to Rolls Royce for trials (June 1943 to May 1946)
LR418 to R.A.E (July 1943 to April 1944)
B Mk IX LR475-7, LR495-513 (22 a/c)
Merlin 72. Delivered 17/4/43 to 10/11/43
LR495 to A&A.E.E for trials 17/4/43, destroyed 29/1/44
LR503 highest mission (213) tally, went on good-will tour of Canada in 1945

59 (Leavesden)
T Mk III LR516-541, LR553-585 (59 a/c)
Merlin 21. Delivered 30/12/43 to 9/10/44

300(Hatfield)
B Mk IX ML896-924 (29 a/c)
Merlin 72. Delivered 10/7/43 to 20/10/43
ML914 used for 4,000lb bomb and Avro six-store carrier trials
B Mk XVI ML925-942, ML956-999, MM112-156, MM169-179, MM181-205, MM219-226 (151 a/c)
Merlin 72/73. Delivered 24/11/43 to 4/12/44
NOTE MM170 NOT DELIVERED
ML926 used for radar bombsight, *Oboe* repeater and *H2S* trials at Defford
ML932 used on rouge aircraft trials
ML937 to A&A.E.E for performance and load tests
ML994 used for 200 gallon drop tank and Mk VIII airborne mine drop trials
MM133 passed to the Netherlands
MM175 used for *H2S* trials at Defford
ML935, 956, 974, 980, 995 & MM112, 117, 142, 156, 177, 192 converted by General Aircraft Ltd to TT Mk 39 for Royal Navy
PR Mk IX MM227-236 (10 a/c)
Merlin 72. Delivered 28/8/43 to 19/11/43
MM229 fitted with Merlin 67
MM230 used by D.H. on exhaust shroud trials
MM235 used by A7 and A.E.E on Hamilton Standard 'paddle' propeller trials (12/43)
B Mk IX MM237-8 & 241 (3 a/c)
Merlin 72. Delivered 11/43
PR Mk IX MM239-240, MM243-257 (17 a/c)
Merlin 72. Delivered 7/10/43 to 3/11/43
PR Mk XVI MM258, MM271-314, MM327-371, MM384-397 (104 a/c)
Merlin 72/73. Delivered 24/11/43 to 4/5/44
MM258 used as Target Indicator (T.I) aircraft
MM308 fitted with H2X 'Mickey' radar in revised nose - Issued to USAAF in UK
MM310, 337, 338, 340, 342, 344, 345, 346, 364, 367, 368, 370, 371, 384, 375, 386, 388, 391 & 393 issued to the USAAF in the UK. NOTE MM370, 371, 384, 385 & 386 were tropicalised versions
MM273, 293, 309, 342, 346, 361, 364 & 368 issued to the Royal Navy (1945)
MM328 Target Indicator aircraft
MM363 used on asymmetric load and drop tanks trials at A&A.E.E
FB Mk VI MM398-423, MM426-431 (32 a/c)
Merlin 25. Delivered 6/1/44 to 9/3/44
MM424 & MM425 converted to FB Mk XVIII (Merlin 25)

300(Leavesden)
NF Mk XIII MM436-479, M491-534, MM547-590, MM615-623 (126 a/c)
Merlin 25. Delivered 23/1/44 to 12/5/44
MM439 & MM462 issued to the Royal Navy
NF Mk XIX MM624-656, MM669-685 (50 a/c)
Merlin 25. Delivered 17/4/44 to 27/5/44
MM626, 630, 635, 636, 638, 642, 644, 651, 656, 670, 675, 682 & 685 to Sweden 1948
MM631 to Belgium
NF Mk 30 MM686-710, MM726-769, MM783-822 (109 a/c)
Merlin 72. Delivered 28/4/44 to 1/9/44
MM764, 765 & 821 issued to the USAAF in North Africa, later they were returned to the RAF

MP469 (Hatfield)
Pressurised cabin bomber prototype, later modified to become NF Mk XV prototype

45 (Leavesden)
NF Mk 30 MT456-500 (45 a/c)
Merlin 76. Delivered 30/8/44 to 29/9/44
NOTE MT480 not delivered
MT462, 464, 465, 478 & 479 issued to No.416 Sqn. USAAF in N.W. Africa
MT477 issued to the Royal Navy
MT466 fitted with Merlin 113 engines 10/44 for NF.36 development programme

50 (Leavesden)
NF Mk 30 MV521-570 (50 a/c)
Merlin 76.
MV569 to MAC

Although the original negative has been damaged this picture nonetheless does show an interesting experimental fitment of drop tanks to a B Mk XVI. The aircraft seems to be carrying metal tanks of a capacity in excess of 200 gallons. The wings and outer faces of the nacelles have been painted white, and there is a datum line on each tank, probably to assist during wind tunnel or flight trials (BAe)

500 (Hatfield) Ordered 17/3/43
PR Mk XVI NS496-538, NS551-596, NS619-660, NS673-712,
NS725-758, NS772-816 (250 a/c)
Merlin 72/3 or 76/77. Delivered 24/3/44 to 31/12/44
NS586-9 Delivered as PR 32 (13/9/44 to 18/10/44)
NS538 & 584 fitted with H2X 'Mickey' radar and issued to USAAF in UK.
NS538 was the prototype H2X machine
NS508, 509, 512-6, 518-9, 533-5, 537, 551-9, 568-70, 581-3, 590-6,
619-20, 625, 630, 635, 638, 650-1, 676, 686, 707, 709, 711-2, 725, 730,
740, 742-5, 748, 752-4, 756-8, 772-5, 782-3, 785, 792-4, 796, 804, 811-
2 issued to the USAAF in the UK.
Eleven machines issued to Royal Navy
Converted for civil use (Israel); NS811 (G-AIRU), NS812 (G-AIRT), NS735
(G-AOCK), NS639 (G-AOCI)
NS561 used on camouflage trails with special grey-green/grey finish applied
mid-1944
NS729 fitted with arrestor gear 9/44
FB Mk VI NS819-859, NS873-914, NS926-965, NS977-999,
NT112-156, NT169-207, NT219-238 (250 a/c)
Merlin 25. Delivered 25/1/44 to 19/5/44
NT220, 224 & 225 delivered as FB Mk XVIIIs
NT220 fitted with B Mk IV nose, torpedo rack and rocket projectiles and
used for trials by R.A.E
NT181 used by F.I.U for *Monica IIIE* and radar ranging trials 1/7/44

300 (Leavesden) Ordered March 1943
NF.30 NT241-283, NT295-336, NT349-393, NT415-458,
NT471-513, NT526-568, NT582-621 (300 a/c)
Merlin 76. Delivered 4/11/44 to 2/5/45

245 (Percival)
B Mk XVI PF379-415, PF428-469, PF481-511, PF515-526,
PF538-579, PF592-619 (195 a/c)
Merlin 72/73. Delivered 15/5/44 to 5/12/45
PF489 Converted to TT Mk 39 as 2nd prototype
PF439, 445, 449, 452, 481-3, 560, 562, 569, 576, 599, 606 & 609
converted to TT.39
PR.34 PF620-635, PF647-680 (50 a/c)
Merlin 76/77. Delivered 6/9/45 to 26/7/46
PF652, 656, 662, 669, 670, 673, 678-80 converted into PR Mk 34A

250 (Hatfield)
FB Mk VI PZ161-203, PZ217-259, PZ273-316, PZ330-358,
PZ371-419, PZ435-476 (241 a/c)
Merlin 25. Delivered 16/5/44 to 19/6/45
PZ251, 252, 300, 301, 346, 467-70 delivered as Mk XVIIIs
PZ196, 200 (ZK-BCY), 237, 254, 297, 310, 313,330, 403, 4134, 444 (ZK-
BCW), 447, 474 (ZK-BCV) to Royal New Zealand Air Force
PZ281 to Vickers-Armstrong for *Highball* development work 16/4/45 to
12/3/48
PZ202 for rocket projectile and drop tank trials at A&A.E.E (1945)
PZ467 from RAF Pershore (9/4/45) to USA (27/4/45), arrived NAS Patuxent
River 30/4/45

300 (Standard Motors)
FB Mk VI RF580-625, RF639-681, RF695-736, RF749-793,
RF818-859, RF873-915, RF928-966 (300 a/c)
Merlin 25. Delivered 16/12/44 to 5/6/45
RF597 (ZK-BCU), 595, 709, 719, 753, 837, 849, 856, 857, 885, 903, 908,
910 & 935 to Royal New Zealand Air Force

200 (Hatfield)
PR Mk XVI RF969-999, RG113-158, RG171-175 (82 a/c)
Merlin 76/77. Delivered 12/12/44 to 3/5/45
PF979, 982, 996 & RG113, 145-6 & 156-7 to USAAF in UK
RG171-173 issued to Royal Navy
PR Mk 34 RG176-215, RG228-269, RG283-318 (118 a/c)
Merlin 113/114. Delivered 6/1/45 to 10/1/46
RG176 to A&A.E.E for trials (as a PR Mk 34)
RG176-8, 181, 189, 194, 195, 198, 201-2, 205, 207, 231, 233, 236, 238,
240, 252, 259, 262, 265, 268, 300, 302 & 314 modified to PR Mk 34A
standard

365 (Leavesen)
NF Mk 30 RK929-954 (27 a/c)
Merlin 76. Delivered 27/4/45 to 12/6/45
RK945/G to Vickers at Wisley (30/8/45 to 28/12/45)
NF36 RK955-960, RK972-999, RL113-158, RL173-215,
RL229-268 (163 a/c)
Merlin 113. Delivered 16/5/45 to 23/3/47
RL248 converted to become the NF Mk 38 prototype
NF 36 RL269-273, RL288-329, RL345-390 (92 a/c)
Merlin 113. Cancelled

50 (Leavesen)
T Mk III RR270-319 (50 a/c)
Merlin 25. Delivered 12/10/44 to 25/7/45

109 (Hatfield)
FB Mk VI RS501-535, RS548-580, RS593-633 (109 a/c)
Merlin 25. Delivered 13/10/44 to 22/1/45

300 (Leavesen)
FB Mk VI RS637-680, RS693-698 (50 a/c)
Merlin 25. Delivered 8/4/45 to 7/6/46
RS646 (NZ2375), RS670 (NZ2357) & RS693 (NZ2348) to Royal New
Zealand Air Force
RS657 fitted with arrestor hook and used by the Royal Navy (14/8/47 to
31/3/49)
B Mk 35 RS699-723 (25 a/c)
Merlin 113/114. Delivered 28/2/46 to 11/4/47
RS701-2, 704, 706-10, 712-3, 715, 717, 719 & 722 converted to TT Mk 35
RS700 converted into PR Mk 35
B Mk 35 RS724-5, RS739-779, RS795-836, RS849-893,
RS913-948, RS960-999, RT105-123
Merlin 113/114. Cancelled

A good shot of B Mk XVI ML963 during a pre-delivery flight. This machine was operated by No.571 Squadron as part of the Light Night Striking Force and this aircraft was to take part in the squadron's first operational sortie on the 21/22nd March 1945 to Berlin (C.E.Brown)

60 (Hatfield)
B Mk XVI RV295-326, RV340-363 (56 a/c)
Merlin 76/77. Delivered 12/11/44 to 21/3/45
RV248-50 delivered as B Mk 35s (Merlin 113A) 29/3/45 to 3/4/45
RV295-6, 303 and 308 converted to TT Mk 35 and issued to Royal navy
B Mk 35 RV364-7 (4 a/c)
Merlin 113A/114. Delivered 29/3/45 to 9/4/45
RV365-7 converted to TT Mk 35

500 (Hatfield)
FB Mk VI SZ958-999, TA113-122 (52 a/c)
Merlin 25. Delivered 4/1/45 to 23/3/45
SZ994 to Royal New Zealand Air Force
NF Mk XIX TA123-156, TA169-198, TA215-249, TA263-308,
TA323-357 (180 a/c)
Merlin 25. Delivered 27/9/44 to 19/9/45
TA343 to Flight Refuelling Ltd 21/2/49 (G-ALGU)
TA229 later became G-ALGV
FB Mk VI TA369-388 (20 a/c)
Merlin 25. Delivered 9/3/45 to 10/4/45
TA373, 383 & 385 to Royal New Zealand Air Force. TA385 later allocated
NZ2376
NF Mk XIX TA389-413, TA425-449 (50 a/c)
Merlin 25. Delivered 20/6/44 to 25/11/45
FB Mk VI TA469-508, TA523-560, TA575-603 (107 a/c)
Merlin 25. Delivered 12/4/45 to 15/12/45
TA488 to ASWDU for camera trials
TA502 to A&A.E.E for rocket projectile trials
TA491 (NZ2370), TA577 (NZ2371) TA578 (NZ2360) and TA597 to Royal
New Zealand Air Force
PR Mk XVI TA614-6 (3 a/c)
Merlin 76/77. Delivered 11/3/45 to 14/3/45
TA614 registered G-AOCN
B Mk 35 TA617-8. TA633-70, TA685-724 (80 a/c)
Merlin 113/114. Delivered 29/3/45 to 16/7/45
TA633-4, 637, 639, 641-2, 647, 649, 651, 660-2, 664, 669, 685, 68, 699,
703, 705, 710-1, 718-20, 722 & 724 converted into TT Mk 35s
TA650 converted to PR Mk 35

320 (Standard Motors)
FB Mk VI TE587-628, 640-669, 683-707, 708-725, 738-780,
793-830, 848-889, 905-932 (266 a/c)
Merlin 25. Delivered 27/5/45 to 21/12/45
TE739-40, 746, 751-2, 755, 757,-8, 765-6, 830, 856, 861-4, 874-6, 878,
880-1, 883, 885, 887-8, 905, 910-13, 925 & 927 to Royal New Zealand Air
Force
TE701, 704, 708, 710-1, 717, 719-25, 741-2, 813, 823, 826 & 829 to
Royal Navy

70 (Hatfield) Ordered 24/5/44
B Mk XVI TH976-999, TJ113-158 (70 a/c)
Merlin 76/77. Delivered 11/7/45 to 9/11/45
NOTE All delivered as B Mk 35s (Merlin 113/114)
TH977-8 980-1, 987, 989, 990-2, 996, 998, TJ113-4, 116, 119-20, 122-3,
125-8, 131, 135-6, 138, 140, 147-9 & 153-7 converted to TT MK 35
TH985,989 and TJ124 & 145 converted to PR Mk 35

94 (Hatfield) Ordered 3/7/44
NF Mk 30 TK591-635, TK648-679, TK691-707 (94 a/c)
Merlin 76.
NOTE Only TK591-635 and TK648-656 completed, delivered as B Mk 35s
(Merlin 113/114) 11/10/45 to 12/5/46
TK591-4, 596, 599, 603-10, 612-3 & 616 converted to TT Mk 35
TK615, 632 & 650 converted to PR Mk 35

300 (Leavesden)
B Mk 35 TN466-497, TN510-530, TN542-590, TN608-640,
TN652-674, TN690-736, TM750-789, TM802-838, TM850-864
(300 a/c)
Merlin 113. Cancelled

2 (Leavesden)
Special Prototypes TS444 & TS449 (2 a/c)
Merlin 25. Delivered 1946
Prototypes for TR Mk 33 used by Royal Navy in service trials

50 (Leavesden)
T Mk III TV954-984, TW101-109 (50 a/c)
Merlin 25. Delivered 20/7/45 to 21/5/46

100 (Leavesden) Ordered January 1945
TR Mk 33 TW227-257, TW277-295 (100 a/c)
Merlin 25. Delivered 1946-47
TW227-239 had non-folding wings
TW240 later converted to TF Mk 35 prototype
TW228 used for trials with Card (*Highball* development)
TW230/G used in *Highball* II trials
TW277 to 295 Cancelled

50 (Leavesden)
T Mk III VA871-94, VA923-948 (50 a/c)
Merlin 25. Delivered 6/6/46 to 1/47
VA871-76, VA882-894 & VA923-8 to RAF
VA877-881 to Royal Navy
VA929-948 cancelled

13 (Hatfield)
PR Mk 34 VL613-625 (13 a/c)
Merlin 113/114. Delivered 16/1/46
VL621 & 623 fitted with H2S
VL621 to Met Res. Flt. 1/2/52 to 29/5/55
VL625 converted to PR.34A

70 (Airspeed)
FB Mk VI VL727-96 (70 a/c)
Merlin 25. Delivered July 1946
VL727-32 delivered only

25 (Airspeed)
B Mk 35 VP178-202 (25 a/c)
Merlin 113A/14A. Delivered 14/3/47 to 3/10/47
VP178, 181, 191 & 197 converted to TT Mk 35
VP183 converted to PR.35

14 (Hatfield)
T Mk III VP342-355 (14 a/c)
Merlin 25. Delivered 1944 to 6/6/47

40 (Hatfield)
T Mk III VR330-379 (50 a/c)
Merlin 25. Delivered 11/46 to 4/48
Only VR330-349 built

15 (Airspeed)
B Mk 35 VR792-806 (15 a/c)
Merlin 113/114. Delivered 10/7/47 to 13/2/48
VR802 converted to TT Mk 35
VR793 used as banner towing prototype

44 (Hatfield)
T Mk III VT581-596, VT604-631 (44 a/c)
Merlin 25. Delivered 6/6/47 to 10/48
VT595, 611, 615-6, 619, 623 & 627-31 to Royal Navy

50 (Hatfield)
NF Mk 38 VT651-683, VT691-707 (50 a/c)
Merlin 113/114. Delivered 2/48 to 1/50
21 passed to Yugoslavia

14 (Chester)
TR Mk 37 VT724-737 (14 a/c)
Merlin 25
VT724-737 to Royal Navy

51 (Chester)
NF Mk 38 VX860-879, VX886-916 (51 a/c)
Merlin 113/114. Delivered 2/50 to 12/50
33 passed to Yugoslavia
Remainder of order cancelled
VX916 completed November 1950, 7,781st and last Mosquito built

Mosquito Bibliography

Appendix X

Mosquito
C. Martin Sharp & Michael J. F. Bowyer
Faber & Faber Ltd. ©1967, 1971
ISBN 0 571 04750 5 & 0 571 09531 3

Mosquito at War
Chaz Bowyer
Ian Allen Publishing © 1973
The Promotional Reprint Company Ltd. © 1995
ISBN 1 85648 227 8

Mosquito Squadrons of the RAF
C. Bowyer
Ian Allen Publishing © 1984

The Mosquito Manual
Arms & Armour Press© 1977
Aston Publications Ltd. © 1988
ISBN 0 946627 32 0

De Havilland Mosquito in RAF, FAA, RAAF, SAAF, RNZAF, RCAF, USAF, French & Foreign Service. Aircam No.28
Francis Mason, R. Ward & M. Roffe
Osprey Publications Ltd. © 1972

De Havilland Mosquito Portfolio
Brooklands Book Distribution Ltd..
ISBN 0 948 207 914

Mosquito Survivors
Stuart Howe
Aston Publishing © 1986
ISBN 0 946627 11 8

Mosquito - A Pictorial History of the DH98
Philip Birtles
Janes Publishing Company Ltd. © 1980.
ISBN 0-531-03714-2

Mosquito Portfolio
Stuart Howe
Ian Allen Ltd. ©1984.
ISBN 0 7110 1406 X

Mosquito - The Wooden Wonder
Edward Bishop
Max Parrish & Co. Ltd.. © 1959
Pan/Ballantine © 1971
Airlife Publishing Ltd.. © 1980 & 1995.
ISBN 1 85310 708 5

De Havilland Mosquito - J.30, NF Mk XIX
Mikael Forslund
Allt om Hobby AB © 1997
ISBN 91-85496-42-1

The De Havilland Mosquito
M. J. Hardy
David & Charles Ltd. © 1977
ISBN 0 7153 7367 6

The De Havilland Mosquito - An Illustrated History
Stuart Howe
Aston Publications Ltd. © 1992
ISBN 0-946627-63-0

De Havilland Mosquito
Martin W. Bowman
Crowood Press ©1997
ISBN 1 86126 075 X

Mosquito - Classic Aircraft No.7
Michael J. F. Bowyer and Bryan Philpott
Patrick Stephens Ltd.. © 1980
ISBN 0 85059 432 4

The Mosquito 50 Years On
GMS Enterprises/Hatfield RAeS © 1991
ISBN 1 870384 11 3

The De Havilland Mosquito Mk's I-IV - Profile No.52
P. J. R. Moyes
Profile Publications Ltd.. ©1965

The De Havilland Mosquito IV - Profile No.209
C. Bowyer
Profile Publications © 1971

Mosquito
B. Sweetman & R. Watanabe
Janes Publishing Co. Ltd.. ©1981

Mosquito In Action Part 1 - 'In Action' No.127
Jerry Scutts
Squadron/Signal Publications Ltd.. ©1992
ISBN 0 89747 283 7

Mosquito In Action Part 2 - 'In Action' No.139
Jerry Scutts
Squadron/Signal Publications Ltd.. ©1993
ISBN 0 89747-305-5

Mosquito Victory
J.Currie
Goodall Press © 1983

Official Publications

Air Publication 2019B De Havilland Mosquito F Mk II
Air Publication 2019C De Havilland Mosquito T Mk III
Air Publication 2019D De Havilland Mosquito Mk IV
Air Publication 2019E De Havilland Mosquito FB Mk VI
Air Publication 2019G De Havilland Mosquito N.F. Mk XII
Air Publication 2019H De Havilland Mosquito NF Mk XIII
Air Publication 2019K De Havilland Mosquito N.F. Mk XVII
Air Publication 2019N De Havilland Mosquito B Mk XX
Air Publication 2019R De Havilland Mosquito NF Mk XIX
Air Publication 2019T De Havilland Mosquito FB Mk 26
Air Publication 2653A De Havilland Mosquito B Mk IX
Air Publication 2653B De Havilland Mosquito PR Mk IX
Air Publication 2653M De Havilland Mosquito PR Mk 34
Air Publication 2653N De Havilland Mosquito B Mk 35
Air Publication 2653P De Havilland Mosquito NF Mk 36
Air Publication 2653Q De Havilland Mosquito NF Mk 38
Air Publication 2653S De Havilland Mosquito TT Mk 35
Air Publication 4088A De Havilland Sea Mosquito TR Mk 33
Air Publication 4088B De Havilland Sea Mosquito TR Mk 37

General Titles

Aircraft of the Royal Air Force since 1918
Owen Thetford
Putnam Publishing Ltd. © 1957, 58, 62, 68, 71, 76, 79 & 1988
ISBN 0 85177 810 0

British Bombers of WWII - Volume 1
P. J. R. Moyes & J. Goulding
Hylton Lacy Publications Ltd.. © 1969

Camouflage & Markings No.6
Ducimus Books Ltd.

Camouflage & Markings No.21
Ducimus Books Ltd.

Famous Fighters of WW2
William Green
MacDonald & Jane's

Pathfinder at War
Chaz.Bowyer
Ian Allen Ltd.

Bomber Squadrons of the RAF
P. J. R. Moyes
MacDonald & Jane's

Fighter Squadrons of the RAF
J. Rawlings
MacDonald & Jane's

Warplanes of the Second World War
William Green
MacDonald & Jane's

Flying Colours
W. Green & G. Swanborough
Salamander Books Ltd.. ©1981

Aircraft of World War 2
B. Gunston
Octopus Books Ltd.. ©1980

Fighting Colours
M. J. F. Bowyer
Patrick Stephens Ltd. © 1969, 1970, 1975
ISBN 0 85059 191 0

Bombing Colours
M. J. F. Bowyer
Patrick Stephens Ltd. © 1973
ISBN 0 85059 128 7

Camouflage & Markings; RAF 1939-45
M. Reynolds
Argus Books. ©1992

The Belgian Air Force
John Pacco
JP Publications © 1986, 1987, 1989, 1990 & 1996

The Aircraft of 100 Group
Martin Streetly
Robert Hale Ltd. ©1984
ISBN 0 7090 1043 5

Confound and Destroy - 100 Group and The Bomber Support Campaign
Martin Streetly
Macdonald & Jane's Publishers Ltd. ©1978
ISBN 0354 01180 4

World Aircraft - World War II Part 2
E. Angelucci & R. Matricaldi
Sampson & Low © 1978

Periodicals & Journals

Air Enthusiast 75 & 76
Air International July 1976
Air International 1-3/1983
Aircraft Illustrated September 1975
Airfix Magazine June 1967
Airfix Magazine July 1968
Airfix Magazine March & April 1973
Airfix Magazine November 1973
Airfix Magazine November 1976
Airfix Magazine Vol 2 No4 1990
Aviation News 30 May - 12 June 1986
Historie a plastikové modelárství 6/1992
IPMS (USA) Quarterly 3/1975 (Vol 10)
Plastic Kits Revue 4/1991
Scale Aviation Modeller Vol 2 Iss 7 July 1996
Scale Aviation Modeller Vol 2 Iss 8 August 1996
Scale Aviation Modeller Vol 2 Iss 9 September 1996
Scale Aviation Modeller Vol 2 Iss 10 October 1996
Scale Aircraft Modelling 3/1986
Scale Aircraft Modelling 3/1990
Scale Models 9/1972
Scale Models 1/1973
Scale Models 8/1974
Scale Models 11 & 12p 0 /1995
Scale Modeller August 1979
Wingspan February 1991
Zlinek 1992

Index

Please note, this index does not reference the appendices.

HJ685 is pictured here in a line-up of other types which were operated by the Empire Tests Pilot's School. The photograph was probably taken at Boscombe Down before the unit moved to Cranfield (via S.Howe)

A

A.&A.E.E.: 11, 13, 15–17, 19–20, 28, 30, 114, 158
A.I. Radar: 13, 16–19, 25, 27, 29, 31, 33–34, 42, 55, 86, 96, 113, 117
Aarhus University: 21
Acklington: 51
Admiralty: 32
AEAF: 133
Aero Space Museum Association of Calgary: 44
Aeroclub: 61, 64
AeroMaster: 117, 120, 122–124, 139, 140
Aerospace Museum, Cosford: 84
Air Fighting Development Unit: 16
Air Kit Enterprises: 120, 127
Air Ministry: 9–10, 15–16
Air Staff: 7, 9
Air to Surface Home: 29, 33–34, 46, 105, 140
Air to Surface Vessel: 33
Airfix: 59–62, 64, 91, 115–117, 120–122, 126–127
Airparts: 60
Airspeed Oxford: 9–10
Airwork Ltd: 46
Aitken, Max, Gp. Cpt.: 30
Alberta Aviation Museum: 44
Alconbury: 137
Alipore: 36
Allahabad: 8
Alten Fjord: 26
Amiens: 20
Andrews, Sqn. Ldr.: 36
Anjeskutan: 45
Arbroath, RNAS: 33
Armament Practice School: 149
Armstrong Whitley: 10
Ashfield, Sqn. Ldr.: 17
Atkinson, R.A., Wg. Cdr.: 30
Augsburg: 14
Australian Survey Corp.: 47
Avro Anson: 47
Avro Lancaster: 21
Avro Manchester: 8

B

B Mk 23: 37
B Mk 25: 37, 49, 68
B Mk 35: 5, 39–40, 42–43, 48, 52, 64, 68–69, 83–85, 90–91, 93–94, 96–97, 101, 105, 110, 125, 131
B Mk IV: 15–17, 19, 21–22, 26–29, 49, 52, 57, 59, 61–66, 94, 107–108, 111, 115–116, 121, 130–131, 141, 145, 152
B Mk IX: 22, 23, 60, 67, 114
B Mk V: 16, 19, 36, 66
B Mk VI: 24, 111
B Mk VII: 35, 36, 66
B Mk XVI: 22–24, 33, 34, 40–41, 56, 58, 67, 98, 100, 106, 110, 155–156
B Mk XX: 23, 36–37, 68, 103, 108, 134
Baedeker Raids: 17
Ball, H.W., Wg. Cdr.: 25
Banff: 31, 62, 78
Bangkok: 39
Bankstown: 38
Barkaby: 28
Barranquilla Airport: 43
Bateson, Gp. Cpt.: 21
Bateson, R.N., Wg. Cdr.: 21
Bay of Biscay: 24
Bayley, K.H., Flt. Lt.: 21
Belgian Air Force: 45, 50, 136, 140
Belgian Air Force Museum: 46
Bell Aircraft: 37

Bell X-1: 42
Bendix Trophy Race: 48
Bengal: 35
Bergen: 14
Berlin: 23, 37
Berne: 15
Bishop, R.E.: 27
Bixby, Mr and Mrs: 48
Black Magic: 8
Blackbushe: 39
Blair, K.H., Wg. Cdr.: 20
BOAC: 28, 54, 72
Boeing 247: 8
Bogotá: 43
Boulton Paul Defiant: 27
Bomb Carriers: 94
Bomb Sight: 88, 89
Bomber Command: 9, 11, 14, 20, 23, 29, 37, 129, 131
Bomber Support Development Unit: 29
Bonneuil Matours: 21
Boozer: 22, 23
Borneo: 38
Bourn: 49
Brawdy, RNAS: 33
Bristol B Mk XI: 12
Bristol Beaufighter: 20, 28–31, 35–36
Bristol Beaufort: 26
Bristol HE 1M: 8
Bristol Blenheim: 10, 24
British Air Forces of Occupation: 39, 40
British Aviation Services Ltd: 46
British European Airways: 40, 129
Broadley, J.A., Flt. Lt.: 21
Brockbank, J.R., Plt. Off.: 18
Brooklands Aviation Ltd: 42
Brown, Eric 'Winkle', Lt. Cdr.: 32
Budapest: 22
Bullnose: 18, 19
Bunting, Flt. Lt.: 18
Burley, F.A., W/O: 39
Bussart, Don: 48

C

Cabourg-St Aubin: 22
Caen: 24
Cairo: 48
Calais: 29
Calcutta: 35
Cambel, Don: 43
Cambodia: 39
Campbell-Black, Tom: 0
Canadian Aviation Historical Society: 44
Canadian Minister of Munitions and Supply: 36
Canberra: 40
Cape Town: 40
Capitol Airways Inc.: 48
Card: 33
Carpena: 118
Casein: 35
Catania: 22
Celle: 40, 131
Centennial Planetarium Museum, Calgary: 44
Central Bomber Establishment: 40
Central Fighter Establishment: 42
Channer, Sqn. Ldr.: 17
Cheshire, Leonard, Gp. Cpt.: 21
Chester: 160
Chiang Kai-shek, General: 48
China National Aviation Corp.: 48
Chinese Nationalist Air Force: 48, 53, 136, 140
Christmas Island: 40
Churchill, Manitoba: 43
Civilian Anti-Aircraft Co-Operation Units: 41–42, 44, 124, 128
Clarkson, R.M.: 9

Clear-air turbulence: 40
Clerke, Sqn. Ldr.: 14
Cleveland, Ohio: 48
Coastal Command: 30
Coastal Strike: 133
Cocos Islands: 39
Colerne: 16
Cologne: 22, 29, 37
Comilla: 35
Compucolor: 139, 140
Control Surfaces: 93
'Cookie': 22, 23, 39, 126, 141, 152
Cowell, Roberta: 43
Coxyde: 50
Crail: 27
Cranfield: 40, 158
Cuidad Trujillo Airport: 43
Cundall, H.J., Wg. Cdr.: 23
Cunningham, Flt. Lt.: 29
Cunningham, J., Wg. Cdr.: 18
Czechoslovakian Air Force: 136, 140

D

D-Day: 24, 132, 133
D.H.106 Comet: 40
D.H.4: 7
D.H.Fox Moth: 7
D.H.Gipsy Moth: 7
D.H.Hornet Moth: 7
D.H.Leopard Moth: 7
D.H.Moth: 7
D.H.Moth Minor: 9
D.H.66 Hercules: 8
D.H.82 Tiger Moth: 7
D.H.84 Dragon: 7
D.H.88: 7–8, 39
D.H.89 Rapide: 7
D.H.90 Dragonfly: 7
D.H.91 Albatross: 7–8
D.H.95 Flamingo: 8–9, 12
D.H.96: 8
D.H.97: 8
D.H.98: 7–10
Dale RNAS: 51
Dallachy: 30
Dambusters: 26
Day Ranger: 24
De Havilland Aircraft of Canada Ltd: 36
De Havilland Vampire: 44
de Havilland, Geoffrey: 7, 9, 11–12, 30
de Havilland, John: 25
Deelen: 23
'Deep Sky': 25, 119
Depth-charge: 20
Derby Aviation Ltd: 43
Dillon, P.F., Fg. Off.: 23
Dominican Air Force: 46, 115
Dornier Do 217: 17–18, 24
Douglas: 8
Douglas Boston: 24
Douglas DC-2: 8
Douglas Havoc: 27
Downsview: 36, 38
Duisburg: 23
Düsseldorf: 22–23, 141
Dutch Central Population Registry: 21

E

E-boat: 31
Eagle Aviation Ltd: 46, 140
Edwards, A.O.: 7
Ejdsfjord: 30
El Cuerpo de Aviacion Militar: 46
Empire Tests Pilot's School: 158
Escadrille de Remorqueurs: 50
Evreux: 18
Exeter Airport Ltd: 42

F

F Mk II: 10, 12–13, 27, 35, 38, 59, 62, 151
F-8-DH: 36, 37, 63, 64, 137
F.24 Camera: 87
Fairey Aviation Co. Ltd: 44, 46
Fairey Barracudas: 27
Falcon Industries: 59
Far East: 133
FB Mk 21: 37, 78
FB Mk 26: 37–38, 43, 48, 78, 110, 112, 136
FB Mk 40: 37–38, 47, 78
FB Mk 42: 47
FB Mk VI: 6, 18–22, 27–28, 30, 31–32, 35–39, 44–47, 50–51, 53–54, 59, 61–63, 77, 96, 108, 114–115, 117, 122, 124, 132, 134, 136–138, 140–141, 154, 159
FB Mk XVIII: 26–28, 30, 51, 78, 126, 133
Fighter Interception Unit: 18, 25, 29
Fillingham, Pat: 36
Firebash: 29
Firestreak missile: 97
Fishpond: 23
Fleet Air Arm: 51, 54
Fleet Requirements Units: 34, 37
Flight: 7
Floquil: 139, 140
Flygvapnet: 44
Flying Tiger Line: 48, 50
Focke Wulf Fw 190: 17, 28
Focke Wulf Fw 190A-3: 16
Focke Wulf Fw 200: 12
Ford, RNAS: 20, 29, 33
Formaldehyde: 35
Foulsham: 29
Frape, F., R/O: 28
Freeman, Sir Wilfred: 9–10
French Air Force: 45–46, 115, 123
FROG: 61–62
Fürth: 39

G

Gaffney, R/O: 29
Gee: 13, 22, 23, 24, 40
Gee-H: 23
General Aircraft Ltd: 33–34
General Electric Co.: 27
Gestapo: 17, 21
Gibbs, James K.: 48
Gibson, Guy P., Wg. Cdr.: 36–37
Gloster Gladiator: 9
Gloster Meteor: 41
Gneisenau: 14
Goose Bay: 43–44
Gothenburg: 29
Green, Sqn. Ldr.: 18
Green, F.A., Sqn. Ldr.: 22
Griffon, Rolls Royce: 9
Grosvenor House: 7–8
Guerleden: 20
Gunnis, Bert, Sqn. Ldr.: 31
Gunze Sangyo: 139–140
Gust Research Unit: 40

H

H2S Radar: 22–23, 40
H2X Radar: 137
Hagg, A.E.: 8
Hague: 21
Halford: 139
Hamilton Standard: 8, 22, 137
Handley Page: 11
Handley Page Halifax: 8
Hankow: 48, 53
Harris, Sir Arthur: 29
Hartford Bridge: 24
Hassell, Fg. Off.: 23
Hatfield: 9–13, 15–16, 30, 36, 39–40, 44, 47, 151
Hawker Siddeley: 129
Hearle, F.T.: 8
Heathrow Airport: 40, 47
Heinkel He 111: 24
Heinkel He 177: 52
Helmorel, A.C.W.: 27
Hemswell: 40, 52
Heston: 26–27
Heston Aircraft Ltd: 18
Hi-Tech: 59, 61, 120, 122
High Altitude Flight: 25
Highball: 16, 26–28, 33, 66, 127
HMS Bonaventure: 26
HMS Daedalus: 33
HMS Fencer: 27
HMS Indefatigable: 32
HMS Peregrine: 33
HMS Striker: 27
Holdaway, A., Flt. Lt.: 23
Home Command Examining Unit: 42
Houlder, C.B., Capt.: 28
Howe, Hon. C.D.: 36
Howitt, Flt. Lt.: 18
Hudson: 20
Hughes, G.E., Sqn. Ldr.: 21
Humbrol: 122, 125, 139–140
Hunsdon: 20–21
Huntor, W.D.: 36
Hurn Airport: 43
Hurricane: 10, 20, 27, 30, 129

I

Iceland: 36, 46
Imperial Airways: 8
India: 35, 39
Indo-China: 45
Ingolstadt: 15
Instep: 29
Institute of Aviation Medicine: 147
IREX Survey Co.: 40
Irvine, Flt. Lt.: 36
Israeli Air Force: 45–46, 53, 140

J

J 30: 33, 44, 46, 53, 60, 75, 115, 117, 120–122, 124, 128, 135
Jack Amman Photogrammetric Engineers Inc: 40
Jacks, Eddy: 48
Johnston, Plt. Off.: 16
Junkers Ju 188: 18
Junkers Ju 86: 24–25
Junkers Ju 88: 18
Junkön: 45
Jutland: 21
Juvisy: 21

K

K-24 Camera: 87
Kabrit: 42
Kanchrapara: 35
Karachi: 35
Kattegat: 31
Kattergat: 31
Keflavik: 43, 44
Keil: 14
Kendall Model Company Inc.: 63, 115–117, 120–123
Kennard, Plt. Off.: 16
Kiel: 23, 31
Koksijde: 45
Krystal Klear: 120, 124

L

Labuan: 50, 159
Leatham, E.G., Flt. Lt.: 25
Leavesden: 41
Lee-on-Solent, RNAS: 33, 54
Letar-2 Torpedo: 47
Lichtenstein, Radar: 19, 29
Light Night Striking Force: 23, 156
Lindesberg: 45
Lindesnes: 30
Linz: 22
Loch Cairbawn: 26
Lockheed: 8, 32–33
Lockheed Hudson: 47
Lockheed Lodestars: 28
London Air Charter Ltd: 43
Loomis, Richard E.: 48
Loran: 23
Lord Beaverbrook: 10
Lowry, W.E.M., Wg. Cdr.: 39
LRF Mk VI: 19
Luftwaffe: 24
Luleå: 45

M

Maastricht: 20
MacRobertson Trophy: 7–8
Magwe: 35
Mahmoud: 29
Majer, J.G., Fg. Off.: 20
Malta: 13–14, 20, 24, 34
MAN: 14
Mandalay: 35
Manners, J.R., Flt. Lt.: 39
Mao Tse-tung: 48
Maquire, Sqn. Ldr.: 18
Marshall of Cambridge: 18
Marshall supercharger: 22
Marshall's Flying Services Ltd: 18, 26, 39–40, 42
Marstrand: 17, 24
Martin, H.B., Sqn. Ldr.: 39
Mascot, Sydney: 38
Matchbox: 60–62, 119–120, 122, 127
McKeard, Flt. Lt.: 23, 141
McRitchie, Sqn. Ldr.: 21
Mediterranean Air Command: 35
Melbourne: 7, 27
Mergui: 47
Merlin, Rolls Royce: 8–9, 18–19, 20, 22–24, 26, 29, 32, 36–40, 42, 47, 59, 64, 93–94, 118, 123, 125, 129, 144
Merrifield, Flt. Lt.: 22

Messerschmitt Bf 109: 9
Messerschmitt Me 163B 'Komet': 41
Messerschmitt Me 410: 18
Met Mk 35: 42
Met Mk 36: 42
Met Mk 38: 73
Met Mk IX: 73
Middle East: 39–40, 129
Mildenhall: 7
Miles M.52: 41, 42
Miles Martinet: 45
Milliput: 62
Mine: 20
Ministry of Aircraft Production: 10–11, 27, 37, 38
Ministry of Supply: 40–41
ML Type G Winch: 42, 95, 113, 123, 124
ModelMaster: 139–140
Molins: 28, 59
Mollison, Amy: 7
Mollison, James: 7
Moncton: 43
Monica, Radar: 19, 29, 57, 114
Monogram: 62
Mont Joli Airport, Quebec: 44
Montdidier: 24
Moore, V.S., Flt. Lt.: 23
Mosquito Museum: 23, 46, 129, 154
Mosquito Squadron: 44
Mr Color: 139, 140
München Gladbach: 23
Muntz, Alan: 27
Musgrove, J.G., Flt. Lt.: 19

N

Napalm: 29
NAS Patuxent River: 28
Neubiburg: 29
NF Mk 30: 6, 18–19, 29, 42, 45–46, 54, 57, 60, 76, 113, 114, 132, 136–137, 150
NF Mk 36: 6, 39, 42, 76, 113–114
NF Mk 38: 42, 46–47, 76, 114, 137–138, 140
NF Mk II: 13–14, 16–18, 24–25, 27, 29–30, 35, 52, 55, 60, 62, 73, 99, 103, 115, 117
NF Mk II (Intruder): 13, 19, 20, 24, 74, 132
NF Mk VI: 19, 59
NF Mk VIA: 19
NF Mk VIB: 19
NF Mk XII: 18, 25, 27, 60, 74, 132
NF Mk XIII: 18, 74, 127, 132
NF Mk XIV: 19
NF Mk XIX: 18–19, 44, 60, 75, 113, 120, 133, 135
NF Mk XV: 24–25, 115, 118, 119
NF Mk XVII: 19, 75, 132
NF Mk XVIII: 59
NF XV: 75
Night Fighters: 132
Night Ranger: 24
Niot, Jacque: 119
Nitrous-oxide injection: 18
No.1 Photo Reconnaissance Unit: 13–15, 21–22, 25, 38, 49, 133
No.1 Sqn. (RAAF): 38, 50, 59, 61, 134, 141, 159
No.1 Sqn. (SAF): 44, 135
No.10 Sqn. (BAF): 45–46
No.105 Sqn.: 16–17, 22–23, 28, 49, 60–63, 130–131, 145
No.107 (Polish) Sqn.: 20, 39
No.108 Sqn.: 20
No.109 Sqn.: 22, 23, 40, 131
No.11 Sqn. (BAF): 45
No.110 Sqn.: 36, 39, 50
No.128 Sqn. (RCAF): 37
No.13 MU: 36
No.13 Sqn.: 40
No.138 Wing: 20
No.139 (Jamaica) Sqn.: 17, 23, 37, 40, 49, 52, 63, 145
No.14 Sqn.: 40
No.140 Sqn.: 22
No.140 Wing: 20–21
No.1409 Flight: 22
No.141 Sqn.: 29, 42, 52
No.142 Sqn.: 37
No.143 Sqn.: 30–31, 62, 133
No.1474 Flight: 29
No.1477 (Norwegian) Flight: 30
No.151 Sqn.: 18, 24–25
No.157 Sqn.: 17–19, 24, 29, 60, 118
No.162 Sqn.: 49
No.1672 Conversion Unit: 35
No.192 Sqn.: 29, 49
No.2 Sqn. (SAF): 44, 60, 135
No.21 Sqn.: 20, 39
No.211 Sqn.: 36
No.219 Sqn.: 19
No.22 MU: 43
No.22 Squadron: 72
No.23 Sqn.: 20, 24, 29, 42, 59, 62, 132
No.235 Sqn.: 30–31
No.239 Sqn.: 29
No.24 Bomber Regiment: 136
No.248 Sqn.: 26, 28, 30–31, 51, 59
No.249 Sqn.: 38
No.25 Sqn.: 18, 24, 42
No.254 Sqn.: 28, 59
No.256 Sqn.: 18
No.264 Sqn.: 24, 42, 52
No.27 MU: 43
No.29 Sqn.: 42
No.3 Sqn.: 44
No.3 Sqn. (SAF): 60, 135
No.305 (Polish) Sqn.: 20
No.307 (Polish) Sqn.: 150
No.32 MU: 17
No.333 (Norwegian) Sqn.: 30
No.333 Sqn.: 31
No.334 (Norwegian) Sqn.: 46
No.36 OTU: 17
No.375 Servicing Squadron: 37
No.39 Sqn.: 42
No.400 Sqn.: 22
No.404 (Buffalo) Sqn.: 31
No.404 Sqn.: 31
No.410 (Cougar) Sqn.: 18
No.410 Sqn.: 19, 51
No.416 Sqn.: 137
No.418 (City of Edmonton) Sqn.: 20, 62
No.418 Sqn.: 44
No.45 Sqn.: 35
No.456 Sqn. (RAAF): 151
No.464 Sqn.: 20–21
No.464 Sqn. (RAAF): 20
No.47 Sqn.: 39
No.487 Sqn.: 20–21
No.487 Sqn. (RNZAF): 19–20, 62
No.489 Sqn. (RNZAF): 18
No.5 Operational Training Unit: 38
No.515 Sqn.: 29
No.540 Sqn.: 21–22, 25, 39–40
No.544 Sqn.: 22, 25, 39
No.571 Sqn.: 23, 156
No.58 Sqn.: 40–41
No.60 Sqn.: 134
No.60 Sqn. (SAAF): 22, 46
No.604 Sqn.: 24
No.605 (County of Warwick) Sqn.: 20, 29
No.605 Sqn.: 19
No.608 Sqn. (RCAF): 23, 37
No.613 Sqn.: 21, 39
No.616 Sqn.: 54
No.617 Sqn.: 21, 26
No.618 Sqn.: 26, 28
No.619 Sqn.: 40
No.627 Sqn. (RCAF): 23, 36, 37
No.653 Sqn.: 137
No.654 Sqn.: 137
No.680 Sqn.: 22, 40, 54, 133
No.681 Sqn.: 22
No.684 Sqn.: 35–36, 39
No.69 Sqn.: 40
No.692 Sqn.: 23, 52, 141
No.703 Sqn.: 33
No.711 Sqn.: 54
No.75 Sqn.: 47
No.762 Sqn.: 33, 51
No.771 Training Sqn.: 33
No.772 Training Sqn.: 33
No.778 Sqn.: 33
No.790 Sqn.: 33
No.81 Sqn.: 39, 40
No.811 Sqn.: 33
No.82 (United Provinces) Sqn.: 39
No.82 Sqn.: 35, 39
No.84 Sqn.: 36, 39
No.85 Sqn.: 19, 24–25, 29, 42, 60
No.87 Sqn. (RAAF): 38
No.92 Sqn. (RAAF): 134
No.94 Sqn. (RAAF): 38
No.96 Sqn.: 18
No.98 Sqn.: 40, 125
Nock, Peter: 43
Norwegian Air Force: 46, 77, 137

O

Oakington: 22
Oakshott, Sqn. Ldr.: 16
Oates, A.J.R., Sqn. Ldr.: 47
Oboe: 22–23, 131
Obrestad: 30
Operation Firedog: 40
Operation Jericho: 20
Orton, B.W.B., Capt.: 28
Oslo: 145
Osnabrück: 23
Oxtail: 26
Ozubski, Marian: 43

P

Packard Motor Co.: 36–38, 47
Pactra: 139–140
Palestine: 40
Palmerston North: 47
Pancevo: 47
Paragon Designs: 59, 61–65, 115–118, 120–123
Paris: 21, 29
Pateman, Flt. Sgt.: 39
Pathfinder: 26
Pearl Harbour: 38
Pennington, Flt. Lt.: 17
Percival Aircraft Ltd: 39
Perfectos: 19
Perth Airport: 47
Phipps, Weldy: 43
Pickard, P.C., Grp. Cpt.: 21
Pisa: 137
Plumb, Fred: 25
Polly-S: 139, 140
Pont-Château: 20
Povey, Harry: 36
PR Development Unit: 25
PR Mk 32: 25, 72
PR Mk 34: 39, 40, 42, 56, 72, 122, 128
PR Mk 34A: 39, 72, 115, 123, 124, 134
PR Mk 35: 40–41
PR Mk 40: 38, 47, 73
PR Mk 41: 38, 47, 73
PR Mk I: 13–15, 70
PR Mk II: 70
PR Mk IV: 14–15, 21, 49, 70
PR Mk IX: 21–22, 36, 71, 114, 133
PR Mk VII: 21
PR Mk VIII: 21–22, 70
PR Mk XVI: 21–22, 25, 27, 36–39, 45–47, 53–54, 71, 115, 123, 134–135, 137, 140
Predannack: 28, 30
Prestwick: 36, 43

R

R.1155 Receiver: 86
R.A.Short Aviation: 46
Rabat: 45
Radio Warfare Establishment: 40
RAE: 15
RAF Benson: 14, 21, 22, 25, 39
RAF Castle Camps: 17, 20, 150
RAF Colerne: 45
RAF Duxford: 16
RAF Farnborough: 9
RAF Fayid: 42
RAF Finningley: 54
RAF Foggia: 22, 54, 133
RAF Ford: 25
RAF Halton: 153
RAF Hendon: 146
RAF Henlow: 36
RAF Horsham St Faith: 16–17
RAF Hunsdon: 25
RAF Kasfarit: 35
RAF Leuchars: 15, 28, 54
RAF Lossiemouth: 46
RAF North Coates: 28, 30
RAF Northolt: 25
RAF Operations: 129
RAF Pembrey: 16
RAF Pershore: 47
RAF Scampton: 16
RAF Schleswigland: 42
RAF Shawbury: 41, 43
RAF Silloth: 43
RAF Wyton: 22
Random Range: 35
Ranger: 24
Rangoon: 35
Ratier: 8
RATO: 32–33
RCAF: 37–38
Rebecca H: 22
Reculver: 26
Regensburg: 22
Replicolor: 139
Revell: 60–61, 63–64, 124, 139–140
Richter, Karel: 12
Rio Cuarto: 43
Robertson, Sir MacPherson: 7
Rocket projectile: 28, 30, 59, 113
Rogers, Carl: 28
Rose Bros: 16
Rose, Bruce: 38
Rose, C.F., Sqn. Ldr.: 26, 28
Rowe, N.E.: 25
Royal Air Force Museum: 85, 136
Royal Australian Air Force: 38–39, 47, 50, 134–135, 139
Royal Navy: 31–32, 37, 46–47, 134
Royal New Zealand Air Force: 47
Royal Norwegian Air Force: 140
RSAAF: 134
Rubin, Bernard: 7

S

Sabre: 8–9
Saigon: 39
Salisbury Hall: 9–10, 12, 83, 129, 145
Sarbono: 22
Scale Aviation Modeller International: 5, 115, 118, 123
Scharnhorst: 14
Schweinfurt: 28
SCI: 20
Scott, C.W.A.: 8
SCR 720/724, Radar: 57
SCR 720/729, Radar: 19, 86, 120
SEAC: 134
Seletar: 6
Serrate: 19, 29
Shellhaus: 21
Simpson, R.W., Flt. Lt.: 21
Singapore: 6, 36
Sismore, E.B., Sqn. Ldr.: 39
Skv.334 (RNAF): 51
Slade, G., Wg. Cdr.: 17
SM-1 engine: 97, 114
Sola: 51
Sondestromfjord: 43
South African Air Force: 46
Spanish Civil War: 9
Sparrow, Flt. Off.: 25
Spartan Air Services Ltd: 43, 69
Specialtryck: 121
Spradbrow, Ralph: 35
St Eval: 41
St Leu d'Esserent: 37
St Nazaire: 14
Standard Identification Characters: 130
Starsborg: 15
Stavanger: 14
Steenbergen: 37
Stewart, George: 48
Stockholm: 28, 54
Strömsholms: 45
Sturgeon: 34
Suez Canal: 40, 42
Sukarno, Dr: 39
Supermarine Spitfire: 10, 16, 24–25, 40, 129
Svartklubben: 45
Swain, H., Flt. Lt.: 47
Swedish Air Force: 44, 53, 60, 121, 135, 140
Swissair: 15

T

T Mk 22: 37, 80, 136
T Mk 27: 38, 80, 136
T Mk 29: 35, 38, 53, 80
T Mk 39: 98
T Mk 43: 38, 47, 80
T Mk III: 6, 17, 24, 28, 37–38, 42, 45–48, 51, 80, 100, 103, 130, 135–138, 140, 146–147, 149
T.1154 Transmitter: 86
Tamblin, W.A.: 9
Tamiya: 63, 139, 140
Tappin, H.E., Flt. Lt.: 18
Target Indicators: 37
Target Tug: 42, 95, 133
Tärna: 45
Tengah: 40
Testors: 139–140
Texel: 29
TF Mk 37: 33–34, 44, 79
The Aeroplane: 7
The College of Aeronautics: 40
'Thimble' Radome: 25, 29, 60, 126
Thruxton: 46
'Tiger Force': 131
Tikedo: 36
Timmins Airport, Ontario: 44
Tirpitz: 15, 26
Torpedo: 32–33
TR Mk 33: 26, 32–34, 44, 46–47, 54, 79, 105, 110, 126–127, 134, 137, 140
TR-45/A Torpedo: 47
Transport Command: 39
Trier: 22
True Detail: 59, 63
TT Mk 35: 34, 41–42, 44, 79, 91, 101, 113, 115, 124, 128, 133
TT Mk 39: 33–34, 80, 98, 106
TT Mk VI: 136
TT.3: 45
TT.6: 45
Tunisia: 24
Turbinlite: 27
Turkish Air Force: 46, 77, 136, 140
Tuttle, G., Wg. Cdr.: 14
Tweedale, Sqn. Ldr.: 29

U

U-boat: 24, 28, 31
Uncle Tom Rocket: 97, 114
'Universal' Radome: 120
Upkeep: 16, 26
Uplands: 43
USAAF: 28, 33, 37, 48, 123, 137, 139

V

V-1: 19–20, 22, 29, 37
V-2: 22
Valskog: 45
VE-Day: 36
Vickers-Armstrong Ltd: 26, 41
Victoria, Australia: 7
Vienna: 22
Viet-Minh: 45
VIP Associations Ltd: 46
VJ-Day: 36, 38
Vultee Vengeance: 35
Vulture, Rolls Royce: 8

W

W.2/700 Power Jets: 41
W4050: 10–12, 65, 81, 115, 117, 129, 145
W4051: 11, 13–14, 133
W4052: 10–11, 13
W4053: 12
W4055: 13
W4057: 12
W4060: 14
W4061: 14
Wahn: 40
Wain, Plt. Off.: 17
Walker, C.T.: 9, 15
Walker, E.: 11
Wallis, Sir Barnes: 16, 26
Walther 109-509: 41
Wanne Eickel: 37
Warick, J.B., Sqn. Ldr.: 36
Watton: 37, 53, 137
Westland Welkin: 25
White Waltham: 42
White, Capt.: 29
Wilhelmshaven: 14
Williamson F.52 Camera: 15, 88
Wings: 91
Woodhall Spa: 36
Woods, J., Capt.: 47
Wooldridge, J., Wg. Cdr.: 61
Wooll, Flt. Lt.: 15
Wright Field: 36
Wright, Rudolph Bay, Capt.: 43
Würzburg: 23
Wykeham, P.G., Gp. Cpt.: 21

X

Xtracolor: 119, 125, 139, 140
Xtradecal: 120

Y

Yeager, Capt. Charles 'Chuck': 42
Yeates, Gerry, Flt. Lt.: 31
Yellahanka: 35
Youngman: 13
Ystad: 45
Yugoslavian Air Force: 42, 46, 137–138, 140

Z

Zalesky, Ed & Rose: 43
Zegrab: 47

10/Groupe de Chasse 'Corse' (Corsican): 45
100 Group: 29, 132
103rd Reconnaissance Regiment: 47
184th Reconnaissance Regiments: 47
25th (Recce) Bomber Group: 53, 137
2nd Tactical Air Force: 20
32nd Bomber Division: 47
3rd Photo Group (Recon): 63
47th Air Regiment: 136
482nd Bomb Group: 137
633 Squadron: 44
97th Air Regiment: 47

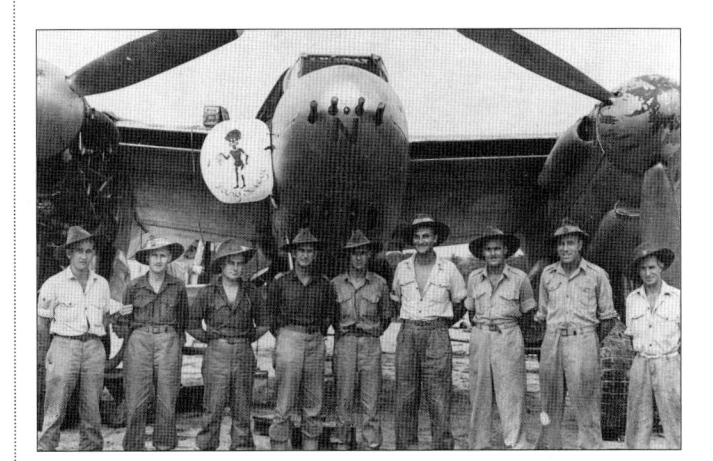

Members of No.1 Squadron line up in front of British-built FB Mk VI A52-506 (NA•N) at Labuan during mid-1945. The aircraft shows a neat piece of artwork ('Young Savage') on the entrance hatch *(F.Smith)*

The Last Mosquito
The 7,781st and last Mosquito (VX916) is seen outside the production hangar
at Chester on November 15, 1950, with some of those who built her.

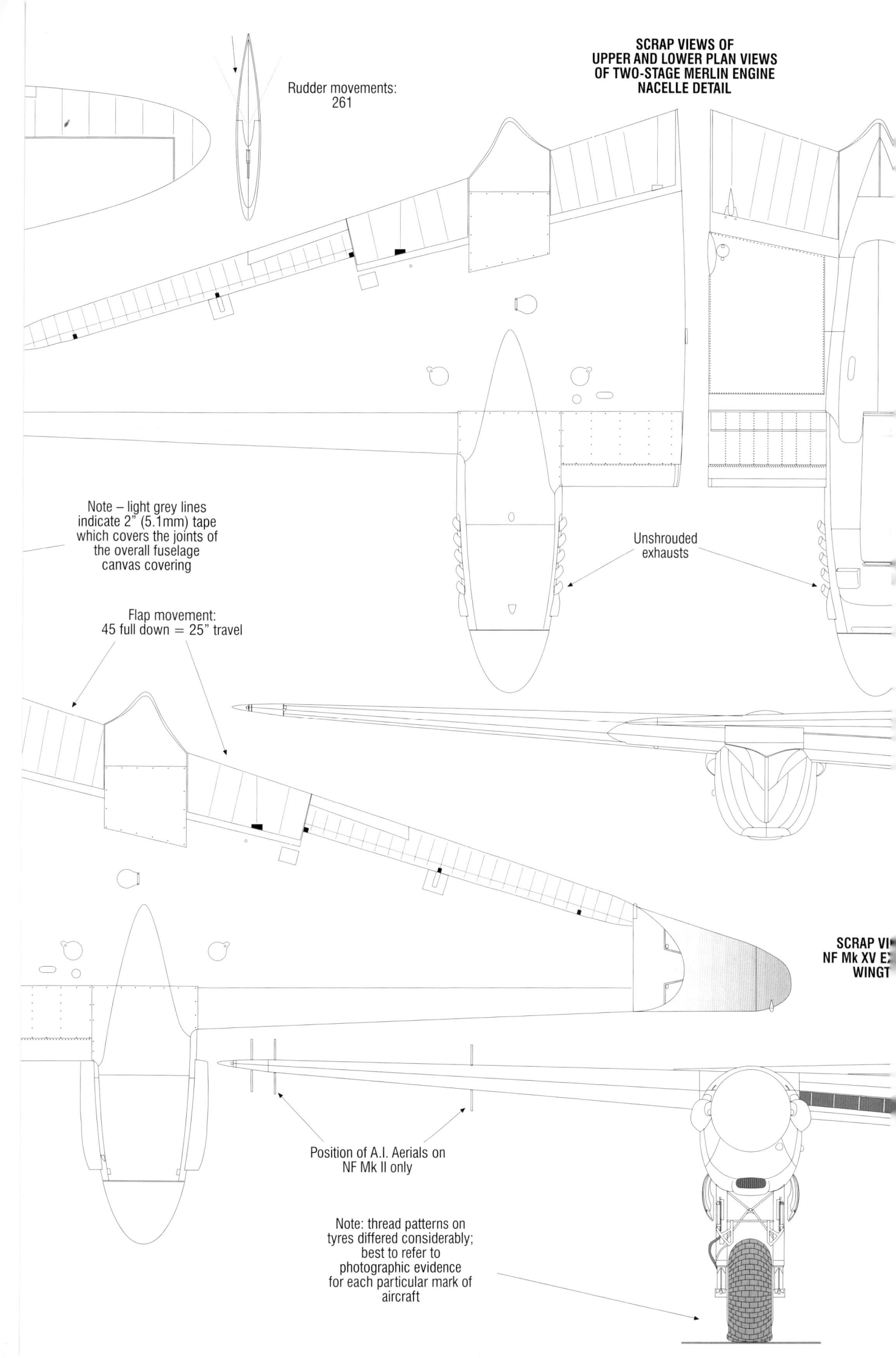

SCRAP VIEWS OF UPPER AND LOWER PLAN VIEWS OF TWO-STAGE MERLIN ENGINE NACELLE DETAIL

Rudder movements: 261

Note – light grey lines indicate 2" (5.1mm) tape which covers the joints of the overall fuselage canvas covering

Unshrouded exhausts

Flap movement: 45 full down = 25" travel

SCRAP VIEW NF Mk XV EXTENDED WINGTIP

Position of A.I. Aerials on NF Mk II only

Note: thread patterns on tyres differed considerably; best to refer to photographic evidence for each particular mark of aircraft

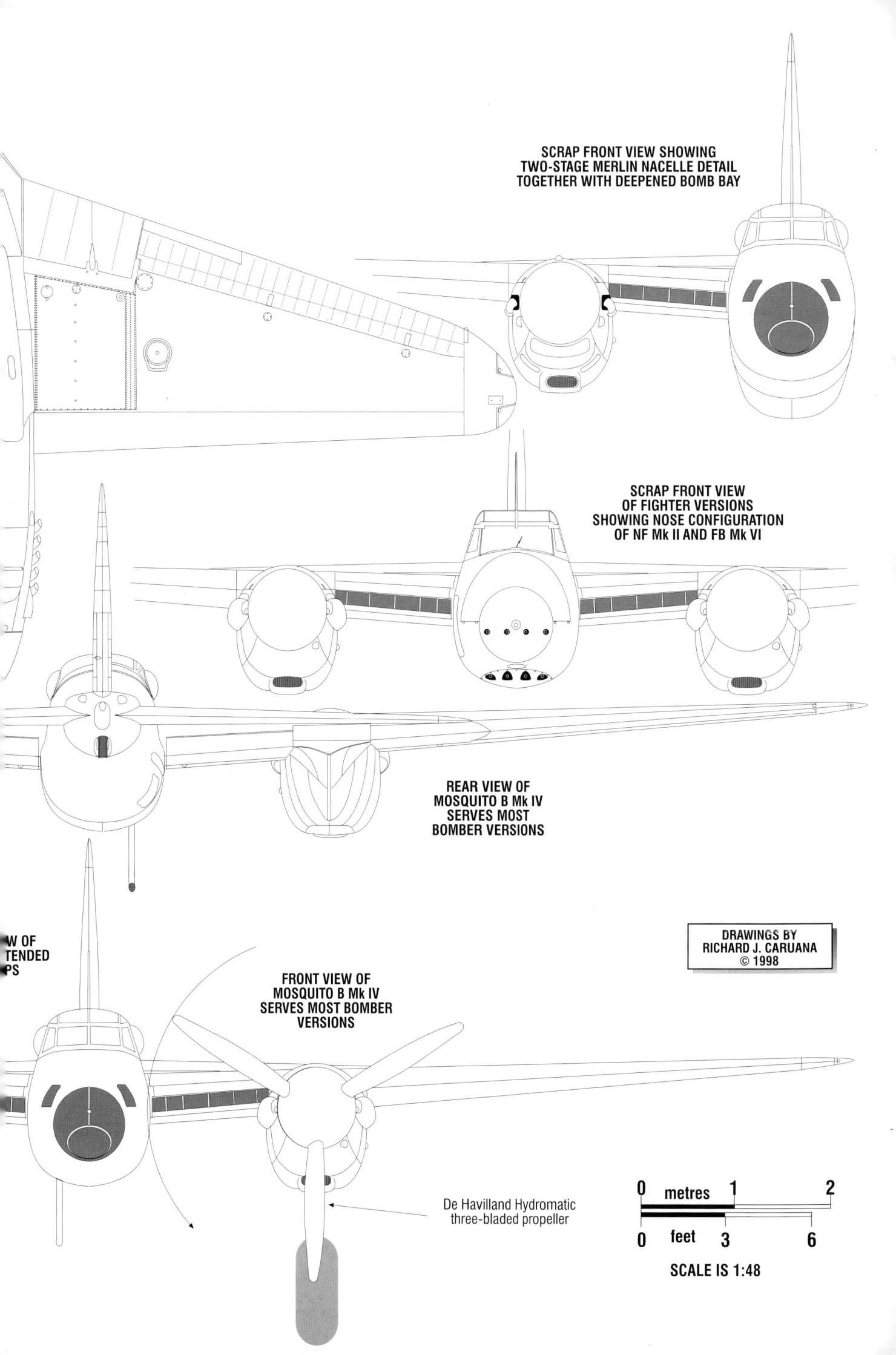

SCRAP FRONT VIEW SHOWING TWO-STAGE MERLIN NACELLE DETAIL TOGETHER WITH DEEPENED BOMB BAY

SCRAP FRONT VIEW OF FIGHTER VERSIONS SHOWING NOSE CONFIGURATION OF NF Mk II AND FB Mk VI

REAR VIEW OF MOSQUITO B Mk IV SERVES MOST BOMBER VERSIONS

DRAWINGS BY
RICHARD J. CARUANA
© 1998

FRONT VIEW OF MOSQUITO B Mk IV SERVES MOST BOMBER VERSIONS

De Havilland Hydromatic three-bladed propeller

SCALE IS 1:48